PAGANS AND CHRISTIANS IN THE LATE ROMAN EMPIRE

CEU MEDIEVALIA 18

Series Editor: József Laszlovszky

Pagans and Christians in the Late Roman Empire

New Evidence, New Approaches (4th–8th centuries)

Edited by
Marianne Sághy and Edward M. Schoolman

CEU Department of Medieval Studies
&
Central European University Press
Budapest · New York
&
University of Pécs
Specimina Nova Supplementum X

Budapest, 2017

© Editor and Contributors 2017
1st edition
Cover design for the series by Péter Tóth
Cover Illustration:
The Burial Chamber with the Jar
(Burial Chamber II, XXX/Pécs)

Joint publication by:
Central European University
Department of Medieval Studies
Nádor u. 9, H-1051 Budapest, Hungary
Telephone: (+36-1) 327-3051, Fax: (+36-1) 327-3055
E-mail: medstud@ceu.hu, Website: http://medievalstudies.ceu.hu

Central European University Press
Nádor utca 11, H-1051 Budapest, Hungary
Tel: +36-1-327-3138 or 327-3000
E-mail: ceupress@ceu.hu
Website: www.ceupress.com
224 West 57th Street, New York NY 10019, USA
Tel: +1-732-763-8816
E-mail: meszarosa@press.ceu.edu

University of Pécs

All rights reserved. No part of this publication may be reproduced,
stored in a retrieval system, or transmitted,
in any form or by any means, without the permission
of the Publisher.

ISSN 1587-6470 CEU MEDIEVALIA
ISBN 978-963-386-255-1

Library of Congress Control Number: 2017955098

Printed in Hungary by Prime Rate Kft.

TABLE OF CONTENTS

List of Illustrations vii

Introduction: Marianne Sághy and Edward M. Schoolman 1

Lives

Maël Goarzin The Importance of the Practical Life for Pagan and Christian Philosophers 11

Linda Honey Religious Profiling in the Miracles of Saint Thecla 27

Margarita Vallejo-Girvés Empress Verina among the Pagans 43

Anna Judit Tóth John Lydus, Pagan and Christian 59

Juana Torres Marcus of Arethusa, Heretic and Martyr 69

Identities

Monika Pesthy Simon Imitatio Christi? Classical and Scriptural Literary Models of Martyrdom in Early Christianity 83

Levente Nagy Ascetic Christianity in Pannonian Martyr Stories? 97

Jérôme Lagouanère Uses and Meanings of 'Paganus' in the Works of Saint Augustine 105

Ecaterina Lung Religious Identity as seen by Sixth-Century Historians and Chroniclers 119

Cults

Branka Migotti The Cult of Sol Invictus and early Christianity in Aquae Iasae 133

Miriam Adan Jones Conversion as Convergence: Gregory the Great confronting Pagan and Jewish Influences in Anglo-Saxon Christianity 151

Edward M. Schoolman Religious Images and Contexts: "Christian" and "Pagan" Terracotta Lamps 165

Landscapes

Hristo Preshlenov Believers in Transition: from Paganism to Christianity along the Southwestern Black Sea Coast (4th–6th centuries) 181

Józef Grzywaczewski and Daniel K. Knox, Glory, Decay and Hope: Goddess Roma in Sidonius Apollinaris' Panegyrics 203

Luciana Gabriela Soares Santoprete Tracing the Connections between "Mainstream" Platonism and "Marginal" Platonism with Digital Tools 217

Tombs

Ivan Basić Pagan Tomb to Christian Church: The Case of Diocletian's Mausoleum in Spalatum 241

Zsolt Visy Christian Topography in Sopianae's Late Antique Cemeteries 273

Olivér Gábor and Zsuzsa Katona Győr Sopianae Revisited: Pagan or Christian Burials? 295

Elizabeth O'Brien Impact beyond the Empire: Burial practices in Ireland (4th – 8th centuries) 341

List of contributors 357

Index of Personal Names 363

Index of Geographical Names 369

LIST OF ILLUSTRATIONS

Cults
Branka Migotti

Figure 1. Map of the location of Aquae Iasae (after Pirnat Spahić 2014, p. 14) 137
Figure 2. Inscription to Sol – Apollo, Zavičajni muzej Varaždinske Toplice / Varaždinske Toplice Local History Museum (photo: Nenad Kobasić) 139
Figure 3. Plan of Aquae Iasae (after Nemeth-Ehrlich and Kušan Špalj 2011, p. 212) 138
Figure 4. Fresco in the narthex of the basilica in Aquae Iasae (photo: Ante Rendić-Miočević) 140
Figure 5. Fresco of a saintly head from the basilica in Aquae Iasae, Arheološki muzej u Zagrebu / The Archaeological Museum in Zagreb (photo: Nenad Kobasić) 140
Figure 6. Plan of the basilica in Aquae Iasae in its Constantinian phase (after Migotti 1999, p. 69) 140

Edward M. Schoolman

Figure 1. 167
Figure 2. 168
Figure 3. 171
Figure 4. 171

Landscapes
Hristo Preshlenov

Figure 1. Tabula Peutingeriana. The Western Black Sea coast, rev. after ad 330 (after Атанас Орачев [Atanas Orachev], "Приноси към историята, археологията и географията на Анхиало [Contribution to the history, archaeology, and geography of Anchialo," in *Поморие: древност и съвремие* [*Pomorie: Past and Present*], ed. Атанас Орачев [Atanas Orachev] et al. (Бургас: Геопан [Burgas: Geopan], 2011), 162–163). 182

Figure 2. Therma. A marble column (author). 185
Figure 3. Karabyzie. A pagan dedication plate of the Heros Karabazmos
(after *IGBulg*, I², no. 287). 188
Figure 4. Karabyzie. The early Christian basilica and the pagan sanctuary of the Heros
Karabazmos (after Мирчев, "Разкопки на тракийското селище край с.
Галата," План 1). 189
Figure 5. Mesembria. The northwestern urban zone (after Прешленов,
"Християнизация и архитектурна среда в Несебър и Паницово," fig. 1).
.... 190
Figure 6. Mesembria. A relief of the Mesambrian *strategoi* (afterW. Welkow,
Nessebar (Sofia: Sofia Press, 1989), *s. p.* 191
Figure 7. Scatrae. A wall painting of the early Christian basilica (author). 194
Figure 8. Durostorum. A wall painting of the late Antique tomb (after Pillinger,
Corpus der spätantiken und frühchristlichen Wandmalereien Bulgariens,
Abb. 30). 195
Figure 9. Odessos, vicinity. The pagan Thracian god-rider onto the wall of a late
Roman tomb (after Мирчев, "Паметници на гробната архитектура
в Одесос," Fig. 16). 197
Figure 10. Odessos. Christian symbols onto the walls of an early Christian tomb
(after Мирчев, "Късноримският некропол на Одесос," Fig. 144). 198
Figure 11. Gerania. Walls and vault painting of the late Antique tomb (after
Pillinger, *Corpus der spätantiken und frühchristlichen Wandmalereien
Bulgariens*, Abb. 2). 200
Figure 12. Gerania. An altar slab of the early Christian basilica (after Овчаров and
Ваклинова, *Ранновизантийски паметници*, Fig. 84). 201

Tombs
Ivan Basić

Figure 1. Split, Diocletian's mausoleum, reconstruction of original appearance
(Marasović-Marasović-Perojević 2006, fig. 9) 246
Figure 2a. Split, Early Christian fragments found in the surroundings of the
cathedral, 6th c. (Mirnik 1989, Pl. 15) 260
Figure 2b. Split, Early Christian fragments found in the surroundings of the
cathedral, 6th c. (Mirnik 1989, Pl. 8) 260
Figure 3a. Split, Archaeological Museum, Early Christian pilaster (left) found at
the cathedral, 6th c. (photo: I. Basić) 260

Figure 3b. Split, cathedral, Early Christian pilaster, 6th c. (photo: I. Basić) 260
Figure 4. Split, cathedral, Early Christian relief with the depiction of a cantharos, 6th c. (Ivanišević 1987, fig. 2) 260
Figure 5. Split, Archaeological Museum, architrave with an inscription mentioning SS. Cosmas and Damian, 9th c. (photo: I. Basić 265

Zsolt Visy

Figure 1. Brick grave with gabled roof and plastered interior. The grave was broken into in a later period. © O. Gábor 277
Figure 2. Burial Chamber XX, secondary burial with painted interior, trellis motif and a Christogram in a triangle, above the head of the deceased. © Zs. Visy 278
Figure 3. The single buried sarcophagus discovered in the cemetery of Sopianae. © Zs. Visy 279
Figure 4. Burial Chamber II, surviving foundation walls of the burial chapel built above the crypt. © A.Török 279
Figure 5. Burial chamber XX was plastered, but unpainted. The grave is against the back wall, two secondary graves to the right and left made with different building methods. © Zs. Visy 280
Figure 6. Ground plan and reconstruction of Burial Chamber XXXI (cella trichora.) © Janus Pannonius Múzeum 281
Figure 7. Burial Chamber V with two secondary columns in the middle of the octagonal space, showing the brick foundation in the opposite corner and the vaulting rib partially covering an earlier wall niche. © Zs. Visy 282
Figure 8. Reconstruction of Burial Chamber XXXII (cella septichora). The building extends into the hillside to a depth of 2 to 5 meters. The drawing shows the 1.5-meter stairway down to the entrance on the western side. © Zs. Visy– K. Szijártó 282
Figure 9. Burial Chamber XXXII (cella septichora), during excavation. The limestone floor is was created during the construction. On the left, the pile of lime in the apse was intended for plastering the interior, but this was never done. © Zs. Visy 283
Figure 10. Burial Chamber I (Saint Peter and Saint Paul burial chamber), back wall with niche and remains of the grave's side walls (later destroyed). The wall is decorated with garlands, in the center the Christogram is celebrated by Saint Peter and Saint Paul with outstretched arms.© A. Török 284

Figure 11. Burial Chamber I (Saint Peter and Saint Paul burial chamber), ceiling. The Garden of Eden with a Christogram in the middle and medallions with male busts in the four corners, amidst evergreens, vine and floral motifs, peacocks and doves.© A.Török 285

Figure 12. Burial Chamber II, back wall of the crypt with false marble, floral motifs, a jar and a cup.© I. Füzi 286

Figure 13. Burial Chamber XXXIII (mausoleum) northern wall, Adam and Eve under the Tree of Life with the snake.© I. Füzi 287

Figure 14. Burial Chamber XXXIII (mausoleum), northern wall, Daniel in the lions' den. © I. Füzi 288

Olivér Gábor and Zsuzsa Katona Győr

Figure 1. Map of the cemeteries in Sopianae Pécs 301
Figure 2. Urn From Nagy Lajos School 2-3rd Century 301
Figure 3. Cremated Pagan Grave (Bustum) No 20 InSzéchenyi Tér 2nd Century 302
Figure 4. Mausoleum – Burial Chamber XXXIII 302
Figure 5. Mausoleum – Burial Chamber XXXIII 302
Figure 6. The Burial Chamber with the Jar 303
Figure 7. Brick Grave (No25) In Széchenyi Tér 4th Century 304
Figure 8. Cemetery Building From Apaca Street 4th Century 304

Elizabeth O'Brien

Figure 1. Map of the Roman Empire 341
Figure 2. Places named in text 343
Figure 3a. Burial in slab-lined cist 349
Figure 3b. Burial in unprotected dug grave 349

INTRODUCTION

Marianne Sághy and *Edward M. Schoolman*

Revisiting 'pagans' and 'Christians' in Late Antiquity has been a fertile site of scholarship in recent years. A rich crop of new studies on religious identity, conflict and coexistence demonstrates how difficult it is to grasp individual or group identities and model the religious transformation of the Late Roman Empire—the dominant master narrative of European historiography.[1] The paradigm shift in the interpretation of the relations between 'pagans' and 'Christians' replaced the old 'conflict model' with a subtler, complex approach and triggered the upsurge of new explanatory models such as multiculturalism, cohabitation, cooperation, identity, or group cohesion.

This collection of essays, originating from an international conference organized by Marianne Sághy at CEU Budapest in cooperation with the University of

---

[1] Anders Klostergaard Petersen- George van Kooten (edd.), *Religio-philosophical discourses in the Mediterranean world: from Plato through Jesus to Late Antiquity*, (Leiden-Boston: Brill, 2017); H. C. Teitler, *The last pagan emperor: Julian the Apostate and the war against Christianity*, (New York: Oxford University Press, 2017); Stéphane Ratti, *L'Histoire Auguste: Les païens et les chrétiens dans l'Antiquité tardive*, (Paris: Les Belles Lettres, 2016); Éric Rebillard, Jörg Rüpke (ed.), *Group Identity and Religious Individuality in Late Antiquity*, (Washington, D.C.: The Catholic University of America Press, 2015); Christopher P. Jones, *Between Pagan and Christian*, (Cambridge, MA.: Harvard University Press, 2014); Birgitte Secher Bøgh (ed.), *Conversion and Initiation in Antiquity: Shifting Identities – Creating Change*, (Frankfurt am Main; New York: Peter Lang, 2014); Rita Lizzi Testa (ed.), *The Strange Death of Pagan Rome: Reflections on a Historiographical Controversy.Giornale Italiano di Filologia: Bibliotheca, 16*. (Turnhout: Brepols Publishers, 2013); Stéphane Ratti, *Polémiques entre païens et chrétiens*, (Paris: Les Belles Lettres, 2012); Éric Rebillard. *Christians and their many identities in late antiquity, North Africa, 200–450 CE*, (Ithaca; London: Cornell University Press, 2012); Peter Brown - Rita Lizzi Testa (edd.), *Pagans and Christians in the Roman Empire: The Breaking of a Dialogue (IVth–VIth Century A.D.)*, (Zürich-Berlin: LIT Verlag, 2011); Alan Cameron. *The Last Pagans of Rome*. (Oxford; New York: Oxford University Press, 2011); Stéphane Ratti. *Antiquus error. Les ultimes feux de la résistance païenne. Scripta varia augmentés de cinq études inédites*, (Turnhout: Brepols, 2010); Stephen Mitchell - Peter Van Nuffelen (ed.), *Monotheism between Pagans and Christians in Late Antiquity*, (Leuven: Peeters, 2010); Maijastina Kahlos, *Debate and Dialogue: Christian and Pagan Cultures, c. 360–430*, (Farnham: Ashgate, 2007).

Pécs on 7-10 March 2013, inscribes itself into the revisionist discussion of pagan-Christian relations. The Budapest-Pécs conference was a follow-up of a very successful and truly delightful 2012 colloquy in the Hungarian Academy in Rome commemorating the Edict of Milan that focused on Constantine and the ways his political vision impacted the fourth-century *Vrbs*.[2] To move the analysis forward, we extended the geographical and chronological scope of investigation to the territory of the Roman Empire from the fourth to the eighth century. The conference had a rich program with two keynote lectures, thirty speakers, nine student posters, a field trip to the Late Antique cemetery in Pécs, and a record attendance. Keynote speakers Hartwin Brandt and Alan Cameron inspired,[3] the presence of iconic figures of the discipline, Wolf Liebeschuetz, Raffaella Cribiore and Giorgio Bonamente stimulated the conference.[4] The Pécs section took place in the Late Roman burial chambers, where participants felt like asking for a spade to do some more excavating! We celebrated Alan Cameron's 75th anniversary with good cheer and an erudite Neo-Latin poem composed by Zoltán Rihmer for the occasion.

The main question our speakers addressed concerned the validity of the concepts 'pagan' and 'Christian.' Do the terms 'pagan' and 'Christian,' 'transition from paganism to Christianity' still hold as explanatory devices to apply to the political, religious and cultural transformation experienced Empire-wise? In this set of papers, Constantine's conversion recedes in the background to give place to power networks, social interaction, practices of worship, literary and philosophical models. While 'paganism' had never been fully extirpated or denied by the multiethnic educated elite that managed the Roman Empire, 'Christianity' came to be presented by the same élite as providing a way for a wider group of people to combine true philosophy and right religion. The speed with which this happened is just as remarkable as the long persistence of paganism after the sea-change of the fourth century that made Christianity the official religion of the State. For a long time afterwards, 'pagans' and 'Christians' lived 'in between' polytheistic and monotheist traditions and disputed Classical and non-Clas-

---

[2] Michele R. Salzman, Marianne Sághy, Rita Lizzi Testa (ed.), *Pagans and Christians in Late Antique Rome: Conflict, Competition and Coexistence in the Fourth Century*. Cambridge: Cambridge University Press, 2016.

[3] Cameron's contribution, "Were Pagans Afraid to Speak Their Minds in a Christian World? The Correspondence of Symmachus" is included in the previous conference volume, Michele R. Salzman, Marianne Sághy, Rita Lizzi Testa (ed.), *Pagans and Christians in Late Antique Rome: Conflict, Competition and Coexistence in the Fourth Century*. Cambridge: Cambridge University Press, 2016: 64–115.

[4] For short reviews of the conference, see Andrea-BiankaZnorovszky – Johanna Rákos-Zichy, "Pagans and Christians in the Late Roman Empire: New Evidence, New Approaches. An International Conference: Budapest, 7–10 March 2013." *Bollettino distudilatini* 43 (2013): 599–602; Marianne Sághy, "Pagans and Christians in the Late Roman Empire: New Evidence, New Approaches. An International Conference in Budapest, 7–10 March." *Annual of Medieval Studies at CEU*, vol. 20 (2014): 283–290.

sical legacies.[5] This is the coexistence of various religious cultures that our conference sought to explore.

The lives of those who lived on the boundaries between pagans and Christians in Late Antiquity allow for the finest levels of resolution in understanding the relationships between the two communities and the intellectual and spiritual mindsets they represented, as well as new approaches to evaluating their interconnectivity. Opening this volume, Linda Honey's work on the life and miracles of the great martyr and healer Thecla raises the possibility of using hagiography to explore socio-religious boundaries in Late Roman Asia Minor. Careful examination of the recipients of Thecla's healing and those described in her fifth-century *vita* unveils the ways in which Christians within her community understood the delineation between religious groups, and furthermore underscores a rare undercurrent of religious tolerance for non-Christians, especially those who sought to regain wellbeing from the saint.

Beyond intercommunal tolerance, the developing Christian traditions owed significantly to their Roman precursors. Maël Goarzin's study on the formation of pagan and Christian biography uses the case studies of Porphyry of Tyre's late third-century biography of his teacher, the Platonic philosopher Plotinus, and Gregory of Nyssa's *Life of Macrina* written almost a century later to celebrate the piety and lifestyle of his own sister, to emphasize the shared intentions of those who were elevated through their biographies. Although there are significant differences in the details of Plotinus and Macrina's careers and contexts, both accounts offered their readers idealized examples of those who strove to lead contemplative lives, practical lifestyle oriented towards action and other people; lives that were also entirely and ideally compatible with intellectual or spiritual pursuits. The depictions of their attitudes and daily activities are far from identical, but echo the widespread value of a lifestyle that transcended the division between pagan philosophy and Christian asceticism.

On the other hand, in the Eastern Roman Empire of the fifth century, even political revolts could make visible the survival and importance of pagans and paganism to a culture now dominated by Christianity (although one divided by Christology). The political career of the Isaurian general Illus, and in particular his actions again the emperor Zeno and his supposed support from pagans, and the role of his one-time court rival and later ally, the dowager empress Verina (and mother-in-law of Zeno) serve as a compelling lens into how notional religious affiliation could play crucial roles in political disputes. Margarita Vallejo-Girvés' analysis of the episode restores Verina's overtly Christian position, both within Illus' revolt and in her proclamation of the general Leontius as the new emperor. While hagiographic texts often depicted Verina positively,

---

[5] For a discussion of the notion 'being in between' see Maijastina Kahlos, *Vettius Agorius Praetextatus: Senatorial Life in Between*. Roma: Acta Instituti Romani Finlandiae, 2002.

especially concerning her piety, concern for the imperial family, and interest and veneration in the cult of the *theotokos*, on the other hand her role in various usurpations, such as that of Basilicus, gave some authors the capacity to also vilify her. By tracing her relationship with Illus, and his vocal pagan advisor Pamprepius, Vallejo-Girvés concludes that Verina was central to the rejection of a possible pagan resurgence during the crisis of the revolt.

The episode of Illus was not the only instance where paganism was associated with those working within the administration of the empire. Anna Tóth reviews the writing of John Lydus, a student of Neoplatonic philosophy before beginning his imperial service in Constantinople under Anastatius and Justinian a generation after the failure of Illus's rebellion, for keys to understanding how his own religious convictions may have been shaped. While his own surviving writings offer few indications that he was Christian, evidence taken primarily from *De mensibus* suggests that his identity was driven by his position as a magistrate in the service of the Roman state. This allowed him to offer a perspective on the development of religious continuity; even in the sixth century, the connections between the pagan cults and Christian practices and beliefs could be emphasized, following the notion that in religions, as in customs, the old are reborn as new.

The flexibility demonstrated by John Lydus, whose writings were likely never designed for distribution, stands in parallel to individuals who bridged the contentious divides among Christians in the fourth century. One such example was Mark, the Bishop of Arethusa from the 340s to the 360s, who was tortured for his refusal to rebuild (or pay for) a pagan temple during the short reign of Julian; following his death, even pagans admitted grudging admiration for his steadfast bravery, and he became celebrated as a champion of Nicene orthodoxy by writers like Gregory Nazianzus and Theodoret. In her chapter, Juana Torres raises the key problem: Christian apologists entirely overlook Mark's pro-Arian (and heretical) beliefs, distorting his life to fit the narrative of a martyr-saint and ultimately serve as a tool to discredit the pagan emperor Julian.

The variations in pagan and Christian belief were often important features of late antique identities, and like the lives of individuals, aspects of identity offer compelling ways to see the connections and friction between them. Monika Pesthy-Simon examines the act of martyrdom, typically argued as an imitation of Christ, but draws the clear inheritance to other earlier models. Taking the examples of Polycarp of Smyrna and Ignatius of Antioch, she reveals that the narratives of their martyrdoms were clearly shaped by Jewish and philosophical paradigms: Ignatius's viewed his own impending death not simply an imitation of Christ's passion, but with eagerness patterned on the Classical noble death; the death of Polycarp, on the other hand, was couched in terms derived from the *Book of the Maccabees*, but to an ever greater degree seems to parallel the stoic death of Seneca.

Following the end of large-scale Christian persecution in the early fourth century, the models of martyrs, such as those of Polycarp and Ignatius, gave way to those who practiced ascetic Christianity. Levente Nagy's contribution explores this evolution through the case study of Pannonia, where the martyrs' struggles against persecution were transformed and replaced by struggles to maintain chastity. In two texts in particular, the *Passio* of Synerus and the *Passio* of Pollio, the saints are depicted not only in respect to their fates as martyrs, but also in their adoption of monastic values, new emphasis that reflected the changing status and attitudes of Christianity.

Transformations and variations in rhetoric over facets of identity were not limited to genres, but also could be found in the writings of individuals. For example, in Augustine's treatment of *pagani*, these "others" served as foils and adversaries, neighbors and interlocutors, and even possibly models and exemplars of virtue. This close reading by Jérôme Lagouanère outlines these instances, and cautions us against viewing Augustine as uniform in his severe reproach of pagans, in whose rejection of Christianity Christians themselves might be compelled for higher virtue.

While pagans could still be seen as relatively commonplace in Augustine's early fifth century, the sixth century marked a far more complex period. Although pagan religious identity had receding significantly, writers, including historians, sought to affirm the identity of the groups to which they belonged. To some degree, sixth-century historians like Procopius, Agathias, John Malalas, and Gregory of Tours offered subjective views that minimized the importance of pagan religion or non-orthodox Christian beliefs held by others. The chapter by Ecaterina Lung sets these as functions related to forging group identity, however that can serve to also distort the narratives these authors crafted.

After the issue of personal identities, several chapters of this book explore cultic practice. A clear differentiation of pagan and Christian layers in cultic performances, objects and beliefs is, in certain cases, well-nigh impossible. The most notable of these is Constantine's apparent flexibility in the worship of Sol Invictus and/or Christ. Branka Migotti lucidly asks the question of why one would expect Constantine to have been able to tell Sol from Christ when Christian theology had already equated these two, producing Christ the Sun as representative of a monotheistic solar cult. Examining the theology of Solar Christology and archaeological evidence at Aquae Iasae in Pannonia Superior, Migotti suggests that this cosmopolitan spa center simultaneously hosted the worship of Sol and Christ during the rule of Constantine: the hot spring baths still in use, the basilica already on its way to become a church, the worship of the pagan gods on the Capitolium had not yet ceased.

Other instances show the fusion of pagan ritual and Jewish tradition. Miriam Adan Jones probes into the theology behind Gregory the Great's idiosyncratic instructions to his missionaries among the Anglo-Saxons. While exhorting King Æthelbert to repress paganism, Gregory advised Augustine of Canterbury to establish Christian festivals with *tabernacula* reminiscent of the Jewish Sukkot celebration. This attitude suggested he thought pagans needed a gradual introduction to Christianity, rather than instant or violent conversion. Progress in the true religion driven by divine *condescensio* mirrored the slow revelation of God in providential history. This is the reason why Gregory, who otherwise sought to root out Jewish remnants from Christianity, found it useful to apply these very customs to help pagans make progress in their new faith. The preservation of both Jewish and pagan rituals, however, could only be provisional until the attainment of a Christian spirituality at its fullest.

Beyond texts, humble everyday objects such as terracotta lamps used mythological, Jewish and Christian motifs as central to their decoration. Did these objects have a religious, or even missionary message? Edward Schoolman argues otherwise. The main purpose of the images was to sell the lamps. Diverse types of lamps, however, shed light on their various functions and contexts as well as changing religious demographics across the Late Antique Mediterranean. The use of pagan motifs until the sixth century may indicate religious preferences, continuity of traditions, as well as utilitarian considerations. In certain cases, oil lamps were simply regarded as sources of light, in other instances (religious) community preferences dictated their designs. Taking actively part in religious service from liturgy to funerals as suppliers of light, these common objects were far from being filled with religious activism even if serving in a ritual practice.

The Christianization of the Classical landscape is among the most difficult and most exciting questions to treat. Hristo Preshlenov's synthetic survey presents a vast panorama of recent research on the Christianization of Scythia, Moesia Secunda and Haemimontus along the southwestern Black Sea coast. The new faith was preached in the region by the apostles Andrew and Paul, yet few early Christian traces remained before the fourth century. The bishops of the coastal cities were regular attendees at church councils and eagerly promoted the construction of basilicas imitating Byzantine models, often by appropriating earlier, pagan temples, sites, or cult-places. Pagan traditions were, however, slow to disappear. If distinctly pagan burials with gifts in tombs under a tumulus, the heroization of the deceased, and the burials with cremation vanished, others such as post-mortal mutilation, the use of purifying fire, protective amulets, and "Charon's fee" long survived. The cities of the Pontic coast may have "gone Christian," but the faithful still lived in a world of transition, sticking to ancient traditions while embracing new hopes of salvation.

Cityscapes and personifications of the cities could be used for precise political ends. This is what József Grzywaczewski and Daniel K.Knox show in Sidonius Apollinaris' representation of Rome. Their paper is the result of a fruitful collaboration generated after the conference by shared interest in the work and networks of the Gallic poet-bishop. Despite generic optimism and bombast, Sidonius' panegyrics allude to the decline of goddess *Roma* and thus to the fall of Roman power. The authors decipher new meanings created by a reverse reading of the poems in which *Roma* is transformed from a strong and active character to one worn out and broken with the effort of defending herself. Voicing fears of the fall of Rome in the fifth century, the poet-bishop, strangely, fails to see Christianity as a savior of Roman civilization.

Intellectual landscapes are at once swiftly changing and resolutely change-resistant. Luciana Gabriela Soares Santoprete presents three ambitious projects of digitization that provide the scientific community with new tools to study the relationships between Classical and Late Antique philosophical traditions, particularly Plato, Middle- and Neo-Platonism, and "marginal" philosophical-religious currents from the early Christian period—the "underworld" of Platonism. Epistemological problems that philosophers encounter when dealing with the relationship between Plotinus' thought and Gnostic teachings result from a "cleavage" between the work of historians of religion and that of historians of philosophy. Soares' projects reveal at once a new intellectual landscape in Late Antiquity—the interaction of philosophical and religious thought that has been treated so far in separate compartments by scholars – and establish a new field of modern interdisciplinary study, fusing philosophy and religion. As a result, scholars will be able to examine the way certain marginal (religious) doctrines were incorporated in mainstream (philosophical) Platonism to refute other marginal positions, such as Gnosis.

The last contributions to this book offer a series of case studies with a focus on tombs. As funeral rites and edifices are the most conservative of all traditions, they are sound indicators of continuity as well as of change. In a broad interdisciplinary perspective and using new interpretive paradigms, Ivan Basić revisits evidence about the transformation of Diocletian's mausoleum in Spalatum into a cathedral. Challenging earlier theories about the Christianization of the pagan emperor's tomb, Basić compellingly argues that the building, just like the majority of classical monuments in Late Antiquity, underwent a gradual process of alteration rather than a one-time conversion. The same is true for entire cemeteries in Late Antiquity—as it is well illustrated by Zsolt Visy's survey of the Christian graveyards in Sopianae, a task made exceptionally difficult due to the staggering lack of inscriptions. In the same cemetery, Olivér Gábor and Zsuzsa Katona Győr revisit the thorny problem of distinguishing pagan and Christian burials, testing earlier as well as recent excavation material against a set of select scholarly criteria. Elizabeth O'Brien examines burials in Ireland and their contacts with the Roman world over a long time-span. Using archaeological evidence in combination with primary documentary sources, she demonstrates the persistence of cremation, the expansion of inhumation and the impact of Roman customs, such as "Charon's fee" – a borrowing particularly stunning, as Ireland did not have a coin-based currency. Christian traditions, such as west-east extended supine inhumation were also adopted. Migration affected burials in unusual ways: newcomers sought out indigenous ancestral burial monuments (*ferta*) for their tombs to create an impression of uninterrupted continuity. O'Brien claims that it is impossible to differentiate between Christian and pagan burials during the fifth to eighth centuries in Ireland because all graves looked alike and the

Church did not seek to actively influence burial practices until the early eighth century, three centuries after the introduction of Christianity.

Surveying evidence from a large territory over a long time-span and addressing a variety of significant issues in pagan-Christian relations, the individual chapters of this volume dialogue with each other, providing fresh assessment of the meaning and experience of religious transition from North Africa to Pannonia, from Hibernia to Scythia, from Britain to Byzantium.

The conference and the publication of its proceedings reflect the long-standing collegial cooperation between CEU's Medieval Studies Department and the Archaeology Department of the University of Pécs. The publication of the conference proceedings concurs with the 650th anniversary celebrations of the foundation of a *studium generale* at Pécs by King Louis the Great in 1367 and thus benefits from the jubilee year grant offered by its Rector Magnificus. The financial contribution of the two Hungarian universities was generously supplemented by the Office of the Vice President for Research and Innovation of the University of Nevada, Reno (USA).

We want to offer special thanks to Professor Zsolt Visy (University of Pécs) for his collegial support, impeccable scholarship, dry wit, and infectious enthusiasm that triggered further collaboration between CEU and the University of Pécs at two unforgettable summer universities in the following summers. We are grateful to Mgr. György Udvardy, bishop of Pécs for opening our conference and for his interest in our work and to Her Excellency Maria Assunta Accili Sabbatini, ambassador of Italy in Hungary for her kind invitation to her Rózsadomb residence near the Veronika Street villa where the late Robert A. Markus was born and lived as a child. Fellow organizers Michelle R. Salzman (University of California Riverside), Rita Lizzi Testa (University of Perugia) and Levente Nagy (University of Pécs) assured international endorsement and high scholarly standards for the conference that was smartly and smoothly coordinated by Andrea-Bianka Znorovszky (CEU) and Johanna Rákos-Zichy (ELTE Budapest). This volume could not exist without the help of Ralph W. Mathisen (University of Illinois at Urbana-Champaign) and Matheus Coutinho Figuinha (University of São Paulo), who provided critical feedback on the submissions. Karen L. Stark and Stephen L. Pow, Ph.D. students at CEU's Medieval Studies Department, did an excellent job of proofreading the papers written by authors from all over the world: many thanks for their contribution.

Budapest, 29 June 2017

Lives

THE IMPORTANCE OF THE PRACTICAL LIFE FOR PAGAN AND CHRISTIAN PHILOSOPHERS

Maël Goarzin

Pagan and Christian literature in Late Antiquity have one major point in common, the importance they set on biography. Defined very generally as the narration of someone else's life,[1] biography flourishes in the fourth century in tandem with the rise of the sage and the holy man. The success of biographical discourse reflects authorial agenda,, the "worship" that surrounded philosophical, religious, and political figures,[2] as well as the expectations of the audience, readers seeking to discern in the lives of great people examples or ideals that they themselves might follow.[3]

---

[1] Biographical discourse, as opposed to biography and hagiography, is not limited to a specific literary genre. It is a type of discourse used in various types of texts—focusing on the life of an individual or not—to provide the narration, by a third party, of the life of a historical or legendary individual. In this paper, I use the term 'biographical discourse' rather than biography or hagiography, following Marc van Uytfanghe, 'L'hagiographie: un «genre» chrétien ou antique tardif ?', *Analecta Bollandiana* 111 (1993), 135–188. For Michael Stuart Williams, *Authorised Lives in Early Christian Biography: Between Eusebius and Augustine* (Cambridge: Cambridge University Press, 2008), pp. 8–9, Christian biographical texts 'exist on the margins of the more familiar genres of biography and hagiography.' On the success of biographical discourse in Late Antiquity, see Mark J. Edwards, 'Epilogue', in *Portraits: biographical representation in the Greek and Latin literature of the Roman Empire*, ed. Mark J. Edwards and Simon Swain (Oxford: Clarendon Press, 1997), pp. 227–31.

[2] Peter Brown, 'The Rise and Function of the Holy Man in Late Antiquity', *Journal of Roman Studies*, 61 (1971), 80–101; idem, 'The Saint as Exemplar in Late Antiquity', *Representations*, 2 (1) (1983), 1–25; idem, *Genèse de l'Antiquité tardive*, trans. by Aline Rousselle (Paris: Gallimard, 1983), pp. 39–40.

[3] Maël Goarzin, 'Diffuser l'autorité morale. Le discours biographique dans l'Antiquité tardive', in *Les mises en scène de l'autorité dans l'Antiquité*, Nancy: Etudes Anciennes 60, A.D.R.A. / Paris: Editions de Boccard, 2015, pp. 159–71 and idem, 'Presenting a Practical Way of Life through Biographical Discourse: the Examples of Gregory of Nyssa and Marinus', forthcoming. For the exemplary function of biographical discourse, see Charles H. Talbert, 'Biographies of Philosophers and Rulers as Instruments of Religious Propaganda in Mediterranean Antiquity', *ANRW*, II.16.2 (1978): 1619–51; Patricia Cox, *Biography in late Antiquity: a quest for the holy man*, (Berkeley: University of California Press, 1983), 9–11; Van Uytfanghe, p. 151; Simon Swain, 'Biography and Biographic in the Literature of the Roman Empire', in Edwards and Swain, pp. 32–35; Gillian Clark, 'Philosophic Lives and the Philosophic Life', in *Greek biography and panegyric in late antiquity*, ed. To-

Pagan philosophical and Christian ascetic tradition share a common reflection on the perfect life andd distinguish between 'active' and 'contemplative' life.[4] Philosophical tradition concerning the best way of life goes back to the Presocratics[5] and Plato,[6] and continues with Aristotle[7] and his followers.[8] Christian thinking on choosing the best life to live is symbolized by the biblical figures of Martha and Mary, one standing for active, the other for contemplative life.[9]

Scholarship on Late Antique biographical texts correlated the lives of ancient philosophers and Christian saints.[10] Comparing the ideal way of life in Porphyry's *Life of Plotinus* with Gregory of Nyssa's *Life of Macrina*, this paper highlights the significance they attribute to the involvement in the world of their heroes. Anthony Meredith suggested that Plotinus' life—in contrast to Macrina's—was devoted to contemplation at the expense of the practical dimension of daily life.[11] If Porphyry's text is centered on the philosophical activity of Plotinus and on his contemplation of the Intellect, he does not neglect the philosopher's action and the external circumstances in which he lives. I wish to show that Plotinus shares with Macrina a care for the other and for the city. Recent studies on Plotinus and Platonism have shown that the practical dimen-

---

mas Hägg, Philippe Rousseau and Christian Høgel (Berkeley: University of California Press, 2000), p. 31; Luc Brisson, 'Le maître, exemple des vertus dans la tradition platonicienne: Plotin et Proclus', in *Exempla docent. Les exemples des philosophes de l'Antiquité à la Renaissance*, ed. Thomas Ricklin (Paris: Vrin, 2006), p. 55; Tomas Hägg, *The art of biography in Antiquity*, (New York: Cambridge University Press, 2012), p. 93, 282 and 300.

[4] Christian Trottmann, 'Vita activa/vita contemplativa', in *Historisches Wörterbuch der Philosophie*, ed. by Joachim Ritter and others, 12 vols (Basel, Schwabe, 1971–2007), 11 (2001), pp. 1071–75.

[5] Robert Joly, *Le thème philosophique des genres de vie dans l'Antiquité classique* (Bruxelles: Palais des Académies, 1956), Chapters I and II. Presocratic philosophers Pythagoras, Prodicus and Isocrates also distinguished the active and the contemplative life.

[6] On the distinction between the philosopher's contemplative life and the political man's active life: Plato, *Republic*, VII. 520a–b. The pre-eminence of the contemplative life is recurrent in Plato's dialogues, despite his consideration of the necessity of the active life: *Republic*, VI. 486a and 496d–497a.

[7] Aristotle, *Nichomachean Ethics*, X. 6–8 compares the active or practical life and the contemplative or theoretical life. Without depreciating the active life, Aristotle gives to the contemplative life the first place in order to reach happiness: *Nichomachean Ethics*, X. 7, 1177a11–18.

[8] See *Theoria, Praxis, and the Contemplative Life after Plato and Aristotle*, ed Thomas Bénatouïl and Mauro Bonazzi (Leiden-Boston, Brill, 2012) on the distinction between the active and the contemplative life in Neoplatonic tradition, such as Plotinus's *Enneads*, VI 9 (9) and I, 4 (46).

[9] Luke 10. 38–42; Christian Trottmann, 'Marthe et Marie', in *Christianisme: Dictionnaire des temps, des lieux et des figures*, ed. André Vauchez et al. (Paris, Editions du Seuil, 2010), pp. 365–67.

[10] Brown, 'The Saint as Exemplar in Late Antiquity'; Cox; Richard Goulet, *Etudes sur les vies de philosophes de l'Antiquité tardive* (Paris: Vrin, 2001); Derek Krueger, *Writing and Holiness: The Practice of Authorship in the Early Christian East* (Philadelphia: University of Pennsylvania Press, 2004); Williams and Hägg.

[11] Anthony Meredith, 'A comparison between the *Vita Sanctae Macrinae* of Gregory of Nyssa, the *Vita Plotini* of Porphyry and the *De Vita Pythagorica* of Iamblichus', in *The biographical works of Gregory of Nyssa*, ed. by Andreas Spira (Cambridge, Mass.: Philadelphia Patristic Foundation, 1984), pp. 181–95.

sion of the philosopher's life is consistent with the contemplative ideal.[12] I argue for the close relationship between the contemplative and the practical life in the *Life of Plotinus* and the *Life of Macrina*. Plotinus' contemplation does not negate the practical dimension, the care for others, and the involvement with quotidian concerns. Macrina's life exemplifies Christian perfectioon characterized by both action and contemplation. The exemplary lives presented in these biographical discourses are not simply contemplative examples, turned towards God or the intelligible world, but also examples of practical life, oriented towards action and the neighbor.

Porphyry, *The Life of Plotinus, 8–9*

Porphyry wrote *The Life of Plotinus* at the beginning of the fourth century, thirty years after the death of his Platonic teacher and master.[13] Placed at the beginning of Porphyry's edition of the complete works of Plotinus, the biography is linked to the *Enneads* and its intended audience is a narrow group of philosophers interested in Plotinus's thinking.[14] Porphyry introduces the reader to the *Enneads* by presenting its author and the context in which Plotinus taught and wrote.[15] Philosophy in antiquity was not a scholarly discourse, but a way of life—not just speaking about philosophy, but living

---

[12] As opposed to John Dillon, 'An Ethic for the Late Antique Sage', in *The Cambridge Companion to Plotinus*, ed. Lloyd P. Gerson (Cambridge, England: Cambridge University Press, 1996), pp. 315–35, K. McGroarty, 'The Ethics of Plotinus', in K. McGroarty (ed.) *Eklogai: Studies in Honour of Thomas Finan and Gerard Watson* (Maynooth: National University of Ireland, Department of Ancient Classics, 2001), pp. 20–34. argues that Plotinian ethics was not directed towards the sensible world and towards others. Recent studies re-evaluated the Neoplatonic way of life. On the political dimension of Neoplatonism see Dominic O'Meara, *Platonopolis : Platonic Political Philosophy in Late Antiquity* (Oxford: Oxford University Press, 2005). On the social work of the philosopher see Alexandrine Schniewind, *L'éthique du sage chez Plotin*, (Paris: Vrin, 2003; idem, 'The social concern of the Plotinian sage', in *The philosopher and society in late Antiquity: essays in honor of Peter Brown*, ed. Andrew Smith (Swansea: Classical Press of Wales, 2005), pp. 51–64). The Neoplatonic way of life thus needs to be nuanced: it is not only turned towards contemplation and the intelligible world, separating one self from the body and the sensible world, but also takes into account the philosopher's place in society and his everyday work.

[13] Porphyry, *On the life of Plotinus and the order of his books*, in Plotinus, *Enneads*, Greek text ed. by Paul Henry and Hans-Rudolf Schwytzer, editio minor (Oxford : Oxford Classical Texts, 1964–1982) and trans. by Arthur H. Armstrong, The Loeb Classical Library 440–445, 6 vols (London: William Heinemann, 1966–88), I (1966), pp. 2–87.

[14] For a discussion of the polemical context in which the edition of the *Enneads* took place, see Henri Dominique Saffrey, 'Pourquoi Porphyre a-t-il édité Plotin ? Réponse provisoire', in *Porphyre. La vie de Plotin*, ed. by Luc Brisson and others, 2 vols (Paris: Vrin, 1982–92), vol. 2 (1992), pp. 31–64.

[15] The historical and social context in which Plotinus lived and worked is described with great precision by Marie-Odile Goulet-Cazé in this article: 'L'arrière-plan scolaire de la *Vie de Plotin*', in *Porphyre. La vie de Plotin*, ed. by Luc Brisson and others, 2 vols (Paris: Vrin, 1982–92), vol. 21(1982), pp. 231–327.

philosophy.[16] The credibility of the *Enneads* was in close relation with the issue of how virtuous a life Plotinus led. The legitimacy of Plotinus's philosophy depended entirely on Porphyry's ability to promote his master's life as an exemplar.

In this prism, *The Life of Plotinus* is but a realization of the practical and contemplative virtues described in *Enneads* I, 2 (19) *On the virtues*.[17] Plotinus' biographer to demonstrate that the philosopher practiced the virtues (including the lower virtues) that he taught his disciples. From practical to paradigmatic virtues, the *Life* exemplifies different levels of virtue described in the *Enneads*. It is, then, a praise of virtuous life, first practiced by Plotinus himself and now presented to the reader as an example.

Recent studies focus on the nature of the ideal way of life in Plotinus' *Enneads*, particularly the compatibility between action and contemplation in the life of the sage.[18] According to Plotinus, contemplative life is not only compatible with action, but directly influences the everyday activity of the sage living in the sensory world. Plotinus's way of life is a perfect example of this duality.[19]

The double aspect of the ideal life is discussed in chapters 8 and 9 of the *Life of Plotinus*. These chapters reveal the way the philosopher combines the perfectly contemplative and the wholly practical on a daily basis, in his attitude towards himself and the others.

Contemplative Life: Being present to oneself

Chapters 8 and 9 of the *Life of Plotinus* describe the way Plotinus lived and taught in Rome. Contemplation thrives even in simplest everyday practice, such as

---

[16] Pierre Hadot, *Philosophy as a Way of Life*, (Oxford: Blackwell's, 1995).

[17] Brisson, 'Le maître, exemple des vertus', pp. 49–60.

[18] Dillon, p. 315 and McGroarty, p. 26 argue that the only aim of Plotinus's ethics is contemplation. Dillon, pp. 331–32 writes that action is valuable only if it leads to the Intellect. Other scholars demonstrate that it is possible for the sage to live in the sensible world while contemplating the Intellect. Action and contemplation are compatible, and the contemplative life of the sage influences his activity in the sensible world: Andrew Smith, 'The significance of practical ethics for Plotinus' in *Traditions of Platonism: Essays in Honor of John Dillon*), ed. J. J. Cleary (Aldershot: Ashgate, 1999), pp. 227–36; Schniewind, *L'éthique du sage chez Plotin*, pp. 191–97; Schniewind, 'The social concern of the Plotinian sage', especially p. 58; Andrew Smith, 'Action and Contemplation in Plotinus', in *The Philosopher and Society in Late Antiquity: Essays in Honour of Peter Brown*, ed. by A. Smith (Swansea: Classical Press of Wales, 2005), pp. 65–72; James Wilberding, 'Automatic action in Plotinus', *Oxford studies in ancient philosophy*, 34 (2008), pp. 373–407; Alessandro Linguiti, 'Plotinus and Porphyry on the contemplative life', in *Theoria, Praxis, and the Contemplative Life after Plato and Aristotle*, pp. 183–97, especially pp. 187–88.

[19] McGroarty, pp. 20–24 and 29 thinks that Plotinus' practical life in Porphyry's biography is incoherent with the philosopher's contemplative life described by Plotinus in the *Enneads*. The *Life of Plotinus* is often cited to exemplify Plotinus's description of the sage living a double life, both active and contemplative: Smith, 'The significance of practical ethics for Plotinus', pp. 228–230; Wilberding, p. 389–93 and Linguiti, pp. 187–89. A. Meredith's opinion, pp. 185–86 about the *Life of Plotinus* is isolated.

sleeping and eating: "He never relaxed his self-turned attention except in sleep: even sleep he reduced by taking very little food, often not even a piece of bread, and by his continuous turning in contemplation to his intellect."[20]

Whatever Plotinus does during the day, he is always turning inwardly towards himself (τήν πρὸς ἑαυτὸν προσοχὴν), that is, towards his intellect (πρὸς τὸν νοῦν). For Plotinus, intellect is the divine part of the human soul, detached from the rest of the soul that contemplates the Platonic Forms contained in the divine Intellect, the second hypostasis of the metaphysical system.[21] By turning towards his intellect (ἡ πρὸς τὸν νοῦν αὐτοῦ ἐπιστροφή), the sage experiences the contemplation of the Intellect.[22] This is the main goal of the philosophical life for Plotinus and Porphyry.[23]

What is interesting here is that Plotinus's contemplative life does not belong to a specific time of the day, but it is continuous (διαρκής), as long as the philosopher is awake.[24] Although restricted by physiological needs related to the incarnation of the human soul, the continuous noetic activity of Plotinus echoes the continuous contemplation of the divine Intellect.[25] Plotinus's life is full of details revealing the link between action and contemplation. At presenting Plotinus as a teacher, Porphyry comments on his physical appearance as well: "When he was speaking, his intellect visibly lit up his face: there was always a charm about his appearance, but at these times he was still more attractive to look at: he sweated gently, and kindliness shone out from him, and in

---

[20] Porphyry, *The Life of Plotinus*, 8. 19–22: καὶ τήν γε πρὸς ἑαυτὸν προσοχὴν οὐκ ἄν ποτε ἐχάλασεν, ἢ μόνον ἐν τοῖς ὕπνοις, ὃν ἂν ἀπέκρουεν ἥ τε τῆς τροφῆς ὀλιγότης—οὐδὲ γὰρ ἄρτου πολλάκις ἂν ἥψατο—καὶ ἡ πρὸς τὸν νοῦν αὐτοῦ διαρκὴς ἐπιστροφή. Greek text and English translation in Porphyry, *On the life of Plotinus and the order of his books*, pp. 30–31.

[21] The first hypostasis is the One, the third hypostasis being the Soul. It is important to notice with Pierre Hadot, 'Les niveaux de conscience dans les états mystiques selon Plotin', *Journal de psychologie normale et pathologique*, 77 (1980), 243–65, that the soul's contemplation of the hypostatic Intellect is different from the mystical union with the One. In this paper, I only refer to the contemplation of the Intellect Porphyry refers to in the passages mentioned. In the *Life of Porphyry*, the mystical union with the One is mentioned in Chapter 23.

[22] On contemplation in Plotinus and the Plotinian doctrine of the undescended soul, see Linguiti, pp. 183–97, especially pp. 184–90.

[23] The last words of Plotinus (*The Life of Plotinus*, 2. 23–34), or the interpretation of Apollon's oracle about the life of Plotinus in Chapter 23, 3–7, 14–16 and 22–24. In these passages it is clear that the contemplative life is the primary focus of the philosopher's life. Porphyry thus confirms Plotinus's opinion about life in philosophy.

[24] The restriction of Plotinus' continuous contemplation is reiterated in the next chapter: *The Life of Plotinus*, 9. 16–18.

[25] Platonic contemplation is timeless because the intelligible contemplated by the sage is not situated in time. If the undescended soul is able to contemplate the Intellect eternally, the incarnate soul is only able to do so by turning itself towards the divine part of its soul. This can only be done when the philosopher is awake. The loss of his full intellectual strength by Plotinus at the end of his life is due to the incarnate condition of the philosopher: *The Life of Plotinus*, 6. 26–37.

answering questions he made clear both his benevolence to the questioner and his intellectual vigour."[26]

The physical expression of Plotinus's contemplation is visible in his daily activities, from his way of teaching to his way of speaking.[27] His face radiates his inner qualities—benevolence, kindliness, and gentleness—as a result of Plotinus's contemplative activity. The verbs used by Porphyry to describe Plotinus's appearance (ὁρώμενος; διέλαμπε; ἐδείκνυτο) highlight the external expression of Plotinus's contemplation. The philosopher's contemplation impacts his physical appearance and his daily activity, confirming Plotinus's notion of the automatic action of the sage, and the compatibility between these two modes of life.

Chapter 8 is often cited by scholars as an example of simultaneous action and contemplation in Plotinus's life, along with the interpretation of the following anecdote:[28]

> "He worked out his train of thought from beginning to end in his own mind, and then, when he wrote it down, since he had set it all in order in his mind, he wrote as continuously as if he was copying from a book. Even if he was talking to someone, engaged in continuous conversation, he kept his train of thought. He could take his necessary part in the conversation to the full, and at the same time keep his mind fixed without a break on what he was considering. When the person he had been talking to was gone he did not go over what he had written, because his sight, as I have said, did not suffice for revision. He went straight on with what came next, keeping the connection just as if there had been no interval of conversation between."[29]

---

[26] Porphyry, *The Life of Plotinus*, 13. 5–10: Ἦν δ' ἐν τῷ λέγειν ἡ ἔνδειξις τοῦ νοῦ ἄχρι τοῦ προσώπου αὐτοῦ τὸ φῶς ἐπιλάμποντος· ἐράσμιος μὲν ὀφθῆναι, καλλίων δὲ τότε μάλιστα ὁρώμενος· καὶ λεπτός τις ἱδρὼς ἐπέθει καὶ ἡ πραότης διέλαμπε καὶ τὸ προσηνὲς πρὸς τὰς ἐρωτήσεις ἐδείκνυτο καὶ τὸ εὔτονον.. Greek text and English translation in Porphyry, *On the life of Plotinus and the order of his books*, pp. 38–39.

[27] On Plotinus's way of speaking and its link to contemplative activity: *The Life of Plotinus*, 2. 13–14.

[28] Smith, 'The significance of practical ethics for Plotinus', pp. 228–30 and Linguiti, pp. 187–88.

[29] Porphyry, *The Life of Plotinus*, 8. 12–19: Συντελέσας γὰρ παρ' ἑαυτῷ ἀπ' ἀρχῆς ἄχρι τέλους τὸ σκέμμα, ἔπειτα εἰς γραφὴν παραδιδοὺς ἃ ἐσκέπτετο, συνεῖρεν οὕτω γράφων ἃ ἐν τῇ ψυχῇ διέθηκεν, ὡς ἀπὸ βιβλίου δοκεῖν μεταβάλλειν τὰ γραφόμενα· ἐπεὶ καὶ διαλεγόμενος πρός τινα καὶ συνείρων τὰς ὁμιλίας πρὸς τῷ σκέμματι, ὡς ἅμα τε ἀποπληροῦν τὸ ἀναγκαῖον τῆς ὁμιλίας καὶ τῶν ἐν σκέψει προκειμένων ἀδιάκοπον τηρεῖν τὴν διάνοιαν· ἀποστάντος γοῦν τοῦ προσδιαλεγομένου οὐδ' ἐπαναλαβὼν τὰ γεγραμμένα, διὰ τὸ μὴ ἐπαρκεῖν αὐτῷ πρὸς ἀνάληψιν, ὡς εἰρήκαμεν, τὴν ὅρασιν, τὰ ἑξῆς ἂν ἐπισυνῆψεν, ὡς μηδένα διαστήσας χρόνον μεταξὺ ὅτε τὴν ὁμιλίαν ἐποιεῖτο. Greek text and English translation in Porphyry, *On the life of Plotinus and the order of his books*, pp. 28–31.

The detailed description of Plotinus's way of writing, highlighting his power of concentration when examining a philosophical question and putting in writing the result of discursive activity, provide a concrete example of the philosopher's intellectual life. Despite holding a conversation with someone, Plotinus does not lose sight of the examined problem. When his interlocutor leaves, he immediately resumes writing. Edifying as it may be, the passage is not an example of simultaneous action and contemplation, as suggested by J. Wilberding.[30] because Porphyry's vocabulary in describing Plotinus' reflection (τὸ σκέμμα; τὴν διάνοιαν) denotes a discursive dimension absent from contemplation.[31] Parallel to his noetic activity, discursive thought, writing, conversation, and everyday actions are part of Plotinus' life. If—in contrast with the first two passages cited above—this anecdote is not an example of simultaneous action and contemplation –– it is nonetheless a good example of Plotinus' active life. Plotinus' availability for conversation reveals the importance of another, external kind of life in his daily schedule: a practical life, turned outwardly, towards action and towards others.

Practical Life: Being present to others

Chapter 9 emphasizes the practical aspects of Plotinus' life, particularly his social behavior:[32]

> "Many men and women of the highest rank, on the approach of death, brought him their children, both boys and girls, and entrusted them to him along with all their property, considering that he would be a holy and god-like guardian. So his house was full of young lads and maid-

---

[30] According to Wilberding, pp. 391–93, this passage shows that action and contemplation are not always simultaneous in the philosopher's life. They are compatible, but in another sense: "The idea here is not that Plotinus can actively be making progress in both the human and the noetic arenas at precisely the same moment. Rather, they are both present to him in the sense that he never loses touch of either, and for this reason he can alternately pursue the one without losing track of where he is in the other." This counterexample does not refute automatic action but limits its extent. It is correct to say that the Plotinian sage sometimes performs automatic action, but it is also correct to maintain that the sage's action is compatible with contemplation in the sense of doing the former without forgetting that the most important is the latter. The conclusion of Chapter 8 confirms Wilberding's position: Plotinus's availability for others does not prevent him from being present to himself, constantly turned towards the Intellect (8. 19–22).

[31] On the difference between discursive and non-discursive thought in Plotinus, see Henry Jacob Blumenthal, *Plotinus' Psychology* (The Hague: Nijhoff, 1971), Chapter 8, 'The discursive reason', pp. 100–11; idem, 'On soul and Intellect', in *The Cambridge Companion to Plotinus*, ed. L. P. Gerson (Cambridge/New-York: Cambridge University Press, 1996), pp. 82–104 and Eyjdfur Kjalar Emilsson, *Plotinus on Intellect*, (Oxford: Oxford University Press, 2007), Chapter 4, pp. 176–213.

[32] On the social dimension of the sage in Plotinus's philosophy, see Schniewind, "The social concern of the Plotinian sage."

ens, including Potamon, to whose education he gave serious thought, and would even listen to him revising the same lesson again and again. He patiently attended to the accounts of their property when their trustees submitted them, and took care that they should be accurate; he used to say that as long as they did not take to philosophy their properties and incomes must be kept safe and untouched for them. [...] He was gentle, too, and at the disposal of all who had any sort of acquaintance with him. Though he spent twenty-six whole years in Rome and acted as arbitrator in very many people's disputes, he never made an enemy of any of the officials."[33]

Plotinus's care for others is illustrated by his roles as warden, educator, and arbitrator. First, Porphyry explains Plotinus's dedication towards the orphans he took in his house. Not only does he educate them (παιδεύσεως), but he also takes care of their accounts. Porphyry's insistence on Plotinus's constant attention (ἠνείχετο, ἐπεμελεῖτο) in supervising the accounts reveals the importance given to practical life and daily tasks by the philosopher (9. 12–14). The fact that Plotinus consented to take role of arbitrator reinforces this idea (9. 20–22).[34]

Plotinus's availability for others is summarized by the Greek word πρᾶος (mild, gentle, or meek) that defines the philosopher's attitude towards others. Plotinus is not concerned exclusively with a self-centered contemplative life, but he truly cares for others and helps them in concrete, functional ways on a daily basis. Gentle (πρᾶος) and at the disposal of those who need it (ἐκκείμενος), Plotinus does not hesitate to take responsibility for the worries and cares of ordinary life (τὰς εἰς τὸν βίον φροντίδας τε καὶ ἐπιμελείας).[35]

A careful reading of chapters 8 and 9 of *The Life of Plotinus* reveals that Plotinus accorded its due importance to the active life, the moral and civic virtues, besides

---

[33] Porphyry, *The Life of Plotinus*, 9. 5–14 and 18–23: Πολλοὶ δὲ καὶ ἄνδρες καὶ γυναῖκες ἀποθνῄσκειν μέλλοντες τῶν εὐγενεστάτων φέροντες τὰ ἑαυτῶν τέκνα, ἄρρενάς τε ὁμοῦ καὶ θηλείας, ἐκείνῳ παρεδίδοσαν μετὰ τῆς ἄλλης οὐσίας ὡς ἱερῷ τινι καὶ θείῳ φύλακι. Διὸ καὶ ἐπεπλήρωτο αὐτῷ ἡ οἰκία παίδων καὶ παρθένων. Ἐν τούτοις δὲ ἦν καὶ Ποτάμων, οὗ τῆς παιδεύσεως φροντίζων πολλάκις ἓν καὶ μεταποιοῦντος ἠκροάσατο. Ἠνείχετο δὲ καὶ τοὺς λογισμούς, ἀναφερόντων τῶν [ἐν] ἐκείνοις παραμενόντων, καὶ τῆς ἀκριβείας ἐπεμελεῖτο λέγων, ἕως ἂν μὴ φιλοσοφῶσιν, ἔχειν αὐτοὺς δεῖν τὰς κτήσεις καὶ τὰς προσόδους ἀνεπάφους τε καὶ σῳζομένας. [...] Ἦν δὲ καὶ πρᾶος καὶ πᾶσιν ἐκκείμενος τοῖς ὁπωσοῦν πρὸς αὐτὸν συνήθειαν ἐσχηκόσι. Διὸ εἴκοσι καὶ ἓξ ἐτῶν ὅλων ἐν τῇ Ῥώμῃ διατρίψας καὶ πλείστοις διαιτήσας τὰς πρὸς ἀλλήλους ἀμφισβητήσεις οὐδένα τῶν πολιτικῶν ἐχθρόν ποτε ἔσχε. Greek text and English translation in Porphyry, *On the life of Plotinus and the order of his books*, pp. 30–33.

[34] Plotinus' role as arbitrator nuances Meredith's comments (p. 186) about the philosopher's lack of political concern: his interest in politics is shown by his proposal to found a city ruled by philosophers called Platonopolis (*The Life of Plotinus*, 12).

[35] Porphyry, *The Life of Plotinus*, 9. 16–17. Greek text and English translation in Porphyry, *On the life of Plotinus and the order of his books*, pp. 30–31.

contemplative life and the practice of virtue.³⁶ The practical dimension of the ideal life exemplified by Plotinus in this text does not stand in contradiction with the pre-eminence of theory in the life of the mind. In a chapter almost entirely devoted to Plotinus' practical activities, Porphyry does not neglect to reiterate the philosopher's unceasing contemplation to show that contemplative and practical life are closely interrelated: "Yet, though he shielded so many from the worries and cares of ordinary life, he never, while awake, relaxed his intent concentration upon the intellect."³⁷ This synthetic sentence echoes chapter 8, where the double aspect—contemplative and active at the same time—of the ideal life is summarized as follows: "In this way he was present at once to himself and to others."³⁸ Continuously turned towards himself (ἑαυτῷ) and towards the Intellect (πρὸς τὸν νοῦν), Plotinus is also turned towards others (τοῖς ἄλλοις) in everyday praxis. The active and the contemplative life are compatible, and the practical life should not be excluded from the philosopher's ideal lifestyle.

Gregory of Nyssa, *The Life of Macrina*

Gregory of Nyssa (c. 330–c. 395 AD) wrote *The Life of Macrina* at the end of the fourth century, sometime in 381 or 382–383. It is a letter narrating the life of Gregory's sister Macrina who died a few years earlier.³⁹ The addressee of the letter is a monk named Olympius, and the text was probably meant to his monastic community. Letters were rarely private in Late Antiquity, and were often read in public, particularly in monasteries.⁴⁰ At the time of writing, Gregory was bishop of Nyssa, thus in a legitimate position to give advice to a monk and to promote Christian perfection in a monastic

---

36 On the coexistence of the different degrees of virtue and the double dimension of the sage's life, see Plotinus, *Enneads* I 2 (19) 7. 13–21. On the link between this passage from the *Enneads* and *The Life of Plotinus*, see Linguiti, pp. 188–89. On the double aspect of the ideal way of life for Plotinus: Schniewind, *L'éthique du sage chez Plotin*, especially pp. 191–97.

37 Porphyry, *The Life of Plotinus*, 9. 16–18: "Καὶ ὅμως τοσούτοις ἐπαρκῶν τὰς εἰς τὸν βίον φροντίδας τε καὶ ἐπιμελείας τὴν πρὸς τὸν νοῦν τάσιν οὐδέποτ' ἂν ἐγρηγορότως ἐχάλασεν" Greek text and English translation in Porphyry, *On the life of Plotinus and the order of his books*, pp. 30–31.

38 Porphyry, *The Life of Plotinus*, 8. 19: "Συνῆν οὖν καὶ ἑαυτῷ ἅμα καὶ τοῖς ἄλλοις." Greek text and English translation in Porphyry, *On the life of Plotinus and the order of his books*, pp. 30–31.

39 Gregory of Nyssa, *The Life of Saint Macrina*, English translation by Anna M. Silvas, in *Macrina The Younger, Philosopher of God* (Turnhout: Brepols, 2008), pp. 109–48. For the Greek text, see Grégoire de Nysse, *Vie de sainte Macrine*, ed. and trans. by Pierre Maraval, Sources chrétiennes, 178 (Paris: Éditions du Cerf, 1971), pp. 136–266.

40 On the public dimension of letters in Late Antiquity, see Alan Cameron, "Were Pagans Afraid to Speak Their Minds in a Christian World? The Correspondence of Symmachus" in *Pagans and Christians in Late Antique Rome: Conflict, Competition, and Coexistence in the Fourth Century*, ed. Michele Renee Salzman, Marianne Sághy and Rita Lizzi Testa (Cambridge: Cambridge University Press, 2016), pp. 88–89.

community. *The Life of Macrina* is usually interpreted as an example of the ideal ascetic life.[41] Olympius might have triggered the genesis of the work:

> "Whereupon you were convinced that it would be a benefit if the story of her noble qualities were told, because then such a life would not be forgotten with the passage of time, and she who had raised herself by philosophy to the highest summit of human virtue would not have passed by ineffectually, veiled in silence. Accordingly, I thought it well to obey you and, in a few words, to tell her story as best as I can, in an unstudied and simple narrative.[42]

Gregory draws attention to the benefit (κέρδος) of his text for the reader: by recording the virtuous life of Macrina, the biographer not only commemorates her holy life, but also gives an example of the perfect life for others to imitate.[43] Narrating the life of the saints would be otherwise useless (ἀνωφελής). Does the *Life of Macrina* argue for the double aspect of contemplation and action as did the *Life of Plotinus*?

Gregory's account of Macrina's life begins with her birth and education,[44] and continues with her choice to remain a virgin.[45] Dedicating her life to God, Macrina nonetheless decides to stay with her mother and take care of her until her death.[46] She makes a monastery out of their villa and works with her hands for the household. Thus summarized, Macrina's life reveals the duality of the contemplative and the active life: turned towards God, she lives in constant contemplation and prayer, but nonetheless

---

[41] On biographical discourse as a way to present an example of the good way of life, see Derek Krueger, 'Writing and the Liturgy of Memory in Gregory of Nyssa's *Life of Macrina*', *Journal of Early Christian Studies* 8 (2000), pp. 483–510. About Macrina's life as a model of the ascetic life, see also Arnaldo Momigliano, 'The *Life of St. Macrina* by Gregory of Nyssa', in *Ottavo contributo alla storia degli studi classici e del mondo antico*, ed. Arnaldo Momigliano, (Roma: Edizioni di Storia e Letteratura, 1987), p. 345; Susanna Elm, '*Virgins of God': The Making of Asceticism in Late Antiquity*, (Oxford: Oxford University Press, 1994), p. 39 and Williams, p. 59. On the ideal way of life presented by Gregory of Nyssa, see Pierre Maraval, 'Introduction', in Grégoire de Nysse, *Vie de sainte Macrine*, pp. 90–103 and Elm, pp. 39–47 and 78–102.

[42] Gregory of Nyssa, *The Life of Macrina*, 1.5, pp. 110–11. Greek original Grégoire de Nysse, *Vie de sainte Macrine*, 1. 24–31, pp. 140–43 : Ἐπεὶ οὖν ἐδοκίμασας φέρειν τι κέρδος τὴν τῶν ἀγαθῶν ἱστορίαν, ὡς ἂν μὴ λάθοι τὸν μετὰ ταῦτα χρόνον ὁ τοιοῦτος βίος μηδὲ ἀνωφελὴς παραδράμοι διὰ σιωπῆς συγκαλυφθεῖσα ἡ πρὸς τὸν ἀκρότατον τῆς ἀνθρωπίνης ἀρετῆς ὅρον ἑαυτὴν διὰ φιλοσοφίας ἐπάρασα, καλῶς ἔχειν ᾠήθην σοί τε πεισθῆναι καὶ δι' ὀλίγων, ὡς ἂν οἷός τε ὦ, τὰ κατ' αὐτὴν ἱστορῆσαι ἐν ἀκατασκεύῳ τε καὶ ἁπλῷ διηγήματι.

[43] In his *Life of Moses*, I. 13, Gregory explicitly justifies his use of biographical discourse by stating that the narration of virtuous lives gives the reader an example to imitate. According to P. Maraval, Grégoire de Nysse, *Vie de sainte Macrine*, p. 141, footnote 6, this is a literary *topos* used by Gregory in other biographical texts as well.

[44] Gregory of Nyssa, *The Life of Macrina*, 2–4, pp. 111–14.

[45] Gregory of Nyssa, *The Life of Macrina*, 5–6, pp. 114–16.

[46] Gregory of Nyssa, *The Life of Macrina*, 7, pp. 116–17.

stays in contact with the temporal world, in which she never stops working with her hands or caring for others.

Contemplative life: turning to God

The protagonist of the *Life of Macrina* is an ascetic woman devoted to contemplation, singing hymns, and prayer[47]. As a child, Macrina recites Psalms all day long, her daily life is already punctuated by contemplative activities:

> "Indeed there was nothing whatever of the Psalter that she did not know, since she recited each part of the psalmody at its own proper time. When she rose from bed, or began her duties or rested from them, or sat down to eat or retired from table, when she went to bed or rose from it for prayers, she kept up the psalmody wherever she went, like a good travelling companion that never left her at any time."[48]

The anecdote from Macrina's childhood prefigures her contemplative life, first characterized by constant prayer, which is one of the three dimensions of monastic perfection. Prayer gives rhythm to her actions until the end of her life.[49] Combined with prayer and hymn singing, ontemplation is an important aspect of Christian perfection.[50] When comparing Macrina to Job, for example, Gregory applauds on her way of dealing with pain through contemplation: "It was some such case that I saw in the great Macrina. Fever was consuming her vital force and impelling her towards death, yet she refreshed her body as with some kind of dew, and so kept her mind unimpaired in the contemplation of the higher things, in no way hindered by her great weakness."[51]

---

[47] The three main contemplative activities of the ideal monastic life: *The Life of Macrina*, 13.5, pp. 121–22.

[48] Gregory of Nyssa, *The Life of Macrina*, 4.3, pp. 113–14. Grégoire de Nysse, *Vie de sainte Macrine*, 3. 19–26, p. 150 : Ἀλλὰ καὶ τῆς ψαλμῳδουμένης γραφῆς οὐδ' ὁτιοῦν ἠγνόει καιροῖς ἰδίοις ἕκαστον μέρος τῆς ψαλμῳδίας διεξιοῦσα τῆς τε κοίτης διανισταμένη καὶ τῶν σπουδαίων ἁπτομένη τε καὶ ἀναπαυομένη καὶ προσιεμένη τροφὴν καὶ ἀναχωροῦσα τραπέζης καὶ ἐπὶ κοίτην ἰοῦσα καὶ εἰς προσευχὰς διανισταμένη, πανταχοῦ τὴν ψαλμῳδίαν εἶχεν οἷόν τινα σύνοδον ἀγαθὴν μηδενὸς ἀπολιμπανομένην χρόνου.

[49] According to Krueger, 'Writing and the Liturgy of Memory', p. 487, Macrina's life is a prayer and her daily actions are part of a liturgy.

[50] For Meredith, pp. 188–92), contemplation is only one of the three dimensions of the perfect life of virtue exemplified by Macrina. Elm, p. 99 however argues that the contemplative life is the pre-eminent dimension of the ideal way of life exemplified by Macrina. My examples support this opinion.

[51] Gregory of Nyssa, *The Life of Macrina*, 20.4, p. 129, Greek text in Grégoire de Nysse, *Vie de sainte Macrine*, 18. 7–12, p. 200: τοιοῦτόν τι καὶ ἐπὶ τῆς μεγάλης ἑώρων ἐκείνης, τοῦ πυρετοῦ πᾶσαν τὴν δύναμιν αὐτῆς καταφρύγοντος καὶ πρὸς τὸν θάνατον συνελαύνοντος, καθάπερ δρόσῳ τινὶ τὸ σῶμα ἑαυτῆς ἀναψύχουσα, οὕτως ἀπαραπόδιστον εἶχεν ἐν τῇ περὶ τῶν ὑψηλῶν θεωρίᾳ τὸν νοῦν, οὐδὲν ὑπὸ τῆς τοσαύτης ἀρρωστίας παραβλαπτόμενον.

Her ability to forget physical pain preceding her death derives from contemplation of higher things (ἐν τῇ περὶ τῶν ὑψηλῶν θεωρίᾳ). Macrina is like a Platonic philosopher: the vocabulary used by Gregory (θεωρίᾳ; νοῦν) and the idea of a contemplative life exceeding every other aspects of daily life evoke the Platonic distinction between the intelligible and the (despised or mistrusted) sensory world.[52] The ascetic life that Macrina lived together with her mother is primarily contemplative that seems to reject any concern for earthly matters:

> "Such was the order of their life, so lofty their philosophy and the dignity of their way of life as they lived it day and night, that it surpasses description in words. For just as souls freed by death from their bodies are freed at the same time from the cares of this life, so too their life was far removed from these things, divorced from all earthly vanities and attuned to the imitation of the angelic life. [...] They were not occupied with the pursuits of this life, or rather, not preoccupied, but solely with meditation on divine things, unceasing prayer and uninterrupted hymnody, which was extended evenly over the whole time, throughout the night and day, so that it became for them both work and respite from work."[53]

The three aspects of Macrina's and Emmelia's contemplative life are constant prayer (τὸ τῆς προσευχῆς ἀδιάλειπτον), continuous hymnody (ἡ ἄπαυστος ὑμνῳδία), and contemplation of the divine (ἡ τῶν θείων μελέτη). Once again, it is important to stress that contemplative activity is continuous (ἀδιάλειπτον, ἄπαυστος). It does not stop day or night (διὰ νυκτὸς καὶ ἡμέρας πάσης). It is the primary aspect of Christian perfection. For Gregory, the contemplative life is both work and respite from work (ὥστε αὐταῖς καὶ ἔργον εἶναι τοῦτο καὶ ἔργου ἀνάπαυσιν), thus encompassing life.[54]

---

[52] On the platonic aspects of Gregory's description of Macrina's contemplative life, see Grégoire de Nysse, *Vie de sainte Macrine*, pp. 96–97, especially footnote 2, p. 96. On Macrina's life as an example of the philosophical, and therefore contemplative, life, see Elm, pp. 39, 44–45 and 99.

[53] Gregory of Nyssa, *The Life of Macrina*, 13.3 and 13.5, pp. 121–22, original Greek: Grégoire de Nysse, *Vie de sainte Macrine*, 11. 13–20 and 27–33, pp. 176–78: Καὶ τοιαύτη τις ἦν ἡ τοῦ βίου τάξις καὶ τοσοῦτον τὸ ὕψος τῆς φιλοσοφίας καὶ ἡ σεμνὴ τῆς ζωῆς πολιτεία ἐν τῇ καθ' ἡμέραν τε καὶ νύκτα διαγωγῇ, ὡς ὑπερβαίνειν τὴν ἐκ τῶν λόγων ὑπογραφήν. Καθάπερ γὰρ αἱ διὰ θανάτου τῶν σωμάτων ἐκλυθεῖσαι ψυχαὶ καὶ τῶν κατὰ τὸν βίον τοῦτον μεριμνῶν συνεκλύονται, οὕτως κεχώριστο αὐτῶν ἡ ζωὴ καὶ ἀπῴκιστο πάσης βιωτικῆς ματαιότητος καὶ πρὸς μίμησιν τῆς τῶν ἀγγέλων διαγωγῆς ἐρρυθμίζετο. [...] ἔργον δὲ τῶν μὲν κατὰ τὴν ζωὴν ταύτην σπουδαζομένων οὐδέν, ὅτι μὴ πάρεργον, μόνη δὲ ἡ τῶν θείων μελέτη καὶ τὸ τῆς προσευχῆς ἀδιάλειπτον καὶ ἡ ἄπαυστος ὑμνῳδία, κατὰ τὸ ἴσον παντὶ συμπαρατεινομένη τῷ χρόνῳ διὰ νυκτὸς καὶ ἡμέρας πάσης, ὥστε αὐταῖς καὶ ἔργον εἶναι τοῦτο καὶ ἔργου ἀνάπαυσιν.

[54] Krueger, 'Writing and the Liturgy of Memory', p. 487 considers manual work a form of prayer.

It seems from the reading of this passage that the only valuable work (ἔργον) of the Christian saint is her contemplation, and that manual work or any other earthly occupation (πάσης βιωτικῆς ματαιότητος) are vain. *The Life of Macrina*, however, excludes reductionist interpretations. Constant prayer and contemplation embrace all other necessary activities of daily life, but do not exclude them. Scholars concur that manual work and earthly concerns are accessory or subordinate (πάρεργον) compared to contemplative activities, the only real work (ἔργον).[55] Consequently, passages in *The Life of Macrina* that refer to her constant prayer and contemplation are often highlighted as a proof of the contemplative aspect of the ideal way of life at the expense of the practical aspect of the ascetic lifestyle.[56] Thus, the passage is interpreted as emphasizing the contemplative dimension of Macrina's ideal monastic life.[57] Macrina, however, worked with her own hands from childhood to death: the active part of her life is just as significant as the contemplative. She lived a contemplative life centered on God, without neglecting the active life, working and caring for her mother and for her neighbors.

Practical life: Manual work and care for others

The first chapters of *The Life of Macrina* are particularly interesting in regard to the practical aspect of the ideal ascetic life, because they describe Macrina living with her mother and thus taking care of her everyday needs.[58] After a failed marriage, Macrina decides to live alone, devoting herself to God.[59] At the same time, however, she devotes her life to her mother.[60] In choosing to offer herself to God, she lives a contemplative life, in working constantly to take care of her mother, she lives a practical life:[61]

---

[55] For Maraval, 'Introduction', p. 101, manual work, virginity, solitude, and poverty are not valuable in themselves, but only as a way to achieve contemplation. Meredith, p. 192 claims that prayer is more central to *The Life of Macrina* than work. Elm, p. 99 describes manual work as a preparation for contemplation, as does A. M. Silvas, Gregory of Nyssa, *The Life of Macrina*, p. 121, footnote 54.

[56] Peter Brown, *The Body and Society*, (New York: Columbia University Press, 1988), pp. 259–304, especially pp. 263, 272 and 298. Brown refers to Macrina as an example of women ascetics who chose to devote their life to the divine by avoiding marriage, childbirth, and bereavement, three distinctive aspects of women's lives. On the avoidance of social and domestic constraints by women ascetics, see Gillian Clark, 'Women and Asceticism in Late Antiquity: The Refusal of Gender and Status', in *The Ascetic Dimension in Religious Life and Culture*, ed. Vincent L. Wimbush and Richard Valantasis (New York: Oxford University Press, 1995), pp. 34–39.

[57] Maraval, 'Introduction', p. 101 quotes this passage in reference to Macrina's contemplative way of life.

[58] Gregory of Nyssa, *The Life of Macrina*, 1–15.

[59] Gregory of Nyssa, *The Life of Macrina*, 6.1, p. 115: 'She resolved from then on to remain by herself.' On the traditional meaning of this expression (ἐφ' ἑαυτῆς) indicating solitary, philosophical life, see Elm, pp. 44–45.

[60] Gregory of Nyssa, *The Life of Macrina*, 7.1, p. 116: 'She determined on one safeguard for her noble decision: never to be separated from her own mother, not even for a moment of time.'

[61] For Arnaldo Momigliano, pp. 339 and 342–43, Macrina is the example of the active saint, firmly rooted in everyday life. M. Williams, p. 81 is on the same opinion. For S. Elm, pp. 46, 82–83 and 125, manual work is

"For the mother looked after the girl's soul, and she her mother's body, fulfilling in all other respects the required service, even to frequently preparing the bread for her mother with her own hands. Not that she made this her primary occupation. But when she had lent her hands to the mystic services—deeming that the zeal for this matter befitted the purpose of her life—from what was left over she furnished food for her mother by her own labours. This was not all, but she also helped manage all her mother's pressing responsibilities. [...] In all these affairs she shared her mother's toils, dividing the responsibilities with her and lightening the heavy load of her sorrows."[62]

Macrina is described as taking great care of her mother, sharing her worries and cares (τὰς φροντίδας), but also making bread for her with her own hands. A possible interpretation of this passage is that Macrina used to make bread for liturgical purposes, and then would make bread for her mother.[63] It is to be noted that manual work and the making of bread in particular were deemed lowly activities in Antiquity, reserved to slaves.[64] Making bread with her own hands (τῷ ταῖς ἰδίαις χερσὶ), Macrina deliberately opts for manual work and active life. Her primary occupation is turned towards God and the contemplative life, materialized here by her preparation and participation in the Eucharist, but manual work and daily chores are presented as an important part of her life.

Macrina's attitude towards her mother echoes Plotinus's attitude towards the orphans. Apart from contemplation, both philopsophers care for others, and both enter the active life because of this care—by making bread for others, taking care of their accounts, or sharing their daily cares (τὰς φροντίδας) in general. Again, the example given here by Gregory suggests that while liturgical purposes and prayer should come first, there is no contradiction between the contemplative and the practical life. On the

---

an integral part of the ascetic way of life exemplified by Macrina. Beside prayer, poverty and frugality, manual work is an external indicator of the holiness of a life.

[62] Gregory of Nyssa, *The Life of Macrina*, 7. 2–4, pp. 116–17 ; Grégoire de Nysse, *Vie de sainte Macrine*, 5. 27–37 and 41–43, p. 158 : Ἡ μὲν γὰρ τὴν ψυχὴν τῆς νέας, ἡ δὲ τὸ σῶμα τῆς μητρὸς ἐθεράπευεν, ἔν τε τοῖς ἄλλοις πᾶσι τὴν ἐπιζητουμένην ὑπηρεσίαν ἀποπληροῦσα καὶ ἐν τῷ ταῖς ἰδίαις χερσὶ πολλάκις τῇ μητρὶ παρασκευάζειν τὸν ἄρτον· ὅπερ οὐ κατὰ τὸ προηγούμενον αὐτῇ διεσπουδάσθη, ἀλλ' ἐπειδὴ ταῖς μυστικαῖς ὑπηρεσίαις τὰς χεῖρας ἑαυτῆς ἔχρησε, πρέπειν ἡγησαμένη τῷ ἐπιτηδεύματι τοῦ βίου τὴν περὶ τοῦτο σπουδὴν ἐκ τοῦ περιόντος τῇ μητρὶ παρεχορήγει τὴν ἐκ τῶν οἰκείων πόνων τροφήν. Καὶ οὐ ταῦτα μόνον, ἀλλὰ καὶ πᾶσαν αὐτὴ συνδιῳκονόμει τὴν ἐπικειμένην φροντίδα· [...] ἐν πᾶσι τούτοις κοινωνὸς ἦν τῇ μητρὶ τῶν πόνων συνδιαιρουμένη τὰς φροντίδας καὶ τὸ βαρὺ τῶν ἀλγηδόνων ἐπικουφίζουσα.

[63] On the three different interpretations of this passage, see Gregory of Nyssa, *The Life of Macrina*, pp. 116–17, footnote 35.

[64] Elm, pp. 46 and 87, and Grégoire de Nysse, *Vie de sainte Macrine*, p. 48–49, especially footnote 1, p. 49.

contrary, the manual work and daily care for her mother and, later, the whole monastic community, are appropriate to the best way of life.[65] And indeed, in a biographical discourse inserted in Gregory's biographical text,[66] Macrina herself recounts her life to Gregory, telling her brother of the joy she had because she had worked all her life:

> "Under God's provision, her life became such that her hands never ceased to be active in respect to the commandment. Macrina neither looked for help from men, nor did human benefit give her a pretext for a comfortable life. Yet neither were those who petitioned her ever turned away, nor did she ever look for benefactors, since God, by his secret blessings, caused the modest resources of her works to grow as from seeds into abundant fruit."[67]

The stress laid on manual work and Macrina's care for others goes beyond the first fifteen chapters and includes her whole life, before and after her mother's death. This passage emphasizes the necessity of work, accepted by Macrina as a commandment coming from God, but also as a grace.[68] Gregory's narration of his sister's life emphasizes not only the contemplative life of the Christian saint, a life turned towards God, but also its complement, the practical life, the importance of which Macrina reveals here.

Conclusion: Practical aspects of the ideal life in Late Antiquity

The conflict between pagans and Christians in Late Antiquity ceased to dominate historiography as recent scholarship broke with oversimplified interpretations. The complex relations between different religions and philosophies in the Roman Empire require more nuanced approaches that enables scholars to discover hitherto hidden, multifaceted aspects of the historical coexistence of pagans and Christians. One of these

---

[65] On Macrina's particular dedication towards her mother and her community, as a 'mother, father, teacher and guide' (pp. 101–102), see Elm, pp. 79, 95 and 101–02. On her familial commitment, see Williams, p. 68.

[66] Gregory of Nyssa, *The Life of Macrina*, 22.1, p. 130: „When we again came before her eyes—for she did not allow us to spend too leisurely a time by ourselves—she began to recall the events of her youth, describing it all in order as in a narrative, what she could remember of the life of our parents, and what happened before and after my birth."

[67] Gregory of Nyssa, *The Life of Macrina*, 22.5–6, pp. 130–31; Grégoire de Nysse, *Vie de sainte Macrine*, 20. 23–31, p. 208 τὸν δὲ βίον αὐτῇ τοιοῦτον ἐκ τῆς τοῦ θεοῦ χορηγίας γενέσθαι, ὡς μηδέποτε λῆξαι τὰς χεῖρας εἰς ἐντολὴν ἐνεργούσας μηδὲ πρὸς ἄνθρωπον ἀποβλέψαι ποτὲ μηδὲ διά τινος ἀνθρωπίνης εὐεργεσίας γενέσθαι αὐτῇ τὰς πρὸς τὴν εὐσχήμονα διαγωγὴν ἀφορμάς, ἀλλὰ μήτε τοὺς αἰτοῦντας ἀποστραφῆναι μήτε τοὺς διδόντας ἐπιζητῆσαι, λεληθότως τοῦ θεοῦ καθάπερ τινὰ σπέρματα τὰς βραχείας ἐκ τῶν ἔργων ἀφορμὰς εἰς πολύχουν καρπὸν ταῖς εὐλογίαις ἐπαύξοντος

[68] Psalms 118. 48 and Genesis 3. 17–19.

is a common reflection on the double nature—active and contemplative—of the ideal life. In *The Life of Plotinus* and the *Life of Macrina*, the good and happy life is a life turned towards oneself and the divine, but also towards others. Contemplation, even if central to both the philosopher and the saint, does not mean withdrawal from the world. Pagan philosopher and Christian saint alike combine in their everyday life contemplation and activity. Pagan and Christian biographical discourse reveal that Platonic sages did not depreciate active life in the sensory world—social concern and practical activities were subjects to be taken seriously as part of the ideal way of life—and that Christian ascetics did manual work beside contemplative activities. Biographies describe the daily lives of the philosopher and the saint in detail, down to its most mundane aspects. Down-to-earth, concrete examples of the biographical discourse allow pagan and Christian authors to refine thinking on the dual nature of the ideal life. If the preeminence of contemplation is undeniable in pagan and Christian theory, biographical discourse presents the ideal life in a more nuanced way and shows practical activity in a more favourable light.[69] The pagan *Life of Plotinus* and the Christian *Life of Macrina* both reserve an important place to involvement in quotidian chores when presenting the dual—active and contemplative—nature of the life of the philosopher and the saint. Thus, the link between the two sides of the perfect life was established well before the rise of the monk-bishop[70] and Eugippius' sixth-century *Life of Severinus of Noricum*.[71]

---

[69] For the combination of the active and contemplative in the ideal life, see Francis Gautier, 'L'idéal de vie mixte de Grégoire de Nazianze', in *Vie active et vie contemplative au Moyen-Age et au seuil de la Renaissance*, pp. 67–88.

[70] Andrea Sterk, *Renouncing the World Yet Leading the Church: The Monk-Bishop in Late Antiquity*. Cambridge, Mass.: Harvard University Press, 2004. Marianne Sághy, "Should Monks become Bishops? A Debate on Asceticism and Episcopal Power in the Fourth-Century West."*Church, Society, Monasticism*. Roma: Pontificio Ateneo S. Anselmo, 2008: 39–45.

[71] Eugippe, *Vita Severini*. Ed. Philippe Régerat. (Paris: Les Éditions du Cerf, 1991); *Eugippius und Severin. Der Autor, der Text und der Heilige*. Szerk. Walter Pohl-Max Diesenberger. (Wien: Verlag der Österreichischen Akademie der Wissenschaften, 2001).
In this biographical text, Eugippius explicitly describes an ideal way of life in which the necessity of active life is accepted and recognized.

RELIGIOUS PROFILING IN THE *MIRACLES OF THECLA*

Linda Honey

Examining the socio-religious relations as revealed in healing accounts from the fifth-century *Miracles of Thecla*,[1] this paper argues that the terms "pagan," "Christian," and "Jew" were recognized, accepted, and actively employed in Seleucia of Rough Cilicia and the surrounding region in Late Antiquity and are not, as some would argue, a result of historiographical construction.

Thecla, a young Iconian woman of noble birth, thought to have been converted by Saint Paul during his first missionary journey, shortly after her conversion and under divine imperative, traveled to Seleucia of Rough Cilicia (present day Silifke, Turkey), a city in which the legacy of Greece and Rome united with Asia Minor in a kaleidoscope of peoples and races resulting in a unique religious and cultural milieu.[2] Thecla took up residence a short distance from the bustling seaport city, spending the rest of her life preaching, instructing, baptizing, performing miracles, and ministering to the needs of the people (*Life* 28). Others joined her and a Christian community, Hagia Thecla, took root.[3]

---

[1] All translations from the *Miracles of Thecla* (hereafter, the *Miracles*) and from *The Virtuous Deeds of the Holy Apostle and Protomartyr Thecla in the Myrtle Wood* (hereafter, *Myrtle Wood*) are my own from the Greek texts provided by G. Dagron, *Vie et miracles de Sainte Thècle. Texte grec, traduction et commentaire*. Subsidia Hagiographica 62. (Brussels: Société des Bollandistes, 1978). The Greek text of the *Myrtle Wood* is contained in Dagron, *Vie et miracles de Sainte Thècle* , Appendix, 216–21. All biblical quotations are taken from the New American Standard Version, First Edition. For a detailed study on Thecla and a complete translation of the *Miracles*, see Linda Honey, "Thecla: Text and Context with a First English Translation of the *Miracles*" (doctoral dissertation, University of Calgary, 2011) Ann Arbor, MI: ProQuest/UMI.

[2] Mercedes Lopéz-Salvá, "Los *Thaumata* de Basilio de Seleucia," *Cuadernos de Filologia Clásica* 3 (1972), p. 217 and 219 : Seleucia was a *mosaico de culturas, razas, y costumbres*.

[3] Initially, it was women who joined Thecla, however, the community grew to include both men and women. Egeria, upon her visit to Hagia Thecla (c. 381–84), records in her *Itinerarium* that the community was composed of a great number of women and men: "*monasteria sine numero vivorum ac mulierum*" and "*visis etiam sanctis monachis vel aputactitis tam viris quam feminis, qui ibi erant*." For Egeria's account, see *Itinerarium Egeriae*, ed. by A. Francheschini and R. Webber, *Itineraria et alia Geographica. Itinerarium Hierosolymitana. Inter-*

Over time, the site achieved city-like proportions.[4] From the fifth- to the mid-seventh century, Hagia Thecla flourished as a major pilgrimage center. The community of Hagia Thecla claimed witness to countless posthumous miracles of the saint.[5]

In the mid-fifth century, one of Thecla's devotees, a local rhetor, whose name may have suffered *damnatio* or was simply lost with time,[6] and to whom, hereafter, we shall refer as Pseudo-Basil, was unabashedly desirous of climbing the ecclesiastical *cursus honorum*. He sought to gain distinction by styling himself as the personal biographer of Saint Thecla as well as the authorized archivist of her miracles. Pseudo-Basil invested up to forty years of his life investigating Thecla's thaumaturgical activity. After interviewing 'reliable' individuals, both recipients of and witnesses to the miracles, he documented and recorded his findings, finally compiling them in a forty-six miracle corpus, commonly known as the *Miracles of Thecla* that function as a companion piece to the *Life of Thecla*, which itself is an amplification of the much earlier *Acts of Thecla* adapted and recast by Pseudo-Basil as a foundation legend for Seleucia.[7] Throughout the remainder of this paper, I shall refer to these texts simply as the *Miracles*, the *Life*, and the *Acts*, respectively, along with the *Myrtle Wood*.[8]

Pseudo-Basil presented his work as having been authorized by the saint herself.[9] He underscored his claim to "authorization" by noting both Thecla's assistance with and her expressed approval for his work (*Mir.* 41). According to Pseudo-Basil, so great was Thecla's interest in his project, that at one juncture, when his enthusiasm had con-

---

  aria Roman. Geographica. Corpus Christianorum, Series Latina 175, ed. by P. Geyer et al. (Turnhout: Brepols, 1965), 37–90, (section 66. 23. 12, 32).

[4] *Life of Thecla*, Dagron's edition, 28. 15–16.

[5] According to Pseudo-Basil (*Mir.* 10. 31-2*)*, the number of Thecla's miracles, like snowflakes, is unfathomable (ἀνεξρεύοντος). His observation evokes that of the Apostle John in regard to the activity of Christ (John 21. 25).

[6] See Derek Krueger, *Writing and Holiness: The Practice of Authorship in the Early Christian East* (Philadelphia, PA: Divinations, 2004), 92; Honey (2011), 353.

[7] Dagron (17–19) suggests a series of redactions for the *Miracles* from approximately 430 to 470. These dates roughly correspond to the tenures of four Seleucian bishops who all are mentioned in the text. A summary of Dagron's argument is provided by S. F. Johnson, *The Life and Miracles of Thecla. A Literary Study.* Hellenic Studies Series 13. (Cambridge, MA: Harvard University Press, 2006), 5–6, n. 18. Scholarly consensus suggests a tentative *terminus ante quem* in that there is no mention of the benefactions by Zeno to the *temenos* in 476. An even earlier *ante quem* is suggested for the work in that several ancient historians including Malalas, note that the sophist Isokasios—who is cited in *Mir.* 39 as having rejected conversion—in 467 avoided punishment by submitting himself to baptism. See slso Lopéz-Salvá, 222, and Honey (2011), 16–17.

[8] For the *Myrtle Wood*, see n. 1 above. All line numbering used in this study for the *Life*, the *Miracles*, and the *Myrtle Wood* follow that of Dagron's edition.

[9] Pseudo-Basil may have been motivated by a subtle battle for textual supremacy with both the traditional *Acta* and a poem about Thecla, composed by his arch nemesis, Bishop Basil of Seleucia. The poem, no longer extant, was catalogued by Photius, (*Bibl.* 168) in the tenth-century codex *Florentinus Laurentinus pluteus*. See J. M. Tevel, "The Manuscript Tradition of Basilius of Seleucia and some Deductions Concerning the Early Development of Liturgical Collections," in *Studia Patristica* 20, ed. by E. Livingstone, (Leuven: Peeters, 1989), 369–401.

fessedly waned and he found himself yawning over his writing tablet, the saint appeared to him, expressing her delight in his work and urging the completion of the collection (*Mir.* 31). His fatigue may well be attributed to his unflagging attention to validation and verification. Pseudo-Basil explicitly employed a precise research methodology—choosing to anchor his findings with specific "people, places, and names" (προσώπων, τόπων, and ὀνομάτων)

> "...in order that it might not be possible for those who come across them [the miracles]to disbelieve...but rather that they might harvest belief from the miracles being performed now and from those already performed....For this reason, we have mentioned persons, places, and names so that our readers (ἐντυγχάνοντας) will ....be able to have close at hand <the evidence> and to examine for themselves the truth of what we have said."[10]

For the most part, Pseudo-Basil restricted his collection to miracles performed during or close to his own day and to those that occurred geographically "nearby." He may be regarded as a knowledgeable on-the-ground reporter.

The arena of Thecla's activity, as identified in the *Miracles,* stretched north into the Isaurian hinterland; south, to Cyprus; as far west as Selinous; and east to Aigai; symbolically imprinting the *signum crucis* as a seal for Christ on the Rough Cilician landscape and delineating Thecla's divinely-appointed territory (χώρα).[11]

Despite the author's claim to accuracy, the reception of the *Life* and *Miracles* was unremarkable. There are only four known manuscripts of the *Miracles,* none of which stand independently from the extant manuscripts of the *Life* of which there are but twelve. Several factors may be attributed to its poor reception, two of which—the distinctly regional character of the work and its unusual degree of religious tolerance often noted by scholars—make the text all the more useful a resource for our study.[12] Precisely *because* of these characteristics, we can be all the more confident that the text paints a reliable picture of this specific region in regard to social relations and one less

---

[10] *Mir.* prologue, 15–21.

[11] For a map of Thecla's activity and a detailed discussion of her territory, see Linda Honey, "Topography in the *Miracles of Thecla:* reconfiguring Rough Cilicia," in *Rough Cilicia: New Historical and Archaeological Approaches.* Proceedings of an International Conference held at Lincoln, Nebraska, October 2007, ed. by Michael C. Hoff and Rhys F. Townsend (Oxford and Oakville, CT: Oxbow Books, 2013), 252–259.

[12] Lopéz-Salvá, 223 describes the degree of religious tolerance displayed in the *Miracles* as "totalmente excepcional en este género literario and that "la inusitada tolerancia religiosa que vemos en los Thaumata a diferencia de otras colecciones cristianas de milagros." For a detailed discussion of the reception of the text, see Honey (2011), 352–357.

likely skewed by religious polemic and also that information contained therein is a faithful expression of the author's perception of Seleucian society.

While Pseudo-Basil carefully crafted the *Miracles* to elicit wonder for the saint with an eye to the expansion of her cult,[13] the text also provides a window onto the quotidian concerns, especially those related to health, of this multi-ethnic, polytheistic region. In particular, the healing miracles provide insight into the sometimes volatile and often humorous socio-religious relations of Thecla's clientele.

There are eighteen healing miracles in the collection: one performed on behalf of an entire city and the rest for individuals among whom are numbered four women, eleven men, and two boys. There are no miracles performed for girls. Pseudo-Basil himself and Dexianos, a guardian of Thecla's *temenos*, are the recipients of healing on two different occasions. For twenty-six percent of those healed, information is not given as to their religious persuasion. Forty-seven percent of the healings were performed for those who were explicitly Christian. Four individuals, one woman and three men, were explicitly not Christians when they experienced healing: Hypsistios, Aba, and the two sophists, Isokasios and Aretarchos.[14] The first two received both physical and spiritual healing while the sophists rejected conversion.[15] Faith healing, such as occurred at Hagia Thecla, was but one of many health care options for individuals in Late Antiquity.

Fifth-century health care was multifaceted, comprised of several different branches that variously interacted with one another. Hippocratic (scientific) medicine and temple ('sacerdotal') medicine are two branches that enjoyed a respectful and symbiotic relationship in that they held complementary ideologies. Edelstein and Edelstein describe the two as "friendly allies."[16] But neither was Christianity hostile to Hippocratic medicine.[17] In fact, Hippocratic medicine played an important role both in the

---

[13] This is a primary premise of Johnson, intro. esp. 13. The argument is further substantiated by the frequency (over one hundred fifty times) that θαῦμα the word for *wonder* or *marvel* and its cognates are used in the *Miracles*.

[14] See *Mir.* 14, 18, 39, and 40, respectively. All four of these individuals were of high social standing. There is a general notion that the aristocratic class was resistant to religious change but, in our text, two of the four became Christians.

[15] See n. 6 above.

[16] E. J. Edelstein and L. Edelstein, *Asclepius: Collection and Interpretation of the Testimonies.* 2 vols. (Baltimore, MD: Johns Hopkins University Press, 1945; repr. 1998), vol. 2, 139.

[17] See D. W. Amundsen, "Medicine and Faith in Early Christianity," *Bulletin of the History of Medicine* 56 (1982), 326–50; and Vivian Nutton, 'From Galen to Alexander: Aspects of Medicine and Medical Practice in Late Antiquity', in *Symposium on Byzantine Medicine*, ed. by John Scarborough, *DOP* 38 (1984), 1–14. For a discussion of miracles, medicine, and incubation in Late Antiquity and of the individual healing miracles perfomed by Thecla, see Honey (2011), 286–349.

monastic medical care system and in Christian hospitals that emerged in Late Antiquity. Nevertheless, an inherent, *underlying* tension existed between Hippocratic medicine and Christianity because the latter emphasized Christ as the Ultimate Healer.[18]

Not surprisingly, the monastic medical care system also worked in cooperation with that of Christian faith healing with which it shared the same ideology. However, as attested in the *Miracles*, between temple ('sacerdotal') medicine and Christian faith healing there existed virulent antagonism and competition. Christian faith healing should not be understood as a derivative or a linear development of the former. Despite surface similarities between the two systems, between theurgy and thaumaturgy, there were great differences, and the enmity was palpable.

But, at times, the individual desperately in search of medical care disregarded these boundaries. It is in this quest for health that interaction between various socio-religious groups can be noted. Gary Vikan addresses the complexities and connections between the various aspects of late antique Graeco-Roman medicine with this insightful comment:

> "One's local bishop, town doctor, and neighborhood sorceress were almost certainly at odds…the patient, however, did not indulge in the luxury of subtle differentiations. If need be, he would call on all in one breath."[19]

As Kötting has succinctly observed, "It was a cure-seeking world."[20] That is precisely the world we enter upon reading the *Miracles*. A survey of the *Miracles* indicates that despite religious persuasion, people sought medical help from a wide range of health practitioners. According to the text, the medical community of Seleucia and its environs included doctors *(iatroi)*,[21] physicians of the school of Asclepius (*Mir.* 11.7,

---

[18] For example, see Cassidorus, *Instit.* 31. 1; Ecclesiasticus 38. 1–3; and St. Theodore of Sykeon, trans. by Elizabeth Dawes and Norman Baynes, *Three Byzantine Saints. Contemporary Biographies of St. Daniel the Stylite, St. Theodore of Sykeon and St. John the Almsgiver.* (Crestwood, NY: St. Vladimir's Seminary Press, 1977), 88–192 (182–83, section 146). Nutton (5) differentiates between the two, the peculiarly Christian type of healing and that of doctors: "This 'Christian healing' succeeded where the 'doctors' had failed, often over many years and at great expense; it was accessible to all; it was simple. It was a medicine of prayer and fasting, or of anointing and the laying on of hands."

[19] Gary Vikan, "Art, Medicine, and Magic in Early Byzantium," in: *Symposium on Byzantine Medicine*, ed. by John Scarborough. *DOP* 38 (1984), 65–86 (86).

[20] Bernhard Kötting, *Peregrinatio religiosa. Wallfahrten in der Antike und das Pilgerwesen in der alten Kirche.* (Münster: Regensberg, 1950), 316.

[21] For doctors, see *Mir.* 4. 34; 11. 10, 46; 12. 4, 9, 35; 14. 26; 23. 6; 24. 42; 25. 12; and 38. 4.

18.40 Ἀσκληπιάδες), the oracular *daimon* Sarpedon,[22] Jewish healers (ἰουδαίων) (*Mir.* 18.29), enchanters (ἐπαοιδῶν) (*Mir.* 18.29), menders (ἀκεσταῖς) of bodies (*Mir.* 25.7), and even menders of horses (20.28).[23]

The adaptability of patients from one type of health practitioner to another can be explained by Wolf's observation that syncretism occurs and should be expected among "first-order concerns" which he identifies as "traditional practices related to healing, death, and family, things that speak to common fears and concerns."[24] In regard to similarities between the various systems, Walton writes: "Who is to say whether the customs are 'heathen' or 'Christian'? They are neither; they are intensely human.[25]

The non-Christians, however, in our text seem to have exhausted other avenues of medical assistance before turning to Thecla for assistance which Pseudo-Basil portrays as a last ditch effort, even an act of desperation.[26] When a person passed into Thecla's sacred precinct *(temenos)*, s/he entered into the world of faith healing, a world that could only be entered by choice, however hesitant or reluctant that choice might be.

---

[22] According to Diodoros, Sarpedon was a chthonian hero especially associated with Apollo in Seleucia and its environs. Thecla's first act in the *Miracles* was to displace Sarpedon, the oracular *daimon* thought to occupy the mountain vastness outside Seleucia. Pseudo-Basil refers to him in *Life* 27 and *Mir.* 1, 11, 18, and 40. For further discussion in regard to Sarpedon's name and its variants and the development of his cult, see *Mir.* 1, 11, 18 and 40, trans. Honey (2011), 365–66, 378–80, 394–95, and 429–30 respectively; Dagron, pp. 83–88 and 91–94; Johnson, 123–25; Lopéz-Salvá, 260–63, and H. W. Parke, *The Oracles of Apollo in Asia Minor* (London: CroomHelm, 1995), 194–96.

[23] The Asclepiades are thought to have been itinerant medical practitioners who claimed descent from Asclepius. See Darrel W. Amundsen and Gary B. Ferngren, "Medicine and Religion: Pre-Christian Antiquity," in: *Health/Medicine and the Faith Traditions: An Inquiry Into Religion and Medicine*, ed. by Martin E. Marty and Kenneth L. Vaux (Philadelphia, PA: Fortress Press, 1982), 53–92 (76–77); Dagron (93), describes the Jewish healers as those "qui sont sans doute des médecins, mais dont les pratiques gardent une certaine connotation religieuse." Primary source references to enchanters *qua* those engaged in song or poetry are generally nuance-free. See H. Remus, "Magic or Miracle? Some Second Century Instances." *The Second Century: A Journal of Early Christian Studies* 2 (1982), 127–56 (145–46). Socrates refers to respectable midwives who employ epodes during the birth of a child: Plato, *Theatetus* 149c–150a). When used negatively, as in the *Miracles*, the term refers to those who use incantations, spells, and chants.

[24] Wolf, as cited by T. E. Gregory, "The Survival of Paganism in Christian Greece," *American Journal of Philology* 107, no. 2 (1986) 229–242 (241–42).

[25] A. Walton, *The Cult of Asklepios*. (New York: Ginn & Co., 1894), 76.

[26] *Mir.* 11 provides an account of a young boy suffering from scrofula who had received no help from doctors. His pagan grandmother then invoked the *daimon* Sapedon on his behalf who disappointingly did not help either. Thecla, however, intervened and the boy was delivered from the malady. *Mir.* 23 relates the account of a manual laborer who had suffered with an eye disease resulting in blindness due to "the negligence or the incompetence of the doctors" and who finally implored Thecla with loud lamentations for help and was healed. Pseudo-Basil himself, in *Mir.* 12, was facing the amputation of a finger due to anthrax, the doctors' medications having already failed. Thecla ministered to him in a dream by night. The doctors arrived the next morning "with their scalpels in hand." Seeing the miraculous cure, they were amazed but a bit upset as well because they "went away unpaid" due to Thecla's ministrations! The inefficacy of doctors is a common *topos* in miracle collections of Late Antiquity.

It is important to note that the text is not primarily about healing nor is it primarily a collection of healing miracles. More than half of the miracles, fifty-four percent, address concerns other than health (e.g., prescient warning, restoration of stolen goods, protection of cities or individuals). Nevertheless, healing *is* the single, largest category of miracle in the text. We find the same phenomenon in the New Testament. Thecla's ministry echoes that of Christ. While Christ performed various types of miracles, the most numerous are those of healing.

The healings effected by Christ were done so to help suffering individuals and as a demonstration of His divine power. "Which is easier," He asks, "to say to the paralytic, "Your sins are forgiven,' or to say, "Get up, take up your mat and walk? But that you may know that the Son of Man has the authority on earth to forgive sins..." He said to the paralytic, "I tell you, get up, take your mat and go home." He got up, took his mat, and walked out in full view of them all. This amazed everyone and they praised God, saying, "We have never seen anything like this." (Mark 2. 6–12) Healing miracles were physical, tangible expressions of greater, intangible transactions. Augustine recognized the inherent value of miracles as "advertisements for God" and engaged himself in recording those accomplished by Saint Stephen at Hippo and including the accounts, perhaps the earliest model for *libelli miraculorum* in Book XXII of the *De civitate Dei*. Augustine wrote:

> "We cannot deny that many miracles were wrought to confirm that one grand and health-giving miracle of Christ's ascension to heaven with the flesh in which He rose."[27]

Basil of Caesarea in his Long Rule (55) expressed similar thoughts referring to "medicine's chief end and purpose" as "a model for the cure of the soul" and as "a parallel to the care given to the soul."[28] That Pseudo-Basil shared the same persuasion is clear by the rationale that he sets forth for his own collection in the prologue of the *Miracles*. He compiled the work "...in order that it may not be possible for those who come across them to disbelieve...but rather that they may harvest belief from the miracles."

Two miracles (14 and 18) in the collection in which unbelievers are physically cured and converted highlight this phenomenon. In the first miracle, Hypsistios- who was a most disagreeable and blasphemous person to the degree that all attending him,

---

[27] Augustine, *De civitate Dei*. 22. 8, *NPNF* Series 1, vol. 2, 484. *Nam facta esse multa miracula, quae attestarentu rill iuni grandi salubrique miraculo, quo Christus in caelum cum carne in qua resurrexit, ascendit, negare non possumus.*

[28] See Darrel W. Amundsen and Gary B. Ferngren, "Medicine and Religion: Early Christianity Through the Middle Ages," in Marty and Vaux (1982) 93–131 (108–9).

including his wife, were hoping for his imminent death—benefitted from Thecla's ministrations.

> "[She] breathed out <into him> some <kernel> of salvation and of strength and grace. All <these things> happened to him together at one and the same time, the faith, the grace, the initiation, and in addition to all these blessings he was made well and healed and <was able to> discern beautiful things and to enjoy truly noble things of which the most excellent is to become a Christian..." [29]

Similarly, the pagan woman Aba was healed of a broken foot but, as Pseudo-Basil notes:

> "Better still is that she became a Christian as a result of this miracle.... The cure for the foot also caused a similar cure to blossom forth for her spirit and so both <cures> resulted from this one miracle." [30]

It is interesting to note that healing is the only type of miracle performed by Thecla for those who are explicitly identified as non-Christians.[31]

Faith healing and medicine are not necessarily co-terminous in the *Miracles*. While medical terminology is abundant in the text, the remedies that Thecla prescribes are, like those of Christ, neither rare, complicated, expensive, nor difficult to obtain.[32] According to Pseudo-Basil, efficacy is invested in the power of the prescriber rather than in that of the prescription.[33] There is no mention of medical staff at the *temenos*. Nor does Egeria, the fourth-century pilgrim to the Holy Land and beyond, make any reference in her travel journal to medical facilities at Hagia Thecla. Thecla is never referenced as a doctor nor does she appear in the guise of a doctor as do several later healing saints, such as Cosmas and Damian or Cyrus and John, or Artemios.[34] Instead, she is

---

[29] *Mir.* 14.

[30] *Mir.* 18.

[31] See *Mir.* 14, 18, 39, and 40. The healing miracles are among the less spectacular and dramatic of the entire miracle collection and might well be regarded as 'entry-level' miracles.

[32] *Mir.* 8. 6–14 and *Mir.* 18. 39–44. In the Old Testament case of Naaman the Leper and his quest for healing, the simplicity of the cure proved to be an offense to his pride. (2 Kings 5. 1–14). Arnobius, a third century rhetor and Christian apologist, persuaded his listeners as to the superiority of Christ's healing to that of Asclepius because Christ's is "without drama and incantations." (Arn. *Adv. nat.* 7. 1. 63–5 (*CSEL* 4, 1875), 43–6). The notion persisted in the twelfthcentury; Byzantine Theodore Prodomus refers to the "unadorned healing of the Savior." (Prodomus, *Ep.* 6 (*PG* 133).

[33] *Mir.*8.6–14.

[34] According to A. J. Festugière, there are two categories of miracle collections: 1) those of saints who are exclusively healers such as Cosmas and Damian, Cyrus and John, Artemios, Therapon, and Isaiah, and 2) collections

presented as "the true healer of humankind" (ἀλεξητήριαν).³⁵ an honor that she defers to Christ when she says, "I am not the healer but rather God is, the One who lives in the heights and watches over the humble." ³⁶

Nevertheless, people sought relief from Thecla for their various ailments. The cases brought to Thecla as recorded in the *Miracles* include four broken legs, all resulting from falls—three from a horse or mule and one from a scaffold, variously treated by the saint; four eye diseases (including blindness) also with diverse cures; three unspecified illnesses, one case of misaligned vertebrae, kidney problems, scrofula, anthrax, disfigurement of a woman's face by deleterious drugs, an ear infection, and a pregnant woman's discomfort which led to attempted suicide.³⁷ For our purposes, we will turn our attention to *Miracle* 18 which records Thecla's care-giving for two women both suffering from broken legs. In the conversion narrative of *Miracle* 18, Pseudo-Basil departs from his general pattern of one story per chapter and juxtaposes two women within the account—the Christian Tigriana of Tarsus and the agnostic Aba of Seleucia,³⁸ both from well-to-do families and both visited by trouble, for trouble is no respecter of persons or religious persuasion. In this account, both women meet with the same trouble. They both fall from their mules and sustain injuries. In this miracle, Pseudo-Basil also draws distinctions between various religious groups—pagans, Christians, and Jews—thereby, injecting the notion of religious profiling into the text. Let us now turn to Miracle 18 in its entirety.

Translation of Miracle 18

"This same miracle was performed also for two other women: one who was named Aba from the city of Seleucia, of an illustrious and famous family; the name of the other was Tigriana, from the city of Tarsus, also of an illustrious family. But the lat-

---

of saints who are devoted to various interventions and not only healing, such as Theodore, Menas, Thecla, and Demetrius. See Festugière, *Collections grecques de miracles: Sainte Thècle, saints Côme et Damien, saints Cyr et Jean (extraits), saint Georges,* (Paris: A. et J. Picard, 1971), 7.

35 *Mir.* 25.8.
36 *Myrtle Wood* 143.
37 For broken legs, see *Mir.* 8 and 17, and two incidents in *Mir.* 18; for eye ailments, *Mir.* 23, 24, 25, and 37; for unspecified illnesses, *Mir.* 14, 38, and 39; for slipped vertebrae, *Mir.* 7; for kidneys, *Mir.* 40; for scrofula, *Mir.* 12; for anthrax, *Mir.* 12; for disfigured face, *Mir.* 42; for ear infection, *Mir.* 41; and for pregnancy, *Mir.* 19. For a discussion of each of these cases as they occur in the *Miracles*, see Honey (2011), 315–28. Later healing collections include lists of quite different illnesses with frequent cases of demonic possession. In contrast, there are no cases of possession by demonic spirits recorded in the *Miracles of Thecla*, and only two of demonic attack.
38 Aba may well have been Isaurian. During Cleopatra and Antony's governance of the region there was a pirate princess named Aba. The name is well attested in the region; 'Tigriana' (Τιγριανή), however, is not. See Dagron, 339, n. 1. According to Liddell and Scott, the adjective τίγρῄος means 'tiger-like', which our Tigriana certainly was in her misdirected anger with Thecla in regard to the mishap.

ter of these was a Christian, and while traveling from Tarsus and hurrying to the Martyr herself, she fell off her mule and broke her leg.[39] And making many complaints against the Martyr as if she were the cause for her suffering this <injury>, she experienced the following miracle. And the Martyr with no delay whatsoever made a visitation by night; she did not order her to do this or that, nor to use this medicine or that, but only to rise up from her bed and to walk to whatever place she was heading for without any delay, since the normal shape and strength of her foot had returned again. The woman arose, as if she did not believe in such a miracle and she tested her foot, but then receiving that which was contrary to her expectations, she did not mount her mule again at all but walking with praises and prayers and hymns, she reached the *neos* of the Martyr.[40] At one and the same time she both rejoiced at the miracle, and tested it for herself by the length of time and of the journey whether this was perhaps not a dream but a true vision.[41] For every miracle of the Martyr is and will be true, authentic, and complete.

Aba, on the other hand, was still a pagan (ἕλληνις) neither loathing the Jews nor avoiding the Christians; she was undecided about all people and all matters. And so she, too, fell from a mule and thus was badly wounded in her leg; the broken bone pierced the flesh around it forcefully on the foot<and> went through to the outside so that the damage appeared to exceed <any> remedy thereafter. Over the course of time, the trouble worsened and she was immobile. At one time some of the Jews, at another time, some enchanters, together with the excellent <oracular *daimon*> Sarpedon toyed (παίζω) with her, promising a cure or even doing something but unable even to do anything and, in the end, they were ineffectual. And so, acting whether upon the advice of others or upon her own advice, the woman was transported to the *naos*. She besought the Martyr with tears <and> with many voluble laments to win over the Virgin. Not even three whole days had passed when the woman, walking on her own two feet, descended no longer needing a helper, and went <towards her> home with sprightly

---

[39] Throughout this miracle, Thecla is repeatedly referred to as 'the Martyr' and once as 'the Virgin'. Pseudo-Basil addresses Thecla in the *Miracles* as 'Thrice-blessed One' (*epilogue*, line 24). The epithet 'Thrice-blessed' refers to Thecla in three different aspects—those of Virgin, Martyr, and Apostle. 'Apostle' refers to Thecla's authority and divine assignment; 'Virgin', to her manner of life and intercessory work; and 'Martyr', to her miracles and thaumaturgical activity. 'Martyr' is the most frequently employed epithet for Thecla in the *Miracles*. For a detailed discussion of these terms, see Honey (2011), 69–77.

[40] In the course of my translation of the *Miracles*, it became apparent that for Pseudo-Basil some words, particularly architectural and building terminology, have semantic fields that do not directly align with our usual translation of them: *naos*, *neos*, and *daimon* among others. I have chosen to simply transliterate these words until such time as a detailed semantic analysis can be done. In this way, other scholars who access this translation will not be misguided. For a discussion of the terms *naos/neos* (perhaps which refer to 'church building' or 'sanctuary') in the *Miracles*, see Honey (2011), Appendix A, "Excavation of the Text: The Archaeology of the Site," 490–97 (496–97).

[41] The distinction between illusions, dreams, and true visions is a common *topos* in Late Antique hagiography and in miracle collections. See Dagron, 105–06.

step, as they say. What kind of medication was used for this therapy? Surely you wish to know this as well! It was nothing expensive, or complicated, or an ingenious invention of the quackery of the Asclepiades. For the Martyr said, "Scraping off the grime (τόνρύπον) from the surrounding latticework in my chamber (θαλάμος), plaster it on the affected part of your foot and immediately you will stop the suffering and you will use your feet for what one ought to use feet." And <the Martyr> spoke; so <Aba> acted; and, indeed, the miracle is proclaimed still to the present day by her and by those who saw her walking, running, and being active with her foot. Better still is that she became a Christian as a result of this miracle and such a Christian as is befitting one after such an experience. The cure for the foot also caused a similar cure to blossom forth for her spirit, and so both <cures> resulted from the one miracle."

* * *

Pseudo-Basil economizes and energizes the narrative by setting forth the two stories in one. The narrative is lexically infused with the ideas of energy and efficacy. Tigriana is "hurrying" to Hagia Thecla when the accident occurs. Not even waiting for daybreak, Thecla comes to her aid 'with no delay whatsoever'. She does not bother with prescriptions or remedies but simply instructs Tigriana to rise up and to proceed on her journey "without delay." Tigriana rejoices and tests the miracle "at one and the same time."

The narrative slows, however, when it turns to Aba. She was "still" a pagan; she was "undecided" about religious matters. "Over the course of time," her condition deteriorated and sundry therapies failed. Pseudo-Basil enumerates the various but unsuccessful health care practitioners whom Aba consulted. But then suddenly, Aba becomes proactive and decides to seek help from Thecla. At once, the narrative accelerates. "Not even three whole days passed" (a common biblical *topos*) before Aba was healed by a simple but efficacious cure. Thecla instructed her to plaster grime scraped from the latticework of Thecla's chamber onto the injured foot. A structurally succinct sentence reinforces the brevity of their interaction: "And <the Martyr > spoke; so <Aba> acted." "With sprightly step," Aba returned home, praising the Martyr. The economy and energy does not end there: *two* cures resulted from the one miracle. The physical cure precipitated a spiritual cure "to blossom or sprout forth" (συνβλαστάνω) and Aba "became a Christian."

An astute reader may have anticipated such an outcome having noted a potential analogy between the grime (τόνρύπον) and the scraping away and polishing associated with the verb περιξέω and the process of spiritual conversion. While Thecla was not alone in prescribing such medical therapy,[42] the grime might also have been regarded as symbolic of the state of Aba's heart. Both Tigriana and Aba are invigorated by their encoun-

---

[42] Dioscorides (c. 60) prescribed "grime from gymnasium walls" for the treatment of tumors (φύματα) (*De materia medica* 1. 30). See John M. Riddle, "High Medicine and Low Medicine in the Roman Empire," in: *Aufstieg und Neidergang der Römischen Welt* II. 37. 1 (1993), 102–220 (110).

ters with Saint Thecla, abandoning their previous means of conveyance by mules in favor of travelling under their own energy. Even those watching the events are enlivened, becoming a proclamation chorus of sorts. Pseudo-Basil rounds out the narrative with a touch of literary flourish by his choice of the verb συνβλαστάνω to describe both the physical and spiritual healing that Aba received and, at the same time, injects into the account a breath of springtime, of freshness, renewal, and rebirth so reflective of Aba's new life.

For the purposes of our inquiry, it would have been interesting had Pseudo-Basil included Aba's thoughts about Jews after her conversion. Apart from *Mir.* 18 (lines 22 and 29), Jews are referenced only two other times in the *Miracles*.

1) *Miracle* introduction, lines 94–6.
Already [Thecla] has appeared both to the Jews (ἰουδαίοις) and to the Greeks (ἕλλησιν) many times and has manifested the same power to them.

2) Miracle 14.10-15.
And so, always running off to the church of the Martyr, "[the wife of Hypsistios] imitated the carriage of Hannah who is of such great fame in the Holy Scripture: her posture, her prayers, her tears, and her perseverance in her prayers and entreaties, but not for the sake of having children—the request of Jewish "vulgarity" (ἰουδαικῆς ἀπειροκαλίας) but so that she might see her husband [as] a Christian and a believer (χριστιανὸν and πιστόν)."[43]

Though the references are fleeting, they support the archaeological record, which includes funerary inscriptions, testifying to a Jewish presence at Seleucia. The necropolis at Seleucia was an area specifically for Jewish burial within the Christian cemetery. According to Dagron, the references in the *Miracles* to the Jews display a latent hostility on the part of Ps.-Basil.[44] At the same time, however, they serve as an additional witness to a Jewish presence in Seleucia and its attendant medical activity.[45]

---

[43] The phrase "a Christian and a believer" implies a certain distinction between the two words, suggesting that they are not analogous. Perhaps it is a matter of degree. In a recent trip to Iraq, I noted that Iraqi Christians make the same distinction, often posing the question, "Are you a Christian or are you a believer?" to those to whom they have been introduced and with whom they presumably share the same faith.

[44] Dagron, 156 and 327, n. 4.

[45] For an extant letter from the twelfth century written in Arabic by an Egyptian Jewish doctor residing at Seleucia to his brother-in-law in Egypt, inviting him to bring his family and join him in Seleucia, see S. D. Goitein, "A Letter From Seleucia (Cilicia) Dated 21 July 1137," *Speculum* 39 (1964), 298–303. In the letter, the doctor refers to a town approximately seventy-five miles away from Seleucia, perhaps Isaura Palai, and to the community of fifty Jewish families residing there. According to Steven Muir, "The Eastern Church at the Synod in Trullo (692 CE) passed a number of canonical decrees including a prohibition against receiving medicine from Jews." See Steven C. Muir, "Mending yet Fracturing: Healing as an Arena of Conflict." In: *The Changing Face*

The presence of a Jewish community contributed to the multi-culturalism for which Seleucia was noted.

While Seleucia itself was a cosmopolitan cross-roads and largely Hellenistic ranking only slightly behind the great centers of Alexandria, Constantinople, and Syrian Antioch, numbered among its populace were the Isaurians, a proud, indigenous, and pagan people, who also required medical assistance. Often characterized in primary source documents as pirates and brigands greatly feared by the general populace,[46] the Isaurians represent a distinctly different type of pagan than that of Seleucia's sparkling, classically-educated circle of local literati. Although Thecla's divine assignment given through Saint Paul was specifically polis-centric, to the "yet uninstructed cities", here and there Isaurians appear implicitly in the narrative.[47] A particularly vivid account of the interaction between Christians and the pagan Isaurians in the context of healing at Seleucia is related by yet another anonymous author in his account of Thecla's life and ministry in the *Myrtle Wood*, a much shorter and somewhat later work than that of Pseudo-Basil.[48]

It includes the story of a married couple of the Isaurian aristocracy with concerns about the future of their twenty-two year old daughter, Theonilla, afflicted at birth with a crippling disease that affected her hands and her feet. Cognizant of Thecla's healing ministry, the mother, Androklea, suggests to her husband, Proklianos, that they take their daughter to Thecla. Proklianos, however, is reticent and replies:

> "You know, My Lady, that I am a leader of the city and I am afraid to go off <to Thecla>, for I think she happens <to be one> of the

---

of *Judaism, Christianity and other Greco-Roman Religions in Antiquity*, ed. by Ian H. Henderson and Gerben S. Oegema, (Gutersloh/ Munich: Gutersloher Verlagshaus, 2006), 57–71 (66).

[46] See Brent Shaw, "Bandit Highlands and Lowland Peace: The Mountains of Isauria-Cilicia." *Journal of the Economic and Social History of the Orient*, 33. 2 (1990), 199–233; 33. 3 (1990) 237–70.

[47] See *Life* 26 for Thecla's divine commission, and n. 10 above. For polis-centricity, see Dagron, 10–11; Shaw, 245; and Johnson, p. 139. The Isaurians are implied in *Mir.* 19, in the account of Bassiane, one of the "noble women of the Ketis" who was held hostage at Hagia Thecla "because of certain covenants that promised peace instead of plundering." Dagron (341, n. 1) explains that the Ketis is the upper Calycadnus region, home to the Isaurians. Again, Ps.-Basil is likely referring to the Isaurians in *Mir.* 32: "Once the bandits, who are our neighbors and live among us, were overrunning our country and were plundering everything here." The Isaurians also inhabited Seleucia's outlying areas and mountain fastnesses as well as other cities that comprised that which Constantine Porphyrogenitus would later identify as the Isaurian Decapolis of which Seleucia was the chief city. For more on the Isaurians, see Linda Honey, "Justifiably Outraged or Simply Outrageous: The Isaurian Incident of Ammianus Marcellinus 14. 2." In: *Violence in Late Antiquity. Perceptions and Practices*, ed. by H. A. Drake, (Aldershot: Ashgate Publishing, Ltd., 2006), 47–55; Dagron, 113–23; and Egeria's account of Isaurian attacks on Hagia Thecla, *Itinerarium Egeriae*, XXIII 4. 19-25.

[48] For the English translation of the Greek text of the *Myrtle Wood* as provided by Dagron, see Honey (2011), 440–46. Internal evidence from the text suggests a provenance of the early iconoclast period.

Galileans, and if I go off to her, the city <will> learn and they <will> hand me over to the fire; but rather seat her [Theonilla] on a litter and two slaves will carry her; and transport her by night!" (*Myrtle Wood* 130–1)

When the Isaurian mother and daughter supplicate Thecla for the healing, she asks whether they have the "holy baptism." They answer that they "happen to be of the pagan manner of life" (βίου ἑλληνικοῦ) (*Myrtle Wood* 140) using the same term to denote 'pagan' as does Pseudo-Basil in the *Miracles*. In this context, the term clearly should be understood as 'not Christian' rather than 'Greek'.[49] The terms that Pseudo-Basil employs in the *Miracles* to denote religious persuasion include pagan (ἑλληνίς), unbeliever (ἄπιστος), Christian (χριστιανός), believer (πιστός), and Jew (ἰουδαῖος). In *Mir.* 14, Thecla makes a visitation to a certain Hypsistios, an "enemy" (πολέμιος) of Christ and "a friend of demons" (φίλος δαιμόνων), to rid him of his "unbelief" (ἀπιστίας) since he was "burning with the fire borne of impiety (ἀσεβείας)."

The charge of impiety is an interesting one in that it was often levied against Christians. A grandmother who sought help from the *daimon* Sarpedon for her ailing grandson is described as doing so in such a way "as would a woman who is the acolyte/follower of a *daimon*." While this certainly is a religious designation, the exact meaning is obscure. In the *Myrtle Wood*, we learn that Thecla found those in Seleucia, "the metropolis of the Isaurians", to be 'pagan' (ἕλληνας) and 'lawless' (ἀνόμους); and Thecla was regarded by them as one of the 'Galileans' (Γαλιλαίων). The lascivious priest whom Thecla encountered in the Myrtle Wood is described as "the priest of the pagans" (τὸν ἱερέα τῶν ἑλλήνων).[50] The phrase, "to become a Christian", in current usage today to describe a person who chooses conversion is literally the same term employed by both Pseudo-Basil and the author of the *Myrtle Wood*: γενέσθαι χριστιανός.[51]

In summary, the healing accounts in the *Miracles of Thecla* and the *Myrtle Wood* prove to be a rich resource for highlighting socio-religious relations in this unique region of the Eastern Roman Empire. In the *Miracles*, Pseudo-Basil unapologetically, but sparingly, references pagans, Christians, and Jews, indicating his definite perception of and delineation between these socio-religious categories. And the authors of both

---

[49] In the introduction of the *Miracles*, Pseudo-Basil notes that Thecla had appeared to both the Jews and the Greeks (ἰουδαίοις καὶ ἕλλησιν) (lines 94–96).

[50] For example, for ἑλληνίς, see *Mir.* 18. 22; for ἄπιστος, (a term used twenty-three times in the New Testament), see *Mir.* 11. 53 and 56, *Mir.* 17. 23; for χριστιανός, *Mir.* 4. 13, 14. 17. 32, 19. 7, 32. 21; for πιστός, *Mir.* 13. 9, 15. 2 and 35, 14. 15, 30. 3; ἰουδαῖος, *Mir.*intro. 94–96, *Mir.* 18. 22 and 29.The passage in regard to the grandmother is found in *Mir.* 11. 13 and reads ὡςἂν δαίμων παρὰ δαιμονώσης γυναικός. For the citations from the *Myrtle Wood* see, respectively, lines 18, 130–31, and 24.

[51] See *Mir.* 17. 32, 18. 48–49 and *Myrtle Wood*, line 83.

the *Miracles* and the *Myrtle Wood* portray the individuals as self-identifying in regard to their respective religious designation. In the *Miracles,* an individual's socio-religious affiliation is often ascertained by his occupation (*e.g.* bishop, priest, temple guardian, etc.) rather than by religious designation. In the case of women, however, who were often without an occupation, Pseudo-Basil necessarily provides a designation as to their religious persuasion. The *Miracles* and the *Myrtle Wood* do not so much depict interactions between individuals (between pagans, between Christians, or between pagans and Christians) as they do between individuals, whether pagan or Christian, and Saint Thecla herself. In general, Thecla treats transgressive behavior exhibited by Christians, in particular, that of lack of faith, with swift and exacting severity but that of pagans with charitable equanimity and forbearance (with a pinch of derision now and then), irrespective of the attitude or response of the particular pagan.[52] Pseudo-Basil's attitude, as revealed in the text, closely mirrors that of Thecla. As we noted at the outset, this religious tolerance extended to those who were not Christians is unusual in miracle collections of Late Antiquity and raises the question as to whether this may reflect the collective response of Christians to the pagan population of fifth-century Seleucia. Pseudo-Basil presents Thecla as generally tolerant but some pagans as intolerant, even combatively so.

In Pseudo-Basil's day, the pagan population of Seleucia, composed of various social strata from the war-like Isaurians to the classically-educated elite, was still ascendant. A broad spectrum of pagans is presented in the *Miracles*. Some individuals, like the two sophists, Aretarchos and Isokasios, were philosophically pagan; some, like Aba, were nominal pagans, not girded by personal conviction; and others, like the grandmother, a follower of Sarpedon, were devoutly pagan.[53]

From the *Miracles,* we learn that it was Pseudo-Basil's perception that general public opinion, largely pagan, considered Christians as best 'avoided' and Jews as 'loathsome'. The avoidance of Christians is again highlighted in the *Myrtle Wood* by the Isaurian leader's fear of punishment if he were to approach the 'Galilean' Thecla in regard to healing for his daughter.

The notion of a general repulsion for Jews is reinforced in that Pseudo-Basil employs the word "vulgar" in his own (Christian) assessment of Jewish practices. The Jewish community, however, continued as a presence in Seleucia and on Cyprus and, by

---

[52] In *Mir.* 11, Thecla sharply upbraids Dexianos, her temple guardian, for his hyper-vigilance equating it with lack of faith. In *Mir.* 10, she prevents an Arian bishop from defacing the creed on consubstantiality inscribed on a wall of her *neos*. He fell from his ladder and was badly crushed and as a result converted from his heretical doctrine to the true faith. In *Mir.* 14, as Thecla interacts with Hypsistios who is described as "an enemy of Christ," and by whom she had been constantly insulted and maligned, she extends saving grace to him saying, "For I am by nature disposed to answer insults with gifts such as these."

[53] See *Mir.* 39, 40, 18, and 11, respectively.

the twelfth century, its thriving and expanding medical practice contributed positively to the socio-economic climate of Seleucia. The Christian community grew as well, welcoming into the fold the Isaurian people who experienced wide-scale conversion in the sixth century.[54]

As we noted, health is numbered among 'first order concerns' and, as such, is an arena of life in which socio-religious boundaries are sometimes suspended, if only temporarily. The pursuit of health and its attendant consumer culture exploded from the mid-fifth to seventh centuries, contemporaneously with the flourishing of the cult of Saint Thecla and the ministry of faith healing. In the *Miracles*, Christians are not presented as picture perfect and, at times, are even characterized as disbelieving while, in some instances, non-Christians exercised belief. The healing accounts in Pseudo-Basil's miracle collection showcase individuals who, in search of relief and regardless of religious persuasion, received healing and became members of an overarching community—a community of health pilgrims –by a salutiferous suspension of disbelief.

---

[54] See Honey (2006), p. 55 and n. 38.

EMPRESS VERINA AMONG THE PAGANS[1*]

Margarita Vallejo-Girvés

The long and complex relationship between Emperor Zeno and the Isaurian general Illus, the latter's rebellion, and Empress Verina's participation in it were recorded in varying detail by many Late Antique authors, and by historians in the subsequent centuries.[2] Nonetheless, scholars such as A. Laniado have noted how fragmentary the ancient accounts are, making it difficult to know precisely how these events actually unfolded.[3] Malchus, Candidus, Zacharias Scholastikos[4], Liberatus of Carthage, Malalas, Evagrius Scholasticus, John of Antioch, and Theophanes Confessor portray Illus's revolt as a political showdown with Zeno—a power struggle amongst the Isaurians. However, it can be surmised from their works that they perceived Illus as leaning more toward Dyophisitism than Miaphysitism or to the ideas set forth in the Henotikon, issued by Zeno in 482, two years before the rebellion. These had failed to satisfy all Dyophisites, both eastern and western.[5] The Christian Zacharias Scholastikos and the pagan Damascius both allude to the hopes harbored in pagan circles for the success of Illus's revolt. In two saints' lives, Zacharias even mentions that Pamprepius, Illus's main adviser, was a pagan, and,

---

[1] *Research for this paper was conducted in the framework of the project "Contextos históricos de aplicación de las penas de reclusión en el Mediterráneo Oriental (ss. V–VII)" [HAR2014-52744-P], supported by the Spanish Ministry of Economy and Competitiveness. Part of the paper was completed in Munich at the *Kommission für Alte Geschichte und Epigraphik*.

[2] The exception would be Ps. Joshua the Stylite, *Chronicle*, § 244–246 and Victor of Tunnuna, *Chronicon ad a.* 483. Although they discuss the rebellion, they do not allude at any time to Verina's participation in it.

[3] Avshalom Laniado, "Some problems in the sources for the reign of the emperor Zeno," *Byzantine and Modern Greek Studies (BMGS)*, 15 (1991): 147–173.

[4] With respect to this being the correct identity of the author, rather than Zacharias of Mytilene, see: Sebastian Brock and Brian Fitzgerald, *Two Early Lives of Severos, Patriarch of Antioch*, (Liverpool: Liverpool University Press, 2013), 15–7.

[5] Ariane Kiel-Freytag, "Betrachtungen zur Usurpation des Illus und des Leontius (484–488 n. Chr.)," *Zeitschrift für Papyrologie und Epigraphik*, 174 (2010), 291–301.

furthermore, that some pagans had considered the possibility that paganism could regain its dominance, with Christianity fading away if Illus were victorious.⁶

Rebellions against imperial power, logically, tended to feature a political component, but at that time it was also common for their leaders to seek support from schools of Christianity struggling to propagate their ideas. It should come as no surprise, then, that as Zeno was more amenable to Miaphysitism, Illus should have attempted to gather Dyophisite support. More perplexing is the relationship which, as we have seen, some authors posit between Illus and the Empire's pagan intellectual circles.⁷

All this has led to Illus's revolt being studied based on profiles of religious affiliations. There have been examinations, for example, of what the relationship between Illus and the Dyophisites leaders of the Eastern Church might have been like.⁸ Illus's potential paganism has also been studied, as well as accounts that he had striven to secure pagan support, or that he was effective in securing it.⁹ Following this line, my intention here is to analyze how the participation of Verina in some episodes of that rebellion—mainly her proclamation of Leontius as the new emperor—is key to the argument that a Christian agenda, rather than a pagan one, was behind the insurrection of Illus. In addition, following the line proposed by Liz James, I shall contribute to the analysis of Verina's activity in greater depth.¹⁰

---

6   Zach.,*Vit. Sev.* § 54; Zach.., *Vit. Isaiae*§ 10; Damasc., *Hist. Phil.* § 77 b. *Cf.*The horoscope of Pamprepius in *Catalogus Codicum Astrologorum Graecorum*(*CCAG*) 8, 4, 221–224, 20, f. 139v; on the authorship of Rhetorius, see Otto Neugebauer and Henry B. Van Hoesen, *Greek Horoscopes* (Philadelphia: American Philosophical Society 1959), 140–41, 187; David Pingree, "Political Horoscopes from the Reign of Zenon," *DOP*, 30 (1976) 133–150 (pp. 144–46); *cf.* Armandus Delatte and Paul Stroobant, 'L'horoscope de Pamprépius', *Bulletin de l' Académie Royale de Belgique, Classe des Lettres*, 9 (1923), 58–76.

7   To garner support for his rebellion Illus may have turned to all of Zeno's enemies: Ps. Joshua the Stylite, *Chron.* § 246; Iohan. Antioch.,*fr.* 306 (for this author we follow the edition of Umberto Roberto, *Ioannis Antiocheni, Fragmenta ex Historia Chronica. Introduzione, edizione critica e traduzione.*Texte und Untersuchungen zur Geschichte der altchristlichen Literatur (Berlin-New York: de Gruyter, 2005); *cf.* Sergei Mariev, *Ioannis Antiocheni fragmenta quae supersunt*. CFHB (Berlin-New York: de Gruyter, 2008, 425–43); see, on this controversy, P. Van Nuffelen, 'John of Antioch, inflated and deflated, or: How (not) to collect fragments of Early Byzantine Historians', *Byzantion*, 82 (2012), pp. 437–50).

8   E. Stein, *Histoire du Bas-Empire. II. De la disparition de l'Empire d'Occident à la mort de Justinien (476–565)* (Paris-Bruxelles-Amsterdam: Desclée de Brouwer, 1949), 19–33; *cf.* Umberto Roberto, 'Sulla tradizionestoriografica di CandidoIsaurico', *Mediterraneo Antico*, 3 (2000), 2, 685–727 (pp. 709–10).

9   Rudolf Asmus, 'Pamprepios, einbyzantinischerGelehrter und Staatsmann des 5. Jahrhunderts', *BZ*, 22/2 (1913), 320–47; Delatte -Stroobant, 'L'horoscope de Pamprépius', pp. 60-61; Pierre Chauvin, *Chronique des derniers païens. La dispariton du paganisme dans l' Empire romain du règne de Constantin à celui de Justinien* (Paris: Les Belles Lettres, 1990), pp. 96–100; Christopher Haas, *Alexandria in Late Antiquity. Topography and Social Conflict* (Baltimore-London: John Hopkins University Press, 1997), pp. 326; Cf. PolymniaAthanassiadi, 'Persecution and Response in Late Paganism: The evidence of Damascius', *JHS*, 113 (1993), 1–29 (p. 19–21).

10 Liz James, 'Goddess, Whore, Wife or Slave: Will the Real Byzantine Empress Please Stand Up ?' in *Queens and Queenship in Medieval Europe. Proceedings of a Conference held at King's College, London, April 1995)*, ed. by Anne J. Duggan (Woodbridge: Boydell Press, 1997; repr. 2002), pp. 123–40 (pp. 133–34). We have also studied the pres-

There are numerous sources providing us with information on Verina's Christian faith and the nature of it: saints' lives, chronicles, histories, *patria*, poems, and even laws demonstrate her conviction. Most mention her activity during the reign of Leo I, and some even date from the reign of Zeno. Verina is portrayed as a "lover of God" by the author of the *Vita Matronae*. This work chronicled her visit, during the life of Leo I, to the ascetic Saint Matrona who is recorded to have refused to accept anything which Verina offered her. It is interesting to note, however, that Verina beseeched Saint Matrona to pray for her, her children, and the emperor.[11] There is no doubt that we are dealing with a hagiographic *topos* when we read of visits by important imperial figures to saintly men and women, especially when these visits occurred in the vicinity of the capital. Other recurring themes are the saints' constant rejection of what is offered them and their being asked to intercede for Divine help.[12] That said, there is no doubt that Verina could have made such a request of Saint. Matrona, not only because the author used contemporary sources for the composition of her *vita*,[13] but also because there are ample accounts that strongly link Verina to the Christian faith.

In the *Life of Daniel the Stylite,* mention is made several times of the protagonist's relationship to members of the court during the reigns of Leo I, Basiliscus, and Zeno. There is broad consensus that the *vita* is the work of a disciple of Daniel, who was witness to some of the events he relates, and who employed oral sources which originated with those who experienced them first-hand.[14] Obviously the author ascribes significant political activity and influence to Daniel: his relations with Leo and Zeno were amicable[15]. In contrast, he rejected Basiliscus, the usurper, and his imperial pretensions[16].

It is in the context of the reign of Leo I that we see Verina linked to Daniel the Stylite. Verina and Leo entreat him for Divine intervention to conceive an heir and for the people of Constantinople to overcome their fear after suffering a terrible fire.[17]

---

ence of Verina in the political scene of Constantinople in Margarita Vallejo Girvés, 'Ad Ecclesiam Confugere, tonsuras y exilios en la familia de León y Verina', in *Movilidad forzada entre la Antigüedad Clásica y Tardía*, ed. by Margarita Vallejo Girvés, Juan Antonio Bueno Delgado, Carlos Sánchez-Moreno Ellard (Alcalá de Henares, Servicio de Publicaciones, 2015), pp. 137–160, and in 'The Triumphal Return of Verina, the Exiled Empress', forthcoming.

[11] *Vit. Matr.* §XXXII; *Versio Metaphras.* §XXVIII; *PG* CXVI, 920–953; *AA.SS.*,nov. III, 813–822.

[12] *Vit. Matr.* §XXXIII: during that same period Matrona received a visit from Euphemia, the wife of Anthemius, who had been the emperor of the *Pars Occidentis*.

[13] Cyril Mango, 'Life of Matrona of Perge' in *Holy Women of Byzantium: Ten Saints' Lives in English Translation*, ed. by Alice-Mary Talbot, (Washington: Harvard University Press 1996), pp. 14–66 (p. 16).

[14] Robin Lane Fox, 'The Life of Daniel', in *Portraits: Biographical Representations in the Greek and Latin Literature of the Roman Empire*, ed. by Mark J. Edwards and Simon Swan (Oxford: Clarendon Press, 1997), pp. 175–225 (pp. 202–05 and 210).

[15] *Vit. Dan. Styl.* § 38, 46, 91. *Vid.* Laniado, 'Some problems in the sources', pp. 166–68.

[16] *Vit. Dan. Styl.* § 68, 69, 76; *cf.* Theoph.,*Chron. a. m.* 5967, *ad a.* 474/475.

[17] *Vit. Dan. Styl.* § 38 and 46.

Along with mentioning Verina's participation in the plot which made possible Basiliscus's usurpation, the *vita* also suggests that the empress was politically manipulated by the conspirators.[18] Except for this, there is nothing critical of Verina in the account; she is even called "the blessed empress" by the author.[19] But we find in it an interesting fact for our analysis: Verina, who feared that Basiliscus would attempt to take her life, took refuge in the *Hagia Soros*, one of the buildings of the *Theotokos* church in Blachernae.[20] Of course, as was a common occurrence during that tumultuous period, many invoked the right of asylum to save their lives, and Verina would seem to be no exception.[21] The reason why Verina chose this church, however, is significant: she and Leo had contributed to the construction of the *Hagia Soros*, a large chapel to house the relics of the *Theotokos*.[22] It was not her only intervention sinceVerina appears in the literature as an active Christian benefactor.[23]

Whether alone or in the company of Leo, she is credited with the foundation or completion of various religious buildings. In addition to *Hagia Soros*, she is linked to the *Hagia Eirene* in Perama,[24] the *Chalkopratia*[25] and perhaps with the *Theotokos*

---

[18] *Vit. Dan. Styl.* § 69: "....περιέστησαν αὐτῇ καὶ ἀπατήσαντες ἔπεισαν συμπνεῦσαι αὐτοῖς, τοῦ ἀπώσασθαι τῆς βασιλείας Ζήνωνα... Ἡ οὖν προλεχθεῖσα βασίλισσα Βηρῖνα ἀνταρτικῇ ἀγωγῇ τὴν βασιλείαν τῷ ἀδελφῷ αὐτῆς Βασιλίσκῳ ἐνεχείρισεν".

[19] *Vit. Dan. Styl.* § 69: "τὴν μακαρίαν Βηρῖναν", also used for her husband, emperor Leo I (*Vit. Dan. Styl.* § 22, 38, 42, 44, 46, 54 y 60). On the other hand, Zeno is treated in a more neutral tone, in difference to Basiliscus, defined as the man with a "name of ill omen" (*Vit. Dan. Styl.* § 70: "ὄρμα ὁ δυςώνυμος", and § 71).

[20] *Vit. Dan. Styl.* § 69: "...ἥτις φυγὰς γενομένη ἐν τῷ εὐκτηρίῳ τῆς ἀειπαρθένου Μαρίας ἐν Βλαχερναις, ἐκεῖ διετέλεσεν ἄχρι τῆς ζωῆς Βασιλίσκου".; *cf.* Cand., *fr.* 1; Phot., *Bibl.* 79, I, 161-166, summarizing Candidus, alludes to his refuge in a church, but does not specify its name.

[21] Vallejo Girvés, '*Ad ecclesiamconfugere*, tonsuras y exilios', pp. 143–44.

[22] Jonathan Bardill, *Brickstamps of Constantinople, vol. I. Text*, Oxford Monographs of Classical Archaeology (Oxford: Oxford University Press, 2004,) p. 33. *Cf.*, based on the new appreciation for the *Vita Virginis* by Maximus Confessor, Stephen J. Shoemaker, 'The Georgic Life of the Virgin attributed to Maximus the Confessor: Its authenticity and importance,' *Scrinium*, II (2006), 307–28; Stephen J. Shoemaker, 'The Cult of Fashion: The Earliest *Life of the Virgin* and Constantinople's Marian Relics', *DOP*, 62 (2008), 53–74 (p. 56 and 60–1); J. Wortley, "The Marian Relics in Constantinople", *GRBS* 45 (2005), 171–187, (p. 177–81).

[23] *Paras. Synt. Chron.* § 89, relates a legend according to which Verina was responsible for bewitching the island of Kranos, near Constantinople: "Τῆς λεγομένην Κράνον νῆσον ἐστοιχειώσατο Βερίνα, καθ' ἣν οὐδεμία εὑρίσκεται φροντίς, τίνος χάριν ταύτην στοιχειοῦται". This owing to her reputation as a schemer in much of the era's literature (*cf. infra*); we should, however, mention the observation by Averil Cameron and Judith Herrin ed., *Constantinople in the Early Eighth Century: The Parastaseis Syntomoi Chronikai*, Columbia Studies in the Classical Tradition X (Leiden: Brill, 1984), p. 277, that the Greek word used to indicate "bewitch" is very similar to that for "build," and the legend may have distorted Verina's actualbuilding constructions.

[24] *Vit. Markiani* 276a, 31–43 (*BHG* 1033); 269, 4–12 (*BHG* 1032); 448D–449A (*BHG* 1034). See Martin Wallraff, 'Markianos – Ein Prominenter Konvertit vom Novatianismuszur Orthodoxie', *VChr*, 52, 1, (1998), 1–29. On the relationship between Verina and this church, see Bardill, *Brickstamps*,32–3.

[25] *NovIust*.3. 1 (a. 535): '*Postea vero et venerabilis domus sanctae gloriosaque virginis et dei genitricis Mariae, iuxta sanctissimae maioris ecclesiae vicinitatem posita, aedificataest a piae memoriae Verina*'. Vid. Martin Jugie, 'L'Église de

in Curator.²⁶ This activity of Verina's was likely the origin of another literary tradition about her life; while some portrayals present her as a schemer and rebel, others point to her pious side, as we can read in the *ekphrasis* which tenth century author, Constantine of Rhodes, dedicated to Constantinople and the Church of the Holy Apostles. Her depiction as devout would seem to stem from her support for Christian construction projects and her link to the cult of the Virgin.²⁷

The association of Verina—and Leo I—with the *Theotokos* cult seems beyond doubt. During this period, the Holy Virgin's relics reached Constantinople and important shrines were erected in her honor.²⁸ The faith which the imperial couple had in the intercession of the Mother of God was so great that they even symbolically offered their grandson, the future Leo II, to the Virgin, an act which they represented iconographically in a mosaic which they placed in the apse of the *Hagia Soros*. Unfortunately the piece has been lost, but a tenth-century manuscript provides a description of what it depicted: *Theotokos* enthroned and surrounded by Leo, Ariadne, and Verina, who, performing *proskynesis* before the Virgin, offered her their grandson: Leo II. The mosaic included an inscription which alluded to the imperial couple's faith that the Virgin would intercede to preserve the empire.²⁹ It is interesting to note the possibility that one of the motivations spurring Leo and Verina to support worship of the Virgin may have been a desire to repudiate Homoian Arianism, the faith of Aspar who had placed them on the throne and whom Leo ultimately ordered to be executed.³⁰

Chalcopratia et le culte de la ceinture de la Sainte Vierge à Constantinople', *Échos d'Orient*, XVI (1913), 308–12 (p. 308);Shoemaker 'The Cult of Fashion', p. 62.

[26] Augustus S. Mordtmann, *Esquisse topographique de Constantinople* (Lille: Desclée de Brouwer et Cie, 1892), p. 70; Bardill, *Brickstamps*, p. 33.

[27] Const. Rhod., *Ekphrasis* §109–110. *Vid.* Liz James, *Constantine of Rhodes. On Constantinople and the Church of the Holy Apostles with a new edition of the Greek text by Ioannes Vasis*, (Farnham: Ashgate, 2012), pp. 27 and 104. *Cf.* James 'Goddess, Whore', pp. 133–34.

[28] Judith Herrin, 'The Imperial Feminine in Byzantium', *Past and Present*, 169 (2000), 3–35 (p. 14–15); Brian Croke, 'Dinasty and Ethnicity: Emperor Leo I and the Eclipse of Aspar', *Chiron*, 35 (2005), 147–203 (pp. 173–74); Shoemaker, 'The Cult of Fashion', pp. 55–66.

[29] Antoine Wenger, 'Notes inédites sur les empereurs Théodose I, Arcadius, Théodose II, León I', *REB*, 10 (1952), 47–59 (pp. 51–2). *Cf.* Liz James, 'The Empress and the Virgin in Early Byzantium: Piety, Authority and Devotion', in *Images of the Mother of God: Perceptions of the Theotokos in Byzantium*, ed. by Maria Vasilake (Aldershot: Ashgate, 2005), pp. 145–52 (148–51); Henry Maguire, 'Byzantine domestic art as evidence for the early cult of the Virgin', in *Ibid*, pp. 183–94 (p. 186).

[30] James, 'The empress and the Virgin in early Byzantium', 148; cf. Philip Wood, 'The Invention of history in the Later Roman World: The conversion of Isauria in "The Life of Conon', *Anatolian Studies*, 59 (2009), 129–38 (p. 131).

After the ascent to the throne of Leo II—and his father Zeno—the references to Verina's Christianity diminish but do not disappear.[31] The *Parastaseis Syntomoi Chronikai* indicates that when Zeno fled Constantinople and Verina crowned Basiliscus as emperor, the Green faction hailed her, saying: "Long life to Verina, the Orthodox Helena."[32] The association of Helena with Verina has been ascribed not only to Verina's profound Christianity, but might also demonstrate a preference for her at a time of intense confrontation between Dyophisites and Miaphysitism. Probably for this reason the author of the *Oracle of Baalbek*, clearly Dyophisite, associated the empress with the evil Scylla of Classical mythology.[33] Some authors, however, have contended that this allusion to Verina's orthodoxy should not be understood as a reference to her preference for one of these two positions in Christianity, but to a defense of her imperial legitimacy[34] and her activity as a Christian benefactor.[35] In any case it seems clear that, in addition to the above, her association with Helena confirms Verina's strong Christian convictions, but also her opposition to paganism, as we shall see while analyzing her controversial relation with her son-in-law, the new emperor Zeno.

During the series of fluctuations which characterized relations between Zeno and Verina there was a moment when their interests coincided, and they agreed to expel a certain pagan from Constantinople: Pamprepius of Panopolis.[36] As Verina would be forced to share the last months of her life with Pamprepius, circumstances that we will investigate at the end of this article, it is necessary to introduce this character, mentioned by pagan and Christian authors alike. Thanks to those sources, we know that Pamprepius was originally from the Egyptian city of Panopolis. He must have acquired training as a *grammaticus* there, although it seems that he did not distinguish himself in this capacity. After leaving Egypt he settled in Athens, where he was admitted to the school of the Sophist, Proclus. Theagenes, a powerful pagan magistrate of the city, became his benefactor.[37] A series of clashes with Theagenes spurred him to abandon Ath-

---

[31] *Vit. Dan. Styl.* § 67; Cand.,*fr.* 1; Iord., *Rom.* § 340; Vict. Tun., *Chron. ad a.* 474.2; Evagr.,*HE* II, 17; *Chron. Pasch.* § 474; Theoph.,*Chron. a. m.* 5966, *ad a.* 473/474.

[32] *Paras. Synt. Chron.* § 29: "'Βερίνης ὀρθοδόξου Ἑλένης πολλὰ ἔτη'". See Gilbert Dagron, *Constantinople Imaginaire. Études sur le recueil des 'Patria* (Paris: PUF, 1984), p. 173.

[33] Paul J. Alexander, *The Oracle of Baalbek. The Tiburtine Sybill in Greek Dress* (Washington: Dumbarton Oaks, 1967), l. 140–141 (p. 17): "ἀναστήσαται δὲ Σκύλλα, γυνὴ τοῦ θηρείου τοῦ βασιλεύοντος"; *cf.* pp. 82 and 110. See Dagron, *Constantinople Imaginaire*, p. 328 n. 56.

[34] Diliana Angelova, 'The Ivories of Ariadne and Ideas about Female Imperial Authority in Rome and Early Byzantium', *Gesta*, 43/1 (2004), 1–15 (p. 4).

[35] James, 'The empress and the Virgin', p. 151.

[36] Malch.,*fr.*23.

[37] Malch.,*fr.* 23: "φένος μὲν ὢν Ξηβαῖος τῶν κατὰ τὴν Αἴγυπτον, φύσει δὲ πρὸς ἅπαντα δεξιὰ χρησάμενος ἔρχεται εἰς Ἀθήνας, καὶ παρὰ τῆς πόλεως γραμματικὸς αἱρεθεὶς συχνά τε ἐπαίδευσεν ἔτη καὶ ἐπαιδεύθη ὁμοῦ, ὅσα ἦν σοφώτερα, ὑπὸ τῷ μεγάλῳ Πρόκλῳ"; Sud., *Π*, 137. *Cf.* Robert A. Kaster, *Guardians of Language. The Grammarian and*

ens and to settle in Constantinople. There he came into contact with Marsus, an Isaurian friend of Illus, thanks to whom Pamprepius was admitted into Illus's circle. A discourse on the soul which Pamprepius delivered before Illus, on the prompting of Marsus, was what definitively fused their destinies.[38] Pamprepius's presence and attitude, however, aroused more antagonism than goodwill. All authors, pagans and Christians alike, agree on this point. Even all the physical portraits of Pamprepius which have survived are very negative, his appearance presented with a clearly disdainful slant. His personality and behavior arousing dislike, he was described as arrogant and self-assured by Malchus, Damascius, and by Rhetorius, the supposed author of his horoscope.[39]

Pamprepius openly proclaimed his paganism in Christian Constantinople, and also boasted his prophetic powers,[40] convincing Illus that the general's power would increase in the near future.[41] His prophecies and personality earned him such fame as a seer in Constantinople that he was ultimately expelled from the imperial capital. The circumstances of this dismissal merit our attention, as it marks the first incident linking Verina to Pamprepius.

On one of the occasions (prior to the rebellion) on which there was a clash between Zeno and Illus, the latter left the city.[42] Strangely, Pamprepius did not accompany his patron but remained in Constantinople. It is very possible that Pamprepius believed his position in the city to be so secure that he did not require Illus's presence and political clout. However, Malchus' account reveals that Pamprepius was mistaken. Illus's departure from Constantinople led to the inexorable decline of Pamprepius, who was then expelled from the city. This same author claims that this was due to his arro-

---

Society in Late Antiquity (Berkeley: Cambridge University Press, 1988), p. 329–32, and Elzbieta Szabat, 'Teachers in the Eastern Roman Empire (Fifth to Seventh century): A Historical Study and Prosopography', in *Alexandria: Auditoria of Kom el-Dikka and Late Antique Education*. Journal of Juristic Papyrology. Suppl. 8, ed. by Tomasz Derda, Tomasz Markiewicz and Ewa Wypszycka (Warsaw: Warsaw University, 2007), pp. 285–86.

[38] Malch.,*fr.* 23: "σθσταθέντα δὲ αὐτὸν ὁ Ἴλλους μάγιστρος ἡδέως δέχεται, καὶ τι καὶ δημοσίᾳ ποίημα ἀναγνόντα λαμπρῶς τε ἐτίμησε καὶ σύνταξιν ἔδωκε"; Cand.,*fr.* 1: "ὡς Παμπρεπίῳ τῷ δυσσεβεῖ διὰ Ἴλλους φιλωθείς"; Damasc., *Hist. Phil.* § 77 d: "ἀχθεὶς οὖν παρὰ Μάρσου πρὸς Ἴλλουν". Damascius, *Hist. Phil.* § 112a and Marinus of Neapolis, *Vita Procli* § 15, compare him to Typhon, a furious and rabid beast. *Vid.* Alan Cameron, 'Wandering Poets: A Literary Movement in Byzantine Egypt', *Historia*, 14 (1965), 470–509 (pp. 471–73 and 485–86).

[39] Cand.,*fr.* 1; Damasc., *Hist. Phil.* § 66 a; 112a and 113e; *CCAG* 8, 4, 221–224. 20, f. 139v; Neugebauer and Van Hoesen, *Greek Horoscopes*, 140–41. *Vid.* Roberto, 'Sulla tradizione storiografica', p. 710.

[40] Malch.,*fr.* 23: "ὡς δὲ ἐν Χριστιανοὺς πάντας ἐχούσῃ πόλει τὸ Ἑλληνικὸν αὐτοῦ τῆς θρησκείας οὐκ ἔχον ὑπόκρισιν, ἀλλὰ μετὰ παρρησίας προδήλως δεικνύμενον, εἰς τὴν τοῦ καὶ ἕτερα τῆς ἀρρήτου σοφίας εἰδέναι ὑπόνοιαν ἦγε"; *Sud.,Π,* 137. *Vid.*Asmus, 'Pamprepios, ein byzantinischer', pp. 329–36 and Alan Cameron, 'Poets and pagans in Byzantine Egypt', in *Egypt in the Byzantine World. 300–700*, ed. By Roger S. Bagnall (Cambridge: Cambridge University Press, 2007), pp. 21–46 (35–6).

[41] Malch.,*fr.* 23; Ps. Joshua the Stylite, *Chron.* § 236.*Sud.,Π,* 137.

[42] Theoph.,*Chron. a. m.* 5972, *ad a.* 479/480; we should note that Theophanes summarizes the events in this way, confusing the time and persons in question. *Vid.* Roberto, 'Sulla tradizione storiografica', p. 702 and *infra*.

gance in openly espousing paganism. These circumstances convinced Zeno and Verina—who is expressly mentioned—of the need to cast him out of the city.[43] But Malchus also suggests that their decision was influenced by their belief that his prophecies were harmful to the interests of the emperor which, incidentally, at the time were the same as Verina's.[44] Both Zeno and Verina must have suspected that Pamprepius was an agent of Illus and decided to remove him. That the reason advanced for his expulsion was his paganism should come as no surprise; it seems likely that at that moment, Zeno and Verina shared Emperor Leo's position of tolerating pagan beliefs, provided that they remained in the private sphere and were not openly expressed.[45]

We know that the expulsion of Pamprepius was carried out, as he left Constantinople and settled in Pergamon from which he was summoned by Illus – an undeniable indication of the high regard in which he held him.[46]

As previously indicated, relations between Zeno and Illus were not smooth. At times they collaborated and other times they squared off.[47] But it is indisputable that Zeno, convinced of Illus's power (who also had as a hostage for some time Longinus, brother of the Emperor),[48] preferred to keep him close, whether to draw him to his side, control him, or so that he could aid him in the event of a feared Ostrogothic attack.[49] Thus, around 477/478 the emperor asked Illus to return to Constantinople, which he did on condition that the emperor consented to Pamprepius accompanying

---

[43] Malch., *fr.* 23: "πείθουσι τὸν Ζήνωνα καὶ τὴν Βερίναν τότε μέγιστα δυναμένην τῆς πόλεως ἐκπέμψαι".

[44] Malch., *fr.* 23; *Sud.,Π,* 137. Theoph.,*Chron. a. m.* 5972, *ad a.* 479/480, mentions that he had been accused of practicing magic: "καὶ Παμπρέπιον τὸν συγκλητικόν, τὸν ἐπὶ μαγγανείᾳ διαβαλλόμενον"; Iohan. Antioch.,*fr.* 303 only indicates that Zeno expelled Illus's friends and family from Constantinople, without providing names.

[45] *Cf.* the cases of pagan philosopher Isocasius (Mal., *Chron.* § 370–371; *Chron. Pasch.* s. a. 467; Iohan. Nik., *Chron.* § LXXXVIII, 7; Theoph., *Chron. a. m.* 5960, *ad a.* 467/468. See Kaster, *Guardians of Language,* 301–2), and the rebel Severianus (Damasc., *Hist. Phil.* § 108. See Athanassiadi, 'Persecution and Response in Late Paganism', p. 17.

[46] Malch.,*fr.* 23: "καὶ ὁ μὲν ἐς Πέργαμον ἔρχεται τῆς Μυσίας· Ἴλλους δὲ πυθόμενος κατὰ τὴν αὐτοῦ πρόφασιν ἐληλάσθαι τὸν ἄνδρα, πέμψας ἀναλαμβάνει αὐτὸν ἐς Ἰσαυρίαν καὶ σύμβουλόν τε αὐτὸν καὶ σύνοικον ποιεῖται"; *Sud.,Π* 137; *cf.* Theoph., *Chron. a. m.* 5972, *ad a.* 479/480, who believes that Pamprepius joined him immediately.

[47] Ernest W. Brooks, 'The Emperor Zenon and the Isaurians', *EHR* XXX (1893), 209–38; William D. Burgess, 'Isaurian Factions in the Reign of Zeno the Isaurian', *Latomus*51, 4 (1992), 874–80; Hugh Elton, 'Illus and the Imperial Aristocracy under Zeno', *Byzantion,* 70 (2000), 393–407; Karl Feld, *Barbarische Bürger. Die Isaurier und das Römische Reich* (Berlin/New York: de Gruyter, 2005), pp. 244–76; Bruno Pottier, "Banditisme et révolte en Isaurie au IVe. et Ve. siècles vus par les Isauriens eux-mêmes. La Vie de saint Conon", *MedAnt.* VIII, 2 (2005), 443–74 (pp. 465–74); Vicent Puech, "'Élites urbaines et élites imperiales sous Zénon (474–491) et Anastase (474–518)', *Topoi* 15/1 (2007), 379–96 (pp. 382–85); Kiel-Freytag, 'Betrachtungen zur Usurpation', pp. 291-301.

[48] Mal., *Chron.* § 385; Theoph.,*Chron. a. m.*5975, *ad a.* 482/483.

[49] Brooks, 'The Emperor Zenon', p. 218; Feld, *Barbarische Bürger,* 264–65.

him, and to Verina's acting in the role of hostage;[50] according to most authors, Illus held her responsible for the problems he had suffered in the city.[51]

In 477/478 Verina was brought to Tarsus, made a nun, and confined to Dalisandus.[52] It seems clear that a woman like Verina, the first empress depicted carrying the scepter (as she appears on the bronze coins alongside Leo),[53] and one particularly interested in the political scene, would consider her confinement a great humiliation, especially given the remoteness of the location. Meanwhile her two enemies, Illus and Pamprepius, enjoyed the splendor of Constantinople.[54] Verina's anger is clear in her request which, according to Malalas, John of Nikiu, and Theophanes Confessor, she sent to Ariadne, pleading for permission to return to Constantinople.[55] In this way Verina was reduced to recognizing the authority of a woman who was not only her daughter but, on many occasions, her rival.[56]

---

50   Iohan. Antioch.,*fr.* 303: "...ἐξαιτεῖ τὴν Βηρίναν"
51   Malch.,*fr.* 1; Cand., *fr.* 1; Iohan. Antioch.,*fr.* 302; Theoph., *Chron. a. m.* 5972, *ad a.* 479/480: Iord., *Rom.* § 349–350, attributes them to Ariadne and the jealousy which she harbored toward Illus. Kiel-Freytag, 'Betrachtungen zur Usurpation', p. 297, has proposed a modification to the chronology of the attempts on Illus which, consequently, affects the moment after which Verina was delivered to him. This author holds that this took place in 480. In any case, this chronological proposal does not affect the fact that Verina was confined by Illus for many years.
52   Iohan. Antioch.,*fr.* 303: "...ἐκεῖθέν τε ἐς Δαλίσανδον ἐφρούρει". On the location of Dalisandus in Isauria or Lyaconia, see Brent D. Shaw, 'Bandit Highlands and Lowland Peace: The Mountains of Isauria-Cilicia', *JESHO*, 23 (1990), 199–233 (pp. 200–03), and Scott Fitzgerald Johnson, *The Life and Miracles of Thekla. A Literary Study*, Hellenic Studies 13 (Washington: Harvard University Press, 2006), pp. 141–42. Cand.,*fr.* 1; Mal., *Chron.* § 385. 12 had presented wide areas for her confinement: Cilicia and Isauria, while in Theoph. Conf., *Chron. a. m.* 5972, *ad a.* 479/489 it was in the fortress of Papirius.
53   *RIC* 10, 718= R. A. G. Karson, P. V. Hill and J. P. C. Kent, *Late Roman Bronze Coinage*, (London: Spink and Son), 1960, vol. II, 2274/2275. *Vid.* Angelova, 'The Ivories', p. 4.
54   Mal., *Chron.* § 387.13; Iohan. Nik.,*Chron.* LXXXVIII, 65–68; Theoph., *Chron. a. m.* 5972, *ad a.* 479/480. Another rebellion against Zeno, in this case led by Marcianus, husband to Leontia, the youngest daughter of Verina, represented, among other things, according to some authors a protest against the widowed empress's confinement; thus, for example, Evagr., *HE* III, 26, citing that this information was taken from the work of Eustathius of Epiphania. It is worth mentioning another of the bases upon which Marcianus advanced his claim: Theoph., *Chron. a. m.* 5971, *ad a.* 478/479, states that Marcianus argued that Leontia was the only living daughter of Leo and Verina who had been born after the imperial proclamation; thus, she had been born "in the purple" and was, along with her mother, the only person transmitting the legitimacy of the throne. It was denied that Ariadne was capacitated for it, such that Zeno was an illegitimate emperor. From other authors, due to the fragmentary nature of the transmission, we have received news of the rebellion, but not the reasons driving it; for example, Malch.,*fr.* 22 or Cand., *fr.* 1. With respect to those "born in the purple" prior to the official use of the title "Porphyrogenitus", *vid.* Gilbert Dagron, 'Nés dans le pourpre', *T&M*, 12 (1994), 105–42 (pp. 107–9). On the rebellion of Marcianus, who was also the grandson of Emperor Marcianus: *vid.* Vicent Puech, ''Élites urbaines', pp. 380–81; Cristian Olariu, 'Legitimacy and Usurpation in the Age of Zeno', *Poemerium*, 6 (2007–2008), 100–05 (p. 102–03); Vallejo Girvés, '*Ad Ecclesiam confugere,* tonsuras y exilios', pp. 153–57.
55   Mal., *Chron.* § 387.13; Iohan. Nik.,*Chron.* LXXXVIII, 68; Theoph., *Chron. a. m.* 5972, *ad a.* 479/480.
56   Kiel-Freytag, 'Betrachtungen zur Usurpation', pp. 293–94; Vallejo Girvés, '*Ad Ecclesiam confugere,* tonsuras y exilios', pp. 151–53.

Illus and Pamprepius's stay in Constantinople ended a few years later. In 482, in response to a new plot against his life—this time orchestrated by Ariadne who apparently decided to act in favor of her mother—Illus abandoned the city, accompanied by Marsus and Pamprepius.[57] Verina, however, did not return, but remained confined and ever beholden to Illus, whom, possibly in an attempt to avoid greater evils, Zeno had appointed *magister militum per Orientem*.[58]

In 484 the strained relations between Zeno and Illus reached a breaking point, and the latter rebelled, joined by his brother Trocundes, his brother-in-law Matronianus, and his fellow Isaurian Marsus Leontius, Zeno's *magister militum per Thracias*, whomIllus had managed to lure away from the emperor, and the pagan Pamprepius, also joined.[59] Literary sources mention that Illus enjoyed great support among the Dyophisites in the Eastern provinces, and that his rebellion might have been well received by the empire's pagans.[60]Authors such as Damascius allude to certain attempts to regain tolerance for paganism in the empire. On one occasion he states that Severianus's attempt to restore paganism failed due to the betrayal of his supporters; among these traitorous allies he expressly names Illus and Marsus.[61] Furthermore, Damascius indicates that Pamprepius had managed to reconcile Illus and Leontius in their ideas, that is, they had converted to paganism.[62]Illus's purportedly pagan sympathies are also indicated in a passage of the *Vita Isaiae Monachi* by Zacharias Scholastikos.[63]

It is difficult to accept the paganism of Illus, however, for reasons which we shall see.First of all, while there are known cases of cryptopagans,[64] Christian conversions to paganism were virtually unheard of. In addition, the story of the conversion of a renowned Christian to paganism has preceding parallels,[65] always false but used for the same purposes that, in my opinion, Illus's conversion was alleged.[66] Illus's paganism, asserted primarily by the Miaphysite author Zacharias Scholastikos, was an instrument

---

[57] Marc. Com., *Chron.* a. 484. 1; Josh. Styl.,*Hist.* § 244–245; Iord., *Rom.* § 351; Mal., *Chron.*§ 387. 13; Evagr., *HE* III, 27; Theoph., *Chron. a. m.* 5972, *ad a.* 479/480. *Vid.* Kiel-Freytag, "Betrachtungen zur Usurpation,"294.

[58] *Cf.* Hugh Elton, "Illus and the Imperial Aristocracy."398.

[59] Theoph.,*Chron. a. m.* 5972, *ad a.* 479/480.

[60] *Vid. supra.*

[61] Damasc.,*Hist. Phil.* § 115 a: "Πρὸςοἱς Μάρσοςκαὶ Ἴλλους".*Vid.* Athanassiadi, 'Persecution and Response in Late Paganism', p. 17.

[62] Damasc.,*Hist. Phil.* § 77 b: "ὅτι καὶ Ἰλλοθν οὗτος καὶ Λεόντιον ὃν ἐκεῖνος ἀντιχειροτονεῖ Ζήνωνι Βασιλέα, τὰ αὐτὰ καὶ φρονεῖν καὶ Βούλεσθαι πρὸς ἀσέβειαν, Παμπρεπίου πρὸς ταύτην αὐτοὺς ἑλκύσαντος διακείνεται". *Cf.* Phot., *Bibl.* 242.109 and 111.

[63] Zach.,*Vit. Isaiae*§ 10.

[64] Raymon van Dam, 'From Paganism to Christianity at Late Antique Gaza', *Viator*, 16 (1985):3.

[65] *Cf.*Ruph., *HE* I, 34, during the reign of Emperor Julian.

[66] *Cf.* Edward Watts, 'Winning the Intracommunal Dialogues: Zacharias Scholasticus' Life of Severus', *JECS*, 13/4 (2005), 437–64 (p. 449, n. 46).

to demonize Illus, and the Dyophisites along with him, as it seems clear that the rebel was more amenable to the latter Christian viewpoint. It is worth mentioning that accusations against Christians said to have gone over to paganism were not only leveled by Miaphysites at Dyophisites, but vice versa: Pope Felix III, a Dyophysite, sent Zeno a letter accusing the Miaphysite Patriarch of Alexandria, Peter III Mongus, of working to restore paganism.[67] However, in the *Vita Severi*, the Miaphysite Zacharias Scholastikos writes that the patriarch had actually overseen the destruction of pagan temples in Kanopos.[68]

The second reason why we consider Illus's conversion to paganism unlikely is related to his personal life, infused with Christian faith. His daughters were baptized with the name of two revered saints of Isauria and Tarsus: Thecla and Anthusa. Nearing death, he asked that Anthusa be buried in the Sanctuary of the Three Children of Tarsus, and that Thecla and his wife also be protected inside this sacred ground.[69] In itself, this request does not suffice to demonstrate Illus's Christian faith. He may have made that decision in an attempt to save their lives, fearful that Zeno would eliminate them.[70] That said, his daughter's naming after the Isaurian saint, and his request for her to receive a Christian burial, do demonstrate Illus's Christian convictions.

Several sources mention Illus' friendship with the Dyophisite Patriarch of Alexandria, John Talaia. This relationship predated the rebellion; Liberatus of Carthage alludes to the fact that, when this bishop was appointed, he sent delegates to Constantinople in order to report this to his *amicus* (friend) Illus,[71] making allegations of Illus's paganism difficult to believe.

Illus's belief in the accuracy of Pamprepius's prophecies could be seen as a sign of paganism, but it is not necessary to reach this conclusion. Other Christian emperors whose Christianity is not doubted, such as Zeno, also believed in prophecies to the

---

[67] Felix Pontif., *Epistola* II (*PL* 58, 599-904). *Cf.* Christopher Haas, 'Patriarch and People: Peter Mongus of Alexandria and Episcopal Leadership in the Late Fifth Century', *JECS*, 1 (1993), 297-316 (pp. 309-10).

[68] Zach.,*Vit. Sev.* § 34-48. *Vid.* Frank R. Trombley, *Hellenic Religion and Christianization. c. 370-529*, II, (Leiden: Brill, 1994), 10-15; Watts, 'Winning the Intracommunal', pp. 263-64, and, by the same author, *Riot in Alexandria* (Berkeley: University of California Press 2010), pp. 235-50.

[69] Iohan. Antioch.,*fr.* 306. *Vid.* Pierre Maraval, *Lieux saints et pèlerinages d'Orient. Histoire et géographie des origines à la conquête árabe* (Paris: Cerf, 1984), 356.

[70] We can cite some similar cases. For example, the wife and daughter of Rufinus, *Praefectus Praetorium* of Arcadius, survived by seeking refuge in a convent in Jerusalem. *Vid.* M. Vallejo Girvés, 'La mujer como víctima de la práctica política: los exilios familiares en la tardoantigüedad', in *Toga y Daga. Teoría y praxis de la política en Roma*, ed. by Gonzalo Bravo and Raúl González Salinero, (Madrid: Signifer, 2010), pp. 229-45.

[71] Lib., *Brev.* XVII: "... haben senimamicum Ellum ... magistrum, ei de sua quide mordinatione scripsit".*Cf.* Zach., *HE* III, v, 6; Evagr.,*HE* III, 12. *Vid.* Puech, ''Élites urbaines, p. 385.

point that they even ordered executions based upon them.[72] Illus does certainly appear to be a lover of classical learning, philosophy, meditation, and reading,[73] but this was not a quality peculiar to paganism at the time, as is shown in the case of his contemporary Candidus, author of a work possibly dedicated to Illus himself. Candidus, of Isaurian origin, was classically trained, an admirer of the classical legacy, while at the same time a fervent Dyophisite Christian.[74]

The alleged direct collaboration with the rebellion of the pagans of Gaza, Aphrodisias, and Alexandria merits separate analysis. In the *Vita Isaiae Monachi*, Zacharias Scholastikos mentions that the pagans of Gaza were hopeful that Illus's victory would allow them to worship openly, a prospect that sparked anxiety among the city's Christians. In this context, Zacharias presents his hero, Isaiah, who calms the Christians by arguing that this was not going to come about.[75] Though this text does make reference to the pagans' hopes, nothing in it indicates that the pagans of Gaza directly supported the rebel Illus.

In the *Vita Severi*, also by Zacharias Scholastikos, the author writes that the pagans of Aphrodisias in Caria, headed by the philosopher Asklepiodotos, had practiced rituals peculiar to their religion in order to determine if Illus's rebellion would succeed. In order to reveal the futility of their rites, Zacharias Scholastikos indicates that they were all useless and nothing was obtained from them.[76] We cannot firmly conclude from this passage that the pagans of Aphrodisias openly supported Illusin his revolt. The fact that they carried out these rituals only indicates their desire to know whether Illus would be their new ruler—one perhaps less injurious to their interests. Perhaps it was Illus's love for classical knowledge, rather than Pamprepius's presence beside him, which led them to believe this.

Damascius alludes to Pamprepius's arrival in Egypt and his attempt to convince the philosophers of Alexandria to support Illus.[77] However, as it cannot be deduced from these passages that it was Illus who had sent him, we find it more probable that Pamprepius undertook this visit on his own initiative, convinced that he could sway the

---

[72] For example, the imprisonment and execution of the pagan Pelagius, who Zeno considered a potential rival after believing a prophecy issued by the *comes* Maurianus; Malch.,*fr.* 2; Mal., *Chron.* § 390.16; *Chron. Pasch.* 490; Iohan. Nik., *Chron.* LXXXVIII, 92; Theoph., *Chron. a. m.* 5982, *ad a.* 489/490 and *a. m.* 5983, *ad a.* 490/491. On this see Alan Cameron, 'Wandering Poets', pp. 506–07 and Roberto, 'Sulla tradizione storiografica', p. 688 n. 6.

[73] Iohan. Antioch.,*fr.* 306, mentions that when he was under siege by Zeno's troops Illus turned over the defense to others and dedicated himself to reading.

[74] Phot.,*Bibl.* 79, in his summary of Cand.,*fr.*1. *Vid.* Roberto, 'Sulla tradizione storiografica', p. 696–97.

[75] Zach.,*Vit. Isaiae*§ 10. *Vid* Van Dam, 'From Paganism', p. 18–9.

[76] Zach.,*Vit. Sev.* § 54. *Vid.*, on this point, Watts, 'Winning the Intracommunal', p. 454. *Cf.* Trombley, *Hellenic Religion* I, 21–2; Trombley, *Hellenic Religion* II, 81–83 and 92–94; Haas, 'Patriarch and People', 325–26.

[77] *Cf.* Damasc., *Hist. Phil.* § 112 a and 113 c: "Οἱ δὲ πλεῖστοι ὠρθοῦντο πρὸς τὰ ἀρχαῖα ταῖς ἐλπίσιν".

pagans to his cause. Damascius does make it clear that the pagan Alexandrians considered Pamprepius so unreliable that they distanced themselves from him, even considering his presence alongside Illus to be detrimental to the rebel's interests.[78] Therefore, these passages also fail to substantiate clear support for Illus from the Egyptian or Alexandrian pagans.

Following Rudolf Asmus, scholars recognize that pagan Egyptians supported Illus's revolt. This conclusion is based on evidence of Zeno's persecution of the pagans after the rebellion's failure and on the text of Rhetorius's horoscope of Pamprepius.[79] However, as some authors have already pointed out, these are not firm foundations upon which to base this supposition.[80] First, because the persecution does not necessarily imply that the pagans openly supported Illus, but rather that they were interested in knowing if he could succeed and whether, in that case, their situation would improve, which surely must have vexed Zeno. In addition, it is well known that the mere act of consulting an oracle or making sacrifices in order to divine the emperor's political future constituted a crime of high treason.[81] Secondly, because in addition to the existing doubts as to the existence of an author named Rhetorius, it seems beyond question that the horoscope was not produced until the sixth century.[82] The pagans' undeniable interest in the rebellion, and their subsequent persecution by Zeno might have led the author of the horoscope to assume, incorrectly, that they openly supported Illus and that he had sought to enlist their help.

In short, the pagans might have taken an interest in Illus's revolt, pondered whether its success would benefit them, and concluded that, compared to Zeno, Illus was their best option. But the truth is that at Illus's side in Antioch and Tarsus there is evidence of only one pagan, Pamprepius, while Christians abounded, apparently all of them Dyophysites.[83] Without doubt, the decisions which Zeno, in collaboration with

---

[78] Damasc., *Hist. Phil.* § 113 k: "Ὁδὲ Παμπρέπιος τούτοις ἀμφίβολος ὀφθείς Βραχὺ παπεωτάτο", and 113 o-p: "Ὁ δὲ Παμπρέπιος κατὰ τὴν Αἴγυπτον παραγεγὼς Ἰσιδώρῳ παρέσχεν ἐκ τῶν λόγον αἴσθησιν ὡς οὐκ ὑγιαίνοι πρὸς Ἴλλιοω. Ἀλλ' ἡδὺ προδωσείοντι ἔοικε καὶ μέντοι καὶ περιορωμένῳ τὴν Ῥωμαίων Βασιλείαν". *Vid.* Alan Cameron, 'Poets and pagans', pp. 21-2.

[79] Asmus, 'Pamprepios', pp. 332-33. *Vid.* also, Trombley, *Hellenic Religion*, I, p. 81-4 and 92-4; Trombley, *Hellenic Religion* II, pp. 21-2; Haas, 'Patriarch and People', 326 and 342-43.

[80] *Cf.* R. von Haehling, 'Damascius und die heidnische Opposition zu einem Kaloghednischer Widersacher in der *Vita Isidori*', *JAChr.*, 23 (1980), 82-95 (p. 92-4); Polymnia Athanassiadi, *Damascius. The Philosophical History. Text with translation and notes* (Athens: Apamea, 1999), 33; Alan Cameron, 'Poets and pagans', p. 35-6.

[81] Trombley, *Hellenic Religion* II, 65-6.

[82] David Pingree ed., *Dorothei Sodonii Carmen Astrologicum* (Leipzig: Teubner, 1976), pp. xii-xiii.

[83] E. Stein, *Histoire*, II, 19-33, believed that Illus received clear support from this group, clearer than any he may have received from the pagans. *Vid.* also, Philippe Blaudeau, 'Ordre religieux et ordre public. Observation sur l'histoire de l'Église post-chalcédonienne d'après le témoignage de Jean Malalas', in *Recherches sur la Chronique de*

the Patriarch Acacius of Constantinople, had taken in matters of faith with the *Henotikon* of 482 pushed the Dyophisites towards Illus.[84]

As we have already mentioned, the previous relationship between Illus and John Talaia leads us to believe that the rebel's sympathies were with Dyophisitism.[85] In addition, the episcopal see of Antioch, one of the cities from which Illus waged his rebellion, was occupied at the time by the other major Dyophisite figure: Bishop Calandion, whose decision with regards to the proclamation of a new emperor is worthy of analysis and brings us, finally, to the issue of Verina's participation in this episode.[86]

Instigator of several rebellions, Illus opted to place puppets on the throne. Thus, he chose Leontius, the Isaurian *magister militum* of Thrace and the first agent sent by Zeno to put down the rebellion.[87] It was at this time that Verina played an active role. Whether forced or convinced by Illus, she proclaimed Leontius emperor, crowning him in Tarsus, and communicating, via *sacra*, her decision to Antioch and the eastern provinces.[88] The activity of Verina at this precise juncture leaves no doubt that if the revolt of Illus had a religious backdrop, it was a Christian and not a pagan one.

There has been much debate about whether Verina was forced to act by Illus, who was interested in proclaiming a new emperor once the rebellion broke out. The ancient authors are not clear about the circumstances under which Verina joined the rebellion. As a result, the theories are diverse. Some believe that she had no choice since, had she resisted, she would have run the risk of being killed by Illus. Others, however, contend that the rebellion offered her a chance to return to the political scene and to take revenge on Zeno, who had allowed her confinement for such a prolonged period.[89] Whatever the legitimacy achieved through Verina's proclamation of Leontius as emperor, the ceremony featured a

---

Jean Malalas. I, ed. by Joëlle Beaucamp *et al.*, (Paris: Centre de recherche d'histoire et civilisation de Byzance, 2004), pp. 243–56 (pp. 246–47).

[84] Kiel-Freytag, 'Betrachtungen zur Usurpation', pp. 291–93.

[85] *Vid. supra*, Blaudeau, 'Ordre religieux, pp. 246–48 and Alan Cameron, 'Poets and pagans', pp. 35–36.

[86] Roberto, 'Sulla tradizione storiografica', p. 709.

[87] Josh. Styl.,*Hist.* § 245; Iord., *Rom.* § 352 and also Evagr., *HE* III, 27. Although most authors believe that Zeno sent Leontius on that particular mission, others, such as Mal., *Chron.* § 388 or Theoph., *Chron. a. m.* 5972, *ad a.* 479/480, believe that Leontius joined Illus when the latter abandoned Constantinople.

[88] Cand., *fr.* 1: "ὡς εἰς τὸ ἐμφανὲς Ἴλλους ἐπαναστὰς Ζήνωνι βασιλέα Λεόντιον σὺν Βηρίνῃ ἀνεῖπεν"; Iohan. Antioch.,*fr.* 306: "πρὸς ἅπερ Ἰλλοῦςἐν Ταρσῷ ἀγαγὼν τὴν Βηρίναν, στολῇ χρήσασθαι βασιλικῇ παρεσκεύασε καὶ, οἷα κυρίαν οὖσαν τῆς Βασιλείας, Λεόντιον ἀναγορεῦσαι Βασιλέα στᾶσαν ἐν βήματι"; Theoph., *Chron. a. m.* 5973, *ad a.* 480/481. Interesting, in this regard, is Ps. Joshua the Stylite, *Chron* § 246, as in a neutral tone he affirms that Leontius was proclaimed emperor in Antioch, without mentioning Verina; however, he attributes all the responsibility to Illus, as does Vict. Tun., *Chron. ad a.* 483.

[89] Brooks, 'The Emperor Zeno', p. 225–27; Miroslaw J. Leszka, 'Empress-Widow Verina's Political Activity during the Reign of Emperor Zeno', in *Mélanges d'Histoire Byzantine offerts à Oktawiusz Jurewicz à l'occasion de son soixante-dixièmeanniversaire*, ed. by Waldemar Ceran (Łódz: Wydawn, 1998), 128–36 (pp. 135–36); Feld, *Barbarische Bürger*, pp. 262–71; Kiel-Freytag, 'Betrachtungen zur Usurpation', p. 300.

markedly Christian tone, to which the empress was party. Freed from her confinement, Verina proclaimed Leontius in Saint Paul's Church in Tarsus, and accompanied him to Antioch.[90] From there she wrote *Sacra* to the city of Antioch and the eastern provinces, where she presented Leontius as emperor.[91] The text of the *Excerpta de Insidiis* and that of Theophanes evince from the outset that she was a Christian empress addressing people who were also Christian to proclaim a Christian emperor.[92] The new emperor was surely a Christian Dyophysite,[93] and it seems that it was along such lines that the city of Antioch, or at least its Dyophisite Bishop Calandion, perceived him. After the ceremony, the bishop erased Zeno's name from the diptychs of the Church, replacing it with that of Leontius.[94]

In the coronation ceremony of Leontius, we find no echoes of paganism. The preparation of a horoscope to determine the most suitable day for Leontius's coronation

---

[90] Mal., *Chron.* § 388: "καὶ καταγαγὼν τὴν δέσποιναν Βηρίναν ὑπὸ τοῦ καστελλίου ἐποίησεν αὐτὴν στέψαι βασιλέα εἰς τὸν ἅγιον Πέτρον ἔξω τῆς πόλεως Ταρσοῦ τῆς Κιλικίας τὸν πατρίκιον Λεόντιον"; Theoph.,*Chron. a. m.* 5973, *ad a.* 480/481: "καὶ ἐξαγαγὼν Βερίναν τὴν αὐγούσταν εἰς Ταρσὸν τῆς Κιλικίας ἐποίησεν αὐτὴν στέψαι ἔξω τῆς πόλεως εἰς τὸν ἄφιον Πέτρον βασιλέα Λεόντιον τὸν πατρίκιον". Iohan. Antioch.*fr.* 306, does not indicate that the ceremony had a Christian meaning: "πρὸς ἅπερ Ἰλλοῦς ἐν Ταρσῷ γαγὼν τὴν Βηρίναν, στολῇ χρήσασθαι βασιλικῇ παρεσκεύασε καὶ, οἷα κυρίαν οὖσαν τῆς Βασιλείας, Λεόντιον ναγορεῦσαι Βασιλέα στᾶσαν ἐν βήματι". Evagr.,*HE* III, 27, only mentions that the proclamation took place in Tarsus.

[91] Theoph., *Chron. a. m.* 5973, *ad a.* 480/481: "καὶ ἔγραφεν ἡ δέσποινα Βερίνα σάκραν τοῖς Ἀντιοχεῦσι Σύροις εἰς τὸ δέξασθαι τὸν Λεόντιον Βασιλέα, καὶ πρὸς πάντας δὲ τοὺς τῆς νατολῆς ἄρχοντας καὶ τῆς Αἰγύπτου καὶ Λιβύης ἐποίησε σάκρας, ὥστε δέξασθαι Λεόντιον βασιλέα καὶ μὴ ντιστῆναι"; *cf.* Mal., *Chron.* § 388: "καὶ ἐποίησεν ἡ αὐτὴ Βηρίνα θείας κελεύσεις κατὰ πόλιν καὶ σάκρας πρὸς τοὺς ἄρχοντας καὶ πρὸς τοὺς στρατιώτας ὥστε δέκασθαι αὐτὸν καὶ μὴ ἐναντιωθῆναί τινα, γράφασα δὲ σάκραν ἔχουσαν πολλὰ κακὰ περὶ Ζήνωνος".

[92] *Excerpta De Insidiis* § 147: "' Αἰλία Βηρίνα ἡ εἰ Αὐγούστα Ἀντιοχεῦσι πολίταις ἡμετέροις. ἴστε, ὅτι τὸ βασίλειον μετὰ τὴν ποβίωσιν Λέοντος τοῦ τῆς θείας λέξεως ἡμετέρου ἐστίν. προεχειρισάμεθα δὲ βασιλέα Στρακωδίσσεον τὸν μετὰ ταῦτα κληθέντα Ζήνωνα, ὥστε τὸ ὑπήκοον βελτιωθῆναι καὶ πάντα τὰ στρατιωτικὰ τάγματα. ὁρῶσι νῦν τὴν πολιτείαν ἅμα τῷ ὑπηκόῳ κατόπιν φερομένην ἐκ τῆς αὐτοῦ πλησίας ναγκαῖον ἡγησάμεθα βασιλέα ὑμῖν στέψαι εὐσεβῆ δικαιοσύνῃ κεκοσμημένον, ἵνα τὰ τῆς Ῥωμαϊκῆς πολιτείας περισῴζῃ πράγματα καὶ τὸ πολέμιον ἥσυχον ἄξει, τοὺς δὲ ὑπηκόους ἅπαντας μετὰ τῶν νόμων διαφυλάξῃ. ἐστέψαμεν Λεόντιον τὸν εὐσεβέστατον, ὃς πάντας ὑμᾶς προνοίας ξιώσει'. καὶ εὐθέως ἔκραξεν ὁ δῆμος τῶν Ἀντιοχέων ἅπας ὑφ᾿ ἓν ναστάς· 'μέγας ὁ θεός,' καὶ 'κύριε ἐλέησον, τὸ καλὸν καὶ τὸ συμφέρον παράσχου'"; Theoph., *Chron. a. m.* 5974, *ad a.* 481/482: "Βερίνα αὐγούστα τοῖς ἡμετέροις ἄρχουσι καὶ φιλοχρίστοις λαοῖς χαίρειν. ἴστε ὅτι τὸ βασίλειον ἡμέτερόν ἐστιν, καὶ ὅτι μετὰ τὴν ποβίωσιν τοῦ ἐμοῦ ὑδρὸς Λέοντος προεχειρισάμεθα βασιλέα Τρασκαλισσαῖον, τὸν μετακληθέντα Ζήνωνα, ὥστε τὸ ὑπήκοον ἐπιβελτιωθῆναι. ὁρῶντες δὲ νῦν τὴν πολιτείαν κατόπιν φερομένην ἐκ τῆς αὐτοῦ πλησίας, ναγκαῖον ἐλογισάμεθα βασιλέα ὑμῖν στέψαι χριστιανὸν εὐσεβείᾳ καὶ δικαιοσύνῃ κεκοσμημένον, ἵνα τά τε τῆς πολιτείας περισῴζῃ πράγματα καὶ τὸ πολεμικὸν ἡσυχως ἄξῃ. ἐστέψαμεν δὲ Λεόντιον τὸν εὐσεβέστατον βασιλέα Ῥωμαίων, ὃς πάντας ὑμᾶς προνοίας ξιώσει". *Cf.*, Mal., *Chron.* § 388–389 and Bernard Flusin, 'Les *Excerpta* Constantiniens et la *Chronographie* de Malalas', in *Recherches sur la Chronique de Jean Malalas*. I, ed. by Joëlle Beaucampe *et al.*, (Paris: Centre de recherché d'histoire et civilisation de Byzance, 2004), pp. 119–36 (p. 131), who believes that the *Excerpta De Insidiis* § 147 proceeds from the *Chronographia* of Malalas.

[93] Blaudeau, 'Ordre religieux', pp. 246–47 and n. 26.

[94] Zach.,*HE* V, 9c; Evagr., *HE* III, 17 and Theoph., *Chron. a. m.* 5982, *ad a.* 489–490. *Vid* .Feld, *Barbarische Bürger*, pp. 274–75; Blaudeau, 'Ordre religieux', p. 246–47.*Cf.* Kiel-Freytag, 'Betrachtungen zur', p. 292, n. 14, as she believes that in this document of Verina's there is nothing contrary to Zeno's religious attitude.

cannot be considered as such; it was drawn up *a posteriori*, when the failure of the enterprise was already a fact, indicating that the man crowned that day would not succeed in his revolt.[95] Neither do the *sacra* which Verina sent to the eastern provinces contain anything leading us to believe that Illus was going to openly tolerate pagan practices.

There is no indication that any pagan, apart from Pamprepius, formed part of the rebel's inner circle at that time. It was Christianity, the faith of Verina, which triumphed. Pamprepius, who openly professed paganism, helped to install a Christian emperor and took part at his coronation.[96]

---

[95] *CCAG* 6, 66, 16–67, 7; Neugebauer and Van Hoesen, *Greek Horoscopes*, 147–48.

[96] The rebellion, however, failed and Verina was exiled once again, this time to Papirius, where she was joined by Marsus, the usurper Leontius, Pamprepius, Illus and his family (Iohan. Antioch.,*fr*306; Theoph., *Chron. a. m.* 5976, *ad a.* 483/484. *Cf.* Evagr., *HE* III, 27). Many of them died in Papirius. Sometime later, Verina's body was transferred to Constantinople and buried, befitting to an Augusta, in the sarcophagus of Leo I in the Church of the Holy Apostles (Iohan. Antioch.,*fr*306; Theoph., *Chron. a. m.* 5976, *ad a.* 483/484, only mentions that Ariadne transferred her mother's body to the imperial capital after her death; *Cf.* Vallejo Girvés, "The Triumphant Return of Verina"(forthcoming). The pagan Pamprepius was executed by the soldiers of Illus (Cand.,*frag.* 1; Ps. Joshua the Stylite, *Chron.* § 246; Damasc., *Hist. Phil.* § 77d; Suda, *Π*, 137. See Roberto, 'Sulla tradizione storiografica', p. 710). After another four years, the rebels, Illus and Leontius, were seized and beheaded by the soldiers of Emperor Zeno.

JOHN LYDUS—PAGAN AND CHRISTIAN*

Anna Judit Tóth

In the first part of *The Last Pagans of Rome,* Alan Cameron emphasizes how misleading it can be to divide the society of Late Antiquity into two easily separable categories, pagans and Christians—with a broad red line of demarcation between these hostile parties—while at the same time disregarding a great proportion of society, perhaps the majority, who cannot be classified unambiguously. He cites the famous story of Marius Victorinus in Augustine's *Confessions*.[1] Having read the Bible, Victorinus declared himself Christian, but his friend Simplicianus doubted his sincerity unless he came to the Church. This proved to be the most demanding task for the convert, but finally Victorinus gave in. Why was public confession of faith so crucially important? It made conversion irrevocable, demonstrating that the convert had burned his bridges. Simplicianus, however, might have had other considerations in mind in this particular case. He may have wondered what Victorinus or any other pagan intellectual understood and learned about Christianity merely out of their reading books alone in their studies. For converts with a philosophical background, joining a Christian community meant to accept the authority of the Church that fought against the danger of syncretism. It is hard to tell how effective the episcopal control of syncretism was, because over the centuries of Christianization it proved riskier to be too interested in theological finery than to be a bad Christian. In Late Antiquity, not only the clergy, but also laymen discussed with enthusiasm theological problems;[2] circus factions

---

* This research benefited from funding from OTKA project number K 101503.
[1] Alan Cameron, *The Last Pagans of Rome,* (Oxford: Oxford University Press, 2011), p. 175; Augustine, *Confessions* VIII. 2. 3–6.
[2] See Gregory of Nyssa, "De deitate filii," *Patrologia Graeca* 46, col. 557 for shopkeepers on the *homousion*: "Everywhere, in the public squares, at crossroads, on the streets and lanes, people would stop you and discourse at random about the Trinity. If you asked something of a moneychanger, he would begin discussing the question of the Begotten and the Unbegotten. If you questioned a baker about the price of bread, he would answer that the Father is greater and the Son is subordinate to Him. If you went to take a bath, the Anomoean bath attendant would tell you that in his opinion the Son simply comes from nothing." *Gregory of Nyssa : The Minor Treatises on Trinitarian Theology and Apollinarism.* eds. V. H. Drecoll - M. Berghaus. (Leiden: Brill, 2011.)

supported theological trends and street fights broke out after the investiture of allegedly heterodox bishops. The people's fervent interest in orthodoxy, however, does not betray the depth of their theological knowledge, unrelated with the outburst of emotional reactions.

Marius Victorinus' example may help explain the religious peculiarities of a sixth-century author, John Lydus. A century passed between Augustine and Lydus, during which fundamental changes occurred in society. The legal status of pagans or heterodox Christians gradually worsened and under the reign of Justinian the first persecutions took place.[3] Under these circumstances, it is remarkable how many of the authors of the age are thought to have been pagans by modern philologists;[4] one of these imputed pagans is John Lydus.[5] Not counted among the most prominent authors of his time, he attracted relatively little scholarly attention until as recently as the last decades.[6] What makes him and his religious views so arresting is the fact that he was not an independent scholar but a bureaucrat, a member of the imperial administration. Thus, his life and works give an insight into the life strategies of a social layer that completely depended on the Christian Empire but—because of their education, ancestry, and social class—traditionally tended to steer away from the Christian religion.

---

[3] J. A. S. Evans, *The Age of Justinian. The Circumstances of Imperial Power*, (London and New York: Routledge, 2000) p. 249; Michael Maas, *John Lydus and the Roman Past*, (London and New York: Routledge, 1992) pp. 70–72.

[4] Prokopios: J.A.S. Evans, 'Christianity and Paganism in Procopius of Caesarea', *Greek, Roman and Byzantine Studies*, 12 (1971), 81–100, pp. 81–83.; Agathias: Anthony Kaldellis, 'The Historical and Religious Views of Agathias: A Reinterpretation', *Byzantion*, 69 (1999), 206–252.

[5] Anthony Kaldellis, 'The Religion of John Lydus', *Phoenix*, 57 (2003), 300–316, p. 302.; cf. Maas, pp. 4–5.; Averil Cameron, *Procopius and the Sixth Century*,(London and New York: Routledge, 1996) p. 246. Kaldellis drew attention to the possibility that Lydus's Christianity was nothing more than mere pretence, Averil Cameron and M. Maas tend to accept that he was a Christian even if a non-conformist and unconventional one. For Maas (p. 4.): 'It is possible that in the course of a single day he might read Plato, be healed at a saint's shrine, deliver a panegyric in Latin, praise or criticise the emperor, and sing the Trisagion hymn—without any sense of contradiction.' According to Maas, Lydus's peculiar religious views are only products of a syncretic culture but not a syncretic religion. What was endangered by Christianity, however, was Hellenic religion, not culture: Platonism has never become a sign of paganism. In Maas' interpretation, the keyword is indifference. Lydus, presumably, was indifferent towards both Christianity and Hellenic religion. This attitude contradicts Lydus's writings: ancient religion, for him, is essential part of Tradition, its annihilation is a source of sorrow.

[6] Anastasius C. Bandy, *Ioannes Lydus on Powers or the Magistracies of the Roman State*. Introduction, critical text, translation, commentary and indices, (Philadelphia: The American Philosophical Society, 1983); James Caimi, *Burocrazia e diritto nel De magistratibus di Giovanni Lido*, (Milano: Dott. A. Giuffrè Editore, 1984); T. F. Carney, *Bureaucracy in Traditional Society. Romano-Byzantine Bureaucracies Viewed from within*, 3 vols. (Lawrence, Kansas: Coronado Press, 1971); Maas, *John Lydus and the Roman Past*; C. N. Tsirpanlis, 'John Lydus on the Imperial Administration', *Byzantion*, 44 (1974), 479–501.; A. J. Tóth, "Ióannés Lydos és a történelem megújítása." [John Lydus and the renewal of history]. *Orpheus Noster* 1 (2009), 75–82; Sviatoslav Dmitriev, "John Lydus and His Contemporaries on Identities and Cultures of Sixth-Century Byzantium," *Dumbarton Oaks Papers* 64 (2010), pp. 27–42. Lydus is frequently quoted because of the data his books contain, but he is not appreciated as an author for his own sake. The *De magistratibus* with its highly personal and subjective tone can be regarded as an early example of the memoir-literature under the mask of an antiquarian work; this ambition to report on a life and a milieu that did not fit into the topics of the traditional historical genres makes his book interesting despite all its faults.

Born in Philadelphia, Lydia, John Lydus studied Platonic philosophy in Constantinople before beginning his service at the office of the praetorian prefect.[7] His career coincided with the gradual decline of the use of the Latin language in the administration, as well as the rise of John the Cappadocian who—if we believe his portrayal by Lydus—must have been almost illiterate. In his disappointment with the prevailing situation, Lydus escaped into literary activities and wrote books on antiquarian subjects.[8] All three of his extant works have some significance regarding his faith. His chief work on religious themes is on the months on the Roman calendar *(De mensibus)* and a fragmentary piece on celestial signs *(De ostentibus)*; but his *On offices (De magistratibus)* must be also taken into account as it reveals his personal beliefs, mentality and social relationships.

Lydus was a deeply conservative Roman, and the purpose with his books was to at least preserve the memory of a dying tradition—the old ways as they related to religion, administration, the military, and all aspects of ancient culture. For him the present was but decay and decadence, lack of culture and barbarism. He may not have been out of touch with the general feeling of his epoch, but he felt so. Lydus' desperate mood is not simply *fin-de siècle,* but almost post-apocalyptic.[9] Desperation and premonition of cultural decline does not necessarily go hand in hand with pagan sympathies, and writing on ancient religion is not the same as believing in the old gods. However, Lydus' readers—starting with Photius— cannot refrain from suspecting that the author believed in what he wrote. According to Photius: "In matters of religion he seems to have been an unbeliever. He respects and venerates Hellenic beliefs; he also venerates our beliefs, without giving the reader any easy way of deciding whether such veneration is genuine or hypocritical."[10] Several arguments can be brought up against Lydus' being a Christian. His personality, the subjects of his works, his obvious nostalgia for, and fascination with, the pagan past all suggest that he was no sincere Christian. He greatly admired his chief-of-office, Phocas, the praetorian prefect, twice accused of secret paganism and eventually forced to commit suicide.[11] Lydus knows almost nothing about Christianity; there is hardly any hint or allusion to the State religion. He inter-

---

[7] The best source for Lydus's life is his autobiography in *De magistratibus,* III. 26–30. C.f. Carney, II, pp. 3–20.; Bandy, pp. IX–XXVI.

[8] Editions of the texts: Bandy; Carney; Ioannes Lydus, *Des magistratures de l'État romain,* ed. by Michel Dubuisson (Paris: Les Belles Lettres, 2006-); Wuensch, R. (ed.): *Ioannis Lydi De magistratibus populi Romani libri tres.* Stuttgart, 1967;Ioannes Lydus, *Liber de mensibus,* ed. by R. Wuensch, (Leipzig: Teubner, 1898); *Liber de Ostentis et Calendaria Omnia,* ed. Curt Wachsmuth, (Leipzig: Teubner, 1897).

[9] Lydus waxes emotional about decline : *De mag.* III.25; *De mag.* III 12; *De mag.* III. 11; III.43; III.20, on the decline of Latin education and the decay of his office. For him, however, decay is connected with oppression: Book III of *De magistratibus* gives a long and sad list of murder, torture, and despoliation of whole provinces.

[10] Kaldellis, *The Religion of John Lydus,* p. 301; Photius, *Bibliotheca,* Cod.180.

[11] Evans, *The Age of Justinian,* p. 249; Maas, pp. 71, 78-82; Kaldellis, *The Religion of John Lydus,* p. 304.

prets Roman religion in a Platonic framework—and all prominent Neoplatonist philosophers were pagan, many of them expressed open hostility towards the new religion.[12]

At the same time, there are arguments for Lydus' Christianity, too. Officer of high rank in Constantinople, teaching philosophy at the imperial court: it is hardly imaginable without at least a *pro forma* Christianity. Lydus was very proud of the imperial favour he received, but what may be the strongest argument for his Christianity is that he did not arrive to Constantinople as a *homo novus*, but as a member of a Lydian patrician clan, supported by his uncle and the Lydian praetorian prefect, Zoticus. Thanks to their support, he received a position otherwise impossible for a young man. They also found him a wife with a considerable dowry.[13] If these high-ranking officials found Lydus a trustworthy and reliable person, we must suppose that either Lydus was Christian, or the entire clan was pagan—but this is practically impossible.

These considerations confirm the obvious fact that there would have been strong, external pressure for him to espouse Christianity, though this says nothing about his inner conviction. However, we must assume that when Lydus says "*we*" he means "we Christians,"[14] and refrains from expressing personal views incompatible or hostile to Christianity. The question is how he reconciled his presumed personal sympathy towards the old religion with the standards required by his office and social status. Photius simply concluded he was a hypocrite. This is, undoubtedly, the easiest answer. But lying throughout one's life is very taxing psychologically. In fact, it is not easy to find traces of hypocrisy, since Lydus does not make any effort in his writing to come across as a Christian. Lydus's texts suggest that his convictions were more complex, irreducible to 'paganism' or 'Christianity', and he does not even hide his syncretic views. Lydus' references to religion are tale-telling. This is what I survey in the next section.

Lydus' silences

The following subjects are conspicuously absent from Lydus' works:

Doctrinal statements. Lydus is a monotheist and sometimes he mentions God, but the relevant passages can be interpreted in a Platonic context as well to refer to the transcendent *Monas* or the idea of the Good.[15]

The Church. Controversies within the Church, heresies, theological problems are virtually non-existent issues.

---

[12] Malalas praises his teacher, Agapius, a disciple of Proclus, in the *De magistratibus*: Kaldellis, *The Religion of John Lydus*, p. 305; Maas, p. 31. The religious views of master and disciple can diverge, as in the case of Hypatia and Synesius of Cyrene: the latter questioned his own orthodoxy, but not his Christian faith.

[13] Lydus, *De magistratibus*, III. 26–27.

[14] Lydus, *De mensibus,* I. 20, IV.31.

[15] For example *De mensibus* III.8.; IV.47.; *De magistratibus*, III. 69.; III. 76.

Christian or Jewish tradition.[16] This lack of information is not surprising, regarding that the themes of Lydus's books have nothing to do with the Bible. Occasionally he indicates that the Church condemns pagan customs, e.g. in the case of the Saturnalia (*De mens.* IV.158.). The omission of these topics shows that Lydus was no fervent Christian (this comes as no surprise). Yet these omissions may have other motives besides paganism: lack of piety, caution in answering theological questions, the historic subjects of his works, etc. Lydus clearly indicates that the omission of such themes is deliberate in treating the significance of the number three: "ἡ γὰρ νοητὴ ὑπερβέβηκε τὴν παροῦσαν ἐξέτασιν."[17] Discussing the transcendent meanings of the number three at length, he actually indicates that he should mention the Holy Trinity, but he is cautious enough to avoid such a delicate problem.

A lack of Christian sources. Lydus quotes Moses in the *De mensibus* IV. 54 once and the *Septuagint* five more times.[18] At the same time, there are seventeen citations of the Chaldean Oracles,[19] six mentions of the Orphic texts, and a longer chapter on the Sibyls.[20] These pagan authorities were to some extent acceptable for Christians because of their alleged prophecy about the Trinity and the Incarnation of Christ—Lydus' contemporary, the Christian chronicler John Malalas also refers to these texts.[21]

Lydus' portrayal of a true Christian: Phocas

In the last chapters of the *De magistratibus*, Lydus gives a eulogy to the late Phocas, his chief-of-office, who committed suicide after being accused of secret paganism.[22] Lydus probably wrote this chapter with the intention of refuting the accusations, but it ended up becoming a veritable encomium rather than an apology.[23] Lydus praises Phocas' Christian virtue. What are these virtues? Mercy combined with tactfulness, politeness, and a deeply emotional urge to help others: Phocas gave away all his fortune, ransomed Roman prisoners from Persian slavery, and supported financially the Church. This list of virtues contain little typically 'Christian' piety, such as participation at the

---

[16] Lydus, *De mensibus* II.2.; III. 11; III.22.: remarks on the Jewish calendar; IV. 91: prohibited foods; IV. 109: under the reign of Nero (sic), the governor of Palaestina erected a statue of the emperor in the Temple of Jerusalem, the result was the Jewish war. IV. 154. For him, the creation of man in Moses I is an 'allegory.'

[17] *De mensibus* II, 8.

[18] Maas, p. 135.

[19] Maas, p. 123.

[20] Lydus, *De mensibus,* IV. 47.

[21] Ioannes Malalas, *Chronographia*, ed. by H. Thurn. (Berolini: De Gruyter, 1998) on Orpheus: IV.7; on Iulianus Chaldaeus: XI. 30; on the Sibyls: IV.5; IV. 10; IX. 8.

[22] Cf. note 11. Kaldellis, *The Religion of John Lydus*, p. 304: *De magistratibus*, III.72–76: Kaldellis emphasizes that Lydus uses more religious term in this passage than anywhere in the book.

[23] Lydus, *De magistratibus*, III. 72–76.

liturgy, or reading of the Scriptures. Yet the encomium does not follow ancient patterns alone. Phocas' virtues, his extravagant generosity and charity that went far beyond his means, are presented as Christian. If Lydus sought to represent Phocas's Christianity with these examples, it might mean that this was the Christian ideal he appreciated most: a good and generous person with no dogmatic hairsplitting.

Lydus' representation of Roman religion

He takes the old gods as allegories—no methodological innovations here. His hypothetical "Roman theology" is based on Platonism and Pythagorean mysticism. What is new with Lydus is that he applies the methods of Neoplatonic theology to a new material, unknown to the majority of his Greek contemporaries, the calendar of Roman holidays. Neoplatonic principles were highly adaptable for monotheisms, each of the creating their own variation. Lydus's aim is to prove that Roman religion was compatible with Neoplatonism, both are a symbolic-allegorical system reflecting the transcendent world (ruled, presumably, by One God), and the structure of the immanent world. For Lydus, Roman gods represent principles, mechanisms that make the world go around.

The continuity between cults and religions

Lydus makes unusually radical assumptions. Instead of accepting the apparent fact that there are fundamental differences between the old and the new religion, he supposes a continuity between various cults. The relevant passages are the following:

1. *De magistratibus*, II. 28.: (Justinian) ἀλλ' αὐτὸν Αὔγουστον τῇ περὶ θεὸν εὐσεβείᾳ καὶ τρόπων μετριότητι (...) παρώθησεν. With this strange statement, Lydos praises the emperors Augustus and Justinian suggesting that they worshipped the same God. What is even more surprising is that we can find a similar wording in Justinian's *Novels*.[24]

2. *De mensibus*, I. 20.[25] The text is slightly corrupted, but the meaning is clear: ritual ribbons used by pagan priests are connected with Christian liturgical vestments.

---

[24] *Corpus Iuris Civilis, Novella* 105. praef. on the consuls: ὕστερον δὲ ὁ χρόνος εἰς τὴν τῶν εὐσεβεστάτων αὐτοκρατόρων μεταστήσας τὸ πολεμεῖν τε καὶ εἰρήνην ἄγειν ἐξουσίαν. The text is about the consular title, so it implies that all emperors, even pagans or the persecutors, were 'pious'.

[25] *De mensibus*, I. 20."Ὅτι ἴδιον ἀεὶ γέγονε τῶν ἀρχιερέων τὴν κεφαλὴν σκέπειν ἢ διαδεσμεῖν ταινίᾳ· καὶ τοῦτο δῆλον ἐκ τοῦ μέχρι τήμερον τὴν τοῦ καθ' ἡμᾶς ἀρχιερέως ταινίαν τοῖς ὤμοις αὐτοῦ περιθέσθαι, τὴν ὡς ἔφην ἐπὶ τῆς κεφαλῆς τιθεμένην πάλαι· ὡς † καικαφόριον ἔτι καὶ νῦν καλεῖσθαι.

3. *De mensibus*, IV. 31.[26] Lydus describes traditional libations offered to the shades of the dead, adding slightly blasphemously that the Eucharist has kept some traces of this *choe*. The statement implies that Christ is dead, a notion hardly reconcilable even with a superficial Christianity. Lydus probably did not sense the real weight of what he was implying, focusing as he was on the ritualistic aspect.

4. *De mensibus*, IV. 67.[27] Lydus assumes a connection between pagan wreath and monastic tonsure.

5. *De mensibus*, IV. 158.[28] In a passage similar to *De mensibus* IV. 31., but less provocatively phrased, Lydus draws the same conclusion: sacrifices to the gods did not cease, they survive in the liturgical practices of the Church. Certain elements of the old religion did survive, transformed in folklore and superstition, but Lydus does not speak about such phenomena. He is searching for direct links between the old cults and the liturgy of the Christian Church. These theories may sound ridiculous, yet they express a wish for cultural continuity, permanence in change, a central motif of Lydus' work.

6. *De mensibus*, IV. 53. The topic of the chapter is a debate between "theologians" on the identity of the Hebrew God. The last passage is the most bizarre. Who are these theologians and what are their opinions?
   a.) According to the Egyptians and Hermes, the Hebrew God can be identified with Osiris.
   b.) He is the one of whom Plato states in the *Timaeus* that he is always existing, without beginning.
   c.) According to the "Hellenes," he is the Dionysus of Orpheus, because a golden cluster of grapes fastened the curtains of the Sanctuary in Jerusalem.

---

[26] *De mensibus*, IV. 31. αἱ γὰρ χοαὶ παραψυχή τις εἰσεφέρετο τοῖς εἰδώλοις τῶν τετελευτηκότων, γάλα, αἷμα καὶ οἶνος, καὶ σεμίδαλις, καὶ κόγχος, καὶ ἑτεράτινα. χοὰς δὲ αὐτὰς ὠνόμαζον ἐκ τοῦ ἐπεκχεῖσθαι τοῖς τάφοις. σώζεται δὲ καὶ νῦν ἴχνος· ἐν γὰρ τοῖς ἱεροῖς ἄρτον καὶ οἶνον προσφέρομεν.

[27] *De mensibus*, IV. 67. ὁ δὲ στέφανος τελειότητος δεῖγμά ἐστι· διὸ δὴ θεοῖς καὶ βασιλεῦσι καὶ ἱερεῦσιν ἐδίδοτο πρώτως. τῆς δὲ τύχης ἀφελομένης παρὰ τῆς ἀρετῆς τὸν στέφανον, οἱ ἱερεῖς τὸ λοιπὸν ἀποκειρόμενοι τὴν κόμην κύκλον τινὰ τριχῶν ἀντὶ στεφάνου τῇ κεφαλῇ περιποιοῦσι.

[28] *De mensibus*, IV. 158. οἱ δὲ γεωργικοὶ πρὸς θεράπειαν Κρόνου καὶ Δήμητρος ἔσφαττον χοίρους· ὅθεν καὶ νῦν φυλάττεται κατὰ τὸν Δεκέμβριον ἡ χοιροσφαγία. ... οἱ δὲ πολιτικοὶ καὶ τὰς ἀπαρχὰς τῶν συγκλεισθέντων καρπῶν, οἶνον καὶ ἔλαιον, σῖτον καὶ μέλι καὶ πάντα τὰ ἀπὸ δένδρων ὅσα διαμένουσι καὶσ ᾠζονται, ἐποίουν ἄρτους ἄνευ ὕδατος καὶ ταῦτα προσῆγον τοῖς ἱερεῦσι τῆς Μητρός· φυλάττεται δὲ ἤτοι αὕτη συνήθεια ἔτι καὶ νῦν καὶ κατὰ τὸν Νοέμβριον καὶ Δεκέμβριον ἄχρι τῶν αὐξιφωτίων προσφέρουσιν αὐτὰ τοῖς ἱερεῦσιν.

d.) According to Livius and Lucanus, the Hebrew God is unknown.
e.) Numenius says he is the father of the gods, who refused to be worshipped with other gods.
f.) The uneducated cite Julian the Apostate who called him the Highest God; because of this and the practice of circumcision, they identify him with Cronus. This view is faulty, because according to Hebrew mystics, circumcision is not a Cronian initiation. Nomads (*skenitai*) and Ethiopians have the same custom, but they worship Astarte and Apollo. At this point, Lydus refers to Origen.
g.) Porphyrius' *Commentary to the Chaldean oracles* suggests he is the *dis epekeina* and the creator of the universe, so he is secondary to the *hapax epekeina*, the transcendent One.
h.) According to Iamblichus, Syrianus, and Proclus, he is the God of the four elements.
i.) According to Varro, he is Iao of the Chaldeans. According to Herennius, Iao is the *phos noetos*, the intelligible light.

Lydus concludes with the most plausible opinion, that the Hebrew God is unknown *(adelos)*. Yet the text comes off as highly provocative. Lydus pretends not to know that the Jewish and the Christian God are the same and tries to resolve the issue with the good old *interpretatio Romana*. He quotes from Julian the Apostate, and does not refute him. Nevertheless, he cautiously rejects all arguments and his conclusion is secure: God is the *adelos* God. Without naming Saint Paul, it seems to me that the choice of the "the unknown God" as solution is not haphazard. It is not the most plausible for Lydus, but he knows that this has a solid Scriptural basis. Consequently, Lydus must have had some knowledge of the New Testament, no matter how much he sought to conceal it. The problem is rather in the question itself, a question that in itself is blasphemous—it sounds like a deliberate provocation. This is, however, unlikely —in contrast with Procopius' *Historia arcana*, Lydus' *De mensibus* was written for publication. Lydus might have composed it before his retirement, that would explain that he had little to lose. It is difficult to assess to what kind of readership he wrote. Justinian's anti-Jewish and anti-Samaritan policy would have prevented potential critics from objecting his strange arguments; perhaps he wrote to an audience who thought similarly, or trusted his patrons defending him against accusations. These alternatives seem all realistic.

What was Lydus' purpose with these remarks? He was walking on thin ice—and he might have found it amusing. *De mensibus* is too fragmentary to reconstruct Lydus' line of thought. In the extant text, he does not develop a coherent and elaborated theory of religious continuity; there are only allusions, hints to what he has in mind. In *De magistratibus*, Lydus presents his theory of change and development in the following way:

"All the things that exist both come into being and exist conformably to the nature of the good. The things that exist exist, as they exist, while the things that come into being do not exist perpetually, nor do they exist in the same manner, but they revolve through generation to corruption, then from the latter to generation, and with respect to existing they are perdurative, but with respect to undergoing change they are somewhat different; for, whenever they retire into themselves, they exist by means of substance but come into being by means of corruption because nature preserves them with itself and brings them forth again into manifestation in accordance with the conditions of existence set down by the Creator. Reason asserts these principles with reference to the original form of our state, in which we know that the office of cavalry commander came into being, as I have said before any magistracy…'[29]

This sounds like a philosophical bluff. It quotes Platonic terms and expressions, but the conclusion does not fit the doctrines of any one philosophical school. Lydus' claims that there is no definitive change and no real corruption in the immanent world. Yet he does not refer to human beings or the life of any living thing, but to history, more precisely to the history of Roman administration. The magistrates of the Roman Empire rise and fall, but in the next phase of the cycle, they are reborn. This text reveals how Lydus understands continuity between paganism and Christianity: he believes in eternal return, in the cyclical rebirth of everything, not in an astrological or eschatological sense, but as an historical process. He repeats this idea again and again in *De magistratibus*: old customs sadly disappear, but they happily survive as new customs. This stands for religions, too. The old religion might have died, but it survives in the new religion. Lydus' idiosyncratic philosophy made possible his survival as an intellectual. He chose the same outlook as Giuseppe di Lampedusa's hero in "*The Leopard*," facing a similar historical situation: "For things to remain the same, everything must change."

---

[29] *De magistratibus*, II. 23: Πάντα μὲν τὰ ὄντα καὶ γίνεται καὶ ἔστι κατὰ τὴν τοῦ ἀγαθοῦ φύσιν· τὰ μὲν ὄντα, ὡς ἔστιν, τὰ δὲ γινόμενα, οὐκ ὄντα μὲν ἀεὶ οὐδὲ ὡσαύτως ἔχοντα, διὰ δὲ τῆς γενέσεως ἐπὶ τὴν φθοράν, εἶτα ἐξ ἐκείνης ἐπὶ τὴν γένεσιν ἀναστρέφοντα, καὶ τῷ εἶναι μὲν ἀθάνατα, τῷ δὲ μεταβάλλεσθαι ἀλλοιότερα· εἰς ἑαυτὰ γὰρ ἀναχοροῦντα τῇ μὲν οὐσίᾳ ἐστί, τῇ δὲ φθορᾷ γίνεται, τηρούσης αὐτὰ τῆς φύσεως παρ' ἑαυτῇ προαγούσης τε αὖθις εἰς τοὐμφανὲς κατὰ τοὺς ὑπὸ τοῦ Δημιουργοῦ τεθέντας ὅρους. ταῦτά φησιν ὁ λόγος διὰ τὴν ἀρχέτυπον τῆς καθ' ἡμᾶς πολιτείας ὄψιν, ἐφ' ἧς ἴσμεν πρὸ πάσης ἀρχῆς τὴν τοῦ ἱππάρχου δύναμιν, ὡς εἴρηται, γενέσθαι.

RHETORIC AND HISTORICAL DISTORTION: THE CASE OF MARK OF ARETHUSA*

Juana Torres

Christian authors cultivated different literary genres, some of them from pagan traditions and others newly created, choosing in each case the one they deemed most suitable for their purposes. Thanks to their excellent training in rhetoric, they composed works of high literary quality, which therefore seemed extremely convincing. Indeed, most early Christian authors received a comprehensive education and finished their schooling in prestigious rhetorical schools.[1] Having acquired great rhetorical skills, they produced highly persuasive discourses.

This paper argues that patristic texts must be subjected to severe philological critique before the historical reconstruction of what they have to say. The predominance of rhetoric in these works, whatever their literary genre, forces us to analyse information they convey with great care, as it is often distorted. This will be shown by one example from many possible in patristic texts: the case of Bishop Mark of Arethusa in Syria, who lived during the reigns of the Emperors Constantius II and Julian. Despite his inclination towards Homoian beliefs, Mark has paradoxically passed into history as a defender of the Nicene faith and a martyr, and thus is included in the Constantinopolitan *Synaxarion*. The events that the sources have transmitted will be analysed to seek a possible explanation for why Nicene scholars overlooked the bishop's obvious pro-Arian position and turned him into a martyr of Julian's policies.

---

* Research for this paper has been carried out within the Project FFI2015–65453-P of the Spanish Ministry of Science and Innovation.
[1] The classic work on the educational system in Late Antiquity is Henri-Irénée Marrou, *Histoire de l'éducation dans l'Antiquité* (Paris: Éditions du Seuil, 1965) (chap. 9). Also useful: Max Ludwig Wolfram Laistner, *Christianity and Pagan Culture in the Later Roman Empire* (New York-Ithaca: Cornell University Press, 1967); Marguerite Harl, *Le déchiffrement du sens. Études sur l'herménéutique chrétienne d'Origène à Grégoire de Nysse* (Paris: Institut des études augustiniennes, 1993), 417-431; and Gilles Dorival, "L'apologétique chrétienne et la culture grecque", in *Les apologistes chrétiens et la culture grecque*, ed. Bernard Pouderon, & Joseph Doré (Paris : Beauchesne, 1998), 423–465.

The first reference to Mark of Arethusa signals his presence at the Council of Antioch in 341, when Bishop Julius of Rome accused the delegates of modifying the dogma established at the Council of Nicaea, and reproached them for not inviting him in breach of Church canons.[2] Mark was a member of the delegation of Eastern bishops—Narcissus of Neronias in Cilicia, Theodore of Heraclea in Thracia, Maris of Chalcedon—from the Eusebian party[3] sent by Constantius in 342 to appear before Emperor Constans in Trier. These bishops defended the decisions of the Synod of Tyre (335) which had deposed Athanasius of Alexandria and Paul of Constantinople and sought to persuade the emperor that the trial at the synod had been fair. When they were asked about their faith, they altered the formula defined at Antioch and proclaimed another that was equally dissimilar to the Nicene faith.[4] Therefore, although the effort was presented before the western authorities as a form of reconciliation, it did not achieve success. Nonetheless, the Eastern delegation had sought peace and tried to attenuate or even end the situation of hostility between the Eastern and Western churches.[5] It was unsuccessful because Emperor Constans dismissed their embassy without accepting their version, but in any case, he understood that Athanasius of Alexandria, the great defender of orthodoxy, was deposed not because of his behaviour but as a result of the reservations of the eastern bishops concerning the Nicene dogma.

In 351, Mark of Arethusa attended the Council of Sirmium convened by Emperor Constantius II to put a halt to a new heresy led by Photinus, the bishop of that city.[6] The Eastern and Western bishops gathered in Sirmium deposed Photinus for his Sabellianism, and Paul of Samosata for his Monarchianism.[7] Following this synod, three

---

[2] Socrates Scholasticus, *Historia Ecclesiastica* II. 17, ed. and trans. by Günther C. Hansen, Pierre Périchon, and Pierre Maraval, *Socrate de Constantinople. Histoire Ecclésiastique, livres II–III*, (Paris: Éditions du Cerf, 2005); Sozomen, *Historia Ecclesiastica* III. 10. 1, ed. and trans. by Joseph Bidez, Günther C. Hansen, André M. Jean Festugière, and Guy Sabbah, *Sozomène. Histoire Ecclésiastique, livres V–VI*, (Paris: Éditions du Cerf, 2005), 98, note 2. Until the Council of Sardica in 343, it was not recognised that the bishop of Rome had the right to be consulted as an act of deference over other sees. The Church historians Socrates and Sozomen may have misinterpreted Bishop Julius of Rome's letter in which he stated that "it was necessary to write to us all", probably referring to all the Western bishops.

[3] The group took their name after Eusebius of Nicomedia, the leader of the pro-Arian party.

[4] It is known as the "fourth Antioch formula"; cfr. Sozomen, III. 10. 5, note 3; and Socrates, II. 18. 2, note 3.

[5] Manlio Simonetti, *La crisi ariana nel IV secolo* (Roma: Institutum Patristicum Augustinianum, 1975), 164.

[6] Socrates, II. 18. 7; II. 29. 1–5; and Sozomen, IV. 6. 1–6. They both mix up the councils and names of the delegates: Hansen, Périchon, and Maraval, *Socrate de Constantinople,* 134–135, note 1; and Simonetti, 246, note 79.

[7] Simonetti, 202–206; and Richard P. Crossland Hanson, *The Search for the Christian Doctrine of God. The Arian Controversy 318–381*, (Edinburgh: Baker Book House, 1988), 235–238, on the doctrine of the various versions of Arianism and especially Photinus' version.

further councils were held in 357,[8] 358 and 359, each with their corresponding Creed, each steadily becoming more radically pro-Arian.[9] In the council of 359, Mark of Arethusa was responsible for drafting a new version in Greek, called the "fourth Sirmium formula" or the "dated Creed" as it gives the date of its publication: 22 May 359. This version was a compromise attempting to situate theological thought midway between pro-Arianism and anti-Arianism.[10]

After Emperor Constantius II's death and the return to Hellenism under Emperor Julian "the Apostate" Mark of Arethusa, who had destroyed a pagan temple, became the victim of anti-Christian persecutions encouraged, or at least permitted, by the new emperor.[11] The great theologian and orator Gregory of Nazianzus was the first patristic author to write about Mark and later Church historians largely depend on him. On Julian's death, Gregory wrote two speeches (*Oratio* IV and V) against the emperor, two veritable invectives aimed at discrediting the emperor by exaggerating the measures Julian took against Christianity. In *Oratio* IV Gregory describes in great detail the torments Mark suffered at the hands of the inhabitants of Arethusa for refusing to rebuild a pagan temple he had destroyed. Gregory remarks that what was permitted in Constantius' time was persecuted when Julian came to power: despite express statements against the use of force and violence, the emperor consented or encouraged the repres-

---

[8] It seems this was the council attended by Ossius of Cordoba and not the 351 Council, as Sozomen claims. He was already very old and at it he subscribed to the Arian creed, but without condemning Athanasius of Alexandria. Cf. Jean Remy Palanque, Gustave Bardy, Pierre de Labriolle, *De la paix constantinienne à la mort de Théodose*, t. 3, (Paris: Bloud & Gay, 1950), 153–154.

[9] Sozomen, IV. 6. 7–16; and Socrates, II. 30.

[10] Socrates, II. 37. 18–24; Sozomen, IV. 22. 6–8; Simonetti, p. 246: "una formula politica, i cui sostenitori -capeggiati da Marco di Aretusa e Acacio di Cesarea- possono per comodità essere definiti Omei (Homoians) dal termine distintivo (*homoios*) de la formula stessa."

[11] Gregory of Nazianzus himself alluded to the ambiguity of the emperor's religious policy and his indecision between persuasion and force because of his clear wish not to create martyrs: "He begrudged the honour of martyrdom to our combatants, and for this reason he contrives now to use compulsion, and yet not seem to do so. That we might suffer, and yet not gain honour as though suffering for Christ's sake. What folly in the first place if he thought it would be unknown on whose account these dangers were run, and that he could hide the truth by his cunning devices! But the more he plotted against our honours so much the greater and more conspicuous was he making them." (*Or.* IV. 58, ed. and trans. by Jean Bernardi, *Grégoire de Nazianze. Discours 4–5*, (Paris: Éditions du Cerf, 1983); English translation by Roger Pearse (Ipswich, UK, 2003). The Church historians Socrates (III. 12. 5–6) and Sozomen (V. 4. 7) make the same comments. Much has been written about Julian's supposed intolerant attitude towards Christians, despite his express wish of getting adherents with conviction rather than violence: Iulianus, *ep.* 114. 438b. See Juana Torres, "Actitudes de intolerancia político-religiosa: el emperador Juliano y el obispo Juan Crisóstomo en conflicto," in *Tolerancia e intolerancia religiosa en el Mediterráneo antiguo: Temas y problemas*, ed. by Mar Marcos, Ramón Teja, (Madrid: Trotta, 2008), 101–121; Juana Torres, "Emperor Julian and the Veneration of Relics," *Antiquité Tardive* 17: *L'Empereur Julien et son temps*, (Brepols Publishers: 2009), 205–214; and Mar Marcos, "'He forced with gentleness' Emperor Julian's Attitude to Religious Coercion," *Antiquité Tardive* 17: 7–20.

sion and persecution of Christians. This case was especially striking to Gregory not so much because Mark' venerable old age was not respected, but because the bishop was apparently one of the people who rescued and sheltered Julian during the massacre suffered by Constantine's family.[12] The veracity of this information cannot be ascertained, but later sources agree that Mark had saved and hidden "the villain" when his relatives were slaughtered.[13] According to the information in *Oratio* IV, the bishop fled initially, but when he heard that he was sought to rebuild the temple or pay for the cost of the repairs, he returned and surrendered himself to avoid that others be punished in his place. Gregory gives a detailed account of the different tortures inflicted on "an elder, priest, and voluntary fighter" (*géron, hiereús, athletés ethelontés*).[14] However, he states that Mark bore all the tortures gladly (*medè gàr en tois deinois tò phaidròn apolipein allà kai entryphan tais basánois*), despising his torturers as if he looked on it all as a holiday and not as a disgrace (*pompé all'u symphorà*).[15] As Mark obstinately refused to give any money to pay for the repairs to the temple, in the end the prefect (*hyparchos*), despite being a pagan, took pity on him and applied to the emperor (*basileus*) to obtain his release.[16] It appears that these events took place in the spring of 363, when Julian began his campaign against the Persians.[17] As a consequence of the dignity of his attitude and his scorn of suffering he had shown, Mark of Arethusa became a highly respected figure, as Libanius of Antioch remarked with certain vexation: despite been hung up, whipped, with his beard pulled out, he bore it all bravely, and later he became similar to a god, judging from the honours he was paid (*isótheós esti tais timais*).[18]

The description of Mark' martyrdom given by Sozomen is clearly based on Gregory of Nazianzus' text, and agrees on the main points with Theodoret of Cyrrhus' version. Sozomen says that due to the old man's (*gennaíos*) nobility and brav-

---

[12] Gregory of Nazianzus, *Or.* IV. 91. 5–7.
[13] Theophanes *Chronographia* 48. 9–12; and Theophylactus, *Histori martyrii XV martyrum* 10. These fragments appear as an appendix (ap. 7, 33g and 33h) in an English translation of Phocius' epitome on Philostorgius' Church History: Philip R. Amidon, S.J., *Philostorgius. Church History*, (Atlanta: Society of Biblical Literature, 2007). See also Michael di Maio, Duane W. H. Arnold, "*Per vim, per caedem, per bellum*: A Study of Murder and Ecclesiastical Politics in the year 337 AD", *Byzantion* 62 (1992): 158–211.
[14] Gregory of Nazianzus, *Or.* IV. 89. 1.
[15] Gregory of Nazianzus, *Or.* IV. 89. 29–31.
[16] Gregory of Nazianzus, *Or.* IV. 91. 10–26. We cannot be sure if by the term *hyparchos* he is referring to the provincial governor or the praetorian prefect, but it seems likely that he means the praetorian prefect of the East, Saturninus Secundus Sallustius, very close to the Emperor Julian; cf. Bernardi, 229, not. 2; and Bidez, Hansen, Festugière, and Sabbah, *Sozomène*, 142, not. 1. Marcus' torture is described by Sozomen, *HE*, V. 10. 8–14; by Theodoret of Cyrrhus, *HE*, III. 7. 6–10; and by Libanius, *ep.* 819: "To Belaeus", (ed. Ricardus Foerster, *Libanii Opera, IX–X: Epistulae* (Lipsiae 1921, 1922). According to Libanius, Julian allowed Marcus to live so as to avoid the increase of his fame he had gained with his resistance to torture.
[17] Cf. Bidez, Hansen, Festugière, and Sabbah, *Sozomène*, 138–139, not. 2; and Bernardi, 221, not. 2.
[18] Libanius, *Ep.* 819. 6.

ery, even pagans praised him (*epainethénai ton auton Helleniston*).[19] Theodoret adds a highly interesting information: "they were converted and learnt from his lips the doctrines of religion" (*eis tanantía metatethentes dià gàr tes ekeinu glótes metémathon tèn eusébeian*).[20] From this information, it can be deduced that Mark of Arethusa did not die of torture but devoted himself to converting heathens to Christianity until his death in the following year in 364, although this might have been a consequence of the physical violence he suffered.[21] Another brief note added by the Bishop of Cyrrhus seems to me significant. He criticises the torturers' lack of compassion and respect for Mark' great age and his virtue:

> "These men showed neither pity for his age nor respect for his virtues. Notwithstanding his holy course of life and his admirable mode of teaching, they seized him, stripped him naked, and lacerated him with scourgings."[22]

The reference to his way of life (*bíos*) and doctrine (*lógos*) is of particular interest; the meaning of the first term is clear, but several versions are given of the second. In Bagster's English translation, given above, it is interpreted as "admirable mode of teaching. Canivet's French version says : *Cet homme dont la vie et la parole faisaient la parure* [...]. Finally, Gallico's Italian translation gives: *Ma prima tormentarono quell'uomo che era adorno di un retto modo di vivere e di una retta dottrina* [...].[23] Although it is true that the Greek word *lógos* means "word", it also has other meanings, such as "teaching and doctrine" when used in a religious context. In this way, it can be concluded that Theodoret, like Gregory of Nazianzus, not only skips over any reference to his previous

---

[19] Sozomen, *HE* V. 10. 14.

[20] Theodoret, *HE* III. 7. 10, (ed. and trans. Leon Parmentier et Günther C. Hansen, Jean Bouffartigue, Annick Martin, and Pierre Canivet, *Théodoret de Cyr. Histoire Ecclésiastique*, t. II (Paris: Éditions du Cerf, 2009); English translation: *Ecclesiastical History. A History of the Church*, (London: Samuel Bagster & sons, 1843). The explanation for the differences between one and another author is that Theodoret did not depend on Gregory of Nazianzus whereas Sozomen did: Hanns Christoph Brennecke, *Studien zur Geschichte der Homöer. Der Osten bis zum Ende der homöischen Reichskirche*. Beiträge zur historischen Theologie 73 (Mohr, Tübingen, 1998), 135, not. 110; and Federico Fatti, *Giuliano a Cesarea. La politica ecclesiastica del principe apostata* (Rome: Herder 2009), 158, not. 31.

[21] Simonetti, 355, not. 4: "*Nel contesto delle violenze anticristiane favorite o tollerate da Giuliano in tante città d'Oriente fu crudelmente ucciso Marco di Aretusa, l'estensore della formula sirmiese del 22 maggio 359*". This is a *lapsus* of this great scholar of Christianity, perhaps due to the vast amount of information he mobilized in his work.

[22] Theodoret *HE*. III. 7. 8 : *Hoi dè labóntes úte ókteiran hos presbýten úte edésthesan hos aretes phrontistén, allà kaì bíō kaì lógō tòn ándra kosmúmenon proton mèn ekísanto, tò soma gymnósantes kaì tois mélesin hapasin epithéntes tàs mástigas*

[23] *Teodoreto di Cirro. Storia Ecclesiastica*, trans. Antonino Gallico, (Roma, 2000).

Homoian tendencies but even goes further and assures that his faith was congruent with orthodoxy.

Some researchers have put forward a theory about the Christian martyrs in Julian's time, suggesting that they were mostly Homoians, those who would have supported the political and religious project of his predecessor Constantius II, as a reaction against him. Another circumstance common to all the martyrs under Julian is that they destroyed temples and idols, and therefore seem to have adopted a provocative attitude against paganism. According to this theory, Nicenes did not suffer persecutions[24] but enjoyed a more sympathetic treatment as demonstrated by the emperor's edict calling those banished by Constantius return from their exile.[25] According to Federico Fatti, this theory fits Julian's ecclesiastical policy. To support his case, he cites the example of Caesarea in Cappadocia, where the *Tycheion* was destroyed; of Arethusa in Syria, where another temple was pulled down; and of Daphne in Antioch, where the temple of Apollo was burnt down. The respective martyrs—Eupsychius of Caesarea, Mark of Arethusa, and the leaders of the Church in Antioch—would have been Homoian and Julian would have persecuted them for that reason.[26] This theory is not very convincing as the martyrs "attributed to" Julian (some of them falsely), were not all Homoians. Actually, only three of them were: George of Cappadocia, Mark of Arethusa and Artemius *dux Aegypti*. In contrast, others like Basil, the presbyter of the Church of Ancyra, who in Constantius' time spoke in favour of orthodoxy and against the Arians, was arrested, tortured and given up for dead in Julian's reign.[27] In the case of Mark of Arethusa, the authorities took pity on him and spared his life, despite his clearly identifying himself as Homoian and challenging authority.

Paradoxically, two fourth-century bishops, who took part in several actions connected with the Arian heresy in different cities in the Western Empire, became respected as saints in the Eastern Church. Historiography tried to find an explanation for this paradox putting forward various hypotheses. In the sixteenth century, the great Cesare Baronio, responsible for the reappraisal of Roman martyrology, explained that Mark were excluded from it due to reasons of orthodoxy.[28] Some years later, he suggested in his book *Ecclesiastical Annals* that the bishop may have abandoned impiety and returned to the

---

[24] Brennecke, 87–91; 96–107.

[25] Ammianus Marcellinus, *Res Gestae* 22. 5. 2; and Sozomen, V. 5. 1.

[26] Fatti, *Giuliano a Cesarea*, 157–183; and Federico Fatti, "Il príncipe, la *Tyche*, i cristiani: Giuliano a Cesarea," in *Pagans and Christians in the Roman Empire: The Breaking of a Dialogue (IVth– VIth century A.D.)*, ed. Peter Brown and Rita Lizzi (Zürich-Berlin: Wien Zürich Berlin Münster Lit, 2011), 121–129.

[27] Sozomen, V. 11. 7 and 9–11; another interesting and useful work is: Francesco Scorza Barcellona, "Martiri e confessori dell'età di Giuliano l'Apostata: dalla storia alla legenda," in *Pagani e cristiani da Giuliano l'Apostata al sacco di Roma*, ed. Franca Ela Consolino (Soveria Mannelli-Messina: Rubbettino Editore 1995), 53–83.

[28] *Martyrologium Romanum… accesserunt notationes atque tractatio de Martyrologio Romano auctore Caesare Baronio Sorano* (Roma 1586), 143.

communion of the Church at the end of his life.[29] This hypothesis would explain the solemn and laudatory tone in which Gregory of Nazianzus wrote about him, in addition to his lack of precise knowledge of the facts. The suggestion was taken up by the Bollandists in their *Acta Sanctorum* in the seventeenth century. In the eighteenth century, Lenain de Tillemont acknowledged that Arianism was widespread in Julian's time and that the boundaries between orthodoxy and heresy were indistinct. However, the principles of faith would not allow anyone who had been clearly associated with heresy to be regarded as a martyr.[30] Among these cases, he cites Maris of Chalcedon, Artemius *dux Aegypti* and Mark of Arethusa as former leaders of Arianism. Indeed, the sources provide information about all the others that largely agrees with the case of the bishop of Arethusa.[31] Maris of Chalcedon was a supporter of Arianism during the Council of Nicaea, but later subscribed the Nicene Creed out of pure convenience. Socrates and Sozomen mention him among the delegation of Eastern bishops sent by Constantius to the Emperor Constans in 342.[32] In the Council of Constantinople of 360, Maris belonged to the Homoian group, together with Acacius of Caesarea.[33] Both authors ignore this fact in describing an episode involving Julian, when Maris encountered him as he was offering a sacrifice in the *Tycheion* of Constantinople. Maris publicly insulted the emperor, calling him impious, atheistic and apostate. Julian defended himself by mocking Maris' blindness, as he was elderly and suffered from cataracts; he said ironically that not even the Galilean God could cure him. The bishop replied that he thanked God for depriving him the power of beholding the emperor's face, degenerate with impiety. The emperor left without replying, imagining that he would defend paganism better by remaining patient and moderate.[34] Artemius, the prefect of Egypt was an Arian and follower of George of Alexandria. The sources do not make clear what Julian's reasons were for having him beheaded in 362. Ammianus Marcellinus affirms that he had committed numerous terrible crimes, without specifying further. Theodoret of Cyrrhus states that in the course of his duties, he had ordered the destruction of a large number of idols. This is confirmed by Julian himself, in his epistle to the Alexandrians, where he states that Artemius had cast the army against

---

[29] "Haec profecto Gregorius si novisset de Marco Arethusio, numquam eum "virum eximium" appellasset, nec tamen tam multa de eo honorifice praedicasset. In Marco Arethusio igitur Gregorius, perinde atque in Constantio Augusto, ignoratione facti erravit. Vel postmodum audierat, Marcum ante finem vitae impietatem abjurasse, et ad Ecclesiae fideliumque communionem rediisse, quod arbitratur Baronius" (*Annales Ecclesiastici*, 4, Roma 1593, 66C).

[30] M. Lenain de Tillemont, *Mémoires pour servir à l'histoire ecclésiastique des six premiers siècles*, t. 7 (Paris 1706), 731 : "Mais pour ceux qu'on voit avoir été certainement engagés dans l'hérésie il semble que les principes de la foi ne nous permettent point de les regarder comme des martyrs."

[31] Socrates 2, 18, 1; Sozomen 3, 10, 4; Socrates 1, 8, 13; Sozomen 1, 21, 1; y 4, 24, 1.

[32] Socrates, II. 18. 1; Sozomen, III. 10. 4.

[33] Socrates, I. 8, 13; Sozomen, I. 21. 1; Sozomen, IV. 24. 1.

[34] Socrates, III. 12. 1–6; Sozomen, V. 4. 8–9.

the people and had seized the temple of God, sacking the images and adornments of the shrines.³⁵ He was regarded as a martyr first by the Homoians and later by all Christians. A *Martyrium Artemii* presents him as a victim of martyrdom for having opposed the emperor by supporting two Antiochian priests, Eugene and Macarius; later *Passiones* support this account. To explain the curious circumstance that an Arian and an adversary of Athanasius of Alexandria should become a saint for the Nicene Church, an attempt was made to differentiate between Artemius, the defender of Eugene and Macarius, and the *dux Aegypti*, but he was doubtless one and the same person.³⁶ As for Mark of Arethusa, Tillemont keeps to the initial idea that anyone implicated in heresy cannot be considered a martyr. Thus, Tillemont supports Baronio's decision not to give him a place in the Roman martyrology, despite the praise of Christian writers like Gregory of Nazianzus and Theodoret of Cyrrhus, and despite the fact that the Greek Church venerated him as a saint.³⁷ On the basis of the same sources, Edward Gibbon interprets Mark's story from a different point of view. He places much of the blame on the bishop. According to him, Mark must have provoked his torturers, first because of the intolerant means he used in converting the populace to Christianity, more effective than mere persuasion, and then for his stubbornness in refusing to compensate the population for the loss of the pagan temple. Gibbon refers to the magistrates as responsible for the torture, in fulfilment of their obligation to obtain the determined fine to rebuild the temple, but he does not blame Emperor Julian:

> "Under the preceding reign, Mark, bishop of Arethusa, had laboured in the conversion of his people with arms more effectual than those of persuasion. The magistrates required the full value of a temple which had been destroyed by his intolerant zeal: but as they were satisfied of his poverty, they desired only to bend his inflexible spirit to the promise of the slightest compensation."³⁸

What is more important, Gibbon identifies Mark with the Arians when he calls him "their pious confessor":

> "From this lofty station, Mark still persisted to glory in his crime, and to insult the impotent rage of his persecutors. He was at length res-

---

35   Ammianus XXII. 11. 2 ; Theodoret HE., III. 18. 1; Socrates, III. 3. 10–12.
36   A full explanation can be found in Barcellona, 63–66.
37   Lenain de Tillemont, 731 : „Baronius a eu sans doute raison de ne vouloir point donner place à Marc d'Arethuse dans le martyrologue Romain, quoiqu'il a été loué par S. Grégoire de Nazianze & par Theodoret & qu'il soit honoré comme un Saint par l'Eglise grecque."
38   Edward Gibbon, *Decline and Fall of the Roman Empire,* Vol. 2, cap. 23, (1781), 128–129.

cued from their hands, and dismissed to enjoy the honour of his divine triumph. The Arians celebrated the virtue of their pious confessor; the Catholics ambitiously claimed his alliance."[39]

Gibbon does not agree with Gregory of Nazianzus in attributing full responsibility for the events to Julian's intolerance, but makes Mark himself responsible because of his stubbornness and excessive zeal against idols. As opposed to Baronio and Tillemont, Gibbon has no doubts about Mark's belonging to Arianism in the last period of his life.

In the nineteenth century, the Benedictine editor of the works of Gregory of Nazianzus expresses his belief that Gregory must have been misinformed when he called Mark an "extraordinary man," and when he spoke about him with so much deference, as there is reliable evidence for his support of the Arians.[40] In the twentieth century, Jean Bernardi, the editor of Gregory's speeches, is surprised to find him portraying Constantius as a model of an orthodox emperor,[41] and that he chose Mark of Arethusa as an example of the persecutions carried out during Julian's reign. Bernardi is equally surprised that Gregroy should have devoted such a lengthy and verbose account to Mark' martyrdom.[42] Bernardi undoubtedly is aware of the different hypotheses that have been offered to find an explanation for why the Bishop of Arethusa was considered a heretic by the Western Church and a defender of Nicene orthodoxy by the Eastern Church. In any case, the justification he puts forward is different from the rest; he thinks that Gregory deliberately decided to present Mark of Arethusa as a paradigm of a Christian concerned with the unity of the faith before suffering martyrdom. According to Bernardi, Gregory did not choose Mark as an example out of ignorance of the facts or by chance, but because he believed that the true danger for the faith did not lie with the Homoians but with paganism, against which Christians should fight.[43]

The bending of history that rhetoric often achieves is striking, as we have seen in the case of Mark of Arethusa. Let me quote another two cases, obviously not the only ones.

The fourth-century Latin *Libellus precum,* signed by the Roman presbyters Faustinus and Marcellinus, asks for protection from the attacks by the followers of Lucifer of Cagliari. The petition is addressed to Emperors Valentinian II, Theodosius, and

---

[39] Edward Gibbon, *Decline and Fall of the Roman Empire,* Vol. 2, cap. 23, (1781), 128–129.
[40] D.A.B. Caillau and D.M.N.S. Guillon, *Collectio selecta SS. ecclesiae patrum,* vol. 79 (Paris, 1835), 151 : "In errorem facti lapsus videtur Gregorius, qui "virum eximium" appellat Marcum Arethusanum, quem Arianis partibus fuisse addictum certis monumentis constat".
[41] He did this only to contrast Constantius with Emperor Julian, as explained below.
[42] Bernardi, *Grégoire de Nazianze,* 31.
[43] Bernardi, *Grégoire de Nazianze,* 32–33 :"Il s'agissait de rappeler que la vraie menace contre la foi ne venait pas de ces homéousiens qui comptaient de belles figures de martyrs, mais du paganisme toujours vivant et redoutable, contre lequel les chrétiens avaient pour premier devoir de s'unir, car tel etait le sens de l'épreuve envoyée par Dieu. Faire l'éloge de Marc c'etait plaider pour l'unité face aux enragés de l'orthodoxie [...]"

Arcadius, and contains a very significant example of the interested use of half-truths, which turn into complete fallacies.[44] Due to Constantius II's religious policy favourable to Arianism, Faustinus calls him the *patronus haereticorum* ("protector of heretics") and states that after his death, Julian had revoked the order of banishment and made all the exiled bishops return. In this way Julian became the great defender of Christianity.[45] It is true that he gave that order, but it is very unlikely that the aim was to favour the integration of the bishops. In any case, the author did not hesitate to praise Julian with the object of denigrating Constantius for favouring Arians. To circumvent the paradox that the "apostate" emperor, who attempted to restore Hellenism, was the benefactor of exiled Christian bishops, Faustinus adds: "Divinity often acts in that way and even takes care of the Christian religion through its adversaries, so that those who honour Christ do the same for the faithful".[46]

The opposite is found in Gregory of Nazianzus' *Oratio* IV and V. Gergory expressed great admiration for Constantius, as he needed to transmit the image of an ideal Christian emperor to contrast him with the impious sovereign Julian. Gregory ignored Constantius II's doctrinal orientation, despite being himself a supporter of orthodoxy, and presented this emperor as the counterpart of his successor:

> "Oh, most religious and Christ-loving of princes; [...] thou art placed at the side of God, and hast inherited the glory that is there; [...] thou who didst so far surpass all in sagacity and understanding, not only the princes of thy own times, but also those who preceded thee; [...] thou that were led by God's own hand in every action and purpose; whose prudence was admired more than his valour, and his valour again more than his prudence, and yet more admirable than his glory in both was his piety."[47]

---

[44] Juana Torres, "Falacias persuasivas en la literatura cristiana antigua: retórica y realidad," in *Fraude, mentira y engaño en el Mundo antiguo*, in , *Fraude, mentiras y engaños en el Mundo antiguo*, ed. Francisco Marco Simón, Francisco Pina Polo and José Remesal Rodríguez, (Collecció Instrumenta, Barcelona: Universitat de Barcelona, 2014), 209–224.

[45] *Libellus precum*, 51. 1–3. Aline Canellis ed. and trans., *Faustin et Marcellin. Supplique aux empereurs. Libellus precum et Lex augusta*, (Paris: Éditions du Cerf, 2006): "Sed mortuo Constantio patrono haereticorum, Iulianus solus tenuit imperium, ex cuius praecepto omnes episcopi catholici de exiliis relaxantur."

[46] *Libellus precum*, 51. 4–6 : *Solet hoc facere Divinitas, ut etiam per adversarios Christianae religioni suae consulat, ut tanto magis, qui cultores sunt Christi pro fidelibus elaborent.*

[47] Gregory of Nazianzus *Or.*, 4. 34 : ὦ θειότατε βασιλέων καὶ φιλοχριστότατε [...], μετὰ Θεοῦ τεταγμένον, καὶ τῆς ἐκεῖ δόξης κληρονομήσαντα, [...] πάντων συνέσει καὶ ἀγχινοίᾳ κατὰ πολὺ διαφέρων, οὐ τῶν ἐπὶ σοῦ βασιλέων μόνον, ἀλλὰ καὶ τῶν ἔμπροσθεν; [...] ὁ χειρὶ Θεοῦ πρὸς πᾶσαν καὶ βουλὴν καὶ πρᾶξιν ὁδηγούμενος· οὗ μᾶλλον μὲν τῆς χειρὸς ἡ σύνεσις, μᾶλλον δὲ τῆς συνέσεως ἡ χεὶρ ἐθαυμάζετο· πλέον δὲ τῆς ἐν ἀμφοτέροις εὐδοκιμήσεως ἡ εὐσέβεια. See Ramón Teja, "Constantino frente a Constancio II: la deformación de la memoria histórica entre "arrianos" y "nicenos," in *Constantinus: ¿el primer emperador cristiano? Religión y política en el siglo IV*, ed. Josep Vilella, (Barcelona, 2015), 473–484; Ramón Teja, "Constancio II, modelo de emperador cristiano en las *Orationes IV*

The Eastern Church venerates Saint Mark, bishop of Arethusa in the Constantinopolitan *Synaxarion*, on 28 March, together with Cyril, deacon of Phoenicia, and the Palestinian martyrs of Gaza and Ascalon. Mark' confession of faith is considered untarnished. If any deed in his life was understood as heretic, this is because it was interpreted wrongly. Moreover, the praise of Gregory of Nazianzus, Theodoret and Sozomen describing his suffering shows that if at any time Mark allied with Arianism, he soon returned to strict orthodoxy and fully atoned for any previous doubts. The *Passiones* of Mark of Arethusa, legends written in the Middle Ages including the passions of Cyril and the Palestinian martyrs, have been published and interpreted in the same direction.[48]

These various hypotheses often reflect confessional points of view. I believe the key to interpretation lies in the apologetic nature of the portrayal of Mark of Arethusa that Gregory of Nazianzus drew in his *Oratio* IV. Chronologically, this text is he first to refer to the bishop, and thus the source on which later works have drawn. The purpose of Gregory's invectives against Julian was to discredit an impious emperor. Gregory did not hesitate to use all possible means and dialectic strategies to achieve that aim. In addition to the numerous rhetorical figures for stylistic adornment, the techniques of linguistic persuasion were also used to present certain people as being endowed with excellent qualities and, in contrast, others as full of defects. Thus, in his desire to attribute the greatest possible number of whims, injustices and errors of all kind to the "apostate" emperor, he preferred to overlook the irregular behaviour of other individuals to make the responsibility fall solely on Julian. Hence, in his discourses, Gregory presented Mark of Arethusa as a martyr-saint, victim of the emperor's evil, and ignored his heretical inclinations. Ultimately, he aimed to blame the emperor for the largest possible number of innocent victims despite his express wish not to provide the Christians with more martyrs. In this way, Gregory was able to reveal the falseness and incoherence of Julian's religious policy.

Rhetoric distorts reality and consequently historians can be mistaken in their historical reconstruction of events if the texts are not subjected to strict critical analysis. The case of Mark of Arethusa helps, in the words of Ramón Teja, "to show the enormous importance of rhetoric in Christian writers and the great ideological load conditioning their opinions [...]; at the same time, it explains the reason for the "exegetic" analysis modern historians are forced to apply to ancient sources if we wish to attain a minimum of historical objectivity untouched by controversies and apologies.[49]

---

y *V* de Gregorio de Nacianzo," in *Officia oratoris. Estrategias de persuasión en la literatura polémica cristiana (ss. I-V)*, ed. Juana Torres, (Madrid: 'Ilu, Revista de Ciencias de las Religiones. Anejos, 2013, XXIV), 167–177.

[48] *Bibliotheca Hagiographica Graeca (BHG)* 2249, ed. Basilius Latysev, *Menologii anonymi byzantini saec. X quae supersunt*, I, (Petersburg, 1911); *BHG* 2248 and 2250. See François Halkin, "La Passion de S. Marc d'Aréthuse", *Analecta Bollandiana* 103, fasc. 3–4 (1985), 217–229.

[49] Ramón Teja, "Constantino frente a Constancio II," 484.

Identities

IMITATIO CHRISTI? LITERARY MODELS FOR MARTYRS IN EARLY CHRISTIANITY

Monika Pesthy-Simon

Martyrs are not born but made. To become a "martyr" in early Christianity, it was not enough—and sometimes not even necessary—to die for Christ. Rather, the essential part of martyr creation was the martyr story compiled by a hagiographer presenting the (actual or fictive) death of a (real or imaginary) person as a heroic public act accomplished for Christ. New hero, the martyr had to replace all preceding models. For this purpose, hagiographers had recourse to various devices. This paper concentrates on a special aspect of the hagiographer's work: the models employed in order to present the protagonist in as heroic a light as possible.

It is commonly accepted that the Christian martyr imitates Christ. Examining two early martyrial texts, the *Letters of Ignatius of Antioch* and the *Martyrdom of Polycarp*, I wish to argue that in the majority of cases, the real model used by the hagiographer in composing his account of a martyr's execution, and the events leading to it (arrest, tribunal, imprisonment, torture, etc.), is not Christ, even if the martyr actually declares to follow Christ and even if certain details are taken from the Gospel accounts of Jesus' death. If Christ is the theological and literary model for the martyr, the martyr is presented by hagiographers as surpassing His heroism in a variety of ways.

First, I sum up the main differences between Christ and the martyrs in Late Antique Christian literature. On the basis of the martyrdom of Ignatius and Polycarp, I then attempt to show that even in the case of the martyrs generally considered prototypes of the *imitatio Christi*, Christ is not the only literary model and perhaps not even the most important one. Finally, I briefly survey and summarize the variegated models used in Christian martyrology.[1]

---

[1] The material of this paper is partly incorporated into my book *Isaac, Iphigeneia, Ignatius: Martyrdom and Human Sacrifice* (Budapest–New York: CEU Press, 2017), pp. 119–31, 157–69.

Christ and the martyrs: different attitudes

The difference between the martyr's death and that of Christ is obvious with regard to their respective behaviour. The martyrs' aggressive and provocative activity, their zeal to promulgate their convictions and to insult their enemies as much as possible, is the opposite of the passive and reserved attitude of Christ. Let us briefly summarize the differences with the help of some examples taken in a somewhat haphazard way.

- Jesus does not want to die (Matthew 26.36–44; Mark 14.32–44; Luke 22.39–44). The martyrs, without exception, want to die. "This we long for, this we desire" – answer the saints to the threats of the magistrate in the *Acts of Justin and his companions*.[2] Desire for death attains pathological measures in the case of Ignatius: he wants to die (ἐρῶν τοῦ ἀποθανεῖν) and admonishes the Christians in Rome not to do anything to save him. If the beasts fail to kill him, he will provoke them to do so (cf. *Letter to the Romans* 4.7).

- Jesus does not want to suffer. The martyr, on the contrary, wants to suffer so as to achieve higher glory. Thus Saturninus "insisted that he wanted to be exposed to all the different beasts, that his crown might be all the more glorious".[3]

- Jesus is sad (Matthew 26.38; Mark 14.34). The martyrs, in contrast, rejoice. Fructuosus is "glad (*gaudens*) that he would receive the Lord's crown";[4] Marian and James are unable to control their overflowing joy (*gaudia cumulata frenare*) when they are arrested;[5] Perpetua and her companions go happily (*hilares*) to their execution;[6] Agathoniké throws herself joyfully (ἀγαλλιωμένη) upon the stake;[7] Carpus is smiling while he is nailed to the stake, etc.[8]

- Jesus waits to be arrested. Christians denounce themselves voluntarily before Roman authorities to become martyrs. In 185, a group of Christians showed up before Arrius Antoninus, proconsul of Asia to be executed. The proconsul executed some of them and advised the others to kill themselves by ropes and

---

[2] 4.6 (Recension C), (Herbert Musurillo, *The Acts of the Christian Martyrs* (Oxford: Clarendon Press, 1972), p. 59).
[3] *The Martyrdom of Perpetua and Felicitas* 19.2 (Musurillo, *The Acts of the Christian Martyrs*, p. 127).
[4] *The Martyrdom of Fructuosus and Companions* 1.4 (Musurillo, *The Acts of the Christian Martyrs*, p. 177).
[5] *The Martyrdom of Marian* 4.5 (Musurillo, *The Acts of the Christian Martyrs*, p. 199).
[6] *The Martyrdom of Perpetua* 18.1 (Musurillo, *The Acts of the Christian Martyrs*, p. 125).
[7] *Martyrdom of Carpus* (Rec. A) 44 (Musurillo, *The Acts of the Christian Martyrs*, p. 29).
[8] *Martyrdom of Carpus* (Rec. A) 38 (Musurillo, *The Acts of the Christian Martyrs*, p. 27)

cliffs.⁹ It is not known whether the would-be martyrs followed his advice. The desire for martyrdom, however, often triggered suicide. Agathoniké, seeing other Christians martyred, throws herself upon the stake;¹⁰ Germanicus drags the beast on top of himself;¹¹ Perpetua guides "the trembling hand of the young gladiator to her throat";¹² Euplus presents himself before the prefect shouting: "I want to die; I am a Christian!";¹³ Agnes and Eulalia, two young girls, escape from home in order to get martyred.¹⁴ Not every martyr appears on his own volition before the authorities to denounce him- or herself a Christian—in most cases they are probably denounced by someone else: in the first centuries, however, voluntary martyrdom is common and its practitioners, such as Agnes, are venerated, up to this day as true martyrs.¹⁵

- After his arrest, Jesus is passive and peaceful throughout the judicial process. The martyrs behave in a provocative and aggressive manner. Pionius and his companions walk around in chains;¹⁶ others refuse to give their names; Martiana, an African saint mutilates the statue of Diana; Valentina of Caesarea overturns the altar.¹⁷

- Jesus remains silent instead of defending his case before Pilate according to the synoptic Gospels, while in John he answers Pilate's questions in a brief and quite dignified way (John 18.33–38; 19.11) The martyrs deliver long speeches expounding their convictions and unveiling the errors of their persecutors, such

---

⁹ Tertullian, *Ad Scapulam* 5.1.

¹⁰ *Acts of Carpus* 42–44 (Musurillo, *The Acts of the Christian Martyrs*, p. 29). For the dating of this event see Musurillo, *The Acts of the Christian Martyrs*, pp. XV–XVI.

¹¹ *Martyrdom of Polycarp* 3.1 (Musurillo, *The Acts of the Christian Martyrs*, p. 5).

¹² *Martyrdom of Perpetua* 21.9 (Musurillo, *The Acts of the Christian Martyrs*, p. 131).

¹³ *The Acts of Euplus* 1 (Musurillo, *The Acts of the Christian Martyrs*, 311). The Greek and Latin versions agree on this point.

¹⁴ Ambrose, *Hymn VIII*; *De viriginibus* 2; Prudentius, *Peristephanon* 3. See Marie-Françoise Baslez, *Les persécutions dans l'Antiquités. Victimes, héros, martyrs* (Paris: Fayard, 2007), pp. 199–230. I do not agree with the conclusions of Baslez who limits the Christians' suicidal disposition to extreme cases. See also Arthur J. Drodge and James D. Tabor, *A Noble Death. Suicide and Martyrdom among Christians and Jews in Antiquity* (San Franciso: Harper, 1992) pp. 138–40; 152–55.

¹⁵ Clement of Alexandria protests against seeking death voluntarily, cf. *Stromata* IV.4.17.3.

¹⁶ *Martyrdom of Pionius* 3,5.

¹⁷ For further examples see Baslez, *Les persécutions*, pp. 206–10.

as Pionius[18] or Apollonius, whose *passio* basically consists of the speeches Apollonius delivered before the proconsul.[19]

- Jesus is forgiving (Luke 23.34). The martyrs are vengeful. Saturus wants to be revenged;[20] Marian in his vision participates in the work of the heavenly tribunal and watches as his persecutors are tried.[21]

- Suffering on the cross, Jesus feelsforsaken by God in the synoptic Gospels (Matthew 27.46; Mark 15.34), while in John he endures everything calmly (John 19.28–30). The martyr, even amidst the most savage tortures, feels no pains because Christ is with him or suffers instead of him. Blandina, when gored by a bull, feels nothing "because of her intimacy with Christ".[22] Felicitas declares: "… then another will be inside me who will suffer for me, just as I shall be suffering for him".[23]

- Jesus suffers and dies as an ordinary vulnerable human being. The martyrs gain superhuman strength. Polycarp remains untouched by fire;[24] wild beasts are unwilling to attack Thecla and a lioness even defends her;[25] after the tortures the martyr miraculously recovers, even if all the limbs of his/her body were torn apart. The climax of this literary device is reached in the sixth century martyr stories, where the hero resuscitates several times.[26]

- Jesus dies for the others. The martyr dies for individual reasons, to receive his/her heavenly reward.[27]

---

[18] *Martyrdom of Pionius* 16–17.

[19] *Martyrdom of Apollonius* (Musurillo, *The Acts of the Christian Martyrs*, p. 90–105), These speeches are obviously construed, see H. F. von Campenhausen, *Die Idee des Martyriums in der alten Kirche* (Göttingen: Vandenhoeck&Ruprecht, 1964²), p. 151.

[20] *Martyrdom of Perpetua* 17.2; Tertullian *On spectacles* 30.

[21] *Martyrdom of Marian and James* 6.10–11.

[22] *Martyrdom of the Martyrs of Lyons* 56 (Musurillo, *The Acts of the Christian Martyrs*, p. 81).

[23] *Martyrdom of Perpetua* 15.6 (Musurillo, *The Acts of the Christian Martyrs*, p. 125).

[24] *Martyrdom of Polycarp* 15 (Musurillo, *The Acts of the Christian Martyrs*, p.15).

[25] *Acts of Paul and Thecla* 33.

[26] In the Coptic version of his martyrdom, Julius of Aqfahs resuscitates five times and dies only at the sixth occasion: Victor Saxer, 'Jules d'Aqfahs', in: *Dictionnaire encyclopédique du christianisme ancien*, vol. 2, (Paris: Cerf, 1990), p. 1369.

[27] The idea that the martyr's death serves as an atonement for the others, though presentin some Acts, is elaborated by the Church Fathers, first of all by Original Prudentius. The martyr's death is considered useful for others primarily as an example.

This sketchy comparison makes it clear that,in the hagiographer's literary construction, the martyr shows much more heroism and intrepidity than Jesus in the Gospels and even surpasses Him in heroism. Christ as a model plays a relatively small role in the early martyr acts and no role at all in the later ones: few would insist that Agnes imitates Christ.

What are then the models that Late Antique hagiographers imitated? Scholars have made considerable efforts to demonstrate that Christian martyrology as a literary genre derives its origins from Jewish martyrology and/or from the Greco-Roman tradition of "noble death." It is debated which of them influenced more Christian authors. Delehaye suggested that late martyrological legends incorporated motives from all possible sources.[28] I argued elsewhere that Agnes, and subsequently virgin martyrs, were modelled after Euripidean heroines.[29] On the basis of two early martyrial texts, the *Letters of Ignatius of Antioch* and the *Martyrdom of Polycarp* this paper suggests that Christian martyr literature from its beginnings was modeled on Jewish and/or Classical literary paradigms. While the *imitatio Christi* perhaps actually motivated the martyrs, the Gospels were only one among the many literary models of martyrdom narratives.

Ignatius of Antioch

Bishop Ignatius of Antioch left seven letters, apparently composed between 100 and 118, while being transported to Rome to be cast to the wild animals in the arena. Scholarship accepts the authenticity of the letters.[30] They differ from other martyrological texts in that they are written by the very person who was about to be martyrized and thus reflect his thoughts and feelings. As to Ignatius' martyrdom, nothing is known about it. Ignatius is considered a "follower of Christ," as he effectively declares himself to be one. Nonetheless, when writing about his impending death, he has recourse to other models, too.

Ignatius and Christ

As a follower of Christ, Ignatius considers that to die for Christ is the apex of becoming Christian (*Rom.* 3.2; cf. *Magn* 5.2). He wants to become a true disciple of

---

[28] Hippolyte Delehaye, *The Legends of the Saints. An Introduction to Hagiography* (London: University of Notre Dame Press. 1961).

[29] Monika Pesthy-Simon, 'From Euripides to the Christian Martyrs',*Acta Classica Univ. Scient. Debrecen.*, 49 (2013), pp. 337–346.

[30] The so-called 'middle collection': Candida Moss, *The Other Christs. Imitating Jesus in Ancient Christian Ideologies of Martyrdom* (Oxford: Oxford University Press, 2010), p. 41.

Christ (*Rom.* 4.2; 5.3) and to be the imitator (*mimētēs*) of Christ's passion (*Rom.* 6.3).[31] His burning desire for death, however, has nothing to do with the attitude of Christ, nor does the manner of his death resemble to that of Christ.

Ignatius and the Maccabees

Scholars sought to prove the dependence of Ignatius on *4 Maccabees*. William argues this first of all on the basis of the expression ἀντίψυχον, "substitute, fee"[32] (*Eph.* 21.1; *Smyrn.* 10.2; *Polyc.* 2.3; 6.1), a rare word that occurs in *4 Maccabees* (6.29; 17.22). Williams stresses also other similarities, such as the endurance of the martyr and his designation as an athlete. The description of the instruments of torture given by Ignatius in *Rom.* 5.3 evokes for Williams the tortures suffered by the Maccabean martyrs.[33] Glen Bowersock, however, denies that Ignatius used *4 Maccabees* because this text, according to him, was written somewhat later than the earliest Christian martyrological texts. He proposes that both were written in Asia Minor and argues that the occurrence of ἀντίψυχον in Ignatius originates from Classical literature, namely from Lucian and Cassius Dio.[34] The expression means, just as for the Classical authors, that Ignatius "will free the Christians by assuming their bondage and death."[35] Lucian and Cassius Dio, however flourished after Ignatius, therefore the argument is not very convincing. It nevertheless shows that it is worthwhile to look for Classical parallels.

Ignatius and the Classical tradition

Several scholars situate Ignatius in the line of the Classical "noble death" tradition. George Heyman compares his death to Decius' *devotio*: "Reminiscent of Roman *devotio*, Ignatius employed an overt sacrificial metaphor when asked to be 'poured out as an offering to god' (*Romans* 2.2) and 'found worthy to be a sacrifice *thusia*' (*Romans* 4.2)."[36] Ignatius' eagerness to die also evokes for Heyman the "noble death." For Brent: "Ignatius' procession to martyrdom reflected the Christian counterpart to the imperial

---

[31] David Seeley, *Noble Death. Graeco-Roman Martyrology and Paul's Concept of Salvation* (Sheffield Academic Press, 1990), p. 130.

[32] *A Patristic Greek Lexicon.* Ed. G. W. H. Lampe (Oxford: Clarendon Press, 1984), p. 162.

[33] Sam K. Williams, *Jesus' Death as Saving Event. The Background of a Concept* (Missoula, Montana: Scholars Press, 1975), pp. 236–38.

[34] Glen W. Bowersock, *Martyrdom and Rome* (Cambridge: Cambridge University Press, 1995), pp. 80–81.

[35] *Martyrdom and Rome*, p. 81.

[36] George Heyman, G., *The Power of Sacrifice. Roman and Christian Discourses in Conflict* (Washington, D. C.: The Catholic University of America Press, 2007), p. 184.

procession that ended with a sacrificial offering on an imperial altar".[37] There are other parallels. In *Rom.* 5.3 we read: "Let there come on me fire, and cross, and struggles with wild beasts, cutting, and rearing asunder, racking of bones, mangling of limbs, crushing of my whole body, cruel tortures of the devil..."[38] Ignatius, however, knows that he will be cast before the beasts, the enumeration of these instruments of torture makes little sense. Seneca's *Letter 24*, the crucial Roman account of noble death, gives a better clue. Seneca exhorts his friend Lucius to despise pain and death: "Why dost thou hold up before my eyes swords, fires and a throng of executioners raging about thee? ... Why dost thou again unfold and spread before me, with all that great display, the whip and the rack? Why are those engines of torture made ready, one for several members of the body, and all the other innumerable machines for tearing a man apart piece-meal?"[39]

Yet another parallel is provided by Lucian: Demonax gives no order concerning the fate of his body and wants it to be devoured by birds and dogs so that in his death he could be "a service to living things."[40] Ignatius hopes that the beasts will completely devour him, leaving no trace of his body, so that in death he would not be burdensome to anyone.[41] This is not to claim that Ignatius was directly influenced by Seneca, or Lucian by Ignatius. Yet it is possible to presume that these *topoi* were known to everyone with a good Classical education-- Seneca attests that the topic of "despising death" and its related examples were repeated incessantly in all the schools.[42]

It comes as no surprise, then, that the cultivated Ignatius conceived of his death not (only) in the terms of the biblical narratives about Jesus' death, but also in terms of the Classical "noble death" tradition.

Polycarp of Smyrna

The *Martyrdom of Polycarp* is considered to be the first Christian account of a martyr's death[43] and the bishop of Smyrna is the first to be called a "martyr". The authenticity of the text is debated and controversy rages both about the date of its composition and its historical kernel. Dating Polycarp's death between 156–160, Boudewijn Dehandschutter argues that the *Martyrdom* was written shortly afterwards

---

[37] Allen Brent, *The Imperial Cult and the Development of Church Order* (Leiden: Brill, 2000); Heyman, *The Power of Sacrifice*, p. 184.
[38] Cf. Drodge and Tabor, *A Noble Death*, p. 130.
[39] *Ep.* 24.14, quoted by Seeley, *The Noble Death*, p. 118.
[40] Lucian, *Demonax* 66; cf. Seeley, *The Noble Death*, p. 141.
[41] *Rom.* 4.1; Seeley, *The Noble Death*, p. 130.
[42] *Ep.* 24.6.
[43] Candida Moss, *The Myth of Persecution. How Early Christians Invented a Story of Martyrdom* (New York: Harper Collins, 2013), p. 94.

and accepts the reliability and historicity of the text.[44] Accepted by the majority of scholars, this opinion has been repeatedly questioned,[45] recently by Candida Moss.[46] Without addressing this controversy, I focus on the models that the author of *Martyrdom of Polycarp* chose to construct his hero and the literary devices employed in the text. The narrative was apparently written to edify the Christians in Philomelium. Whatever its historical value, the text does not restrict itself to reporting the events, but also interprets them.

Polycarp and Christ

Polycarp is considered as the prototype of the *imitatio Christi,* and indeed the *Martyrdom* account follows closely the Gospel narratives. It has long been observed that in many details Polycarp imitates Christ: he is a witness "in accordance with the Gospel" (2.1; 19.2); "just as the Lord did, he too waited that he might be delivered up" (1.2); he is betrayed by someone close to him; he is arrested by a police captain named Herod (6.2); he enters the city on a donkey (8.1), etc.[47] For Dehandschutter,[48] however, the imitation of Christ does not reside in the (often only superficial) similarity of details, but in Polycarp's very attitude: just like Christ, the bishop fulfils the will of God (*MPol.* 2.1). The expression "martyrdom in accordance with the Gospel" must be understood in this way. Dehandschutter is right in calling these similarities superficial: Polycarp follows Christ in his own way. His death, in my opinion, is intentionally *not* modelled after that of Christ.

Polycarp and the Maccabean Martyrs

Sam K. Williams argued that the author of the *Martyrdom of Polycarp* knew *4Macc* and made liberal use of it to construe the plot line of Polycarp's death. He highlights the following similarities:[49]

---

[44] Boudewijn Dehandschutter, 'Le Martyre de Polycarpe et le développement de la conception du martyre au deuxième siècle', in Dehandschutter, *Polycarpiana. Studies on Martyrdom and Persecution in Early Christianity* (Bibliotheca EphemeridumTheologicarumLovannensium 205) (Leuven: Univ. Pr. – Peeters, 2007), pp. 93–104 (93–94).

[45] Jan de Boeft and Jan Bremmer, 'Notiunculae martyrologicae V', *Vigiliae Christianae,* 49/2 (1995), pp. 146–64, (146–51).

[46] *The Myth of Persecution,* pp. 94–104.

[47] Moss, *The Myth of Persecution,* p. 63.

[48] Dehandschutter, 'Le Martyre de Ploycarpe', pp. 93–95.

[49] Williams, *Jesus' Death,*pp. 234–36.

- the martyr's endurance in suffering (*MPol.* 2.2–4; 3.1; 13.3);
- the authorities' attempt to dissuade the martyrs by appealing either to their youth or old age (*MPol.* 3.1; 9.2);
- the martyrs endure horrible tortures (*MPol.* 2.2; 13.3);
- they demonstrate courage;
- the ἀγών motif expresses the martyrs' struggle and reward;
- the cultic language of Polycarp and Eleazar's prayers;
- the impact of the martyrs' deaths.

The first, second, and fourth point are commonplaces observable in every description of noble death. Polycarp does not endure horrible tortures, and compared to the descriptions of executions in *4Macc*, his death is simple and fast; the ἀγών motif has no importance in the *Martyrdom of Polycarp*;[50] the cultic language used in the prayer of Polycarp and the impact of the martyr's death also have New Testament antecedents.

Polycarp and the philosophers

While acknowledging the parallels between the Gospels and the *Martyrdom of Polycarp*, Candida Moss maintains that on several points Polycarp resembles Socrates, who willingly accepts death for his convictions and remains composed until the end:

> "Both Polycarp and Socrates are described as 'noble' and both are charged with atheism. Neither was willing to persuade others to save his life. Socrates took control of his death by requesting the hemlock rather than waiting for it to be administered to him. Polycarp took control of his death by removing his own clothes and standing on the pyre without being nailed to the stake. Both Socrates and Polycarp prayed before dying, and the accounts of both of their deaths explicitly interpret their deaths as sacrifices. Socrates refers to Asclepius and

---

[50] The devil plays little role in *MPol.* Certain references to Satan belong to later redactions: Moss, *The Other Christs*, p. 95. The devil's main concern is to prevent Christians from recuperating the saint's body (ch. 17).

pours out the hemlock as a libation offering, and Polycarp is described as being like a ram bound for sacrifice... Both men are elderly... Finally their deaths are described as being models for others."[51]

Polycarp's self-control also makes him resemble Stoic philosophers: "Like Zeno and Anaxarchus, Polycarp takes control of the torture and demonstrates with his words that he is both manly and self-controlled".[52] These arguments are not compelling: Moss' parallels are either too general (such as praying before death), or forced (requesting the hemlock and taking off clothes). Unsurprisingly, the description of Polycarp's death does show similarities with "noble death" stories in Classical literature because these stories had already impacted earlier Jewish and Christian writings.

Polycarp and Isaac

I wish to suggest that the narrative of Polycarp's martyrdom was predominantly modelled after the sacrifice of Isaac *(Aqedah)*.

1. Polycarp does not let himself to be nailed to the pyre: a significant difference from the death of Christ. For Moss, the *imitatio Christi* does not break down at this crucial moment. In my view, by refusing to be nailed down, Polycarp "overdoes" Christ.[53] If "overdoing" constitutes an important motive in the *Martyrdom of Polycarp* (and in martyrology in general), it certainly makes the story different from the Gospel narratives.

2. Instead of being nailed, Polycarp is bound down; a detail which evokes naturally the binding of Isaac. The similarity is emphasized by the expression "bound like a noble ram" (προσδεθεὶς ὥσπερ κριὸς ἐπίσημος). The animal caught in the bush and offered by Abraham instead of Isaac (Gen 22.13) is called by the *Septuagint* ram(κριός). By using the same word, the *Martyrdom* establishes a parallel between the death of Polycarp and the *Aqedah* while avoids any allusion to the Lamb (ἀμνός) of God.

3. Polycarp wants to become an "acceptable holocaust" (ὁλοκαύτωμα δεκτόν) for God (14.1), the only form of sacrifice not identified with Christ. Polycarp

---

[51] *The Myth of Persecution*, p. 64.
[52] *The Myth of Persecution*, p. 65.
[53] *The Other Christs*, p. 58.

previously learned from a vision that he would be burnt. This is all the more interesting because in the end he dies by a dagger, not by fire—a fact that does not seem to bother the author of the *Martyrdom of Polycarp*, for whom Polycarp apparently *is* a holocaust. Isaac, similarly, is considered by Jewish tradition a perfect holocaust, even though he was not burnt at all.[54]

4. Polycarp is placed on the pyre to be burnt (*MPol*. 14.1) just like Isaac (Gen 22.2, 3,7, 8, 13). He is bound, just like Isaac and before dying he also makes a speech (ch. 14), as Isaac does according several Jewish writings, in which he not only gives his assent to be sacrificed, but also praises God for having accorded him this favour.[55]

5. The fire does not touch him. This reminds us of Daniel 3, especially in its Greek version (Dan 3. 49–50).

6. Jewish tradition often mentions the blood of Isaac even if not a single drop of it was spilled. Yet there is no expiation without blood. Polycarp is killed at the end by a dagger and from the wound comes such a quantity of blood that it extinguishes the fire (16.1).

7. Williams has remarked that Polycarp's prayer (14.1–2) shows similarities with that of Eleazar in *4Macc*.[56] This is true, but the parallels between the words of Polycarp and that of Isaac according to *Liber Antiquitatum Biblicarum (LAB)* are even more compelling. For instance:

"his offering was acceptable before my face"[57] (*facta est oblatio in cospectum eo acceptabilis*) (*LAB* 18.6) – "May I be received this day before your face as a rich and acceptable sacrifice" (προσδεχθείην ἐνώπιόν, σου σήμερον ἐν θυσίᾳ πίονι καὶ προσδεκτῇ) (*MPol*. 14.2);

"If a lamb of the flock is accepted as sacrifice to the Lord with an odor of sweetness"[58] (*Si agnus ex pecoribus acceptatur in oblatione Domini in odorem sua vitatis...*)

---

[54] Géza Vermes, 'Redemption and Genesis XXII. The Binding of Isaac and the Sacrifice of Jesus', in Vermes, *Scripture and Tradition in Judaism. Haggadic Studies* (Leiden: Brill 1961), pp. 193–227 (205).
[55] The earliest known example of this is Pseudo Philo's *Liber Antiquitatum Biblicarum* 32.2–4.
[56] Williams, *Jesus' Death*, p. 236.
[57] Transl. Daniel J. Harrington, in James H. Charlesworth (ed.), *The Old Testament Pseudepigrapha*, vol. 2, (Garden City, N. Y.: Doubleday, 1985), p. 325.
[58] Transl. Harrington, in Charlesworth, *OT Pseudepigrapha*, vol. 2, p. 345.

(*LAB* 32.3) – "He was bound like a noble ram chosen for an oblation from a great flock, a holocaust prepared and made acceptable to God"⁵⁹ (κριὸς ἐπίσημος ἐκ μεγάλου ποιμνίου εἰς προσφοράν, ὁλοκαύτωμα δεκτὸν τῷ θεῷ ἡτοιμασμένον) (*MPol.* 14.1), cf. *MPol.* 15. 2: "...we perceived such a delightful fragrance..."⁶⁰ (εὐωδίας τοσαύτης ἀντελαβόμεθα);

> "...have I not been born into the world to be offered as a sacrifice to him who made me? ... the Lord has made the soul of man worthy to be sacrificed"⁶¹ *(Quid si non essemnatus in seculo, ut offerer sacrificium ei qui me fecit? ... quoniam dignificavit Dominus animam hominis in sacrificium)* (*LAB* 32. 3) – "...I bless you because you have thought me worthy of this day and this hour..."⁶²(εὐλογῶ σε ὅτι ἠξίωσάς με τῆς, ἡμέρας καὶ ὥρας ταύτης) (*MPol.* 14. 2).

The description of Polycarp's death is best situated within the framework of Jewish martyrology. It seems deliberately to avoid any identification with the passion of Christ. It is true that Polycarp partakes of the cup of Christ (14.2), but he does so according a Jewish model. His death is an expiatory sacrifice, just like the death of the Maccabean martyrs, and the result is the same: the cessation of persecution (*MPol.* 1.1; 19.2 ; cf. *4Macc.* 1.11; 17.20-22; 18.4-5).⁶³ The similarities with Isaac clearly connect the death of Polycarp to human sacrifice.

The *Martyrdom of Polycarp* follows an ancient paradigm present both in the Old Testament and in Classical sources. God stops the calamity (in this case the persecution) which He launched because of the sins of the people/the Christians after having received an adequate quantity of human blood—naturally innocent blood. Blood sacrifice plays an important role in the *Martyrdom of Polycarp*.

Conclusions

Ignatius of Antioch wants to die the way philosophers were expected to die, and the author of the *Martyrdom of Polycarp* presents the death of his hero as a new

---

[59] Musurillo, *The Acts of the Christian Martyrs*, p. 13.
[60] Musurillo, *The Acts of the Christian Martyrs*, p. 15.
[61] Transl. Harrington in: Charlesworth, *OT Pseudepigrapha*, vol. 2, 345.
[62] Musurillo, *The Acts of the Christian Martyrs*, 13.
[63] Cf. Williams, *Jesus' Death*, 168-70; 236.

Aqedah, a prefect holocaust offered by Christ as the high priest (cf. *MPol.* 14).[64] Yet other Christian writers chose yet other models: Agnes dies as Iphigeneia and Polyxena died in Euripidean drama; Thecla, the "protomartyr", behaves in the apocryphal *Acts of Paul and Thecla* like the heroines of Hellenistic novels,[65] participating in a love-story where *erōs* is replaced by *agneia* (Thecla is spellbound by Saint Paul, not by Christ);[66] the literary predecessors of Perpetua, who acts against family will and kills herself by directing the gladiator's dagger to her throat,[67] are African heroines such as Elissa, founder of Carthage[68] or the wife of General Hasdrubal.[69] Tertullian displays these women—along with other Classical examples of "noble" suicide such as Lucretia, Heracleitus, Empedocles, and even Cleopatra—to his Christian readers to spur them to martyrdom.[70] Origen exhorts his readers to martyrdom by evoking the self-sacrifice of Jephthah's daughter.[71] The *Acts of Montanus and Lucius* praise the martyr Flavianus' mother as a "Maccabean mother".[72] Dasius' story is pieced together from historical, mythical, literary elements: the feast of Saturnalia with its king, the descriptions of Sakaia and of the *pharmakos* ritual, and the myth of the hero sacrificing himself for his country.[73]

---

[64] Moss, *The Other Christs*, p. 84: 'The author of Polycarp uncomfortably constructs his death so that he dies at the hand of Jesus as a preordained sacrifice to God'.

[65] The *Apocryphal Acts of the Apostles (AAA)* resemble to Hellenistic novels; Gail P. C. Streets, *Redeemed Bodies: Women Martyrs in Early Christianity* (Louisville, Kentucky: Westminster John Knox Pr., 2009), p. 3.calls them 'Christian popular novels,' and Peter Brown, *Body and Society. Men, Women, and Sexual Renunciation in Early Christianity* (New York: Columbia Univ. Pr., 1988), p. 155.describes them as follows: 'The Christian authors of the Apocryphal Acts had only to replace a manifest destiny to the wedding bed ... by the Apostle's call to continence.'

[66] Eung Chun Park, 'ΑΓΝΕΙΑ as a Sublime Form of ΕΡΩΣ in The *Acts of Paul and Thecla*', in Holly E. Hearon (ed.), *Distant Voices Drawing Near: Essays in Honor of Antoinette Clark Wire*, (Michael Glazier Book) (Saint John's Abbey, Minn.: Liturgical Pr., 2004), pp. 215–26.

[67] *Martyrdom of Perpetua* 21.9, Musurillo, *The Acts of the Christian Martyrs*, p. 131.

[68] Elissa (known also as Dido, ca. 800 BCE) chose death rather than to marry a local chieftain: she prepared a pyre as if to offer a sacrifice to her deceased husband before marrying again, then she herself stepped on the fire and killed herself with a sword; cf. Justin, *Epitome* 18.6; cf. Joyce E. Salisbury, *Perpetua's Passion, The Death and Memory of a Young Roman Woman* (New York and London: Routledge, 1997), p. 34. Tertullian knows the story: *Ad Martyras* 4.5. In Virgil, Dido dies out of love for Aeneas.

[69] Appian *Historia Romana* 8.131 and Tertullian *Ad Martyras* 4.5: at the end of the third Punic war, when Carthage was already burning, she reproached Hasdrubal his cowardice, called him a traitor, and finally slew their children and threw them along with herself into the fire.

[70] *Ad Martyras*, 4.4.

[71] *ComJoh* 6.54.276–78.

[72] Ch. 16, similarly *The Acts of Marian and James* 13.

[73] *Martyrdom of Dasius* (Musurillo, *The Acts of the Christian Martyrs*, pp. 272–79), see Monika Pesthy-Simon, 'Human Sacrifices and/orMartyrs', *Classica et Christiana* 9/1 (2014), pp. 213–25.

These examples suffice to prove that hagiographers, so as to optimize the heroism of the martyr and make the story as interesting as possible, recycled all available heroic models of the past, Jewish, Greek, Roman, Egyptian, Carthaginian history, myth and legend about people who died in a "noble" way—meaning anything from human sacrifice to suicide. Christ in the Gospels was one among the many literary heroes of Antiquity—and for the authors of martyrdom narratives apparently not the most interesting one.

ASCETIC CHRISTIANITY IN PANNONIAN MARTYR STORIES?

Levente Nagy

Pannonia had a rich crop of martyrs in the Great Persecution.[1] Archaeology and martyrology offer graphic evidence of the strength of Christianity in the province.[2] Reconstructing the context of early Christianity in Pannonia, however, is far from easy due to the destruction of the ecclesiastical structure and the lack of sources. This paper argues that passion stories, compiled as late as a century after the persecution, reflect new Christian concerns besides concentrating on martyrdom. Possibly influenced by the fourth-century "ascetic revolution," the martyrdom narratives of Saint Syneros and Pollio reveal features of the martyr that can be seen as 'ascetic.' The *Passio Synerotis* retroprojects the rise of the "monk" into early fourth-century Sirmium, while the *Passio Pollionis* praises virginity, defends bodily integrity and extols celibate priesthood. I argue that these texts show the speed with which the martyr merged with the monk.

The Monk in the Garden: Temptation and Marriage

The Greek monk (*monachus*) Synerus took up a gardener job in Sirmium.[3] One day, in the sixth hour, a married woman walked into the garden. Synerus reminded

---

[1] Special thanks to Marianne Sághy for her invaluable help in refining the argument of this paper.
[2] Noël Duval, "Sirmium „ville impériale" ou „capitale?" *Corso di cultura sull'arte ravennate e bizantina* 26 (1979): 83–84; Miroslav Jeremić, "Adolf Hytrek et les premières fouilles archéologiques à Sirmium,"*Starinar* 55 (2005): 120–123; Miroslava Mirković, "Kontinuität und Diskontinuitätbei der Entwicklung der Stadt Sirmium," in *Keszthely-Fenékpuszta im Kontext spätantiker Kontinuitätsforschung zwischen Noricum und Moesia*, ed. Heinrich-Tamáska Orsolya. (Rahden: Verlag Marie Leidorf GmBH, 2011), 87–89; Henrik Hildebrandt, "Early Christianity in Roman Pannonia – facts among fictions?" *Studia Patristica* 39. Ed. Frances Margaret Young, Mark J. Edwards, and Paul N. Parvis (Leuven: Peeters Publishers, 2006), 59–64.
[3] *Passio Synerotis*, BHL 7595–7596; Péter Kovács, ed., *Die antiken Quellen zu Pannonien in der Spätantike.Teil I: 284-337 n. Chr.* (Vienna: Phoibos, 2014), 45–49 (hereafter Kovács, *Die antiken Quellen*); Levente Nagy, *Pannóniai városok, mártírok, ereklyék. Négy szenvedéstörténet helyszínei nyomában [Cities, Martyrs and Relics in*

her that it was inappropriate for a wife to leave her husband's house so late and walk alone after sunset. At this, the woman denounced him at her husband, a bodyguard of Emperor Galerius. The husband accused Synerus of adultery and had him thrown to prison. Synerus successfully cleared himself from adultery, but when accused of Christianity, he freely admitted the charge:

> „Upon hearing the holy man's answer, the governor mused: 'The man must be a Christian if he does not suffer women leaving the house in unbefitting hours.' So he asked him: 'Who are you?' He replied without delay: 'I am a Christian.' 'Where did you hide? How did you avoid sacrificing to the gods?' 'God saved my body. I was like the foundation stone rejected by the builders. Now, however, the Lord needs me for the building of his house. As he wanted to stand here outright, I am ready to suffer for His name, in order to be in His kingdom together with the saints."

Refusing to sacrifice, Synerus was executed on 22 February 307.[4]

The shorter Latin version of the *Passio Synerotis* (version B) is generally dated to the end of the fourth century as the term *monachos* first appears in papyri dated to 324 or 323,[5] and the Latin form *monachus* spread in the Latin West thanks to Saint Jerome from the mid-370s.[6] The figure of the "wandering monk" may seem anachronistic at the beginning of the fourth century. The ascetic revolution, however, reached the Latin West in the second half of the fourth century: urban asceticism was practiced by the

---

Pannonia. Discovering the Topography in Four Pannonian Passion Stories]. (Pécs: Pécsi Történelemtudományért Kulturális Egyesület, 2012), 56–61 (hereafter Nagy, *Pannóniai városok*).

[4] Nagy, *Pannóniai városok,* 61–66; Hippolyte Delehaye, *Les legends hagiographiques.*(Bruxelles: Société des Bollandistes, 1955), 101–118; Mirja Jarak, "Martyres Pannoniae – The Chronological Position of the Pannonian Martyrs in the Course of Diocletian's Persecution," in *Westillyricum und Nordostitalien in der spätrömischen Zeit*, ed. Rajko Bratož (Ljubljana: Narodnimuzej, 1996), 268–269 (hereafter Jarak, "Martyres Pannoniae").

[5] Edwin A. Judge, "The Earliest Use of Monachos for Monk (P. Coll. Youtie 77) and the Origins of Monasticism,"*Jahrbuch für Antike und Christentum* 20 (1977): 77, 79; Malcolm Choat, "The Development and Usage of Terms for 'Monk' in Late Antique Egypt," *Jahrbuch für Antike und Christentum* 45 (2002): 7 (hereafter Choat, *The Development and Usage*).

[6] Tibor Nagy *A pannoniai kereszténység története a római védőrendszer összeomlásáig [The History of Pannonian Christianity until the Collapse of the Roman Defence System]*. (Budapest: Pázmány Péter Tudományegyetem, 1939), 59, note 50, based on letter no. 14 of Jerome, chapter 6 (hereafter Nagy, *A pannoniai kereszténység története*); Jarak, "Martyres Pannoniae," 269; Péter Tóth, "Szent Szinerótasz szerzetesvértanú (St. Synerotas, a martyr monk)," in *Magyarság és ortodoxia. Ezer esztendő (Hungary and Orthodoxy. Thousand Years)*, ed. Tibor Imrényi (Miskolc: Magyar Orthodox Egyházmegye – Miskolci Orthodox Múzeumért Alapítvány, 2000), 37; Kovács, *Die antiken Quellen*, 49.

Christian elite of Aquileia and Milan as early as in the 360s–370s.[7] The existence of suburban eremitism in Pannonia cannot be excluded at the beginning of the fourth century, even if these ascetic were not yet called *monachoi*.

The scene of a gardener confronting a lascivious woman is as old as the Book of Genesis, where Joseph meets Potiphar's wife in a garden.[8] The biblical *topos* of the temptation of the chaste male by deviant females reappears and becomes extremely popular in Late Antique ascetic biographies.[9] Synerus' story, like that of Joseph, is about rejected women who seek to avenge the injury by persuading their powerful husbands to punish the virginal heroes. But, as Monika Pesthy showed, it is hard to draw a dividing line between moral proof tests coming from God and physical temptations coming from evil conceded by God.[10] Avoiding adultery is not yet proof of asceticism. Synerus' story is less about the monk's fight to preserve his chastity than about a righteous person rejecting adultery. The gardener/*monachus* is adamant that married women must stay home at night. The proper place of little women (*levis muliercula*) is not in the holy man's garden, a delightful place (*locus amoenus*) with paradisiacal associations, but in her husband's house. Synerus is a staunch defender of marriage. In his eyes, the social order based on marriage is far from being "a sandcastle touched by the ocean-flood of the Messiah."[11]

The Lector's Lecture: Chastity as Integrity

Pollio's martyrdom begins with a striking summary of the persecution of Christians in Pannonia. Following the execution of Bishop Irenaeus of Sirmium and Montanus of Singidunum in 303/4, Probus, governor of Pannonia Secunda is unsatisfied with his record as a persecutioner and raids the neighboring towns in search of Christians. On his official visit in Cibalae (Vinkovci, Croatia), he arrests Pollio, *lector* of the local Christian congregation for blaspheming pagan gods and emperors.[12] The

---

[7] Nagy, *A pannoniai kereszténység története,* 167; Rajko Bratož,"Die Geschichte des frühen Christentums im Gebiet zwischen Sirmium und Aquileia im Licht der neueren Forschungen,"*Klio* 72 (1990/2): 548; Rajko Bratož,"Christianisierung des Nordadria- und Westbalkanraumes im 4. Jahrhundert," in *Westillyricum und Nordostitalien in der spätrömischen Zeit,* ed. Rajko Bratož, *Situla* 34 (1996): 350–351; Neil B. McLynn, *Ambrose of Milan. Church and Court in a Christian Capital* (Berkeley: University of California Press, 1994), 61–62.

[8] *Genesis* 39, 7–23.

[9] Monika Pesthy, "Ördögi kísértés vagy asszonyi csábítás? (Evil temptation or female seduction?),"*Studia Patrum*, ed. Péter Nemeshegyi and Zoltán Rihmer (Budapest: Szent István Társulat, 2002), 183–188.

[10] Monika Pesthy-Simon, *Die Theologie der Versuchung im frühen Christentum.* (Bern: Peter Lang, 2011).

[11] Peter Brown, *The Body and Society. Men, Women and Sexual Renunciation in Early Christianity* (New York: Columbia University Press, 1988), 32 (hereafter Brown, *The Body and Society*).

[12] *Passio Pollionis,* BHL 6869; Hajnalka Tamás,"Passio Pollionis (BHL 6869) Introduction, Critical Text and Notes. "*Sacris Erudiri* 51 (2012): 9–35 (hereafter Tamás, "Passio Pollionis").

passio's representation of the Great Persecution—the governor's failure to round up Christians in Sirmium; his razzia in the province; his incapacity to find more than one Christian; the accusation with blasphemy (a minor crime)—betrays a rather low-key implementation of the fourth edict of the tetrarchs against Christians in Pannonia.[13]

At his arrest, Pollio delivers a long monologue to the governor about Christian doctrine and Christian lifestyle,[14] explaining that the foundation stone of Christian theology is belief in one God and the renunciation of idols, complemented with the ethical precepts taught by the apostles. Moral obligations affect all classes of late Roman society—women, slaveholders, slaves, secular rulers—and include family relations and attitudes towards the poor.[15] Refusing to commit idolatry, Pollio is burnt on the stake a mile away from the town on 27/28 April,[16] on the feast of the martyr Bishop Eusebius of Cibalae.[17]

In 2012, Croatian archaeologist Hrvoje Vulić found an early Christian basilica complex surrounded by a cemetery in Vinkovci-Kamenica exactly a mile from the town. Geophysical research revealed the ground plan of a possible *martyrium* with adjacent cemetery and mausolea.[18] The findspot was interpreted as the place where Pollio (and perhaps also Eusebius of Cibalae) was killed and where the feasts commemorating the martyr (or the martyrs) were held.[19] The basilica complex is dated to the last quarter of the fourth century, to reign of Valentinian I. Born in Cibalae, it was possibly Valentinian who commissioned the construction of the basilica.[20] Pollio's martyrdom must have been compiled around the same time. The *terminus post quem* of the composition of the *Passio Pollionis* is given by its use of the term *christianissimus imperator*[21] addressing Emperor Valentinian I. As Hajnalka Tamás has shown, this vocative first appears in a

---

[13] Nagy, *Pannóniai városok,* 32. For the Great Persecution in Pannonia: Kovács, *Die antiken Quellen,* 100–103.
[14] *Passio Pollionis* III.
[15] Tamás, "Passio Pollionis," 13.
[16] Tamás, "Passio Pollionis," 11–12.
[17] *Passio Pollionis* IV.5–V.
[18] Hrvoje Vulić, "Kamenica. An Early Christian Complex," in *Neue Forschungen zum frühen Christentum in den Balkanländern,* ed. Renate Johanna Pillinger. Österreichische Akademie der Wissenschaften, Philosophisch-Historische Klasse, Denkschriften, 484. Band – Archäologische Forschungen 26 (C=Vienna: Verlag der Österreichischen Akademie der Wissenschaften, 2015), 69–72. I thank Hrvoje Vulić for information about new research results in Kamenica.
[19] Branka Migotti, *Evidence for Christianity in Roman Southern Pannonia (Northern Croatia): A Catalogue of Finds and Sites.*(Oxford: Archaeopress, 1997), 22; Tamás, "Eloquia Divina Populis Legere," 180, note 3.
[20] Vulić, "Kamenica," 71.
[21] *PassioPollionis* II.2.

letter of Ambrose of Milan to Emperor Gratian in 380.²² Unfortunately, the author and the date of the *Passio Pollionis* remain unknown.

Pollio's long monologue is impregnated with ascetic ideas, demonstrating up-to-date theological ideas worked out in the great ascetic centers of Northern Italy (Aquileia, Milan) and Rome. Pollio praises integrity in virgins and reserve *(pudica conscientia)* in married women.²³ Governor Probus provokes Pollio when he asks whether Christians prefer virginity to marriage for their daughters: "Are they [the Christian lectors] the ones who are said to forbid little women to marry, and who persuade them to keep useless chastity?"²⁴

The concept of bodily integrity is crucial in Ambrose of Milan's theology of virginity.²⁵ His *De virginibus*, compiled in 377, presents chastity *(integritas)* as the opposite of intercourse with harmful effects *(contagio)*;²⁶ his *De institutione virginis*, written in 393, shows the Virgin Mary raising the standard of integrity;²⁷ his *Exhortatio virginitatis*, written in 394 defines virginity as a particular disposition to "modesty that guards the integrity of the genitals" *(quae signaculum pudoris et claustrum integritatis genital custodit.)*²⁸ Bodily integrity *(integrum corpus)* appears *De officiis* written in the late 380s in connection with the priests' obligation of sexual abstinence before the holy service,²⁹ and his letter 63, written to the Christian community of Vercelli in 396, "integrity" marks the Church as virgin and bride of Christ.³⁰

---

[22] Tamás, "Passio Pollionis," 14–16; Hajnalka Tamás, "Valentinian I, *christianissimus imperator*? Notes on a passage of the Passio Pollionis (BHL 6869)," *Vigiliae Christianae* 68 (2014): 82–97 (hereafter Tamás, "Valentinian I, *christianissimus imperator*?"); Tamás, "Eloquia Divina Populis Legere," 186–187; Tamás, "Passio Pollionis," 14.

[23] *Passio Pollionis* III.7..

[24] *Passio Pollionis* III.3: "*Probus dixit: 'Illi, qui leves mulierculas vetant ne nubant ac pervertere et ad vanam castitatem suadere dicuntur?'*" (ed. Tamás, "Passio Pollionis", 28.)

[25] Brown, *The Body and Society*, 354–361. David Hunter, "Helvidius, Iovinian, and the Virginity of Mary in Late Fourth-Century Rome," *Journal of Early Christian Studies* 1/1 (1993): 47–71 (hereafter Hunter, "Helvidius, Iovinian").

[26] Ambrosius, *De virg.* I, 5, 21: *Quid autem est castitas virginalis, nisi expers contagionis integritas? De virginibus*: I, 2, 5: *Natalis est virginis, integritatem sequamur*; I, 3, 10: *Invitat nunc integritatis amor*; II, 4, 22: *Itaque sancta virgo, ne diutius alerentur potiendi spe cupiditatis, integritatem pudoris professa*. [Jacques-Paul Migne (ed.), *Ambrosius: De virginitate liber unus*. Patrologiae Cursus Completus. Series Latina XVI (Paris: Vrayet, 1845) 265-302B.]

[27] Ambrosius, *De inst. virg.*5, 35.[Jacques-Paul Migne (ed.), *Ambrosius: De institutione virginis et Sanctae Mariae virginitate perpetua*. Patrologiae Cursus Completus. Series Latina XVI (Paris :Vrayet, 1845) 305-334B.]

[28] Ambrosius, *Exhort. virg.* 6, 35.[Jacques-Paul Migne (ed.), *Ambrosius: De institutione virginis et Sanctae Mariae virginitate perpetua*. Patrologia Latina XVI (Paris: Vrayet, 1845) 335-364B.]

[29] *De officiis* I, 249.[Ivor J. Davidson (ed.), *Ambrose: De officiis: Volumes One and Two* (Oxford: Oxford University Press, 2002)]

[30] Ambrosius, *Epist.* 14 (63) 37. Michaela Zelzer (ed.), *Ambrosius: Epistularum liber decimus, Epistulae extra collectionem, Gesta Concilii Aquileiensis*. Corpus Scriptorum Ecclesiasticorum Latinorum 82/3 (Vienna: Austrian Academy of Sciences Press, 1982)]; John Moorhead, *Ambrose. Church and Society in the Late Roman World* (London: Longman, 1999), 40–41; David G. Hunter, *Marriage, Celibacy, and Heresy in Ancient Christianity* (Oxford: Oxford University Press, 2007), 197, 201, 225 (hereafter Hunter, *Marriage, Celibacy, and Heresy*).

Hajnalka Tamás, who regards the apocryphal *Acts of Peter* as the literary antecedent of Pollio's speech,[31] takes the *Passio*'s use of "integritas" for a simple hagiographical *topos*, without insinuating the superiority of virginity over marriage. Close comparison with Ambrose's works about virginity, however, compels us to posit that the anonymous author of the *Passio* knew the thoughts of the bishop of Milan on the topic and used the term in Ambrose's meaning. Even without direct textual borrowing and exact citations, the subject matter and the connotations in the *Passio Pollionis* betray knowledge of the works (and concerns) of Ambrose about virginity. Young girls were advised to take the veil of virginity instead of marriage by Jerome and Ambrose, even against the will of the family.[32] Pollio's answer to the governor's question about male-female relations among Christians is telling: "Christianity teaches virgins how to obtain the highest grade of integrity, and wives, how to preserve their chaste conscience in procreating children (*virgines integritatis suae docent obtinere fastigia, coniugem pudicam in creandis filiis conscientiam custodire*.) The interpretation of this sentence is not easy, particularly with regard of the grades of sexual abstinence in the case of lay Christian couples. Christian married couples in the Late Roman Empire understood *castitas* as periodical abstincence (during menstruation, breast-feeding, or before taking the Eucharist) and as faithfulness. At the height of the Jovinian controversy in 396,[33] Ambrose encouraged the congregation of Vercelli to live a life of chastity, avoid sexual contacts in marriage, and choose celibate spiritual directors.[34] The emphasis on bodily integrity in the *Passio Pollionis* suggests deep familiarity with Ambrose's works. The divine commandments recited by Pollio correspond to the *Decalogue* and to the Letters of Saint Paul. If it is right to say that Pollio does not extol asceticism over marriage, at least not for lay Christians,[35] his advice on *pudica conscientia* for women, however, challenges the teachings of Saint Paul to the Ephesians and Corinthians, for whom husband and wife form a single body.[36] This difference is not accidental: the *Passio Pollionis* reflects Ambrose's theology of virginity and the promotion of sexual abstinence by the "new ascetics."

Another indication of the anonymous author's ascetic agenda is the introductory paragraph of the *Passio Pollionis* on the Great Persecution in Pannonia that lists Montanus as the first martyr in the region. The priest Montanus figures here alone, while in the *Martyrologium Hieronymianum* he suffers martyrdom together with his

---

[31] Tamás, "Eloquia Divina Populis Legere," 196.
[32] Brown, *The Body and Society*, 357; Kelly, *Jerome*, 91–115.
[33] Hunter, "Helvidius, Iovinian," 47–71; Kelly, *Jerome*, 180–189.
[34] Ambrosius: *Epist.* 14 (63) 32 (ed. Zelzer, *Ambrosius*); Brown, *The Body and Society*, 362.
[35] Tamás, "Eloquia Divina Populis Legere," 197.
[36] *1 Cor.* 7:1-16; *Eph* 5: 21-33.

wife, Maxima.[37] It might simply be that the redactor of the *Passio* ranks Montanus among the martyrs in the male clergy,[38] but even in this case, the omission of his wife (as well as of seven virgins executed in Sirmium on 9 April 307, all listed in the *Martyrologium Hieronymianum*) is obvious. I argue that Maxima's obliteration from the passion story reflects the advocacy of sexual abstinence among the married clergy and the promotion of celibacy in the 380s.[39] Clerical chastity is praised by Ambrosiaster in the early 380s, by the decretal of Pope Damasus to the Gallic clergy in 384, and by Pope Siricius in his letter to Himerius around 384–385.[40] Ambrose advises priestly celibacy and asceticism in his *De officiis,* where he contrasts the behavior of married priests practicing sexual intercourse with the abstinence of laymen who do not visit their wives for two-three days before taking the Eucharist. According to Ambrose, ancient liturgical customs, when a longer time passed between each Eucharistic celebration, made married life possible for the priests. Everyday celebration of the Eucharist, however, excludes it. Priests should follow the example of laymen and avoid intercourse with their wives.[41] The "new asceticism" made a huge impact in the Western Empire in the 380s despite the critique of "old-fashioned" Christian laymen and clerics.[42] Married clerics are advised to avoid intercourse with their wives, and not to engender sons.[43] The superiority of virginity in the hierarchy of Christian virtues was acknowledged in early Christianity, and it became the cornerstone in fourth-century patristic theology.[44] This paper argues that chastity and ascetic ideas impregnated martyr literature. The passion stories of the martyrs Synerus and Pollio reflect the ascetic ideal in their representation of the martyr as a "monk" *avant la lettre,* gently guiding frivolous women onto the path of (married) virtue and in their obliteration of the martyr's married status.

---

[37] Kovács, *Die antiken Quellen*, 37; Nagy, *Pannóniai városok*, 42.

[38] Tamás, "Passio Pollionis," note 21

[39] Canon 3 of the Synod of Elvira in 306? and canon 29 of the Synod of Arles in 314 prohibit priests to have sexual intercourse with their wives. The authenticity of these canons is debated, later interpolations are possible: Hunter, *Marriage, Celibacy, and Heresy*, 214.

[40] Brown, *The Body and Society*, 358–359; Hunter, *Marriage, Celibacy, and Heresy*, 213–217. Ambrosiaster affirms that the Christian priest who celebrates the Eucharist should be as pure as it is required in the Bible for Jewish priests. As the Eucharistic celebration took place every day, priests were supposed to be constantly pure. 1Cor. 7:5 requires temporary marital abstinence during common prayer.

[41] Ambrosius: *De offic.* I, 248-249. (ed. Davidson, *Ambrose*)

[42] Rajko Bratož, "Die kirchliche Organisation in Westillyricum (vom späten 4. Jh. bis um 600) – Ausgewählte Fragen," in *Keszthely-Fenékpuszta im Kontext spätantiker Kontinuitätsforschung zwischen Noricum und Moesia.* Ed. Orsolya Heinrich-Tamáska. (Budapest: Marie Leidorf, 2011), 211–219.

[43] Brown, *The Body and Society*, 357–358; Hunter, *Marriage, Celibacy, and Heresy*, 213–223.

[44] John Norman Davidson Kelly, *Jerome: his Life, Writings and Controversies* (Peabody, MA: Hendrickson, 1998), 102; Marianne Sághy, *Isten barátai. Szent és szentéletrajz a későantikvitásban [The Friends of God. Holy Men and Holy Biography in Late Antiquity]* (Budapest: Kairosz, 2005), 65–147.

While this elevates Synerus onto the rank of the first "monk" in Sirmium, Maxima, the priest Montanus' deliberately obliterated wife becomes the first victim of the ascetic revolution in Pannonia. Apart from the profession of Christ as God, the preservation of virginity, the rejection of temptation and the protection of integrity are clearly the main concerns of these texts. The prevalence of these issues show not only the rapid spread of the monastic ideal and the vivid intellectual contacts among ascetic centers in the Late Antique West, but also the determination of ascetic authors to appropriate the past for their ascetic agenda.

USES AND MEANINGS OF 'PAGANUS' IN THE WORKS OF SAINT AUGUSTINE

Jérôme Lagouanère

Augustine of Hippo employs the term "pagan" (*paganus*) in special ways. A quick search in the Brepols *Library of Latin Texts* shows that the plural *pagani* is more frequent in his works than the singular *paganus*: the latter occurs in his sermons, often in negative sense.[1] Just like *iudaeus* and *haereticus, paganus* is an opponent of *Christianus* as persecutor of the Church (*persecutor ecclesiae*),[2] enemy (*inimicus*),[3] and adversary of Christ (*hostis Christi*).[4] Only occasionally are pagans assessed less negatively, when, for example, Augustine reminds his flock of the reality of conversion: "Today he is pagan, but how do you know that he is not Christian tomorrow?"[5] For Augustine, "pagan" is a typological figure in the construction of Christian identity, rather than a socio-historical group.[6]

Vigorous defender of the Catholic Church and talented polemicist, Augustine of Hippo would rank among "committed Christians" in the categories set up by Alan Cameron.[7] Being a "committed Christian," however, does not mean that Augustine

---

[1] *Paganus* rarely turns up in the *De ciuitate Dei*: Paul C. Burns, "Augustine's use of Varro's *Antiquitates Rerum Diuinarum* in his *De Civitate Dei*," *Augustinian Studies* 32/11 (2001), 37–64, esp. 44–45.

[2] Augustine, *In Iohannis euangelium tractatus*, 5, 13, l.3.

[3] Augustine, *Sermones* 56, ed. *Revue Bénédictine* 68, p.36, l.279.

[4] Augustine, *Sermones* 71, ed. *Revue Bénédictine* 75, p.68, l.77.

[5] Augustine, *Sermones* 71, ed. *Revue Bénédictine* 75, p. 86, l.464: *Paganus est hodie: unde scis, utrum sit futurus crastino Christianus?*

[6] For the Christian construction of the notion of *paganus*: James J. O'Donnell, "Paganus," *Classical Folia*, 31 (1977): 163–169; Id., "The Demise of Paganism", *Traditio* 35 (1979), 45–88; Alan Cameron, *The Last Pagans of Rome* (Oxford-New York: Oxford University Press, 2011), 14–32.

[7] Alan Cameron, *The Last Pagans of Rome*, 176 distinguishes five categories: "committed Christians" (Ambrose, Augustine); "center Christians" (Ausonius); "neither Christian nor pagan" (Bacurius); "center pagans" (Servius) "committed pagans" (Praetextatus, Symmachus). These categories become problematic when arguing that "Augustine and other rigorists" (*The Last Pagans*, 801) seek to purge Christian literature from Classical references, but accepting that Augustine was an educated Christian immersed in the Classical tradition: *The Last Pagans*, 385.

meets paganism in polemics alone. Augustine's complex relation with pagans is not to be reduced to controversy. The bishop does not exclusively perceive pagans as adversaries. Throughout his episcopate, Augustine is in constant contact with pagans such as Maximus of Madaura,[8] Nectarius,[9] Longinianus,[10] or Volusianus.[11] Augustine's sermons (including the Dolbeau Sermons[12]) show that pagans came to Augustine's church to hear him preach. Besides, Augustine was an educated man impregnated with Classical culture, who did not hide his love for Platonic philosophy or Virgil.[13]

This paper explores the social and historical background as well as the rhetorical context in which the figure of the *paganus* appears in Augustine's works to show that the pagan is not only an adversary, but also a brother in the eyes of the bishop of Hippo. I examine three representations of the *paganus* in Augustine—adversary, interlocutor, exemplar – to show that contacts with self-professed pagans such as Volusianus made a huge impact on Augustine's thought and inspired him to write *The City of God* and, more importantly, to argue that rhetorics notwithstanding, the bishop of Hippo preaches the love of God and neighbour towards the "pagans."

The pagan as adversary

Augustine's writings contain a good number of treatises *contra paganos*[14] demonstrating that the fight against paganism was one of the chief agendas of the bishop of Hippo—even after 399, when idolatry was prohibited in North Africa by Stilicho.[15] Is the preponderance of this topic in Augustine a sign of a "pagan resistance" in Africa

---

[8] Augustine, *Letters* 16 & 17.
[9] Augustine, *Letters* 103 & 104.
[10] Augustine, *Letters* 233, 234 & 235.
[11] Augustine, *Letters* 132, 135 & 137.
[12] *Sermones Dolbeau* are found in: François Dolbeau, *Augustin d'Hippone. Vingt-six sermons au peuple d'Afrique*, (Paris, Collection des Études Augustiniennes, 1996 ; repr. 2009). See for instance Augustine, *Sermones Dolbeau*, 24 and 26.
[13] Recent scholarship on "pagans and Christians" invalidates this categorization as inaccurately describing specific situations: Hervé Inglebert, Sylvain Destephen, Bruno Dumézil ed., *Le problème de la christianisation du monde antique*, (Paris: Picard, 2010); Peter Brown, Rita Lizzi Testa ed., *Pagans and Christians in the Roman Empire: The Breaking of a Dialogue (IVth-VIth Century A.D.)*, (Münster: Lit, 2011); Éric Rebillard, *Christians and Their Many Identities in Late Antiquity, North Africa, 200–450, CE*, Ithaca: Cornell University Press, 2012); *Id.*, "Religious Sociology: Being Christian in the Time of Augustine", in *A Companion to Augustine*, ed. Mark Vessey (Oxford: Blackwell, 2012), 40–53.
[14] *De ciuitate Dei contra Paganos libri uiginti duo*; *Quaestiones expositae contra Paganos*; Sermon Dolbeau 24: *De testimoniis scripturarum contra Donatistas et contra Paganos*; Sermon Dolbeau 25: *Cum Pagani ingrederentur*; Sermon Dolbeau 26: *Tractatus Augustini Episcopi Contra Paganos*.
[15] Augustine, *Letter* 97, 2.

Proconsularis?[16] Or does it show that Augustine lumped all non-Christians under the umbrella term of "paganism"? His correspondence and sermons, including *Dolbeau* 24 and 26, show otherwise. The paganism Augustine fought was a socio-cultural phenomenon, a paganism of daily habits of the ordinary man as well as of the municipal elite.[17] Examples of popular paganism condemned by Augustine's *sermons* are endless, because "paganism" thus understood was practiced not only by "pagans," but also by Christians. Thus, for example, Christians too worshiped the *Genius* of Carthage and, in so doing, prevented the conversion of heathen according to Augustine.[18] On 1 January 404, the bishop of Hippo delivered an inordinately long homily in Carthage to bar his flock from rushing out of church to see the gladiatorial games (*munera*) starting after mass.[19] His homily reveals the difficulty to distinguish between popular paganism and popular Christianity.[20] Another form of "pagan resistance" that Augustine criticized was that of the African municipal elites as Lepelley[21] and Lancel[22] have convincingly shown. The urban riots in Sufes (summer of 401) and in Calama (June 408), where Bishop Possidius almost lost his life, enjoyed the silent support of the municipal leaders.[23] Augus-

---

[16] Claude Lepelley, "L'aristocratie lettrée païenne: une menace aux yeux d'Augustin (à propos du sermon Dolbeau 26 – Mayence 62)," in *Augustin prédicateur (395–411). Actes du Colloque International de Chantilly (5–7 septembre 1996)*, ed. Goulven Madec (Paris: Collection des Etudes Augustiniennes, 1998), 327–345. The notion of pagan resistance is challenged by A. Cameron, *The Last Pagans*, 3–13.

[17] Claude Lepelley, "L'aristocratie lettrée païenne."

[18] Augustine, *Sermo* 62, 6, 9; Éric Rebillard, "Augustin et le culte des statues," in *Ministerium sermonis : a philological, historical and theological studies on Augustine's Sermones ad populum*, ed. Gerd Partoens, Anthony Dupont, Mathijs Lamberigts (Turnhout: Brepols, 2009), 299–325.

[19] *Dolbeau Sermon* 26; Claude Lepelley, "L'aristocratie lettrée païenne."

[20] Michel-Yves Perrin, "*Creuit hypocrisis*. Limites d'adhésion au christianisme dans l'Antiquité tardive: entre histoire et historiographie", in, *Le problème de la christianisation du monde antique*, ed. Hervé Inglebert, Sylvain Destephen, Bruno Dumézil (Paris: Picard, 2010), 47–62 ; Jean-Marie Salamito, "Ambivalence de la christianisation, frontière de l'Église, identité chrétienne », in *ibid.*, 63–75 ; Cl. Lepelley, "Augustin face à la christianisation de l'Afrique romaine: le refus des illusions", in *ibid.*, 269–281 ; É. Rebillard, *Les chrétiens de l'Antiquité tardive ; Id.*, "Religious Sociology: Being a Christian in the Time of Augustine".

[21] Claude Lepelley, "L'aristocratie lettrée païenne".

[22] Serge Lancel, *Saint Augustin* (Paris: Fayard, 2001), 430–453.

[23] I follow here Lepelley against Cameron, *The Last Pagans*, 797–801. É. Rebillard (*Les chrétiens de l'Antiquité tardive*, 146–154; "Religious sociology: Being a Christian in the Time of Augustine," 52–53) points out the role of Augustine's letters in the elaboration of the notion of a "pagan resistance." B. Shaw (*Sacred Violence: African Christians and Sectarian Hatred in the Age of Augustine*, Cambridge-New-York: Cambridge University Press, 2011, ch. V) stresses the role of Christian bishops in the riots, criticized by M. Dulaey, *Bulletin Augustinien 2013-2014*, 435–439). For the riots of Calama: Erika T. Hermanowicz, "Catholic Bishops and Appeals to the Imperial Court: A Legal Study of the Calama Riots in 408", *JECS* 12 (2004), 481–521. For a general survey: Anna Leone, *The end of the pagan city. Religion, economy, and urbanism in late antique North Africa* (Oxford: Oxford University Press, 2013); John F. Matthews, *Western Aristocracies and Imperial Court A.D. 364–425*, (Oxford: Clarendon Press, 1975); Michele Salzman, *The Making of a Christian Aristocracy: Social and Religious Change in the Western Roman Empire* (Cambridge MA: Harvard University Press, 2002).

tine denounced in harsh terms "the magistrates, leaders and elders of the Colony of Suffectum."[24] In *The City of God*, Augustine says that the propertied class defends pagan cults out of material interests, to protect their wealth and riches. Under the guise of the defense of pagan tradition, they defend the established order that Christianity threatens to overturn:

> "But the worshippers and the lover of these gods, whom they are even delighted to copy in their evil deeds, are not concerned to prevent the republic from sinking to the lowest level of wickedness and profligacy. "Only let it stand," they say, "only let it flourish with abundant resources, glorious in victory or, and that is better, secure in peace. And how does it concern us? No, no! It interests us more that the individual should constantly increase his wealth to support his daily extravagance, and to enable the more powerful individual thereby to make weaker men his subjects. Let the poor court the rich to fill their bellies and to enjoy under their patronage an undisturbed idleness; let the rich misuse the poor as clients and to minister to their pride".[25]

What kind of "paganism" do the pagans practice? Augustine denounces, above all, the rituals contrary to the true religion, and the false conception of mediation between the true God and humankind.[26] These are the leitmotifs of *Sermons Dolbeau* 6, 24, and 26, where the bishop of Hippo reiterates the prohibition to honour the statues of pagan gods, handiwork of the devil, contrary to the worship of God.[27] *Sermon Dolbeau* 26 comprises a long refutation of the pagan theology of mediation elaborated by

---

[24] Augustine, *Letter* 50.

[25] Augustine, *De ciuitate Dei*, II, 20, éd. Loeb (trad. George E.McCracken) : *Verum tales cultores et dilectores deorum istorum, quorum etiam imitatores in sceleribus et flagitiis se esse laetantur, nullo modo curant pessimam ac flagitiosissimam non esse rem publicam. 'Tantum stet, inquiunt, tantum floreat copiis referta, uictoriis gloriosa, uel, quod est felicius, pace secura sit. Et quid ad nos? Immo id ad nos magis pertinet, si diuitias quisque augeat semper, quae cotidianis effusionibus suppetant, per quas sibi etiam infirmiores subdat quisque potentior. Obsequantur diuitibus pauperes causa saturitatis atque ut eorum patrociniis quieta inertia perfruantur, diuites pauperibus ad clientelas et ad ministerium sui fastus abutantur'.*

[26] Nonetheless we must recognize that the link between traditional cults and paganism in the Late Antiquity is much discussed, and it seems that only the state cults provided the last resistance to Christianity; on this point, see: A. Cameron, *The Last Pagans*, 132–172.

[27] Éric Rebillard, "Augustin et le culte des statues"; *Id.*, "The Christian mob and the destruction of pagan statues", in É. Rebillard, *Transformation of Religious Practices in Late Antiquity*, (Ashgate: Farnham, 2013), 73–87.

Porphyry and Apuleius.[28] Remarkably, these homilies delivered in 403–404 contain the germs of arguments later developed in *The City of God*.[29]

The pagan as interlocutor

In the eyes of Augustine, the "pagan" is not only an opponent but, first and foremost, a neighbour to be converted. Once again, the sociological dimension of the question is significant: pagans live among us, they must be converted by examples of the virtuous Christian life, by fasting and penance, as well as by divine providence.[30] "Philosophical" pagans, on the other hand, must be convinced by philosophical arguments about the Christian truth. The commonalty of Christianity was obstacle to conversion, well summed up in *Sermon Dolbeau* 26: "They say to themselves: 'And will I be what my doorkeeper is, not rather what Plato was, what Pythagoras was?'"[31]

Augustine had many pagan correspondents: his letters shed light upon their views on Christianity as well as on Augustine's understanding of them. His archetypal interlocutor, who played a crucial role in Augustine's life is Rufius Antoninus Agrypnius Volusianus.[32] Their correspondence deserves attention for several reasons. Member of the prestigious Ceionii clan, Volusianus, prefect of Rome in 428–429, was a socially important partner of Augustine's. His father, prefect of Rome in 389, was pagan, but the womenfolk of his family—his mother, sister, and niece, the celebrated Melania the Younger—was Christian.[33] Their correspondence is more extensive than it seems at first glance: to one surviving letter of Volusianus and two of Augustine, we can add the letter of Marcellinus and Augustine's response, and *Letter* 102 addressed to Deogratias in response to the objections of "a pagan".[34] This pagan is either

---

[28] Jean Pépin, "Falsi mediatores duo. Aspects de la médiation dans le sermon d'Augustin *Contra Paganos* (*S. Dolbeau* 26)", in *Augustin prédicateur (395–411). Actes du Colloque International de Chantilly (5–7 septembre 1996)*, ed. by Goulven Madec (Paris: Collection des Études Augustiniennes, 1998), 395–417.

[29] See Jean Pépin, "*Falsi mediatores duo*", 407–413.

[30] Aimé Solignac, "Le salut des païens d'après la prédication d'Augustin", in *Augustin prédicateur (395–411). Actes du Colloque International de Chantilly (5–7 septembre 1996)*, ed. by Goulven Madec (Paris: Collection des Études Augustiniennes, 1998), 419–428.

[31] Augustine, *Sermon Dolbeau* 26, 59 (F. Dolbeau, *Vingt-six sermons au peuple d'Afrique*, 137): *Sibi dicunt: 'Et hoc futurus sum quod est ostiaria mea, ac non potius quod fuit Plato, quod Pythagoras?'*

[32] Madeleine Moreau, *Le Dossier Marcellinus dans la correspondance de saint Augustin* (Paris: Collection des Études Augustiniennes, 1973), 47–9, 123–129 ; Serge Lancel, *Saint Augustin*, 443–449 ; Alan Cameron, *The Last Pagans*, 196 sq. Cameron, *The Last Pagans*, 197, the response of Volusianus was "the response of a catechumen rather than a pagan"; this statement, unsupported by any evidence, is not convincing. I follow the traditional view: Volusianus was a pagan, baptized on his deathbed.

[33] Nicole Moine, "Melaniana", *Recherches Augustiniennes*, 15 (1980), 3–79.

[34] Isabelle Bochet, "The Role of Scripture in Augustine's Controversy with Porphyry", *Augustinian Studies*, 41/1 (2010), 7–52.

Volusianus,[35] or the objection emanated from the "circle of Volusianus".[36] Indeed, from the end of 410, following the Gothic sack of Rome, a "circle of Volusianus" was active in Carthage, reminiscent of the "circle of Symmachus." Members of the Roman aristocracy fleeing Rome gathered in this "salon" to talk eloquently about politics and culture. In Augustine's *Letter* 135, Volusianus describes perfectly this educated pagan universe immortalized by Macrobius' *Saturnalia*.[37] The aristocrats discussed the merits of rhetoric, poetry, and philosophy, and took pleasure in quoting the Classics—Virgil, Aristotle, Isocrates or Epicurus.[38] Volusianus' style, his choice of words, sounds, proper names, and citations highlights the superiority of pagan culture, but also creates a rhetorical *persona*. The letter revels that religion was also discussed among the pagans, including the foundations of Christianity: the dogma of the Incarnation. One of them, perhaps Volusianus, expresses doubt about the Incarnation:

> "In the midst of this, the memory of our conversation lingered with me, and one of many asked: 'Who is endowed with wisdom to the perfect measure of the Christian; who can solve the doubts in which I am entangled (*haereo*); who can enlighten (*firmare*) my doubting faculties (*dubios assensus*) and strengthen them with true (*uera*) or probable (*uersisimili*) systems of belief?' We were struck dumb. Then he rushed on of his own accord, in this fashion: 'I wonder whether the Lord and Ruler of the world filled the womb of the chaste Virgin; whether that mother bore the long weariness of ten months, and nevertheless brought Him forth as a virgin according to the usual method of birth, and afterwards was reputed an inviolate virgin.' He added other objections to these. He to whom the universe can scarcely be compared lies hid within the tiny body of a wailing infant; He endures the years of childhood, He grows to be a youth, His strength develops into manhood, and so long a time that Ruler is absent from His throne, and all the care of the whole world is transferred into one small body! Moreover, He relaxes in sleep, He is nourished by food, He is subject to all the feelings of mortals, and gives no clear indication of such great

---

[35] Anne-Marie La Bonnardière, *Biblia Augustiana. A.-T. – Les douze petits prophètes* (Paris: Collection des Études Augustiniennes, 1963), 29.

[36] Goulven Madec, *Introduction aux 'Révisions' et à la lecture des œuvres de saint Augustin* (Paris: Collection des Études Augustiniennes, 1996), 99; Madeleine Moreau, *Le Dossier Marcellinus*, pp. 49–77, 123–129.

[37] Christian Tornau, "Die Heiden des Augustinus: das Porträt des Pagan gebildeten in *De civitate Dei* und in den *Saturnalia* des Macrobius", in *Die christlich-philosophischen Diskurse der Spätantike: Texte, Personen, Institutionen*, ed. by Therese Führer (Stuttgart: Steiner, 2008), 299–325.

[38] Augustine, *Letter* 135, 1.

majesty by any suitable signs. As for driving out evil spirits, cure of the sick, life restored to the dead, if you consider other men, these are small things for a god to do.'[39]

This objection repeats recurring pagan critique against Christianity, stressing the incompatibility between the pagan conception of the divine implying power but rejecting the body, and the affirmation of the God who became man.[40] Volusianus' critique is very smart: he uses the vocabulary of the New Academy and recycles the dialogues of Cicero (*haereo, dubius, assensus, uerum, uerisimilis, firmare*) – a clever allusion to Augustine's *Cassiciacum Dialogues*, setting a similar *mise-en-scène* and exploiting the same philosophical schools, it compels Augustine to answer him in a philosopher's way. Deference and courtesy towards Augustine notwithstanding, Volusianus argues for the incompatibility between philosophy and Christianity, and thus for the philosophical inferiority of Christianity. He does so by opposing a positive vocabulary to qualify God and a pejorative vocabulary concerning the body, with the subtle allusion to Virgil's *Eclogues* 4, 61.

Marcellinus' *Letter* 136 presents "Volusianus' circle' in a less irenic light. In recounting the unsuccessful efforts of Volusianus' mother, Melania the Elder to guide her son towards conversion, it exposes that the aristocrats in Hippo challenged not only Augustine's episcopal, but also intellectual authority: "the excellent landlord and ruler of the countryside of Hippo was present when these questions were raised, and he praised your Holiness with sarcastic flattery, insisting that he had not been at all satisfied when these queries were made."[41]

Marcellinus' letter makes it plain that Volusianus' objection against the Christian faith is not limited to the Incarnation, but affects miracles and the incompatibility

---

[39] Augustine, *Letter* 135, 2, trad. Ludwig Schopp, Augustine, Letters, volume III, in *The Fathers of the Church* (Washington: Catholic University Press, 1953): *Dum in his confabulatio nostra remoratur, unus e multis: Et quis, inquit, est sapientia ad perfectum Christianitatis imbutus, qui ambigua in quibus haereo possit aperire, dubiosque assensus meos uera uel uerisimili credulitate firmare? Stupemus tacentes. Tunc in haec sponte prorumpit: Miror utrum mundi Dominus et rector intemeratae feminae corpus impleuerit, pertulerit decem mensium longa illa fastidia mater, et tamen uirgo enixa sit solemnitate pariendi, et post haec uirginitas intacta permanserit. His et alia subnectit : Intra corpusculum uagientis infantiae latet, cui par uix putatur uniuersitas; patitur pueritlitatis annos, adolescit, iuuentute solidatur; tam diu a sedibus suis abest ille regnator, atque ad unum corpusculum totius mundi cura transfertur; deinde in somnos resoluitur, cibo alitur, omnes mortalium sentit affectus; nec ullis competentibus signis tantae maiestatis indicia clarescunt, quoniam larualis illa purgatio, debilium curae, reddita uita defunctis, haec, si et alios cogites, Deo parua sunt.*

[40] Pierre Courcelle, "Propos antichrétiens rapportés par S. Augustin", *Recherches Augustiniennes*, 1 (1958), 149–186.

[41] Augustine, *Letters* 136, 3, trad. Ludwig Schopp, Augustine, *Letters*, volume III, in *The Fathers of the Church* (1953): *a eximius Hipponensis regionis possessor et dominus praesens aderat which Sanctitatem tuam et sub ironiae adulatione laudaret et sibi, cum his quaereret, minimal satisfactum esse contenderet.*

of Christian morality with the administration of the Roman State. Marcellinus' remarks give a better information about "Volusianus' circle." It comprised not only Roman aristocrats in exile, but also the North-African landowner élite at the head of the municipalities, with whom Augustine had a difficult relationship from the beginning of his episcopate. These aristocrats were troubled by the Christian ethical teaching on sharing wealth and refusing retaliation because they felt this would undermine their status within Roman society and question their role in the Roman State. A comparison between the letters of Marcellinus and Volusianus reveals important shifts in their Classical references: while Volusianus *explicitly* refers to the authority of Cicero, Virgil, Aristotle and Epicurus, his circle *implicitly* thinks of Apuleius and Apollonius of Tyana and compare their wonderworking with those of Christ.[42] The unnamed master of thought of "Volusianus' circle" is clearly Porphyry, author of the Contra Christianos whose preserved pages contain this particular reference to Apollonius of Tyana.[43] He is the target of Augustine's refutation in Letter 102.[44] "Volusianus' circle" must have been the intended audience of Augustine when writing The City of God, as Marcellinus reported that Volusianus "believes, even if he says nothing on this score, that all those points can be related to this same question, that at least to this extent it is evident that great evils befall the state when Christian rulers generally observe the Christian religion."[45]

Augustine's answer first to Volusianus then to Marcellinus are, indeed, the "first drafts" of *The City of God*.[46] It is worth noting, however, that Augustine wrote first to Volusianus, in all likelihood at the bidding of his mother.[47] Their exchange is quite remarkable. Augustine urges Volusianus to read the Apostles and the Prophets;[48] Volusianus makes no reference whatsoever to these books of the Bible in his answer and his questions are completely unrelated to these. In other words, Volusianus did not follow the advice of the bishop. Augustine, at the same time, clearly tells him about his prefer-

---

[42] Augustine, *Letters* 136, 1: *Apollonium siquidem suum nobis et Apuleium, aliosque magicae artis homines in medium proferunt, quorum maiora contendunt extitisse miracula.*

[43] Cameron, *The Last Pagans*, 547sq. Jerome, *Letter* 53, 1 showing that Porphyry's reference to Apollonius of Tyana has an anti-Christian function.

[44] Isabelle Bochet, "The Role of Scripture"; *Le traité de Porphyre contre les chrétiens. Un siècle de recherches, nouvelles questions. Actes du colloque international de Paris, 8–9 septembre 2009*, ed. Sébastien Morlet (Paris: Collection des Études Augustiniennes, 2011).

[45] Augustine, *Letter* 136, 2, trad. Ludwig Schopp, Augustine, *Letters*, volume III, in *The Fathers of the Church* (1953): *Haec ergo omnia ipsi posse adiungi aestimat quaestioni, in tantum ut per christianos principes, christianam religionem maxima ex parte seruantes, tanta (etiamsi ipse de hac parte taceat) reipublicae mala euenisse manifestum sit.*

[46] Gerard O'Daly, *Augustine's City of God. A Reader's Guide*, (Oxford, Oxford University Press, 2009) 27–33.

[47] Augustine, *Letter* 132 : *De salute tua, quam et in hoc saeculo, et in Christo esse cupio, sanctae matris tuae uotis sum fortasse etiam ipse non impar.*

[48] Augustine, *Letter* 132 : *Praecipue Apostolorum linguas exhortor ut legas ; ex his enim ad cognoscendos Prophetas excitaberis, quorum testimoniis utuntur Apostoli.*

ence to continue their debate in written form, rather than in personal conversation, to avoid the curious crowd that loved such confrontations to reveal the truth.[49] This may actually be an allusion to "Volusianus' circle" about which Augustine held no illusions. Augustine's answer to Volusianus is different in tone from his answer to Marcellinus: he is much tangier with Volusianus. Since Augustine suggested to Volusianus an immersion in the apostles, it is hard to miss the irony when he says "so I have decided to spend my leisure in dictating your answer, and I have delayed as little as possible in the belief that it is not fair to put off someone who appeals to me when I had personally invited him to appeal."[50] Likewise, reference to "proud little minds who make no account of grace, who make a great show of their ability, but can do nothing either to cure their own faults or even to check them"[51] sounds like a critique of "Volusianus' circle." Augustine demonstrates that he knows the psychology of his interlocutor who considers that Christianity is an impediment to power. As Volusianus displayed his knowledge by accumulating names and references, including the *Eclogues* of Virgil, Augustine answers him that Christ's birth was predicted by Virgil in the fourth *Eclogue*[52]—a topic taken up again in *The City of God*.[53] Reference to the *Eclogues* and to Cicero's *Tusculanes* are polemical, because it shows not only that Augustine lives up to his reputation as a highly educated man who knows his Classics, but that the Classics themselves refute the ideas of fourth-century pagans!

The bishop uses a different, more neutral style in his answer to Marcellinus in *Letter* 138, partly because Marcellinus was not the addressee of the letter, but the intermediary between Augustine and "Volusianus' circle." *Letters* 137 and 138 are tailored to the addressee's identity, even in their Scriptural quotes. The nature of Christ in *Letter* 137 is presented as a summary on the sources of knowledge with quotes from Virgil, peppered with Porphyry's notions on the union of soul and body taken from

---

[49] Augustine, *Letter 132, Si quid autem, uel cum legis, uel cum cogitas, tibi oritur quaestionis, in quo dissoluendo uidear necessarius, scribe ut rescribam Magis enim hoc forte Domino ad iuuante potero, quam praesens talia loqui tecum ; non solum propter occupationes uarias et meas et tuas (quoniam non cum mihi uacat, occurrit ut et tibi uacet), uerum etiam propter eorum irruentem praesentiam, qui plerumque non sunt apti tali negotio, magisque linguae certaminibus, quam scientiae luminibus delectantur.*

[50] Augustine, *Letter 137*, 1, trad. Ludwig Schopp, Augustine, *Letters*, volume III, in *The Fathers of the Church* (1953): *Quibus autem hoc dictandis otium statueram impendere, paululum distuli, Nequaquam iustum esse ad quem arbitratus quaerendum exhortatus ipse fueram, differre quaerentem.*

[51] Augustine, *Letters 137*, 1, trad. Ludwig Schopp, Augustine, *Letters*, volume III, in *The Fathers of the Church* (1953): *animulae superbae [...] quae nimis affecting plurimum posse, et ad sua uitia sananda uel etiam refrenanda nihil possunt.*

[52] Pierre Courcelle, "Les exégèses chrétiennes de la quatrième Eglogue" *Revue des Études Anciennes*, 59 (1957), 294–319; Guillermo Pons Pons, "La égloga IV de Vergilio y san Agustín", *Revista agustiniana*, 52 (2011), 747–774.

[53] Augustine, *De ciuitate Dei*, X, 27.

his *Zetemata*[54] and *Sententia*.[55] *The refutation of the incompatibility between Christianity and the State in Letter* 138 musters a survey of Roman Republican virtues with references from Sallust, Cicero's *Pro Ligario* and Juvenal's *Satires*. The issue of the miracles and the prophets is presented with a close reading of pagan texts, a critique of Apuleius' *Apology* and some acknowledgement of Apollonius of Tyana's achievement.

Reference to pagan texts and models obviously form part of a polemical strategy. Augustine disproves the arguments of the pagan interlocutor on his own ground, while he promotes his image as a man of *paideia*. Quotes from the Classics are not merely an "embellishment:"[56] they play a rhetorical function in the technique of reversal (*retorsio*). I explain Augustine's ample references to pagan authors and the length of these letters both by a pastoral concern and by a respect of Classical culture. The pagan is a neighbor (*proximus*) and the duty of the bishop is to convert him: this is why Augustine, at the first place, starts his correspondence with Volusianus, writes him detailed answers, and uses the conventional form of dispute: because even intelligent men, accustomed to disputation may be unable to recognize the truth, hence the importance of meeting them on their level.[57] The recognition of Apollonius of Tyana[58] reflects Augustine's affection for Classical culture that he does not want to eradicate from Christian literature and education.

The pagan as exemplar?

This leads us to consider a paradoxical figure: the pagan as a possible "model" for Christians. *A priori*, this is impossible: pagans cannot be exemplars for Christians. Yet Augustine does not deny that pagans may play a positive role in society. Quoting Sallust, he makes the following remark:

> "So, what use is it for me to labour the point; rather, why not ask them how those early patriots were able to govern and enlarge the state which they had changed from a small, 'poor one to a great, rich one,'"[59]

---

[54] Ernest Fortin, *Christianisme et culture philosophique au Vème siècle. La querelle de l'âme en Occident* (Paris: Collection des Études Augustiniennes, 1959), 111–161.

[55] Goulven Madec, *Le Christ de Saint Augustin. La Patrie et la Voie* (Paris: Desclée, 2001), pp. 192–197.

[56] Danuta Shanzer, "Augustine and the Latin Classics", in *A Companion to Augustine*, ed. by Mark Vessey (Oxford: Blackwell), 161–174, especially 169–170.

[57] Augustine, *Letter* 138, 4, 20: *Video me fecisse prolixissimam epistolam, nec tamen de Christo dixisse omnia quae uel eis qui uel ingenio diuina non ualent assequi, uel eis quos, licet acute moueantur, contentiosum tamen studium et praeoccupatio diuturni erroris ab intellegendo impedit, possint utcumque sufficere.*

[58] Augustine, *Letter* 138, 4, 18: *Multo enim melior, quod fatendum est, Apollonius fuit, quam tot stuprorum auctor et perpetrator, quem Iovem nominant.*

[59] Sallust, *Catilina*, 9, 5.

when 'they preferred to pardon the wrongs they had suffered rather than avenge them'"[60];[61]

To bring out the hypocrisy of cultivated pagans, he adds:

"When men read of these traits in their authors, they publish and applaud them; such conduct as is described and praised seems to them worthy of the beginning of a state which was to rule over so many nations, as when they say that 'they preferred to pardon wrongs suffered rather than avenge them'. But, when they read the command of divine authority that evil is not to be returned for evil, when this advice is preached from the pulpit to congregations of people, in these universal schools of both sexes and of every age and rank, religion is charged with being an enemy of the state."[62]

Thus, *Letter* 138 advances the argument of Book V of *The City of God* on pagan virtue. Augustine quotes Sallust to show that there were virtuous pagans under the Republic.[63] There is ample scholarship on the question of pagan virtue in *The City of God*[64] and in the *Contra Iulianum*.[65] Augustine changes considerably his views on this issue between *Letter* 138, written in 412, and Book V of *The City of God*,[66] written in 413–414 Augustine recognizes that pagan virtues have merits, even if lesser than Christian virtue, and reminds his flock that pagan virtues are examples to follow. By

---

[60] Sallust, *Catilina*, 52, 19.

[61] Augustine, *Letter* 138, 2, 9, trad. Ludwig Schopp, Augustine, *Letters*, volume III, in *The Fathers of the Church* (1953): *Vnde quid opus est ut diutius laboremus, ac non ipsos potius percontemur quomodo poterant gubernare atque augere rempublicam, quam ex parua et inopi magnam opulentamque fecerunt, qui accepta iniuria ignoscere quam persequi malebant.*

[62] Augustine, *Letter* 138, 2, 10, trad. Ludwig Schopp, Augustine, *Letters*, volume III, in *The Fathers of the Church* (1953): *Haec cum in eorum leguntur auctoribus, exclamatur et plauditur; describi atque praedicari mores uidentur, quibus dignum esset exsurgere ciuitatem quae tot gentibus imperaret, quod accepta iniuria ignoscere quam persequi malebant. Cum uero legitur praecipiente auctoritate diuina, non reddendum malum pro malo; cum haec tam salubris admonitio congregationibus populorum, tamquam publicis utriusque sexus atque omnium aetatum et dignitatum scholis, de superiore loco personat, accusatur religio tamquam inimica reipublicae!*

[63] Augustine, *De ciuitate Dei*, V, 6.

[64] Joseph Wang Tch'ang-Tche, *Saint Augustin et la vertu des païens* (Paris: Beauchesne, 1938); Terence H. Irwin, "Splendid Vices ? Augustine For and Against Pagan Virtues", *Medieval Philosophy and Theology*, 8 (1999), 105–127; Brian Harding, *Augustine and Roman virtue*, (New York: Continuum, 2008); Brett Gaul, "Augustine on the Virtues of the Pagans", *AugStud*, 40/2 (2009), 233–249.

[65] Mickaël Ribreau, "La culture profane et les auteurs classiques dans le *Contra Iuliainum* d'Augustin," *R.É.L.*, 89 (2011), 200–231, especially 218sq.

[66] Augustine, *De ciuitate Dei*, V, 11–17.

420, however, Book XIX of *The City of God*[67] and the *Contra Iulianum*[68] are much more critical about pagan virtue, fruit of pride and vice. Augustine's attitude towards the pagans remained unchanged. What changed was the tenor of the debate during the Pelagian crisis. Julian of Eclanum's references on pagan, especially Stoic virtue against the Augustinian theology of grace[69] compelled the bishop of Hippo to point out the evil roots of pagan virtue.

Despite all this, Augustine believes that salvation is possible for pagans. *Letters* 137 and 138, the *Dolbeau Sermons* and the *Enarrationes in Psalmos* discuss this issue.[70] Augustine understands Christianity as the "best of" pagan culture.[71] This idea, central in *The City of God*, is already expressed in his first works and in *Dolbeau Sermon 26* of 1 January 404 in an exegesis of Romans 1: 18–25.[72] Augustine recognizes the great achievement of Platonic philosophy, a pure knowledge of the divine, but denounces its ignorance of salvation and its preference for false mediation, such as theurgy—this will be an argument in Book X of *The City of God*. The theme surfaces in *Letters* 137 and 138. Both in *Dolbeau Sermon 26* and in *Letter 137*, Augustine mentions Pythagoras in positive terms, implying that he might have had, indirectly, a revelation of the Saviour.[73] In *Letter 137*, the bishop explains to Volusianus that Christian revelation completes Platonic philosophy with its distinction of the physical, logical and ethical powers. The same idea is summarized in *The City of God*:[74]

> "What arguments, what works of any philosophers, what laws of any states can be compared in any way with the two commandments on which Christ says the whole Law and the Prophets depend? 'Thou shalt love the Lord thy God with thy whole heart and with thy whole soul and with thy whole mind; and thou shalt love thy neighbour as thyself' (Matthew 22:37–39). Herein is natural science, since all the causes of all natures are found in God, the Creator; herein is ethics, since the good and honourable life is formed in no other way than by

---

[67] Augustine, *De ciuitate Dei.*, XIX, 10.

[68] Augustine, *Contra Iulianum*, IV, 3, 21; IV, 3, 30.

[69] Robert Dodaro, "Augustine's Revision of the Heroic Ideal", *AugStud*, 36/1 (2005), 141–157.

[70] A. Solignac, « Le salut des païens ».

[71] Isabelle Bochet, « *Le Firmament de l'Ecriture* ». *L'herméneutique augustinienne* (Paris: Collection des Études Augustiniennes, 2004), pp. 333–413.

[72] Augustine, *De uera religione*, 3, 3–5; *Sermon Dolbeau 26*, 30–37 (F. Dolbeau, *Vingt-six sermons au peuple d'Afrique*, 388–394).

[73] Augustine, *Letter* 137, 3, 12; *Sermon Dolbeau 26*, 36 (F. Dolbeau, *Vingt-six sermons au peuple d'Afrique*, 394).

[74] Augustine, *De ciuitate Dei*, VIII, 4–10 et XI, 24–25. About this point, see I. Bochet, « *Le Firmament de l'Écriture* », 415–500.

loving what ought to be loved as it ought to be loved, that is, God and our neighbour; herein is logic, since there is no other truth and light for the rational mind than God."[75]

Augustine here reiterates what he had written to Deogratias in *Letter* 102: revelation and salvation through Christ are not limited to Christian times, for the Son is the Eternal Wisdom,

"by whom universal nature was called into existence, and by participation in whom every rational soul is made blessed. Therefore, from the beginning of the human race, whosoever believed in Him, and in any way knew Him, and lived in a pious and just manner according to His precepts, was undoubtedly saved by Him, in whatever time and place he may have lived."[76]

Conclusion

This paper sought to nuance the image of Augustine, the "committed Christian."[77] The writings of the bishop of Hippo attest that he opposed relentlessly any survival of popular, municipal, and aristocratic paganism in North Africa. His treatises and sermons against the pagans, however, do not construct pagans exclusively in terms of enemies: if they cannot be exemplars for Christians, pagans may compel Christians for higher virtue. What is more, the pagan is always a neighbour, a brother in hope for Augustine. The *Dolbeau Sermons* and the correspondence with Volusianus and Marcellinus demonstrate that the main arguments of *The City of God* are already formulated in these sermons and letters. "Volusianus' circle" is undoubtedly the addressee of Augus-

---

[75] Augustine, *Letter* 137, 5, 17, trad. Ludwig Schopp, Augustine, *Letters*, volume III, in *The Fathers of the Church* (1953): *Quae disputationes, quae litterae quorumlibet philosophorum, quae leges quarumlibet ciuitatum, duobus praeceptis, ex quibus Christus dicit totam Legem Prophetasque pendere, ullo modo sint comparandae: Diliges Dominum Deum tuum ex toto corde tuo, et ex tota anima tua, et ex tota mente tua; et, diliges proximum tuum tamquam teipsum (Mt 22, 37–39)? Hic physica, quoniam omnes omnium naturarum causae in Deo creatore sunt. Hic ethica, quoniam uita bona et honesta non aliunde formatur, quam cum ea quae diligenda sunt, quemadmodum diligenda sunt, diliguntur, hoc est Deus et proximus. Hic logica, quoniam ueritas lumenque animae rationalis, nonnisi Deus est.*

[76] Augustine, *Letter* 102, 11–12: *per quam creata est uniuersa natura, et cuius participatione omnis rationalis anima fit beata. Itaque ab exordio generis humani, quicumque in eum crediderunt, eumque utcumque intellexerunt, et secundum eius praecepta pie et iuste uixerunt, quandolibet et ubilibet fuerint, per eum procul dubio salui facti sunt.*

[77] A. Cameron, *The Last Pagans*, 176.

tine's *magnum opus et arduum* as it is shown by the final words of *Letter* 137 ushering in the great theological vision of *The City of God* of saving grace:

> "But God does not act as a mortal king or ruler of a state acts, *in leaving unpunished offenses committed by everybody*.[78] His mercy and grace, preached to men by the Man, Christ; imparted by God and the Son of God, the same Christ, do not forsake those who live by faith in Him and who worship Him devoutly; whether they bear the evils of this life patiently and bravely, or make use of His good gifts charitably and temperately; in both cases they will receive their reward in the heavenly and divine City. There we shall no longer have to bear painful trials or curb our passions with laborious effort, but there we shall possess the pure love of God and neighbour, without any trouble, and with perfect freedom."[79]

---

[78] Lucan, *De bello ciuilo*, 5, 260, éd. D.R. Shackleton Bailey (Teubner, 1988).

[79] Augustine, *Letter* 137, 5, 20, trad. Ludwig Schopp, Augustine, *Letters*, volume III, in *The Fathers of the Church* (1953): *Non autem sicut regi homini, uel cuilibet principi ciuitatis, ita etiam Deo quidquid a multis peccatur inultum est. Misericordia uero eius et gratia praedicata hominibus per hominem Christum, impartita autem per Deum Deique filium eumdem ipsum Christum, non deserit eos qui ex eius fide uiuunt, eumque pie colunt, siue mala huius uitae patienter fortiterque experiantur, siue bonis eius misericorditer ac temperanter utantur; aeternum pro utroque praemium recepturi in ciuitate superna atque diuina, ubi iam non sit moleste toleranda calamitas, nec laboriose frenanda cupiditas, sed sola sine ulla difficultate, et cum perfecta libertate retinenda Dei et proximi caritas.*

RELIGIOUS IDENTITY AS SEEN BY SIXTH-CENTURY HISTORIANS AND CHRONICLERS

Ecaterina Lung

In recent decades, the problem of identity has become central in the research on Late Antiquity, a period characterized by the disruption of existing political structures through large scale migrations. In order to decipher the process of creating new identities in this period which formed the foundation of medieval identities, the historical narratives are of primary importance. This paper exploits these sources to explain the construction of religious identity.

The concept of collective or group identity refers to the group's members' shared "conception of its enduring characteristics and basic values, its strengths and weaknesses, its hopes and fears, its reputation and conditions of existence, its institutions and traditions, its past history, current purposes, and future prospects."[1] Identity can be defined from various ethnic, social and cultural points of view, but historians and anthropologists look mainly at ethnic identity because ethnicity is to them the most important reference point.[2] Furthermore, these ethnic identities are considered as irrevocably established from the time when peoples are first mentioned in historical sources. Only in the 1960s did scholars begin to challenge this assertion: historian Reinhard Wenskus and anthropologist Fredrik Barth stressed the fluid character of identities.[3] In the 1980s, Benedict Anderson persuasively argued that intellectuals in the "century of nations" projected onto the past a reality of their own time, the nation, an "imagined

---

[1] Herbert C. Kelman, *"The Place of Ethnic Identity in the Development of Personal Identity: A Challenge for the Jewish Family"* in Peter Y. Medding, ed., *Coping With Life and Death: Jewish Families in the Twentieth Century.* (Oxford: Oxford University Press, 1998), p. 16.

[2] Piere Bonte, Michel Izard, dir., *Dictionnaire de l'ethnologie et de l'anthropologie.* (Paris: PUF, 2004), p. 799.

[3] Reihard Wenskus, *Stammesbildung und Verfassung: Das Verden der frühmittelalterlichen Gentes.* (Köln, 1961); Fredrik Barth, *Ethnic Groups and Boundaries. The Organisation of Social Difference,* (Oslo: Universitetsforlaget, 1969).

community."[4] Ethnic identity is now linked to possessors of political power, elites who imposed on their subjects their family traditions.[5] Ethnicity is thus shown as a social and cultural construct, a form of mobilization to achieve political goals.[6]

Due to the concentration on ethnic identity in the last decades, less attention was paid to religious identity in Late Antiquity and the Early Middle Ages, even though the issue of Christianity was quite often taken into consideration by the historians dealing with questions of identity.[7] In the words of Denise Kimber Buel, "religion remains surprisingly under theorized in relation to ethnicity."[8] This may be explained by the idea that the link between ethnic identity and religion was somehow obscured by Christian monotheism and its pretension to universalism.[9] Social psychology gave more attention to religion being "at the core of individual and group identity" and contributing to its stabilization.[10]

This paper examines the ways religion was used by sixth-century historians as a tool to forge and secure the identity of the group to which they belonged (the *in-group identity*), in contrast to the identity of *others*. Throughout, I will use the terms 'Christians' and 'pagans', ignoring different Christian persuasions competing with each other during the Christological debates.

Sixth-century Byzantine and Latin historians and chroniclers preserve popular myths and legends that are remarkable sources for the study of the mentality and world-view of the period. As Ian Wood states, "Communities often fantasize about their origins, which can provide a crucial element in the construction of their self-identity."[11] Self-identity has a strong religious component. Historical writings of the time were either political and military-centered histories, or universal chronicles, written from

---

[4] Benedict Anderson, *Imagined Communities. Reflections on the Origin and Spread of Nationalism*, London, 1983.

[5] Patrick J. Geary, *Mitul naţiunilor. Originile medievale ale Europei*, (Romanian translation of *The Myths of Nations*), (Târgovişte: Editura Cetatea de Scaun, 2007), p. 17.

[6] Florin Curta, *Apariţia slavilor. Istorie şi arheologie la Dunărea de Jos în veacurile VI–VII* , Târgovişte, Editura Cetatea de Scaun, 2006.

[7] See, for example, Walter Pohl, Clemens Gantner, Richard Payne (eds.), *Visions of community in the Post-Roman World. The West, Byzantium and the Islamic World, 300–1100*, Ashgate, 2012. A recent survey presenting the problem of religion connected with other kinds of identity: Marilyn Dunn, *Belief and Religion in Barbarian Europe c. 350-700*. (London, New York, Bloomsbury, 2013).

[8] Denise Kimber Buell, *Why This New Race: Ethnic Reasoning in Early Christianity*. (Columbia University Press, 2005), p. 35.

[9] Bas Ter Haar Romeny (ed.), *Religious Origins of Nations? The Christian Communities of the Middle East*, (Leiden: Brill, 2010), p. XIV.

[10] Jeffrey R. Seul, "'Ours is the Way of God': Religion, Identity, and Intergroup Conflict", *Journal of peace research* 36 (1999), p. 558.

[11] Ian Wood, "Barbarians, Historians and the Construction of National Identity", *Journal of Late Antiquity*, nr. 1, 1, 2008, p. 61.

a Christian perspective.[12] These categories offer better insight into the mentality of ordinary people than theological treaties or Church histories, representative of clerical perspectives, not consistently or entirely shared by the society at large. Herbert Hunger rightly considered these historical narratives, especially chronicles, as Late Antique and early medieval equivalents of "Sex und Kriminalgeschichte." These literary products intended not only to instruct, but also to entertain their readers or listeners.[13] It is useful to keep in mind that different kind of narratives had different functions which were related to theirs authors' intentions and cultural background.[14]

Even those sixth-century historians who wrote history in an attic—the 'pagan' manner of writing inspired by Thucydides – could not escape the impact of Christianity. Procopius of Caesarea is a case in point. He has been accused of religious indifference as well as of heresy for the simple reason of avoiding Christian terminology in his *Histories*, until Averil Cameron argued that Procopius was an orthodox Christian, forced by the literary conventions of the genre of classical history to translate Christian terminology into a language which had developed about a millennium before the advent of Christianity.[15] Procopius worked like an anthropologist trying to explain to his contemporaries the practices of an unknown tribe of Amazonia. Writing about monks, he describes them as "those of the Christians who are more careful in their observance, whom they call monks."[16] All the same, Procopius refers many times to God, and gives credit to Christian miracles, for example when asserting that Saint Peter protected the walls of Rome during the Gothic siege.[17] Another miracle that he did not seem to disavow was the protection given to the city of Apameea by the piece of the True Cross kept there, thus expressing the idea that God preserved Apameea.[18]

I am inclined to think that Procopius was not a pagan but a "conventional" Christian irritated by the Christological controversies of his time – a person who would have preferred a Christianity with less doctrinal conflicts. His attitude on this score is palpable when writing about the Tetraxite Goths living in the North-Eastern region of

---

[12] The classification of medieval narratives is debated, see Bernard Guénée, *Histoire et culture historique dans l'Occident medieval*. (Paris: Aubier Montaigne, 1980); B. Roest, "Medieval Historiography: About Generic constraints and Scholarly Constructions" in B. Roest, H. Vanstiphout (eds), *Aspects of Gender and Type in Pre-Modern Literary Cultures*, COMERS/ICOG Communications, 1, Groningen, 1999, pp. 47–61; Deborah Mauskopf Deliyannis, (ed.), *Historiography in the Middle Ages*, Leiden, Brill, 2003, pp. 1–13.
[13] Hunger, Herbert, *Hochsprachliche profane Literatur der Byzantiner*, vol. I. (München: Aschenbach 1977), p. 12.
[14] Justin Lake, "Authorial Intention in Medieval Historiography", *History compass*, 12/4, 2014, p. 346.
[15] Averil Cameron, *Procopius and the sixth century*. (Berkeley-Los Angeles: University of California Press, 1985. According to Anthony Kaldellis, *Procopius of Caesareea: Tiranny, History and Philosophy at the End of Antiquity*. (Philadelphia: University of Pennsylvania Press, 2004), Procopius was pagan.
[16] Procopius, *The History of the Wars*, ed. H. H. Dewing, (London, New York, 1914),, I, VII, 22.
[17] Procopius, *Wars*, V, XXIII, 4–8.
[18] Procopius, *Wars*, II, XI, 17–18; 28.

the Black Sea,[19] of whom he did not know whether they were formerly pagans or Arians: "But at the present time they honor the faith in a spirit of complete simplicity and with no vain questionings."[20]

On occasion, Procopius takes stand against the doctrinal fights of his time e mentioning religious dispute between members of Christian clergy and stating that although he knows well the points in discussion he will "maintain a discreet silence concerning these matters."[21] Anthony Kaldellis argues that this fragment is proof that Procopius did not speak about the Christian god but expressed a Platonic point of view and a skeptical position.[22] I think that there is a good amount of overinterpretation here. The context suggests that Procopius did not support constant questioning about the nature of God, so prominent during his lifetime. The core of the problem is that we do not really know how laypeople in sixth-century Byzantium expressed their religious views, because only the works of theologians and churchmen serve as the basis for our interpretations. Is the theological definition of faith applicable to everyone? Is not it rather that in sixth-century Byzantium, like in any other society, different levels of religiosity were specific to different groups of people, without implying that these differences were pagan or heretical?

Agathias, who continues the history of Byzantine wars at the point where Procopius stopped, also writes in Classicizing style, considered as a proof that he was pagan, or worse, atheist.[23] In a well-known passage, Agathias states that he would prefer to call a place by its ancient name, Onogouris, instead of the new, Christian name of Saint Stephen, because "such a practice is more in keeping with the style of historiography."[24] This has been used as an argument for proving Agathias' paganism, along with the argument that he opposes Christian names despite the pretext that he mentions them.[25]

If the religious confession of sixth-century Byzantine historians must remain open to debate, Classical style cannot be taken for proof of their paganism. Classical

---

[19] Igor O. Gavritukhin, Michel Kazanski, "Bosphorus, the Tetraxite Goths and the Northern Caucasus Region During the Second Half of the Fifth and the Sixth Centuries", in Florin Curta, dir., *Neglected Barbarians*. (Turnhout: Brepols, 2010), p. 86.

[20] Procopius, Wars, VIII, III, 9.

[21] Procopius, *Wars*, V, III, 6–9.

[22] Anthony Kaldellis, *Procopius of Caesareea: Tiranny, History and Philosophy at the End of Antiquity*, pp. 170–172.

[23] "Pagan" refers to a practitioner of civic cults in the pre-Christian Graeco-Roman World; see Alan Cameron, *The Last Pagans of Rome*. (Oxford- New York: Oxford University Press, 2011), p. 783. Anthony Kaldellis, "The Historical and Religious Views of Agathias. A Reinterpretation", *Byzantion* 69 (1999), pp. 206–252 argues that Agathias was pagan. See also Anthony Kadellis, "Agathias on History and Poetry", *Greek, Roman and Byzantine Studies* 38 (1997), p. 300, note 16.

[24] Agathias, *The Histories*, ed. Joseph D. Frendo, Berlin, New York, Walter De Gruyter, 1975, III, 5,7.

[25] Anthony Kaldellis, "Things Are Not What They Are: Agathias *Mythistoricus* and the Last Laugh of Classical Culture." *Classical Quarterly*, 53 (2003), p. 300.

education meant that they knew by heart the writings of the ancient authors and so they were able to use, at any moment, references taken from these models. Their audience shared with them respect and knowledge of the ancients, not necessarily in contradiction with Christian faith. An oblique criticism of the excesses of the Church or of a Christian emperor made by Procopius, does not imply the rejection of Christianity. Following Alan Cameron, I continue to doubt that Classical style and a preference for Classical conventions are correlated with the religious allegiance of the writers who used them.[26] To assume that in the sixth century the use of rhetoric and of classical authors is proof of paganism is to forget the extent to which in Byzantium, "Hellenic culture infected Christian thought and expression."[27]

Christian belief is overtly and exaggeratedly flagged in chronicles written by clerics or devout laypeople. Even these authors, however, do not limit themselves to a providential explanation of events alone. Their Christian self-definition is no distorting lens describing historical events. Gregory of Tours starts his universal chronicle with a confession of his Catholic faith.[28] We can rarely find an affirmation which seems to contradict the strong Christian attitude of the chronicler, but there is something idiosyncratic in his account of the destruction of a pagan temple by a barbarian invader, Chrocus. The king of the Alemans invaded Gaul at the end of third century and destroyed all the pagan temples including one in Clermont which had been built and adorned "with wonderful skill."[29] In this passage, appreciation for a pagan work of art and regret for its destruction shine through, even if Gregory was dedicated to eradicating the pagan traces from Frankish society without any regret for the destruction of the ancient temples. A possible explanation of this apparent contradiction is in this particular situation, the aesthetic beauty of the pagan temple served to underline the barbarity of the Alamannic invader.

Another apparent contradiction between religious faith and attitude towards pagans appears in the work of the Byzantine chronicler John Malalas. He shows real sympathy for the pagan philosopher Hypatia, killed by Christians incited by the Patriarch Cyril. Malalas expresses his regret for what happened by stating that Hypatia "had a great reputation and was an old woman."[30] Just like in the case of Procopius or Agathias, Malalas' Christian faith cannot be doubted, but this sympathy for a pagan person does raise questions. In fact, in his work, Malalas often tried to reconcile three streams that

---

[26] Alan Cameron, *The Last Pagans of Rome*. (Oxford, New York, Oxford University Press, 2011).
[27] Vasilios Makrides, *Hellenic Temples and Christian Churches: A concise History of the Religious Cultures of Greece from Antiquity to the Present*. (New York University Press, 2009), p. 162.
[28] Gregorii episcopi Turonensis *Historiarum Libri Decem*. Ed. R. Buchner. (Berlin: 1957), 25.
[29] Gregory of Tours, *History of the Franks*, ed. and transl. Ernest Brehaut, New York, 1916, I, 32.
[30] John Malalas, *The Chronicle*. English translation by Elisabeth Jeffreys, Michael Jeffreys and Roger Scott, with Brian Croke, Jenny Ferber, Simon Franklin, Alan James, Douglas Kelly, Ann Moffatt, Ann Nixon. (Melbourne: Byzantina Australiensia IV, 1986), XIV, 12.

constituted the Roman past: Greek mythology, Roman law and Judeo-Christian Scripture.[31] Moreover, he often took fragments from his sources and inserted them in his work with a kind of "copy paste method." This may account for different and even contradictory ideological trends in his chronicle.[32] At the same time, his Christian identity did not prevent Malalas from appreciating pagan personalities such as Hypathia.

Any analysis of the eventual role of the historian's own religious belief has to be very cautious and nuanced. It cannot be assumed that Christian historians would present facts and interpretations only from a strictly Christian point of view. The complexity of each personality prevents such an interpretation.

How do sixth-century historians present the role of religion in shaping individual or groups identity? More than a century and a half after Christianity became the State religion in the Roman Empire, historians and chroniclers felt the need to justify their confession in opposition to that of others. It is useful to explore the way they affirmed their own religious identity and classified others.

Gregory of Tours is a case in point: "As I am about to describe the struggles of kings with the heathen enemy, of martyrs with pagans, of churches with heretics, I desire first of all to declare my faith so that my reader may have no doubt that I am Catholic." Gregory presents by a theological description his Catholic faith, summarizing the Apostles' Creed: "I believe, then, in God the Father omnipotent. I believe in Jesus Christ his only Son, our Lord God, born of the Father, not created. [I believe] that he has always been with the Father, not only since time began but before all time. For the Father could not have been so named unless he had a son; and there could be no son without a father."[33] The consequences of the chronicler's Catholicity are various. Gregory casts the Merovingian kings to resemble Old Testament kings and prophets and thus scholars often (rightly) doubt the accuracy of his narrative.[34] He judges the Frankish kings (and the queens) on the basis of their attitude towards the servants of the Christian God—priests like him.[35]

Other authors do not clearly profess their belief. Iordanes relates almost cryptically that before his conversion he was a secretary for Gunthigis-Basa, a Byzantine general of Barbarian origin: "To his sister's son Gunthigis, also called Baza, the Master of

---

[31] Elizabeth Jeffreys, "Writers and Audiences in the Early Sixth Century", in *Greek Literature in Late Antiquity: Dynamism, Didacticism, Classicism*, eds. Scott Fitzgerald Johnson, James George. (Ashgate Publishing, 2006), p. 133.

[32] Peter Wood, "Multiple Voices in Chronicle Sources:The Reign of Leo I (457–474) in Book Fourteen of Malalas", *Journal of Late Antiquity*, 4.2, 2011, pp. 298–299.

[33] Gregory of Tours, *History of the Franks*, I, 1.

[34] Yitzhak Hen, "The uses of the Bible and the perception of kingship in Merovingian Gaul", *Early Medieval Europe*, 1998, 7, 3, p. 278.

[35] Martin Heinzelmann, *Gregory of Tours: History and Society in the Sixth Century*, Cambridge University Press, 2001, p. 37.

the Soldiery, who was the son of Andag the son of Andela, who was descended from the stock of the Amali, I also, Iordanes, although an unlearned man before my conversion, was secretary.[36] It is hard to imagine that around the middle of the sixth century a Goth was still pagan, as the Goths converted to Arian Christianity in the fourth century.[37] Therefore, this may be information about Iordanes' change of confession (renouncing Arianism for Nicene orthodoxy) or about converting to asceticism, as "conversio" signified at the time the choice of a monastic way of life.[38]

Yet others discuss their religion through a neutral affirmation of their belief in an omnipotent God. Refusing to take part in the confessional struggles of his time, Procopius of Caesarea says: "As for the points in dispute, although I know them well, I shall by no means make mention of them; for I consider it a sort of insane folly to investigate the nature of God, enquiring of what sort it is. For man cannot, I think, apprehend even human affairs with accuracy, much less those things which pertain to the nature of God. As for me, therefore, I shall maintain a discreet silence concerning these matters, with the sole object that old and venerable beliefs may not be discredited. For I, for my part, will say nothing whatever about God save that He is altogether good and has all things in His power."[39]

Beyond the authors' declarations, we have to analyze how their own religious, Christian identity filters their understanding and representation of *others*. There are different ways to use Christianity as a mark of identity: it confers superiority on one's own community and helps to place the others in an inferior position. For sixth-century historians and chroniclers, it does not mean that the world is divided between 'us' and 'them,' between Christians and pagans. As Christians are divided, each author favors his own confession, framed as the correct, orthodox one. Pagans are arranged into different categories: Gentiles before the advent of Christianity, including ancient Greeks and Romans; barbarians to be converted; rival Zoroastrians. Within this hierarchy, historians employ other elements than religion, such as ethnic belonging, moral values, and cultural traits as well, showing how complex the construction of identity was.

The historical change of religions is a question raised by sixth-century historians. Byzantines as well as and the barbarian kingdoms in the Western Empire had a pagan past—a past that had to be presented and justified. As Rosamond McKitterick

---

[36] Iordanes, *The Origin and Deeds of the Goths*, translated by Charles C. Mierow, Princeton, 1915, L, 266.
[37] Iordanes was anti-Arian: Walter Goffart, "Iordanes's *Getica* and the Disputed Authenticity of Gothic Origins from Scandinavia." *Speculum* 80 (2005), p. 394.
[38] Walter Goffart, *The Narrators of Barbarian History*. (Princeton, Princeton University Press, 1988), p. 44; Arne Søby Christensen, *Cassiodorus, Iordanes and the History of the Goths*. (Museum Tusculanum Press, 2002), pp. 91–94; a summary of the recent discussions in Marcus Cruz, "Gregório de Tours e Jordanès: a construção da memória dos 'bárbaros' no VI século", *Acta Scientiarum*, vol. 36, no. 1, 2014, p. 21.
[39] Procopius, *Wars*, V, III, 6–9.

notes, a fundamental element in the formation of both individual and group identity was the communication with the past.[40] Many different strategies of communication exist in Byzantine historiography, starting with those writers who simply ignore the past together with the religious problems and events of their time, because they write political and military history. In the work of Procopius, it is very rare to find a reference to ancient gods. An exception is when he describes that during the siege of Rome by the Goths, the citizens returned to ancient religious practice by opening the doors of the Temple of Janus.[41] It is very difficult to analyze his attitude towards this event that he does not entirely embrace, neither condemns.[42]

Another strategy is the minimization of the importance of pagan gods. Malalas claims the gods were mortals later deified: Kronos "was a strong man who was the first to practice ruling" as a king in Assyria, and that he "had a son, named Picus, who was called Zeus by his parents."[43] Malalas applies to the ancient gods the rational method of interpretation (euhemerism) claiming that mythological characters were originally human beings.[44] In doing so, Malalas follows an early Christian tradition adopted by the Church Fathers. Euhemerism competed with another tradition that considered the gods demons – this remained the winning solution.[45] Malalas shares the commonly accepted idea that the ancient religion was wrong: the Justinian Codex calls it "Hellenic error."[46] Nevertheless, in the first six of the eighteen books of his chronicle, Malalas seeks to reconcile classical mythology with Biblical history, quoting Hermetic and Orphic (pagan) writings to support Christianity.[47]

Iordanes, writing about the Goths who never renounced the Arian heresy, is clearly embarrassed by this fact. He therefore highlights the heathenism of the Goths as something that gives this people equal dignity with that of the Romans. Iordanes thinks that Mars is the god of war only in the "fables of poets," and proudly asserts

---

[40] Rosamond McKitterick, "Introduction: Being Roman after Rome." *Early Medieval Europe*, 22 (4), 2014, p. 387.

[41] Procopius, *Wars*, V, XXV, 24.

[42] For Anthony Kaldellis, *Tyranny*, pp. 165–166, this indicates that Procopius shared pagan belief in the ancient gods.

[43] Malalas, *The Chronicle*, I, 8.

[44] Franco de Angelis and Benjamin Garstad, "Euhemerus in context." *Classical Antiquity* 25 (2006), pp. 211–242.

[45] Peter Brown, *L'essor du christianisme occidental*, French translation by Paul Chemla. (Paris: Seuil, 1997), p. 42; Alan Cameron, *The Last Pagans of Rome*. (Oxford- New York: Oxford University Press, 2011), p. 797.

[46] Simon Corcoran, "Anastasius, Justinian, and the Pagans: A Tale of Two Law Codes and a Papyrus", *Journal of Late Antiquity* 2.2, 2009, p. 194.

[47] Wolf Liebeschuetz, "The View from Antioch: from Libanius via John Chysostom to John Malalas and beyond." In: *Pagans and Christians in the Roman Empire: The Breaking of a Dialogue, (IVth–VIth Century A.D.)*, Proceedings of the International Conference at the Monastery of Bose, 2008, eds. Peter Brown, Rita Lizzi Testa. (Wien- Berlin: LIT, 2011), p. 336.

that the god of war was born among the Goths. His Virgilian quote in fact refers to the Getae, an ancient people living in the territory of Dacia, not to the Goths, but the confusion between the Getae and the Goths was longstanding, at least dating from the fourth century when the Goths entered the Roman Empire. What is interesting here is the way Iordanes fused their histories together.[48] Incorporating stories about the Getae into the Gothic history gave the Goths a proper Classical past that was able to compete, symbolically, with that of the Romans.[49] Iordanes states: "Now Mars has always been worshipped by the Goths with cruel rites, and captives were slain as his victims. They thought that he who is the lord of war ought to be appeased by the shedding of human blood. To him they devoted the first share of the spoil, and in his honor arms stripped from the foe were suspended from trees. And they had more than all other races a deep spirit of religion, since the worship of this god seemed to be really bestowed upon their ancestor."[50] Even though Iordanes formally condemns human sacrifice as cruel rite, he also regards it as proof of a profound religiosity, which has value, notwithstanding its pagan character. He tells a curious story about witches called *haliurunnae*. Exiled from the Gothic tribe by King Filimer, they mated with demons and gave birth to the race of Huns:

"Filimer, king of the Goths [...] found among his people certain witches, whom he called in his native tongue Haliurunnae. Suspecting these women, he expelled them from the midst of his race and compelled them to wander in solitary exile afar from his army. There the unclean spirits, who beheld them as they wandered through the wilderness, bestowed their embraces upon them and begat this savage race.[51]

Herwig Wolfram argued that this story might reflect a change of religion, the ancient, matriarcal agrarian cult being replaced by a newer, more warlike, patriarcal one.[52] Considering that Iordanes tries sought to forge a positive identity for the Goths to make them equal with the Romans, one wonders if this episode does not have another meaning, too. It is possible that Iordanes intends to show that despite being pagans, the Goths avoided practices such as witchcraft, repugnant from a Christian point of view. The episode's main purpose is to explain the genesis of the Huns as kins-

---

[48] Brian Swain, "Iordanes and Virgil: A Case Study of Intertextuality in the *Getica*." *Classical Quarterly* 60 (2010), p. 246.
[49] J.H.W.G. Liebeschuetz, "Making a Gothic History: Does the *Getica* of Iordanes Preserve Genuinely Gothic Traditions?" *Journal of Late Antiquity* 4.2 (2011), p. 198.
[50] Iordanes, *Getica.*, L, 41.
[51] Iordanes, *Getica*, XXIV, 121-122.
[52] Herwig Wolfram, "Origo et religio. Ethnic traditions and literature in early medieval texts." *Early Medieval Europe* 1994, pp. 19-38.

men of the Goths.[53] A large Ostrogothic group was under Hunnic domination from about 376 until the death of Attila in 453.

Categorical, yet formal, condemnation of pagan religion is to be found in the works of Gregory of Tours. Preoccupied with the Arian heresy, Gregory was not overtly troubled by the issue of paganism. In a well-known description of the baptism of Clovis, he condemns the former religious beliefs and actions of the pagan king: "Gently bend your neck, Sigamber; worship what you burned; burn what you worshipped."[54] The widely accepted translation of the Latin *"mittis depone colla Sigamber"* has been debated for some time. The alternative interpretation is that Bishop Remigius simply asked Clovis to take off his collar decorated with the magical symbols of pagan royalty.[55] Recently, scholars questioned Clovis' paganism asking whether he had not been influenced by Christianity before his conversion or whether he was not an Arian catechumen or at least impacted by Arianism.[56] Doubt about the accuracy of the story of Clovis' baptism is based on the observation that Gregory of Tours models Clovis on Constantine the Great to the extent of rearranging the chronology of the reign so as to be able to present military success after conversion.[57] For Gregory, Clovis must have been a pagan, like Constantine, at the moment of his conversion, and his baptism must have taken place exactly in the middle of a thirty-year reign. The probability that we are dealing with a hugely biased presentation of the foundational moment of Frankish history is seldom refuted today, when the trustworthiness of Gregory of Tours is questioned.[58] Gregory sought to orchestrate the baptism as the founding moment of Clovis' reign, when the king "underwent ideological transformations, with attendant benefits for his kingdom and himself."[59]

What is the attitude of historians towards those who maintained their pre-Christian beliefs in Byzantium after Christianity became the official religion of the

---

[53] J.H.W.G. Liebeschuetz, "Making a Gothic History: Does the *Getica* of Iordanes Preserve Genuinely Gothic Traditions."*Journal of Late Antiquity* 4.2 (2011), p. 191.

[54] Gregory of Tours, *History of the Franks*, II, 31.

[55] Jean Hoyoux, „ Le collier de Clovis." *Revue belge de philologie et d'histoire* 21 (1942) pp. 170–171.

[56] Ian Wood, "Gregory of Tours [and Clovis]", *Revue Belge de Philologie et d'Histoire*, 63, 1985, pp. 249–272 hypothesised that Clovis was an Arian catechumen. For Clovis' pre-baptismal Arianism see Danuta Shanzer, "Dating the baptism of Clovis: the bishop of Vienne vs the bishop of Tours." *Early Medieval Europe* 7 (1998) pp. 29-57.

[57] Claude Carozzi, „Le Clovis de Grégoire de Tours." *Le Moyen Age* XCVIII, 2 (1992), pp. 169–185.

[58] Alexander Callander Murray, "Chronology and the Composition of the *Histories* of Gregory of Tours." *Journal of Late Antiquity* 1.1, 2008, pp. 157–196; see also Felice Lifshitz, "The Vicissitudes of Political Identity: Historical Narratives in the Barbarian Successor States of Western Europe",„ in *The Oxford History of Historical Writing*, vol. 2, 400–1400, eds. Sarah Foor, Chase T. Robinson. (Oxford: Oxford University Press, 2012), pp. 374–375.

[59] Jonathan Barlow, "The Morality of the Franks." *Bulletin of the Institute of Classical Studies* 50/91 (2007), p. 111.

Roman Empire? The Byzantine historians speak about "Hellenes," distinguishing them from other pagans called "barbarians." In a curious passage, Malalas calls those who fought Constantine after his vision of the Cross "barbarians."[60] Malalas may mistakenly mix different events, but here barbarians" actually signify "pagans." This became the standard meaning of the term at the time when the earlier 'Romans' and 'barbarians' dichotomy gave way to the new opposition between' Christians' and 'pagans'.[61]

The attitude towards Hellenes differs from author to author. Agathias is more empathetic toward them when he narrates that the philosophers of the School of Athens closed by Justinian in 529 sought refuge at King Chosroes of Persia, a reputed lover of philosophy and philosophers: "They had come to the conclusion that, since the official religion of the Roman Empire was not to their liking, the Persian state was much superior."[62] The philosophers did not stay too long in Persia. They returned to the Byzantine Empire in 532, when the Persian-Byzantine treaty granted them freedom of religion.[63] Sympathizing with the philosophers, Agathias nonetheless opines that they were misled into naively believing that a Persian king like Chosroes would understand Classical philosophy. Agathias' object of criticism is not the philosophers' paganism, but their credulity. Speaking of the paganism of the *other*—the paganism of the barbarians—Agathias becomes more severely condemning. He calls Zoroastrianism is "a false religion."[64] Accessing first-hand sources of the Persian religion and customs, Agathias shows heightened criticism towards King Yazgard—a ruler praised by Procopius and earlier writers.[65] Agathias' better knowledge of the Persians' religion does not lead to a better understanding, just the opposite.

At a first glance, Procopius seems to be neutral, even sympathetic to the Abasgi people living in the Caucasus, when describing their pagan practices and beliefs: "These barbarians even down to my time have worshiped graves and forest; for with a sort of barbarian simplicity they supposed the trees were gods."[66] He writes that "during the reign of the present Emperor Justinian the Abasgi have changed everything and adopted a more civilized standard of life," having begun to live "in a state of freedom" because

---

[60] Malalas, *The Chronicle*, XIII, 2.
[61] Peter Hoppenbrouwers , "Such Stuff as Peoples are Made on: Ethnogenesis and the Construction of Nationhood in Medieval Europe." *The Medieval History Journal* 9 (2006), p. 197.
[62] Agathias, *Histories*, 2.30.3–4.
[63] Edward Watts, "Where to live the Philosophical life in the Sixth Century? Damascius, Simplicius and the Return from Persia."*Greek, Roman and Byzantine Studies* 45 (2005), p. 286.
[64] Agathias, *Histories.*, 26, 6.
[65] Scott Mc Donough, "A Second Constantine? The Sassanian King Yazgard in Christian History and Historiography." *Journal of Late Antiquity* 1/1 (2008), pp. 127–141.
[66] Procopius, *Wars*, VIII, III, 13–14.

"they espoused Christian doctrine."[67] This is a convincing piece of evidence for the positive attitude of Procopius towards Christianity: he sees it as an intrinsic component of civilization where freedom is a defining characteristic.

I am aware that a single category of sources does not offer deep insight into the complexity of religious issues in the sixth century. I have not intended to analyze entire societies, but an intellectual group, that of the historians, who formulated and spread ideas and opinions concerning religious difference in their writings. Without referring to all historians and chroniclers of the period, I selected the most representative ones. Avoiding generalization, I sought to demonstrate that as much as religious confession may be a distorting lens for historians, it does not function the same way each time when an author deals with religion. The personal interests and goals of the historian and the autonomy of the historical craft yield to a more nuanced picture of religion in the historiography of the sixth century.

---

[67] Procopius, *Wars*, VIII, III, 18–20.

Cults

THE CULT OF *SOL INVICTUS* AND EARLY CHRISTIANITY IN AQUAE IASAE

Branka Migotti

The subject of this paper is related to Emperor Constantine's (306–337 AD) religious policy, an issue that has recently witnessed considerable increase of scholarship related to the commemoration of the seventeen hundred years of the Edict of Milan.[1] Recent academic discussion has shifted the focus of research from the emperor's Christian belief to the framework within which his religious policies unfolded.[2] Nevertheless, scholarship cannot entirely rid itself of the burden of the (essentially unanswerable) question related to the sincerity (or lack thereof) of Constantine's Christian affiliation and his attitude towards Christianity versus pagan religions, most evidently reflected in his wavering between the Sun god, Sol, and Christ.[3] Some commentators still dwell on Constantine's hostility, or at least his lack of leniency towards pagan religions, but such interpretations seem to lack balance and objectivity.[4] It is beyond the scope of this paper to discuss this issue in detail, especially with regard to the vast body of scholarship. Let it suffice to recall that Constantine did remain *pontifex maximus* and that Constantinople, praised by some contemporary sources as a Christian city in the time of Constan-

---

[1] Richard Flower, "Visions of Constantine" (review article). *Journal of Roman Studies* 102 (2012), 287–305 (hereafter: Flower, Visions).

[2] Flower, Visions, 304.

[3] Augusto Fraschetti, "Costantino e la sua famiglia." In: Angela Donati - Giovanni Gentili (eds.), *Costantino il Grande. La civiltà antica al bivio tra Occidente e Oriente.* (Milano: Silvana Editoriale, 2005), pp. 16– 25 (hereafter: Donati .Gentili); Marta Sordi, "La conversione di Costantino." In: Donati- Gentili, pp. 36–43; Marianne Bergmann, „Konstantin und der Sonnengot. Die Aussagen der Bildzeugnisse." In: Alexander Demandt - Joseph Engemann (eds.), *Konstantin der Grosse: Geschichte – Archäologie – Rezeption.* (Trier: Rheinischen Landesmuseums, 2006), pp. 143–162 (hereafter: Demandt-Engemann) ; Clauss 2006; Klaus Martin Girardet, "Konstantin und das Christentum: die Jahre der Entscheidung 310 bis 314." In: Demandt-Engemann, pp. 69–82; Franz Alto Bauer, „Konstantinopel – Kaiserresidenz und künftige Hauptstadt." In: Demandt-Engemann, pp. 165–172; Manfred Clauss, „Die alten Kulte in konstantinischer Zeit." In: Demandt-Engemann, pp. 39–48; Flower, Visions, 291–292, 303.

[4] Flower, Visions, 290, 294.

tine, and often perceived as such in scholarship, had a newly built Capitolium, and the city was embellished with a host of pagan religious sculptures. "New Rome" was not the only city where such policy prevailed.[5] Constantine, then, can hardly be accused of general religious intolerance, even if his leniency in religious matters seems to have been more at work in the Western part of the Roman Empire than in the East, and not particularly evident in the Holy Land.[6] Religious syncretism seems to be the guiding principle of Constantine's religious policy throughout his reign.[7] His attitude towards Sol Invictus epitomizes this phenomenon. Whatever theological and chronological nuances and uncertainties scholars detect in the emperor's religion, it remains unquestioned that Constantinian legislation protected Christians from 313 at the latest.[8] It is against this background that archaeological evidence from Aqua Iasae (present day Varaždinske Toplice in North-Western Croatia), is analysed. Examining the theology of Solar Christology and archaeological findings, this paper argues for the possibility that the spa centre of cosmopolitan Aquae Iasae simultaneously hosted the worship of Sol and Christ during the rule of Constantine.

From Solar Henotheism to Solar Christology

In the early third century, Emperor Elagabalus (218–222 AD) strove to impose the Syrian version of the god Sol as the head of the Roman pantheon. Elagabalus failed for two reasons: the revolutionary and premature nature of his action and his moral and political untrustworthiness.[9] Aurelian's (270–275 AD) introduction of the cult of Sol Invictus as a henotheistic God to the Roman Pantheon was more successful. The circumstances were different, thanks to the Aurelian's respectable personality. Sol Invictus was an "occidentalised" version of Sol, closer to the Emperor Augustus' Apollonian solar divine aspect than to the oriental and Mithraic mysteries with their ecstatic rituals. Aurelians's religious policy favouring a henotheistic conception of Sol Invictus was con-

---

[5] Marina Falla Castelfranchi, "Costantino e l'edilizia cristiana in Oriente." In: Donati – Gentili, p. 113; Clauss 2006; Bauer 2007; Clauss 2007; Marcello Ghetta, Das Weiterleben der alten Kulte in Trier und Umgebung. In: Demandt- Engemann, 220–227.

[6] Flower, Visions, 299. The site of Golgotha in Jerusalem is one of the exceptions to the rule of Constantine's tolerant approach to pagan religious sites.

[7] Manfred Clauss, „Die alten Kulte in konstantinischer Zeit,". In: Demandt-Engemann, p. 211.

[8] Klaus Martin Girardet, "Konstantin – Wegbereiter des Christentums als Weltreligion. In: Demandt- Engemann, 237–238; Flower 2012, 294.

[9] Gaston H. Halsberghe, *The Cult of Sol Invictus*. (Leiden: Brill, 1972), pp. 42–43; Helga Von Heintze, "Sol Invictus." In: Herbert Beck - Peter C. Bol (eds.), *Spätantike und frühes Christentum*. (Frankfurt am Main: Liebighaus Museum alter Plastik, 1983), p. 145 (hereafter Beck-Bol); Robert Turcan, *The Cults of the Roman Empire*. Translated by Antonia Neville. (Oxford: Blackwell, 1996), pp. 176–183; Marianne Bergmann, „Konstantin und der Sonnengot. Die Aussagen der Bildzeugnisse." In: Demandt -Engemann, 146–147.

vincing enough to survive through changing religious trends under the Tetrarchs. Imperial policy under the Tetrarchs equated Sol and Christ as sources of light, victory, and celestial supremacy.[10] Aurelian's Sol Invictus thus served as the basis for Constantine's religious shift from Sol to Christ, from Solar henotheism to Solar Christianity.[11] The emperor's affiliation to Solar Christology was presented in historiography as an original and almost revolutionary concept, provoking the unsolvable and torturous debate over the emperor's wavering between Sol and Christ, and the sincerity of his Christian persuasion up to the present.[12]

Solar Christology, however, was no invention of Constantine. In Christian theology, Tertullian (160–225) was the first to stress the solar component of Christianity.[13] The concept of Christ the Sun came to be established by Origen of Alexandria (185–253) in his lunar cosmological theology, originating from Hellenistic-Asiatic cosmological mythology and supported by Biblical quotations endowing God with metaphorical astral attributes. Origen's cosmological theology that produced the concept of Christ as Sun[14] was not only Christianity's answer to the enormous popularity of solar cults in the second and third centuries, but also the predecessor of fourth-century Solar Christology.

What was the true meaning of Emperor Constantine's Sun-Christ devotion? When did he turn from henotheistic paganism, symbolized by Sol Invictus, to monotheistic Christianity? To believe that Constantine was able to truly divorce these two components of his monotheistic religious persuasion is perhaps to overrate his philosophical powers and, at the same time, to underestimate his political pragmatism. Why

---

[10] Cf. Flower 2012, 303.

[11] On Aurelian's religious policy see Halsberghe, 130–171; Von Heintze, 145; Turcan, 183; Maria Vittoria Cerutti, "La crisi del mondo religioso tardoantico." In: Sandro Piussi (ed.), *Cromazio di Aquileia 388–408 al crocevia di genti e religioni*. (Milano: Silvana Editoriale), 176. On the terms *henotheism* and *monotheism* in the context of late Roman religion see Girardet, 70; Cerutti, 181. See also Noel Lenski, "The Sun and the Senate: The Inspiration for the Arch of Constantine," in E. Dal Covolo and G. Gasparro Sfameni, eds. *Costantino il Grande alle radici dell'Europa*. Atti del Convegno Internazionale di Studio in occasione del 1700 anniversario della Battaglia di Ponte Milvio e della conversione di Costantino (Libreria Editrice Vaticana: Vatican City, 2014), pp. 153–93.

[12] Günter Ristow, Passion und Ostern im Bild der Spätantike. In: Beck -Bol, 360; Fraschetti, 17; Sordi, 39–43; Clauss, 39–40; Girardet, 69–72; Flower 2012, 291–292, *passim*.

[13] See note 26.

[14] Origen, *Homilia in Numeros* XXIII, 5 (*Patrologiae Cursus Completus: Series Graeca*, ed. J.-P. Migne, vol. 12, Paris 1857): Sol iustitiae Christus est (Christ is the Sun of Justice). See Hugo Rahner, *Symbole der Kirche. Die Ekklesiologie der Väter*. (Salzburg: Müller, 1964), pp. 104–114; Dorothea Forstner, *Die Welt der christlichen Symbole*. (Innsbruck – Wien – München: Tyrolia Verlag, 1982), pp. 100–102. There is an uninterrupted line of Solar Christology from the Biblical quotations to Origen to the fourth and fifth century Christian theologians, such as Ambrose of Milan, Athanasius of Alexandria, John Chrysostom, Augustine of Hippo, Jerome of Stridon who identified Christ with the conception of the overwhelming universal power through syntagms such as *lux mundi*, *Sol iustitiae*, and *Sol salutis*: Migotti Branka Migotti, „Sol iustitiae Christus est (Origenes). Odrazi solarne kristologije na ranokršćanskoj građi iz sjeverne Hrvatske.[Sol iustitiae Christus est. (Origenes). Elements of Solar Christology in the Early Christian Objects from North Croatia.] *Diadora* 16–17 (1994–95), Zadar, 263–265.

should anyone expect Constantine to have been able to tell Sol from Christ when Christian theology had already equated these two, producing Christ the Sun as representative of a monotheistic solar cult? Christians were equally unable to tell Sol from Christ.[15] Constantine might have been influenced by Origen's theology that conceived of the emperor as an instrument of Divine Providence—which comes close to defining the cosmological aspect of the emperor's religious philosophy.[16] Be it as it may, the chronology and the theological nuances of Constantine's religious profile are less important for the present context. What matters is the fact that the emperor's religious policy, based on the conception of Christ the Sun, was such as to allow for a contemporary worship of Sol–Apollo alongside Christ, as presumably occurred in Aquae Iasae.

People and Religion in Aquae Iasae

Aquae Iasae was a well-known spa and rehabilitation site in Pannonia Superior (from 197, Pannonia Savia), close to the border with the province of Noricum (fig. 1). Healing thermal waters, as well as the location on the crossroads connecting two important main highways that ran from Italy towards the Danubian provinces and further east (Emona–Sirmium, and Poetovio–Sirmium), gave impetus to the development of Aquae Iasae as an important bath, trade, and religious centre for the wider Norico-Pannonian region.[17] Epigraphic evidence from the site shows that it attracted not only common soldiers, higher echelons of military and administrative officials, but also the emperor.[18] In the first two decades of his rule, Constantine visited Pannonia on a more or less yearly basis; in 315 he returned from Sirmium to Rome via Poetovio.[19] Presumably, this was not the only such imperial visit to the site that evidently charmed Constantine enough

---

[15] Paul Johnson, *A History of Christianity*. (Harmondsworth: Penguin, 1982), p. 67.

[16] ibid, 69.

[17] Dorica Ehrlich Nemeth and Dora Kušan Špalj, "The Roman Settlement Aquae Iasae – Findings of Archaeological Excavations in the Area of the Varaždinske Toplice Municipal Park." In: Nina Pirnat Spahić (ed.), *Aquae Iasae. Recent Discoveries of Roman Remains in the Region of Varaždinske Toplice*. (Ljubljana : Cankarjev dom, Collegium graphicum, 2014), p. 36; (hereafter Pirnat Spahić) Dora Kušan Špalj, "History of the Roman Settlement Aquae Iasae." In: Pirnat Spahić, 53–54; (hereafter Kušan Špalj 2014 a) Dora Kušan Špalj, "Aquae Iasae – a Centre of Health, Cult and Oracle". In: Pirnat Spahić, 82–106. (hereafter Kušan Špalj 2014 b)

[18] Marcel Gorenc - Branka Vikić, "Das fünfundzwanzigjährige Jubiläum der Untersuchungen der antiken Lokalität Aquae Iasae (Varaždinske Toplice)." *Archaeologia Iugoslavica* XVI (1975), 32; Duje Rendić-Miočević, "O akvejasejskoj epigrafskoj baštini i o posebnostima njenih kultnih dedikacija."[On the epigraphic heritage of *Aquae Iasae* and the peculiarities of its cult dedications.] VAMZ XXIV-XXV (1992) 67–76; Dora Kušan Špalj, "Aquae Iasae – a Centre of Health, Cult and Oracle". In: Pirnat Spahić, 82–106.

[19] András Mócsy, "Pannonia." *Realencyclopädie der Classischen Altertumswissenschaft*. Georg Wissowa- August Friedrich Pauly eds. Suppl. 9. (Stuttgart: J. B. Metzler), p. 572. Jenő Fitz, *Die Verwaltung Pannoniens in der Römerzeit*, vol. III. (Budapest: Encyclopedia, 1994), 1182, 1259–1260 (hereafter Fitz, *Verwaltung*) dates the emperor's visits to Poetovio between 314 and 316.

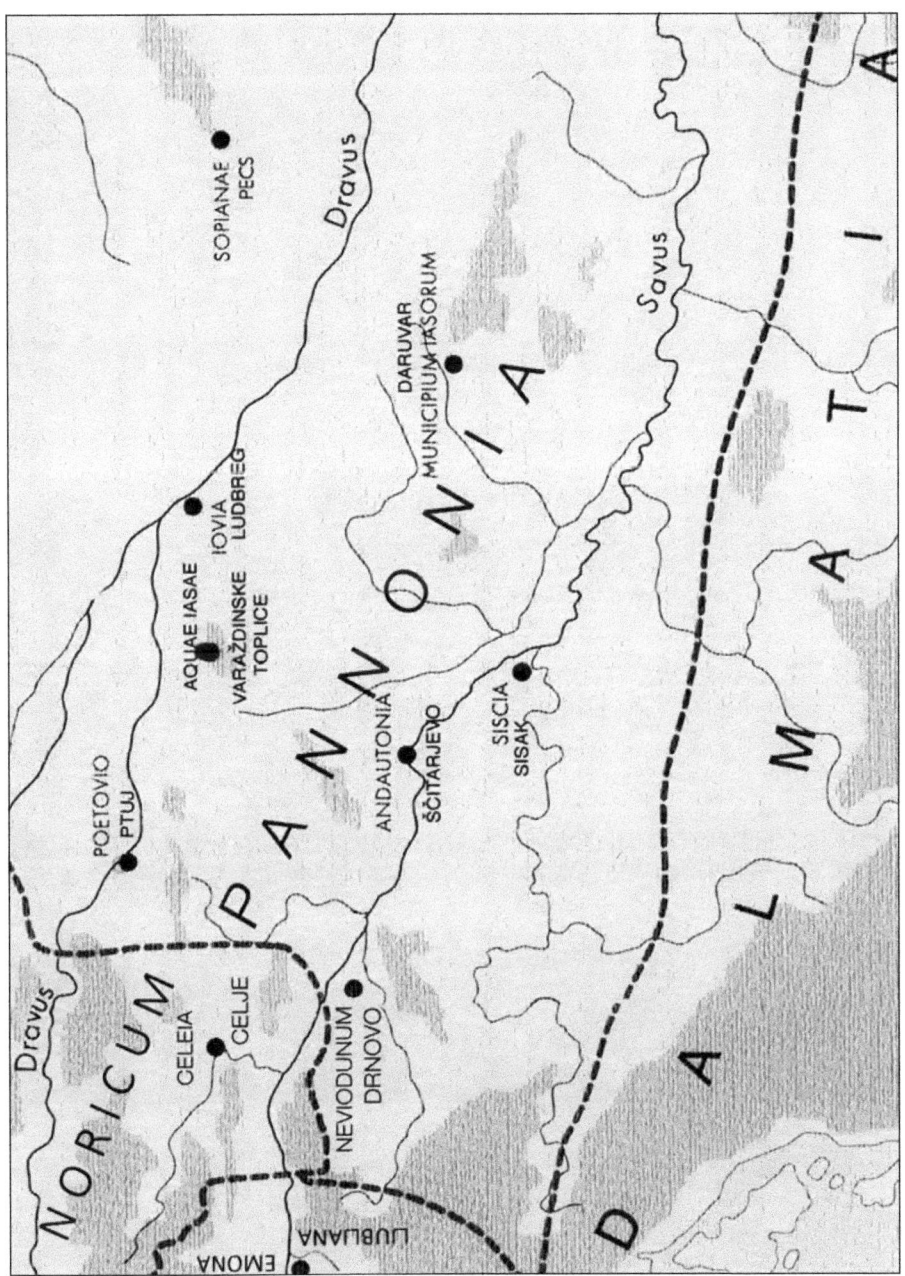

Fig. 1. Map of the location of Aquae Iasae (after Pirnat Spahić 2014, p. 14).

Fig. 2. Inscription to Sol – Apollo, Zavičajni muzej Varaždinske Toplice / Varaždinske Toplice Local History Museum (photo: Nenad Kobasić).

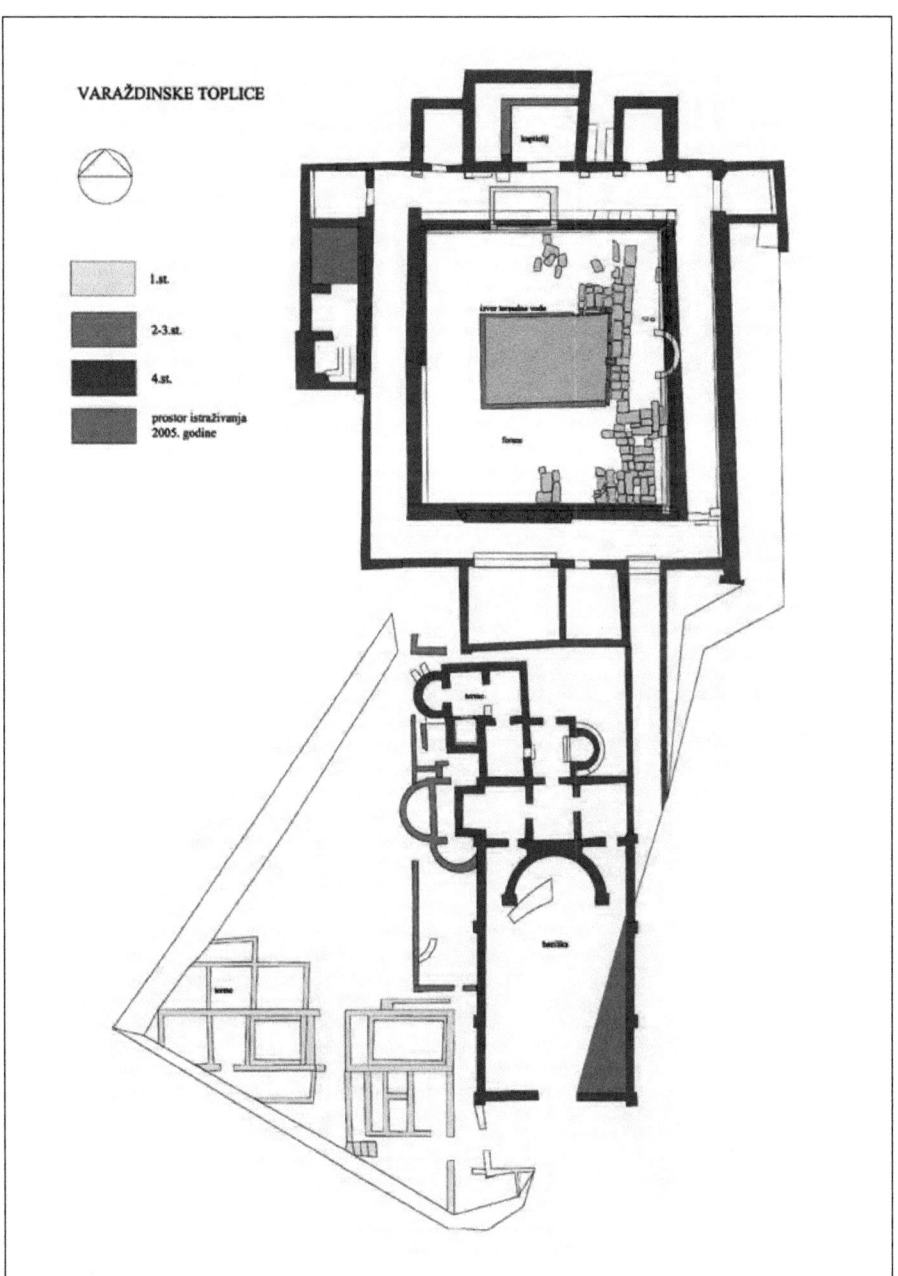

Fig. 3. Plan of Aquae Iasae (after Nemeth-Ehrlich and Kušan Špalj 2011, p. 212).

Fig. 4. Fresco in the narthex of the basilica in Aquae Iasae (photo: Ante Rendić-Miočević).

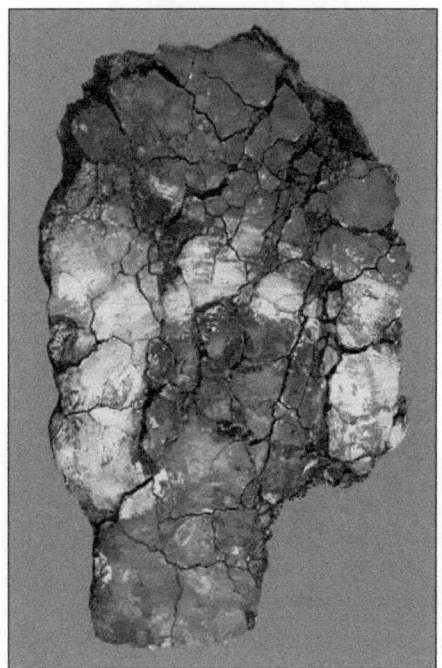

Figure 5. Fresco of a saintly head from the basilica in Aquae Iasae, Arheološki muzej u Zagrebu / The Archaeological Museum in Zagreb (photo: Nenad Kobasić).

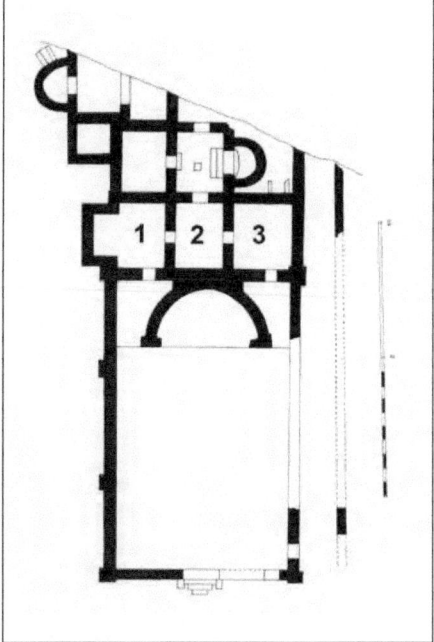

Figure 6. Plan of the basilica in Aquae Iasae in its Constantinian phase (after Migotti 1999, p. 69).

to compel him to spend his own resources on a reconstruction of the town, after it had been consumed in a fire (CIL III 4121). The town never achieved municipal status, it retained its cultic (healing, commercial, and religious) profile instead of donning a political and administrative role.

The merger of religion with trade and healing is a well-known phenomenon in Classical and Late Antiquity, pertaining to pagan and Christian worship alike.[20] It was exactly these circumstances that made Aquae Iasae a religious, trade, and healing site in the region, as is clear from its rich epigraphic and sculptural evidence. The site has produced quite a number of dedicatory and votive inscriptions and reliefs to various gods and divinities dating from the first to fourth centuries. All of this evidence was produced by itinerant visitors who had stopped by Aquae Iasae in search of health and pleasure. They mostly belonged to various strata of the military and civil administrations and had diverse ethnic and provincial background. The share of Oriental visitors among them was negligible, and no Jews have been attested from the findings; the majority originated from the western provinces. Predominant among the gods recorded in the inscriptions were those belonging to the so-called salutary deities in the narrow sense of the word. The most frequently attested are thermal nymphs, addressed as *salutares, augustae,* and *Iasae*. Furthermore we observe the cognate salutary deities Diana-Luna, Diana and Silvanae, as well as Fortuna and Isis-Fortuna, Iuno, Minerva, Polux, Hercules, Apollo, Aesculapius, Hygeia (Salus), Serapis, and finally, Sol syncretised with Apollo.[21]

The inscription celebrating the settlement's renovation reads as follows:

Imp(erator) Caes(ar) Fl(avius) Val(erius) Constantinus Pius Felix Maximus Aug(ustus) / Aquas Iasas olim vi ignis consumptas cum porticibus / et omnib(us) ornamentis ad pristinam faciem restituit / provisione etiam pietatis su(a)e nundinas / ⁵die Solis perpeti anno constituit / curante Val(erio) Catullino v(iro) p(erfectissimo) p(rae)p(osito) p(rovinciae) P(annoniae) Super(ioris).

---

[20] On the relationship between religion and recovery from illness, especially through healing waters, see Vivian Nutton, "From Galen to Alexander, Aspects of Medicine and Medical Practice in Late Antiquity." *Dumbarton Oak Papers* 38 (1984), pp. 1–19; Fikret Yegül, *Baths and Bathing in Classical Antiquity.* (New York – Cambridge, Mass., – London: The MIT Press, 1992), pp. 124–127; Klára Póczy, "Pannonian Cities." In: Alfonz Lengyel - George T. Radan (eds.), *The Archaeology of Roman Pannonia.* (Lexington, KY: University Press of Kentucky, 1998), pp. 239–274; Stacey Lynne McGowen, *Sacred and Civic Stone Monuments of the Northwest Roman Provinces.* (London: BAR 2010), pp. 23–24. On the religious aspect of trading in fairs and markets, see Luuk de Ligt, *Fairs and Markets in the Roman Empire. Economic and Social Aspects of Periodic Trade in a Pre-industrial Society.* (Amsterdam: J. C. Gieben, 1993), pp. 243–255; Peter Salway, *The Oxford Illustrated History of Roman Britain.* (Oxford – New York: Oxford University Press, 1993), p. 194; Sean A. Kingsley, "Late Antique Trade: Research Methodologies and Field Practices." In: Luke Lavan - William Bowden, *Theory and Practice in Late Antique Archaeology.* (Leiden – Boston: Brill, 2003), pp. 113–138; McGowen 2010, 13–14.

[21] See the articles of Rendić-Miočević and Kušan Špalj quoted above.

[Flavius Valerius Constantinus, pious, happy, the greatest, venerable emperor, restored Aquae Iasae, previously consumed by fire, to its erstwhile appearance with porticoes and all decoration, and established, with the provision of his piety, the weekly market on Sunday during the whole year, through the care of Valerius Catullinus, a most excellent man, governor of the province of Pannonia Prima Superior].

This inscription offers a convenient introduction to the religious atmosphere of Aquae Iasae at the time of Emperor Constantine, due to a statement that must have held special significance not only to the adherents of Sol, but equally to Christians: *Provisione etiam pietatis suae nundinas die Solis perpeti anno constituit.* The meaning of *nundinae* here is weekly markets, which were to take place in Aquae Iasae always on the same day, Sunday.[22] Any intentional Christian overtone to this sentence or the inscription on the whole, dated variously to between 314 and 326, has already been rejected in scholarship.[23] Though this issue deserves a more careful and nuanced approach as some religious overtone is indeed suggested by the phrase *pietatis suae*, whether this piety was Solar or Christian remains an open question. It is true that this problem is not at all crucial here, given that in the fourth century the syntagms *dies Solis* and *dies dominica* were both in use alternately, the former imbued with the same meaning for the worshippers of Sol as for Christians, that is: the day for the worship of God.[24] Despite reservations towards the possibility of establishing clear chronological steps in Constantine's religious drive towards Christianity, some details concerning his attitude towards Sunday should still be pinpointed. Thus, it is significant that the ruling of 321 that manumissions, but no other legal business, could take place on *dies Solis*, which was to become the day of rest, were taken as a proof that Christianity was brought into official practice across the Empire by the partisans of the emperor's Christianity.[25] In any case, the inscription's Christian connotations seem convincing, suggesting a fairly consistent development from the second century to the end of Antiquity in establishing Sunday as the day of Christian day of rest,

---

[22] On weekly markets in the Roman world, de Ligt, 117–122.

[23] For Peter Barton, *Die Frühzeit des Christentums in Österreich und Südmitteleuropa bis 788.* (Wien – Köln – Graz: Hermann Böhlau, 1975), p. 54 Constantine's act was spurred by devotion to Sol, but meant no harm to Christians either, while Rajko Bratož, "Christianisierung des Nordadria- und Westbalkanraumes im 4. Jahrhundert. In: Rajko Bratož (ed.), Westillyricum und Nordostitalien in der spätrömischen Zeit." *Situla* 34 (1996), p. 305, n. 19 remarked that the inscription in question lacked any reference to possible Christian structures in Aquae Iasae. Fitz, *Verwaltung,* 1182, 1259–1260 dated the inscription to 314–324 on the basis that it does not mention Pannonia Savia, created in 314–324. Nevertheless, as the most plausible date he offered 314–316, when Constantine sojourned in Poetovio after the war with Licinius.

[24] On Sunday as the day of Sol Invictus and Christianity in the light of the 321 Constantine's edicts, see Henri Dumanie, „Dimanche." In: *Dictionnaire d'archéologie chrétienne et de liturgie.* Henri Leclerc -Fernand Cabrol eds. Vol. 4/1. (Paris: Letouzey et Ané, 1920), pp. 858–994; Barton, 54; Girardet, 70; Flower, "Visions," 292, 298.

[25] Flower, "Visions," 292, 298.

and the week as ultimately a Christian conception of measuring periods of time, despite the pagan origin of the days' names.[26] Therefore, the turn from a pagan to Christian significance of *dies Solis* in its shift from the second to the first day in the week represented an absolute novelty in the Classical world.[27] In tandem with the market taking place in Aquae Iasae on Sunday, it furnishes the inscription with Christian connotations. If Jenő Fitz's dating of the inscription ro 314 or 316 is accepted, it could be well placed in the context of the 313 ruling on the freedom of the Christian religion.

Worship of Sol – Apollo and the «henotheisation» of the Capitolium

The worship of the god Sol in Aquae Iasae is recorded through a single marble votive inscription (fig. 2) and a single statue. At first glance, such modest evidence does not illustrate the true importance of this worship and its special role in the concept of Christ the Saviour as Sol Salutis, which seems conveniently suited within the atmosphere of a spa.[28] Tellingly, in both cases Sol is syncretised with Apollo, in the tradition of a western, "Constantinian" guise.[29] The Sol–Apollo syncretism is proved by a radiate crown on the head of the statue,[30] while the inscription, partially restored, suggests something along the same lines. The inscription (67.5 x 58.5. x 22 cm) was found in the 1960s excavations, built into the pavement of the eastern portico of the forum.[31] The

---

[26] Christian connotations of the phrase *dies Solis* are clearly suggested in authors as early as Justin Martyr and Tertullian. The former, in his First Apology 67, 7 (*S. Justini philosophi et martyris, Apologia prima pro Christianis, Patrologia Graeca* 6. (Turnhout: Brepols, 1978) relates that Sunday (*dies solis*) is the day on which the Christians held their assemblies, because on that day God made the world and on the same day Jesus Christ rose from the dead. Equally, Tertullian in his Apology XVI, 11 (*Tertulliani Liber Apologeticus, Patrologia Latina* 1, ed. Jacques-Paul Migne, Paris 1879) states: *Aeque si diem solis laetitiae indulgemus, alia longe ratione quam religione solis, secundo loco ab eis sumus, qui diem Saturni otio et victui decernunt, exorbitantes et ipsi a Iudaico more, quem ignorant* (). The continuity between Tertullian and Jerome is clear, cf. Jerome, Easter Homily 550, 1, 52 (*In die dominica Pashae, S. Hieronimi presbyteri opera, Pars II, Opera homiletica, Corpus Christianorum, Series Latina* LXXVIII. (Turnhout: Brepols 1958): *Dies dominica, dies resurrectionis, dies Christianorum, dies nostra est. Unde et dominica dicitur: quia in ea Dominus victor ascendit ad Patrem. Quod si a gentilibus dies solis vocatur, et nos hoc libentissime confitemur: hodie enim lux mundi orta est, hodie sol iustitiae ortus est, in cuius pennis est sanitas*. Jerome's words demonstrate the quintessential of merging Sol and Christ in their most conspicuous elements: light, justice, and salvation.

[27] Girardet, 238.

[28] As early as the second century the concept of *salus* as physical health acquired the meaning of metaphorical salvation: Jérôme Carcopino, *Daily Life in Ancient Rome. The People and the City at the Height of the Empire*. Translated from the French by Henry T. Rowell. (London: Penguin, 1991), p. 151. Its fourth-century continuation is best epitomised in the words of Jerome (see note 26). See Rahner, 175–181; Halsberghe, 83, *passim*; Póczy, 33–34.

[29] Girardet, 72; Bergmann; Clauss, 212; Flower, "Visions," 287–288, *passim*. The Sol – Apollo syncretism is omnipresent in the third century: Halsberghe, 110, 113–114.

[30] The statue of Sol – Apollo was found in the 2011 excavations: Kušan Špalj, 2014 b, 100–101.

[31] Rendić-Miočević 1992, 73, n. 36; Migotti 1999, 55.

surface of the stone and the inscription are quite worn out, so the text remains partly unreadable, but a partial restoration of its most important point allows for Sol–Apollo syncretism. It reads:

Soli
[---]ra[--]niis-
simo
[A]pollini
[---

The second line was tentatively restored as *radiantissimo* (who shines most brightly).[32] This remains conjectural, but would conveniently correspond with an added pictorial embellishment to the text. The inscription is adorned by five sunrays streaming obliquely toward the right from the lower part of the letter *o*, as if towards the reader. Very likely, this particular letter was chosen for its association with the shape of the sun. Given that the rays are thinner and cut more sharply than the letters, there should be no doubt that they were incised subsequently, but still within the Roman period, as Aquae Iasae did not survive into the Middle Ages. As there are no clear palaeographic indicators for the inscription's chronology, it can tentatively and rather hypothetically be dated on the basis of the general development of Solar worship, with tentative additional support based on the syncretic nature of the dedication. On balance, the original inscription could be dated to the third century, and its pictorial addition somewhat later, possibly to the turn of the third and fourth centuries.[33] My guess is that this stone might have played a role in the reconstruction of the Capitolium during Constantine's renovation of the whole complex, as will be argued below.

There is some doubt whether the main temple of Aquae Iasae was a true Capitolium (fig. 3). The building initially comprised three detached rooms, with the central one only slightly larger than the two at its sides. The doubt is based on the fact that only dedications to Juno and Minerva were found in the side rooms, no statue or a dedication to Jupiter. Furthermore, the two goddesses were not represented in the typical Capitolium guise, but with attributes pointing to their independent divine character: *Juno regina* in tandem with Fortuna, and *Minerva augusta*. Contrary to standard practice, Juno took the right temple and Minerva the left one. In Constantine's reconstruction, the central temple was considerably enlarged with all three buildings placed under the same roof.[34]

---

[32] Lučić 2014, 234, no. 27, with incorrect statement on the material (sandstone instead of marble).
[33] Halsberghe, IX, 147; Branka Migotti, "Od kulta Sola do kršćanstva u Varaždinskim Toplicama (*Aquae Iasae*)." [From the Cult of Sol to Christianity in Varaždinske Toplice (Aquae Iasae).] *Radovi Filozofskog fakulteta u Zadru* 37 (24) (1998), p. 57. (hereafter Migotti, From the Cult)
[34] Gorenc and Vikić, 39; Nemeth-Ehrlich, 11–13; Migotti, From the Cult, 59–62.

Evidently, the idea behind this procedure was to stress the importance of one god over those in the side temples: Constantine's conception of *summus deus* or *summa divinitas* comes straight to mind.³⁵ However, no trace of Jupiter has ever been found in the central temple, nor has any trace of the worship of Jupiter been identified anywhere at the site.³⁶ With this in mind, would it be too bold to suggest the worship of Sol in the central temple? If one's answer is to the affirmative, the question remains; until what point was such worship able to continue? The researchers of the site had previously been convinced that the traces of Jupiter in the central temple have simply failed to appear until now, while recently, with the find of the Sol Apollo statue, they have opened discussion on the importance of this god to the religious life of Aquae Iasae without, however, discarding the possibility that the worship of Jupiter was conducted in the Capitolium.³⁷ On balance, they do not see Sol–Apollo, for all his importance, as a possible substitute for Jupiter. According to the archaeological evidence, both the statue of, and the inscription to, Apollo–Sol could have been destroyed in the fire preceding Constantine's refurbishing of Aquae Iasae and ended up as discarded material dumped in remote spots during the works of reconstruction. Thus, while the inscription was built in the pavement of the forum's eastern portico, the statue was buried with a lot of other discarded stones in the ground north of the main pool.³⁸ This has been taken as a proof that the worship of Sol was extinguished by the time of Constantine, with even a possible suggestion that his votive monuments were deliberately destroyed in the course of the reconstruction works.³⁹ Contrary to this, the possibility should still be allowed that both the statue, and especially the inscription, survived through Constantine's reconstruction of the settlement. Owing to Constantine's inscription on the renovation of Aquae Iasae after its collapse in a fire, all archaeological evidence of destruction has customarily been ascribed to this event.⁴⁰ Yet, Aquae Iasae saw some reconstructions in the second half of the fourth century, and there are hints in scholarship about the uncertainties of the phases of destruction and renovation in the settlement during that time.⁴¹ The inscription to Sol–Apollo could have been placed in the pavement of the eastern portico in the second half

---

35   Sordi; Girardet, 239.
36   Migotti, From the Cult, 59; Dora Kušan Špalj, "Reconstruction of the Area Around the Natural Thermal Spring – Rituals and Utilization." In: Pirnat Spahić 2014,119.(hereafter: Kušan Špalj 2014 c).
37   Gorenc and Vikić, 39; Nemeth-Ehrlich, 11; Kušan Špalj 214 c, 118.
38   On the inscription see notes 31 and 32, and on the statue see Ehrlich Nemeth and Kušan Špalj 2014, 45; Kušan Špalj 2014 b, 99.
39   Kušan Špalj 2014 b, 101. The latter is unlikely with regard to Constantine's general attitude towards pagan religion (see notes 6 and 7)
40   Gorenc and Vikić, 40–41; Nemeth-Ehrlich, 11; Ehrlich Nemeth - Kušan Špalj 2014, 48.
41   Gorenc and Vikić, 41–43; Ehrlich Nemeth - Kušan Špalj 2014, 40–45

of the fourth century, especially in view of the renovations of the basilica at that time.[42] The find-spot of the Sol–Apollo statue is likewise problematic in terms of the chronology of its collapse. It was found in the collapsed layers to the north of the pool, that is, in the area behind the north wall of the pool that was most vulnerable and exposed to landslides.[43] On account of all this, we should remain open to the possibility that the two monuments to Sol–Apollo survived the fire mentioned in Constantine's inscription, and were, either together or singly, placed in the central temple of the Capitolium, standing for the main deity in keeping with a henotheistic attitude. This hypothesis is perhaps more likely for the inscription than the statue, as it would be very tempting to connect the adding of sun-rays with a new role of the inscription, standing perhaps for the *divinitas* or *summus deus* of Constantine's religious vocabulary. Although this hypothesis remains highly tentative at this stage, it should be remembered that a triad composed of Sol–Apollo, Juno, and Minerva is known from the Syrian context in the period of Emperor Elagabalus (218–222), with Elagabal as the supreme God.[44]

From Bath Basilica to Christian Church

The connection between thermal sites and Christian buildings is attested in the archaeological record at two levels: a – adaptation of thermal complexes for Christian purposes, especially as concerns baptismal infrastructure; b – a continuous use of the existing baths, or even the building of new ones, adapted to the needs and mentality of Christian communities.[45]

In Croatian archaeology, it is commonplace that the *basilica thermarum*, the most spacious N-S oriented room of the baths, was turned into a Christian church in the second half of the fourth century, following the baths' alleged disuse.[46] Contrary to this "canon", I argue that the basilica was probably used as a church already in the time of Constantine, with the baths partially still in use and, furthermore, the worship in the Capitolium still taking place.

---

[42] Gorenc and Vikić, 37–38; Migotti, From the Cult, 73–77; Ehrlich Nemeth - Kušan Špalj 2014, 39–40.

[43] Ehrlich Nemeth - Kušan Špalj 2014, 43. On natural destruction and renovation in spa settlements, see the example of Bath / *Aquae Sulis*, Barry C. Burnham and John Wacher, *The Small Towns of Roman Britain*.(Berkeley – Los Angeles: University of California Press, 1990), p. 175.

[44] Turcan, 180. Another unorthodox Orientalizing triad, composed of Jupiter Heliopolitanus, Venus and (probably) Mercury, was established in Carnuntum, the capital of Pannonia Superior, with the peak of worship in the Severan period: Manfred Kandler *et al.*, „Carnuntum." In: Marjeta Šašel Kos - Peter Scherrer (eds.), "The Autonomous Towns of Noricum and Pannonia II." *Situla* 42 (2004), p. 59.

[45] Migotti, From the Cult, 65; Giuliano Volpe, Caterina Annese, Pasquale Favia, "Terme e complessi paleocristiani. Il caso di San Giusto. In: Marie Guérin-Beauvois- Jean-Marie Martin (eds.), *Bains curatifs et bains hygiéniques en Italie de l'antiquité au Moyen Age*. (Rome: École française de Rome, 2007.)

[46] See note 42.

According to the initial hypothesis, the most spacious room of the baths, the N-S oriented *basilica thermarum*, was, during Constantine's renovation, given an interior apse raised 20 cm above the remaining floor, but this would not alter the basilica's use and function (fig. 3). Such a shift would have happened only in the second half of the fourth century, when a narthex-like adjacency was attached to the building's southern facade, and the interior redecorated, with two frescoes still surviving. Faint traces of one, showing a fragment of a stylised paradisiac fence (a red saltire cross on a background of pale yellow with green nuances), are still visible on the south narthex wall (fig. 4). The other one, featuring a slightly tilted nimbate head of an anonymous saint with beard, moustache, and fairly short hair, had fallen from the collapsed ceiling of the main room and was found in the fill (fig. 5). My arguments for interpreting Constantine's restructuring of the bath basilica in terms of its «Christianisation» rests on several grounds: the adding of a raised apse, the inner arrangement of the whole thermal complex, and the juxtaposing of the two frescoes. With the raised apse newly added, the thermal basilica should have experienced a shift in its basic use as a venue for social gatherings, leisure, and sports recreation. The most plausible guess seems to be that it was adapted for religious gatherings presided over by a chairman in the raised apse serving as the presbytery; judicial or administrative events do not seem likely, given that Aquae Iasae was not an autonomous town. On balance, it can be presumed that the raised apse provided the building in question with the capacity to hold Christian services, either exclusively or even alternately with some other function, which would be completely in line with Emperor Constantine's complex religious affiliations and his tolerant religious policies.[47] A further argument for this is the fact that in the process of restructuring the three small thermal rooms immediately north of the basilica, the two presumed apodyteria and a space between them became more detached from the rest of the baths. Some of the previously existing doors in two of them (1 and 3) were walled up so that the three rooms communicated with the northern section of the baths only through the opening in room 2, while at the same time the two more important rooms 1 and 3 remained connected to the basilica by means of doors (fig. 6). Their function can tentatively be interpreted as something similar to *pastophoria*.[48] On balance, the basilica as a whole, with the mentioned northern adjacencies, became a unit detached from the rest of the thermal complex. It is important to notice that when the narthex was added to the southern facade in the second half of the fourth century, the northern rooms remained unchanged both in ground plans and in terms of internal communication. Therefore, the adding of the narthex can safely be considered as the

---

[47] See notes 6 and 7. A suggestive coincidence is found from almost a century later when John Chrysostom (344–407) for political reasons celebrated Mass in a room of one of the Constantinople's baths instead of the Cathedral: Dumaine 1925, 63.

[48] Migotti, From the Cult.

second Christian phase of the Iasean thermal basilica. Finally, the two frescoes, initially both dated to the second half of the fourth century,[49] also seem to bolster the theory of two Christian phases. In spite of all uncertainties of chronologies based on art-historical criteria, and notwithstanding the fact that several artists with different styles and capacities often worked simultaneously on smaller surfaces,[50] the two frescoes from Aquae Iasae call for an interpretation based on chronology, not only because of different styles, but also on account of their phased architectural settings.[51] Soft and melancholy features of the saintly head show an air of a classical or classicizing style, which is theoretically ascribable to several so-called classicizing renaissances of fourth century painting, starting in the time of Constantine and closing with the so-called Theodosian revival.[52] Nevertheless, the Iasean fresco significantly differs from the majority of Pannonian fresco portraits of the later fourth century, even those that are maintained to be examples of classicising, such as those from Sopianae. [53] In spite of some common traces, such as the gentle bow of the head, the classicism of the fresco discussed here differs from those from Sopianae in that the latter are characterised by a more expressionistic air, certain schematism, light-shadow effects, and dark contours. As a matter of fact, the Iasean fresco has more in common with utterly classicizing third century faces from the Hypogeum of the Aurelii in Rome than with any of the fourth-century Pannonian paintings.[54] Therefore, the fresco of a saint from Aquae Iasae should be dated to the early rather than the later fourth century, thus supporting the idea of Constantine's phase in the «Christianisation» of the thermal basilica. On the other hand, the fresco still *in situ* in the subsequently added narthex corresponds to the second Christian phase (second half of the fourth century) of the basilica not only on the basis of its position, but also in terms of style and execution. It takes the motif of a saltire cross in the form of two obliquely crossed red lines on a background of pale yellow with greenish nuances,

---

[49] Branka Vikić-Belančić, "Elementi ranog kršćanstva u sjevernoj Hrvatskoj." [Les éléments du christianisme primitif en Croatie septentrionale/] *Arheološki vestnik* 29 (1978), p. 590.

[50] Krisztina Hudák, "The Iconographical Program of the Wallpaintings in the Saint Peter and Paul Chamber of Sopianae (Pécs)." *Mitteilungen zur Christlichen Archäologie* 15 (2009), p. 62, n. 57. (hereafter: Hudák, "The Iconographical Program.")

[51] Branka Migotti, *Evidence for Christianity in Roman Southern Pannonia (Northern Croatia). A catalogue of finds and sites.* (London: BAR, 1997), pp. 33–35. (hereafter Migotti, *Evidence for Christianity*). On the difficulties in attributing fourth- century frescoes to the period of Constantine, and the importance of an individual and topographic approach in establishing such chronologies, Fabrizio Bisconti, "Affreschi estremi. La fine della pittura nelle catacombe Romane." *Mitteilungen zur Christlichen Archäologie* 20 (2014), pp.37–38.

[52] Wladimiro Dorigo, *Pittura tardoromana.* (Milano: Feltrinelli, 1966), p. 67, *passim*; Harald Mielsch, "Zur stadtrömischen Malerei des 4. Jahrhunderts n. Chr." *Mitteilungen des Deutschen Archäologischen Instituts, Römische Abteilung* 85 (1978), pp. 151–207. Hudák, "The Iconographical Program," p. 52, n. 21; 62, n. 57.

[53] Hudák, "The Iconographical Program," 47–76.

[54] On the frescoes from the Aurelii Hypogeum see Dorigo, 103–106, especially fig. 75.

and was evidently part of a continuous line of equal patterns representing lattice rails and symbolising the paradisiac fence. Its late date is suggested by the rendering through unassuming schematic outlines and a notable simplification of the well-known motif.[55]

Evidence seems to indicate that Christian services were taking place in Aquae Iasae already under the reign of Constantine, simultaneously with the worship in the Capitolium and with the baths still in use. In addition to the Constantinian inscription on the renovation of the settlement, Aquae Iasae has another important verse inscription, composed in hexameters and iambs, from the same period that tellingly conveys the religious and intellectual atmosphere of the settlement. In a sophisticated religious, philosophical, and poetic language, it addresses the higher spirits of nature, with water as the supreme power. The inscription has not yet been fully published, but commentators detected a blend of pagan and Christian components in its subtle intertwining of metaphors and allegories.[56] In principle, there is nothing unexpected in identifying such peaceful religious coexistence within the lofty Constantinian intellectual atmosphere of the Aquae Iasae spa. What makes its case special is the fact that Constantinian church architecture can hardly ever be identified outside important centers of Christianity. Poor in early Christian architecture, Pannonia province falls quite far from these centers.[57] On the basis of the archaeological evidence for the worship of Sol–Apollo, one may hypothesize that Aquae Iasae is one of the settlements where local Christianity stemmed from the cult of Sol Invictus, rather than from Judaism and/or oriental mystery cults. If the reconstruction of the Iasean religious architecture suggested in this paper is correct, the early appearance of Christianity, its coexistence with the cult of Sol Invictus and the worship of pagan deities are to be ascribed to Constantine's religion and his general tolerance in religious matters.

---

[55] It corresponds to the so-called green and red linear style typical of third-century Christian painting, but revived in the second half of the fourth century mainly in the provinces: Dorigo, 227. On the parallels from Sopianae, see Krisztina Hudák - Levente Nagy, *A Fine and Private Place. Discovering the Early Christian Cemetery of Sopianae/Pécs*. Translated by Marianne Sághy. (Pécs: Örökség Ház Kft. 2009), pp. 34–37.

[56] Bruna Kuntić-Makvić, Ante Rendić-Miočević, Marina Šegvić, and Igor Krajcar, "Integracija i vizualna prezentacija ulomaka monumentalnog natpisa iz V. Toplica." [Integration and visual presentation of the fragments of a metrical inscription from Varaždinske Toplice.] In: Jacqueline Balen- Marina Šimek (eds.), *Arheologija varaždinskog kraja i srednjeg Podravlja / Archaeology of the Varaždin Region and the Middle Drava Area*. (Varaždin: Gradski muzej Varaždin, 2012), pp. 285–295.

[57] On Constantinian church building see Guntram Koch, *Early Christian Art and Architecture. An Introduction* Translated by John Bowden. (London: SCM Press, 1996), pp. 20–28; Bisconti 2005; Paolo Liverani, "L'edilizia costantiniana a Roma: il Laterano, il Vaticano, Santa Croce in Gerusalemme." In: Donati - Gentili, 74–81. On Pannonian early Christian architecture see Migotti, *Evidence for Christianity*; Dorottya Gáspár, *Christianity in Roman Pannonia. An Evaluation of Early Christian Finds and Sites from Hungary*. (London: BAR, 2002).

CONVERSION AS CONVERGENCE: GREGORY THE GREAT CONFRONTING PAGAN AND JEWISH INFLUENCES IN ANGLO-SAXON CHRISTIANITY

Miriam Adan Jones

In a famous letter written in July 601, Gregory the Great offers two pieces of advice to the party of Roman missionaries working in Anglo-Saxon England, regarding how they are to deal with the pagan past of their (prospective) converts. First, with regard to places of worship, Gregory proposes that pagan temples ought to be rid of their idols and consecrated as churches; second, with regard to religious celebration, that the pagan custom of ritual slaughter and feasting should be retained with certain adjustments.[1] Particularly striking is the advice to include in the festivities the building of huts (*tabernacula*), from the boughs of trees, in which the worshipers may sojourn while feasting at the site of their converted church.[2] Far from being a concession to English pagan usage, this seems to have been inspired by the Jewish festival of *Sukkot*, the feast of tabernacles, as described in the Old Testament and practiced by early-medieval Jews.[3]

Gregory's letter, addressed to Abbot Mellitus and meant to be relayed by him to the missionaries, goes on to argue that the Anglo-Saxons will be more receptive to Christianity if the change is incremental: "For there is no doubt that it is impossible to cut away everything at the same time from hardened minds, because anyone who strives

---

[1] *S. Gregorii Magni Registrum epistularum*, ed. Dag Ludvig Norberg, 2 vols, Corpus Christianorum Series Latina (hereafter CCSL) 140, 140A (Turnhout: Brepols, 1982), XI.56 (hereafter *Reg. ep.*).

[2] It is not clear whether Gregory's advice was ever put into practice. David Wilson, *Anglo-Saxon Paganism* (London; New York: Routledge, 1992), 29–43, finds no indication in the literature that pagan sites of worship were converted into churches. Flora Spiegel, "The *tabernacula* of Gregory the Great and the Conversion of Anglo-Saxon England," *Anglo-Saxon England* 36 (November 14, 2007): 6–10 (hereafter Spiegel, "The *tabernacula*"), on the other hand, offers archaeological and literary evidence that Gregory's instructions to construct *tabernacula* may have been carried out in at least some cases.

[3] Spiegel, "The *tabernacula*," 4–5.

to ascend to the highest place, relies on ladders or steps. He is not lifted up in one leap."[4] But in other letters Gregory's attitude is markedly different: "hunt down the worship of idols, and overturn the building of temples" (*Idolorum cultus insequere, fanorum aedificia euerte*), he writes to King Æthelbert of Kent only a few weeks earlier.[5] This harsher approach accords better with what we know of Gregory's missionary strategy in other regions: where paganism is found in Sicily, Sardinia, and Francia, we find him encouraging bishops and aristocrats alike to repress it forcefully.[6] There is also support for the use of force to aid Christianization in Gregory's theological works: in his *Moralia*, Gregory compares the power wielded by temporal rulers to the strength of the rhinoceros—just as the rhinoceros breaks up the earth enabling it to be cultivated, the Christian ruler crushes the wicked and allows the church to flourish.[7] This makes Gregory's leniency towards English paganism in his letter to Mellitus surprising.

Surprising also is his deliberate importation of a Jewish custom into the English context. Not only because there was no precedent for such an appropriation, but because Gregory would normally balk at the idea of Christians applying the letter of the Law to themselves in such a manner. His preference for a spiritual understanding of the Hebrew scriptures expresses itself throughout his exegetical works. An extended argument for the spiritual reading of the Old Testament opens his commentary on the Song of Songs. To heed only the literal sense, he writes, is like noticing only the colors

---

[4] "Nam duris mentibus simul omnia abscidere impossibile esse non dubium est, quia is qui summum locum ascendere nititur gradibus uel passibus, non autem saltibus eleuatur." *Reg. ep.*, XI.56; John R.C. Martyn, trans., *The Letters of Gregory the Great*, Mediaeval Sources in Translation 40 (Toronto: Pontifical Institute of Mediaeval Studies, 2004), 803 (hereafter Martyn, *Letters*).

[5] *Reg. ep.* XI.37; Martyn, *Letters*, 783; George Demacopoulos, "Gregory the Great and the Pagan Shrines of Kent," *Journal of Late Antiquity* 1, no. 2 (2008): 353–69 (hereafter Demacopoulos, "Gregory and the Pagan Shrines"), suggests Gregory's letter to Æthelbert should not be read as literally instructing the king to oversee the destruction of pagan shrines. Its focus, he reasons, is on the king's spiritual formation, rather than on his people's conversion, and this document therefore cannot be read as a programmatic statement of Gregory's wishes for the Anglo-Saxon mission. I remain unconvinced that Gregory never meant his instructions in this letter to be followed.

[6] Maymó i Capdevila, "Gregory the Great and Religious Otherness: Pagans in a Christian Italy," *Studia Patristica* 48 (2010): 328–330 (hereafter Capdevila, "Gregory and Religious Otherness"); Robert A. Markus, "Gregory the Great and a Papal Missionary Strategy," in *The Mission of the Church and the Propagation of the Faith: Papers Read at the Seventh Summer Meeting and the Eighth Winter Meeting of the Ecclesiastical History Society*, ed. G.J. Cuming, Studies in Church History 6 (Cambridge: Cambridge University Press, 1970), 31–32 (hereafter Markus, "Papal Missionary Strategy").

[7] *S. Gregorii Magni Moralia in Job*, ed. Marcus Adriaen, 3 vols., Corpus Christianorum Series Latina 143, 143A, 143B (Turnhout: Brepols, 1979), xxxi, 4-7 (hereafter *Moralia*); David Hipshon, "Gregory the Great's 'Political Thought,'" *The Journal of Ecclesiastical History* 53, no. 3 (2002): 441; Carole E. Straw, "Gregory's Politics: Theory and Practice," in *Gregorio Magno E Il Suo Tempo. XIX Incontro di studiosi dell'antichità cristiana in collaborazione con l'École Française de Rome, Roma, 9-12 Maggio 1990*, vol. 1 (Rome: Institutum Patristicum "Augustinianum," 1991), 56–57.

of a painting and paying no attention to the objects it depicts. Changing the metaphor, he compares the literal sense to the husk in which the kernel of the spiritual sense is hidden; to approach the text only in a literal way is to eat the husks as animals do.[8] Turning from his exegesis to his correspondence, we find Gregory working to "prevent encroachments of Jews and Judaism on Christianity" and "respond[ing] vehemently to reports of Judaizing among Christians."[9] In several letters he renounces Jewish ownership of Christian slaves, because this situation provides "opportunity for simple souls to be slaves [...] to the Jewish superstition" (*occasionem, ut superstitioni iudaicae simplices animae [...] deseruirent*).[10] In a letter to the citizens of Rome, Gregory objects to Christians observing the Sabbath, a practice he connects to the coming of the antichrist who "compels the people to live like Jews [...] so that he may recall the external rite of the law and subject the perfidy of the Jews to himself" (*iudaizare populum compellit, ut exteriorem ritum legis reuocet et sibi iudaeorum perfidiam subdat*).[11] Gregory impresses upon his addressees that "after the appearance of the grace of almighty God, our Lord Jesus Christ, the precepts of the law that were said figuratively could not be observed to the letter" (*postquam gratia omnipotentis dei domini nostri iesu christi apparuit, praecepta legis, quae per figuram dicta sunt, iuxta litteram seruari non possunt*).[12]

Given that in his other writing Gregory tends to resist pagan and Jewish influences on the Christian church, his suggestion in his letter to Mellitus, that a space be created for such influences within the life of the new English church, requires explanation.

July 601: A Turning Point

Scholars have sought that explanation in the context of the letter. Dated 18 July 601, it is Gregory's latest surviving statement on the English mission. That mission had been underway for several years by the time the letter was written; the missionary

---

[8] *Sancti Gregorii Magni Expositiones in canticum canticorum in librum primum regum*, ed. Patrick Verbraken, CC SL 144 (Turnhout: Brepols, 1963), §4 (hereafter *In canticum canticorum*). On Gregory's exegetical method, see Stephan C. Kessler, "Gregor der Grosse und seine Theorie der Exegese: Die Epistula ad Leandrum," in *L'esegesi dei padri latini: Dalle origini a Gregorio Magno: XXVIII Incontro di studiosi dell'antichità cristiana*, vol. 2, Studia Ephemeridis "Augustinianum" 68 (Rome: Institutum Patristicum Augustinianum, 2000), 691–700; Stephan C. Kessler, "Gregory the Great: A Figure of Tradition and Transition in Church Exegesis," in *Hebrew Bible, Old Testament: The History of Its Interpretation: Volume 1: From the Beginnings to the Middle Ages (Until 1300), Part 2: The Middle Ages*, ed. Magne Sæbø (Göttingen: Vandenhoeck & Ruprecht, 1996), 135–47; Robert A. Markus, *Signs and Meanings: World and Text in Ancient Christianity* (Liverpool: Liverpool University Press, 1996), 48–51 (Markus, *Signs and Meanings*).

[9] Jeremy Cohen, *Living Letters of the Law: Ideas of the Jew in Medieval Christianity* (University of California Press, 1999), 78 (hereafter Cohen, *Living Letters*).

[10] *Reg. ep.*, IV.21; Martyn, *Letters*, 303.

[11] *Reg. ep.*, XIII.1; Martyn, *Letters*, 822.

[12] *Reg. ep.*, XIII.1; Martyn, *Letters*, 822.

Augustine and his party had arrived in Kent and been welcomed there by King Æthelbert and Queen Bertha in 597. In the spring of 601, the priest Laurence and monk Peter returned to Rome from the mission field with news, and Gregory sent them on their way again in June, after what appears to have been a short stay of only a few weeks.[13] They departed with a second party of missionaries under the leadership of Abbot Mellitus. This party carried, among other things, a *pallium* for Augustine, instructions for the organization of two archdioceses in Britain, and letters to Æthelbert and Bertha, praising their reception of the first mission party and exhorting them to continue Christianizing their subjects.[14] These letters are dated 22 June. The letter to Mellitus, which strikes such a discordant note with Gregory's policy until then, follows less than a month later, while Mellitus is still "in Francia" (*in franciis*). Robert Markus and others have seen it as a belated response to Gregory's receipt of news from the mission field: once the flurry of activity involved in sending off the new missionary party had passed, Gregory had the chance to reconsider the information he had received from Peter and Laurence, and came to realize its implications for his missionary approach.[15] The insight gained by Gregory tends to be envisioned as political in nature: the authority of the papacy in Anglo-Saxon England was somewhat less, and the court of Æthelbert somewhat more reluctant, than anticipated. Since Gregory was unable to gain the necessary support from the local aristocracy, it is argued, he was unable to use his preferred coercive methods, and had to advocate a milder strategy.[16]

But does Gregory's advice to Mellitus really represent the abandonment of his usual principles for the sake of expediency?[17] Gregory was not only an administrator, but

---

[13] Markus, "Papal Missionary Strategy," 33.

[14] To Bertha: XI.35, to Æthelbert: XI.37, to Augustine: XI.36 and XI.39. Letters were sent at the same time to several bishops the missionaries would encounter on their way through Gaul (XI.34, XI.38, XI.40, XI.41, XI.42 and XI.45), Kings Theoderic (XI.47), Theodebert (XI.50), and Clothar (XI.51) and Queen Brunichild (XI.48).

[15] Markus, "Papal Missionary Strategy," 35–36; Robert A. Markus, "Augustine and Gregory the Great," in *St Augustine and the Conversion of England* (Stroud: Sutton, 1999), 47; Ian Wood, "The Mission of Augustine of Canterbury to the English," *Speculum* 69, no. 1 (1994): 12 (hereafter Wood, "Mission of Augustine"); Fabrizio Conti, "Gregorio Magno e gli Anglosassoni. Considerazioni sullo sviluppo di una strategia missionaria," *Studi romani: Rivista trimestrale dell'Istituto di studi romani* 53, no. 3–4 (2005): 479–480 (hereafter Conti, "Gregorio Magno e gli Anglosassoni").

[16] Robert A. Markus, "Gregory the Great's Pagans," in *Belief and Culture in the Middle Ages: Studies Presented to Henry Mayr-Harting*, ed. Richard Gameson and Henrietta Leyser (Oxford; New York: Oxford University Press, 2001), 31–32; Capdevila, "Gregory and Religious Otherness," 331; Spiegel, "The *tabernacula*," 12.

[17] Clare Stancliffe, "Kings and Conversion: Some Comparisons between the Roman Mission to England and Patrick's to Ireland," *Frühmittelalterliche Studien* 14 (1980): 60 n.12, points in a helpful direction by noting that Gregory often pairs "two apparently contradictory approaches" because to him they are not contradictory, but complementary. The two letters do not represent a complete change of mind, but rather a shifting of focus. Conti, "Gregorio Magno e gli Anglosassoni," 476–477 makes a similar point.

also a theologian with a deep concern for harmony between faith and action.[18] In order to properly understand Gregory's mildness in the letter to Mellitus and its motivations, we must therefore consider his missionary strategy in Anglo-Saxon England against the backdrop of his general understanding of conversion and spiritual formation.[19]

Gregory's Theology of Spiritual Progress

Gregory's views on conversion and spiritual progress are intimately tied to his ideas about human nature and the processes by which God draws human beings to himself. His missionary strategy and pastoral approaches are informed by the dealings of God with mankind from the beginning of the world to its end, as described in the Old and New Testaments. Gregory's understanding of the human condition begins with the fall of Adam and the expulsion of man from Paradise. Ever since, humanity has been blind, cold, and lost. It chases after empty philosophies, false gods, and material goods.[20] But divine grace seeks humanity out, meeting human beings where they are, condescending to speak to them in the terms of their limited and wayward hearts and minds:

> Divine speech is communicated to the cold and numb soul by means of enigmas and in a hidden manner instills in her the love she does not know by means of what she knows. Allegory provides the soul set far below God with a kind of crane whereby she may be lifted to God. If enigmas are placed between God and the soul, when the soul recognizes something of her own in the language of the enigmas, through the meaning of this language she understands something that is not her own and by means of earthly languages hopes for eternal things.[21]

---

[18] Carole E. Straw, *Gregory the Great: Perfection in Imperfection*, Transformations of the Classical Heritage 14 (Berkeley: University of California Press, 1988), 49–50; Mirjam Schambeck, "Actio und Contemplatio - Überlegungen zu einem Modell bei Gregor dem Großen," *Wissenschaft und Weisheit* 62, no. 1 (1999): 44–46.

[19] Demacopoulos, "Gregory and the Pagan Shrines" presents Gregory's English correspondence against the backdrop of the *Regula Pastoralis*. That the English mission should not be seen apart from Gregory's work as a theologian is also noted by Claude Dagens, *Saint Grégoire le Grand: culture et expérience chrétiennes* (Paris: Etudes Augustiniennes, 1977), 311 (hereafter: Dagens, Saint Grégoire).

[20] *In canticum canticorum*, §1; *Homiliae in Evangelia*, ed. Raymond Étaix (Turnhout: Brepols, 1999), I.2.1 (hereafter *Homiliae in Evangelia*); *Moralia* V.34, VIII.30, IX.33.

[21] "Idcirco per quaedam enigmata sermo divinus animae terpenti et frigidae loquitur et de rebus, quas novit, latenter insinuat ei amorem, quem non novit. Allegoria enim animae longe a deo positae quasi quandam machinam facit, ut per ilam levetur ad deum. Interpositis quippe enigmatibus, dum quiddam in verbis cognoscit, quod suum est, in sensu verborum intellegit, quod non est suum, et per terrena verba separatur a terra." *In canticum canticorum*, §1-2; Mark DelCogliano, trans., *Gregory the Great on the Song of Songs*, Cistercian Studies Series 244 (Liturgical Press, 2012), 109.

Thus by God's speaking the covenant people of Israel is formed, and the books of the Old Testament are written. Jews live by a greater light than pagans: they worship the true God, listening to his words. But their knowledge of God is still limited, the bliss and intimacy of Paradise are not yet regained. Though they have the words of Scripture as their guide, they remain blind to the spiritual meaning of the text, which for Gregory points to Christ.[22] For with the coming of Christ into the world, the union of God with humanity is achieved. Now a direct knowledge of God becomes possible, and the church progresses with confidence towards the perfection that is its eschatological hope.[23] The spiritual history of the world can thus be divided into three stages: paganism, Judaism, Christianity. And this succession is not accidental, but reflects the gradual increase of revelation as divinely ordained. The whole of history leads up to the perfect union of God and man, and each step of the journey is undertaken with this goal in mind.

This movement of humanity as a whole is mirrored in each person's ascent from carnal to contemplative life, a process described over and over again in Gregory's works. He uses many metaphors to describe its stages, for instance the church as a house into which individuals enter, progressing through the rooms one by one as they master the virtues of faith, hope and love, or devotion as movement, with those who do not believe standing still, while immature believers walk, the mature run, and the perfect sprint following Christ.[24] The boundaries between these categories are not hard and fast. It is often very difficult to tell just to whom Gregory is referring, as the images are constantly changing, the numbers of categories ranging from two (perfect/imperfect; elect/reprobate; spiritual/carnal), through threes and fours, to nine in one homily.[25]

---

[22] Gregory believes the problem with Judaism is a failure to progress from the level of the letter to the spirit and to recognize the fulfillment of the Old Testament in Christ. Although he wants contemporary Jews to be allowed to practice their religion in peace, he continues to hope for and work towards their conversion to Christianity. Cohen, *Living Letters*, 73–94; Darius Oliha Makuja, "Gregory the Great, Roman Law and the Jews: Seeking 'True' Conversions," *Sacris Erudiri* 48 (2009): 52–61, 70–72; G. R. Evans, *The Thought of Gregory the Great* (Cambridge; New York: Cambridge University Press, 1986), 135–138. See also Jean Stern, "Israel et l'église dans l'exégèse de saint Grégoire le Grand," in *L'esegesi dei padri latini: Dalle origini a Gregorio Magno: XXVIII Incontro di studiosi dell'antichità cristiana*, vol. 2, Studia Ephemeridis "Augustinianum" 68 (Rome: Institutum Patristicum Augustinianum, 2000), 676–89.

[23] Michael Fiedrowicz, *Das Kirchenverständnis Gregors des Grossen: eine Untersuchung seiner exegetischen und homiletischen Werke*, Römische Quartalschrift für christliche Altertumskunde und Kirchengeschichte, Supplementheft 50 (Freiburg: Herder, 1995), Chapters 4 and 9 (hereafter Fiedrowicz, *Das Kirchenverständnis Gregors des Grossen*).

[24] *In canticum canticorum*, §25-26.

[25] *Homiliae in Evangelia*, II.34.11; Bruno Judic, "Hiérarchie angélique et hiérarchie ecclésiale chez Grégoire le Grand," in *Hiérarchie et stratification sociale dans l'Occident médiéval (400-1100)*, ed. François Bougard, Dominique Iogna-Prat, and Régine Le Jan, Collection haut Moyen Âge 6 (Turnhout: Brepols, 2008), 41–43.

Gregory's main concern is not exactly where a person is on that great continuum between perdition and perfection, but that he should be making constant progress. To this end, both discipline and teaching must be tailored to fit the needs of the situation.[26]

> Now the preacher should realise that he must not overtax the mind of his hearer, lest, so to speak, the string of the soul be strained too much and snap. ... Wherefore, Paul says: *I could not speak to you as unto spiritual, but as unto carnal. As unto little ones in Christ, I gave you milk to drink, not meat.* ... So, the true preacher proclaims aloud plain truths to hearts still in the dark, showing them no hidden mysteries. Then only are they to learn all the profounder things of Heaven, when they approach the light of truth.[27]

We can take three points from this that are helpful to the present discussion. First, the ascent of humanity to divinity is made possible and initiated by the descent of divinity to humanity.[28] God condescends to those he seeks to convert. Secondly, change for Gregory is incremental, so much so that the transition from one stage to the next is often not clearly defined, and it is not always easy to determine where a person sits on the spectrum of spiritual states. And finally, spiritual development and growth are proper to everyone. Not only the heathen must be converted, but the Christian, too, must ever be converted anew.[29]

---

[26] Paul Meyvaert, "Diversity in Unity, A Gregorian Theme," *Heythrop Journal* 4, no. 1 (1963): 148.

[27] "Sciendum uero praedicatori est, ut auditoris sui animum ultra uires non trahat, ne, ut ita dicam, dum plus quam ualet tenditur, mentis chorda rumpatur. ...Hinc paulus ait: non potui uobis loqui quasi spiritalibus, sed quasi carnalibus. Tamquam paruulis in christo lac uobis potum dedi, non escam. ...qui recte praedicat, obscuris adhuc cordibus aperta clamat, nil de occultis mysteriis indicat, ut tunc subtiliora quaeque de caelestibus audiant, cum luci ueritatis appropinquant." *Regula Pastoralis*, ed. Floribert Rommel, Library of Latin Texts (Turnhout: Brepols, 2010), clt.brepolis.net/llta, III.39; Henry Davis, trans., *Pastoral Care*, Ancient Christian Writers 11 (New York: Paulist Press, 1978), 231–232.

[28] Sandra Zimdars-Swartz, "A Confluence of Imagery: Exegesis and Christology according to Gregory the Great," in *Grégoire le Grand: Chantilly, Centre culturel Les Fontaines, 15-19 septembre 1982: actes*, ed. Jacques Fontaine, Robert Gillet, and Stan Pellistrandi (Paris: Editions du Centre national de la recherche scientifique, 1986), 329; Rodrigue Bélanger, "Anthropologie et parole de Dieu dans le commentaire de Grégoire le Grand sur le Cantique des cantiques," in *Grégoire le Grand: Chantilly, Centre culturel Les Fontaines, 15-19 septembre 1982: actes* (Paris: Editions du Centre national de la recherche scientifique, 1986), 248.

[29] Katharina Greschat, *Die Moralia in Job Gregors des Grossen: ein christologisch-ekklesiologischer Kommentar*, Studien und Texte zu Antike und Christentum 31 (Tübingen: Mohr Siebeck, 2005), 243; Dagens, *Saint Grégoire*, 263; Markus, *Signs and Meanings*, 47.

The Gradual Progress of the English

Against this theoretical backdrop, Gregory's comment about the conversion of the English, that progress is made step by step, not by leaps and bounds, makes perfect sense. The ideas of incremental growth and tailored pastoral care are everywhere in Gregory's work, and find their outworking here, too.

The preservation of certain elements of the pagan religion of the Anglo-Saxons becomes for Gregory a way of helping them ascend the ladder to the knowledge and love of Christ one rung at a time. Beginning from complete ignorance of God, the next rung of the ladder for the Anglo-Saxons is one associated in Gregory's mind with a "Jewish" kind of faith: one in which God becomes known as the Lawgiver deserving of obedience and worship, but is not yet known as beloved Savior. Perhaps this explains his appropriation of a Jewish festival in order to begin to steer the Anglo-Saxons from their pagan feasts towards Christian worship: Gregory is seeking in his dealings with the Anglo-Saxons to emulate God's dealings with humanity, leading them to Christ by way of the Old Testament.[30] He makes the comparison between the English and the Israelites explicit in the letter to Mellitus, pointing to biblical precedent for the appropriation and reinterpretation of pagan sacrifices: "Even so, the Lord certainly made himself known to the people of Israel in Egypt, and yet he kept their use of sacrifices, which they used to offer to the devil in worshipping him, for their own sacrifice" (*Sic israelitico populo in aegypto dominus se quidem innotuit, sed tamen eis sacrificiorum usus, quae diabolo solebat exhibere, in cultu proprio reseruauit*).[31]

But it is never Gregory's intention that the spiritual development of the English should be arrested at this level. In the individual, certain vices can be tolerated for a time to facilitate the correction of others, but in the end all vice must be eradicated.[32] Just so, Gregory's hope for the English church is that it will progress towards and ultimately attain the perfection towards which the whole church, indeed all of humanity, strains. He is therefore careful to give what pagan and Jewish elements he allows a Christian interpretation. The slaughter of oxen is to take place "on the day of a dedication, or on the birthdays of holy martyrs" (*die dedicationis uel natalicii sanctorum martyrum*) and is to be done "in praise of God" (*ad laudem dei*). Like the ancient Israelites, they are to offer their sacrifices with "changed hearts" (*cor mutantes*), doing so "for the true God and not for the idols" (*uero deo et non idolis*) so that "they would no longer be the same sacrifices" (*iam sacrificia ipsa non essent*).[33]

---

[30] Dagens, *Saint Grégoire*, 263; Spiegel, "The *tabernacula*," 5–6.
[31] *Reg. ep.*, XI.56; Martyn, *Letters*, 803.
[32] *Regula Pastoralis*, III.38.
[33] *Reg. ep.*, XI.56; Martyn, *Letters*, 803.

Although he thus shows himself open to incorporating elements of non-Christian festival gatherings into the life of the newly formed English church, Gregory makes it clear that he does so by way of concession and that the ultimate goal is precisely not for the English to remain attached to the exteriors of their rituals, but to use them as a way of accessing interior and spiritual truths: "Thus, while some joys are reserved for them externally, they might more readily consent to internal joys" (*ut, dum eis aliqua exterius gaudia reseruantur, ad interiora gaudia consentire facilius ualeant*).[34]

The Threat of Regress

But if this incremental approach to missions fits so comfortably with Gregory's theology, what are we to make of his earlier admonitions to forcefully stamp out pagan worship? What can explain his earlier admonishment to King Æthelbert to "hasten to extend the Christian faith among the races subject to you, ... by terrifying them" (*christianam fidem in populis tibi subditis extendere festina ... terrendo*) and to destroy the temple buildings used in the worship of idols?[35]

Perhaps these admonitions can best be understood as a reaction against backsliding.[36] The very dynamism in Gregory's anthropology that makes spiritual progress possible also opens up the possibility of regress, and Gregory is well aware that some begin to live the Christian life but then stumble and fall to temptation.[37] This is what Gregory fears most for the newly converted English, for to convert to Christianity and then return to Judaism or paganism is even worse than not converting at all.[38] All around him, Gregory sees civilization crumbling; he lives, so he puts it himself, in a barbaric time, which he believed to be the old age of the world.[39] Christ's return and the

---

[34] *Reg. ep.*, XI.56; Martyn, *Letters*, 803.

[35] *Reg. ep.*, XI.37; Martyn, *Letters*, 783.

[36] Cf. Conti, "Gregorio Magno e gli Anglosassoni," 470: "la distruzione degli idoli va legata, in ultima analisi, al proposito di dissuadere coloro che avessero già respinto il paganesimo dal riabbracciarlo nuovamente."

[37] *Moralia*, XIX.27.50 and XII.52.59 indicate that some convert but make no progress and some convert but soon fall back to their old ways. *Homiliae in Evangelia*, II.38.15 gives a specific example of three sisters, two of whom progress in love for God but one of whom sees her love fade over time and eventually returns to the love of the world. Cited in Dagens, *Saint Grégoire*, 264–265.

[38] "Dum enim quispiam ad baptismatis fontem [...] peruenerit, ad pristinam superstitionem remeans inde deterius moritur," *Reg. ep.*, I.45. Likewise, to begin to be converted to Christ and then remain stagnant will ultimately lead to regress. Faith and baptism are sufficient to grant entry to the church, but only those who go on to add the chief virtue of charity to their faith will be allowed to remain inside. *Homiliae in Evangelia*, II.38; Fiedrowicz, *Das Kirchenverständnis Gregors des Grossen*, 289–90.

[39] *Homiliae in Evangelia*, I.17.14; Robert A. Markus, *Gregory the Great and His World* (Cambridge: Cambridge University Press, 1997), 51–54.

final judgment could not be far. It was therefore of the essence that those who had once embraced Christ not grow lax and revert to godless ways.

Until June 601, Gregory seems to have believed that the English were already swiftly advancing in their spiritual journey. Already in his commentary on Job, written before the first departure of his missionaries, he makes mention of recent conversions in England: "see, the tongue of Britain, which knew nothing but barbarous gnashing, has now begun to resound in divine praise with the Hebrew 'alleluia'" (*ecce lingua britanniae, quae nihil aliud nouerat, quam barbarum frendere, iam dudum in diuinis laudibus hebraeum coepit alleluia resonare*).[40] He thus seems to have thought, when he sent Augustine and his companions on their way, that there was already a significant Christian presence in England.[41] To what extent British Christianity survived the *adventus Saxonum* remains a subject of scholarly debate, but it is likely that Gregory was not wrong to expect the English to have some familiarity with Christianity already.[42] Bertha herself was a Christian, and had brought a bishop with her from Francia upon her marriage to Æthelbert, which may indicate a Frankish interest in converting the English.[43] By the time Gregory sent Augustine forth in the summer of 596, he had heard that the English were eager for conversion and had asked "priests from the vicinity" (*sacerdotes e vicinio*) to preach to them, but had been rebuffed.[44] He therefore had every reason to expect Augustine's mission to be a swift success, and indeed the first reports appeared to confirm this expectation. In July of 598, he wrote to Eulogius of Alexandria that

> ... now letters have already reached us about [Augustine's] safety and work, stating that either he, or those who crossed over with him, are ablaze with such great miracles among that same race [of the English], that they seem to be imitating the virtues of the apostles with the proofs they provide. And in the solemnity of our Lord's nativity, which

---

[40] *Moralia*, XXVII.11.

[41] Spiegel, "The *tabernacula*," 3 n.4; Clare Stancliffe, "The British Church and the Mission of Augustine," in *St Augustine and the Conversion of England*, ed. Richard Gameson (Stroud: Sutton, 1999), 111–113.

[42] On the presence of Christianity in Anglo-Saxon England before the Augustinian mission, see Jane Stevenson, "Christianity in Sixth- and Seventh-Century Southumbria," in *The Age of Sutton Hoo: The Seventh Century in North-Western Europe*, ed. Martin Carver (Boydell Press, 1992), 175–83; Rob Meens, "A Background to Augustine's Mission to Anglo-Saxon England," *Anglo-Saxon England* 23 (1994): 5–17. Ian Wood goes so far as to suggest that "Anglo-Saxon paganism was modelled in part on Christianity" in his "Some Historical Re-Identifications and the Christianization of Kent," in *Christianizing Peoples and Converting Individuals*, International Medieval Research 7 (Turnhout: Brepols, 2000), 30.

[43] Liudhard's episcopal status suggests that he may have been expected to work on converting the Anglo-Saxons. Arnold Angenendt, "The Conversion of the Anglo-Saxons Considered Against the Background of the Early Medieval Mission," *Settimane di studio del centro Italiano di studi sull' alto medioevo* 32 (1986): 779–780.

[44] *Reg. ep.*, VI.51; Wood, "Mission of Augustine," 8–10.

was celebrated during this first indiction, it was reported that our brother and fellow-bishop baptized more than ten thousand English.[45]

Even in the middle of June 601, he writes that he is full of joy "because the English race ... now trample[s] the idols [...] to which they were subject before with an insane fear" (*quod gens anglorum* [...] *iam calcat idola, quibus prius uesano timore subiacebat*).[46]

In this context, the continued existence of pagan shrines represented a serious lapse, one that Gregory could not permit in a people otherwise progressing so well. Those who are only just beginning their advance are treated gently, but those who have already made some progress and begin to waver deserve harsher treatment. As Gregory remarks to Augustine: "For in these days the holy Church corrects some things with zeal, and tolerates some things with gentleness [...] for as the sin is in some measure to be tolerated in those who did it through ignorance, so it must be strenuously prosecuted in those who presume to sin knowingly" (*In hoc enim tempore sancta ecclesia quaedam per feruorem corrigit, quaedam per mansuetudinem tolerat, ... quia, sicut in his qui per ignorantiam fecerunt culpa aliquatenus toleranda est, ita in his fortiter insequenda, qui non metuunt sciendo peccare*).[47]

Where Gregory seeks to forcefully curb pagan and Jewish influences in his earlier letters to England and in his other correspondence, he is "strenuously prosecuting" what he perceives as willful disobedience. But the shift in Gregory's approach we witness between the letters to Æthelbert and Mellitus suggests that he found cause to reconsider whether the English were really "sinning knowingly" by continuing the use of their pagan shrines. By the time he wrote to Mellitus, his optimism about the success of the mission had been tempered, and he writes as though dealing with a people not yet so advanced in spiritual matters as to merit stern rebuke. For an essentially pagan people only just beginning their ascent to God, a milder approach was more appropriate.

This shift in Gregory's estimation of the spiritual maturity of the English is also attested in his *Libellus responsionum*, a document that, like the letter to Mellitus, dates

---

[45] "...iam nunc de [Augustini] salute et opere ad nos scripta peruenerunt, quia tantis miraculis uel ipse uel hi qui cum eo transmissi sunt in [Anglorum] gente eadem coruscant, ut apostolorum uirtutes in signis quae exhibent imitari uideantur. In sollemnitate autem dominicae natiuitatis, quae hac prima indictione transacta est, plus quam decem milia angli ab eodem nuntiati sunt fratre et coepiscopo nostro baptizati." *Reg. ep.*, VIII.29; Martyn, *Letters*, 524.

[46] *Reg. ep.*, XI.36; Martyn, *Letters*, 779.

[47] *Bede's Ecclesiastical History of the English People*, ed. and trans. Bertram Colgrave and Roger Aubrey Baskerville Mynors, Oxford Medieval Texts (Oxford: Clarendon Press, 1993), I.27, 84–87 (hereafter *Bede's Ecclesiastical History*).

to July 601.⁴⁸ This lengthy letter is a collection of Gregory's answers to questions put to him by Augustine, and its tone is remarkably consonant with that of the letter to Mellitus. Again and again, Gregory points to the biblical Law as an important source of insight for the Christian community in England, suggesting that Gregory imagines the Anglo-Saxon community as one that is, like the ancient Hebrews, halfway between paganism and mature Christianity.⁴⁹ The writing of this extended reply to questions arising from the mission field may even have been a catalyst for the change in Gregory's thinking about the English mission. His letter to Mellitus certainly suggests that he has spent some time thinking things over—"tell them what I have long pondered over, while thinking about the case of the English" (*dicite ei quid diu me cum de causa anglorum cogitans tractaui*)—and formulating his responses to Augustine would have given him occasion to do so.⁵⁰

Conclusion

Many scholars have pointed out the apparent tension between Gregory's instruction that Roman missionaries fuse and adapt pagan ritual and Jewish tradition into a Christian festival practice involving the construction of *tabernacula* (reminiscent of the Jewish Sukkot celebration) and feasting (with echoes of Germanic pagan sacrifice), and the harsher approach to mission advocated in other letters, both to insular and continental correspondents. Rather than suppose that Gregory would have preferred to use coercion in Anglo-Saxon England, but found it impossible, we can understand Gregory's softer approach as a reflection of his theological ideas about conversion and

---

48   The text exists in three versions. One is included in Bede's *Ecclesiastical History*, I.27, another in *Gregorii I Papae registrum epistolarum: Libri VIII-XIV*, ed. L.M. Hartmann, Monumenta Germaniae Historica: Epistolae 2 (Berlin: Weidmann, 1899), XI.56a. Martyn, *Letters*, 532–545, provides an English translation of the latter. The text's authenticity has been defended by Henry Chadwick, "Gregory the Great and the Mission to the Anglo-Saxons," in *Gregorio magno e il suo ttempo. XIX incontro di studiosi dell'antichità cristiana in collaborazione con l'École Française de Rome, Roma, 9-12 Maggio 1990*, vol. 1, Studia Ephemeridis "Augustinianum" 33 (Rome: Institutum Patristicum "Augustinianum," 1991), 199–212; Paul Meyvaert, "Bede's Text of the Libellus Responsionum of Gregory the Great to Augustine of Canterbury," in *England before the Conquest: Studies in Primary Sources Presented to Dorothy Whitelock*, ed. Peter Clemoes and Kathleen Hughes (Cambridge: Cambridge University Press, 1971), 15–33; Paul Meyvaert, "Le Libellus responsionum à Augustin de Cantorbéry: une oeuvre authentique de Saint Grégoire le Grand," in *Grégoire le Grand: actes de le Colloque international du Centre national de la recherche scientifique, Chantilly, Centre culturel Les Fontaines, 15-19 septembre 1982*, ed. Jacques Fontaine, Robert Gillet, and Stan Pellistrandi (Paris: Editions du Centre national de la recherche scientifique, 1986), 543–50.
49   Bill Friesen, "Answers and Echoes: The Libellus Responsionum and the Hagiography of North-Western European Mission," *Early Medieval Europe* 14, no. 2 (2006): 164, argues that (Bede's version of) the *Libellus* suggests that at the time of writing the English still knew little or nothing about Christianity, and that Gregory's directions make more sense as a "concession to new converts, not lapsed church members."
50   *Reg. ep.*, XI.56; Martyn, *Letters*, 802.

spiritual formation as a single, incremental and continuous process, in which progress is driven by divine *condescensio*. His exhortation that Æthelbert act forcefully against pagan remnants in his domain, on the other hand, flowed from a belief that the English had already made significant strides forward in their spiritual journey, and were now in danger of relapse into their old sins. Both letters can thus be understood from the perspective of Gregory's theology of spiritual progress and regress and his attendant ideas about pastoral practice. Gregory's change of heart in the summer of 601 suggests that he came to a new appreciation of just how far the English still had to come before they reached his Christian ideal. He concluded that this people was in need of a gradual introduction to Christianity, mirroring the slow revelation of God in providential history, and accommodations could be made accordingly. But, as his harsher statements remind us, Gregory considered the preservation of pagan ritual, and the infusion of Jewish elements into it, only a provisional measure. Development towards a fuller Christian spirituality and lifestyle was still expected to lead to the abandonment of such props, and convergence with the wider Christian tradition.[51]

---

[51] I would like to thank Stichting De Honderd Gulden Reis for awarding me a travel grant towards the cost of attending the conference at which this paper was first presented.

IMAGE AND FUNCTION
IN 'CHRISTIAN' AND 'PAGAN' LATE ANTIQUE TERRACOTTA LAMPS

Edward M. Schoolman

Among the various categories and types of clay-based domestic and mercantile objects, such as tableware, cooking vessels, and containers for storage and transport, terracotta lamps are some of the most common objects that survive in archaeological contexts from the Late Roman world. They appear in almost every type of site, from urban to rural, in every type of facility or structure, from domestic to commercial, with contexts that include specific ritual, religious, or funerary activities. In terms of their appearance, lamps varied greatly in size (and could include a number of nozzles for lighted wicks) and their designs and decorations were limited only by social convention and the imaginations of the lamp-makers who made them. Compared to other typical clay wares, their variety is astounding, as evidenced by the collection of more than 1,500 types of lamps published in Oscar Broneer's 1930 catalogue for excavations at Corinth, which has served as an important catalogue of decorative schemes on late Roman lamps in the Eastern Mediterranean, although it covers less than a decade of the excavation and only a fraction of the lamps now uncovered at the on-going excavation.[1] While the volume of excavated and now published lamps from excavations across the Mediterranean suggests the size of the corpus as a whole, those that remain unpublished make up a far greater portion and form the rest of the iceberg we do not see.

The ubiquity of lamps from archaeological contexts stems from their essential function of supplying light in a world of limited other options, the widespread availability of material for their production, and their low cost, as well as the frequency with which they had to be replaced after use.[2] The constant use, and the ease with which the

---

[1] Oscar Broneer, "Terracotta Lamps," *Corinth* 4 (1930). For the late antique period, more recent exactions have exposed sequences for lamps from the fifth through the seventh centuries from Corinth, some of which have been summarized in Katherine W. Slane and Guy D. R. Sanders, "Corinth: Late Roman Horizons," *Hesperia* 74 (2005).

[2] Although terracotta lamps are the most common by far, examples survive in other material, such as glass and the exceptionally durable bronze, the latter preserving both unique forms and those common to their terracotta siblings.

decorations could be altered or modified, make terracotta lamps efficient barometers of public interest and acceptance of elements within decorative schemes. Furthermore, because of the widespread use of lamps in the Roman world, they commonly appear in literary sources that underscore the use of lamps beyond their purpose for illumination, and in Late Antiquity pagans, Christians, and Jews could attach additional religious, cultic, or other social functions to them, visible also in some archaeological contexts.

These contexts in which lamps become important beyond supplying light are almost as varied as the designs they bore. For example, outside of illuminating homes, shops, churches, and other public buildings, lamps often found alternative uses in funerary, devotional, and apotropaic contexts. This has made lamps a point for significant scholarship, with foci on their iconography, inscriptions, forms, and production, as well as their ritual functions. The objective of this chapter is to explore in a few examples the ritual contexts in which lamps appeared as well as the possibilities for religious images or symbols in their decorative schemes as the central foci of investigation. In tying together these diverse types of lamps and their various functions from across the Late Antique Mediterranean, the challenge becomes not an attempt to answer the questions of does the decoration of an everyday object give it (or its owner) a religious designation and what makes a lamp "pagan" or "Christian" in Late Antiquity, but rather an assessment of how new designs and decorations point to changing religious demographics and how everyday objects could take on ritual and religious meanings and functions in specific contexts in the changing social and cultural dynamics of the period.[3]

Lamps with "Pagan" and "Christian" Decoration

Out of the entire corpus of published lamps, it is clear that very few served as vehicles for outwardly religious, apotropaic, and devotional imagery or symbols. Between the fourth and sixth centuries, lamps were decorated with a wide range of motifs and images, and even figural representations were displayed on the disc on the flattened top of lamps. Of all lamps, the most frequent designs were simple and ornamental, such as vegetal or geometric motifs absent of specific iconographic meaning. In the lamps excavated from Athens dating to the third and fourth century, for example, none can be construed to have any decoration derived from overt Christian symbols or images (consistent with the position of Christianity for much of that period).[4] While

---

[3] In addition to questions about religious identity, "decoration on vessels form[ed] a series of elaborate social codes relating to their practical use." Ellen Swift, "Decorated Vessels: The Function of Decoration in Late Antiquity," in *Objects in Content, Objects in Use: Material Spatiality in Late Antiquity*, ed. Luke Lavan, Ellen Swift, and Toon Putzeys (Leiden: Brill, 2007), 407.

[4] Although mythological scenes appear on a number of lamps, very few contain iconography that was demarked as Jewish or Christian, but at the end of the fifth century "potters and lampmakers catered to both factions,

these designs that appeared on the lamps bear no direct connection to religious beliefs, one can could see vines connected to fecundity or plenty or to direct biblical allusions (such as John 15:1, "I am the true vine, and my Father is the gardener"),[5] or to interpret the decoration on the disc of a lamp as the representation of a Catherine Wheel. The context of these lamps in homes and businesses, however, suggests typical uses and once damaged the lamps end up in refuse piles with other common wares.

In other archaeological contexts, some lamps carried far more illustrative images, including those bearing specific pagan mythological motifs, Jewish or Christian symbols, or other representations clearly associated with specific religious practices or ideologies. For example, the menorah was a common feature of lamps produced in areas with Jewish populations, although its appearance was not limited to lamps.[6] While the menorah was the most common form of iconography associated with Late Antique Judaism, images were not limited to *menorot*, and although rare, some extant examples of representations of biblical scenes suggest at least a small market in Jewish communities for lamps featuring Old Testament figures. One of the clearest examples is a unique large fifth-century lamp featuring David and Goliath (likely from Alexandria, although it lacks clear provenance); this 7-nozzle mold-made example features labels in Greek, an indication of the Hellenist-Jewish community for which it was manufactured (fig. 1).[7] Along with other lamps bearing *menorot*, these examples, while associated with locations with

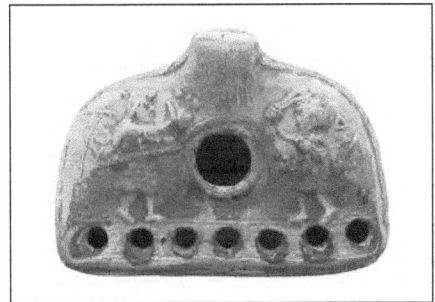

Figure 1.

---

with the same shops offering a choice of Christian symbols and pagan scenes." Alison Frantz, *Late Antiquity: A.D. 267-700*, (Princeton: American School of Classical Studies, 1988), 68–9. Furthermore, "The paucity of Christian lamps in the second half of the 4th century suggests that the Athenians were very slow to adopt Christianity long after it had become the official religion of the empire. It is not until the first half of the 5th century that Christian symbols predominate on Attic lamps." Judith Perlzweig, *Lamps of the Roman Period: First to Seventh Century after Christ*, (Princeton: American School of Classical Studies, 1961), 23.

5   John 15:1 (NIV).

6   "[T]he menorah, especially after the destruction of the Temple, took on particular significance and was depicted on walls of houses and tombs and on lamps, amulets, and rings." Douglas R. Edwards, *Religion & Power: Pagans, Jews, and Christians in the Greek East*, (Oxford: Oxford University Press, 1996), 136. The prevalence of lamps with *menorot* or with multiple nozzles in imitation of *menorot* has been used to address the location of Jewish communities, most visibly in Carthage. John Lund, "A Synagogue in Carthage? Menorah-Lamps from the Danish Excavations," *Journal of Roman Archaeology* 8 (1995).

7   Kurt Weitzmann, *Age of Spirituality: Late Antiquity and Early Christian Art, Third to Seventh Century* (New York: Metropolitan Museum of Art, 1979),384–5; Christopher Haas, *Alexandria in Late Antiquity: Topography and Social Conflict* (Baltimore: Johns Hopkins University Press, 1997), 98.

known Jewish (and sometimes Samaritan) communities in Late Antiquity, did not necessarily mean that they were owned by Jews, or acknowledged to be specifically Jewish.[8] Ultimately, on the one hand lamps could simply be used as sources of light, but on the other community preferences drove the suitability of the designs.

In terms of examples with motifs that could be considered pagan, throughout the Roman Mediterranean numerous lamps featuring mythological figures and scenes are commonly found through the fifth century, and while their production continues in the sixth century (an indication of some level of popularity), they make up a small portion of lamps in this later century. These lamps are often simple mold-made forms, frequently with figures of Asklepios or Zeus (fig. 2); other figures, even rarer in the sixth century, included Eros, Herakles and his Twelve Labors, Poseidon, and Athena.[9] What is striking about these examples is that they were based on figural decoration found on lamps manufactured in the third and fourth century, representing a significant continu-

Figure 2.

---

[8] Excavations in the areas of Late Roman Palestine known to have communities of Samaritans have frequently uncovered lamps that incorporate the menorah in their design: Varda Sussman, "Samaritan Lamps of the Third-Fourth Centuries A.D.," *Israel Exploration Journal* 28 (1978). Ultimately, the problem of ownership of these has long been acknowledged: "there seems to be no way to be sure that a lamp embellished with a menorah was used by Jews rather than by Samaritans, or, for that matter, Jews that had converted to Christianity, Jewish Christians, Christians, or maybe even pagans who simply liked the design." Leonard Victor Rutgers, "Archaeological Evidence for the Interaction of Jews and Non-Jews in Late Antiquity," *American Journal of Archaeology* 96 (1992): 110.

[9] Arja Karivieri, "Mythological Subjects on Late Roman Lamps and the Persistence of Classical Tradition," in *Late Antiquity: Art in Context*, ed. Jens Fleischer, John Lund, and Marjatta Nielsen (Copenhagen: Museum Tusculanum Press, 2001), 179–98.

ity and suggesting perhaps a conservative nature in decorations. The examples from the Agora in Athens from the fourth and fifth century, although hardly fine or detailed, depict representations of Athena, Eros, and Helios, long into the Christian period of the city's history. While these figures were based on pagan mythology, especially from the fifth century on, the context of their manufacture may be classicizing in its intension rather than pagan, where the connection was not to the religious feature but rather to highlighting the link to valued aspects of classical culture (a feature common in reused sarcophagi, for example). For these objects, questions of their survival and their interpretation in newly Christian contexts remain.

With the end of Christian persecution and the change in status of Christianity as an official religion in the Roman Empire by the end of the fourth century, lamps began to appear with clear forms of Christian decoration and iconography: the cross, the Chi-Rho monogram, animals such as doves, lambs, and fishes, and even figural representations, including Christ in various episodes and saints, although these are significantly rarer.[10] Lamps with clear Christian decoration do not become common until the middle of the fifth century, leaving a period of a hundred years in which Christianity became the dominant religion but simultaneously competed with the continued popularity of paganism (and pagan motifs).[11] Perhaps because overtly Christian images do not become a popular decoration until the fifth century and mythological figures continue to be depicted on lamps into the sixth century, it makes sense to underscore that as popular objects lamps reflect the changing interests of their consumers, tracing the rise of Christianity and the decline of paganism over two centuries. In respect to decorations, however, changes in lamps may broadly speak to cultural transitions, but at the individual level cannot be predicative with any certainty (that is, for example, a pagan could own a lamp with a Chi-Rho). On the other hand, with both literary and archaeological contextual evidence, the value of lamps beyond their basic utility, such as their role in burial and funerary rituals, begins to appear.

Lamps and Burial Practices

Lamps are commonly found connected to burials, basic and elaborate, rich and poor, for individuals and for groups, pagan and Christian, throughout the Roman Mediterranean through the sixth century, and served as witnesses to both significant

---

[10] John Herrmann and Annewies van den Hoek, "'Two Men in White': Observations on an Early Christian Lamp from North Africa with the Ascension of Christ," in *Early Christian Voices in Texts, Tranditions, and Symbols*, ed. David H. Warren, Graham Brock, and David W. Pao (Boston: Brill, 2003), 293–318. See also John Lund, "Motifs in Context: Christian Lamps," in *Late Antiquity: Art in Context*, ed. Jens Fleischer, John Lund, and Marjatta Nielsen (Copenhagen: Museum Tusculanum Press, 2001), 201 (hereafter Lund, *Motifs in Context*).

[11] Lund, *Motifs in Context*, 204.

political and cultural transformations.[12] The continuity of such use extends far back into Roman and Hellenistic traditions, where lamps were objects offered for the journey of the deceased into the afterlife, and/or left as mementos during periods of ritual mourning or continued commemoration.[13] The importance and relative prevalence of lamps in pagan and later Christian grave-good assemblages attests to a function as ritual objects beyond their immediate intended use.

Although there are numerous examples, the late Roman cemetery in Pessinus in Asia Minor proves useful in its breadth: it contains 138 graves dating from the first century BC through the fourth century AD, with both cremation and inhumation graves.[14] Across the entire four-century period of the cemetery's active use, a total of nineteen lamps were included as grave goods for both types of burial. While the group comprised both locally made and imported lamps, all bore very simple decorations. An additional fact important for their interpretation is that the lamps were never deposited alone, but were frequently part of a collection with other objects, including common and fine ceramics, rings, and jewelry, and connected directly to the burial, rather than post-burial commemorative rituals. The intended ritual function of lamps for those performing burials in the late Roman tombs in Pessinus would have been quite different from that of the mourners visiting tombs, and along with the other goods provided the dead with tools for the afterlife or objects that connected to their past.

While tastes and conventions changed in burial practices, with cremation giving way to inhumation, and with larger scale group burials appearing frequently in addition to individual tombs, lamps appearing in burial contexts remained a consistent practice. For example, 40 km south of Pessinus in the city of Amorium, the evidence from a sixth-century tomb supports the fact that even in entirely Christian contexts, lamps found use in funerary ritual. The tomb was designed from the outset to hold many individuals, built from Roman funerary doorstones in the form of a rectangle bisected by a cross, and contained the bodies of at least 40 individuals buried over at least a century

---

[12] Lamps were just one of many items frequently associated with the deposition of goods with the deceased in Roman contexts as well as within collections of early medieval grave-goods. On the latter, see Heinrich Härke, "Grave Goods in Early Medieval Burials: Messages and Meanings," *Mortality* 19 (2014). Lamps may even have been included in the funeral pyres of Roman cremation burials, evidenced by signs of secondary firing; many examples from the excavation at Gerulata (on Rome's Pannonian frontier) indicate that this may have been a common practice. Robert Frecer, *Gerulata: The Lamps* (Prague: Charles University Press, 2014), 253–54.

[13] For example, following Roman funerals "provision could be made for the lighting of lamps at the grave on the Kalends, Ides and Nones of every month." J. M. C. Toynbee, *Death and Burial in the Roman World* (London: Thames and Hudson, 1971), 62.

[14] John Devreker, Hugo Thoen, and Frank Vermeulen, *Excavations in Pessinus: The So-Called Acropolis from Hellenistic and Roman Cemetery to Byzantine Castle* (Ghent: Academia Press, 2003), 84–88.

and a mixture small objects and fill (fig. 3).[15] Within the jumble, two lamps were discovered, both intact examples of locally made sixth-century lamps with clear indications of

Figure 3.

use but not of extreme wear, which would have made them suitable objects to leave at the grave of a loved one (fig. 4). Although simple, both lamps feature crosses as part of their decorative schemes: one with a very prominent cruciform handle, and the other

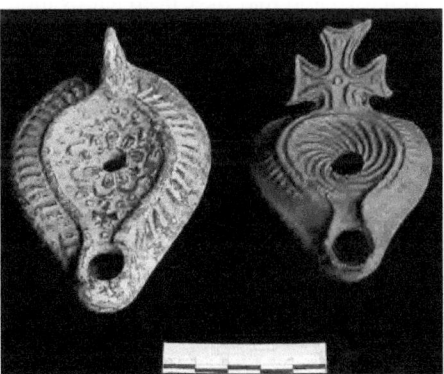

Figure 4.

with a small cross on the disk. Yet when considered in the corpus of all the lamps uncovered in excavations at Amorium and in the region, the ones left at the tomb are simply

---

[15] Research on the tomb, known as MZ94, has not been fully published. On the doorstones of Amorium, see Hüseyin Yaman, "Door to the Other World: Phrygian Doorstones at Amorium", in *Funeral Rites, Rituals and Ceremonies from Prehistory to Antiquity: Proceedings of the International Workshop "Troas and Its Neighbours"*, ed. Onur Özbek (Instanbul: Institut Français d'Études Anatoliennes, 2008), 59–68.

representative of the common locally made forms from the sixth century. Fragments of lamps with similar cross motifs and cruciform handles were recovered in many areas of the excavation and appear in other excavations in the region, and as decorative elements crosses were ubiquitous in late antique Amorium and the eastern Mediterranean.[16]

While remaining common in burials, lamps also seemed to serve in the process of continued commemoration for Christians (and perhaps that may have been the purpose of the lamps at the tomb in Amorium).One excellent example of an elaborate, rich, and single grave featuring lamps as commemorative grave goods might be that belonging to Maria, the wife of Euplous of Corinth, who was interred in a chamber tomb located in a prominent position northwest of the city.[17] Although the dating remains somewhat contested, the tomb was likely put in use for Maria in the sixth century, which further explains two aspects of her burial that are overtly Christian: it was an interment rather than cremation, and her short Greek epitaph contains a number of allusions to her professed faith with the use of crosses to mark the beginning and the end of the text.[18] While it seems clear that nothing was interred with her during her burial in terms of burial goods, six lamps were found during the excavation of her tomb, with three deposited directly over the burial and three adjacent to it.

The group of lamps left directly on Maria's tomb was composed of three locally produced unglazed lamps from either Athens or Corinth. As evidenced by soot deposits on the nozzles, all had been used and may have been left by mourners as funerary offerings or during commemorative visits to the tomb following the burial. In terms of their decoration, the lamps themselves were completely devoid of religious symbols, inscriptions, or images. With respect to the lamps found adjacent to her tomb, we see the same

---

[16] Edward Schoolman, "Middle Imperial, Late Roman, and Early Byzantine Terracotta Oil Lamps: 2002–2005," in *Amorium Reports 3: The Lower City Enclosure*, ed. Chris S. Lightfoot and Eric A. Ivison (Istanbul: Zero, 2012), 193–215; Edward Schoolman, "Kreuze Und Kreuzförmige Darstellungen in Der Alltagskultur Von Amorium," in *Byzanz: Das Römerreich Im Mittelalter, Teil 2,1*, ed. F. Daim and J. Drauschke (Mainz: Römisch-Germanischen Zentralmuseums, 2010), 373–386. A number of cross-handle lamps were produced locally in the Balkans as well; see Florin Curta, "Shedding Light on a Murky Matter: Remarks on 6th to Early 7th Century Clay Lamps in the Balkans,"*Archaeologia Bulgarica* 20, no. 3 (2016): 85–90.

[17] Mary E. Hoskins Walbank and Michael B. Walbank, "The Grave of Maria, Wife of Euplous: A Christian Epitaph Reconsidered,"*Hesperia: The Journal of the American School of Classical Studies at Athens*, 75 (2006) (hereafter Walbank and Walbank, "The Grave of Maria"). Maria's burial was relatively typical as a regional variation on Christian burial, which were incredibly diverse; for example in Gaul, burial goods can be frequently found through the seventh century, when other means of releasing sin for the deceased became more prominent. Bonnie Effros, *Caring for Body and Soul: Burial and Afterlife in the Merovingian World* (University Park, PA: Pennsylvania State University Press, 2002), 139–146.

[18] Walbank and Walbank argue for a sixth-century date, based on elements of the epigraphy and the tone of the plaque as well as the grave goods themselves, although the first study dated the tomb to the fourth century based on the goods found at the tomb. See Theodore Leslie Shear, "The Excavation of Roman Chamber Tombs at Corinth in 1931," *American Journal of Archaeology* 35 (1931), 439–441.

local unglazed lamps, again with signs of use, but with decorations that might connect to the community around Maria. While the first lamp was decorated with geometric stamps and a herringbone pattern on the rim, and the second lamp with vines and clusters of grapes along the outer rim and lion in repose on the disk, the third displayed a figural scene. Abraham's sacrifice of Isaac appears on the disc of the lamp, with the hand of God pointing to the ram.[19] Although exceedingly rare in lamps, this scene may have recalled the act and importance of deliverance, and is also found on overtly Christian sarcophagi, where it appears on the fourth-century tomb of Junius Bassus, for example. Here, although the lamp may also have primarily been used to illuminate the dark catacomb, the scene it portrays could have additionally served either as a suitable gift to the deceased or more likely for the consolation of contemporary visitors to the tomb. In this context, these lamps form part of the assemblage connected to a tomb for a Christian, visited later by presumably Christian friends and family, and while lamps that were left for Maria did not need to be overtly Christian themselves, at least one could possibly serve as a commentary on deliverance appropriate for a Christian audience considering the death of a loved one.

In these three examples of lamps connected to funerary and burial practice, it is difficult to discern if there was an interruption or change in how lamps were deposited or even used in graves in the transition between pagan and Christian, and indeed it seems that "engrained custom ensured the continuous presence of lamps in Christian burials," as in pagan ones.[20] During the pagan Roman Empire, lamps were included as grave goods during burial as well as a result of funerary and commemorative activities after burial, roles they continued to play into later periods, although the religious and ritual impulses were transformed.[21] The continuity in the utilization of lamps includes

---

[19] Walbank and Walbank, "The Grave of Maria," 274. Although rare, lamps featuring the sacrifice of Isaac were not entirely unknown, with one from North Africa and two from the Levant, including a Samaritan example in which the scene is presented without figures, only with representations of the objects associated with the event. Varda Sussman, "The Binding of Isaac as Depicted on a Samaritan Lamp," *Israel Exploration Journal* 48 (1998): 183. More broadly, the scene is common in church decorations, and "is widely known throughout the entire Church during the golden age of paleo-christian art." Isabel Speyart Van Woerden, "The Iconography of the Sacrifice of Abraham," *Vigiliae Christianae* 15 (1961): 221.

[20] Laskarina Bouras and Maria G. Parani, *Lighting in Early Byzantium* (Washington, DC: Dumbarton Oaks Research Library and Colletion, 2008).

[21] In the fourth century, the line dividing Christian and pagan tombs is especially blurry: "No longer is the representation of a fish automatically assumed to be Christian. The presence of the date of death in a funerary inscription is no longer thought to be an exclusively Christian practice while the dedication "Dies Manibus Sacrum" is no longer assumed to be pagan. Archaeologists are no longer surprised when they find obviously pagan or even obscene representations in tombs thought to be Christian." Mark J. Johnson, "Pagan-Christian Burial Practices of the Fourth Century: Shared Tombs?," *Journal of Early Christian Studies* 5 (1997): 50.

the fact that lamps were still placed in some proximity to the deceased.[22] The significance of the lamp featuring the sacrifice of Isaac at the tomb of Maria (or the inclusion of lamps with cross decorations at Amorium) opens the possibility that decorations could matter in funerary and commemorative contexts, yet the other examples indicate that clearly religious decoration was not necessary (or even preferable).

Lamps in 'Pagan' and 'Christian' Cult and Veneration

An interesting parallel to the use of lamps in mortuary culture is in their function as votive or magical offerings in cult practice (both pagan and Christian), or in connection with the veneration of saints. As in the examples above where early Christian burials did not require so-called Christian lamps (even when those with clear Christian iconography were in broad circulation), when lamps were put to use in magical contexts it seems clear that their decoration was of limited importance.

One such example is the deposition of lamps discovered in the remains of a derelict and damaged Roman subterranean bathhouse in Corinth, which had turned into a cult center in Late Antiquity called the "Fountain of the Lamps" by its excavators.[23] During the course of excavation, more than 4,000 lamps from the fifth and sixth century showing a range of about 300 designs were uncovered.[24] The majority of the lamps bore simple or little decoration, while a few others displayed clearly religious iconography, including lamps featuring Chi-Rho as well as patterns with fish. A few unique examples featured the sacrifice of Isaac, Eros and a lyre, and a lion in repose; one lamp even carries a graffito inscription addressed to the angels below.[25] These lamps, placed in the murky and water-filled ruins of a late Roman bath, were left as offerings to subterranean deities or spirits, ignoring the divide between pagans and Christians. The fact that some of the lamps displayed Christian iconography seems to have had little direct influence in their ultimate function as votive offerings; in essence, their images and decorations do not seem to matter or were irrelevant to this function. In a pre-Christian example, the same is true for the early fourth-century lamps used as vessels for lead *defixiones* (sheets

---

[22] "If Roman modes of giving did not simply promote, but actually helped shape individuals' identity, the Christian transformation of euergetism signaled a new way of regarding the self and his or her relationship with the broader collective." Kim Bowes, "Early Christian Archaeology: A State of the Field," *Religion Compass* 2 (2008): 596.

[23] The first publication of the area appeared in James Wiseman, "The Gymnasium Area at Corinth, 1969-1970," *Hesperia: The Journal of the American School of Classical Studies at Athens* 41 (1972).

[24] Karen S. Garnett, "Late Roman Corinthian Lamps from the Fountain of the Lamps," *Hesperia: The Journal of the American School of Classical Studies at Athens* 44 (1975): 184.

[25] Some inscriptions on lamps directly address the Abrahamic God or use language taken directly from scripture and function as vehicles for religious and ritual language and are clear indications of the religious profession of the maker: Joseph Naveh, "Lamp Inscriptiosn and Inverted Writing," *Israel Exploration Journal* 38 (1988).

inscribed with magical formulae and spells) found in the excavation of a sacred spring dedicated to Anna Perenna in Rome.[26]

Even before the practices of the Fountain of the Lamps in Corinth or Anna Perenna, in the first century AD, an intriguing form of worship emerged predominantly in Greek communities perhaps connected to monotheistic Judaizers centered on a deity identified as Theos Hypsistos, "the highest god," in which lamps became essential to ritual practice. Especially as vehicles for fire, they played a central role in the devotional and religious practices of the Hypsistians, primarily evidenced by their appearance in sanctuaries. In Asia Minor, the archaeological and epigraphic evidence suggests that "by dedicating a lamp in the sanctuary it was possible for even the most insignificant devotee to establish a direct link with the eternal heavenly fire," the form of this pagan monotheistic or henotheistic deity.[27]

The surviving cult center for Theos Hypsistos was prominent (or perhaps localized) on the island of Delos, where the practitioners of the cult may have used all or part of a sanctuary from the first century BC to the second century AD, which is remarkable in that it seemed to operate for both the Jewish community as well as the worshippers of Hypsistos. During excavation of the building "it is also significant that over sixty lamps were found... many adorned with pagan, but none with Jewish motifs' or ones which could be connected directly to the cult of Hypsistos."[28] The decoration on many of the lamps or fragments include a centaur, a maenad, a lion ravaging a donkey, Athena, vegetal decoration, a vase with tendrils, and Zeus with an eagle. As in the previous examples from other contexts (funerary and votive), the core function of the lamps as sources of light is relevant for this practice.

---

[26] Attilio Mastrocinque, "Late Antique Lamps with Defixiones," *Greek, Roman, and Byzantine Studies* 47 (2007).

[27] "This is revealed by the only other inscription carved in a similar fashion on the old city wall at Oenoanda, the dedication by a woman, Chromatis, of a lamp to Theos Hypsistos, the highest god. The votive offering was appropriate to the god's divine nature. The lamp stood in a small niche, carved at the top of the low relief of an altar, and the next block of the wall had a ledge cut along its upper edge where a row of lamps could be placed. Chromatis' dedication was the humble earthly counterpart to the deity's divine fire. Lamps and fire were essential to a cult which was associated with the upper air of heaven and with the sun." Stephen Mitchell, "The Cult of Theos Hypsistos between Pagans, Jews and Christians," in *Pagan Monotheism in Late Antiquity*, ed. Polymenia Athanassiadi and Michael Frede (Oxford: Oxford University Press, 1999), 92.

[28] Ibid., 98. Further study on the lamps from Delos underscore their utilitarian purpose: "Numerous lamps were collected near the walls and mostly from under the marble benches; these positions could correspond with the actual use of the lamps, in which case the synagogue would have been abandoned during an instance of use, or they could be the result of a subsequent shifting of the debris, for example when the lime kiln was built. It has often been observed that the Jewish community clearly obtained its lamps exclusively from Roman merchants, and that it was not particular about the decorative motifs on them." Monika Trümper, "The Oldest Original Synagogue Building in the Diaspora: The Delos Synagogue Reconsidered," *Hesperia: The Journal of the American School of Classical Studies at Athens* 73 (2004): 587.

Moving past the pagan world and into one decidedly Christian, a different role for lamps can be found associated with the cults of saints. Gregory of Tours, the sixth-century bishop, historian, and hagiographer, included in his collection of miracles performed by confessors and their relics known as the *Glory of the Confessors* this anecdote about the shrine dedicated to the fourth-century bishop Eusebius of Vercelli:

> Bishop Eusebius of Vercelli was a great supporter of Hilary against heresies. He shows that he is still alive after his burial by his current miracles. For although many ill people are cured on his anniversary day, possessed people dance throughout the entire church in violent spins and believe that they are afflicted with powerful torments. They leap in the air and with their hands strike and break the lamps that are burning as lights. Once they are soaked with the oil from a lamp, immediately the demon leaves and the people are cleansed. Then the congregation knows that the number of ill people who have been healed matches the number of lamps that it sees are broken.[29]

This is a playful story, but the oil-soaked exorcized (*perfusi liquore*) and the broken lamps (*lignos effractos*) point to a crucial contextual element: that under the right circumstance and in the right context, the oil held in lamps becomes the means by which Christians could partake in the healing offered by saints. While holy oil was commonly formed through the direct contact between the liquid and holy relics (demonstrated by the large number of ossuaries drilled with holes for this particular purpose), the simple fact of oil being used in a lamp to illuminate a shrine has imbued the oil with a spiritual property.[30]

But of course Eusebius is neither the only nor the most well-known saint to use lamps and oil as devices for health and sanctity. That title might be long to Egyptian saint Menas, whose cult site at Abu Mina was the epicenter of the production of the

---

[29] *Eusebius vero Vercellensis episcopus magnum huic Helario adiutorium contra hereses fuit, qui vivere se post tumulos praesentibus virtutibus manifestat. Nam in die natalis sui cum multi infirmi salventur, inergumini tamen rotatu valido per totam eclesiam debachantes et nimio confitentes torqueri cruciatu, elevati in aera, lignos, qui ad officium luminis succenduntur, mann verberantes effrangunt. De quo perfusi liquore, ilico, discedente daemone, personae purgantur, scitque tunc populus, tot infirmos esse mundatos, quot videret lignos effractos.*Gregory of Tours, *Liber in gloria confessorum*, ed. Bruno Krusch, MGH SRM I.2 (Hanover, 1885; reprinted 1969), 300. For the English translation see: Gregory of Tours, *Glory of the Confessors*, trans. Raymond Van Dam (Liverpool: Liverpool University Press, 1988) 4.

[30] The Basilica of Dor presents clear archaeological evidence for the industrial collection and distribution of oil having passed through the relics of saints. Claudine Dauphin, "On the Pilgrim's Way to the Holy City of Jerusalem: The Basilica of Dor in Israel," in *Archaeology and Biblical Interpretation*, ed. John R. Bartlett (London: Routledge, 2002), 160–61.

famous pilgrim bottles that bear his image. The connection between Saint Minas and lamps was very strong, and archaeological evidence points to the existence of locally produced oil lamps along with flasks at the site. The likely function of the lamps at the shrine of the saints is that they were offered and purchased as mementos, gaining their power through the image of the saint and the proximity of their manufacture and use to his shrine. The far more common flasks had the same connection, although in addition they were "intended for taking home drops of oil [as *eulogia*] from lamps at the tomb of the saint" and other specified reliquaries and receptacles.[31] In this context, the lamps might also have gained additional value at the shrines of Eusebius and Menas not for their illumination, but in their capacity for holding oil.

Conclusions

The examples of lamps used in funerary or religious contexts in Late Antiquity point to the fact that the value of any lamp was in its function and the context (as a means of illumination, as a vessel for *defixiones*, or in its capacity to hold oil), and not specifically in its decoration, although the slow disappearance of lamps with pagan themes in the fifth and sixth century attests to the changing religious demography. While a lamp with Christian symbols and decoration might appeal to a Christian, the main purpose of such images was likely to sell these common and everyday objects, rather than to inspire specific practices. The end of overtly mythological and pagan motifs on lamps, which may have had just as strong of a draw in the fifth century as a Christogram, takes place in the sixth century, when the vestiges of pagan culture were lost to the onslaught of reform. In their various functions, lamps offer a window into the localized continuities of practice in the fourth, fifth, and sixth century, as objects molded to suit many diverse needs.

These examples of both the slow development of religious decorative schemes and the use of lamps in ritual context in Late Antiquity ultimately build to two conclusions. While it is clear that an image on a lamp cannot be divorced from the object, in burial and votive situations it was in large part from the context that lamps gained their extraordinary functions. The more specific conclusion is that among Christians, Jews, and pagans, parallel contexts suggest deep similarities in the ways various environments and uses could change the underlying function of a lamp, and that commonalities between practices and decorative schemes were features of a society in transition.

---

[31] Peter Grossman, "The Pilgimage Center of Abû Mînâ," in *Pilgimage and Holy Space in Late Antique Egypt*, ed. David Frankfurter (Leiden: Brill, 1998), 299.

Landscapes

BELIEVERS IN TRANSITION: PAGANISM TO CHRISTIANITY ALONG THE SOUTHWESTERN BLACK SEA COAST (4th–6th CENTURIES)

Hristo Preshlenov

This study presents the process of Christianization in the cities along the southwestern Black Sea region between the fourth and the sixth century primarily through the lens of archaeology, but using numismatic, epigraphic and hagiographical evidence as well. The region of the Black Sea coast comprised the Roman provinces of Scythia, Moesia Secunda and Haemimontus that maintained active contacts between the Lower Danube region and the Eastern Mediterranean. Its Roman cities—Tirissa/Acres on Cape Kaliakra, Dionysopolis (now Balchik), Odessos (Varna), the former Roman ro station Templum Iovis (Obzor), Mesembria (Nesebar), Anchialos (Pomorie), Debeltos (Debelt), and Apollonia/Sozopolis (Sozopol)—ministered the coastal border zone and were primary centers of material and cultural exchange (Figure 1).

While the spread of Christianity in these areas is clearly visible in both textual and archaeological records, new Bulgarian archaeological research has uncovered important new findings allowing for innovative hypotheses about the development of new religious practices. Apart from Bulgarian-language scholarship, however, the confrontation between, and coexistence of, pagans and Christians along the Black Sea is hardly known. The aim of this chapter is to offer a synthesis and summary of some of the most important recent work.

The Rise of the Bishop: Conciliar and Administrative Activity

The first Christian communities appeared along the southwestern coast of the Black Sea in the first century as a result of the missionary preaching of the Apostles Saint Paul and Saint Andrew.[1] With the rise of Christianity to the postition of state

---

[1] Николай Кочев [Nikolay Kochev], *Християнството през IV- началото XI в.* [*Christianity during the fourth to the beginning of the eleventh century*]. (София: Хейзъл [Sofia: Heisăl], 1995), 9–10; Венцислав Каравълчев [Ventsislav Karavălchev], "Християнският Анхиало [The Christian Anchialus]," in *Поморие: древност и съвремие* [*Pomorie: Past and Present*], ed. Атанас Орачев [Atanas Orachev] et al. (Бургас: Геопан [Burgas: Geopan], 2011), 199 (hereafter Каравълчев, "Християнският Анхиало").

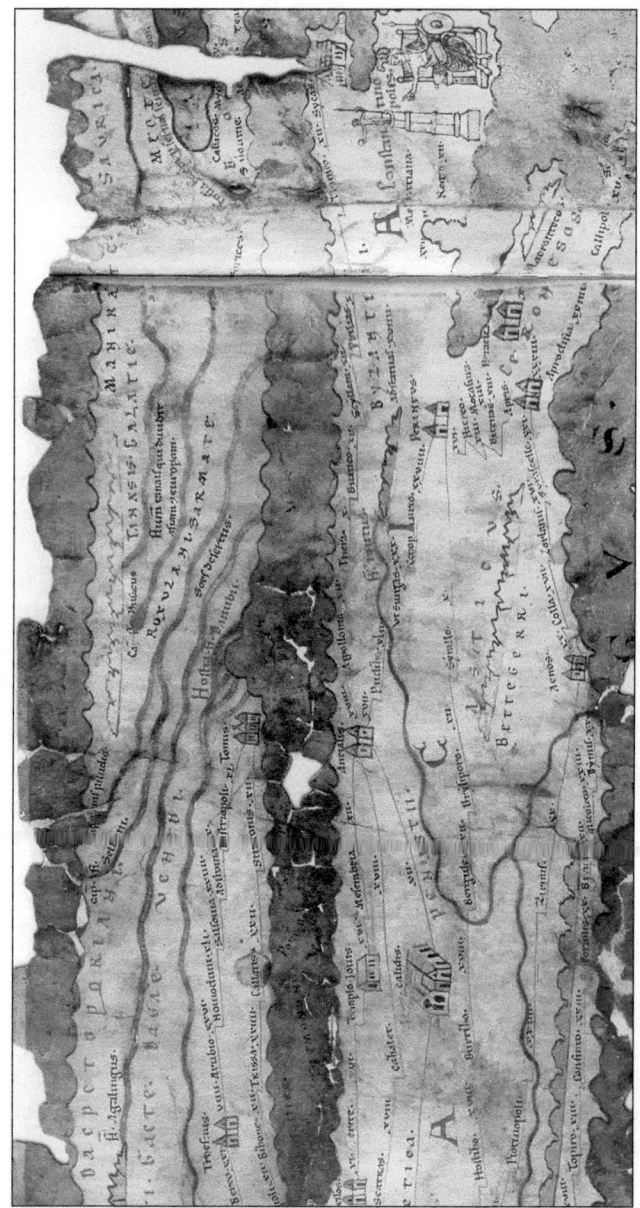

Figure 1. Tabula Peutingeriana. The Western Black Sea coast, rev. after ad 330 (after Атанас Орачев [Atanas Orachev], "Приноси към историята, археологията и географията на Анхиало [Contribution to the history, archaeology, and geography of Anchialo]," in *Поморие: древност и съвремие* [*Pomorie: Past and Present*], ed. Атанас Орачев [Atanas Orachev] et al. (Бургас: Геопан [Burgas: Geopan], 2011), 162–163).

religion in the fourth century, bishops gained new prominence and growing visibility. Their new administrative functions are reflected in Roman legislation. Under these new conditions, a number of regions and cities in the Black Sea region, whose episcopacies claimed an apostolic origin, retained their authority and influence. The bishops of these cities participated at the Church councils in the fourth-, fifth- and sixth-centuries. The bishops of Anchialos and Mesembria were among the 318 Fathers at the First Ecumenical Council of Nicaea in 325.[2] The Christian community of Anchialos was represented at the Council of Serdica in 343 by Bishop Timotheus, who became an Arian at the alternative council in Philippopolis. Bishop Sebastianos of Anchialos participated at the Council of Constantinople in 381.[3] A certain Athanasios took part as the Bishop of Debeltos and Sozopolis at the Council of Ephesus in 431.[4] The two cities were also presented at the Council of Chalcedon in 451, but already as two separate episcopacies. Bishop Iobinos of Debeltos and Bishop Olympius of Sozopolis also participated in the work of this council that condemned Monophysitism.[5] The decisions of the council were supported by Bishop Dizas of Odessos. In 458, together with another 1600 bishops, Dizas signed a letter in response to query of the newly elected emperor, Leo I on the attitude of the bishops of the Eastern and Western church dioceses to the decisions of the council: the bishops condemned Monophysitism.[6] In the following year, at the council of Constantinople convened by Patriarch Gennadius, two bishops of southwestern towns showed up: Sabbatios of Anchialos and Eustratios of Debeltos.[7] At another council in Constantinople, in 518, Johannes of Odessos acted in canonical defense of the decisions of the Council of Chalcedon.[8] At the Council of Constantinople in 553, Paulus of Anchialos did the same.[9] Apart from their conciliar activity, the bishops of the border provinces sought to provide greater protection for their flock

---

[2] Каравълчев, "Християнският Анхиало," 203. Μαργαριτης Κωνσταντινίδης, Ἡ Μεσημβρία του Ευξείου (Αθηναι: Γεωργιος Μεγας, 1945), 128, 131.

[3] Peter Soustal, *Tabula Imperii Byzantini*,6. *Thrakien (Thrakē, Rodopē und Haimimontos)* (Wien: Verlag der Österreichischen Akemie der Wissenschaften, 1991), 175 (hereafter Soustal, *Tabula Imperii Byzantini*) 175; Каравълчев, "Християнският Анхиало," 203.

[4] Soustal, *Tabula Imperii Byzantini*, 234.

[5] Soustal, *Tabula Imperii Byzantini*, 234, 454.

[6] Kazimierz Ilski, *Biskupi Mezji i Scytii* [BishopsofMoesiaandScythia] (Poznań: Vis, 1995), 21, no. 7 (hereafter Ilski, *Biskupi Mezji i Scytii*); Георги Атанасов [Georgi Atanasov], *Християнският Дуросторум-Дръстър* [*The Christian Durostorum-Drăstar*] (Varna: Zograf, 2007), 87 (hereafter Атанасов, *Християнският Дуросторум-Дръстър*).

[7] Каравълчев, "Християнският Анхиало," 203-204; Soustal, *Tabula Imperii Byzantini*, 175, 234.

[8] Михаил Поснов [Mikhail Posnov], *История на християнската църква* [History of the Christian Church] (София: Анубис [Sofia: Anubis], 1993), 283–284 (hereafter Поснов, *История на християнската църква*); Ilski, *Biskupi Mezji i Scytii*, 35–36, no. 17.

[9] Поснов, *История на християнската църква*, 302; Каравълчев, "Християнският Анхиало," 204; Soustal, *Tabula Imperii Byzantini*, 175.

throughout the sixth century. They were able to do this due to the greatly expanded administrative powers within the new public governing bodies formed in the first half of the sixth century by order of Emperor Anastasios I and confirmed in 545.[10]

In the sixth century, the Church of Odessos experienced financial difficulties in fulfilling its social mission and care for "the little people" (*plebs infima*). In 538, Bishop Martinus of Odessos was able to arrange a private meeting with Emperor Justinian I in Constantinople in order to obtain permission to sell church lands and buildings in the town in order to raise money to be used for charitable purposes and to free Christian captives or slaves from pagan owners. As a result of Bishop Martinus's intercession, Justinian issued his 65th novel on 23 March 538.[11] In addition to money, the church would serve other functions, and for some members of *ordo plebeiorum* (urban plebs) in Odessos, the affiliation to the Church community provided spiritual and material support against the attacks of the Trans-Danubian tribes, the rising tax and service obligations to the state and the arbitrariness of the powerful (*homines potentes*). The membership of the *ordo plebeiorum* of Odessos is visible in the city's preserved tombstones from the fifth to the sixth century as group that included furriers, marble-hewers, soap-boilers, candle-makers, and hired workers manufacturing canopies.[12]

The initiative of Bishop Martinus proved timely and had practical application as seen from the emperor's 120th novel from 9 May 544, which re-confirmed the decision from 538.[13] Among the possible reasons for its application are the raids of the Trans-Danubian tribes of the Bulgarians and Kutrigurs, who stayed over the winter in the hinterland of Odessos and Marcianopolis in 540 and 558/559.[14]Durostorum was

---

[10] Велизар Велков [Velizar Velkov], *Градът в Тракия и Дакия през Късната античност (I–VI в.). Проучвания и материали [The City in Thracia and Dacia in Late Antiquity (1ˢᵗ–6ᵗʰ c.). Research and sources]*(София: Българска академия на науките [Sofia: Bulgarian Acemy of Sciences],1959), 69, 70 (hereafter Велков, *Градът в Тракия и Дакия*).

[11] *Imperatoris Iustiniani PP. A. Novellae quae vocantur sive constitutiones quae extra codicem supersunt ordine chronologico digestae, II*, ed. Karl Eduard Zachariae von Lingenthal (Lipsiae: Teubner, MDCCCLXXXI), Nov. LXV (hereafter *Imperatoris Iustiniani PP. A. Novellae)*; Велизар Велков [Velizar Velkov], "Бележки върху социално-икономическото развитие на Одесос през късноантичната епоха [Notes on the social-economic development of Odessos during the Late Antiquity]," *Известия на Варненското Археологическо дружество[Proceedings of the Varna Archaeological Society]*10 (1956): 112–113 (hereafter Велков, "Бележки върху социално-икономическото развитие на Одесос"); Ilski, *Biskupi Mezji i Scytii*, 41–42, no. 23.

[12] Веселин Бешевлиев [Veselin Beshevliev], "Старохристиянските надписи от Варна като исторически извор [The old Chrisitan inscriptions from Varna as historical source],"*Известия на Народния музей – Варна [Proceedings of the National museum - Varna]*, 19 (1983): 26–27 (hereafter Бешевлиев, "Старохристиянските надписи от Варна").

[13] *Imperatoris Iustiniani PP. A. Novellae*, CXX. 4–8; Велков, "Бележки върху социално-икономическото развитие на Одесос," 113.

[14] Димитър Ангелов, Стефан Кашев, and Борис Чолпанов [Dimităr Angelov, Stefan Cholpanov and Boris Kashev], *Българска военна история. От античността до втората четвърт на X в.* [Bulgarian military

conquered and destroyed by the Avars in 587.[15] The bishop of the town Dulcissimus then moved to Odessos, where he lived to the end of his life. His body was buried in the tomb of Bishop Daniel of Odessos, who died before the middle of the century.[16]

Apart from providing financial and physical aid, bishops oversaw the liturgical and pastoral needs of their dioceses with the help of the clergy, whose functions increased and differentiated over time, evidenced by their appearance in the inscriptions from the region. Eutychianus is mentioned as the bishop (most probably of Anchialos) in an inscription on a marble column erected possibly in an early Christian church in Aquae Calidae-Therma (the Roman station near the thermal bath complex fortified under Justinian I, now Burgaski mineralni bani), together with his Deacon Vindemiul, entrusted with the management of church property, and with the auxiliary bishop, the Vicar Philip (Figure 2).[17] There is evidence about a "Stephanus *diak(onus)*," who

Figure 2. Therma. A marble column (author).

---

history. From Antiquity till the second quarter of the 10th c.] (София: Издателство на Българската академия на науките [Sofia: Bulgarian Acemy of Sciences], 1983), 72–75, pl.17–18.

15   Велков, "Бележки върху социално-икономическото развитие на Одесос," 116; Атанасов, *Християнският Дуросторум*, 88.

16   Атанасов, *Християнският Дуросторум*, 88; Veselin Beševliev, *Spätgriechische und spätlateinische Inschriften aus Bulgarien* (Berlin: Akemie Verlag, 1964), 76, no. 107 (hereafter Beševliev, *Spätgriechische und spätlateinische Inschriften*); Ilski, *Biskupi Mezji i Scytii*, 20, no. 6.

17   About the *territorium* of Anchialos and Aquae Calidae-Therma, see Борис Геров [Boris Gerov], "Земевладението в римска Тракия и Мизия (I-III в.)," [Landownership in Roman Thrace and Moesia (1st-3rd c.)] *Годишник на Софийския университет. Факултет класически и нови филологии* [Sofia University Year-book. Faculty of Classical and new Philology], 72, no. 2 (1977): 45, 46, 102-103 (hereafter Геров, "Земевладението в римска Тракия и Мизия"); *Inscriptiones Graecae in Bulgaria repertae I²*, ed. Georgius Mihailov (Serdicae: Acemia Litterarum Bulgarica, MCMLXX), 335-336, nos. 380, 381(hereafter *IGBulg, I²*); Soustal, *Tabula Imperii Byzantini*, 477–478; Veselin Beševliev, *Zur Deutung Kastellnamen in Prokops Werk "De Aedificiis"* (Amsterdam: Hakkert, 1970), 71–72, 90, 142; Велков, *Градът в Тракия и Дакия*, 65–67; *Corpus Iuris Civilis*, I. 3.On AquaeCalidae-Therma, see: *Procopii Caesariensis opera omnia, recognovit Jacobus Haury* (Lipsiae: Teubner, 1905–1906), III, 7, 19–23; Цоня Дражева and Димчо Момчилов [TsonyrazhevaandDimchoMomchilov], "Археологически проучвания на обект „Късноантична и средновековна крепост „Акве Калиде – Терма", Бургаски минерални бани [Archaeological research on the site „Late antique and Medieval fortress "AquaeCalidae – Therma, mineral baths of Bourgas]," in *Археологиски открития и разкопки през* [*Archaeological discoveries and excavations in 2011 г.*], ed. Мария Гюрова [Mariya Gyurova] et al. (София: Авангард [Sofia: Avangard], 2012), 444–446 (hereafter *Археологически открития и разкопки през 2011 г.*). Beševliev, *Spätgriechische und spätlateinische Inschriften*, 118, no. 171.

according to a building inscription from the fortified settlement Bizone on Cape Chirakman, was engaged with the (re)construction of a temple with donations from the believers dedicated to the holy martyrs Cosmas and Damian,[18] much honored during the reign of Justinian I.[19] Other epigraphic evidence only notes their existence: the subdeacon Eutychianus[20] and presbyter Vitalios[21] were buried in Sozopolis; the presbyter Theodore died in a fortified settlement on Cape Saint Athanasius;[22] the presbyter Peter, his son the Reer Bonos,[23] and Abba Marcellus, primate of the Asia Minor Christian community in Odessos[24] all buried in that town; the vicar Marcellus from Odessos died in Tomis.[25]

The Archaeology of Change: Appropriation of Holy Places

Surviving written and epigraphical sources offer only a glimpse into the history of the Church in the region of the southwestern coast of the Black Sea. They underscore the rise of the Christian bishop as a representative, overseer and patron of the urban communities in the area. Archaeological evidence gives a greater resolution picture about

---

[18] Beševliev, *Spätgriechische und spätlateinische Inschriften*, 56, no. 84; Милко Мирчев, Горана Тончева, and Димитър Димитров [Milko Mirchev, Gorana Toncheva, and Dimităr Dimitrov], "Бизоне-Карвуна [Bizone-Karvuna]," *Известия на Варненското археологическо дружество* [*Proceedings of Varna Archaeological Society*] 13 (1962): 25, 30, fig. 1.

[19] Danilo Mazzoleni, "Les inscriptions des martyrs des origines chrétiennes au VIIe siècle," in *Раннохристиянски мъченици и реликви и тяхното почитане на Изток и Запад. Международна конференция* [*Early Christian Martyrs and Relics and their Veneration in East and West. International Conference*](*Варна* [Varna], 20.–23. 11. 2003) (*Acta Musei Varnaensis*, 4), ed. Alexander Minchev et al. (Велико Търново: Абагар [Veliko Tărnovo: Abagar], 2006), 113 (hereafter *Раннохристиянски мъченици и реликви*); Alexander Minchev, "Early Christian double crypt with reliquaries at Khan Krum Street in Varna (ancient Odessos)," in *Early Christian Martyrs and Relics and their Veneration in East and West: International Congress, Varna, November 20th–23rd, 2003*, Acta Musei Varnaensis 4 (Varna, 2006), 253 (hereafter Minchev, "Early Christian double crypt").

[20] Beševliev, *Spätgriechische und spätlateinische Inschriften*, no. 180.

[21] Dan Dana, "Une nouvelle épitaphe grecque tardive de Bulgarie," *Zeitschrift für Papyrologie und Epigraphik* 174 (2010): 107.

[22] Веселин Бешевлиев [Veselin Beshevliev], "Два надгробни старохристиянски надписа от Черноморието [Two early Christian funerary inscriptions from the Black Sea coast]," *Известия на Народния музей – Варна* [*Proceedings of the National museum - Varna*] 9 (1973): 302–303; Валери Йотов and Александър Минчев [Valeri Iotov and Alexandăr Minchev], "Късноантична крепост (V – VI в.) на нос Свети Атанас до град Бяла, област Варна [A late antique fortress (5th–6th c.) on St. Athanasius Cape near city of Byala, Varna district]," in *Археологически открития и разкопки през* [*Archaeological discoveries and excavations in*] 2013 г., ed. Мария Гюрова [Mariya Gyurova] et al. (София: TDG Print [Sofia TDG Print, 2014), fig. 1 (hereafter *Археологически открития и разкопки през 2013 г.*).

[23] Бешевлиев, "Старохристиянските надписи от Варна," 23.

[24] Бешевлиев, "Старохристиянските надписи от Варна," 24.

[25] Ion Barnea, *Les monuments paléochrétiens de Roumanie* (*Sussidi allo studio delle Antichità christiane*, 6) (Città de Vaticano: Pontificio Instituto di Archeologia Christiana, 1977), no. 16; Велков, Градът в Тракия и Дакия, 58.

the process of the institutional and ideological establishment of Christianity as the state religion of the Empire. This process is connected to a changing attitude towards pagan temples and monuments. Following the official imposition of Christianity in the region, the *temene* of pagan temples were repurposed for new religious practice. The option of pre-Christian sacred places was essentially an act of the spiritual reshaping of traditional sacred *topoi* and retaining them as sustainable spiritual foci of the territorial community served as the materialization of the victory of Christianity over pagan cults.[26]

The practice of appropriation of pagan sites is noted in the archaeology of the Black Sea coast in a number of different cases, suggesting its wide-spre acceptance and practice. The earliest date from the second half of the fourth century, when a single-nave church, possibly part of a monastery complex, used the space of a Roman sanctuary near the citadel of the settlement Aphrodision, located approximately six Roman miles to the east of Dionysopolis. Up to the beginning of the sixth century, an atrium and a *narthex* were attached to the temple.[27]

Another early appropriation took place in the early Byzantine unfortified settlement Karabizye, located approximately four and a half Roman miles southeast of Odessos, where a single-apse basilica with side aisles, *narthex* and baptistery was built. Judging by the coin finds on and under its flooring the construction must have been carried out between the reign of Magnentius and Arcius that is, between 350 and 408.[28] In the construction of the basilica, dedication slabs related to a local pagan cult were inserted in the altar and floor. Three of them date from the third century BC, and the rest are from the end of the first to the end of the second century (Figure 3).[29] Origi-

---

[26] Маргарита Харбова [Margarita Harbova], *Три религии, три храма. Една земя, наричана българска* [*Three religions, three temples. A land called Bulgarian*] (София: Академично издателство „Проф. Марин Дринов" [Sofia: Acemic publishing house "Prof. Marin Drinov"], 1999), 13, 16.

[27] Боян Иванов [Boyan Ivanov], "Спасителни проучвания на античен обект при с. Топола, община Каварна [Rescue excavations on ancient site near village of Topola, Kavarna municipality]," in *Археологически открития и разкопки през* [*Archaeological discoveries and excavations in*]*2007 г.*, ed. Дияна Гергова [Diyana Gergova] et al. (София: Фабер [Sofia: Faber], 2008), 499 (hereafter Иванов, "Спасителни проучвания"); Сергей Торбатов [Sergei Torbatov], *Укрепителната система на провинция Скития (края на III–VII в.)* [The fortification system in the province of Scythia (the end of the 3rd–7th c.)] (Велико Търново: Фабер [Veliko Tarnovo: Faber], 2002), 256–257 (hereafter Торбатов, *Укрепителната система на провинция Скития*).

[28] Милко Мирчев [Milko Mirchev], "Разкопки на тракийското селище край с. Галата [Excavations on the Thracian settlement near village of Galata]," *Известия на Варненското археологическо дружество* [*Proceedings of the Varna Archaeological Society*] 9 (1953): 4–8, 11, 21 (hereafter Мирчев, "Разкопки на тракийското селище край с. Галата").

[29] Горана Тончева [GoranaToncheva], "За датирането на светилището край с. Галата [On the dating of the sanctuary near the village of Galata]," *Известия на Народния музей – Варна* [*ProceedingsoftheNationalmuseum – Varna*] 4 (1968): 17–22. IGBulg, I², nos. 284–290; Zlatozara Gočeva and Manfred Oppermann, *Monumenta Orae Ponti Euxini Bulgariae* (*Corpus Cultus Equitis Thracii* (*CCET*), I) (Leiden: E. J. Brill, 1979), nos. 83, 84, 85, 86, 87, 88, 89, 94 (hereafter Gočeva and Oppermann, *Monumenta Orae Ponti Euxini Bulgariae*).

Figure 3. Karabyzie. A pagan dedication plate of the Heros Karabazmos (after *IGBulg*, I², no. 287).

nally, the slabs were used in the sanctuary of the local Thracian deity Heros Karabazmos: the images were erased before the slabs were reused. Furthermore, in the process of building the basilica, the walls and floor of the pagan sanctuary were dismantled, but part of its groundwork has been discovered under the floor of the basilica (Figure 4) during excavations. In the pre-Christian layers, a number of coins were found: civic issues for the city Odessos, those of Marcus Aurelius and minted in Augusta Trajana, and those depicting Maximinus II Daia, Constantine I, Constantius II, and Magnentius.[30] The choice of location for the construction of the Christian church was not accidental in this case: during Hellenistic and Roman times, the Thracian cult of Heros Karabazmos was celebrated in the nearby *polis* Odessos, where in the second century the cult was mingled with Apollo, a deity highly respected in the Ionian city-states.[31] The

---

[30] Мирчев, "Разкопки на тракийското селище край с. Галата," 12–21.
[31] *IGBulg*, I², nos. 78 *bis*, 78 *ter*, 79 *bis*; Gočeva and Oppermann, *Monumenta Orae Ponti Euxini Bulgariae*, nos. 28, 30, 34 and *IGBulg*, I², nos. 79, 162; Gočeva and Oppermann, *Monumenta Orae Ponti Euxini Bulgariae*, nos. 32, 60; Zlatozara Gočeva, "Der Apollonkult in Odessos," in *Studia in honorem Veselini Beševliev*, ed. Vlimir Georgiev et al. (Sofia: Academia Litterarum Bulgarica, 1978), 289–298; Norbert Ehrhardt, *Milet und seine Kolonien Vergleichende Untersuchungen der kultischen und politischen Einrichtungen* (*Europäische Hochschulschriften*, Reihe III: *Geschichte und ihre Hilfswissenschaften, Bd.* 206) (Frankfurt am Main: Peter Lang, 1983), 61, 84, 130, 137.

temples of the two deities in Odessos were built in the coastal zone over the harbor and located about 130 m apart, and had significant historical positions in the city. The temple of Apollo was built no later than the first half of the third century BC in a Doric order, and part of the public archive was kept in the temple.[32] The pagan *templum in antis* (temple with pilaster terminating internal walls) 9 m wide, more than 13.75 m long and 9.20 m high was repeatedly repaired and reconstructed.[33] Probably after the end of the fourth century, the building was destroyed and the *temenos* of Apollo was transformed into an early Christian basilica. In and around the temple Doric capitals and fluting drums, monolithic columns, bases, crowning cornices, and a trapezium-shaped early Byzantine capital with a monogram from the sixth century were found.[34]

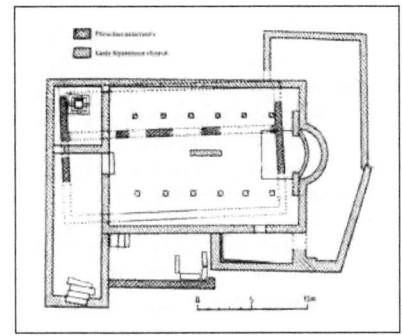

Figure 4. Karabyzie. The early Christian basilica and the pagan sanctuary of the Heros Karabazmos (after Мирчев, "Разкопки на тракийското селище край с. Галата," План 1).

The pagan temple of Cybele in Dionysopolis continued to function through the third quarter of the fourth century. The only Latin inscription in the temple, carved into a marble base, attests to the fact that Emperor Licinius I dedicated, through the governor of the province of Scythia Aurelius Speratianus, a silver statue of the Pontic Mother of Gods after his successful campaign against the Sarmatian tribes in 310. The statue replaced another silver statue of the goddess, mentioned in the temple list of donations and lost during the Gothic raids in the second half of the third century.[35] The cult of the *Mater*

---

32   Hristo Preshlenov, "Urban Spaces in Odessus (6thc. BC – 7thc.)," *Archaeologia Bulgarica* 6, no. 3/3 (2002): 22–24, fig. 1/9, 1/20.*IGBulg*, I², no. 43.

33   Христо Прешленов [Hristo Preshlenov], "Теменосът на Аполон в Одесос: топография и архитектура [The *temenos* of Apollo in Odessos: topography and architecture]," in *Jubilaeus VII*. A Conference in memory of Prof. Margarita Tacheva on the occasion of the 80th anniversary of her birth, ed. Dilyana Boteva et al. (София: Издателство на Софийския университет „Св. Климент Охридски" [Sofia: Publishing house of the "Saint Kliment Ohridski" University], forthcoming).

34   Милко Мирчев [Milko Mirchev], "За античните храмове в Одесос [About the ancient temples in Odessos]," *Известия на Народния музей Варна* [*Proceedings of the National museum - Varna*] 3(1967): 24; Александър Минчев [Alexandăr Minchev], "Ранното християнство в Одесос и околностите му [The Early Christianity in Odessos and its vicinity]," *Известия на Народния музей – Варна* [*Proceedings of the National museum – Varna*] 22 (1986): 35–36.

35   Igor Lazarenko, Elina Mircheva, Rostina Encheva, and Nikolaj Sharankov, "The Temple of the Pontic Mother of Gods in Dionysopolis," in *Ancient Sacral Monuments in the Black Sea*, ed. Elias Petropoulos et al. (Thessaloniki: Kiriakidis Brothers, 2010), 22, 23–24, 27, 37, 39 (hereafter Lazarenko, Mircheva, Encheva, Sharankov, "The Temple of the Pontic Mother of Gods").

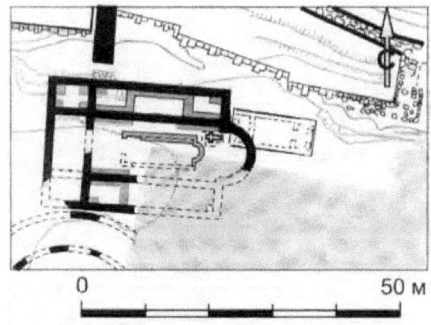

Figure 5. Mesembria. The northwestern urban zone (after Прешленов, "Християнизация и архитектурна среда в Несебър и Паницово,"fig. 1).

deum, one of the few pagan sacred places in Dionysopolis still functioning in the fourth century, also bore dedications to the Thracian Horseman, Apollo, Dionysos, and Pan. The latest coins under the burned roof tiles in the *pronaos* and the *naos* belong to the reigns of Valentinian I and Valens. Before or after the destruction, caused by the earthquake in 366/7–68 and/or by the Gothic raid of 378, some of the temple statues were probably desecrated by Christians as well.[36]

In Mesembria, the basilica at the main gate was built on the square, in which during the Hellenistic and Roman periods the founders and the heroes were celebrated (Figure 5). Its apse was constructed over a temple of Zeus, and next to it a pagan *heroon* stood.[37] There, the tombs *intra muros* of the deified city-founders (*oikistes*) served cult centers where the founders were honored as heroes of the *polis* (Figure 6). Around the *heroon*, citizens who had defended the city were also honored in the late Hellenistic period.[38] In the middle of the fifth century, the basilica had already inherited the sacred place and the existing pagan buildings were demolished. In the altar space, a cruciform vaulted subterranean building has been discovered, as well as pieces of marble sarcophagus and a reliquiary.[39] Despite the questionable link between the cult of the pagan

---

[36] Атанас Орачев [Atanas Orachev], "Земетресения и последици по Добруджанското крайбрежие през III–IV век (предварителни наблюдения) [Earthquackes and their consequences on the Dobrudzha coastline in Dobruja during the 3rd–4th century (preliminary observations)],"in *Сборник в чест на Александър Минчев* [*Collection in honour of Aleksandăr Minchev*]. *Terra Antiqua Balcanica et Mediterranea. Международна конференция, Варна* [*International conference, Varna*], 23. 02. 2007 (*Acta Musei Varnaensis*, VIII.1), ed. Валери Йотов [Valeri Iotov] et al. (Варна: Онгъл [Varna: Ongăl], 2011), 127–128, 129 (hereafter *Сборник в чест на Александър Минчев*); Lazarenko, Mircheva, Encheva, Sharankov, "The Temple of the Pontic Mother of Gods," 27, 37, 39, fig 21).

[37] Христо Прешленов [Hristo Preshlenov], "Теменосите на Зевс в Месамбрия Понтика. Историческа топография и архитектура [*Temenoi* of Zeus in Mesambria Pontica. Historical topography and architecture]," in *Богове и хора. Международна археологическа конференция, Варна* [*Gods and humans. International conference of archaeology, Varna*], 18–20. 09. 2008 (*Acta Musei Varnaensis, IX*), ed. Александър Минчев [Aleksandăr Minchev] et al. (Varna, forthcoming).

[38] Иван Маразов [Ivan Marazov], "Ойкистите" в релефите на стратези от Месамбрия [The *oikistes* on the reliefs of Mesambrian *strategoi*]," *Проблеми на изкуството* [*Problems of art*] 37-A/1 (2004): 20, 25, 27.

[39] Hristo Preshlenov, "Mesambria Pontica in *orbis Romanum*", in *Corpus of Ancient and Medieval Settlements in modern Bulgaria*, 1. *Roman Cities in Bulgaria*, ed. Rumen Ivanov (Sofia: Acemic Publishing House Prof. Marin Drinov, 2012), 515–516, fig. 22 (hereafter Preshlenov, "Mesambria Pontica in *orbis Romanum*").

Figure 6. Mesambria. A relief of the Mesambrian *strategoi* (afterW. Welkow, *Nessebar* (Sofia: Sofia Press, 1989), *s. p.*

heroes and the Christian cult of martyrs, one cannot exclude the possible formation of a memorial complex near the *heroon* before the construction of the basilica where holy relics were (re)buried, perhaps connected to the relics of the martyr Saint Irene, already in the town in the fourth century according to the *Synaxarium Ecclesiae Constantinopolitanae*.[40] Interred in the crypt, it was preserved during the reconstruction of the basilica in the third quarter of the seventh century, which turned it into a cross-dome church.[41]

Similar topographic continuity has also been found on Saint John's Island near Sozopolis. Northwest of the early Christian church, which housed relics of Saint John the Baptist,[42] a Thracian sanctuary from the first millennium BC has been located.[43]

---

[40] Юлия Вълева [YuliyaVăleva], "Погребения *Sanctos* през ранните християнски векове [Burials *Sanctos* over early Christian centuries]," *Проблеми на изкуството*[*Problem sofart*] 33-A/4 (2000): 59; Christian Gnilka, Stefan Heid, and Reiner Riesner, *Blutzeuge – Todund Grabdes Petrusin Rom* (Regensburg: Schnell&Steiner, 2010), 183.A similar regional and local practice, cf. Stéphane Boyjiev, "L' architecture du mausolée de Lozenetz et sa corrélation avec ceux de la Moésie et la Thrace," in*Раннохристиянски мъченици и реликви*, 133–139; Zhivko Aljov, Tsonjrazheva, and Dimcho Momchilov, "The martyrium of "Markeli" fortress by Karnobat," in*Раннохристиянски мъченици и реликви*, 277–278, fig. 2. *Synaxarium Ecclesiae Constantinopolitanae*, 656; Soustal, *Tabula Imperii Byzantini*, 355.

[41] Preshlenov, "Mesambria Pontica in *orbis Romanum*," 517, fig. 23.

[42] Казимир Попконстантинов, Цоня Дражева, Росина Костова, and Даниела Николова [Kazimir Popkonstantinov, Tsonya Drazheva, Rossina Kostova, and Daniela Nikolova], "Средновековен манастир „Св. Йоан Продром" на остров „Св. Иван", Созопол,"[Medieval monastery Saint John the Baptist on Saint Ivan Island, Sozopol] in *Археологически открития и разкопки през* [*Archaeological discoveries and excavations in*] *2010 г.*, ed. Мария Гюрова [Mariya Gyurova] et al. (София: Авангард [Sofia: Avangard], 2011), 500–503.

[43] ИванПетрински [Ivan Petrinski], "Манастирът "Свети Иван Предтеча и Кръстител" на остров Св. Иван [The monastery of Saint John the Baptist on Saint Ivan Island] (1467/71-1629)," *Известия на Народния Музей – Бургас* [*Proceedings of the National museum – Bourgas*], 3 (2000): 178.

On the adjacent Saint Cyriacus Island, topographic continuity of pre- and early Christian sacred places has also been established. Here, a basilica with a necropolis from the fifth to the seventh century inherited the pagan *temenoses*, where late Archaic and early Hellenistic temples, sacral pits with graffiti dedicated to Apollo "the Helper", terracotta associated with the cult to Aphrodite, and Roman votive tablets of the Thracian Horseman were found.[44]

Archaeological findings from the cities along the southwestern coast of the Black Sea indicate that the fourth-century Christianization meant essentially the "secularization" or appropriation of pagan sacred sites, without apparent instances of religious violence.

Christian Architecture and Decoration

Thirty-eight early Christian churches are known today along the southwestern Black Sea coast.[45] They are as follows: one in the fortified area and in the citadel

---

[44] Кръстина Панайотова, Методи Даскалов, Росица Пенчева, and Катя Трендафилова [Krastina Panayotova, Metodi Daskalov, Rositsa Pencheva, and Katya Trendafilova], "Спасителни археологически проучвания на о. Св. Кирик," [Rescue archaeological researches on Saint Cyriacus Island] in *Археологически открития и разкопки през [Archaeological discoveries and excavations in] 2009 г.*, ed. Дияна Гергова [Diyana Gergova] et al. (София: Авангард [Sofia: Avangard], 2010), 295–298 (hereafter *Археологически открития и разкопки през 2009 г.*); Кръстина Панайотова, Маргарит Дамянов, and Теодора Богданова [Krastina Panayotova, Margarit Damyanov, and Teodora Bogdanova], "Храмов комплекс на о-в Св. Кирик, гр. Созопол" [Complex of temples on the Saint Cyriacus Island, city of Sozopol] in *Археологически открития и разкопки през [Archaeological discoveries and excavations in] 2014 г*, ed. Гергана Кабакчиева [Gergana Kabakchieva] et al. (София: Актив Комерс [Sofia: Aktiv Comers], 2015), 344–346).

[45] Hristo Preshlenov, "Frühchristliche Archäologie an der Bulgarischen Schwarzmeer küste (1878–2008)," *Römische Quartal Schrift für Christliche Altertumskunde und Kirchen geschichte* 105/1–2 (2010):86–104; Валери Йотов and Александър Минчев [Valery Iotov and Alexandăr Minchev], "Късноантична крепост на нос Свети Атанас до град Бяла, Варненско [Late Antique fortress on Saint Athanasius Cape near the city of Byala, Varna district]," in *Археологически открития и разкопки през 2009 г.*, 295–298; Александър Минчев and Васил Тенекеджиев [Alexandăr Minchev and Vasil Tenekedzhiev], "Спасителни разкопки на раннохристиянска църква в местността Боровец край Варна [Rescue excavations on the early Christian church in Borovets locality near Varna]," in *Археологически открития и разкопки през [Archaeological discoveries and excavations in] 2012 г.*, ed. Мария Гюрова [Mariya Gyurova] et al. (София: Колбис АД [Sofia"Kolbis], 2013), 205–205 (hereafter *Археологически открития и разкопки през 2012 г*); Цоня Дражева and Димитър Недев [Tsonya Drazheva and Dimităr Nedev], "Спасителни археологически проучвания на обект „Крепостна стена и прилежащите й съоръжения в участъка на пл. Хан Крум, църква „Св.Св. Кирил и Методий" и южна крайбрежна алея, УПИ XIX-523 и 525, УПИ XXII-526 и УПИ XXI-527, кв. 27 по плана на гр. Созопол [Rescue archaeological researches on the site "Fortification wall and justed facility in the area of Khan Krum Square, Saints "Kiril and Metodii" Church, and South coastal lane, ... by the plan of the city of Sozopol]," in *Археологически открития и разкопки през 2012 г.*, 468; Тодор Марваков, Мартин Гюзелев, and Константин Господинов [Todor Marvakov, Martin Gyuzelev and Konstantin Gospodinov], "Спасително археологическо проучване в границите на НААГР „Старинен Несебър", УПИ III-278, кв.

of the settlement Timum[46] five and a half Roman miles west of T(i)rissa/Acres; one in Bizone; another in and near the citadel of Aphrodision;[47] seven churches in Odessos and eight churches in the surrounding area; in Karabyzie; in Erite, the former Roman station at the mouth of the *Panysos* River (now Kamchiya); in the *quadriburgium*-type fortification with a possible primary monastic function at the mouth of the Shkorpilovska River;[48] in the fortified settlement on Cape Saint Athanasius; in Templum Iovis; in the fortified settlement (Scatrina ?) on the Dyulino Pass; seven churches in Mesembria; five churches in Sozopolis. The construction of these churches started at the beginning of the fifth century. Their symmetric composition was influenced by the form of the Hellenistic basilica. The churches have side aisles, a wooden roof, a relatively long nave along the coast north of Odessos, and up to short nave to the south of this city. The attachment of baptisteries and atriums to some churches during the reign of Justinian I was obviously connected with the mass Christianization of the native population.[49]

The inner ratio of the naves' dimensions of the Pontic churches range from 1:1.7 (Bizone),[50] 1:1.6 (Erite),[51] 1:1.4 (Karabyzie),[52] 1:1.3 (the Episcopal basilica in Odessos,[53] and the basilica in the fortified settlement (Scatrina ?) on the Dyulino

---

6; УПИ III-217, кв. 8 и УПИ VII-204, кв. 12 по плана на гр. Несебър, област Бургас [Rescue archaeological researches within the bounds of the NAAGR "Old Nesebär ... by the plan of the city of Nesebär"]," in *Археологически открития и разкопки през 2013 г*, 233–234.

[46] Торбатов, *Укрепителната система на провинция Скития*, 234–237.

[47] Торбатов, *Укрепителната система на провинция Скития*, 253–254, 256–257; Иванов, "Спасителни проучвания," 449.

[48] Венцислав Динчев [Ventsislav Dinchev], *Ранновизантийските крепости в България и съседните земи (в Диоцезите Thracia и Dacia)*[*Early Byzantine fortifications in Bulgaria and the neighboring lands (in the dioceses of Thracia and Dacia)*](*Разкопки и проучвания* [*Excavations and research*] 35)(София: Българска Академия на науките [Sofia: Bulgarian Acemie of sciences], 2006), 49, 87 (hereafter Динчев, *Ранновизантийските крепости в България*); Constantin Băjenaru, *Minor Fortifications in the Balkan-Danubian Area from Diocletian to Justinian* (Cluj-Napoca: Mega, 2010), 138, 170, 175).

[49] Нели Чанева-Дечевска [Neli Chaneva-Dechevska], *Раннохристиянската архитектура в България IV–VI в.* [*Early Christian architecture in Bulgaria 4th–6th c.*] (Sofia: Publishing house of the "Saint Kliment Ohridski" University, 1999), 54, 58, 62, 86.

[50] Мирчев, Тончева, Димитров, 28–30, fig. 6.

[51] Сергей Покровски [Sergei Pokrovski], "Християнска базилика до устието на р. Камчия," [Christian basilica by the mouth of Kamchiya river] *Известия на Българския археологически институт* [*Proceedings of the Bulgarian archaeological institute*], 14, (1940–42): 252, fig. 349; AlexanderMintschev, "Dasfrühe Christentum in Odessos und seinemTerritorium," in *Die BulgarischeSchwarzmeerküsteimAltertum(Xenia, KonstanzerAlthistorischeVorträge und Forschungen,* 16), ed. Wolfgang Schuller (Konstanz: UniversitätVerlag, 1985), 60, Abb. 4 (hereafter Mintschev, "Das frühe Christentum in Odessos").

[52] Мирчев, "Разкопки на тракийското селище край с. Галата," 4–7, pl. 1.

[53] Minchev, "Early Christian double crypt," 230, fig. 1.

Figure 7. Scatrae. A wall painting of the early Christian basilica (author).

Pass[54], 1:1.1 the monastery basilica in the site known as Pirinch Tepe, excavated half Roman mile southwest of Odessos,[55] the basilica in the monastery of Saint Iliya, located eight and a half Roman miles southeast of Odessos,[56] and the basilica next to the western gate of the fortress of Mesembria[57] to 1:1 the basilica in the *quadriburgium*-type fortification at the mouth of the Shkorpilovska river,[58] the episcopal basilica of Saint Sofia,[59] and the monastery church of the Holy Virgin Eleusa[60] in Mesembria.

The architectural patterns of churches along the southwestern coast of the Black Sea indicated the connection between the symbolism of the liturgy with the material environment in which it was celebrated: the Church built of stone was the image of the world, while the *naos* ('the place where the liturgy took place') represented the visible, physical world and the altar - the invisible, spiritual world.

---

[54] Христо Прешленов [Hristo Preshlenov], "Паганизъм и християнство в Източна Стара планина. Проучвания на укрепеното селище при Паницово," [Paganism and Christianity in Eastern Stara Planina Mountain. Excavations on the fortified settlement near Panitsovo]" in *Spartacus*,2. *2075 години от въстанието на Спартак. Трако-римско наследство. 2000 години християнство. Международен симпозиум (Сандански, 1.- 4. 10. 2002)* [*2075 years from the revolt of Spartacus. Thraco-Roman heritage. 2000 years Christianity. Proceedings of the international symposium held in (Sandanski, 1-4. 10. 2002)*], ed. Александра Милчева [Aleksandra Milcheva] et al.) (Велико Търново: Фабер [Veliko Tărnovo: Faber], 2006), 262, fig. 10 (hereafter Прешленов, "Паганизъм и християнство в Източна Стара планина").

[55] Карел и Херменегилд Шкорпил [Karel and Hermenegild Shkorpil], "Одесос и Варна [Odessos and Varna]," *Известия на Варненското археологическо дружество* [*Proceedings of the Varna Archaeological Society*], 3 (1910): 14–21; Mintschev, "Das frühe Christentum in Odessos," 57, Abb. 1.

[56] Горана Тончева [Gorana Toncheva], "Материали за археологическата карта на България [Materials for the archaeological map of Bulgaria]," *Известия на Варненското археологическо дружество* [*Proceedings of the Varna Archaeological Society*], 8 (1951): 107, 108, fig. 161.

[57] Димо Кожухаров [Dimo Kozhuharov], "Базилика в северозападната части Несебра [Basillica in the Northwestern part of Nesebăr]," in *BulgariaPonticaMediiAevi 4–5¹*, ed. VasilGyuzelev (Sofia: Gutenberg, 2003) 372, fig. 1.

[58] Александър Минчев [Alexandăr Minchev], "Нови данни за раннохристиянската базилика с мозайки при с. Шкорпиловци, Варненско [New data about the early Christian basilica with mosaics near village of Shkorpilovtsi, Varna region]," *Известия на Народния музей – Варна* [*Proceedings of the National museum – Varna*], 32–33 (2002): 132, fig. 1.

[59] Dimitar Boyzhiev, "L Ancienne Église Métropole de Nesebăr," *Byzantinobulgarica,* I (1962):322–323, fig. 1.

[60] Димитър Съсълов [Dimităr Săsălov], "Архитектурно проучване на черквата "Богородица Елеуса"," [Architectural survey of the church Mother of God Eleusa] *Музеи и паметници на културата* [*Museums and monuments of the culture*], 12/5–6 (1982): 14–15, 17, fig. 9.

The decorative painting of the fourth-fifth century Christian churches in the region was influenced by Byzantine styles. In the basilica in the fortified settlement (possibly Scatrina) on the Dyulino Pass, geometric and floral motifs are combined with human figures.[61] From the end of the fourth to the beginning of the fifth century, Classical-realistic as well as illusionistic painting styles were popular, using various colors. In the northern aisle on the walls above the brick flooring a continuous edge is painted with white, red, and black paint. Above it rectangles with circles, rhombuses, and triangles inserted in them are painted, as well as framed floral ornaments, wavy, horizontal, and inclined lines around them. The human figures (Figure 7) with their style and colors are similar to the images of servants in a tomb from the end of the fourth century in Durostorum (Figure 8).[62] The overall impression is that decorative-linear schematization and geometrization prevail. The palette of the painters includes red (Fe_2O_3), blue ($2CuCO_3.Cu/OH/_2$), white ($CaCO_3$), black (carbon), and green (insoluble substance) pigments. The wall paintings were completed in a fresco technique. The pigments were mixed with quicklime binder ($CaCO_3$ in the pre-crystallization stage, without protein).[63]

Figure 8. Durostorum. A wall painting of the late Antique tomb (after Pillinger, *Corpus der spätantiken und frühchristlichen Wandmalereien Bulgariens*, Abb. 30).

---

[61] Прешленов, "Паганизъм и християнство в Източна Стара планина," 262, figs. 11, 12.

[62] R. Pillinger et al., eds., *Corpus der spätantiken und frühchristlichen Wandmalereien Bulgariens* (Wien: Verlag der Österreichischen Akemie der Wissenschaften, 1999), 24, Abb. 30, 34 (hereafter Pillinger, *Corpus der spätantiken und frühchristlichen Wandmalereien Bulgariens*).

[63] Петя Пенкова [Petya Penkova], "Аварийна консервация на стенописни фрагменти от раннохристиянската базилика при антично селище "Голямо Еркечко градище" [Emergency conservation of wall paintings from the early Christian basilica in the ancient settlement "Golyamo Erkechko Grishte"]," in *Национална конференция "Консервация и реставрация на музейни и художествени ценности", София, 2–3 януари 2000* [*National conference "Conservation and restoration of museums and fine arts cultural values", Sofia, 2–3 January 2000*], ed. Любен Прашков [Lyuben Prashkov] (София [Sofia], 2003), 157, 158.

Nascent Christianities, Gnostic Communities

Before the fourth century, Christian symbols and artefacts rarely appear in the Roman cities and their necropolises of the Southwestern Black Sea area. However, some evidence of nascent Christian communities can be detected. In the wall of a tomb in the vicinity of Odessos, an iron anchor, typical for the third century, and a sailboat are incised,[64] symbolizing the salvation of the human soul. In the northwest necropolis of Odessos, a sarcophagus from the third century with an image of a sailboat has been discovered.[65] A golden ring with the letters Α Ω incised on the plate was placed in a child's grave between the second half of the second and the beginning of the third century. The ring was made in the second century.[66] In the pagan necropolis of Apollonia third-century burials were found with incised crosses on gravestones.[67]

In the neighboring Roman colony of Deultum there is evidence for the spread of Gnosticism, a syncretic belief system influenced by Christianity and combining evangelical message, theosophy, occultism, and mythology, very popular from the second to the third century. In a chamber of a family tomb in the Roman necropolis of the colony bronze coins of Septimius Severus and Caracalla and two gold double-obverse medallion-amulets, the so-called Abraxas stones, were found.[68] Around the image of Abraxas on one of the obverses of the first gem the letters ΦΡΗΝ (the sun-god Phre) and ΙΑΩ (perhaps from *Yahweh*) were engraved, while on the other obverse the words ΑΒΡΑΣΑΞ (Abraxas) and ΣΕΜΕΣΕΙΛΑΜ (eternal Sun) are visible. Abraxas is also

---

[64] Михаил Лазаров [Mihail Lazarov], *Потъналата флотилия* [*The sunken fleet*] (Варна: Георги Бакалов [Varna: Georgi Bakalov], 1975), 115; Милко Мирчев [Milko Mirchev], "Паметници на гробната архитектура в Одесос и неговата околност [Monuments of the funerary architecture in Odessos and its vicinity]," in *Изследвания в чест на академик Димитър Дечев по случай 80-годишнината му* [*Studies in honour of acemician Dimităr Dechev on the occasion of the 80th anniversary of his birth*], ed. Веселин Бешевлиев [Veselin Beshevliev] (София: Българската академия на науките [Sofia: Bulgarian Acemie of sciences], 1958), 581, 582 (hereafter Мирчев, "Паметници на гробната архитектура в Одесос,"); Димитър Овчаров [Dimităr Ovcharov], "Архитектура и декорация на старохристиянските гробници в нашите земи [Architecture and decoration of Old Christian tombs in ours lands]," Археология [Archeologiya] 19, no. 4 (1977): 23; Димитър Овчаров and Маргарита Ваклинова [Dimităr Ovcharov and Margarita Vaklinova], *Ранновизантийски паметници от България IV–VII век* [*Early Byzantine monuments from Bulgaria 4th–7th century*](София: Септември [Sofia: Septemvri], 1978), 26, 43 (hereafter Овчаров and Ваклинова, *Ранновизантийски паметници*).

[65] *IGBulg*, I², no. 213 bis.

[66] Александър Минчев [Alexandăr Minchev], "Гроб с богат инвентар от римския некропол на Одесос [A furnished grave from the Roman necropolis of Odessos]," *Известия на Народния музей – Варна* [*Proceedings of the National museum - Varna*] 17 (1981): 65, 69.

[67] Acknowledgements for this information to Dimităr Nedev (Archaeological Museum Sozopol).

[68] Красимира Костова [Krasimira Kostova], "Археологически проучвания на обект 'Антична гробница' в НАР 'Деултум-Дебелт'" [Archaeological researches on the site "Ancient Tomb" in NAR "Deultum-Debelt"], in *Археологически открития и разкопки през 2012 г.*, 239–240.

presented on one of the obverses of the second gem, together with ΦΡΗΝ, ΑΒΡΑΣΑΞ, and ΙΑΩ. On the other obverse ΒΟΗΘΕΙ ΜΟΙ ΠΑΝΤΗ (help me in every way) and Ο ΑΝΓΕΛΟΣ (a messenger) were engraved.[69]

Pagan and Christian Burials

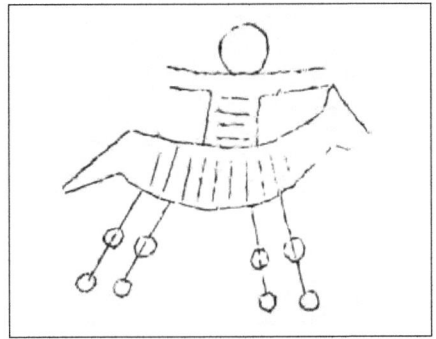

Figure 9. Odessos, vicinity. The pagan Thracian god-rider onto the wall of a late Roman tomb (after Мирчев, "Паметници на гробната архитектура в Одесос," Fig. 16).

The investigation of twenty-one family tombs in Late Roman and Early Byzantine urban necropoles along the Pontic Coast revealed the gradual disappearance of pagan rites and burial practices parallel with the spread of Christianity.[70] Burials with grave goods in tombs under a tumulus,[71] the heroization of the deceased by the reproduction of the Thracian god-rider (Figure 9),[72] and cremations vanished, with only one exception from the fourth century in the area between T(i)rissa/Acres and Callatis.[73] Tumular embankments also disappeared: the last ones found are from the fourth century.[74] The Roman tradition of burials in sarcophagi also ceased with two possible exceptions in Debeltos and Odessos.[75] All this is connected with the Christianization of the local population, especially in the towns. At the same time, in the tombs Christian symbols such as incised crosses, Christogram, saints, and peacocks appear more

---

[69] I would like to thank Krasimira Kostova (Regional Historical Museum - Sredets) and Nikolai Sharankov (Sofia University „Saint Kliment Ohridski") for information about the artifacts and preliminary recension of the inscriptions.

[70] Йордан Гатев [Iordan Gatev], "Погребален обред по Западното Черноморско крайбрежие през късната античност (4-6 в.) [Burial custom on the Western Black Sea Coast during the Late Antiquity 4th–6th c.]," (София: Българска академия на науките [Sofia: Bulgarian Acemie of Sciences], 2004), 5–7. A published abstract of the unpublished doctoral dissertation in National Institute of Archaeology with Museum (hereafter Гатев, "Погребален обред").

[71] Иван Василчин [Ivan Vasilchin], "Каменна гробница от IV в. при с. Горун, Толбухинско [A stone tomb from the 4th c. near village of Gorun, Dobrich area]," Известия на Народния музей – Варна [Proceedings of the National museum - Varna] 14 (1978): 111–116, fig. 1.

[72] Мирчев, "Паметници на гробната архитектура в Одесос," 582.

[73] Гатев, "Погребален обред," 7; Любка Бобчева [Lyubka Bobcheva],Археологическа карта на Толбухински окръг[Archaeological map of Tolbuhin district](София: София Прес [Sofia: Sofia Press], 1973), 46.

[74] Гатев, "Погребален обред," 6.

[75] Гатев, "Погребален обред," 13.

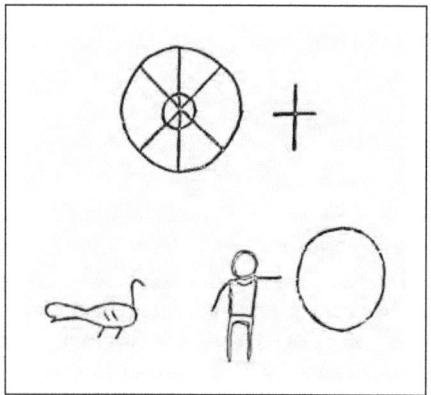

Figure 10. Odessos. Christian symbols onto the walls of an early Christian tomb (after Мирчев, "Късноримският некропол на Одесос," Fig. 144).

frequently, especially in the rapidly Christianizing Odessos. (Figure 10).[76] In the second half of the fourth century, pagan graves were re-used or destroyed (including the human remains and grave inventory) in Odessos when Christian burials were performed. A tomb from the second century was reused and the body was laid in west-east direction.[77] Gravestones with Latin and Greek inscriptions from tombs that had been destroyed after the middle of the third century [78] were built into the chamber of a Christian tomb in the middle of the fourth century.[79] West-east extended supine inhumation—laying the head of the deceased towards the west—is an unmistakeable trend.[80] Deviations from this direction laying the arms next to the body, burial gifts, and "death-coins", such as Charon's fee, reflect the preservation of traditional (pagan) elements in burial rites.[81]

Christianization was a long process, and the continuity of pagan traditions can be retraced on gravestones as well. From the fourth to the sixth century, simultaneous pagan and Christian formulae were in use in funeral inscriptions. In a fortified settlement (Scatrina ?) on the Dyulino Pass, a Greco-Roman inscription from the first half of the fourth century offers an "autobiography" of Φλάβιος Ζηνις, an armorer from the emperor's workshops in the neighboring Marcianopolis.[82] Next to Ἀγαθῇ τύχῃ (good

---

[76] Милко Мирчев [Milko Mirchev], "Късноримският некропол на Одесос [The Late Roman necropolis of Odessos]," *Известия на Варненското археологическо дружество* [*Proceedings of the Varna Archaeological Society*] 8 (1951): 94, 95, figs. 144, 145 (hereafter Мирчев, "Късноримският некропол на Одесос").

[77] Мирчев, "Късноримският некропол на Одесос,"94; Гатев, "Погребален обред," 13.

[78] *IGBulg*, I², no. 228 *bis*; Edward Luttwak, *The grand Strategy of the Roman Empire. From the First Century A.D. to the Third* (Baltimore and London: The Johns Hopkins University Press, 1976), 146, Map 3.1.

[79] Димитър Димитров and Камен Горанов [Dimităr Dimitrov and Kamen Goranov], "Раннохристиянска гробница в Одесос [Early Christian tomb in Odessos]," *Музеи и паметници на културата* [*Museums and monuments of the culture*]10, no. 3 (1970):3, 4, fig. 4; Милко Мирчев [Milko Mirchev], "Епиграфски паметници от Черноморието [Epigraphic monuments from the Black Sea coast]," *Известия на Народния музей – Варна*[*Proceedings of the National museum – Varna*] (1968): 173–177.

[80] Гатев, "*Погребален обред*," 16–17.

[81] Гатев, "*Погребален обред*," 8, 11, 12, 14, 16, 19, 21–22.

[82] Георги Михайлов [Georgi Mikhailov], "Epigraphica," *Известия на Народния музей – Бургас* [*Proceedings of the National museum - Bourgas*] 2 (1965): 150–153.

luck) the Christogram is carved. On the mouth of a clay pot found in the settlement, a cross with πᾱςὑγιής (wishes for health to the believers) is engraved.[83]

Pagan remnants abound in Odessos from the fifth to the sixth century. The pagan formula χερε παρωδῖτα (greetings, passerby!) ends an inscription that begins with the Christian formula ✝ Ἰρ(ήνη) (peace to you).[84] Another epitaph starts in a traditional way with Ἐ]νθάδε κατάκιτε ἡ μακαρία (here rests the blessed) and ends with the pagan greeting χερε παρωδῖτα.[85] The funeral inscription of Augusta,[86] daughter of a serviceman from the division of *Constantini seniores*[87] reads A✝Ω *Gaude legens. Iacet hic felix Augusta* (Be glad, reader. Here rests the happy Augusta). The Latin inscription is a free translation of the Greek model Χαίρε παροδῖτα. Ἐνθάδε κατάκιτε ἡ μακαρία (greetings, passerby! Here rests the blessed). Is this formulaic wording connected with the pagan expression for paradise, known by Hesiodos?[88] On other gravestones the greeting χέρετεπαροδῖτε and the identification of a deceased woman by the name of her husband evidence pagan traditions still alive.[89] The latest Christianized pagan inscription of Odessos dates from 557 and perhaps attests the presence of some pagan population in the city: ✝ Χαίρε πιστὲ παροδῖτα (greetings, faithful passerby!)[90]

Traditions of post-mortem arrangement, alteration, and mutilation of the body—tied to the fear of the reanimation of the corpse – stayed vivid in Christian times. Post-mortal fixation of the corpse, use of the purifying power of fire by scorching the graves and placing coals next to the corpse, as well as the use of protecting amulets are as many rites that served as obstacles to stop the dead come back. In the third and fourth century, "nailed burials" took place in Debeltos. The skulls of the departed, both Christians and pagans, were pierced by large iron nails and stones were placed on their extremities. Purging rites with fire were performed on stone grounds, and tumuli were formed over them.[91] In the fourth century, amulets (a necklace with an apotropaic

---

[83] Archaeological Museum Nesebar, mus. no. 1684 (unpublished).

[84] Бешевлиев, "Старохристиянските надписи от Варна," 24. The same greeting Χαῖρε, παρ(ο)δεῖτα, see in the middle (after 238) 3rd c. pagan funeral epigram, reused in an early Christian tomb (middle of the fourth century) in Odessos(*IGBulg, I²*, no. 228 bis, see also note 90 and 91).

[85] Бешевлиев, "Старохристиянските надписи от Варна," 27.

[86] Бешевлиев, "Старохристиянските надписи от Варна," 21.

[87] For the *Constantini seniores*, see Mihail Zahariade, "The role Tasks of the Roman Army Squads and Personnel on the Western and Northern Black Sea Coast. 1st–3rd Centuries. Some Short Considerations," in *Proceedings of the International Symposium "La Thrace et les Sociétés Maritimes Anciennes", Sozopol, 18–24 September 1994* (*Thracia Pontica, VI.1*), ed. Mihail Lazarov and Christina Angelova (Sozopol, 1997), 383 .

[88] Hesiod, *Theogonia* 1015, ed. Aloisius Rzach, *Hesiodi Carmina* (Lipsiae, 1913), 156–173.

[89] Бешевлиев, "Старохристиянските надписи от Варна," 28.

[90] Бешевлиев "Старохристиянските надписи от Варна," 25.

[91] Petar Balabanov, "Mortuary archaeology in Roman Thrace: the 'Helikon' funerary complex (Debelt Archaeological Reserve)," in *Early Roman Thrace. New Evidence from Bulgaria* (*Journal of Roman Archaeology, Supplementary Series Number 82*), ed. Ian P. Haynes (Portsmouth, Rhode Island: Journal of Roman Archaeology, 2011), 112, 113. On the pagan remnants in the tritional culture until the late Middle Ages, see Бони

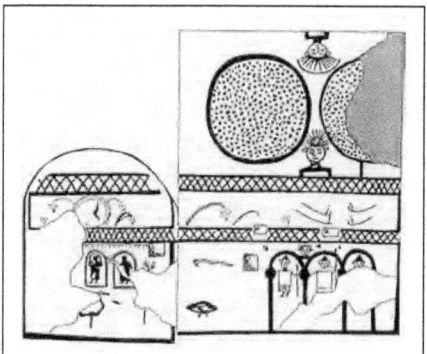

Figure 11. Gerania. Walls and vault painting of the late Antique tomb (after Pillinger, *Corpus der spätantiken und frühchristlichen Wandmalereien Bulgariens*, Abb. 2).

image of Medusa[92]) and "death-coins" were placed in the late Roman necropolis of a settlement near a Roman fortification (*burgus*, medieval Pyrgos, contemporary Burgas) on the coastal road between Debeltos and Anchialos,[93] as a part of the rites connected with the traditional idea of ensuring transition to the world of the dead.[94]

Pagan influences can be also be seen in the semantic and style of paintings, as well as in decorative plastic art and grave reliefs. Such influences have been noticed in a settlement perhaps (Gerania),[95] located on the road along the seashore some ten Roman miles northeast of Odessos. From the end of the fourth to the beginning of the fifth century, a fortified settlement with an area of about 0.85 ha emerged by structural transformation of an earlier fortification of the *quadriburgium*-type (a fort with four towers), with a surface of 0.12 ha, and equipped it with a common defensive wall.[96] In the settlement stone-carvers, sculptors, and painters of local

---

Петрунова [Boni Petrunova], "*Погребални обичаи и обреди в българските земи през XV–XVII век (по данни от християнските некрополи)* [*Funerary rites and customs in the Bulgarian lands in the 15th–17th century (based on the Christian cemeteries)*]" (София: Българска академия на науките [Sofia: Bulgarian Acemie of Sciences], 1996), 15. A published abstract of the unpublished doctoral dissertation in National Institute of Archaeology with Museum (hereafter Петрунова, "*Погребални обичаи и обреди*"). About the presence of the Medieval Deviant Burials in Bulgaria (VII–XIV c.) I am thankful to Petar Parvanov, MA Student, CEU.

[92] Лазаров, "Некропол от IV в. на н. е. в Бургас," 50, fig. 7; Петрунова, "*Погребални обичаи и обреди*," 10, 15.

[93] Константин Господинов [Konstantin Gospodinov], "*Древната картография* [The Ancient cartography]," in *Бургас – вечното пристанище* [*Burgas – the eternal harbour*], ed. Петя Кияшкина [Petya Kiashkina] (Бургас: Понтика Принт [Bourgas: Pontika Print], 2000), 62–63, 65, 73, 75, 76 (hereafter *Бургас – вечното пристанище*); Михаил Лазаров [Mikhail Lazarov], "Некропол от IV в. на н. е. в Бургас [Necropolis from the 4th c. in Bourgas]," *Археология* [*Arkheologiya*] 9, no. 4 (1967): 52 (hereafter Лазаров, "Некропол от IV в. на н. е. в Бургас"); Торбатов, *Укрепителната система на провинция Скития*, 77–78; Геров, "Земевладението в римска Тракия и Мизия," 45; Иван Карайотов [Ivan Karaiotov], "Поемата на Мануил Фил [The poem of Manuil Phil] (1275–1345 г.)," in *Бургас – вечното пристанище*, 77, 78; Soustal, *Tabula Imperii Byzantini*, 418–419, Karte 2.

[94] Лазаров, "Некропол от IV в. на н. е. в Бургас," 49, 51, fig. 8; Гатев, "*Погребален обред*," 16; Петрунова, "*Погребални обичаи и обреди*," 12.

[95] Константин Иречек [Konstantin Irechek], *Пътувания по България* [*Travels in Bulgaria*](София: Наука и изкуство [Sofia: Science and art], 1974), 895 (hereafter Иречек, *Пътувания по България*).

[96] Bulgarian Acemie of Sciences, manuscript archives Karel Shkorpil, arch. no. 425, fols. 8, 10, 12–14; arch. no.543, fol. 25. About the other fortified settlements that developed over an earlier military fortress in Thracia, see Динчев, *Ранновизантийските крепости в България*, 9–11, 19, 33, Appendix I.

origin worked undisturbed by the dominant influence of the Byzantine cultural sphere. In the last third of the fourth century a vaulted tomb was built in the necropolis north of the village.[97] When composing its frescoes, the painters used the motif of the funeral banquet *(cena funebris)*, where they depicted the participants in an expressive style (Figure 11).[98] At the same time, they mixed Christian symbolism with astral and chthonic symbols. The Sun and the Moon on the vault meant to protect the tomb from desecration and represented both astral immortality and the universe grieving for Jesus Christ. The snake symbolized the heroization of the deceased as well as Christian virtue.[99]

Figure 12. Gerania. An altar slab of the early Christian basilica (after Овчаров and Ваклинова, *Ранновизантийски паметници*, Fig. 84).

A small basilica was built in the settlement probably during its fortification between the fifth and the first half of the sixth century,[100] when the blocks of the *bema*'s chancel barrier were crafted.[101] In the technical implementation of the frame of these limestones chancel-screen as well as the peacocks depicted on them, one can find also the influence of late Roman techniques of bone and metal processing (Figure 12).[102] In a local workshop of neighboring Odessos stone-cravers used Greco-Roman models in composing and shaping gravestones architectonically. Certain early Christian gravestones are decorated with architectonic elements such as the *tabula ansata* (a tablet with dovetail handles) and stylized *acroterion* (pediment ornaments) typical for the pagan period.

Christian symbols and artefacts did not stamp out pagan traditions from the cities and their graveyards along the southwestern coast of the Black Sea, even after the demolition of pagan temples and the statues of the gods. This is especially true in the

---

[97] Александър Минчев and Петко Георгиев [Alexandăr Minchev and Petko Georgiev], "Раннохристиянска гробница със стенописи край с. Осеново, Варненско [Ealy Christian tomb with wall paintings near village of Osenovo, Varna region]," *Известия на Народния музей – Варна* [*Proceedings of the National museum – Varna*] 17 (1981): 9–10, 15 (hereafter Минчев and Георгиев, "Раннохристиянска гробница").

[98] Овчаров and Ваклинова, *Ранновизантийски паметници*, 26–28, 43–45; Pillinger, *Corpus der spätantiken und frühchristlichen Wandmalereien Bulgariens*, 14, Abb. 2, 9, 10.

[99] Минчев and Георгиев, "Раннохристиянска гробница," 15; Pillinger, *Corpus der spätantiken und frühchristlichen Wandmalereien Bulgariens*, 12–14, 15, Abb. 2.

[100] Иречек, *Пътувания по България*, 895.

[101] Ива Досева [Iva Doseva], "Релефите от Осеново. За възможната употреба на лъжички за причастие през V–VI в.," [The reliefs from Osenovo. On the possible function of eucharist spoons in 5th–6th c.] in *Сборник в чест на Александър Минчев*,366, 369 (hereafter Досева, "Релефите от Осеново").

[102] Овчаров and Ваклинова, *Ранновизантийски паметници*, 43, figs. 84–85; Досева, "Релефите от Осеново," 360.

cemeteries, where archaeologists excavated protective amulets, Charon's fee, pagan formulae on epithaphs and "nailed burials." The semantic and the style of decorative art – representations of *cena funebris*, *tabula ansata*, astral and chthonic symbols --also attest the survival of pagan traditions.

Conclusion

Christian communities first appear along the southwestern Black Sea coast in the apostolic times, when Christianity was a persecuted sect. The spread of the new faith was promoted by the preaching of Saint Andrew the Apostle in Odessos and the disciples of Saint Paul in Anchialos. Following the legalization of Christianity under Constantine, the ecclesiastical organization in Thracia, Moesia Secunda and Haemimontos followed the administrative model of the East Roman Empire.

The formation of a "Christian society" in the region reduced the differences between the laypeople's "native" Christian culture and that of the clerical and secular elites. The "everyday" archaeology of the faith is of paramount importance in researching the nature, directions, and pace of the Christianization. The establishment and the architectural patterns of the early Christian churches in the coastal zone of the provinces of Scythia, Moesia Secunda and Haemimontos imitate differentiated Constantinopolitan solutions. The abstract geometric shapes in the dominant type of religious construction are perceived by believers through their considerable size, lighting, aggregation of elements, color scheme, and surface textures. The reuse of the pagan *temene* at the end of the fourth to the beginning of the fifth century is essentially an act of spiritual reshaping of traditional sacred places and retaining them as a sustainable spiritual focus of the Christianized population. The construction of the earliest Christian churches *ex nihilo* start at the beginning of the fifth century. Their symmetric composition was influenced by the traditional form of the Hellenistic basilica in the Pontic region.

Physical traces of the early followers of Christ in the urban environment on the West-Pontian coast are barely noticeable until the official imposition of Christianity in the Roman Empire. A clear change occurs in the fourth century, when the burials with gifts in tombs under a tumulus, the heroization of the deceased, and the burials with cremation vanish, pagan graves are reused or destroyed, and the deceased are buried in west-east extended supine inhumation. Pagan rites, such as post-mortal mutilation and the use of purification by fire, protective amulets, and "death-coins," however, resisted suppression for long. Classical influences can be discovered in the arrangement and composition of funeral paintings, the decorative plastic shaping of grave reliefs, and the simultaneous use of pagan and Christian formulae on gravestones. The overlap of these two traditions eventually give birth to a uniform Christian culture, signaling the end of the Classical world along the Black Sea.

GLORY, DECAY AND HOPE:
GODDESS *ROMA* IN SIDONIUS APOLLINARIS' PANEGYRICS

Joseph Grzywaczewski – Daniel K. Knox

Between A.D. 456 and 468, Sidonius Apollinaris, the Gallo-Roman aristocrat and future bishop of Clermont, delivered three panegyrics in honor of three newly appointed emperors.[1] Each poem is marked by a strict adherence to traditional literary forms and conventional styling.[2] Sidonius, though a Christian, packed each poem with pagan motifs and themes that at times seem garish and antiquated.[3] Having received an extensive and traditional literary education, Sidonius was expected to embellish his work with references to pagan mythology and literature.[4] These motifs were not used unwittingly, Sidonius carefully used them to craft political narratives within each panegyric. The key figure in each panegyric is the goddess *Roma*. She is used in each poem as a foil for each of the emperors being lauded. *Roma* is a unifying theme throughout the three panegyrics and her importance goes beyond the original context of each poems initial composition. Sidonius edited and circulated his poems in the 460s prior to becoming Bishop of Clermont in c. late 469–470. In his collection of poetry Sidonius placed the panegyrics in reverse chronological order beginning with the most recently

---

[1] The authors would like to thank Marianne Sághy, Lisa Bailey and Michael Hanaghan for their critiques and suggestions on this article, and for providing access to manuscript versions of soon to be released work.

[2] Sidonius Apollinaris, *Poems and Letters*, vols. 1–2, trans. William Blair Anderson (London: Harvard University Press, 1936) (hereafter Anderson, *Poems and Letters*). All Latin and English quotations are from this translation. Sidonius has recently been the focus of renewed scholarly interest, see in particular: Johannes A. Van Waarden and GavinKelly, eds., *New Approaches to Sidonius Apollinaris* (Leuven: Peeters, 2013) (hereafter Van Waarden and Kelly, *New Approaches*).

[3] For a poetical critique of Sidonius's work see Gerbrandy Piet, "The failure of Sidonius' Poetry," in Van Waarden and Kelly, *New Approaches*, 53–76; Sigrid Mratschek, "Identitätsstiftung aus der Vergangenheit: Zum Diskurs über die trajanische Bildungskultur im Kreis des Sidonius Apollinaris," in *Die christlich-philosophischen Diskurse der Spätantike: Texte, Personen, Institutionen*, ed. Therese Fuhrer(Stuttgart: Franz Steiner Verlag, 2008), 363–380.

[4] Lynette Watson, "Representing the Past, Redefining the Future: Sidonius Apollinaris' Panegyrics of Avitus and Anthemius,"in *The Propaganda of Power: The Role of Panegyric in Late Antiquity*, ed. Mary Whitby (Boston: Brill), 180–81 (hereafter Watson, "Representing the Past").

composed panegyric in honor of Anthemius. In doing so, Sidonius presents a narrative of imperial decay. The goddess *Roma* is the key figure in this narrative, her decline throughout the three panegyrics reflects the political turmoil of the mid-fifth century. In the following discussion, we will review Sidonius's use of *Roma* in each panegyric.[5] This initial review will be carried out in the order of each panegyric's composition. After, we will consider Sidonius's reuse of the panegyrics in his circulated poems and his construction of a coherent narrative of decay across the three poems.

Sidonius can be an enigmatic writer. He has been described as an author focused on "keeping up appearances" whilst ignoring the increasingly troubled world around him.[6] As we will see this was not the case—Sidonius's panegyrics addressed current political themes and concerns. Though a Christian, Sidonius's poetry often appears to be bloated by pagan themes and decoration invoking an age that had long passed:

> Now grant thy presence, Paean Apollo, whose hook-beaked gryphons the well-schooled curb doth constrain with its bond of laurel, whensoever thou wieldest thy leafy reins and guidest their winged shoulders with double-hued ivy! Hither direct thy lyre! It is not now the time to sing of Python's destruction or to hymn the twice seven wounds of the Niobids—victims whose dooms are preserved to thine honour in song, so that their deaths live in deathless poesy.[7]

Partly this was due to the late antique education that he had received, which encouraged deference to authoritative authors' archaic styles.[8] Throughout his corpus Sidonius illustrated the extent of his literary education with numerous references to classical culture and literature, with his verse being heavily influenced by Statius.[9] Yet Sidonius could just as easily reject classical themes in favor of Christian motifs. Compare this passage from *Carmen* XVI to the one above:

---

[5] For a fuller commentary on the political and social concerns behind Sidonius's panegyrics see: Tiziana Brolli, "Writing Commentary on Sidonius' Panegyrics," in Van Waarden and Kelly, *New Approaches*, 93–110; and Watson, "Representing the Past," 175–98.

[6] John Percival, "Desperately Seeking Sidonius: The Realities of Life in Fifth-Century Gaul," *Latomus* 56 (1997): 287.

[7] Anderson, *Poems and Letters*, 35; Sidonius Apollinaris*Carmen* II, 307–315 (hereafter Sid. Ap. *Carm.*): *Nunc ades, o Paean, Lauro cui grypas obuncos/docta lupata ligant quotiens per frondea lora/flectis penniferos hederis bicoloribus armos/huc converte chelyn: non est modo dicere tempus/Pythona exstinctum nec bis septena sonare/ vulnera Tantalidum, quorum tibi funera servat/cantus et aeterno vivunt in carmine mortes.*

[8] Anderson, *Poems and Letters*, xxxiv; Catherine M. Chin, *Grammar and Christianity in the Late Roman World* (Philadelphia: University of Philadelphia Press, 2008), 12–20.

[9] Watson "Representing the Past," 181; for the impact of Virgil in the panegyrics see: Francesco Montone, "'Vergilian' Wolves in the Panegyric on Avitus by Sidonius Apollinaris (Carm. 7.361–368)," *Acta Antiqua Academiae Scientiarum Hungaricae* 53 (2013–2014): 287–300.

> Thrust far from thee, O lyre of mine, Phoebus and the nine Muses together with Pallas as tenth, Orpheus and the fabled water of the horse's spring, and that Theban lute that with its music moved the stones to follow it and raised by its strains the eagerly listening walls. Rather do thou come, O Great Spirit, I pray, to speak of thy pontiff – thou who didst enter into the heart of Miriam in olden times, when Israel seizing their timbrels marched dry-shod through the trough of the suspended sea...[10]

This example comes from *Carmen* XVI, written in honor of his spiritual mentor Faustus of Riez. The comparison with the passage from *Carmen* II could not be starker. Here Sidonius is a committed Christian and readily sheds the pagan clothing of his poetry as necessary.[11] Lynette Watson notes that this is the only poem in which Sidonius explicitly makes reference to his Christianity with the panegyrics and remaining *carmina minora* drawing on classical themes and motifs.[12] Still, the casting out of Apollo shows us that rather than exhibiting a slavish devotion to classical motifs, Sidonius used the lyrical imagery that suited his genres and themes. Rather than accepting that Sidonius relied on pagan imagery solely due to the necessities of the genre that he was working in and as a product of his education, we should consider the deeper purposes that lay behind his inclusion of particular motifs. This is particularly necessary with the figure of *Roma* who as a central figure in all three panegyrics is clearly more than scenery.

Sidonius's portrayal of *Roma* in his three panegyrics was not without precedent. The personification of *Roma* in literature was a venerable motif by the fifth century giving Sidonius ample examples to draw on in his own compositions. It is worth noting that three early fifth-century authors: Claudian Claudianus, Aurelius Prudentius Clemens, and Rutilius Namatianus, all featured personifications of *Roma* in their works.[13] Claudian was a particularly heavy influence on Sidonius's three

---

[10] Anderson, *Poems and Letters*, 241–43; Sid. Ap. *Carm.* XVI,1–9: *Phoebum et terternas decima cum Pallade Musas/Orpheaque, et laticem simulatum fontis equine/Ogygiamque chelyn, quae saxas equacia flectens/cantibus, auritos erexit carmine muros; sperne fidis; magis ille veni nunc spiritus oro/pontificem dicture tuum, qui pectora priscae/intrasti Mariae, rapiens cum tympana siccus/Israel appensi per concava gurgitis iret.*

[11] Sidonius reused Christian topoi and scripture in the same manner that he treated classical themes, for a fuller discussion of this and of Sidonius the Christian see: Lisa Bailey, "Sidonius and Religion," in *Prolegomena to Sidonius*, ed. Johannes Van Waarden and Gavin Kelly (Peeters, forthcoming).

[12] Watson, "Representing the Past," 180.

[13] Michael Roberts "Rome Personified, Rome Epitomized: Representations of Rome in the Poetry of the Early Fifth Century," *The American Journal of Philology* 122, no. 4 (2001): 533–65 (hereafter Roberts, "Rome Personified").

panegyrics.[14] In *de Bello Gildonico* Claudian presents a weak and enfeebled *Roma*, which Sidonius's mirrors in *Carmen* VII honoring Avitus.[15] While Claudian was certainly an influence upon Sidonius, the two wrote under very different circumstances—Claudian under the established and stable reign of Theodosius I, Sidonius during a volatile period that saw four successive regimes over the course of two decades.[16] *Roma* was also a figure used by poets with differing world views: Prudentius was a Christian while Rutilius remained a pagan. Roberts argues that Prudentius's portrayal of *Roma* strips away her pagan past in order to present her as a leading figure in the Christian world.[17] While Sidonius shared Prudentius's Christian outlook, as we shall see he did not remold his *Roma* in a Christian manner. Nor did he adorn his panegyrics with Christian motifs. While the shared iconography and motifs represent a dialogue between Sidonius and his literary predecessors, particularly Claudian, Sidonius' representation of *Roma* in his three panegyrics represents a conscious choice to address the political concerns of his own period.[18]

The Promise of Avitus

In 455 Eparchius Avitus, a Gallo-Roman aristocrat and imperial civil and military official under Aëtius, was proclaimed emperor by the Visigothic king Theodoric in the wake of the death of the emperor Petronius Maximus.[19] For members of the Gallo-Roman aristocracy this was cause for cautious optimism. Many Gallo-Romans had felt neglected byimperial policy, which had favored the retrenchment of Roman strength in Italy while the Visigoths and Burgundians continued to secure increasing power in Gaul. With one of their own in the supreme position Gallo-Roman aristocrats could hope for Gaul to remain a focus of imperial policy during a tumultuous period. Still Avitus was backed by the power of the Visigoths, which was a cause for concern for many.[20] Sidonius had more reason to celebrate the appointment than most; Avitus was

---

[14] For a close analysis of the similarities of Sidonius's portrayal of *Roma* to that of Claudian see:Franca Ela Consolino, "Fra intertestualità e iconografia: le rappresentazioni di Dea Roma nei panegirici di Sidonio Apollinare," in *Présence de Sidoine Apollinaire*, ed. Rémy Poignault and Annick Stoehr-Monjou (Clermont-Ferrand: Centre Recherches A. Piganiol, 2014), 152–60 (hereafter Consolino, "Fra intertestualità e iconografia").

[15] Roberts, "Rome Personified," 534. This similarity is noted by: Consolino, "Fra intertestualità e iconografia," 150; Michael Hanaghan, "Avitus' Characterisation in Sidonius' Carm. 7," *Mnemosyne*70 (2017), 262–80 (hereafter Hanaghan, "Avitus' Characterisation"); Watson, "Representing the Past," 184.

[16] Watson, "Representing the Past," 181–82.

[17] Roberts, "Rome Personified," 538–39.

[18] Watson, "Representing the Past," 181–82, 196.

[19] Theodoric II (426–466).

[20] Philip Rousseau, "Sidonius and Majorian: The Censure in "Carmen" V," *Historia: Zeitschrift für Alte Geschichte*49 (2000): 251–52 (hereafter Rousseau, "Sidonius and Majorian").

GLORY, DECAY AND HOPE

his father-in-law. Sidonius stood to gain personally from Avitus's appointment and rule. In his panegyric Sidonius casts Avitus as the savior of a dejected and disheveled *Roma*. In casting Avitus as the "man of the hour" Sidonius down played his Visigothic support and reaffirmed his commitment to the imperial cause.

In *Carmen* VII *Roma* serves as a foil for Avitus. When we are first introduced to her sheis portrayed in a dejected mood and a shadow of her former glories:

> Lo! Afar, from a lofty tract of sky, came Rome, dragging her slow steps along, with neck bent and head bowed; her hair hung limply down, covered not with a helmet but with dust; at each feeble step her shield knocked against her, and in her spear there was no terror, but only heaviness.[21]

The image is very much one of faded glory and impotent power. *Roma* is shown lacking vigor in step and countenance, lacking proper equipment, and without an aura of menace. Sidonius contrasts *Roma's* current state of ruin with her past glories:

> My spears affrighted Libya's clime, and I laid the yoke even a third time upon the faithless Carthaginian. Ganges of the Indian, Phasis of the colchian, Araxes of Armenia, Ger of the Ethiopians, Tanais of the Getae, all trembled before my Tiber.[22]

While the past is presented as an age of expansion and vigor the present is a time of contraction. Thus, *Roma* laments: "I, who complained aforetime that the world's limits were too narrow, am now not even a boundary to myself."[23] Sidonius presents *Roma* as wrecked and in need of a savior, who might provide new vigor.

Sidonius presents Avitus as the force that will reinvigorate Rome with a necessary dose of Gallic fortitude:

> This man I have given thee, Rome, while Gaul throughout her wild plains thunders with plaudits for Augustus, and the north, now

---

[21] Anderson, *Poems and Letters*, 121–23; Sid. Ap. *Carm.* VII, 45–49: *Cum procul erecta caeli de parte trahebat/pigros Roma gradus, curvato cernua collo/ora ferens; pendent crines de vertice, tecti/pulvere non galea, clipeusque impingitur aegris/gressibus, et pondus, non terror, fertur in hasta.*

[22] Anderson, *Poems and Letters*, 125; Sid. Ap. *Carm.* VII, ln. 72–76: *Libycum mea terruit axem/cuspis et infido posui iuga tertia poeno./Indorum Ganges, Colchorum Phasis, Araxes/Armeniae, Ger Aethiopum Tanaisque Getarum/Thbrinum Tremuere meum.*

[23] Anderson, *Poems and Letters*, 127; Sid. Ap. *Carm.*VII, ln. 96–97: *Cumque prius stricto quererer de cardine mundi,/nec limes nunc ipsa mihi.*

stronger, carries the auspicious clamour to the pale-cheeked south. He shall restore Libya to thee a fourth time in chains—and when a man has recovered the lost Pannonias after so many generations by a mere march 'tis easy to feel sure even now of what he can do by waging war.[24]

Sidonius skirts around the fact that Avitus had not yet achieved any military victories as emperor by celebrating the promise that his reign held.[25] The recapture of Africa from the Vandals was a pressing concern and Sidonius promises its return under Avitus. Sidonius's reference to the return of Pannonia is a false flag. William Blair Anderson argues that *iter* refers to his march from Gaul to Rome—during which Avitus may have received salutations from Gothic leaders in Pannonia.[26] This was far from a return to Roman control over the area, but for Sidonius it represented a chance to enhance Avitus's stature through political spin. Avitus's achievements as emperor lay in the future and so Sidonius was forced to celebrate the promise that Avitus represented. Sidonius compares Avitus to Trajan, who through a geographic technicality sheds his Spanish background in favor of a Gallic origin.[27] *Roma* listing the great leaders of the past wonders aloud: "I know not if anyone can match Trajan—unless perchance Gaul should once more send forth a man who should even surpass him."[28] Sidonius calls forth the image of an expansionist emperor who was active at the periphery of the empire—in doing so he makes a clear statement that the provinces matter. The effect of the political turmoil and conflict on Gaul is referred to on multiple occasions, and is a consequence of *Roma's* inability to exert her will.[29] The broken and dejected *Roma* portrayed in *Carmen* VII is a foil for the invigorated and warlike Avitus, whose efforts his son-in-law Sidonius sought to legitimize in the panegyric.[30] Avitus's image is enhanced by the striking contrast presented by the figure of *Roma*.

---

[24] Anderson, *Poems and Letters*, 169; Sid. Ap. *Carm.* VII, ln. 584–591: *Hunctibi, Roma, dedi, patulisdumGalia/ campis/intonat Augustum plausu faustum que fragorem/portat in exsanguem Boreas iam fortiori Austrum./Hic tibi restituet Libyen per vincula quarta,/et cuius solum amissas post saecula multa/Pannonias revocavit iter, iam credere promptum/est/quid faciat bellis.*

[25] An in-depth consideration of the figure of Avitus in this panegyric is presented in Hanaghan, "Avitus' Characterisation," 262–80.

[26] Anderson, *Poems and Letters*, 168n3–169n3.

[27] Gaul came under the administrative control of the prefecture of Spain—allowing Sidonius to claim Trajan as a part of Gaul.

[28] Anderson, *Poems and Letters*, 127–29;Sid. Ap. *Carm.* VII lns. 116–18: *Traianum nescio siquis/aequiperet, ni forsiterum tu, Gallia, mittas/qui vincat.*

[29] Sid. Ap. *Carm* VII lns. 295–300:*Haec post gesta viri (temet, Styx livida, testor)/intemerata mihi praefectus iura regebat;/et caput hoc sibimet solitis defessa ruinis/Gallia suscipiens Getica pallebat ab ira*; and lns. 319–21: *subito cum rupta tumult/ barbaries totas in te transfuderat Arctos,/Gallia.*

[30] Hanaghan, "Avitus' Characterisation," 262–80.

Roma Bellatrix

Unfortunately for Sidonius, Avitus lacked the support of Emperor Leo I, the senatorial elite, and the Italian army.[31] Avitus was quickly deposed months after his elevation in October 456 by Ricimer and replaced by Majorian.[32] Sidonius found himself caught in the middle of a dangerous political upheaval. As a member of Avitus's camp he was implicated in the subsequent Gallic plot against Majorian.[33] The opportunity to present a panegyric celebrating Majorian was for Sidonius a chance to clear his name from any suspicion. Majorian is portrayed as man of action—rather than a man of promise: "Now a consul holds the imperial power, one whom the hauberk clothes no less than the purple."[34] Sidonius matches his second subject with a mighty and enthroned *Roma*. This is *Roma bellatrix*, Sidononius's sole use of this strong epithet. The image is far more majestic and inspiring than the *Roma* portrayed in Avitus's panegyric: "Rome, the warrior-goddess, had taken her seat. Her breast was uncovered, on her plumed head was a crown of towers, and behind her, escaping from under her spacious helmet, her hair flowed over her back."[35] Here, in contrast with his first panegyric, Sidonius depicts *Roma* as majestic and enlivened. Sidonius returns to the depiction of *Roma's* hair as a symbol of her vitality—in this instance it is flowing forth from under a helmet rather than unkempt as in the previous example. This *Roma* does not seek aid from outside of Italy but sits at the center of the world and looks outwards towards the periphery.

Franca Ela Consolino compares the more robust and glorious *Roma* of *Carmen* V with Majorian's wider support among the senatorial elite at Rome—where Avitus had represented Gaul coming to Rome's help, here Rome once again stands on its own feet with Majorian.[36] For Phillip Rousseau the figure of *Roma bellatrix* is more menacing. Sidonius delivered this panegyric in Lyons after Majorian had defeated the Gallic army of Avitus and put down the subsequent unrest following his accession to power. *Roma bel-*

---

[31] André Loyen, ed.,*Sidoine Apollinaire: Poèmes*(Paris:Budé, 1960), xii (hereafter Loyen,*Sidoine*): "L'empereur d'Orient s'était refusé à reconnaître Avitus comme son collègue. Aussi le règne de l'empereur gaulois sombra-t-il bientôt sous la coalition du *comes domesticorum* Majorien, du magister *utriusque militiae* Ricimer et de l'aristocratie italienne ...Le 17 octobre 456, Avitus, privé du secours de ses alliés wisigoths, était battu à Plaisance, dépouillé de ses attributs impériaux et contraint d'accepter un évêque."

[32] See Guy Lucam, *Ricimer, un barbare au service de Rome* (Paris: Atelier national, reproduction des thèses, Université Lille III, 1986); Guy Lucam, *L'Agonie de Rome : un barbare maître de l'Occident 455-472*(Paris: Klincksieck, 1992).

[33] Rousseau, "Sidonius and Majorian," 251–52.

[34] Anderson, *Poems and Letters*, 61; Sid. Ap. *Carm*V, ln. 2–3: *Imperiumiam consul habet, quem purpura non plus/ quamloricaoperit.*

[35] Anderson, *Poems and Letters*, 61; Sid. Ap. *Carm* V, ln. 13–15: *Sederat exserto bellatrix pectore Roma,/cristatum turrita caput, cui pone capaci/casside prolapses perfundit terga capillus.*

[36] Consolino, "Fra intertestualità e iconografia,"160.

latrix is presented then as a conquering force and her renewed vigor is as much a threat to Gaul as it is a salve for the problems of the Empire.[37] In *Carmen* V *Roma* becomes a vehicle for expressing Gallic fears in the wake of Majorian's deposition of Avitus.

It is on the periphery of the Empire that the action turns next. A personified Libya confronts *Roma* and questions her lack of action in returning Africa to the imperial fold: "Why dost thou delay the fight? Why dost thou fear the sea, when even heaven is wont so oft to battle for thy victories?"[38] In response Sidonius uses *Roma* to voice his own parochial concerns:

> My land of Gaul hath even till now been ignored by the lords of the world, and hath languished in slavery unheeded. Since that time much hath been destroyed, for with the emperor, whoe'er he might be, closely confined, it has been the constant lot of the distant parts of a wretched world to be laid waste.[39]

Where as in the first panegyric Gaul had supplied the answer to *Roma's* problems now she is in need of remembrance. *Roma* voices the concerns of Sidonius and his fellow Gallo-Romans that with the change of government and the accompanying strife, Gaul would be forgotten in favor of other theatres. Sidonius took the opportunity of the panegyric to bridge the divide that had developed between the elite of Gaul and Italy during the conflict between Avitus and Majorian. Reassurance is the overarching theme of this poem. The deposition of Avitus by Majorian had pitted the aristocracies of Gaul and Italy against each other in support of their preferred candidates. *Roma* serves as a vehicle for these concerns.

Majorian, like Avitus, did not live up to the promise that Sidonius ascribed him. After the failure of his campaign against the Vandals in 461, Majorian was deposed by Ricimer and succeeded by Libius Severus. Severus was a puppet of Ricimer and never gained the approval of Leo in the East. In 465 Severus died under suspicious circumstances. After an interregnum, Anthemius was placed on the western throne through a compromise between Ricimer and Leo.[40] Amidst a period of instability and intrigue

---

[37] Rousseau, "Sidonius and Majorian," 253–55.

[38] Anderson, *Poems and Letters*, 69;Sid. Ap. *Carm* V, ln. 98–100: *Quid proelia differs?/Quid mare formidas, pro cuius saepe triumphis/et caelum pugnare solet?*

[39] Anderson, *Poems and Letters*, 93;Sid. Ap. *Carm.* V, ln. 356–60: *Mea Gallia rerum/ignoratur adhuc dominis ignaraque servit./Ex illo multum periit, quia principe clauso,/quisquis erat, piseri diversis partibus orbis/vastari sollemne fuit.*

[40] Peter Heather, "The Western Empire, 425-76," in *The Cambridge Ancient History vol. 14 Late Antiquity, Empire and its Successors, 425-600*, ed. Averil Cameron, Bryan Ward-Perkins, and Michael Whitby (Cambridge: Cambridge University Press, 2001),23–24.The position of Ricimer in the Western Empire may be compared to the position of other men with German origin, like Stilicho or Arbogast, Paul Veyne, *L'Empire gréco-romain* (Paris: PUF, 2005), 724–728.

Sidonius found himself yet again commissioned to compose a panegyric, this time in honor of Anthemius and his new regime (*Carmen* II). For his work Sidonius was granted the title of *patricius Romanus* and appointed *Praefectus Urbi*.[41]

Roma *and the East*

In his opening to his panegyric of Anthemius, Sidonius begins not with *Roma*, but with the laudation of his subject:

> This, my Lords, is the man for whom Rome's brave spirit and your love did yearn, the man to whom our commonwealth, like a ship overcome by tempests and without a pilot, hath committed her broken frame, to be more deftly guided by a worthy steersman, that she may no more fear storm or pirate.[42]

Again Rome is presented as being in need of guidance—in this case at the hands of a skilled sailor. Anthemius is just the man (*hic est!*) to right the ship and correct its course. Importantly Sidonius highlights that Anthemius has the approval of the emperor in Constantinople and thus represents a renewal of ties between East and West and a promise of future stability: "(to Leo) now your government shall be more perfectly one, having thus become a government of two."[43] *Roma* gives voice to this sentiment in her address to *Aurora*:

> All hail to thee, pillar of sceptre power, queen of the East, Rome of thy hemisphere, no longer to be worshipped by the eastern citizen alone, now that thou hast sent me a sovereign prince—O home of Empire, and more precious in that thou appearest before the world as Empire's mother![44]

---

[41] Jean Rougé, *Les institutions romaines: de la Rome royale à la Rome chrétienne*, 2nd ed. (Paris: Armand Colin, 1991), 82: "*Praefectus Urbi*. Doté de pouvoir de police, le préfet a à sa disposition un corps militaire chargé du maintien de l'ordre, les trois cohortes urbaines numérotées de X à XII qui, forte de cinq cents hommes étaient casernées avec les prétoriens."

[42] Anderson, *Poems and Letters*, 7; Sid. Ap. *Carm*. II, ln. 13-17:*Hic est, o proceres, petiit quem Romula virtus/ et quem vester amor; cui se ceu victa procellis/atque carens rectore ratis republica fractam/itulit, ut digno melius flectenda magistro,/ne tempestates, ne te, pirata, timeret.*

[43] Anderson, *Poems and Letters*, 9; Sid. Ap. *Carm*. II, ln. 28-29: *Melius respublica vestra/nunc erit una magis, quae sic est facta duorum.*

[44] Anderson, *Poems and Letters*, 9; Sid. Ap. *Carm*. II, ln. 30-34: *Salve, sceptrorum columen, regina Orientis,/orbis Roma tui, rerum mihi principe/misso iam non Eoo solum veneranda Quiriti,/imperii sedes, sed plus pretiosa quod exstas/imperii genetrix.*

Having introduced the subject of the panegyric, Sidonius moves on to the mythological topoi. Ancient Italy personified as Oenotria makes her entrance:

> Oenotria, when from the crags of towering Apennine she beheld this calamity, hid her to the glassy abode of blue Tiber. She had not encased her cheeks in a helmet (and she wore no hauberk fashioned with stitched rings of tight driven hooks), but bared was her head. Instead of hair there overran her forehead a vine-branch with clustered grapes, binding fast her many towns, and along her shapely shoulders and radiant arms jeweled brooches gripped her flowing robe. The slowness of old age was in her gait, and she held as a staff an elm covered with vine-foliage, and guided her venerable limbs thereby.[45]

Oenotria is a stark contrast to *Roma Bellatrix*, she is unarmed and adorned with symbols of plenty such as clusters of grapes and numerous towns—hers is an image of unprotected wealth. The effects of age are reminiscent of Sidonius's first portrayal of *Roma* in *Carmen* VII, but the emphasis here is on *Oenotria's* venerability not her infirmity. *Oenotria* voices again the growing threat of the Vandals.[46] *Oenotria* makes it clear that the Vandal threat was no longersolely limited to Africa but threatened the heartland of the Empire itself having captured the naval strength of Carthage. The wealthy and venerable *Oenotria* lacks the ability to defend herself from the Vandals, requiring aid from *Roma* and her leaders.

Anthemius is not the only leader praised by Sidonius in *Carmen* II. As well as the duality represented by the partnership of Leo and Anthemius, Sidonius highlights the importance of the generalissimo Ricimer to the continued safety of Italy:

> If the Norican is restraining the Ostrogoth, it is that Ricimer is feared; if Gaul ties down the armed might of the Rhine, it is he that inspires the dread; and because the Vandal foe plundered me while the Alan, his kinsman, swept off what remained, this man took vengeance by the force of his own arms.[47]

---

[45] Anderson, *Poems and Letters*, 35–37; Sid. Ap. *Carm.* II, ln. 318–328: *quem mox Oenotria casum/vidit ut aerei de rupibus Appennini,/pergit caerulei vitreas ad Thybridis aedes,/non galea conclusa genas (nec sutilis illi/circulus inpactis loricam texuit hamis),/sed nudata caput; pro crine faemifer exit/plurima per frontem constringens oppida palmes,/perque umeros teretes, rutilantes perques lacertos/pendula gemmiferae mordebant suppara bullae./segnior incedit senio venerandaque membra/viticomam retinens baculi vice flectit ad ulmum.*

[46] Anderson, *Poems and Letters*, 39; Sid. Ap. *Carm.* II, ln. 348–350: *hinc Vandalus hostis/urget et in nostrum numerosa classe quotannis/militat excidium.*

[47] Anderson, *Poems and Letters*, 41;Sid. Ap. *Carm.* II, ln. 377–380: *Noricus Ostrogothum quod continet, iste timetur;/Gallia quod Rheni Martem ligat, iste pavori est;/quod consanguineo me Vandalus hostis Halano/diripuit radente, suis hic ultus ab armis.*

Within the panegyric to Anthemius is a mini panegyric dedicated to Ricimer. The theme of cooperation is brought up again and again. Throughout the course of the poem we are presented with several sets of pairs: Leo and Anthemius, Anthemius and Ricimer, and *Oenotria* and *Roma*. Despite all of Ricimer's efforts Sidonius notes that he is only one man and that true security can only be gained through a strong partnership. To this end a new man—Anthemius, is required: "We need now an armed prince who in the manner of our sires shall not order wars but wage them."[48] The criticism of Majorian and Avitus is clear. While Avitus was a man of promise, and Majorian a strong force, Anthemius will finally give action to the plans that each had promised.

Finally, Sidonius presents *Roma* in an image that matches his hopes for Anthemius:

> Stern was her look as she bound up her flowing hair; then she shut in her towers and hid them under a helmet; laurel formed her fillet. Her belt, rough with shield-studs taken from enemies, made fast a sword, which rose high on her left side. Her conquering arm was thrust into a shield, whose orb was filled with the twin sons of Mars, with the wolf and Tiber and Love and Mars and Ilia.[49]

The similarity to Majorian's *Roma* is clear; she is well equipped and suitably stern in going about the task at hand. Her hair is once again in good trim and her equipment is well maintained. The key difference is that here action is emphasized. As Sidonius had already stated—intent was not sufficient on its own, action was required too. Hence we are presented with an active *Roma* in the midst of arming herself for the conflict ahead. Anthemius had not yet set forth on his expedition against the Vandals so Sidonius could not present *Roma* in the act of conquest; thus by presenting her preparations he signaled both a willingness to take on the foe and a commencement of the action.Sidonius places a great deal of emphasis on cooperation in *Carmen* II. He celebrates the cooperation between Constantinople and Rome, Leo and Anthemius, and Anthemius and Ricimer. Whereas the *Roma* of *Carm.* VII was in dire need of assistance, and the *Roma* of *Carmen.* V was fiercely independent, in *Carmen*. II *Roma* is shown as looking to the East for instruction and invoking a new age of interdependence between East and West. Furthermore,this *Roma* is not isolated but willing to go to war on behalf of Italy and the provinces.

---

[48] Anderson, *Poems and Letters*, 41;Sid. Ap. *Carm.* II, ln. 382–384: *Modo principe nobis/est opus armato, veterum qui more parentum/non mandet sed bella gerat.*

[49] Anderson, *Poems and Letters*, 43; Sid. Ap. *Carm.* II, ln. 391–396: *laxatos torva capillos/stringit et inclusae latuerunt casside turres;/infula laurus erat. bullis hostilibus asper/applicat a laeva surgentem balteus ensem./Inseritur clipeo victrix manus; ilius orbem/Martigenae, lupa, Thybris, Amor, Mars, Ilia/complent.*

We are presented with three versions of *Roma*—all slight variances on similar themes. Chief among Sidonius's concerns in all three poems is the relationship between the central authority of the Empire and the provinces—particularly Gaul. In each case Sidonius matches the figure of *Roma* to the traits of each emperor that he wishes to celebrate: the renewed hope provided by Avitus; the strength of Majorian; and the cooperation between East and West heralded by Avitus. Sidonius uses other deities such as *Oenotria* to voice provincial concerns and to provide visual comparisons to the figure of *Roma*.

Re-imagining the Past

While the figure of *Roma* is an important motif in each of the three panegyrics individually, it is when the three panegyrics are taken together that her true significance shines through. The order in which we read the poems is important. A chronological reading in order of composition lends itself towards the more political and historical critique. The reader is forced to consider the individual situations that Sidonius wished to address in each instance. Reading the panegyrics in the reverse chronological order that they are presented to us changes our perspective, particularly with regard to the figure of *Roma*. The contexts in which Sidonius's panegyrics were originally composed differed from the context of their subsequent re-use and circulation.

There is no question that, as Watson notes, each panegyric was the result of a particular situation and that the political contexts of each poem's "moment of delivery" shaped their initial form and Sidonius's stylistic choices.[50] Watson argues that it is in the context of each of these political moments that we must primarily consider the motivations behind the panegyrics—chief amongst them being Sidonius's desire for political stability.[51] This desire was expressed clearly, as we have seen, in the hope for cooperation between Anthemius and Ricimer in *Carmen* II. But, as Watson herself notes, the political instability of the 450s and 60s meant that events rapidly outpaced Sidonius's compositions leaving his sentiments outdated.[52] This was certainly the case in the aftermath of Avitus's downfall and Sidonius's subsequent delivery of the panegyric honoring Majorian in the tense recriminatory atmosphere of Lyon in 458.[53] The continuously shifting sands of the political landscape left their mark on Sidonius.

While the moment of delivery is crucial in understanding these works; equally, the reuse and circulation of literature by ancient authors imbues the works with new

---

[50] Watson, "Representing the Past," 196.
[51] Watson, "Representing the Past," 196–97.
[52] Watson, "Representing the Past," 196.
[53] Rousseau, "Sidonius and Majorian," 251–52.

meaning, which, as Andrew Gillett argues, we must take into consideration.[54] Sidonius circulated his own work extensively amongst his literary circle. The panegyrics were circulated soon after the delivery of the panegyric to Anthemius in January 468 and likely before the circulation of the *Carmina Minora* c. 469/70. Sidonius re-ordered the panegyrics so that they were presented in reverse chronological order to that of their original delivery.[55] Anderson introduces his translation of the panegyrics with the suggestion that Sidonius placed the panegyric to Anthemius first as an honor to the current emperor.[56] The importance of placing the current emperor in the position of honor is certainly plausible, but it misses a key connection between the three panegyrics—the figure of *Roma*. While the original portrayals of *Roma* were tied to the political contexts of each panegyric's moment of delivery, the circulation and re-use of the poems imbued them with a new context informed by hindsight of the events Sidonius had lived through. Sidonius had composed three panegyrics in quick succession and in each he lay forth his hopes for a stable and successful ruler, only to see these hopes dashed by repeated outbursts of conflict—between Avitus and Majorian and Anthemius and Ricimer.[57]

While individually each panegyric offers hope for the future in the form of each new emperor, when the poems are read together in reverse order Sidonius presents a less hopeful and more disillusioned narrative—one where we are witness to the decline of *Roma* and thus the decline of Roman power. *Roma* is transformed from a strong and active character to one worn out and broken with the effort of defending herself. *Roma* is at her strongest in *Carmen*. II where Sidonius focuses on the theme of cooperation. Sidonius promotes the harmony between Leo and Anthemius and this is reflected in *Roma*'s relationship with *Aurora*. In contrast the *Roma* of *Carmen*. V, while fierce and warlike, is isolated and many threats compete for her attention—both in Africa and Gaul. Finally, the *Roma* of Carmen. VII is completely broken, disheveled, and appealing for aid.[58] *Roma* provides no strength or hope of her own but completely relies on Avitus for rejuvenation. By reordering the panegyrics Sidonius creates a fresh narrative from his own previous representations of *Roma*. This is a narrative of broken promises and decay. The impact of political instability on *Roma* is clear leaving her a shadow of her former glories.

---

[54] Andrew Gillett, "Communication in Late Antiquity: Use and Re-Use," in *The Oxford Handbook of Late Antiquity*, ed. Scott Fitzgerald Johnson (Oxford: Oxford University Press, 2012).

[55] Watson, "Representing the Past," 180; see also Loyen, *Sidoine*, xxxf; for the publication of the *Carmina Minora* see: Willy Schetter, "Zur Publikation der 'Carmina Minora' des Apollinaris Sidonius," *Hermes* 120 (1992): 352.

[56] Anderson, *Poems and Letters*,liii.

[57] Watson, "Representing the Past," 196.

[58] As Hanaghan notes *Roma* is not only tired—*fessa*—but broken—*fracta* (Hanaghan, "Avitus' Characterisation," 8).

Throughout the panegyrics Sidonius compares the past with the present—in order to make statements about his hoped-for future.[59] An example of this was seen in his comparison of Avitus and Trajan in *Carmen* VII when *Roma* calls out for a new savior from Gaul. At the end of the panegyric Sidonius offers this hope for Avitus's reign: "The fateful sisters spun out a happy time for thy rule, Augustus, and for thy consular year they drew out with their whirling spindles a golden age."[60] Yet the golden age had not materialized and Roman power, particularly in Gaul, was waning. Sidonius had seen first-hand the futility of his own compositions. As we have seen, the reign of his father-in-law Avitus was not a golden age but exceedingly brief. Individually, Sidonius's hopes had been dashed. His comparisons of past and present had been wrong. Yet, in preparing the poems for circulation Sidonius was presented with a chance to salvage his efforts. The re-ordering the poems makes the lines hoping for Avitus's golden age the final lines of all three panegyrics. The effect is jarring and this once hopeful line, in hindsight, becomes one of bitter irony. The reader is forced to compare past and present again by the historical dissonance of these final lines and Sidonius's former hopes are revealed to be empty and his rhetoric the propaganda of failed regimes. If the poems were circulated, as is likely, during the reign of Anthemius then the effect of the re-ordering was two-fold. Anthemius's panegyric was positioned in the place of honor, but Sidonius's rhetoric in favor of his appointment was undercut by the poems that followed. While Anthemius was the man of the moment, the context provided by the panegyrics of Majorian and Avitus leave us in doubt as to how long his moment will last. Finally, by presenting Avitus's panegyric last Sidonius could re-imagine the past and prevent Avitus from being overthrown by Majorian—at least in literature. While *Roma* declined, Avitus might have his golden age—at least in verse.

Sidonius's use and depiction of the goddess *Roma* in his three panegyrics was two-fold. First, *Roma* was used as a foil for the subjects of his panegyrics. In each case her portrayal was matched to the qualities that Sidonius wished to praise in his subjects and the political concerns that he hoped to give voice to. His depictions of *Roma* placed his work in dialogue with that of previous poets, particularly Claudian, but the focus was certainly on the present, not the past. Second, with the recirculation of the panegyrics each individual *Roma* became a part of a larger continuous narrative. Over the course of this narrative *Roma* becomes increasingly enfeebled and the political instability of the period is highlighted. The rhetoric of each poem is undercut by the poem that succeeds it and the hindsight it provides. *Roma* was not then an empty adornment used to provide an antique flavor to his works, but a motif used and re-used by Sidonius to give voice to his concerns and frustrations.

---

[59] Watson, "Representing the Past," 177–78.
[60] Anderson, *Poems and Letters*, 171; Sid. Ap. *Carm.* VII, ln. 600–602: *felix tempus nevere sorores/imperiis, Auguste, tuis et consulis anno/fulva volubilibus duxerunt ssaecula pensis.*

TRACING THE CONNECTIONS BETWEEN "MAINSTREAM" PLATONISM AND "MARGINAL" PLATONISM WITH DIGITAL TOOLS

Luciana Gabriela Soares Santoprete *

This paper presents the three-part digital and collective project *Les Platonismes de l' Antiquité tardive* consisting of a database, a bibliographical index, and a research blog directed by myself in collaboration with Anna van den Kerchove, a specialist on Hermeticism and Gnosticism.[1] These three resources are already available online.[2] The objective of this triple project is to provide the scientific community with new digital resources relating to the study of the relationships between Classical and Late Antique philosophical traditions, particularly Plato, Middle- and Neo-Platonism, and "marginal"

---

* I would like to thank Dr. Stephen Lake for his patient and meticulous work in correcting my English text. I also wish to express my gratitude to the *Labex-Hastec*, the Centre Jean Pépin (CNRS, Paris), and the *Institute for Advanced Studies* at Nantes (France), which have sponsored this research from 2012 to 2014, and to the *Alexander von Humboldt Foundation* and to Professor Dr. Christoph Horn, Institut für Philosophie, *Rheinische Friedrich-Wilhelms-Universität Bonn*, whose support has enabled me to prepare this article. An extended version of this article, including a detailed section on "The Current Status of Research on Platonism in Late Antiquity" will be published with the title "Tracing the Connections between 'Mainstream' Platonism (Middle- and Neo-Platonism) and 'Marginal' Platonism (Gnosticism, Hermeticism, and the Chaldean Oracles) with Digital Tools: the Database, the Bibliographical Directory, and the Research Blog *The Platonisms of Late Antiquity*," in *Theologische Orakel in der Spätantike*, ed. Helmut Seng and Giulia Sfameni Gasparro, Collection Bibliotheca Chaldaica n° 5, Heidelberg, Universitätsverlag Carl Winter: 9–46 (forthcoming).

[1] Cf. Anna Van den Kerchove, *La voie d'Hermès, pratiques rituelles et traités hermétiques* (Leiden: Brill, 2012).

[2] These resources were created during my post-doctoral appointment funded by the LabEx-HASTEC and the Centre Jean Pépin (UPR 76-CNRS) in 2011–2012 and my research contract with the Institute for Advanced Studies in Nantes in 2013–2014; additional funding was provided in 2012–2013 by the LabEx-HASTEC, the Centre Jean Pépin (CNRS), and the Laboratoire d'Études sur les Monothéismes (CNRS). Cf. http://philognose.org and http://philognose.hypotheses.org. The database is currently hosted on the OVH server, but will soon be released and hosted by the "Partage" platform that will be opened at the UPR 76 in collaboration with the project ARTFL University of Chicago (http://artfl-project.uchicago.edu/). The research blog is on the platform of research blogs in the Humanities and Social Sciences "Hypotheses.org" of OpenEdition funded by the Équipex Digital Library for Open Humanities - DILOH. Its editorial board is composed of specialists from different fields and countries (cf. the list on the website under "Crédits").

philosophical-religious currents from the early Christian period—the "underworld of Platonism."[3] These three instruments are:

1. A *database* capable of performing interdisciplinary searches between the philosophical, Gnostic, Hermetic, and Chaldean text corpuses using vocabulary, doctrines, and pertinent bibliographies;

2. A *bibliographical index* specializing in the relationships between philosophy, Gnosticism, Hermeticism, and Chaldean ideas;

3. A *research blog* that presents and discusses current projects, activities, and scientific publications relevant to the relationship between "mainstream" and "marginal" philosophical currents in Late Antiquity.

Because of their complexity and scope, these resources have been conceived as a collective, long-term project. They also benefit from the collaboration of a team of French and foreign researchers from different disciplines for the insertion of additional data and the periodic critical analysis of the data.

Issues and Challenges of a New Digital Approach to the "Underworld of Platonism" Plotinus

My interdisciplinary research on the relationship between the Platonic and Gnostic traditions began on treatises 31 (V 8) and 32 (V 5), respectively, which, following Richard Harder,[4] are considered to be the second and third parts of Plotinus' great anti-Gnostic treatise. I found that there are few previous studies on the anti-Gnostic controversy that is reflected in these treatises (as well as in other Plotinian treatises), and for the most part, those which have been published do not attempt to analyze this polemic by taking into account both the texts of Plotinus and the direct and indirect sources concerning the various Gnostic schools.[5] In other words, they do not adequately

---

[3] To use John M. Dillon's famous expression to denote the Gnostic, Chaldean, and Hermetic currents cf. John M. Dillon, *The Middle Platonists. 80 B.C. to A.D. 220* (Ithaca: Cornell University Press, 1977; ²1996) (hereafter Dillon, *Platonists*). A reluctance to engage in the parallel study of these doctrines is unfortunately common among historians of philosophy.

[4] Richard Harder, "Eine neue Schrift Plotins," *Hermes* 71 (1936): 1–10.

[5] A first version of the complete list of these works was presented in an appendix to my thesis: Luciana Gabriela Soares Santoprete, *Plotin, Traité 32 (V, 5), Sur l'Intellect, que les intelligibles ne sont pas hors de l'Intellect et sur le Bien: introduction, traduction, commentaire et notes*, 2 vol. (PhD diss., École Pratique de Hautes Études, 2009); forthcoming as *Plotin, Traité 32 (V, 5)* (Paris: Vrin) (hereafter Soares Santoprete, *Plotin, Traité 32*); a more complete version will be published: Luciana Gabriela Soares Santoprete, "Bibliographie critique des travaux consacrés à la polémique antignostique dans l'École de Plotin," in *Plotin et les gnostiques. 1. La tétralogie antignostique de Plotin*, ed. Michel Tardieu and Luciana Gabriela Soares Santoprete (Paris: Vrin, forthcoming).

consider the historical context in which these treatises were drafted, and to that extent the arguments used to support their interpretation of the anti-Gnostic character of treatises 31 and 32 are not decisive.

It also became apparent that modern commentaries on lexical and thematic parallels between Plotinus and the Gnostics have typically been compiled by religious historians and not by historians of philosophy; the parallels which they have identified are often merely mentioned, but rarely accompanied by any detailed analysis, and these parallels are scattered through the introductions and notes to the translations of Plotinian and Gnostic texts, instead of being grouped together and examined as a significant element in the interpretation of these texts. Similarly, the authors of these commentaries, whether historians of religion or of philosophy, tend to collaborate very little and are often unfamiliar with each others' work.

It is not easy to identify appropriations of and amendments to Gnostic terms and doctrines made by Plotinus. In fact, he almost never clarifies the identity of his opponents and he often organizes his arguments by giving only brief and fragmentary summaries of theories that he adopts or critiques, so that it requires a sophisticated knowledge of both Plotinus' and the Gnostics' technical vocabulary in order to be able to identify these references. The task of identification is made more difficult by the complexity of the texts of these two bodies of work and by the frequent discrepancies in scholars' interpretations and translations of them.

It therefore seemed that some of the epistemological problems that I have encountered in attempting to interpret the nature of the relationship between Plotinus' thought (and, consequently, that of Platonism more broadly) and Gnostic teachings result from this "cleavage" between the work of historians of religion and that of historians of philosophy. An additional complication stems from the fact that, until the discovery of the Coptic Gnostic manuscripts at Nag Hammadi in 1945 and their publication in facsimile from 1972, researchers attempting to understand the position of the various Gnostic schools in the early centuries AD were necessarily obliged to work almost entirely with indirect sources, namely the great heresiological treatises dating for the most part from this same period, because very few Gnostic writings had previously been available. This fact also helps to explain why many scholars of Plotinus limited their studies of his anti-Gnostic philosophical polemic to an analysis of the critique made by Plotinus, or to juxtaposing Plotinus' criticism with Gnostic positions that could be identified from indirect rather than primary sources. However, such dependence upon Christian anti-heretical writings has meant that scholars have also used stereotypical representations that rarely do justice to the Gnostics.

Indeed, many scholars still seem to assume that Plotinus challenges Gnosticism only in treatise 33 (II 9): *Against the Gnostics*, in which he specifically identifies his opponents and addresses his critique against them; further, that he treats the Gnostics with contempt, refuses to consider their philosophical arguments seriously, and that he views their doctrines as being philosophical "heresies" devoid of any interest. This interpretation in effect excludes the possibility that Plotinus and his school could have had any significant philosophical exchange with the Gnostics, and accepts the attitude espoused by the heresiologists that the Gnostics were amoral, ignorant, and illogical. Scholars thereby acquiesce in the dichotomy established by the heresiological discourse, which simplifies the complexity of the debate by systematically classifying doctrines as either "orthodox" or "heretical." Finally, they ascribe to Plotinus a purified intellectual genealogy that situates him in a direct line of descent from Plato, while ignoring his biography, which includes in particular an education in Egypt, the influence of Numenius, and also the cultural context of Rome in the third century. By ignoring the fact that Gnosticism includes contemporaneously accepted philosophical content, as well as the fact that Plotinus engages with the philosophical problems that Gnosticism raised not only in his anti-Gnostic tetralogy, but throughout his treatises, their interpretation overlooks the possibility that Plotinus in fact takes the philosophical content of Gnosticism seriously and that his engagement with it has also shaped his own philosophy.

It is only possible to resolve these epistemological issues surrounding Plotinus' anti-Gnostic controversy when we view Gnostic thought as having been more integrated within both religious and philosophical currents in the first centuries AD than has been previously supposed, and when we recognize the precise points of convergence and divergence between Gnostic Platonic exegeses and the writings of Plotinus. It is this method that I have adopted in my thesis, in my contributions to the project *Plotin et les Gnostiques,* and in other collective volumes.[6]

Our work employed new elements to help resolve the epistemological problems mentioned above. We have shown in a systematic manner that the dialogue between Plotinus and the Gnostics concerning the definition of the hierarchical levels between material and immaterial reality and the stages by which the soul ascends to know the higher realities constitutes the organizing principle of Plotinus' thought not only in his treatise 32, but through most of the *Enneads.* Much previous research on his relationship with the Gnostics, however, has concentrated only on treatise 33.

It has also been shown that treatises 30–33 can indeed be regarded as a "great anti-Gnostic treatise" (broken up by Porphyry[7]), but also that this same dialogue pervades

---

[6] For the titles of these papers and articles see my CV and my list of publications on the website https://uni-bonn.academia.edu/LucianaGabrielaSoaresSantoprete.

[7] Cf. Pierre Hadot, "Les traités *30* à *33* constituent-il un grand écrit dirigé contre les gnostiques?," in *Plotin et les gnostiques 2. Au-delà la tétralogie antignostique,* ed. Luciana Gabriela Soares Santoprete, Anna Van den Kerchove, Jean-François Balaudé, and Philippe Hoffmann (Paris: Vrin, forthcoming). I disagree with the recent suggestions of Richard Dufour, "*Annexe 1. Les traités* 30 *à* 33: *un grand traité?*," in *Plotin, Traités 30-37,* trans. and notes Luc Brisson and Jean-François Pradeau (Paris: GF Flammarion, 2006), 399–406; and of Jean-Marc Narbonne, *Plotin, Œuvres Complètes,* vol. I, *Traité 1 (I 6) Sur le Beau,* ed., trans., and notes Lorenzo Ferroni, Martin Achard, and Jean-Marc Narbonne (Paris: Les Belles Lettres, 2012), LII, note 1. The recognition of the unity of treatises 30–33 is not incompatible with the idea that Plotinus made reference to the Gnostics before and after the tetralogy.

the remaining corpus of Plotinus' treatises. On the one hand, treatise 33 constitutes a reference point for the identification of Gnostic and anti-Gnostic ideas that appear in the other treatises; on the other hand, the study of those parallel traces of the exchange with the Gnostics is fundamental to an understanding of treatise 33. While Plotinus mentions explicitly in this treatise the principal points of Gnostic doctrine that he is opposing, he interacts with those points, and establishes the theoretical foundation for his critique by means of agreement and demurral, in more discreet and subtle ways, in his other treatises.

It is only in reading treatise 33 that the organization and intention of treatises 30, 31, and 32 are revealed, while these in turn provide detailed foundations for some of the criticisms in treatise 33. In treatises 30–32, Plotinus demonstrates that only three principles of reality exist (the One, the Intellect, and the Soul, or as the Hesiod myth suggests, Ouranos, Kronos, and Zeus). He clarifies his view that all intelligible and sensible realities proceed ultimately from the First Principle in a necessary, natural, and eternal progression, and that the Intellect is to be identified with the Demiurge and still has in itself beings, intelligence, and truth, constituting together with them one single and unique nature. With these explanations in place, Plotinus can then definitively refute what he considers to be the "[Gnostic] doctrine that exceeds all others in absurdity," which is discussed in treatise 33 and which is the origin of the second title of the treatise (*Against those who say that the Maker of the Universe is Evil and the Universe is Evil*). This view comes from the Gnostic idea that "Soul descended to what was beneath it, and with it some sort of Wisdom," and that this descent produced what, according to their interpretation of the *Timaeus*, "they call the Demiurge," from which "they make the world proceed from similitudes in similitudes until the last, as a violent insult to the Demiurge who has designed them," thereby unnecessarily multiplying the number of realities in the intelligible spheres. A detailed interpretation of treatise 33 therefore cannot be undertaken without a parallel analysis of the themes discussed in this treatise as they occur throughout the entire corpus of the *Enneads*, and in the light of that analysis, reconsideration of the evolution of his engagement with Gnosticism and the influence of that engagement on the development of his thought.

It has also been observed[8] that several of Plotinus' critiques could be addressed with equal validity against the Gnostics, Numenius, other Platonists, and/or against

---

[8] Cf. in particular: Luciana Gabriela Soares Santoprete, "La question de la localisation des intelligibles chez les philosophes païens des premiers siècles de l'ère chrétienne," in *Pensée grecque et sagesse d'Orient. Hommage à Michel Tardieu*, ed. Mohammad-Ali Amir-Moezzi, Jean-Daniel Dubois, Christelle Jullien, and Florence Jullien (Turnhout: Brepols, 2009), 637–651; Luciana Gabriela Soares Santoprete, "L'emploi du terme *amphistomos* dans le grand traité antignostique de Plotin et dans les Oracles Chaldaïques," in *Die Chaldaeischen Orakel. Kontext – Interpretation – Rezeption*, ed. Helmut Seng and Michel Tardieu (Heidelberg: Universitätsverlag Winter, 2010), 163–178; Luciana Gabriela Soares Santoprete, "La signification plotinienne du nom d'Apollon," in *Noms barbares*. I. *Formes et contextes d'une pratique magique*, ed. Michel Tardieu, Anna Van den Kerchove, and Michela Zago (Turnhout: Brepols, 2013), 239–251.

the *Chaldean Oracles*. It is therefore essential that an evaluation of polemical elements in Plotinus should be based on comparison not only with direct and indirect Gnostic sources, but also with Middle-Platonic writings (that is, with the tradition that some historians of philosophy persist in elevating into a Platonic "orthodoxy"[9]) and with other supposedly "marginal" Platonizing and religious currents. The primary purpose of such a comparative study is not, at least in the first instance, to establish the relationships of influence and borrowing between the respective currents, inasmuch as this assumes that it has been possible to establish the specificity of each of them; rather, we first wish to discern what is common to all of them, and what by implication then in fact characterizes not simply one given current, but the pervasive religious environment of the period. Only then can we begin to identify the individual character of distinct philosophical and religious currents, and who Plotinus' Gnostic opponents were.

In 1977 and 1980, John M. Dillon and Guy G. Stroumsa respectively observed that "much detailed work is necessary before acceptable conclusions can be reached about the type of Platonism that lies behind the elaborate metaphysical constructions of the Gnostics, Hermetics and the Chaldeans";[10] and, "in order to be properly understood, these various trends must be studied together, as different facets of the same [historical-cultural] reality."[11] These statements remain valid, despite the significant progress that has been made in these areas over the intervening decades. The *Chaldean Oracles* and Hermeticism have "striking similarities with the numerous Gnostic writings..., not [necessarily] due to direct borrowing, but to the fact that they were all shaped by the same intellectual background and responded to analogous spiritual needs of the day [such as] ... the preoccupation with the soul and its salvation [and the] tendency to view the world in relation to the fate of the soul and the fate of the soul in relation to the world."[12]

Numenius of Apamea

As I have also noted, several polemical references in Plotinus' work could have the Platonism of Numenius as their target, rather than or as well as Gnostics and/or the *Chaldean Oracles*. This is the case, for example, with his remarks on the theory of

---

[9] A typical example is the book of Polymia Athanassiadi, *La lutte pour l'orthodoxie dans le platonisme tardif de Numénius à Damascius* (Paris: Les Belles Lettres, 2006); cf. my review of this book in *Apocrypha* 18 (2007): 340–342.

[10] Dillon, *Platonists*, 384.

[11] Guy G. Stroumsa, "*Chaldean Oracles*," *Numen* 27 (1980): 167–172.

[12] Arthur D. Nock, ed. *Corpus Hermeticum*, trans. André-Jean Festugière, *vol. I, Traité VII* (Paris: Les Belles Lettres, 1960), VII (my translation). Cf. also Anna Van den Kerchove, "Le mode de révélation dans les *Oracles Chaldaïques* et dans les traités hermétiques," in *Die Chaldaeischen Orakel. Kontext – Interpretation – Rezeption*, ed. Helmuth Seng and Michel Tardieu (Heidelberg: Universitätsverlag Winter, 2010), 145–162.

the Intellect and on the hierarchical differentiation of the first principles in treatises 13 (III 9) and 30–33. Only when Numenius' thought is carefully examined does it then become possible to identify precisely to whom Plotinus refers—given also that Plotinus rarely names his opponents—as well as possible interaction between him and Numenius, Gnosticism, and the *Chaldean Oracles*. We can then also understand how Numenius may have influenced some Gnostic writings and how he was likewise influenced by Judeo-Christian and Gnostic thought, we can establish the chronological line of influence between him and the *Chaldean Oracles*, and, finally, we can determine the role that he played in mediating knowledge of these "marginal" doctrines to Plotinus and in their assimilation into Neo-Platonism after Plotinus. Further research in these areas would also clarify the relationship of dependency between Numenius, the *Chaldean Oracles,* and Porphyry. Commentators are divided over the question whether or not Porphyry was familiar with the *Oracles* through Numenius' mediation.

Numenius did express a strong interest in doctrines from beyond the Greek cultural heritage, as we can see in the first book of his treatise *On the Good*, where he presented a program of syncretism, a "call to the Orient" as Henri-Charles Puech called it,[13] encouraging those who consider the problem of God to combine the teachings of Plato with those of Pythagoras, and also to invoke as testimony the mysteries and doctrines of the Brahmins, the Jews, Magi, and Egyptians which, he argued, were likewise compatible with Platonism. This syncretistic approach is a trademark of Numenius' thought and, given its strong legacy in Neo-Platonism—Plotinus read Numenius in his courses, and the latter enjoyed considerable prestige with Plotinus' disciples, Porphyry and Amelius—it is possible to imagine not only that Numenius is the missing link to understanding the relationship between the school of Plotinus and "marginal" doctrines, but also that the demarcation that Plotinus sought to establish between his own teaching and that of the Gnostics and/or the *Chaldean Oracles* might be the same or a similar distinction to that which he makes between himself and Numenius, who had influenced (and/or been influenced by) these "marginal" schools of thought.[14] It is arguably not a coincidence that these approaches of Plotinus are mentioned together by Porphyry

---

[13] Henri-Charles Puech, "Numénius d'Apamée et les théologies orientales au second siècle," *Annuaire de l'Institut de philologie et d'histoire orientales et slaves* II (Brussels: 1934): 745–778 [= Henri-Charles Puech, *En Quête de la Gnose*. I *La Gnose et le Temps* (Paris: Gallimard, 1978), 25–54 (hereafter Puech, *Numénius*)].

[14] For bibliographies concerning debates about the direction of these influences, cf. Édouard des Places, ed. and trans., *Numénius, fragments* (Paris: Les Belles Lettres, 1973), 21–22 (for Numenius and Gnosticism, Judaism and Hermeticism); Ruth Majercik, "The *Chaldean Oracles* and the School of Plotinus," *Ancient World* 29/2 (1998): 91–105 (hereafter Majercik, *Chaldean Oracles*); and Michel Tardieu, "Les Oracles chaldaïques 1891-2011," (hereafter Tardieu, *Oracles*), in *Chaldaean Oracles and Theurgy. Mysticism, Magic and Platonism in the Later Roman Empire, Troisième édition par* Michel Tardieu, avec un supplément "Les *Oracles chaldaïques* 1891-2011," ed. Hans Lewy (hereafter Lewy, *Chaldaean Oracles*) (Paris: Institut d'Études Augustiniennes, 2011, ¹1978), 731–766 (in particular 743–744; for Numenius and the *Chaldean Oracles*).

in his *Life of Plotinus* (16–18), and that the principal refutations written by Plotinus' disciples are those of Porphyry against the Gnostic book of *Zoroaster*, and of Amelius against the Gnostic writing of Zostrianos and against accusations of Plotinus' plagiarism of Numenius, which are also mentioned by Porphyry in this section of the *Life*.

Further study of Numenius would therefore benefit from the resumption and pursuit of three previously initiated, but unfinished projects: that begun by Friedrich Thedinga[15] in 1917 and continued by Eric R. Dodds in 1960[16] on references to Numenius in Plotinus' treatises; that commenced by Puech in 1934[17] to investigate Gnostic and Oriental influences on Numenius' thought; and that initiated by Richard T. Wallis in 1992 on the relationship between Numenius and the Nag Hammadi corpus.[18]

Hermeticism

Most of Greek Hermetic literature was written during the first centuries AD, and presents an eclectic combination of Platonism, Aristotelianism, Stoicism, and religious elements of Egyptian, Iranian, and Jewish origin, as has been demonstrated by the several axes of research on these texts.[19] These texts have been transmitted to us in three groups (the *Corpus Hermeticum*, the *Asclepius*, and the thirty-nine fragments extracted from the *Anthology* of Stobaeus); even if they often offer divergent teachings, they all show that the means of salvation for Man is knowledge that can only be obtained through a revelation given by God or a prophet, leading to a spiritual elevation and deification, which occurs through a mysterious initiation and the exercise of piety and asceticism.

The presence of terminologies and themes that are common to other philosophical and religious currents of Late Antiquity,[20] the attestation to Gnostic traits in some of these texts, and the existence of Hermetic treatises in the Coptic language in codex VI of the Gnostic Nag Hammadi library, reinforce the necessity of studying all of

---

[15] Friedrich Thedinga, "Plotin oder Numenios? Erste Abhandlung," *Hermes* 52 (1917): 592–612; Friedrich Thedinga, "Plotin oder Numenios? Zweite Abhandlung," *Hermes* 54 (1919): 249–278; Friedrich Thedinga, "Plotin oder Numenios? Dritte Abhandlung," *Hermes* 57 (1922): 189–218.

[16] Eric R. Dodds, "Numenius and Ammonius," in *Entretiens sur l'antiquité classique V: Les sources de Plotin* (Vandoeuvres-Geneva: Fondation Hardt, 1960), 3–61 (in particular 3–32).

[17] Puech, *Numénius*.

[18] Richard T. Wallis, "Soul and Nous in Plotinus, Numenius and Gnosticism," in *Neoplatonism and Gnosticism*, ed. Richard T. Wallis and Jay Bregman (Albany: State University of New York Press, 1992), 461–482.

[19] Cf. Ilaria Ramelli, "2. Breve panoramica: gli studi sull'ermetismo filosofico nel Novecento," in *Corpus Hermeticum*, ed., trans., and comm., Arthur D. Nock and André-Jean Festugière, trans. into Italian Ilaria Ramelli (Milan: Bompiani, 2005), 1280–1290; Alberto Camplani, *Scritti ermetici in copto* (Brescia: Paideia, 2000) (hereafter Camplani, *Scritti*).

[20] Cf. Boudewijn Dehandschutter, "Théologie négative: la contribution des textes gnostiques et hermétiques," in *Théologie Négative*, ed. Marco Olivetti (Padua: Cedam, 2002), 505–513.

these different literatures together. The Hermetic treatises found in 1945 (*The Prayer of Thanksgiving* and the fragment of *Asclepius* containing chapters 21–29 already known in a very similar form,[21] and the writing, until then unknown, entitled *The Discourse on the Eighth and Ninth*)[22] also show considerable similarities with the mythological group of "Sethian" writings, the least Christianized of the Gnostic groups with which Plotinus and his school debated.[23]

On the other hand, recent research by Claudio Moreschini[24] has shown that Christians themselves appropriated Hermeticism in various ways. Some assimilated philosophical and religious concepts and/or suggested a concordance between these two bodies of work, as in Arnobius' *Against the Pagans* and Lactantius' *Divine Institutes*, even though both of these writings are apologetic treatises against pagan doctrines. Others expressed harsh criticism by equating Hermetic writings with Gnostic doctrines and/or pagan philosophy, as in Tertullian's *Treatise on the Soul*, for which he used the Middle-Platonist Albinus as a source, and his *Against the Valentinians*. The process of integration and marginalization of the Greek "orthodox" philosophical tradition was therefore not a phenomenon to which Christians contributed without reference to the Hermetic tradition.

The Chaldean Oracles

In his survey of studies of the *Chaldean Oracles* and their place in the religious literature of Late Antiquity undertaken up to 1978, Pierre Hadot stated:

"it is obvious that it is necessary to take into account in the study of the *Chaldean Oracles* the enormous progress that has been made in research on Gnosticism following the discovery at Nag Hammadi. As Michel Tardieu clearly showed at the Yale Conference in 1978, it is now possible to analyse the structural similarities between the Valentinian Gnostic school of thought in particular and the "Chaldean" school of thought. We can "consider Valentinus and the *Oracles* as belonging to the same stage of development as the original Platonic

---

[21] Cf. Arthur D. Nock, ed., *Corpus Hermeticum*, trans. André-Jean Festugière, vols. I-IV (Paris: Les Belles Lettres, 1945–1954); André-Jean Festugière, *La révélation d'Hermès Trismégiste* I-IV (Paris: Gabalda, 1949–1954, ²1981).

[22] Jean-Pierre Mahé, *Hermès en Haute-Égypte. Les textes hermétiques de Nag Hammadi et leurs parallèles grecs et latins*, t. I (Louvain/Québec: Peeters/Presses de l'Université Laval, 1978); and Camplani, *Scritti*.

[23] Cf. Jean-Pierre Mahé, "VI. Hermétisme," in *Écrits gnostiques. La bibliothèque de Nag Hammadi*, ed. Jean-Pierre Mahé and Paul-Hubert Poirier (Paris: Gallimard, 2007), LVII–LXII (in particular LXII).

[24] Claudio Moreschini, *Storia dell'ermetismo cristiano* (Brescia: Morcelliana, 2000); cf. also Andreas Löw, *Hermes Trismegistos als Zeuge der Wahrheit. Die christliche Hermetik-rezeption von Athenagoras bis Laktanz*, (Berlin: Theophaneia, 2002).

thought". Here as well, a very wide field of investigation is open to future research."[25]

Indeed, Tardieu explained that "the genesis of the *Chaldean Oracles* can only be understood in relation to the environment in which they were produced, and in that environment, Valentinian Gnosticism had a prominent place,"[26] as W. Kroll had already suggested in 1894[27]. Tardieu further stated that the analysis presented in his essay on the terms and themes used by the two literatures did not aim to find "elements of Gnostic thought in the *Oracles*. Without excluding this method or losing sight of lack of certainty in these areas of synthetic analysis (...) [his investigation tried rather to] capture the movement of thought which led a "traditional" Platonism to become a Platonism of revelation: not so much to demonstrate that Valentinus and the *Oracles* say the same thing, as how they have said it"[28] If Tardieu[29] uses and completes the indices of similarities that, according to him, Kroll rightly perceived to exist between the *Chaldean Oracles*, Numenius, Jewish literature, and the Gnostics, he refuses, however (along with Hans Lewy), to assign to the *Oracles*, as Kroll does, the appellation of "pagan Gnosis" and to speak of the "influence" of the Gnostics on the Chaldeans. He also acknowledges the originality of Lewy in reading the triptych into which Kroll inserted the *Oracles* (Numenius-*Oracles*-Iamblichus and subsequent Neo-Platonists) not only from left to right as Kroll did, but from right to left. This "method has resulted in significantly enlarging the areas of study" and has shown that "the properly mystical transcendent element of the *Oracles* is not to be sought on the side of an oriental Gnosis", as Kroll thought, but rather on the Platonic side of the philosophical and religious-philosophical currents of the time. Three problems remain: "to discover whether or not the 'Chaldean' religion corresponds to the state of pre-Plotinian,[30] Gnostic, or Neo-

---

[25] Cf. Pierre Hadot, "Bilan et perspectives sur les Oracles Chaldaïques," in Lewy, *Chaldaean Oracles*, 703–720 (in particular 720).

[26] Michel Tardieu, "Le congrès de Yale sur le Gnosticisme (28-31 mars 1978)," *Revue des études augustiniennes* 24 (1978): 188–209 (in particular 199–200).

[27] Wilhelm Kroll, *De oraculis Chaldaicis* (W. Koebner: Breslau, 1894).

[28] Michel Tardieu, "La Gnose Valentinienne et les Oracles Chaldaïques," in *The Rediscovery of Gnosticism, vol. I : The School of Valentinus*, ed. Bentley Layton (Leiden: Brill, 1980), 194–237 (in particular 215–216; my translation).

[29] The references and quotations (in my translation) given in this paragraph are taken from the pages 737–739 of the following article of Michel Tardieu: "Les Oracles chaldaïques 1891-2011," in Lewy, *Chaldean Oracles*.

[30] This is the position of Hadot: cf. Pierre Hadot, "Théologie, exégèse, révélation, écriture dans la philosophie grecque," in *Les règles de l'interprétation*, ed. Michel Tardieu (Paris: Éditions de Cerf, 1987), 13–34 (in particular 29). [= Pierre Hadot, *Études de philosophie ancienne* (Paris: Les Belles Lettres, 1998), 27–58 (in particular 46)]; also Pierre Hadot, *Porphyre et Victorinus*, vol. I (Paris: Études Augustiniennes, 1968), 95–98 and 482–485.

Platonic Platonism", to define the points of contact between the *Oracles* and Numenius, and to determine the role played by the latter in the transmission of the *Oracles* to the Neo-Platonists.

These are the tasks now confronting scholars. In order to address them, it is necessary to adopt, as Hadot and Tardieu suggest, a methodology that examines simultaneously the Platonic writings, the Gnostic corpus, and the *Chaldean Oracles*. The importance of such an approach was recently documented in two articles that propose to show the connections between the *Oracles*, the Gnostic writings, and *The Anonymous Commentary on Plato's 'Parmenides.'*

In his article "The *Chaldean Oracles* and the Metaphysics of the Sethian Platonizing Treatises,"[31] John D. Turner emphasizes convergences between these three corpuses through a parallel analysis of the female figures of Hecate and Barbelo in the *Oracles* and in the "Sethian" writings, and of the Father–Power–Intellect triad of the *Oracles*, the Existence–Life–Intellect triad in the *Anonymous Commentary,* and the triadic structure of the One-three-times-powerful in the Platonizing "Sethian" writings, especially in the *Allogenes* treatise which, according to Porphyry (*Life of Plotinus* 16), was known in the circle of Plotinus. Turner's study shows that these female figures and triads appear to be related by a common notion, that of "dynamic emanation," which was very characteristic of the Platonism of the late second and early third centuries.

Luc Brisson analyzes in his article the critique in the *Anonymous Commentary* of a particular interpretation of Plato's *Parmenides* about the knowability or the impossibility of knowing the First One.[32] He notes that the critique in columns IX and X of the *Anonymous Commentary* of this interpretation deploys post-Plotinian Platonic arguments, which have elements in common with Plotinus' treatises 39, 11 and 10, 8. This criticism claims that the First One is unknowable because it is beyond the being and the Intellect, a position different from that assumed by the author of the interpretation that is being disputed, which is based on the authority of the *Chaldean Oracles* and strongly influenced by the Middle-Platonism of Numenius and by Stoicism. Brisson also notes one similarity between the vocabulary used in the critique in the *Anonymous Commentary* and that used by Plotinus against the Gnostics in treatise 33. This similarity is to the "audacious" manner in which these authors present their Platonic exegesis. He therefore suggests that the interpretation that is criticized should be attributed to a Gnostic author. Brisson also relies on the relationship established by John Turner in

---

[31] John D. Turner, "The *Chaldean Oracles* and the Metaphysics of the Sethian Platonizing Treatises," in *Plato's Parmenides and its Heritage, Volume I: History and Interpretation from the Old Academy to Later Platonism and Gnosticism,* ed. John D. Turner and Kevin Corrigan (Atlanta: Society of Biblical Literature, 2010), 213–232 (hereafter Turner and Corrigan, *Plato's Parmenides I*).

[32] Luc Brisson, "A Criticism of the *Chaldaean Oracles* and of the Gnostics in Columns IX and X of the *Anonymous Commentary on the Parmenides,*" in Turner and Corrigan, *Plato's Parmenides I*, 233–241.

2001[33] between the *Anonymous Commentary on Plato's 'Parmenides'* and the Gnostic writings *Allogenes* and *Zostrianos*—criticized by Plotinus and his school—as well as the relationship between *Zostrianos* and Marius Victorinus, which was demonstrated in the book by Michel Tardieu and Pierre Hadot on the relationship between the *Zostrianos*, the sources of Marius Victorinus, and an unidentified common Platonic source.[34]

In that book, Tardieu demonstrates with the aid of other works by Hadot that the passage 1, 49, 7 - 50, 21 of the work *Adversus Arium*, written by Marius Victorinus in 360 AD, shows striking similarities with the passages VIII 63-68.74.75.84 of the Gnostic writing *Zostrianos*. Given that the latter was known and refuted by Amelius, a disciple of Plotinus, Tardieu and Hadot advance the hypothesis that a common source must have existed between Victorinus and *Zostrianos*, namely a Middle-Platonic commentary (written by Numenius according to Tardieu[35] and by Porphyry according to Hadot) on the first series of deductions from the second part of Plato's *Parmenides*. According to Brisson, this Tardieu-Hadot hypothesis is strengthened by identifying, at the beginning of column IX of the *Anonymous Commentary on the 'Parmenides,'* the common source that could have inspired both Marius Victorinus and *Zostrianos*, that is to say, the Middle-Platonic interpretation—in his opinion from a Gnostic author—of the First God influenced by the description of the Father in fragments 3, 4, and 7 of the *Chaldean Oracles*, the latter in turn relying on the representation of the One in the first deduction of the second part of Plato's *Parmenides* (142 a).

These articles by Turner and Brisson appeared in 2010 in the aforementioned volume edited by Turner and Corrigan, which examines the current differentiation between Middle- and Neo-Platonism, specifically by analyzing the *Anonymous Commentary on Plato's 'Parmenides'* and the hypotheses of its dependence on one or several commentaries on the *Parmenides*, which purportedly existed in Platonic pagan and Gnostic circles before Plotinus[36] and was of post-Plotinian origin. These articles illustrate perfectly the importance of interdisciplinary studies for the resolution of questions that are at the heart of the history of Platonism in Late Antiquity.

---

[33] John D. Turner, *Sethian Gnosticism and the Platonic Tradition* (Québec-Louvain: Presses de l'Université Laval-Peeters, 2001).

[34] I am preparing a translation into Portuguese of Michel Tardieu, "Recherches sur la formation de l'Apocalypse de Zostrien et les sources de Marius Victorinus," *suivi* de Pierre Hadot, "Porphyre et Victorinus. Questions et hypothèses," *Res orientales* 9 (Bures-sur-Yvette: GEMCO, 1996) into Portuguese: "A composição do *Apocalypse de Zostriano* e as fontes de Mário Vitorino *seguido* de Porfírio e Vitorino. Questões e hipóteses" (Annablume, forthcoming).

[35] Cf. also Luc Brisson, "The Platonic Background in the Apocalypse of Zostrianus: Numenius and Letter II attributed to Plato," in *Tradition of Platonism. Essays in Honour of J. Dillon*, ed. John J. Clearly (Aldershot: Ashgate, 1999), 173–188.

[36] Cf. also Eric R. Dodds, "The Parmenides of Plato and the Origin of the Neoplatonic 'One,'" *Classical Quaterly* 22 (1928): 129–142.

As Hadot said, once again in 1978, "there is still much work to be done to prepare for the great synthesis [about the *Oracles*] dreamed about by J. Bidez that will unite both the *Chaldean Oracles*, studied in their Neo-Platonic context, and all of those documents which pertain to theoretical and practical theurgy."[37] Such a synthesis cannot be accomplished without extensive research on the relationships between the *Oracles*, Gnosticism, and Platonism before Plotinus, particularly that of Numenius. Notwithstanding the many avenues of research suggested since the 1980s by Hadot and Tardieu in the works mentioned above and the growth of Gnostic studies over recent decades, there has still been very little work devoted to this topic, according to the thematic bibliography recently compiled by Tardieu.[38] All of the works in the bibliography were written after those of Hadot and Tardieu, and so attest to the fruitfulness of their work. Yet it is also apparent that Hellenistic scholars have not completely accepted that these "marginal" currents should be studied together. This is evidenced by the translation of the *Chaldean Oracles* published by Édouard des Places[39] in 1971 and its revised and corrected second edition from 1996, which makes no reference to the relationship between the *Chaldean Oracles* and Gnosticism or to the bibliography related to this field.

Thus, the Platonism of the *Chaldean Oracles* needs to be clarified via two approaches: the comparative study of "marginal" and "mainstream" Platonisms of this period, and the comparative study of different authors and the contexts by which these fragments have come down to us. Research pursued along such lines will also allow us to acquire new insights into possible connections between Ammonius Saccas, Plotinus, and Amelius and the *Chaldean Oracles*, about which specialists are far from being in agreement,[40] as well as better understanding of the defense of the theological oracles against Christianity by Celsus, Porphyry, Iamblichus, and the emperor Julian.[41] These studies will, moreover, contribute to the realization of the vast project conceived so many years ago by J. Bidez.[42]

---

[37] Pierre Hadot, "Bilan et perspectives sur les *Oracles Chaldaïques*," in Lewy, *Chaldaean Oracles*, 703–720 (in particular 720).

[38] More than a dozen other important works have been published in addition to those mentioned in this article. For the complete list see "Oracles chaldaïques et Gnosticisme" at http://philognose.hypotheses.org/category/bibliographies-thematiques.

[39] *Oracles Chaldaïques avec un choix de commentaires anciens*, introduction, texte grec, traduction et notes Édouard des Places (Paris: Les Belles Lettres, 1971).

[40] Cf. Majercik, *Chaldean Oracles*.

[41] Giulia Sfameni Gasparro, *Oracoli Profeti Sibille. Rivelazione e salvezza nel mondo antico*, (Rome: Las, 2002), 28–29 and 72–74.

[42] Joseph Bidez, *La liturgie des mystères chez les Néo-platoniciens*, dans *Bulletin de l'Académie royale de Belgique, Classe de Lettres*, 1919, 415–423, and Joseph Bidez – Franz Cumont, *Les mages hellénisés: Zoroastre, Ostanès et Hystaspe d'après la tradition grecque* (Paris: Les Belles Lettres, 1938) t. I, 163.

The Anonymous Commentary on Plato's 'Parmenides'

Several examples in the preceding pages have shown the importance that the study of extant fragments of an anonymous commentary on the *Parmenides* (137c–143a) has for understanding the relationship between "mainstream" and "marginal" philosophical and religious currents in Late Antiquity; the dating and the identification of the author of these fragments also have implications for our understanding of the history of philosophy and the role that "marginal" religious currents, especially Gnosticism and the *Chaldean Oracles,* played in the development of Platonism.

As Michael Chase has shown,[43] historians are not yet unanimous in their views on the dating and authorship of this text. The difficulty lies in the fact that these fragments demonstrate a pattern of thought that is on some points very close to Plotinus (notably, the correspondence between the first principles as hypostases and the hypotheses of the *Parmenides,* and sketches of a doctrine of three stages of Being, Life, and Thought), while on other points it is very distant (for example, the utilization, with some critical reservations, of the doctrines of the *Chaldean Oracles*). In 1961 and 1968, Pierre Hadot claimed to recognize a sample of a Porphyrian commentary on the *Parmenides* in these fragments. This ascription was supported by W. Beierwaltes, H. J. Blumenthal, A. C. Lloyd, John M. Rist, W. Theiler, R. Wallis, J. Whittaker, Henry Dominique Saffrey, John Dillon, J. Halfwassen, and Marco Zambon, among others, and doubted by Andrey Smith, Marc Edwards, Alessandro Linguiti, and Gerald Bechtle. Therefore, according to Chase, "with regard to the author, Smith, Edwards and Linguiti envision a successor, direct or indirect, of Porphyry, while Bechtle, for his part, situates the author of this commentary in Numenius' circle, implying that its composition would date from at least a century earlier, and that its author would be a Middle-Platonist, rather than Neo-Platonist. In this case, the 'Plotinian' elements of the commentary would in fact be 'proto-Plotinian' elements, that is to say, Middle-Platonic doctrines intended to be developed by Plotinus." Chase also notes the significant impact that Tardieu's abovementioned 1996 discovery had on the question of the attribution of the *Anonymous Commentary.* Indeed, it had "the immense merit of opening the field to a comparative study of the doctrines of Porphyry, Marius Victorinus, and the Gnostics, a domain that without doubt has not exhausted its capacity to produce important discoveries."

The richness of and the continuing interest in these questions concerning the *Anonymous Commentary* are illustrated by the new fields of research opened up by the many recent contributions devoted to the exegesis of the *Parmenides* in Late Antiquity,

---

[43] Michael Chase, "Porphyre de Tyr," in *Dictionnaire des philosophes antiques,* t. V b, ed. Richard Goulet (Paris: CNRS, 2005), 1289–1469 (in particular 1358–1373). The references and quotations (in my translation) given in this paragraph are taken from this article where we can find the complete bibliographical references of the auteurs mentioned here.

which have been collected in the work edited by Turner and Corrigan and published in 2010.[44] In this work, the proposal was made to attribute the *Anonymous Commentary* to Amelius and to "Sethian" Gnostics by Luc Brisson and Tuomas Rasimus, respectively.[45]

Further study of the debate between the school of Plotinus and the "Sethian" texts will permit us to determine what validity the recently advanced hypothesis that the *Anonymous Commentary on Plato's 'Parmenides'* pre-dates Plotinus might have, against the persuasive arguments in favor of a post-Plotinian dating, first presented by Pierre Hadot and subsequently endorsed by other prominent Neo-Platonism scholars. The resolution of this question in turn has consequences for the criteria by which we currently differentiate between Middle- and Neo-Platonism.

New Digital Approaches to the "Underworld of Platonism": Database, Bibliographical Directory, and Research Blog

The triple collective digital project *Les Platonismes de l'Antiquité Tardive. Base de données, répertoire bibliographique et carnet de recherche sur les liens entre médio- et néoplatonisme, gnosticisme, hermétisme et Oracles Chaldaïques* was created in order to address the problems surveyed in the preceding pages. In these three resources, ancient commentaries and modern studies on the interaction between "mainstream" and "marginal" currents in philosophical texts, as well as philosophical references present in the Gnostic, Hermetic, and Chaldean corpuses, will be collected and analyzed in order to answer the following questions: Which polemical viewpoints, vocabulary, and other elements from Gnostic, Hermetic, and Chaldean doctrines can be identified in the works of Middle- and Neo-Platonic authors? Which philosophical doctrines can be found in the Gnostic, Hermetic, and Chaldean texts? What is the current state of research on each of these elements, and what conclusions can be drawn today on the relationships between them?

At issue here is the broad question of whether the conventional scholarly distinction that is made between, on the one side, "philosophy," and on the other side, "religion," which is further sub-divided into "mainstream" and "marginal" or "heretical," in fact accurately reflects the Late Antique cultural reality; or whether instead—as is assumed here—there was a much more porous border between them, and both philosophy and religion cross-fertilized one another. Similarly, as should be apparent, no clear and consistent separation between the "marginal" and the "mainstream" existed.

---

[44] Turner and Corrigan, *Plato's Parmenides I*; and John D. Turner, and Kevin Corrigan, eds., *Plato's Parmenides and its Heritage, Volume II: Its Reception in Neoplatonic, Jewish, and Christian Texts* (Atlanta: Society of Biblical Literature, 2010) (hereafter Turner and Corrigan, *Plato's Parmenides II*).

[45] Luc Brisson, "The Reception of the Parmenides before Proclus," in Turner and Corrigan, *Plato's Parmenides II*, 49–63; Tuomas Rasimus, "Porphyry and the Gnostics: reassessing Pierre Hadot's thesis in light of the second and third-century sethian treatises," in Turner and Corrigan, *Plato's Parmenides II*, 81–110.

Within this context, we may summarize the problems in relation to Plotinus that illustrate this broader challenge, and that will be examined as part of this digital project. Thus: Which specific Gnostic texts constitute the background of Plotinus' treatise 33? Are these texts Valentinian and/or "Sethian"? How is it possible to locate traces of a dialogue with the Gnostics in the remaining *Enneads*? How does the study of treatise 33 help us to identify these traces and how, at the same time, does their identification enable us to better understand treatise 33 itself? Could Plotinus have written his critique against the *Tripartite Tractate*, or was this a Valentinian work written in response to his treatise 33? Is the *Tripartite Tractate* post-Plotinian or pre-Plotinian (as argued by Jean-Daniel Dubois[46], principally because of the similarity between its prologue and that of Origen's *On First Principles*)? Does the recurrence of the triad Being-Life-Thought in treatise 34, chronologically immediately following the tetralogy, indicate that this treatise is also part of Plotinus' anti-Gnostic polemic? Analysis of the definitions of the triad given in treatise 34 would facilitate resolution of the much debated question, whether or not the triad was a Gnostic loan to pre-Porphyrian Neo-Platonism, or a Porphyrian, or a Plotinian *and* Porphyrian loan to Gnosticism. Was the *Untitled Text* in the Bruce Codex known to the school of Plotinus, and can it be identified with the *Apocalypse of Messos* quoted by Porphyry, as Michel Tardieu[47] suggests? Can we say that the *Zostrianos*, the *Allogenes*, and the *Untitled Text* in the Bruce Codex, known to the circle of Plotinus according to Porphyry, are "Sethian" or "non-Christian" treatises, as John Turner[48] claims? Does the use of the classifications coined by modern researchers to catalogue the various Gnostic writings assist or impede the identification of the Gnostic texts known to Plotinus and his circle? What are the philosophical sources of Gnostic writings? What contribution did Peripatetic doctrines make to Gnostic thought? Does Plotinus' assimilation of Plato with Aristotle through the mediation of Alexander of Aphrodisias enable him to distinguish himself from Gnostic currents? Do the Gnostic, Hermetic, and Chaldean texts shed light on the philosophical tradition prior to Plotinus? What was the relationship between Numenius, Plotinus, and Gnosticism? Which ideas emanating from Numenius' syncretism were assimilated within "traditional" Platonism? What role did Numenius play in the transmission of the *Chaldean Oracles* to the Neo-Platonists? Is the Platonism of the *Chaldean Oracles*

---

[46] « Le *Traité des Principes* d'Origène et le *Traité Tripartite* valentinien : une lecture comparée de leurs prologues », dans *Entrer en matière — les prologues*, sous la direction de Jean-Daniel Dubois et Bernard Roussel, (Paris: Cerf, 1998), 53–63 (in particular 54).

[47] Michel Tardieu, « Les gnostiques dans la *Vie de Plotin : Analyse du chapitre 16* », suivi d'un répertoire chronologique (1933-1990) des publications relatives au chapitre 16 de la *Vie de Plotin*, dans *Porphyre. Vie de Plotin*, t. II, Luc Brisson *et alli* (ed.), (Paris: Vrin, 1992), 527 *sq*.

[48] John Turner, *Sethian Gnosticism and the Platonic Tradition* (Québec/Louvain/Paris: Les Presses de l'Université Laval – Éditions Peeters, 2001), 61-64.

pre-Plotininian, Gnostic, or Neo-Platonic? What is the relationship between Hermeticism and Gnosticism? What dating should be ascribed to the *Anonymous Commentary on Plato's 'Parmenides,'* and who was its author: Numenius, a Gnostic writer, Porphyry, or Amelius (depending on arguments presented by Gerald Bechtle, Thuomas Rasimus, Pierre Hadot and Luc Brisson, respectively[49])? And what similarities are there between the theoretical and rhetorical anti-Gnostic arguments deployed in Christian heresiological treatises and in Neoplatonic writings?

The three digital research tools were conceived primarily in order to address the epistemological problems that have been encountered in studying the relationship between Plotinus and the Gnostics. The aim is to identify all of Plotinus' references to the Gnostics by reviewing all studies of the *Enneads* that are pertinent to this topic, beginning with M.-N. Bouillet's annotated translation published in 1857[50], and systematically examining their thematic and lexical parallels in Gnostic texts. This analysis will also clarify the historiography of previous research—the principal terms, themes, and texts which have been examined, the assumptions that scholars have made, and the intellectual context of their own work.

In the database, commentaries in editions and translations of Plotinian and Gnostic writings, which are devoted specifically to the relationship between Plotinus, his school, and the Gnostics, are listed first, followed by published articles on this topic. In order to aid a better understanding of the relationship between Plotinus and Gnosticism, and of the history of Platonism, the scope of these resources will be gradually expanded to include works more broadly concerned with points of contact between "traditional" philosophical and "marginal" philosophical-religious currents from Classical to Late Antiquity. These additions will privilege Plato, Aristotle, Numenius, Epicureanism, Stoicism, Pythagoreanism, Plotinus, and post-Plotinian Neo-Platonism in the area of "mainstream" philosophy, and Hermeticism, Gnosticism, and the *Chaldean Oracles* for "marginal" religious currents.

These three resources will allow the creation of files for each of these fields of study, including data and research tracks previously scattered throughout the introductions, notes, and commentaries of translations and articles. They will also provide a detailed map of the history of studies on the relationship between philosophy and Gnosticism, which will demonstrate the philosophical implications of "marginal" Pla-

---

[49] Cf. Gerald Bechtle, *The Anonymous Commentary on Plato's "Parmenides"* (Bern/Stuttgart/Wien: Paul Haupt, 1999); Thuomas Rasimus, "Porphyry and the Gnostics: Reassessing Pierre Hadot's Thesis in Light of the Second and Third-Century Sethian Treatises", in *Plato's Parmenides II*, 81–110; "Fragments d'un commentaire de Porphyre sur le *Parménide*", *Revue des Études Grecques*, 74: 410–468 et *Porphyre et Victorinus I*, Paris, 102–146; Luc Brisson, "The Reception of the *Parmenides* before Proclus", *Plato's Parmenides II*, 49–63.

[50] Marie-Nicolas Bouillet, *Plotin, Les Ennéades*, traduites, accompagnées de sommaires, de notes et d'éclaircissements, t. I-III (Paris: Hachette, 1857-1861).

tonic currents and the integration of the "underworld of Platonism" into what is conventionally considered as the Platonic tradition. The concentration of and facility of access to this data will afford a foundation for continuing research on a debate that animated Christians and non-Christians alike in Antiquity.

To disseminate the results of this research, I intend to create *Gémina: An International Journal Devoted to Cultural Interaction between Philosophy and Religion in Antiquity*,[51] an electronic journal on OpenEdition's Revues.org devoted specifically to work on the relationship between "mainstream" and "marginal" philosophical currents in this period. The first planned print publication will be an edition of the *Enneads* with a commentary that includes all of the anti-Gnostic citations, references, and allusions that have been identified to date,[52] to appear initially in the form of independent articles dealing with each of the treatises.

The collective research blog *Les Platonismes de l'Antiquité Tardive* has been created in order to supplement the database and the bibliographical directory. The objective of this blog is to list current projects, activities, and scientific publications that are devoted specifically to the relationship between "mainstream" and "marginal" philosophical and religious currents from Classical to Late Antiquity. Its function is to disseminate texts, commentaries, discussion of researchers' methodological approaches, and pertinent references and links. It will provide a forum for continuing exchanges between all of those engaged in these areas.

These resources are innovative: no other database, critical bibliographical directory, or research blog on these themes exists. Specialized directories are available in the field of Plotinian philosophy and on the Gnostic and Hermetic writings, but none of these constitutes an exhaustive resource, insofar as they do not permit interdisciplinary research between the areas of Late Antique philosophy and "marginal" religious currents.

The directory of David Scholer[53] on the Nag Hammadi corpus offers neither a thematic index nor a classification of works that allows the identification of those that are pertinent to my project. It classifies as follows: I. Gnosticism: General; II. Other Gnostic Texts (Non-Nag Hammadi); III. Gnostic Schools and Leaders; IV. New Testament and Gnosticism; V. Nag Hammadi Library. The directory of Richard Dufour does not allow easy identification of work on the relationship between philosophers and

---

[51] This name has the double advantage of indicating the name of the owner of the house where Plotinus lived in Rome, according to Porphyry, *Life of Plotinus* 9, and of deriving from the French verb "géminer" (3rd pers. sing., simple past), meaning "arranged in pairs," "grouped by two."

[52] An explanation of the different types of references that can be identified in Plotinus' writings and in modern commentaries will be given in the sections "Methodological Remarks" and "How to Use this Site" on the home page of the database.

[53] David Scholer, *Nag Hammadi Bibliography*, 1948-1969; 1970-1994; 1995-2006 (Leiden: Brill, 1971, 1997, 2009; four supplements in *Novum Testamentum* 1984, 1993, 1994, 1995).

Gnostics, because it lists all publications only in alphabetical order by author.[54] Only the *Bibliographie rétrospective de Plotin* of Pierre Thillet allows the user to search by theme, but the rubric on "Gnosticism" is far from exhaustive: it takes into account primarily the work of specialists on Plotinus, while largely ignoring research by historians of religion; moreover, it lists only works published between 1947 and 1995.[55] The only directory that exists for Hermetic texts is that created in 1984 by Antonino González Blanco.[56] Other important directories have been consulted,[57] but none list all of the literature on this topic under a separate rubric and so facilitate convenient access to it.

The design and structure of the database for my project are innovative in the field of digital Humanities, and could provide a model for other similar databases. It is multi-disciplinary and multi-lingual, given the inclusion of several conventionally distinct discipline areas (philosophy, philology, history of religions, and computing resources) and the different languages of the authors studied as well as of modern researchers (Greek, Coptic, Latin, French, Italian, Spanish, Portuguese, English, and German); and it is hoped that these resources will be used by scholars and students across these discipline areas. The development of these resources also has broader ambitions: to augment the body of known commentaries, to understand the production of both ancient commentaries and modern scholarship within their intellectual and cultural historical contexts, to promote academic exchanges and the coordination of interdisciplinary research projects, to build up a virtual library of commentaries with bibliographies, thereby making them more accessible and complementing currently available resources, and contribute to the debate on the new prospects for the digital publication of commentaries and their dissemination within the scientific community.

The first stage of this work (November 2011–November 2013) was devoted to the creation of the model database, to the design of search mechanisms, and to their technical implementation in PHP/SQL MyAdmin. It is possible to perform the following searches: by ancient author (e. g. "Plotinus") and modern author (e. g. "É. Bréhier"); by ancient works (e. g. "treatise 33") and modern works (e. g. "É. Bréhier, Plotinus, *Enneads*, t. V, Paris, Les Belles Lettres, 1967 [1931]"); by the date of the ancient or modern work; by keywords in French, Greek, Coptic, and Latin; and by the most

---

[54] Richard Dufour, *Plotinus : A Bibliography 1950-2000* (Leiden: Brill, 2002); "Bibliographie Plotinienne," last modified June 18, 2015, http://rdufour.free.fr/BibPlotin/Plotin-Biblio.html).

[55] Pierre Thillet, "La Bibliographie rétrospective de Plotin," http://upr_76.vjf.cnrs.fr/biblioPlotin.pdf.

[56] Antonino González Blanco, "Hermetism. A Bibliographical Approach," *ANRW* II 17, 4 (1984): 2240–2297; Cf. also Ilaria Ramelli, "Bibliografia degli ultimi cinquant'anni sull'ermetismo filosofico: A. Bibliografia sul 'Corpus Hermeticum'" and "Bibliografia degli ultimi cinquant'anni sull'ermetismo filosofico: B. Bibliografia sull'ermetismo filosofico in copto," in *Corpus Hermeticum*, ed., trans., and comm., Arthur D. Nock and André-Jean Festugière, trans. into Italian Ilaria Ramelli (Milan: Bompiani, 2005), 1549–1572 and 1573–1619.

[57] Such as *L'Année philologique*, le *Répertoire bibliographique de la philosophie*, and *The Philosopher's Index*.

commonly recurring links woven by commentators between ancient authors in relation to the ancient and/or modern commentary. The collection of research material and the cataloguing of commentaries that discuss the relationship between Plotinus and the Gnostics was also completed in this first stage. These commentaries are found in the introductions, notes, and analyses accompanying translations of Plotinus and Gnostic texts into French, English, and Italian.

In December 2013, the database was put online for public use (http://philognose.org). The primary intention is to include in the database evidence relevant to this material, and to list the discussions that are concerned specifically with the debate between Plotinus and the Gnostics that have been found in books and articles in French, English, and Italian. Following this, such discussions in Spanish, Portuguese,[58] and German, as well as material from heresiological literature will also be added. Throughout this process, references to the relationship between Gnosticism and other philosophical and religious-philosophical currents from Classical to Late Antiquity will also be identified in the same primary sources and secondary literature that have been consulted in relation to Plotinus, and included in the database. For each of the authors and currents studied, the body of work present in the database will be systematically listed and found under the tab "Directory of Works."

Conclusions

The triple digital project presented here aims to demonstrate that the various conflicts that animated Platonic circles in Late Antiquity afford fertile ground for the study of the complexity of the dynamic between integration and marginality in the

---

[58] In 2010, I published three articles with a total of 128 pages (http://www.red.unb.br/index.php/archai/issue/view/187/showToc), which contain a comprehensive bibliographical directory of works on Neo-Platonism in Portuguese, which is an outcome of a project on this topic developed in Portugal with the support of the Calouste Gulbenkian: Luciana Gabriela Soares Santoprete, "Primeiro repertório bibliográfico dos estudos em língua portuguesa dedicados ao Neoplatonismo da Antiguidade Tardia. Parte I : Histórico da pesquisa" [First Bibliographical Repertory of the Studies in Portuguese devoted to the Neoplatonism in Late Antiquity. Part I: History of the Research], *Revista Archai: Revista de Estudos sobre as Origens do Pensamento Ocidental* 5 (2010): 151–212; Luciana Gabriela Soares Santoprete, Loraine Oliveira, and Emmannuela Freitas de Caldas, "Anexo à Parte I do Primeiro repertório bibliográfico dos estudos em língua portuguesa dedicados ao Neoplatonismo da Antiguidade Tardia" [Appendix to the Part I of the First Bibliographical Repertory of the Studies in Portuguese devoted to the Neoplatonism in Late Antiquity], *Revista Archai: Revista de Estudos sobre as Origens do Pensamento Ocidental* 5 (2010): 213–231; Luciana Gabriela Soares Santoprete, Loraine Oliveira, and Emmannuela Freitas de Caldas, "Primeiro repertório bibliográfico dos estudos em língua portuguesa dedicados ao Neoplatonismo da Antiguidade Tardia. Parte II : Elenco de autores e títulos" [First bibliographical Repertory of the Studies in Portuguese devoted to the Neoplatonism in Late Antiquity. Part II: List of Authors and Titles], *Revista Archai: Revista de Estudos sobre as Origens do Pensamento Ocidental* 5 (2010): 232–278.

history of Platonism, and illustrates in an exemplary manner how, as a result of that dynamic, this tradition continued to be innovative instead of becoming static. This process can only be understood by employing an interdisciplinary methodology in the study of the philosophical *koinè* and Platonic theology, of the different "mainstream" and "marginal" texts that constitute the Platonic tradition, and of the polemical relations between proponents of diverse interpretations of Plato.

This triple project will allow us to clarify how other doctrines from the philosophical tradition have been appropriated in debates within "mainstream" Platonism in order to refute "marginal" views, as well as how some "marginal" ideas have been incorporated within Platonism in order to refute other "marginal" positions. This discussion will then facilitate the development of a more complex and nuanced conception of the history of Platonism in the Roman period, and the specification of the character of diverse controversies that occurred during that history. Finally, it will highlight how these two different forms of assimilation of ideas have given rise to considerable innovation within Late Antique thought, and in turn thereby marked all subsequent western thought.

One of the most significant examples of this appropriation in a polemical context is the deployment of Aristotelian doctrines through the mediating exegesis of Alexander of Aphrodisias, to a limited degree by Plotinus, but more extensively by Porphyry,[59] as a means of opposing Christianity. In order to oppose Christianity with the appearance of a unified pagan philosophical tradition, Porphyry sought to prove the harmony or complementary relationship between Plato and Aristotle, as well as to combine Plato with the *Chaldean Oracles*. These syncretistic currents were accepted and further exploited by later Neo-Platonists. Furthermore, it was also a Platonized legacy

---

[59] Plotinus, unlike Porphyry, did not attempt to harmonize Plato and Aristotle, and he often took a critical approach to the latter. In contrast, however, we see that in his great anti-Gnostic treatise, he used theses, concepts, and modes of argument inspired by Aristotle and his commentators in order to refute Gnostic teaching, and that this allowed Plotinus to separate his own interpretation of Platonism from that of his "mainstream" and "marginal" interlocutors. This can be attested in the treatise 32 (V 5) where Plotinus' critique of the Gnostics' theory of knowledge and his definition of the Intellect are constructed from Aristotle, *Metaphysics* Λ and *On the Soul* III, and from Alexander of Aphrodisias' commentaries. As I have showed in my doctoral thesis (*Plotin, Traité 32*), these passages, among the most important concerning Plotinus' noetic theory, where he describes the relationship between the First Intelligence and its objects of thought, were written in response to the Gnostics, not the Epicureans and the Stoics, as has always been thought. In combining Plato, Aristotle, and Alexander of Aphrodisias, Plotinus differentiates his noetic theory from that of the Gnostics, who were "heterodox" Christians. Until now, however, such a harmonization with an anti-Christian purpose has only been identified in the works of his disciple Porphyry and in the later Neo-Platonists, who also combined the works of these authors with the *Chaldean Oracles*. Study of "marginal" religious movements thus helps us to better understand how Neo-Platonism developed and responded to the rise of Christianity.

of Aristotelianism from this period that largely defined the Byzantine, Muslim, Latin Scholastic, and Hebrew medieval philosophical traditions.

It is therefore intended that this three-part research project should contribute to a reassessment of the ways in which Middle- and Neo-Platonism developed and of how these are characterized in modern scholarship. As such, it will form part of the new conception of Platonism, at once more unified and diverse, that is now emerging from recent and continuing research.

Tombs

PAGAN TOMB TO CHRISTIAN CHURCH: THE CASE OF DIOCLETIAN'S MAUSOLEUM IN SPALATUM

Ivan Basić

How and when did Emperor Diocletian's tomb in Spalatum (present day Split in Croatia) become a Christian church? Earlier scholarship presented the conversion of Diocletian's mausoleum into a church as a 'one-time' event, taking place in the seventh century, following an earlier step of transformation in the fourth century, when triumphant and revengeful Christians destroyed the persecuting emperor's *domus aeterna* and removed his mortal remains.[1] A reexamination of the evidence in a broad interdisciplinary perspective with new interpretive paradigms reveals a different process and turns traditional theories about the Christianization of Diocletian's mausoleum upside down. Revisiting the data in context, this paper challenges earlier hypotheses about the transformation of the final resting place of "Christianity's greatest mass persecutor." It shows that Diocletian's mausoleum, just like the majority of Classical monuments in Late Antiquity, underwent a gradual process of alteration.

Sources and Scholarship on Diocletian's Mausoleum

Built in around 305 AD, Diocletian's mausoleum is an elevated, two-storey octagonal structure in the center of the emperor's palace. The well-preserved construction is now the Cathedral of Split, dedicated to the patron saints of the city, the Blessed Virgin Mary, Saint Domnius and Saint Anastasius. There are no Late Antique sources on the monument prior to Ammianus Marcellinus, writing some eighty years after Diocletian's death at the end of the fourth century.

---

[1] E.g. Željko Rapanić, *Od carske palače do srednjovjekovne općine* [From Imperial Palace to Medieval Municipality] (Split: Književni krug, 2007), 70–2; Željko Rapanić, "Tri ljubavne anegdote kao povijesni izvor," [Three Love Stories as Historical Sources] in *Scripta Branimiro Gabričević dicata*, ed. Josip Dukić, Ante Milošević, and Željko Rapanić (Trilj: Kulturno društvo Trilj, 2010), 207–12.

When was Diocletian's monumental domed octagon converted into a church? This question of considerable importance triggered a long academic debate with views ranging from the mid-seventh to the ninth century.

Theories on the chronology of the Christianization of Diocletian's mausoleum cluster around two dates: an early dating (shortly after the Edict of Milan, 313), and a later dating (middle of the seventh—closing years of the eighth century). Early daters emphasize the supposed desecration of the emperor's tomb after the Christian triumph (not necessarily involving a conversion into a church); late daters link the event to the move of the archdiocese of Salona to Split after the turmoils of the early seventh century (explicitly linking the move to the tomb's conversion into a church). The move of Salona to Split is variously dated in scholarship, depending on scholarly preconceptions and preferences of various historical contexts best fitting the late medieval narrative on the establishment of the archbishopric in Split. Following Frane Bulić and Ljubo Karaman in the early 20th century, the majority of scholars agreed that the mausoleum was first modified for Christian use when it was transformed into a cathedral.[2] With little or no deviation, the physical and functional transformations of the building were automatically connected with the establishment of the archbishopric––with some ambiguity as to whether this happened in the seventh, the eighth or the ninth century.

Archaeologists, historians, and art historians brought up profuse arguments to date the Christian octagon from a plethora of sources, such as the narrative of the medieval chronicler Thomas of Spalato; early medieval liturgical installations; early medieval architectural sculpture; early medieval sculpture decoration, typology, iconography, and style. The Early Christian sculpture fragments, however, were not seriously discussed,[3]

---

[2] Frane Bulić and Ljubo Karaman, *Palača cara Dioklecijana u Splitu* [The Palace of Emperor Diocletian in Split] (Zagreb: Matica hrvatska, 1927), 70–4, 88–90 (hereafter Bulić and Karaman, *Palača*). This is still predominant in the recent literature, see: Tomislav Marasović, *Dalmatia praeromanica*, vol. 3 (Split-Zagreb: Književni krug, Muzej hrvatskih arheoloških spomenika, 2011), 254–69 (hereafter Marasović, *Dalmatia*). The conversion of Diocletian's mausoleum was not included in comprehensive catalogues and gazetteers of Christianized pagan monuments (such as the ones by Friedrich Wilhelm Deichmann) because Dalmatia and Illyricum were largely by-passed in these studies; another reason is that the mausoleum in Spalatum was not considered by the scholarly literature a temple in the strict sense. A useful review of earlier literature: Tomislav Marasović, "The transformation of Diocletian's Palace in the city of Split as a chronological question," *Acta ad archaeologiam et artium historiam pertinentia* XVIII (N.S. 4) (2005): 115–29 (hereafter Marasović, "The transformation").

[3] To my knowledge, the only ones to tackle the issue of mausoleum's Early Christian phase––albeit in passing–– were: Nenad Cambi, "The cult of the blessed Virgin Mary at Salona and Split from the Fourth till the Eleventh Century in the Light of Archaeological Evidence," in *De cultu Mariano saeculis VI-XI. Acta Congressus Mariologici-Mariani internationalis in Croatia Anno 1971 celebrati*, ed. Karlo Balić (Roma: Pontificia Academia Mariana Internationalis, 1972), 58, Branka Migotti, "Vrste i namjene ranokršćanskih zdanja u Dalmaciji," [Early Christian Buildings in Dalmatia. Types and Functions] *Radovi Filozofskog fakulteta u Zadru, Razdio povijesnih znanosti*, 34/21 (1994-1995): 122, and Goran Nikšić, "Svjetlo u katedrali sv. Duje u Splitu," [Light in the cathedral of St. Domnius in Split] *Kulturna baština* XX/28-29 (1997): 38.

neither were they ever considered as physical indicators of the chronology of the monument. This sharply limited the scope of research and thwarted all other possible solutions.

From the late 1970s onwards, revisionist scholarship on pagan-Christian relations, based on a series of regional studies, demonstrated that temple conversions took place much later than previously thought.[4] The conversion of the temples did not stem directly from religious conflicts. Few pagan temples were destroyed,[5] and out of roughly three hundred recorded temple conversions into churches (this is a generous estimate) only few took place in the fourth and fifth century. The conversion of pagan cult places into churches began in the fifth and culminated in the sixth century, by which time most pagan shrines were not operational and many of them decayed.[6] In Greece, for example, the building of churches in the places of ruined temples happened only after a long timespan, generally not before the late fifth–early sixth century (a notable exception is the church built in Hadrian's Library in Athens). Of about a hundred previously recorded cases of conversion of temples into churches in the territory of Greece, the vast majority dates back to the fifth and sixth centuries. The chronology of conversion of temples into churches is equally late in Italy: none is earlier than the second half of the fifth century. The same goes for Asia Minor, Hispania and North Africa (there, some examples of the transformation of temples into churches can be dated back to the turn of the fifth

---

[4] Luke Lavan, "The end of the temples: towards a new narrative?," in *The archaeology of Late Antique 'paganism'*, Late Antique Archaeology, vol. 7, ed. Luke Lavan and Michael Mulryan (Leiden: Brill, 2011), xxi–xxii, n21 (hereafter Lavan, "The end of the temples"). Until the end of the 1970s, the most influential studies were: Friedrich Wilhelm Deichmann, "Frühchristliche Kirchen in antiken Heiligtümern," *Jahrbuch des Deutschen Archäologischen Instituts* LIV (1939): 105–36 (hereafter Deichmann, "Frühchristliche") and Friedrich Wilhelm Deichmann, "Christianisierung (der Monumente)," in *Reallexikon für Antike und Christentum*, Bd. II (Stuttgart: Hiersemann Verlag, 1954), 1228–41.

[5] Bryan Ward-Perkins, "Reconfiguring sacred space: from pagan shrines to Christian churches," in *Die spätantike Stadt und ihre Christianisierung*, ed. Gunnar Brands and Hans-Georg Severin (Wiesbaden: Reichert, 2003), 285–90 (hereafter Ward-Perkins, "Reconfiguring"); Richard Bayliss, *Provincial Cilicia and the archaeology of temple conversion* (BAR Int. Ser. 1281) (Oxford: Archaeopress, 2004), 45–61, 64–8 (hereafter Bayliss, *Provincial Cilicia*); Béatrice Caseau, "The fate of rural temples in Late Antiquity and the Christianisation of the countryside," in *Recent research on the Late Antique countryside*, ed. William Bowden, Luke Lavan, and Carlos Machado, Late Antique Archeology, vol. 2 (Leiden: Brill, 2004), 122ff. (hereafter Caseau, "Fate").

[6] Béatrice Caseau, "Polemein Lithois. La désacralisation des espaces et des objets religieux païens durant l' Antiquité tardive," in *Le sacré et son inscription dans l'espace à Byzance et en Occident. Études comparées*, ed. Michel Kaplan, Byzantina Sorbonensia, 18 (Paris: Publications de la Sorbonne, 2001), 103, 105–6 (hereafter Caseau, "Polemein"); Jan Vaes, "Christliche Wiederverwendung antiker Bauten. Ein Forschungsbericht," *Ancient Society* 15–17 (1984-1986): 310–13 (hereafter Vaes, "Wiederverwendung") concludes that between 30% and 50% of all Early Christian and early medieval churches were built within pre-Christian (cult and profane) buildings. Deichmann was able to record 89 examples of conversion in 1939: Deichmann, "Frühchristliche," passim.

century, but the dating is rather problematic).[7] Richard Bayliss demonstrated that in the Roman Empire a hundred and twenty (according to his more conservative estimate) temples were converted into churches, only one-third of them before the end of the fifth century.[8] Active destruction of temples was rare, connected with the imperial legislation of Theodosius I at the end of the fourth century. The destruction or desacralization of temples in the Empire shows not only strong regional variations, but also a varying scale of abandon, neglect, decay, demolition, and conversion.[9] In the Western Empire, for example, destruction was rare, and conversion late: almost no temple was recycled as a church prior to the sixth century.[10] Thousands of pagan shrines remain, however, archaeologically invisible, "for not only is an early Christian reuse of a temple or of any

---

[7] Greece: Helen G. Saradi, "Late paganism and Christianisation in Greece," in *The archaeology of Late Antique 'Paganism'*, ed. Luke Lavan and Michael Mulryan (Late Antique Archaeology, 7) (Leiden-Boston: Brill, 2011), 268–70, 273–76, 303 (hereafter Saradi, "Late paganism"); Alison Frantz, "From Paganism to Christianity in the temples of Athens," *Dumbarton Oaks Papers* 19 (1965): 195, 202–04 (hereafter Frantz, "From Paganism to Christianity"); Jean-Michel Spieser, "La christianisation des sanctuaires païens en Grèce," in *Neue Forschungen in griechischen Heiligtümern*, ed. Ulf Jantzen (Tübingen: Wasmuth, 1976), 310–17; Helen G. Saradi, *The Byzantine City in the Sixth Century: Literary Images and Historical Reality* (Athens: Society of Messenian Archaeological Studies, 2006), 360 (hereafter Saradi, *The Byzantine City*); Paavo Castrén, "Paganism and Christianity in Athens and vicinity during the fourth to sixth centuries A.D." in *The idea and ideal of the town between Late Antiquity and the Early Middle Ages*, ed. Gian-Pietro Brogiolo and Bryan Ward-Perkins (Leiden-Boston-Köln: Brill, 1999), 218–19; Vincent Déroche, "Delphes: la christianisation d'un sanctuaire païen," in *Actes du XIe Congrès International d'archéologie chrétienne*, vol. III, ed. Noël Duval, Françoise Baritel and Philippe Pergola (Roma-Città del Vaticano: École française de Rome, Pontificio Istituto di Archeologia cristiana, 1989), 2713–23. Italy: Deichmann, "Frühchristliche," 134–35; Jean-Pierre Caillet, "La transformation en église d'édifices publics et de temples à la fin de l'Antiquité," in *La fin de la cité antique et le début de la cité médiévale de la fin du IIIe siècle à l'avènement de Charlemagne*, ed. Claude Lepelley (Bari: Edipuglia, 1996) 199–200 (hereafter Caillet, "Transformation"). Asia Minor: Deichmann, "Frühchristliche," 129–30; Caillet, "Transformation," 200–01. Hispania: Javier Arce, "*Fana, templa, delubra destrui praecipimus*: the end of the temples in Roman Spain," in *The archaeology of Late Antique 'Paganism'*, Late Antique Archaeology, vol. 7, ed. Luke Lavan and Michael Mulryan (Leiden: Brill, 2011), 198–206 (hereafter Arce, "*Fana*"). North Africa: Gareth Sears, "The fate of the temples in North Africa," in *The archaeology of Late Antique 'Paganism'*, ed. Luke Lavan and Michael Mulryan, Late Antique Archaeology, 7 (Leiden-Boston: Brill, 2011), 246, 249–50, 252–55.

[8] Bayliss, *Provincial Cilicia*, 16–25, 32–49, 50–7, 107–20, 124–29.

[9] Gisella Cantino Wataghin, "*...Ut haec aedes Christo domino in ecclesiam consecretur*: Il riuso cristiano di edifici antichi tra tarda Antichità e alto Medioevo," in *Ideologie e pratiche del reimpiego nell'alto Medioevo. Settimane di Studio del Centro Italiano di Studi sull'Alto Medioevo*, XLVI/2 (Spoleto: Centro Italiano di Studi sull'Alto Medioevo, 1999), 716–17 (hereafter Cantino Wataghin, "Il riuso cristiano di edifici antichi"); Bayliss, *Provincial Cilicia*, 64–9.

[10] Bryan Ward-Perkins, "Re-using the architectural legacy of the past: *entre idéologie et pragmatisme*," in *The idea and ideal of the town between Late Antiquity and Early Middle Ages*, ed. Gian-Pietro Brogiolo and Bryan Ward-Perkins (Leiden: Brill, 1999), 225–44; Ward-Perkins, "Reconfiguring," 286–87; Bayliss, *Provincial Cilicia*, 26–9; Lavan, "The end of the temples," xxxvi.

other building possible without there being any relevant or enduring traces left behind to begin with, but just as possible is a first, profane reuse of a cultic building before it found a new character as a church."[11]

New research on architectural reuse distinguishes three periods of conversion of pagan buildings into churches. In the fourth century, profane, private buildings were reused for liturgical use; in the fifth, public buildings were reutilized; in the sixth, pagan temples and shrines were converted into churches.[12] Diocletian's mausoleum in Split fits this scheme. Great Roman shrines and public monuments (the Temple of Romulus in the Roman Forum, the Pantheon, the Academy in Athens, the *Serapeum* of Alexandria, the temple complex on Philae near Aswan) were converted only after a long process that included several steps. This was even more apparent in the case of structures belonging to the imperial estate, whose arbitrary destruction entailed severe punishment. An imperial tomb standing on imperial property could not be destroyed with impunity. The reuse of pagan cultic buildings was the last phase in the chronological development, because there was a considerable lapse of time from the abandonment of the temple to the alteration of the building into a church. Conversion at this point no longer had an anti-pagan meaning: in other words, recycling was utilitarian rather than ideological.

The transformation of pagan monuments is a manifold process, in which "questions about local religious, social and political configurations within both regional and imperial contexts"[13] need to be taken into consideration. Emperor Constantius II, for example, issued not only edicts prohibiting pagan sacrifices and rites, but also protecting pagan monuments. Physical continuity of pagan shrines must be distinguished from continuity of active use. There is a chronological relationship between the abandonment or closure of pagan shrines and their transformation into Christian churches: "a marked break, with a de-sacralization that was followed, only in a later and separate step, by a re-sacralization of the former cultic space."[14]

---

[11] Stephen Emmel, Ulrich Gotter, and Johannes Hahn, "'From temple to church': Analysing a Late Antique phenomenon of transformation," in *From temple to church. Destruction and renewal of local cultic topography in Late Antiquity*, ed. Johannes Hahn, Stephen Emmel, and Ulrich Gotter (Leiden: Brill, 2008), 10 (hereafter Emmel, Gotter, and Hahn, "From temple to church").

[12] Vaes, "Wiederverwendung," 310–13; Arja Karivieri, "From pagan shrines to Christian churches: methods of conversion," in *Ecclesiae Urbis. Atti del Congresso Internazionale di Studi sulle chiese di Roma (IV-X secolo)*, ed. Federico Guidobaldi and Alessandra Guiglia Guidobaldi, vol. I (Città del Vaticano: Pontificio Istituto di Archeologia Cristiana, 2002), 77 (hereafter Karivieri, "From pagan shrines to Christian churches").

[13] Emmel, Gotter, and Hahn, "From temple to church," 4.

[14] Emmel, Gotter, and Hahn, "From temple to church," 5.

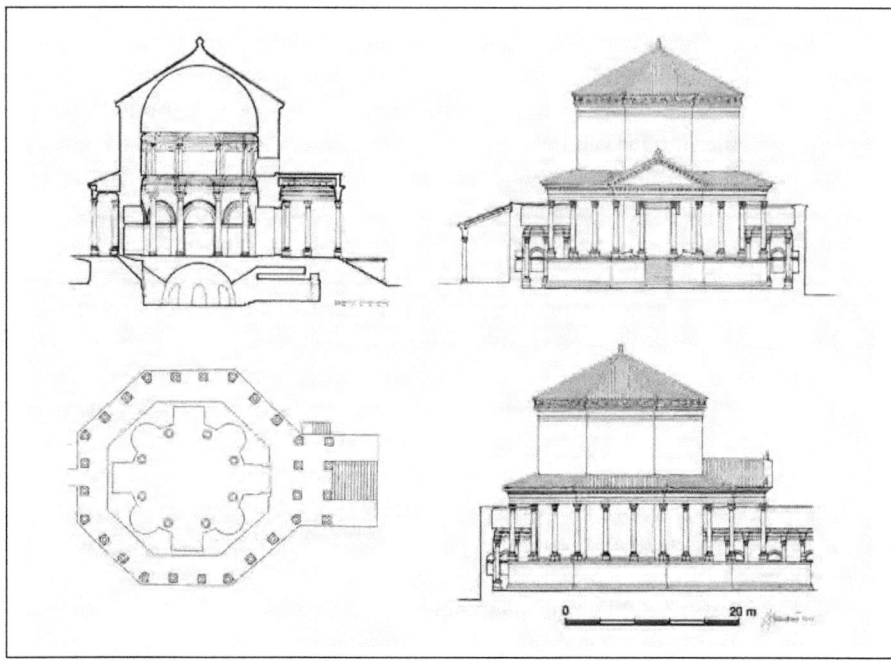

Fig. 1. Split, Diocletian's mausoleum, reconstruction of original appearance (Marasović-Marasović-Perojević 2006, fig. 9).

While considerable attention was devoted to the problem of the original layout and function of Diocletian's mausoleum (Fig. 1),[15] the survival and afterlife of the

---

[15] For an overview of Diocletian's palace see Sheila McNally, "Introduction. State of scholarship," in *Diocletian's Palace. American-Yugoslav joint excavations*, ed. Sheila McNally, Ivančica Dvoržak Schrunk, Jerko Marasović and Tomislav Marasović (Minneapolis: University of Minnesota, 1989), 3–43 (hereafter McNally, "Introduction"); Jerko Marasović and Tomislav Marasović, "Le ricerche nel Palazzo di Diocleziano a Split negli ultimi 30 anni (1964-1994)," *Antiquité Tardive* 2 (1994): 89–106; Wolfgang Kuhoff, "Zwei Altersresidenzen römischer Kaiser: *Aspalathos* und *Romuliana*," in *Humanitas – Beiträge zur antiken Kulturgeschichte. Festschrift für Gunther Gottlieb zum 65. Geburtstag*, ed. Pedro Barceló and Veit Rosenberger (München: Ernst Vögel, 2001), 149–89; Annie Jacques and Noël Duval, "XI – Split, le palais de Dioclétien (E.-M. Hébrard, 1909)," in *Italia Antiqua. Envois de Rome des architectes français en Italie et dans le monde méditerranéen aux XIXe et XXe siècles*, ed. Annie Jacques, Stéphane Verger, and Catherine Virlouvet (Paris: École nationale supérieure des beaux-arts, 2002), 282–304; Joško Belamarić, "The date of foundation and original function of Diocletian's Palace at Split," *Hortus Artium Medievalium* 9 (2003): 173–85 (hereafter Belamarić, "The date"); Joško Belamarić, "Gynaeceum Iovense Dalmatiae - Aspalatho," in *Diokletian und die Tetrarchie. Aspekte einer Zeitenwende*, ed. Alexander Demandt, Andreas Goltz, and Heinrich Schlange-Schöningen (Berlin: Walter de Gruyter, 2004), 141–62 (hereafter Belamarić, "Gynaeceum"); Jerko Marasović, Katja Marasović, and Snježana Perojević, "Le mausolée de Dioclétien à Split: construction

building up until its pre-Romanesque phase in the ninth century remained unexplored due to the lack of sources. During the past few decades, the study of relevant textual and archaeological sources intensified in tandem with a novel approach to the Christianization of pagan buildings.[16] Along with a new reading of textual sources, this paper discusses new archeological evidence to show that Split's major pagan monument did not undergo any substantial modifications prior to the sixth century and that its Christian conversion had several stages. Diocletian's tomb did not become a cathedral overnight.

Diocletian's tomb, anti-pagan legislation, and monument protection under the Constantinian dynasty

The first author to identify the octagonal building in Split as Diocletian's mausoleum is Constantine Porphyrogenitus in his *De administrando imperio* written in the middle of the tenth century.[17] There are no Late Antique descriptions of the monument, thus it is hard to know whether the emperor's remains were buried in the crypt or in the upper cella of the mausoleum. The upper cella may have served ceremonial and

---

et restitution," in *L'architecture funéraire monumentale: la Gaule dans l'Empire romain*, ed. Jean-Charles Moretti and Dominique Tardy (Paris: Édition du Comité des travaux historiques et scientifiques, 2006), 497–506; Sheila McNally, "The Palace of Diocletian at Split," in *Croatia: aspects of art, architecture and cultural heritage*, ed. Jadranka Beresford-Peirse (London: Frances Lincoln, 2009), 48–59 (hereafter McNally, "The Palace"); Wolfgang Kuhoff, "Das tetrarchische Herrschaftssystem und seine Darstellung in der Architektur: Herrscherresidenzen und Altersruhesitze als Ausdruck kaiserlicher Regierung und Repräsentation," in *Diocletian, Tetrarchy and Diocletian's palace on the 1700th anniversary of existence*, (hereafter *Diocletian, Tetrarchy and Diocletian's palace*), ed. Nenad Cambi, Joško Belamarić, and Tomislav Marasović (Split: Književni krug, 2009), 95–116; Tomislav Marasović, "Diciasette secoli di ricerche e restauri nel Palazzo di Diocleziano a Spalato," in *Diocletian, Tetrarchy and Diocletian's palace*, 15–50; Snježana Perojević, Katja Marasović, and Jerko Marasović, "Istraživanja Dioklecijanove palače od 1985. do 2005. godine," [The research of Diocletian's palace from 1985 to 2005] in *Diocletian, Tetrarchy and Diocletian's palace*, 51–94; Goran Nikšić, "Diocletian's Palace – design and construction," in *Bruckneudorf und Gamzigrad. Spätantike Paläste und Großvillen im Donau-Balkan-Raum*, ed. Gerda von Bülow and Heinrich Zabehlicky (Bonn: Rudolf Habelt, 2011), 187–202.

[16] Cantino Wataghin, "Il riuso cristiano di edifici antichi," 676–78; Caseau, "Polemein," 63–6; Bayliss, *Provincial Cilicia*, 24–7; Lavan, "The end of the temples," xix–xxii.

[17] Gyula Moravcsik, ed., Romilly J. H. Jenkins, transl., Constantine Porphyrogenitus, *De Administrando Imperio* (Washington D.C.: Dumbarton Oaks Center for Byzantine Studies, 1967), 136 (29.237–42): "The city of Spalato, which means 'little palace', was founded by the emperor Diocletian; he made it his own dwelling-place, and built within it a court and a palace, most part of which has been destroyed. But a few things remain to this day, e. g. the episcopal residence of the city and the church of St. Domnus, in which lies St. Domnus himself, and which was the resting-place of the same emperor Diocletian". On this, see: Ivan Basić, "*Spalatensia Porphyrogenitiana*. Some issues concerning the textual transmission of Porphyrogenitus' sources for the chapters on Dalmatia in the *De Administrando Imperio*," *Byzantinoslavica* LXXI/1-2 (2013): 91–110.

commemorative functions as a shrine devoted to the cult of the deified ruler.[18] If so, it must have contained statues and an altar dedicated to the deceased emperor. Two Latin authors who mention the monument, Adam of Paris (eleventh century) and Thomas, archdeacon of Split (thirteenth century), refer to it as "a temple of Jupiter" (*templum Iovi* or *templum Iovis*).[19] Do they mean a "temple of Jupiter" or the temple of the Jupiter—like Diocletian (*Iovius Diocletianus*)? The problem of the emperor's mausoleum as a pagan cult place remains unsolved. There is no scholarly consensus on the function of the emperor's octagon. Was it a shrine-mausoleum? Did it serve Diocletian's ritual worship after his death? If so, for how long? In fact, it is not sure that Diocletian became a god. According to Eutropius, he did,[20] but according to Simon Corcoran, Diocletian was not deified.[21] The emperor is mentioned on two milestones from Heraclea-Perinthus in Thrace as *divus Diocletianus* (*Divis Diocletiano et Constantio et Gal. Maximiano Augg.*), but the dating as well as the interpretation of these inscriptions remain problematic. No *consecratio* coins mark Diocletian's deification: such coins are well known

---

[18] McNally, "Introduction," 22; Mark J. Johnson, "From Paganism to Christianity in the Imperial mausolea of the Tetrarchs and Constantine," in *Niš and Byzantium. Fifth Symposium. The Collection of Scientific Works*, V, ed. Miša Rakocija (Niš: Kulturni centar Niš, 2007), 116, 122–23; and Mark J. Johnson, *The Roman Imperial Mausoleum in Late Antiquity* (Cambridge: Cambridge University Press, 2009), 67–8 (hereafter Johnson, *Mausoleum*).

[19] Adam of Paris (attributed to), *Tertia vita S. Domnii*, in Daniele Farlati, *Illyricum sacrum*, vol. I (Venice, 1751), 419: *Ac deinde reversi in Diocletiani aedificio, quod tribus ferme millibus a Salonis distat, Spalatum appellatum, sedem sibi posuerunt, templumque, olim Iovi dicatum, ejectis idolis, per Joannem Archiepiscopum sanctae Dei genitrici Mariae consecrarunt.* Thomas Archidiaconus Spalatensis, *Historia Salonitanorum atque Spalatinorum pontificum - History of the bishops of Salona and Split*, cap. IV, Central European Medieval Texts, 4, ed. Damir Karbić, Mirjana Matijević Sokol, and James R. Sweeney (Budapest: CEU Press, 2006), 20 (hereafter Thomas Archidiaconus, *Historia Salonitana*): *Et quia Dalmatinus erat origine, nobilius edificium prope Salonam edificari iussit in modum urbis munitissime, quasi imperiale palatium, in quo templa facta sunt ydolorum Iovis, Asclepii, Martis, sicut apparet usque in hodiernum diem.*

[20] Hans Droysen, ed., *Eutropi Breviarium ab urbe condita cum versionibus graecis et Pauli Landolfique additamentis*, Monumenta Germaniae Historica, Auctores Antiquissimi, II (Berlin: Weidmann, 1879), 168 (IX, 28): *Diocletianus privatus in villa, quae haud procul a Salonis est, praeclaro otio consenuit, inusitata virtute usus, ut solus omnium post conditum Romanum imperium ex tanto fastigio sponte ad privatae vitae statum civilitatemque remearet. Contigit igitur ei, quod nulli post natos homines, ut cum privatus obisset, inter divos tamen referretur.*

[21] *L'Année épigraphique* 1998 (2001): 440–41, nos. 1180, 1181. This was analyzed by Simon Corcoran in a conference presentation titled "*Divus Diocletianus?*" at the 13th International Congress of Greek and Latin Epigraphy, Oxford, 2007. The inscription lists members of the First Tetrarchy (293–305), but without Maximianus Herculius. Furthermore, it was dedicated to the two Augusti, although three of them are explicitly mentioned (*Augg.* instead of *Auggg.*), whilst Caesars were not mentioned at all. It is also not clear who the title *divus* refers to—to all three of the rulers, or only to some of them? The *terminus post quem* of the inscription is undoubtedly 306, the year of the death of Constantius Chlorus, who was the first to die of the three rulers mentioned on the inscription, and was deified. It is also possible that it was made after the death of Galerius (311) and Diocletian (his death is dated differently, between 311 and 316). Most probable date is 3 December 312; on this, see: Byron J. Nakamura, "When did Diocletian die? New evidence for an old problem," *Classical Philology* XCVIII/3 (2003): 283–89.

in the case of the deified members of the First and Second Tetrarchy and the House of Constantine. Roman religion accorded divine status to the dead only after a formal *consecratio*. Later emperors did not refer to Diocletian as a god on formal occasions, but administrative and legal sources from the early 320s call him *divus Diocletianus*. If Diocletian did not receive *consecratio*, his mausoleum in Split did not function as the temple of the divine Diocletian. But it could have been designed and built as such with appropriate iconographical features during the emperor's life, in the expectation of his posthumous apotheosis.[22]

Scholars assume that the emperor's tomb suffered destruction after the Edict of Milan in 313 and decayed until the 640s, when it became the Cathedral of Split (confusingly called Salona, as it kept the name of the former archbishopric)[23] The transformation is presented as a 'one-stage' event: John of Ravenna, the restorer of the former diocese of Salona in Diocletian's palace in Split after the collapse of Salona at the beginning of the seventh century, dedicated the octagon in Split to the Blessed Virgin Mary and made it his cathedral. This reconstruction is based on Thomas of Spalato's *Historia Salonitana* from 1266. According to Thomas, John of Ravenna, who after the flight of local populace from Salona to Diocletian's palace became the first archbishop of Split,

> ...cleansed the Temple of Jupiter (*templum Iovis*), a building that had been raised so as to tower above others within the imperial palace, of the deceit of its false idols, and fitted it with doors and locks. Then he announced a ceremony of dedication, and a great crowd of people gathered from every side. Thus he turned that famous temple into a church, consecrating it with great devotion to the honor of God and the glorious Virgin Mary, to the jubilation of all who had assembled.[24]

New interpretive paradigms and new archaeological findings, however, challenge the scholarly narrative. Historical sources concur that Christians did not attack and demolish pagan buildings for a considerable time after 313.[25] If Emperor Constan-

---

[22] On these features, see: Duje Rendić-Miočević, "O uništenom središnjem motivu friza Dioklecijanova mauzoleja u Splitu," [On destroyed central motif of the frieze in Diocletian's mausoleum] *Prilozi povijesti umjetnosti u Dalmaciji* 32 (1992): 104, 108, 110, 113–14; Stanislav Živkov, "Varia Diocletianea," in *Diocletian, Tetrarchy and Diocletian's palace*, 515–16. On imperial mausolea as places of cult worship, see Jean-Claude Richard, "Tombeaux des empereurs et temples de « divi » : notes sur la signification religieuse des sépultures impériales à Rome," *Revue de l'histoire des religions* 170, no. 2 (1966): 130–38; and Johnson, *Mausoleum*, 186–90.

[23] E.g. Marasović, "The transformation," 128; Marasović, *Dalmatia*, 254–69.

[24] Thomas Archidiaconus Spalatensis, *Historia Salonitana*, cap. 11, 55.

[25] Helen Saradi Mendelovici, "Christian attitudes toward pagan monuments in Late Antiquity and their legacy in later Byzantine centuries," *Dumbarton Oaks Papers* 44 (1990): 47–61 (hereafter Saradi Mendelovici, "Christian attitudes").

tine issued anti-pagan laws, the destruction of pagan shrines and of polytheistic cult-places began only with the repressive measures of Theodosius in the last decades of the fourth century. Roman legislation in the fourth and fifth centuries is notoriously inconsistent on the matter.[26] Selecting a certain number of anti-pagan laws distorts reality,[27] giving the impression of either a radical, linear suppression of pagan cults with dramatic consequences, or of a more or less peaceful coexistence between pagans and Christians, reflecting the emperors' concern for concord and for the preservation of classical monuments.[28] Up to the 380s, pagan and Christian worship coexisted not only on a daily, but also on a legal basis.[29] Theodosius' legislation distinguished pagan cult buildings from the pagan rites performed in them. While the latter were suppressed, the former were

---

[26] It was prohibited to offer private sacrifices in 320/321 – Theodor Mommsen and Paul M. Meyer, eds., *Theodosiani libri XVI, cum Constitutionibus Sirmondianis, et Leges novellae ad Theodosianum pertinentes* (Berlin: Weidmann, 1905), XVI, 10, 1 (hereafter *CTh.*), which was then extended to all forms of sacrifices in 341 (*CTh.* XVI, 10, 2), and in 356, it was reinforced with the death penalty (*CTh.* XVI, 10, 6). Then followed the official closing down of the temples in 346, 354, or 356 (*CTh.* XVI, 10, 4). The prohibition of sacrifices is repeated in 381 and 382 (*CTh.* XVI, 10, 7; XVI, 10, 8), and then again in 391 (*CTh.* XVI, 10, 10), when the closing of temples was ordered (*CTh.* XVI, 10, 11), followed by the strict prohibition of the ritual practice of any forms of pagan cults, both in public and in private, in 392 (*CTh.* XVI, 10, 12); nevertheless, it was necessary to repeat the prohibition of sacrifices and the closing down of temples in 395 (*CTh.* XVI, 10, 13), followed by the order to systematically and quietly remove all pagan temples located outside cities in 399 (*CTh.* XVI, 10, 16). Finally, in 435, a systematic removal of all temples was ordered, accompanied by the obligatory repetition of the prohibition of sacrifices (*CTh.* XVI, 10, 24.) The same legislature, however, protected temples and pagan festivals outside of the city in 342 or 346 (*CTh.* XVI, 10, 3). In 382 and 399, the emperors protected the statues of the gods in the temples as artistic monuments (*CTh.* XVI, 10, 8; XVI, 10, 15), and in 399 even protected the temple buildings (*CTh.* XVI, 10, 18), called "ornaments of the city" in 401 (*CTh.* XV, 1, 41). In 400, the emperors ordered urban authorities to preserve the temples built on public land (*CTh.* X, 3, 5). Majorian, the Western Roman emperor, prohibited further destruction of temples in 458, because they were beautiful. See Lavan, "The end of the temples," xxii–xxiii; Cantino Wataghin, "Il riuso cristiano di edifici antichi," 735–49.

[27] Caseau, "Polemein," 70: "Le *Code Théodosien* reflète ainsi une situation confuse, ce qui permet à certains historiens de s'imaginer une société empreinte de violence religieuse et à d'autres, au contraire, une société fondée sur le respect des valeurs classiques et le maintien des traditions urbaines." For the imperial laws between 341 and 511 see Christophe J. Goddard, "The evolution of pagan sanctuaries in Late Antique Italy (fourth-sixth centuries A.D.): a new administrative and legal framework. A paradox," in *Les cités de l'Italie tardo-antique (IVe-VIe siècle). Institutions, économie, société, culture et religion*, ed. Massimiliano Ghilardi, Christophe J. Goddard, and Pierfrancesco Porena (Rome: École française de Rome, 2006), 282 (hereafter Goddard, "Evolution"); Yves Janvier, *La législation du Bas-Empire romain sur les édifices publics* (Aix-en-Provence: La Pensée universitaire, 1969); Périclès-Pierre Joannou, *La législation impériale et le christianisation de l'Empire romain (311-476)* (Roma: Pontificum Institutum Orientalium studiorum, 1972), 63–116; and Cantino Wataghin, "Il riuso cristiano di edifici antichi," 735–49.

[28] Saradi Mendelovici, "Christian attitudes," 54; Goddard, "Evolution," 281–84, 286–90. See also Caseau, "Fate," 113, n43. Arce, "*Fana*," 199. Arce points out that the law of 435 gave license to preserve the temples physically, but only if "purified" with a cross.

[29] Laurence Foschia, "The preservation, restoration, and (re)construction of pagan cult places in Late Antiquity, with particular attention to mainland Greece (fourth–fifth centuries)," *Journal of Late Antiquity* 2 (2009): 209, 214. Cf. also Saradi, *The Byzantine City*, 355–84.

considered public monuments to be protected or reused. This is an important shift: pagan shrines were no longer considered sacred, but beautiful. The inalienable property of the emperors (*res privata*), such as shrines and mausolea on imperial estates, enjoyed special legal status: they were inviolable, their destruction was a sacrilege and therefore was severely punished.

Split's coastline was owned by the Roman State as *ager publicus* since the early first century. The area was later absorbed into the imperial fisc and became *res privata* on three grounds: because here stood Diocletian's palace, and because there was an imperial weaving factory for the production of woollen clothing (*gynaeceum Iovense Dalmatiae Aspalatho*) in the palace or in its immediate vicinity,[30] as well as an imperial armory (*fabrica Salonitana armorum*).[31] The Split littoral fell therefore under the jurisdiction of the Roman state, not under the jurisdiction of the nearby city of Salona. After Diocletian's death, the imperial complex reverted to the state as imperial property.

The mausoleum and Constantius II

In 356, a thief named Danus stole the purple drapery covering the tomb of Diocletian.[32] Emperor Constantius II sent an imperial commission of high officials—Ursulus, the *comes sacrarum largitionum*, and the *praefectus praetorio* Mavortius—to

---

[30] Belamarić, "The date"; Belamarić, "Gynaeceum"; Joško Belamarić, "Dioklecijanova palača – razmatranja o okolnostima utemeljenja i izvornoj funkciji" [Diocletian's palace: Reflections on the circumstances of its foundation and on the problem of its original function] (unpublished PhD diss., University of Zagreb, 2009), 82–117 (hereafter Belamarić, "Dioklecijanova palača").

[31] Ivan Basić, "*Spalatum–ager Salonitanus*? Prilog tumačenju pravno-posjedovnoga položaja priobalja Splitskoga poluotoka u preddioklecijanskome razdoblju," [*Spalatum – ager Salonitanus*? An analysis of the property law status of the coastal region of Split peninsula in pre-Diocletian period] *Povijesni prilozi* 42 (2012): 9–42; Ivan Basić, "Poleogeneza Splita na razmeđu kasne antike i ranoga srednjeg vijeka" [Poleogenesis of Split at the turn of Late Antiquity and the Early Middle Ages] (unpublished PhD diss., University of Zagreb, 2013), 471–96 (hereafter Basić, "Poleogeneza"); Ivan Basić, "The inscription of Gaius Orchivius Amemptus," *Vjesnik za arheologiju i historiju dalmatinsku* 108 (2015): 37–77, with references to relevant historical sources. That it was an imperial property is also shown by the relief of Victoria—Nike—above the western gates, the old imperial symbol was replaced in the late sixth century with the new one—a cross of the same type as the one on Byzantine coins of that age, with the legend: VICTORIA AVGVST(i) or VICTORIA AVGG (Augustorum), this time identifying the imperial victory with the symbol of a cross. Both symbols point to the continuity of imperial ownership over the palace. Cf. Nenad Cambi, "The relief on the architrave of the western gate of Diocletian's palace in Split," in *Assaph: Studies in Art History* [*Kalathos. Studies in honour of Asher Ovadiah*], 10–11, ed. Sonia Mucznik (Tel Aviv: Tel Aviv University, Department of Art History, 2005–2006), 143–54.

[32] Wolfgang Seyfarth, ed., *Ammiani Marcellini Rerum gestarum libri qui supersunt* (Leipzig: Teubner, 1978), XVI, 8, 3–7 (hereafter *Amm. Marc.*). On this affair: Hermann Funke, "Majestäts- und Magieprozesse bei Ammianus Marcellinus," *Jahrbuch für Antike und Christentum* 10 (1967): 156; Jan Den Boeft, Jan Willem Drijvers, Daniël Den Hengst, and Hans C. Teitler, *Philological and historical commentary on Ammianus Marcellinus XXVI* (Leiden: Brill, 2008), 161; Belamarić, "Dioklecijanova palača," 118–37, with references to older literature.

Split to investigate the matter.[33] Danus was found guilty for high treason and executed. This incident reported by Ammianus Marcellinus shows that in the mid-fourth century, forty years after the emperor's death, Diocletian's mausoleum remained a protected place as an imperial monument.[34]

In 356, Constantius II's two laws against paganism (19 February and 1 December) prohibited, under penalty of death, offerings to and the worship of idols and ordered the closing down of temples in all cities and places.[35] The emperor issued a law on 13 June 356—precisely around the time when Danus's case was examined—forbidding the desecration of tombs (*aedificia manium, domus defunctorum*).[36] Violators of tombs were blamed for disturbing the dead by robbing the graves and disgracing the living by recycling funerary material. Removal of objects from graves entailed a considerable fine in gold. If it cannot be proven that the violation of Diocletian's tomb triggered this edict, it does demonstrate a high respect towards funerary monuments. It nuances our interpretation of Constantius's laws of 19 February and 1 December 356 on the prohibition of sacrifice and temple cults, with a fine distinction between pagan religion and pious monuments (*res religiosae*). Ten years earlier, Constantius II issued a little quoted edict on the protection of temples: "Although all superstitions must be completely eradicated, nevertheless, it is Our will that the buildings of the temples situated outside the walls shall remain untouched and uninjured."[37] The legislator differentiated between religious "superstition" in the shrines and the actual buildings. While he sought to eliminate the former, he preserved the latter. The new imperial policy is best

---

[33] Arnold H. M. Jones, John R. Martindale, and John Morris, *The Prosopography of the Later Roman Empire, A.D. 260-395* (Cambridge: Cambridge University Press, 1971), 988, s.v. Ursulus 1; 512–14, s.v. Q. Flavius Maesius Egnatius Lollianus signo Mavortius 5.

[34] Frane Bulić, "Il sepolcro di Diocleziano a Split (Spalato)," *Vjesnik za arheologiju i historiju dalmatinsku* XLVI (1923): 4 (hereafter Bulić, "Sepolcro"); Frane Bulić, "L'imperatore Diocleziano. Nome, patria e luogo della sua nascita; anno, giorno, luogo e genere della sua morte," *Bullettino di archeologia e storia dalmata* XXXIX (1916): 48ff. (hereafter Bulić, "Imperatore"); Bulić and Karaman, *Palača*, 70ff.; Emilio Marin, "La tomba di Diocleziano," *Rendiconti della Pontificia Accademia Romana di Archeologia* LXXVIII (2005–2006), 517 (hereafter Marin, "La tomba di Diocleziano"); Johnson, *Mausoleum*, 59.

[35] *CTh*. XVI, 10, 6; XVI, 10, 4. Some authors date the first law to 346. Both are sometimes related to the affair of Diocletian's tomb, e.g. Belamarić, "Dioklecijanova palača," 133–34. On those laws, see: Glen L. Thompson, "Constantius II and the first removal of the Altar of Victory," in *A Tall Order. Writing the Social History of the Ancient World. Essays in honor of William V. Harris*, ed. Jean-Jacques Aubert and Zsuzsanna Várhelyi (München: K. G. Saur, 2005), 87 (hereafter Thompson, "Constantius II").

[36] *CTh*. IX, 17, 4. On this constitution, see: Cezary Kunderewicz, "La protection des monuments d'architecture antique dans le Code Théodosien," in *Studi in onore di Edoardo Volterra*, vol. IV (Milano: Giuffrè, 1971), 143–44. According to the older law issued by the same emperor in 340, the master of the perpetrator will be deprived of his house or villa in which the property, stolen from the tomb, is found (*CTh*. IX, 17, 1). For a more precise dating of the Danus affair: Belamarić, "Dioklecijanova palača," 128.

[37] *CTh*. XVI, 10, 3: *Quamquam omnis superstitio penitus eruenda sit, tamen volumus, ut aedes templorum, quae extra muros sunt positae, intactae incorruptaeque consistant*. The law was first issued in 342, repeated in 346.

summarized by Theodosius in 382: "the statues of ancient gods in temples should be valued for their artistic value, rather than for their divinity."[38] This was already in the air in 357, when Constantius II visited Rome. He filled the vacancies in the pagan priestly colleges,[39] but removed the Altar of Victoria from the Roman Senate. The altar had to go, but the statue of Victoria stayed as a (religiously apparently neutral) symbol of imperial victory.[40] What differentiated the imperial symbol from pagan religion was its function. Severed from its context, rendered materially defective for worship, the pagan statue ceased to be controversial: there was no need to subject it to repressive measures. The difference between imperial symbols (monuments, memory) and the symbols of a pagan cult was that the latter were susceptible to be used for pagan cult practices, while the former were not.

It was the same with Diocletian's mausoleum in Split. At some point—in 356, 407, 408, or 435[41]—the mausoleum ceased functioning as a pagan cultplace, but survived physically as imperial property for centuries to come. The purple cover on the emperor's tomb in 356 reveals continuity of care and respect. The upkeep of the mausoleum had nothing to do with the religion of the State. In the forty years after Diocletian's death, the tetrarchy vanished, a new dynasty rose, Christianity spread. Diocletian's successors, however, preserved the emperor's mausoleum, because the tomb was inviolable and because it was an imperial monument. Not only was the prohibition of touching or carrying dead bodies strictly adhered to, but the repair and partitioning of tombs were forbidden without a special permit from the priestly colleges and the offering of a ritual sacrifice (*piaculum*).[42] Since the late principate, the emperor as *pontifex maximus* arbitrated in matters pertaining to tombs. Imperial rescripts confirm that tombs were not to be sold and were excluded from legal disputes. Notwithstanding Diocletian's negative reputation among Christians, his mausoleum was not demolished. The fact that Diocletian was one of the pagan emperors, with an especially negative reputation amongst Christian inhabitants of the Empire, might have affected the cancellation of rituals related to the cult of the dead emperor, but not the existence of his mausoleum, particularly because it was situated in the center of imperial property. The attitude of the Constantinian dynasty toward Diocletian is best illustrated by Constantine's transfer of Dio-

---

[38] C. Th. XVI, 10, 8: *simulacra feruntur posita artis pretio quam divinitate*. Cf. Goddard, "Evolution," 282 and Yuri A. Marano, "Fonti giuridiche di età romana (I secolo a.C. - VI secolo d.C.) per lo studio del reimpiego," *Antichità Altoadriatiche* LXXIV (2012): 74 (hereafter Marano, "Fonti giuridiche di età romana").
[39] Thompson, "Constantius II," 95.
[40] Thompson, "Constantius II," 91–3, 103. The altar was later returned to the Senate, probably during the short reign of Julian, only to be removed again in 382 by Emperor Gratian.
[41] Belamarić, "Dioklecijanova palača," 133, assumes that the law of 356 was applied to Diocletian's palace, i.e. that the temples of the palace and the mausoleum were closed down at the same time.
[42] Fergus Millar, *The Emperor in the Roman world (31 BC – AD 337)* (London: Duckworth, 1992), 360–61 (hereafter Millar, *The Emperor in the Roman world*).

cletian's statue—along with those of Julius Caesar and Augustus—from Nicomedia to the imperial box (*kathisma*) of the hippodrome in Constantinople.[43] Pagan he might be, Diocletian was above all Constantine's predecessor. The corpse and the tomb of another pagan emperor received similar care. Julian the Apostate was transferred from Tarsus to the imperial mausoleum at the Church of the Holy Apostles in Constantinople and buried with full imperial honors next to Christian emperors. His Christian successor, Jovian, visited and decorated Julian's tomb in Tarsus; Valentinian I and Valens invested considerable care in Julian's mausoleum, sparing no expense and sending architects to Tarsus to make it more monumental. Gregory of Nazianzus' description of Julian's tomb in Tarsus, a combination of mausoleum, temple, and *temenos*, makes it resemble Diocletian's mausoleum in Split and the mausolea of Maximianus and Maxentius in Milan and Rome respectively. The architectural language of the monument shows that Julian's Christian successors allowed typically "pagan" complexes to be built in respect of the deceased emperor's faith and dignity.[44]

Diocletian's grave was doubly sacrosanct: it was an imperial tomb on imperial property. As *senior augustus*, Diocletian retained his honorary and advisory functions after his retirement.[45] His tomb in his palace of Split had an "official" character as the seat of the senior ruler. Any destruction or privatization of major pagan monuments

---

[43] Averil Cameron and Judith Herrin, eds., *Constantinople in the early eighth century: The "Parastaseis Syntomoi Chronikai"* (Leiden: Brill, 1984) 158–59 (cap. 76); Theodor Preger, ed., Πάτρια Κωνσταντινουπόλεως, Scriptores originum Constantinopolitanarum, II (Leipzig: Teubner, 1907), 189 (II, 73). *Parastaseis syntomoi chronikai* is a compilation from the last quarter of the eighth century, compiled of material gathered from the first quarter of the eighth century onwards. Depending on the translation, the statue was placed "in front of the Kathisma" or "in the middle of Kathisma." Sarah G. Bassett, "The Antiquities in the Hippodrome of Constantinople," *Dumbarton Oaks Papers* 45 (1991): 92: "Images of Julius Caesar, Augustus, and Diocletian represented men who had ruled Rome from Republic to Empire and Tetrarchy, and their presence may have been intended to achieve for the Hippodrome what the re-use of the Trajanic, Hadrianic, and Antonine reliefs accomplished for the Arch of Constantine. In the Roman arch a sequence of images of sound rulers from the halcyon days of the empire's past evoked at once the memory of a Golden Age and, by means of comparison, the idea of its resurgence in the present under the enlightened rule of Constantine." For a wider discussion on the problem of attitude of succeeding emperors towards Diocletian: Heinrich Schlange-Schöningen, "Felix Augustus oder αὐτοκράτωρ δείλαιος: Zur Rezeption Diokletians in der konstantinischen Dynastie," in *Diokletian und die Tetrarchie. Aspekte einer Zeitenwende*, ed. Alexander Demandt, Andreas Goltz, and Heinrich Schlange-Schöningen (Berlin: Walter de Gruyter, 2004), 172–92.

[44] On Jovian's visit: *Amm. Marc.* XXV, 10, 5. On Julian's mausoleum: Johnson, *Mausoleum*, 11, 16, 103–4; the author noted that covering imperial sarcophagi with expensive fabrics is mentioned in sources of the twelfth century (the sarcophagus of Constantine the Great). On imperial burials in general: Johnson, *Mausoleum*, 8–16, 180–81; Jocelyn M. C. Toynbee, *Death and burial in the Roman world* (Ithaca: Cornell University Press, 1971), 56–61; Javier Arce, "Imperial funerals in the later Roman Empire: change and continuity," in *Rituals of power from Late Antiquity to the Early Middle Ages*, ed. Frans Theuws and Janet L. Nelson (Leiden: Brill, 2000), 115–29.

[45] A balanced overview of the theories on Diocletian's status after the abdication is given by McNally, "The Palace," 57.

required imperial approval—this was obviously lacking in the case of Diocletian's mausoleum.

From a legal point of view, the temples and sacred places in the Roman Empire were public or private. Roman pontifical law respected the legal status of a sacred place, together with temple lands and the inventory it included in the moment of consecration, from votive offerings and similar movable property that were gained subsequently and that were treated as *res profanae*.[46] Imperial jurisdiction over municipal and private shrines—including desacralization and preservation—was flexible. Public shrines, consecrated in the name of the emperor or of the Roman people, were sacrosanct, inviolable, and inalienable. After 313, their fate depended on a number of factors: their legal status, the architectural context in which they were located, their significance for the urban tissue, the level of Christianization of their surroundings, and on variable intentions and religious orientations of their owners—the emperors. From the reign of Alexander Severus, public, state shrines (*loca sacra*) were under the control of the emperor; according to Libanius's oration *Pro templis* written in 387–90, public temples were considered imperial property. Temple lands (*fundi templorum*) were confiscated in favor of the imperial *res privata* by Emperor Honorius in 415.[47] There was no need to confiscate temple buildings as they were already under imperial control. Temples were gradually closed down, abandoned, and desacralized: the emperor, as *pontifex maximus* (until Gratian), had the supreme authority to translate the *locus sacer* to *locus profanus*.[48] This process was slow, unsystematic, subjective, and varied from region to region.[49] Temples qualified as *loca sacra* until 399 when Honorius relegated them among the *ornamenta*, public buildings without religious connotations, maintained by imperial will.[50]

---

[46] Giannetto Longo, "Sul diritto sepolcrale romano," *Iura* XV (1964): 137–58 and Yan Thomas, "La valeur des choses. Le droit romain hors la religion," *Annales. Histoire, Sciences Sociales* LVII/6 (2002): 1443–44.

[47] *CTh.* XVI, 10, 20; Roland Delmaire, *Largesses sacrées et* res privata. *L'aerarium impérial et son administration du IVe au VIe siècle* (Rome: École française de Rome, 1989), 643 (hereafter Delmaire, *Largesses sacrées et* res privata); Béatrice Caseau, "Sacred landscapes," in *Late Antiquity. A guide to the postclassical world*, ed. Glenn Bowersock, Peter Brown, and Oleg Grabar (Cambridge, MA; London: Belknap Press of Harvard University Press, 2000), 30 (hereafter Caseau, "Landscapes"); Goddard, "Evolution," 283–4. It is important to highlight that Honorius's law applied to *non tam per Africam quam per omnes regiones in nostro orbe positas*.

[48] Millar, *The Emperor in the Roman world*, 360–1; Caseau, "Landscapes," 24–5, 31; Caseau, "Fate," 110–11; Marano, "Fonti giuridiche di età romana," 74. Cf. also the famous essay by Frank R. Trombley, "The Social Context of Temple Conversions" in his book *Hellenic Religion and Christianization c. 370-529*, vol. I (Leiden: Brill, 2014), 108–22.

[49] Sacrificial offerings were forbidden in the years: 341, 346, 353, 356, 381, 385, 391, 392, 395, 399 (twice), and 435; temples were closed down in: 346 and 399; idolatry was forbidden in: 356 and 391; temple properties were confiscated in: 392 and 415; idols were destroyed in: 408. All the laws related to these events are from the sixteenth book of *CTh.*—cf. Saradi Mendelovici, "Christian attitudes," 48, note 13.

[50] *CTh.* XVI, 10, 15.

Scholarship on pagan mausolea standing on imperial estates is scarce, only the shrines on imperial properties were researched.[51] An important constitution from 407 or 408 states that altars and images of gods inside temples were to be removed from all locations, regardless of whether they were being used in pagan rituals currently, or had been worshipped in cult rituals in the past. Temples were to be put to public use, regardless of whether they were located in the city or in the country. If they stood on imperial property, they were to be put to appropriate use, whereas on private property, they had to be destroyed by their owners.[52] This constitution sheds light on pagan cults in the early fifth century. The legislator clearly did not expect that a large number of temples with preserved cult inventory would still be "active"; there is a distinction between cult images (*simulacra*) and temple buildings. Temples pose a threat only if they host cults—altars and images of gods—otherwise they are religiously neutral, when emptied of contents considered dangerous for Christians (pagan statuary, votive offerings, inscriptions). The edict forbids pagan funeral feasts at tombs, as well as all other ceremonies. It authorizes bishops to repress pagan cult practices. If we apply this edict to Diocletian's mausoleum, the emperor's tomb had to cease functioning as a cult-place in 407 (if not earlier, in 356). The building housing the emperor's body, however, remained intact.

Mausoleum to church: sixth and seventh centuries

In the late fifth century, Sidonius Apollinaris' *Carmen XXIII* may contain a reference to Diocletian's tomb "in Salona." Speaking of his friend Consentius's bathing habits in Rome, Sidonius mentions Salona: "Hence to the baths; they were not those of Nero or those given by Agrippa or by him whose tomb Dalmatian Salonae views [Baths of Diocletian], but we were pleased to go to baths fittingly provided for privacy and

---

[51] See, e.g., the state of scholarship in: Steven J. Larson, "What temples stood for: Constantine, Eusebius, and Roman imperial practice" (unpublished PhD diss., Brown University, 2008), 21–70. Some more famous cases (for example Helena's donation of the imperial palace in 326 to the bishop of Trier) were emphasized, see Michael Greenhalgh, *The Survival of Roman Antiquities in the Middle Ages* (London: Duckworth, 1989), 94–5.

[52] *CTh.* XVI, 10, 19: *Simulacra, si qua etiamnunc in templis fanisque consistunt et quae alicubi ritum vel acceperunt vel accipiunt paganorum, suis sedibus evellantur, cum hoc repetita sciamus saepius sanctione decretum. Aedificia ipsa templorum, quae in civitatibus vel oppidis vel extra oppida sunt, ad usum publicum vindicentur. Arae locis omnibus destruantur omniaque templa in possessionibus nostris ad usus adcommodos transferantur; domini destruere cogantur. Non liceat omnino in honorem sacrilegi ritus funestioribus locis exercere convivia vel quicquam sollemnitatis agitare. Episcopis quoque locorum haec ipsa prohibendi ecclesiasticae manus tribuimus facultatem; iudices autem viginti librarum auri poena constringimus et pari forma officia eorum, si haec eorum fuerint dissimulatione neglecta.* Cf. Frantz, "From Paganism to Christianity," 187; Delmaire, *Largesses sacrées et* res privata, 642, 649; Cantino Wataghin, "Il riuso cristiano di edifici antichi," 747 n23; Caseau, "Landscapes," 32; Karivieri, "From pagan shrines to Christian churches," 79; Bayliss, *Provincial Cilicia*, 51; Goddard, "Evolution," 290; Arce, "*Fana*," 198–9.

modesty".[53] Sidonius' verse was written between 461–469. Insignificant Spalatum is replaced by Salona because of her greater renown, but also because Romans regarded the city one and the same as its *ager*; thus, *territorium Salonae* implied the area of Spalatum.[54] Sidonius attests the functioning of Diocletian's mausoleum to the end of the fifth century, thus major alterations must have taken place in the subsequent period.

The Early Christian decorative sculpture in the mausoleum—the earliest layer of post-classical art in the building dating from the early sixth century—provide important information about the Christian conversion of the monument and substantiate written evidence. Diocletian's palace was the residence of the penultimate Western Roman emperor Julius Nepos. Dethroned by Orestes in 475, Julius fled to Dalmatia. Recognized by Constantinople, he nominally ruled from Split for another five years, until he was murdered in 480. The chronicler Marcellinus unambiguously calls Diocletian's palace, where Julius was killed, "his villa" (*villa sua*),[55] i.e. the property of emperor Nepos. This is a clear indication that the palace remained an imperial estate. Odoacer, the new king of Italy captured Julius' murderer and annexed Dalmatia. The province—like Sicily—became private property (*patrimonium*) of Odoacer and his successors, the Ostrogothic kings of Italy.[56] The Ostrogothic ruler disposed of public and impe-

---

[53] Eugène Baret, ed., *C. Soll. Apollinaris Sidonii Opera. Oeuvres de Sidoine Apollinaire* (Paris: E. Thorin, 1878), 592 (*Carmen XXIII*, verse 495–9): *Hinc ad balnea, non Neroniana nec quae Agrippa dedit, vel ille cujus bustum Dalmaticae vident Salonae ad thermas tamen ire sed libebat privato bene praebitas pudori*; William B. Anderson, ed. & transl., Sidonius, *Poems and Letters*, I (Loeb Classical Library 296), (Cambridge, MA; London: Heinemann; Harvard University Press, 1963), 317. Cf. Bulić, "Sepolcro," 4; Bulić, "Imperatore," 49ff., 65; Bulić and Karaman, *Palača*, 71, 182; Marin, "La tomba di Diocleziano," 517; see also Johnson, *Mausoleum*, 59.

[54] Thus Bulić, "Sepolcro", 4–5 and Bulić and Karaman, *Palača*, 70–2. See, e.g., the famous anecdote on Diocletian's response to the tetrarchs in 308: Franz Pichlmayr and Roland Gruendel, ed., *Sexti Aurelii Victoris Liber de Caesaribus praecedunt Origo gentis Romanae et Liber de viris illustribus urbis Romae subsequitur Epitome de Caesaribus* (Leipzig: Teubner, 1970), 164 (39.6): *Qui dum ab Herculio atque Galerio ad recipiendum imperium rogaretur, tamquam pestem aliquam detestans in hunc modum respondit: 'Utinam Salonae possetis visere olera nostris manibus instituta, profecto numquam istud temptandum iudicaretis'.* – Thomas M. Banchich, transl., *Epitome De Caesaribus. A Booklet About the Style of Life and the Manners of the Imperatores, sometimes attributed to Sextus Aurelius Victor* (Canisius College Translated Texts, 1) (Buffalo, NY: Canisius College, 2009), 164: "It was he who, when solicited by Herculius and Galerius for the purpose of resuming control, responded in this way, as though avoiding some kind of plague: 'If you could see at Salonae the cabbages raised by our hands, you surely would never judge that a temptation'". Whether the anecdote is fictitious or not, Diocletian obviously could not have planted cabbages in Salona, but in or near his palace at Spalatum.

[55] Brian Croke, ed., *Marcellini viri clarissimi Chronicon - The Chronicle of Marcellinus. A Translation and Commentary* (Sydney: Australian Association for Byzantine Studies, 1995), 27 (480.2): *His consulibus Nepos, quem dudum Orestes imperio abdicaverat, Viatoris et Ovidae comitum suorum insidiis haut longe a Salonis sua in villa occisus est.* On this, see Ivan Basić, "Diocletian's *villa* in Late Antique and Early Medieval historiography: a reconsideration," *Hortus Artium Medievalium* 20 (2014): 63–76.

[56] Arnold H. M. Jones, *The Later Roman Empire 284-602. A Social, Economic and Administrative Study*, vol. I (Oxford: Basil Blackwell, 1964), 255–6; Delmaire, *Largesses sacrées et* res privata, 693; Mladen Nikolanci, "Die Dalmatinische Dynastie und der Untergang des Weströmischen Reiches," *Vjesnik za arheologiju i historiju dalmatinsku* 77 (1984): 273–92; Penny MacGeorge, *Late Roman Warlords* (Oxford: Oxford University Press, 2002), 62.

rial possessions. Dalmatia, as well as Diocletian's palace, remained under Ostrogothic administration until the Gothic wars in 535–55. After the Justinianic reconquest, it reverted to the fisc. On behalf of the fisc it must have been administered by a fiscal representative (*conductor domus regiae*), while the entire complex (together with dependent land) fell within the *fundi iuris publici*, or under the higher authority of the *comes privatarum*; the latter in turn was subordinate to the *comes sacri patrimonii*.[57] It is not known if the emperor granted certain areas of the palace to the archbishopric of Salona, or if representatives of the state initiated the construction of churches. The saints of Split—Theodore, Martin, Apollinaris, and Anastasia—whose cult flourished after the Gothic rule, are the saints of Ravenna with strong anti-Arian connotations. The saints enhance Justinian's reaffirmation of Catholic orthodoxy.[58] The cults of the saints arrive in Split in the sixth century, and churches are built in their honor above the gates of the palace: in the north, Martin, in the west Theodore, in the east Apollinaris, and in the south Anastasia. The emperors sought to wipe out Gothic Arianism from Diocletian's palace, still an imperial estate and, nominally, an imperial residence. Arianism was exiled and new dedications to unquestionably orthodox and anti-Arian saints were introduced to purify the palace from heretical worship.[59] It was Archbishop Peter of Salona (554–62), the representative of imperial orthodoxy in the Salonitan region, who re-introduced orthodoxy to the city. Regardless of the dilemmas concerning the formal and legal status of churches in the Diocletian's palace, its clergy were certainly the local clergy from Salona. The gradual entry of local ecclesiastical structures into the imperial building and its association with the archbishops of Salona thus takes place in the early sixth century.

Fleeing Avar and Slav invasions, the inhabitants of Salona moved with imperial permission into Diocletian's palace in Split in the seventh century. The palace became a city and the mausoleum a church. The whole affair is described in detail by Thomas of Spalato, saying that the citizens sent a request (*petitio*) to the emperors in Constantinople, receiving in return a sacred rescript (*sacrum rescriptum*) granting them the use

---

[57] Delmaire, *Largesses sacrées et res privata*, 693.
[58] Nikola Jakšić, "Patron saints of the Medieval gates in Diocletian's palace," *Hortus Artium Medievalium* 9 (2003): 187–94 (hereafter Jakšić, "Patron saints"); Nikola Jakšić, "The cults of Byzantine-Ravennate provenance in Diocletian's Palace of Justinian's age," *Bulletin de l'Association pour l'Antiquité tardive* 11 (2002): 79–83.
[59] As was the case in Ravenna: Agnellus qui et Andreas, *Liber pontificalis ecclesiae Ravennatis*, ed. Oswald Holder-Egger, Monumenta Germaniae historica, Scriptores rerum Langobardicarum et Italicarum saec. VI-IX (Hannover: Hahn, 1878), 334 (cap. 85, 86); Arthur Urbano, "Donation, dedication, and *Damnatio memoriae*: the Catholic reconciliation of Ravenna and the Church of Sant'Apollinare Nuovo," *Journal of Early Christian Studies* XIII/1 (2005): 82, 84–5, 92; Deborah M. Deliyannis, *Ravenna in Late Antiquity* (Cambridge: Cambridge University Press, 2010), 167–8, 206–13 (hereafter Deliyannis, *Ravenna in Late Antiquity*).

of the imperial property.⁶⁰ This is further evidence on the continuity of state ownership of the palace.

Sixth-century archaeological finds

Archaeological findings of the earliest post-Diocletianic phase of the mausoleum have received little scholarly attention so far. Fourth–fifth century North African (*African Red Slip Ware*) and Asia Minor ceramics (*Phocaean Red Slip Ware*) found in Diocletian's palace attest thriving life within the walls. Two-thirds of the pottery date to the early fourth–mid-fifth century, the remaining to the mid-fifth to the mid-sixth century.⁶¹ Amphorae, coins, glass, and lamps of the same period were also found. These imported commercial goods show that people living in Diocletian's palace (imperial retinue? high imperial dignitaries?) bought luxury objects.

In the mausoleum, decorative sculpture was found dated to 550 or earlier. Some of these come from archaeological excavations at the octagon and may therefore reasonably be correlated with its conversion into a church. Early Christian reliefs dated to the sixth century were found during excavation works in and around the cathedral.⁶² Southeast of the mausoleum, two Early Christian capitals were found, one of them reutilized as an early medieval wall. These archaeologically ascertained stratigraphic indicators suggest that the construction to which these capitals belonged had been destroyed earlier. The majority of the Early Christian fragments with traceable stratigraphic context within Diocletian's palace come from the northeast and southeast sector in the immediate vicinity around the emperor's octagon, near the baths, with another zone in the southeastern quadrant of the imperial residence, between the *triclinium* and the eastern wall of the palace. These findings include a sarcophagus fragment, part of the lid of another sarcophagus, two impost-capitals decorated with crosses, three smaller simplified capitals with vegetal decorations, two fragments of a *pluteus*, the remains of a simplified *transenna*, and a part of a pilaster with a carved cross (Fig. 2a–b).⁶³ These

---

[60] Thomas Archidiaconus Spalatensis, *Historia Salonitana*, 52 (cap. X). See Radoslav Katičić, "*Vetustiores ecclesiae Spalatensis memoriae*," *Starohrvatska prosvjeta*, ser. III, 17 (1987): 17–51; and Basić, "Poleogeneza," 166–80.

[61] Ivančica Dvoržak-Schrunk, "Dioklecijanova palača od 4. do 7. stoljeća u svjetlu keramičkih nalaza," [Diocletian's palace from the 4th to 7th century in the light of ceramic finds] *Vjesnik Arheološkog muzeja u Zagrebu* 3ʳᵈ ser., XXII (1989): 92–4, note 6.

[62] Stanko Piplović, "Ranokršćanski Split," [Early Christian Split] *Grada i prilozi za povijest Dalmacije* 21 (2008): 141–71 and Basić, "Poleogeneza," 424–69.

[63] Ivan Mirnik, "Roman architectural fragments," in *Diocletian's Palace. American-Yugoslav joint excavations*, vol. VI, ed. Sheila McNally and Ivančica Dvoržak-Schrunk (Minneapolis: University of Minnesota, Kendall/Hunt, Urbanistički zavod Dalmacije, 1989), 6, 25, 35–6 (cat. no. 61–72 and Pl. 8, 14, 15). For our considerations, it is important to emphasize that the *pluteus* (p. 36, cat. no. 68 and Pl. 8) was found in the southwestern yard of the mausoleum's *temenos*.

Fig. 2a. Split, Early Christian fragments found in the surroundings of the cathedral, 6th c. (Mirnik 1989, Pl. 15).

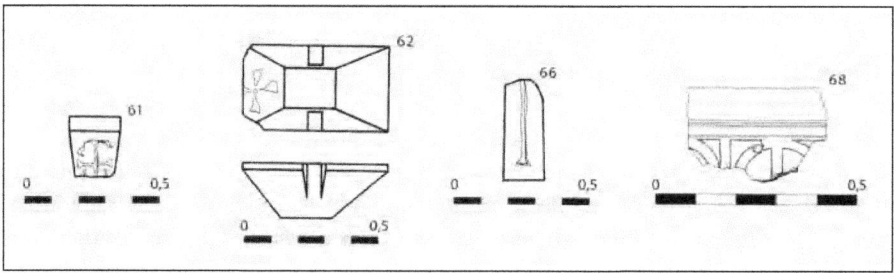

Fig. 2b. Split, Early Christian fragments found in the surroundings of the cathedral, 6th c. (Mirnik 1989, Pl. 8).

Fig. 3a. Split, Archaeological Museum, Early Christian pilaster (left) found at the cathedral, 6th c. (photo: I. Basić).

Fig. 3b. Split, cathedral, Early Christian pilaster, 6th c. (photo: I. Basić).

Fig. 4. Split, cathedral, Early Christian relief with the depiction of a cantharos, 6th c. (Ivanišević 1987, fig. 2).

findings are dated to the sixth century. Three pilasters with crosses (Fig. 3a–b), and a decorative relief with a kantharos (Fig. 4), the latter found in the northeastern niche of Diocletian's mausoleum, iconographically and stylistically also belong to the sixth century.⁶⁴ Except for the sarcophagi, these fragments come from decorative sculpture and liturgical installations—altar rails (*plutei*, pilasters, columns, and capitals), biphora pilasters, and window elements—typical to Justinianic church interiors. Concentrated as they were around the octagon, their topography reveals that these Early Christian reliefs must have decorated the imperial mausoleum. As the oldest layer of Christian sculpture in Diocletian's octagon, they indicate the first Christian reutilization of the pagan cult space. These furnishings and architectural decoration belong to a well documented type datable to the middle of the sixth century. In other words, there is a clear indication that this period comprised an extensive refurbishment of the octagon. Diocletian's octagonal mausoleum was eminently suitable for Christian liturgy, structural changes were minimal: one just had to install the altar in the main apse and to decorate the church with Christian liturgical furniture.⁶⁵

The fragments from the mid-sixth century indicate the first Christian conversion of the mausoleum. The transformation of Diocletian's tomb for Christian use thus took place at least a hundred years before the mid-seventh century. This means that the mausoleum stood intact for a longer period than previously thought.

This can be further corroborated by drawing on a variety of sources, dating from the fourth, fifth and sixth centuries. Apart from Ammianus's report on the affair of 356, particularly important is the evidence provided by Sidonius Apollinaris (*ca.* 430–89), which seems to confirm that the emperor's mausoleum was still in function during the Gallic bishop's lifetime.

This data is well known in scholarship, but its implication concerning the Christianization of the mausoleum has not been taken into consideration. How did the frieze on the top of the interior—portraying Diocletian, his wife Prisca, Hermes Psychopompos, and erotes—survive the Christian appropriation of the monument? How did the most important relief of the frieze above the main niche—tentatively identified as the Diocletian's apotheosis—survive undamaged until the fifteenth or sixteenth century? These remains indicate the lack of Christian violence against Diocletian. The mausoleum's pagan interior stood more or less intact up to the sixth century, when the

---

⁶⁴ Milan Ivanišević, "Stari oltar svetog Staša u splitskoj prvostolnoj crkvi," [The old altar of St. Anastasius in the Split cathedral] *Starohrvatska prosvjeta*, ser. III, 17 (1987): 137–38, fig. 2. It's enough to compare the relief with the *pluteus* from the Basilica of SS. Felice and Fortunato in Vicenza (Gian-Pietro Brogiolo and Monica Ibsen, eds., *Corpus Architecturae Religiosae Europeae (saec. IV-X), vol. II.1: Province di Belluno, Treviso, Padova, Vicenza* [Zagreb: International Research Center for Late Antiquity and the Middle Ages, 2009], 253–54, fig. 11) dated to the first third of the sixth century, not long before the war in 535. For other pilasters, see Basić, "Poleogeneza," 103–4, 434.

⁶⁵ Cf. similar case with the Pantheon in 609: Sible De Blaauw, "Das Pantheon als christlicher Tempel," *Boreas* 17 (1994): 13–26 (hereafter De Blaauw, "Das Pantheon"); Adam Ziolkowski, "Pantheon," in *Lexicon topographicum urbis Romae*, vol. IV, ed. Eva M. Steinby (Roma: Quasar, 1999), 54–61 (hereafter Ziolkowski, "Pantheon"); Arce, "*Fana*," 196.

first functional modifications took place. Unfortunately, it is impossible to know the condition of Diocletian's mausoleum at the time of its reuse in the sixth century. Out of use for two hundred years, it must have shown signs of dilapidation.[66] As we have seen, the survival of pagan structures depended on their legal status in the Christian Roman Empire. Diocletian's mausoleum was imperial property and this guaranteed its upkeep. The "owners" of the mausoleum, the successive emperors, did not care about destroying or reusing it. Supervised by the imperial officials of the *res privata*, Diocletian's mausoleum withstood destruction and spoliation for two centuries.

Tomb to church: the sixth-century conversion

The conversion of Diocletian's tomb into a church took place in the early sixth century—at the time when the Temple of Romulus and its adjacent buildings on the *Forum Pacis* in Rome were converted into the Church of SS. Cosmas and Damian by Pope Felix IV (526–30), with the permission of the Ostrogothic Queen Amalasuntha.[67] It was the first church constructed on the *Forum Romanum* and one of the first that used a pagan monument as its outer shell. The construction of the Basilica of SS. Cosmas and Damian as well as the conversion of the Pantheon into the Church of *Sancta Maria ad Martyres* parallels the transformation of Diocletian's mausoleum. The buildings on the *Forum Pacis* belonged to the *fiscus*, as state property passed from the Roman emperors to Ostrogothic kings, so a special dispensation was needed for it to be obtained and reused by the Catholic church. The imperial allocation of public land

---

[66] Frantz, "From Paganism to Christianity," 201. Cf. also Caseau, *"Polemein,"* 98.

[67] Louis Duchesne, ed., *Le Liber pontificalis. Texte, introduction et commentaire*, vol. 1 (Paris: E. Thorin, 1886), 279 n3 (hereafter Duchesne, *Liber pontificalis*): *fecit basilicam sanctorum Cosme et Damiani in urbe Roma in loco qui appellatur Via Sacra iuxta templum urbis Romae*. See also Richard Krautheimer, *Corpus basilicarum christianarum Romae*, vol. I (Città del Vaticano: Pontificio Istituto di Archeologia Cristiana, 1937), 137–43; Bruno M. Apollonj-Ghetti, "Nuove considerazioni sulla basilica romana dei SS. Cosma e Damiano," *Rivista di Archeologia Cristiana* 50/1-4 (1974): 7–54; Richard Krautheimer, *Rome: Profile of a City, 312-1308* (Princeton: Princeton University Press, 1980), 71, 93ff. (hereafter Krautheimer, *Rome*); Eva M. Steinby, ed., *Lexicon topographicum urbis Romae*, vol. I (Roma: Quasar, 1993), 324–25, s.v. *Ss. Cosmas et Damianus, basilica* (Silvana Episcopo); Jean-Marie Sansterre, "Felice IV, santo," in *Enciclopedia dei papi*, vol. 1 (Roma: Treccani, 2000), 489; Beat Brenk, "Zur Einführung des Kultes der heiligen Kosmas und Damian in Rom," *Theologische Zeitschrift* LXII/2 (2006): 311; Jean Guyon, "La marque de la christianisation dans la topographie urbaine de Rome," in *La fin de la cité antique et le début de la cité médiévale de la fin du IIIe siècle à l'avènement de Charlemagne*, ed. Claude Lepelley (Bari: Edipuglia, 1996), 224; Massimiliano Ghilardi, "Trasformazioni del paesaggio urbano: il *Templum Pacis* durante la guerra greco-gotica (a proposito di Procop., *Goth.* IV 21)," in *Les cités de l'Italie tardo-antique (IVe-VIe siècle). Institutions, économie, société, culture et religion*, ed. Massimiliano Ghilardi, Christophe J. Goddard, and Pierfrancesco Porena (Rome: École française de Rome, 2006), 142–43; Stefania Fogagnolo and Federica Michaela Rossi, "Il *Templum Pacis* come esempio di trasformazione del paesaggio urbano e di mutamenti culturali dalla prima età imperiale ai primi del '900," *Bollettino di Archeologia on line* I (2010): 36.

to the Church for the building of churches had a long tradition in Rome, but the right of the sovereign to the disposal of public assets was scrupulously respected. A request for assigning state property (*petitio, postulatio*) was referred to appropriate state officials (*praefectus urbi*, on whose behalf the public property was disposed by *curator operum maximorum* and *curator operum publicorum*), and ultimately, imperial permission had to be obtained (*concessio*), after which construction could begin. Imperial license could be obtained directly by the personal intervention of the pope, regardless of the usual procedure (*sacra adnotatio*).[68] The best known temple conversion is the Pantheon. Pope Boniface IV was granted permission by the Byzantine Emperor Phocas in 609 to convert the temple into a church dedicated to the Virgin Mary and the martyrs.[69] Emperor Heraclius allowed Pope Honorius I (625–38) to use bronze plates from the Temple of Venus and Rome to repair the Basilica of St. Peter.[70] However, when Heraclius's grandson, Constans II, resided in Rome in 663, he removed the bronze decorations of the urban buildings and sent them to Constantinople. The papal chronicle records that this included the bronze covers of the Pantheon.[71] Constans's action shows that the Byzantine emperors as late as the seventh century reserved supreme rights of ownership over public buildings. In the case of imperial property, not state property, this fell under the jurisdiction of imperial officials (*comes rei privatae*), to whom one was obliged to refer a petition for the allocation of a part of the imperial patrimony. This included the emperor's private property, as well as hereditary crown property of Roman rulers that had been multiplying since the beginning of the principate (*palatia, villae, horti*).[72] The Early Christian conversion of Diocletian's mausoleum must have entailed similar legal steps.

---

[68] It is important to note that, in doing so, the Church used precise legal terminology: public lands on which churches were to be built were not donated to the Church as an institution (*donatio*), but the Church was given permission to build on public soil (*concessio*). Cf. the allocation of land to Sixtus III (432–40) for the Basilica of San Lorenzo given to him by Valentinian III—Duchesne, *Liber pontificalis*, 234: *Fecit autem basilicam sancto Laurentio, quod Valentinianus Augustus concessit*; Julia Hillner, "Le chiese paleocristiane di Roma e l'occupazione degli spazi pubblici," in *Ecclesiae Urbis. Atti del Congresso Internazionale di Studi sulle chiese di Roma (IV-X secolo)*, vol. I, ed. Federico Guidobaldi and Alessandra Guiglia Guidobaldi (Città del Vaticano: Pontificio Istituto di Archeologia Cristiana, 2002), 321–29 (hereafter Hillner, "Le chiese paleocristiane").

[69] Duchesne, *Liber pontificalis*, 317: *Eodem tempore petiit a Focate principe templum qui appellatur Pantheum, in quo fecit ecclesiam beatae Mariae semper virginis et omnium martyrum; in qua ecclesia princeps dona multa optulit*. For more about the conversion see: Deichmann, "Frühchristliche," 135; Krautheimer, *Rome*, 72; De Blaauw, "Das Pantheon," 13; Caillet, "Transformation," 200; Ziolkowski, "Pantheon," 54–61; Tod A. Marder, "The Pantheon after Antiquity," in *The Pantheon in Rome: Contributions*, ed. Gerd Graßhoff, Michael Heinzelmann, and Markus Wäfler (Bern: Bern Studies, 2009), 145–53.

[70] Duchesne, *Liber pontificalis*, 323: *Hic cooperuit ecclesiam omnem ex tegulis aereis quas levavit de templo qui appellatur Romae, ex concessu piissimi Heraclii imperatoris*; Caseau, "Polemein," 106.

[71] Duchesne, *Liber pontificalis*, 343: *XII dies in civitate Romana perseverans, omnia quae erant in aere ad ornatum civitatis deposuit; sed et ecclesiae sanctae Mariae ad martyres quae de tegulis aereis erant discoperuit et in regia urbe cum alia diversa quas deposuerat direxit*.

[72] Hillner, "Le chiese paleocristiane," 325–6.

Under what circumstances did Diocletian's mausoleum become a church? The importance of the palace in Late Antiquity is confirmed by the *Ravenna Cosmography* around 700 that lists *Spalathron, Spalathrum* among the towns (*civitates*).[73] The Anonymous of Ravenna drew his geographical and topographical data from compilations published prior to the 560s. The palace retained its significance up to the sixth century.

Ostensibly, Diocletian's remains were removed from his mausoleum and the building was Christianized sometime between *ca.* 469 (the last mention of the mausoleum in Sidonius Apollinaris's poem) and *ca.* 550 (the first Early Christian cult installations). In this time-span, three possible historical contexts for the conversion of the mausoleum emerge: Julius Nepos as the legitimate emperor ceded Diocletian's mausoleum to the Church between 475 and 480 to use it for daily worship in his residence;[74] the Ostrogothic rulers gave parts of the palace to the Church; Justinian's representatives dedicated churches to Saint Martin, Theodore, Apollinaris, and Anastasia in the guard corridors of the palace to Christianize the freshly reconquered imperial estate.[75]

The events of 526–30 concerning Felix IV and Amalasuntha heralded the popularity of the cult of two saintly brothers, Cosmas and Damian, up until then venerated mainly in the East. From Ravenna, the capital of Byzantine Italy, their cult quickly spread following in the footsteps of Justinian's *reconquista* (Trento, Grado, Poreč),[76]

---

[73] Joseph Schnetz, ed., *Ravennatis Anonymi Cosmographia*, Itineraria Romana, II (Leipzig: B. G. Teubner, 1940), IV, 16; V, 14. About the Anonymous Ravennate see: Ivan Basić, "Najstariji urbonimi kasnoantičkog i ranosrednjovjekovnog Splita: *Aspalathos, Spalatum* i Jeronimov *palatium villae* u svjetlu povijesnih izvora," [The oldest late Antique and early medieval urbonyms of Split: *Aspalathos, Spalatum* and Jerome's *palatium villae* in the light of historical sources)] in *Munuscula in honorem Željko Rapanić*, ed. Miljenko Jurković and Ante Milošević. (Zagreb-Motovun-Split: International Center for Late Antiquity and the Middle Ages, 2012) 143–44. According to Belamarić ("Dioklecijanova palača," 137) the conversion of Diocletian's mausoleum and the temples of Diocletian's palace happened in the early fifth century. Since the author has so far only preliminarily presented his conclusions, while awaiting for him to publish his arguments for this interesting proposition, I am presenting my opinion, which is opposite of the aforementioned.

[74] One might assume that Julius Nepos was buried in the imperial mausoleum; he was murdered in Diocletian's palace and there is no known data about his tomb. It is reasonable to assume that he was buried in an ecclesiastical ambience. In that case, Diocletian's remains could have been removed and the mausoleum could have been converted into a church. However, the circumstances of Nepos's death are far too unclear for such a conclusion. In a similar way, one could assume that Odoacer, after the conquest of Dalmatia in 482, somehow honored Nepos's memory, who presented himself as Nepos's legitimate successor.

[75] Marin ("La tomba di Diocleziano," 500ff.) and Johnson (*Mausoleum*, 58–70) are the two most recent authors to write about the form and function of Diocletian's mausoleum. Marin holds that the destruction of the imperial sarcophagus should be separated from the reutilization of the mausoleum, and speculates that the profanation of the tomb occurred during the Byzantine-Ostrogothic war. Further on in the article, he supports the traditional dating of the conversion of the mausoleum to the seventh century, referring to analogies with the Pantheon.

[76] Sergio Tavano, "Mosaici parietali in Istria," *Antichità Altoadriatiche* 8 (1975): 267–69 (hereafter Tavano, "Mosaici parietali in Istria"); Jean-Pierre Caillet, *L'évérgetisme monumental chrétien en Italie et à ses marges* (Rome: École française de Rome, 1993), 69, 71, 331; Myla Perraymond, "Linee di diffusione del culto dei Santi Anargiri attraverso le testimonianze monumentali ed epigrafiche del VI secolo," in *Acta XIII Congressus Internationalis*

Fig. 5. Split, Archaeological Museum, architrave with an inscription mentioning SS. Cosmas and Damian, 9th c. (photo: I. Basić).

hand in hand with imperial armies. It is of particular importance for our argument that another saint, Theodore of Euchaite in Pontus, was also commemorated in the basilica of Saint Cosmas and Damian. Theodore was popular in the Eastern Empire, venerated together with Cosmas and Damian in Apamea and Gerasa. The introduction, in a representative manner, of the cult of these three carefully chosen saints to the ancient heart of Rome during the pontificate of Felix IV enables us to better understand the common cultural background to the introduction of the cult of Cosmas and Damian into Diocletian's palace, together with the cults of Theodore, Martin, Apollinaris, and Anastasia. The cult of Saint Cosmas and Damian is attested in the cathedral of Split at least since the mid-ninth century. The first mention of them as co-patron saints of the cathedral is in a charter issued by the Croatian Duke Trpimir in 852 or 844 (*coenobium sanctorum martyrum Domnii, Anastasii, Cosmae et Damiani*). An inscription on an architrave fragment (Fig. 5), probably also from the cathedral (around 800), also mentions the saints.[77]

Archaeologiae Christianae, vol. II, ed. Nenad Cambi and Emilio Marin (Città del Vaticano-Split: Pontificio Istituto di Archeologia Cristiana, Arheološki muzej, 1998), 673–86; Giuseppe Cuscito, "Origine e sviluppo del culto dei santi Cosma e Damiano: testimonianze nella 'Venetia et Histria,'" in *San Michele in Africisco e l'età giustinianea a Ravenna. Atti del Convegno «La diaspora dell'arcangelo, San Michele in Africisco e l'età giustinianea», Ravenna, 21-22 aprile 2005*, ed. Claudio Spadoni and Linda Kniffitz (Milano: Silvana, 2007), 105–8 (hereafter Cuscito, "Origine e sviluppo del culto dei santi Cosma e Damiano"). All of these attestations of their cult in the respective churches can be firmly dated to the early sixth century.

[77] For the charter see: *Codex diplomaticus regni Croatiae, Dalmatiae et Slavoniae*, vol. I, ed. Jakov Stipišić and Miljen Šamšalović (Zagreb: Jugoslavenska akademija znanosti i umjetnosti, 1967), 5; for the inscription: Rade Mihaljčić and Ludwig Steindorff, *Glossar zur frühmittelalterlichen Geschichte im östlichen Europa, Beiheft 2: Namentragende Steininschriften in Jugoslawien vom Ende des 7. bis zur Mitte des 13. Jahrhunderts* (Wiesbaden: Franz Steiner, 1982), 67.

Since the cult of Cosmas and Damian probably *did not* reach Spalatum together with the cult of Salonitan martyrs, there is a possibility that their cult preceded the latter, transferred to Diocletian's palace only in the Early Middle Ages.[78] However, the fact that the cult of Cosmas and Damian in the Euphrasian Basilica in Poreč was combined with the cult of Bishop Severus from Ravenna allows us to affirm even further the hypothesis of simultaneous entry of the cult of Cosmas and Damian with the cult of Bishop Severus from Ravenna into Diocletian's palace. In Poreč, the left side apse of the Basilica Euphrasiana is decorated with a mosaic depicting Christ crowning Cosmas and Damian with a martyrdom wreath. In the corresponding right-side apse, Saint Severus and another unidentified saint (probably Apollinaris of Ravenna, whose feast day coincided with Severus's) are represented in the same way.[79] These mosaics can be reliably dated *ca.* 553-557. Once accepted, the cults of Cosmas, Damian, and Severus in Poreč will become in every respect chronologically aligned with their appearance in Split, where, simultaneously, the cult of Apollinaris was recorded. This parallelism indicates the center from where both cults arrived in Split and in Poreč: Ravenna. The saints' arrival in Diocletian's palace was not isolated, but occurred together with other Ravennate cults with a powerful anti-Arian edge. Whether the cult of Saint Cosmas and Damian in the Cathedral of Split represents a survival of an original Early Christian dedication, remains yet to be seen. There is, however, no doubt that the octagon was used by Christians in the sixth century, at the apex of the popularity of the two saints. The elevation of the church to the status of cathedral happened later, in the seventh or eighth century.[80] It was a separate and different process.

---

[78] Joško Belamarić ("The first centuries of Christianity in Diocletian's palace in Split," in *Acta XIII Congressus Internationalis Archaeologiae Christianae*, III, 65 [hereafter Belamarić, "The first centuries"]) refers to the hypothesis by C. Fisković according to which the cult of Cosmas and Damian directly replaced the cult of Aesculapius in the small temple of the palace and was transferred to the mausoleum opposite the temple; Belamarić notes that "even with all the information we currently possess, we are unable to ascertain when SS. Cosmas and Damian became joint protectors of Split." Their cult vanished already in the Late Middle Ages: as co-patrons of Split, they were depicted for the last time on the Romanesque choir seats from the twelfth or thirteenth century. After that, in the Statute of Split from 1312, only Domnius and Anastasius are mentioned as patrons, with no mention of Cosmas and Damian—see Ivan Ostojić, *Benediktinci u Hrvatskoj* [Benedictines in Croatia], vol. 2 (Split: Benediktinski priorat Tkon, 1964), 368.

[79] Tavano, "Mosaici parietali in Istria," 268–69; Cuscito, "Origine e sviluppo del culto dei santi Cosma e Damiano," 106–7. It is equally possible that these are St. Ursus or St. Ursicinus, bishops of Ravenna from the fourth and sixth centuries, respectively.

[80] In my opinion, this happened in the late eighth century, but I cannot elaborate on that here. See Ivan Basić, "New evidence for the re-establishment of the Adriatic dioceses in the late 8th century," in *Imperial Spheres and the Adriatic Byzantium, the Carolingians and the Treaty of Aachen (812)*, ed. Mladen Ančić, Jonathan Shepard, and Trpimir Vedriš (London–New York: Routledge, 2017, 261–287), and Basić, "Poleogeneza," 181–421, for arguments.

In my view, the conversion of the mausoleum into the church of Saint Cosmas and Damian must have taken place under Justinian. Early Christian churches rose above the four gates of Diocletian's palace. With the Ravennate-Byzantine cults there,[81] an Early Christian cult was also present in the most representative building of the palace: the octagon. That the octagon was already an Early Christian church is demonstrated by sixth-century Early Christian sculpture fragments. The cult of Cosmas and Damian was not brought here when the mausoleum was converted into a cathedral (at the time, the cults of the Virgin Mary, Domnius, and Anastasius were introduced), nor is there evidence that Cosmas and Damian were revered at all in Early Christian Salona. It is unlikely that the cult of Cosmas and Damian entered the Cathedral of Split between the eighth and twelfth century, when they are sporadically mentioned and completely disappear after the thirteenth century. The cult of Saint Cosmas and Damian did not appear in the West before 500,[82] thus their veneration in Split cannot be earlier. As their cult is mentioned from the ninth century onward in tandem with the dominant cults of the patron saints of Salona-Split, Domnius and Anastasius, their presence looks like a remnant of the Early Christian dedication of the mausoleum. Following the introduction of the cult of the Salonitan martyrs, the earlier patrons were retained in the dedication of the church, but only in a secondary place. This hypothesis is corroborated primarily by the lack of a material presence of Christian cult in the mausoleum before the sixth century and by the popularity of Saint Cosmas and Damian under Justinian's reign.

The worship of Cosmas and Damian in Diocletian's mausoleum predates the arrival of the inhabitants of Salona to Split in the seventh century and the restoration of its archdiocese in the eighth century. Their cult started in the sixth century, when the mausoleum became a church. At the time of the restoration of the archdiocese and the secondary dedication of the octagon to the saints of Salona, Domnius and Anastasius, the cult of SS. Cosmas and Damian was already several decades old. Two Early Christian reliquaries—one bearing the inscription of Saint Severus, another containing the relics of Saint Domnius, Anastasius, and George—from the sixth century show their cult in Diocletian's palace under Justinian's reign.[83] Severus's relics inevitably suggest contacts

---

[81] Jakšić, "Patron Saints," *passim*. Belamarić, "The first centuries," 57–9 was the first to present the dating of these churches back to the Early Christian period. He believes that the cult of St. Euphemia, whose churches are located in both places next to *Porta Aurea*, originates from Ravenna, too.

[82] The first recorded case is the oratory, built in honor of the two saints by Pope Symmachus (498–514) in Rome next to the church of Santa Maria Maggiore: *qui ad sanctam Mariam oratorium sanctorum Cosmae et Damiani a fundamentis construxit* (Duchesne, *Liber pontificalis*, 262). Cf. Eva M. Steinby, ed., *Lexicon topographicum urbis Romae*, vol. I (Roma: Quasar, 1993), 325, s.v. *Ss. Cosmas et Damianus ad sanctam Mariam Maiorem* (Giuseppe De Spirito).

[83] Arsen Duplančić, "Two Early Christian reliquaries from Split," *Vjesnik za arheologiju i povijest dalmatinsku*, 106 (2013): 205–29.

with Ravenna (previously identified via other cults), where this local holy bishop was particularly revered.[84] Cosmas and Damian, together with Severus, were also venerated in the Basilica Euphrasiana in Poreč. The cults of Saint Cosmas and Damian, Apollinaris, Theodore, Martin, Anastasia, and Severus in Diocletian's palace started simultaneously under Justinian following his triumph over the Goths. The imperial palace in Split was enriched with the typical cults of the saints of the Justinianic reconquest. The churches intended for the Byzantine garrison were manned by the clergy of Salona: the archbishop of Salona must have paid occasional visits to the palace.

The settlement, surely, predated the transition of the populace from the town of Salona that happened during the seventh century. Again, the aforementioned alterations of the palace must have happened during the sixth century and were, most surely, arranged by the then-inhabitants of the palace. The question that remains is who initiated these large-scale interventions. Considering the well-known policy of Justinian I towards the Church after the Gothic wars, it can be assumed that at least some parts of Diocletian's palace were ceded by the Byzantine government to the *Ecclesia catholica Salonitana* under Archbishops Honorius II (528–47) or Peter (554–62).[85] Thus, most of these alterations are to be attributed to them, in close collaboration with the Byzantine military units stationed in the palace at the time.

Church to cathedral: seventh or eighth century?

The transition from the sixth to the seventh century was a time of sudden decline in the Western church. The Lombard invasion shook the dioceses and wiped out churches along the western and eastern Adriatic coasts, especially in the northwestern region of the Adriatic. More than half of the early Christian dioceses documented in the Italian peninsula no longer existed by the turn of the seventh century. In Dalmatia, the barbarian raids and the anarchy of the early seventh century ended urban life of Salona and its status as the province's metropolis. According to Thomas of Spalato, the Salonitan refugees, led by a certain Severus the Great (*Magnus Severus*), fled first to neighbouring islands before settling in Diocletian's palace, the core of the future Split. The move was supported by the Constantinopolitan government that reportedly allowed Salonitans to occupy the imperial buildings and regulated their relationship with neighbouring Slavs. Shortly after the destruction of Salona, the papal legate John of Ravenna arrived in the newly established city of Split, where he reinstated the old archbishopric and metropolitan see of Salona and transferred the relics of the Salonitan

---

[84] Deliyannis, *Ravenna in Late* Antiquity, 213, 274–75.
[85] On these archbishops, see: Jean-Pierre Caillet, "L'église salonitaine à l'epoque des évêques Étienne et Honorius II," in *Salonitansko-splitska crkva u prvom tisućljeću kršćanske povijesti*, ed. Josip Dukić, Slavko Kovačić, and Ema Višić-Ljubić (Split: Crkva u svijetu, Splitsko-makarska nadbiskupija, 2008), 211–19.

martyrs, St. Domnius and St. Anastasius to Diocletian's mausoleum that became the Cathedral of Split.

On the basis of Thomas of Spalato's chronicle, scholars generally accepted that the metropolitan see of Salona was reinstated in nearby Split in the mid-seventh century with John of Ravenna at its head. The account became common among later historiography dealing with the establishment and the rise of the church of Split and other churches of the eastern Adriatic. This narrative has exerted a profound influence on the overall perception of events and continues to be widely accepted, with certain additions and alterations, in scholarly publications. A detailed analysis of the historiography is beyond the scope of this paper.[86] For a long time, the early seventh century was seen as a conventional final date of the collapse of Early Christian dioceses in Dalmatia—that suddenly and inexplicably re-emerged in the sources around 800. The circumstances under which the early medieval bishoprics were founded in Dalmatia and the way they developed remained unexplained. This is not the place to dwell on the issue of the foundation of new bishoprics and the reestablishment of Early Christian episcopal seats in Split and other Adriatic cities.[87] The earliest medieval archaeological findings within the mausoleum date from the late eighth century (a possible trace of John of Ravenna's acitivities according to the late dating), but this has nothing to do with the Christianization of Diocletian's mausoleum. Whether we accept the seventh-century or eighth-century dating for the establishment of the archdiocese, the conversion of the mausoleum into a church has to be differentiated from the later reutilization of the church as a cathedral.

Conclusion

According to Jan Vaes' parameters compiled in 1989, the basic questions that need to be answered in each case of conversion are the following: in what state and shape was the object found prior to its reutilization; what was its function in that moment; when and with what purpose was the object built; for how long did the object

---

[86] A full *status quaestionis* on this issue would exceed the limits of this paper; for a summary of opinions, see: Basić, "Poleogeneza", 181ff. and Basić, "New evidence", 261–265.

[87] Beginning with the possibility that some or all of these cities achieved their episcopal status at the end of the eighth century, I recently tried to connect the historical records of several Dalmatian dioceses from the end of the eighth century with artistic material firmly dated to the same period and preserved in the respective church buildings. The founding of the eastern Adriatic bishoprics should be seen in a different social and chronological context—namely that of the late eighth century—sustaining the thesis with a critical examination of the sources; archaeological and art-historical evidence; and comparison with regional, Adriatic and pan-Mediterranean contexts. See Basić, "New evidence", 266–279.

remain in its original function and with what aim.[88] This paper attempted to give an answer to these questions.

Diocletian's palace was built on an imperial property established in the first century and remained part of the *fiscus* for centuries to come. Overlooking this fact resulted in outdated theories. As a part of unalienable crown property, the palace complex in Split, as well as the mausoleum, were under imperial supervision. Any functional change required imperial decree. The removal of the pagan contents of the palace must have occurred at several stages, during a protracted time-span: suspension of pagan cult practices, desacralization, dissolution of imperial prerogatives attached to the building, followed by the possible exemption of parts of its inventory, and ultimately its Christianization and adaptation for a new use.

A new approach to the written sources and new material evidence corroborate the argument that the pagan mausoleum in Split did not undergo substantial modification prior to the sixth century. I showed that change occurred through several stages. In the first stage, the building was transformed into a simple church, to be transformed into a cathedral centuries later. The case study of the conversion of a pagan monument into a Christian one holds important clues that cast new light on the process of transformation of pagan buildings into churches in general.

No ritual desacralization of the Diocletian's sacred octagon took place in the decades following the emperor's death. The conversion of the building to an Early Christian structure more than two hundred years after the emperor's death, however, must have been an important juncture, as it significantly altered a major imperial monument. The architectural alteration consisted of the removal of Diocletian's remains together with the pagan statuary, the construction of an altar, and the addition of a choir-screen. No radical change took place in the use of space. The decisive archaeological evidence for this change are the fragments of sixth-century decorative sculpture. The mausoleum's conversion into a church was not immediate, and it amounted to a simple refurbishment of the interior with Early Christian church installations.

Like other pagan monuments (Pantheon, Parthenon, Temple of Athena in Syracuse, etc.), Diocletian's mausoleum owes its preservation to church reuse. The fact that it became a cathedral protected the octagon and guaranteed its survival. Its size and integration in the imperial complex further assured its existence in the long run.

---

[88] Jan Vaes, "*Nova construere sed amplius vetusta servare*: la réutilisation chrétienne d'édifices antiques (en Italie)," in *Actes du XIᵉ Congrès International d'archéologie chrétienne*, vol. I, ed. Noël Duval, Françoise Baritel, and Philippe Pergola (Roma-Città del Vaticano: École française de Rome, Pontificio Istituto di Archeologia cristiana, 1989), 299.

The use of Diocletian's funerary octagon as an Early Christian church ultimately does not seem as revolutionary as it has been previously thought. Christians did reuse a monumental space built by a persecuting Roman emperor, but this took place centuries after his death, by which time the conversion seemed more utilitarian than symbolic. It was not a key revolutionary moment of Christian triumph, although it did involve the desacralization of a building associated with a Tetrarch. Once we separate the conversion of a pagan mausoleum into a church from its transformation into a cathedral, the survival of Diocletian's mausoleum as a Christian place of worship suddenly looks less surprising.

CHRISTIAN TOPOGRAPHY IN SOPIANAE'S LATE ANTIQUE CEMETERIES[1]

Zsolt Visy

Sopianae's Roman cemeteries, now a World Heritage Site,[2] constitute a poignant monument of the transition from, and cohabitation of, paganism and Christianity in the fourth century. The tombs, burial chambers and mausolea offer a glimpse into the lively Roman civilization in Pannonia, only decades preceding the collapse of the Roman world. Tombs were the last citadels of Romanitas in a period when the Empire was rapidly disintegrating and Rome receeded into the distance. In the three hundred years since the discovery of the painted burial chambers in 1716, scholars dealt intensely with the question of the religious denomination of the tombs—a difficult task because of the almost complete lack of funerary inscriptions. Inspired by recent theoretical work and new excavation campaigns this paper offers a synthesis of novel scholarly approaches to the Christian funeral topography in Sopianae and indicates avenues of further research.

Sopianae in the Christian Empire

A minor city in Roman Pannonia, Sopianae (Pécs) saw her glory days in Late Antiquity. Prior to the Marcomannic Wars in the first half of the second century, the indigenous settlement composed of several smaller properties and villas was an average provincial vicus. Its spectacular growth started in the Severan period when the small, partially underground homes and workshops were replaced by a Roman city and an organized network of streets with a forum, government buildings, shrines and a bath

---

[1] This paper is an updated version of my „The Late Roman Cemeteries of Sopianae" in E. Tóth – T. Vida – I. Takács (eds.), *Saint Martin and Pannonia. Christianity on the Frontiers of the Roman World. Exhibition catalogue.* (Pannonhalma–Szombathely 2016), 68–76. I thank Marianne Sághy for her revision of the text.

[2] Krisztina Hudák and Levente Nagy, *A Fine and Private Place. Discovering the Early Christian Cemetery of Sopianae/Pécs.*Translated by Marianne Sághy. Pécs: Örökség Kht, 2008. (Henceforth: Hudák-Nagy, A Fine and Private Place.)

in the center. Given the lack of written documents, we can only hypothesize that the settlement must have been raised to the rank of municipium. At the end of the third century, new barbarian attacks on Pannonia Inferior led to Sopianae's partial destruction, followed by ostentatious restoration and recovery in the 270s, evidenced by the repair and construction of urban buildings and by the increasing number of imperial coins issued by Roman emperors originating from neighboring Illyricum.[3] Sopianae became an important transportation hub, best illustrated by the Itinerarium Antonini, a second-third century register of Roman roads. Stemming from the imperial road linking Byzantium (Istanbul) and Augusta Treverorum (Trier), several roads branched out from the city to Pannonian settlements such as Carnuntum (Petronell), Brigetio (Szőny), or Aquincum (Budapest).[4]

In 296, as a result of the Tetrarchy's administrative reform that separated the civil from the military administration, Pannonia Inferior—the eastern region of the former Pannonia provincial—was yet again partitioned along the River Drava to Pannonia Secunda and Pannonia Valeria—named after Emperor Diocletian's daughter, wife of Emperor Galerius. Thecenter of the military administration—presided by a dux of the equestrian order as commander of the provincial army—remained in Aquincum, but the seat of the praeses (also of the equestrian order) must have been transferred to Sopianae. Written evidence is yet again lacking, but two sources offering indirect information support this suggestion. Recent archaeological excavations in the center of Pécs unearthed extensive fourth-century constructions: this led to the hypothesis that the boom of the Roman city—attested by the proliferation of stately villas in the suburbium as well—, must have resulted from Sopianae's political upgrading that caused an influx of administrative officials.[5] Ammianus Marcellinus indirectly reinforces the hypothesis about Sopianae's function as a provincial seat. He mentions Maximinus, a prominent politician executed by Gratianus in 376, who was born in Sopianae (apud Sopianas), to a family of administrators in the office of the praeses (patre tabulario praesidialis

---

[3] Zsolt Visy, "Sopianae története" (History of Sopianae), In: *Pécs története I. Az őskortól a püspökség megalapításáig* (*History of Pécs I. From the Neolithic to the foundation of the bishopric*). (Pécs: PécsTörténete Alapítvány-Kronosz Kiadó 2013), 93–152. (Henceforth: Pécs története).

[4] Endre Tóth, *Itineraria Pannonica. Római utak a Dunántúlon* (Itineraria Pannonica. Roman roads in Transdanubia) (Budapest: Magyar Nemzeti Múzeum, 2006), 53–62.; Magdolna Szilágyi, *On the Road: The History and Archaeology of Medieval Communication Networks in East-Central Europe*. Budapest: Archaeolingua, 2014. It is unlikely that Sopianae replaced Mursa (Osijek) as the seat of provincial assemblies in Pannonia Inferior in the last third of the fourth century, as the city had already some importance.

[5] Excavation reports of Gábor Kárpáti, Zsuzsa Katona Győr, and Olivér Gábor, summarized in: Gábor Kárpáti, "The Roman Settlement of Sopianae," Situla 42 (2004): 279–287.; Gábor Kárpáti and Olivér Gábor, "Régészeti ásatás a Jókai utca 13. számalatt" (Archeological Excavation under Jókai street 13.), Pécsi Szemle VII (2004/3): 11–15.; Visy, "Sopianae".

officii).⁶ The workplace of Maximinus' father must have been also in Sopianae. If so, this means that,in the fourth century, Sopianae was the civil administrative center of Valeria.

Christianity arrived in Pannonia by the second century, but evidence of Christian communities appears only from the mid-third century onwards, particularly during the persecutions of Christians. The acts of the martyrs reveal a great number of Christian congregations whose bishops suffered martyrdom in the cities south of the Drava and attest a large number of Pannonians who were ready to die for Christ. Following the edicts of toleration in 311 and 313, Christianity rapidly spread in Pannonia. Sirmium (Sremska Mitrovica), Poetovio (Ptuj), Siscia (Sisek) and Cibalae (Vinkovci) all had bishops,⁷ but Savaria (Szombathely) and Aquincum (Budapest) also had vigorous Christian congregations. Sopianae' burial chambers and the mausoleum of Iovia (Alsóhetény)⁸ also demonstrate the growing importance of Christianity in the province, a Christianity strongly influenced by Arianism promoted by the emperors in the mid-fourth century. Arius of Alexandria was exiled to Sirmium after the Council of Nicaea in 325, and his teaching quickly spread in the province: the bishops of Mursa (Osijek), Siscia and Singidunum (Belgrade) were the staunchest defenders of the Arian dogma.

If Christian presence in Sopianae is demonstrable from the early fourth century, nothing is known of the city's bishops and ecclesiastical structure.⁹ At the end of the fourth century, when Arianism was on its apex, the representations of Saint Peter and Paul in the burial chambers can be read as markers of the Nicene Catholic "reconquista" of the region led by Damasus of Rome and Ambrose of Milan.¹⁰ No churches were found in Sopianae. A buttressed wall section unearthed near the Roman basilica adjacent to the forum might have been reused in a Christian structure, but the interpretation of the wall is ambiguous. As the wall lays under the main thoroughfare of modern Pécs next to the cardo maximus, it is well-nigh inaccessible. A future excavation may help finding out more about the structure.

---

6   Ammianus Marcellinus, Res gestae XXVIII 1.5.
7   Lajos Nagy, "Pannonia sacra," *Emlékkönyv Szent István király halálának 900. évfordulóján*, ed. Jusztinián Serédi. I. (Budapest: Magyar Tudományos Akadémia, 1938), 31–148; Tibor Nagy, *A pannoniai kereszténység története a római védőrendszer összeomlásáig [History of Christianity in Pannonia until the fall of the Roman limes]*, Dissertationes Pannonicae II/12, Budapest: (1939) 31; Endre Tóth, "Das Christentum in Pannonien bis zum 7. Jahrhundert nach den archäologischen Zeugnissen" in: *Das Christentum im bairischen Raum*, ed. E. Boshof – H. Wolff (Cologne–Weimar–Vienna: Böhlau, 1994), 241–265.
8   Endre Tóth,"Az alsóhetényi 4. századi erőd és temető kutatása, 1981–1986. Eredmények és vitás kérdések" (Excavation of the fourth-century fortress and cemetery in Alsóhetény, 1981–1986. Results and debates), *Archaeológiai Értesítő* 114 (1987–1988) 22–41.
9   Ferenc Fülep, Sopianae. *The History of Pécs during the Roman Era, and the Problem of the Continuity of the Late Roman Population.* Translated by Mrs. István Telegdy. (Budapest: Akadémiai Kiadó,1984), 279–280; Visy, Sopianae.
10 Marianne Sághy, *Versek és vértanúk. A római mártírkultusz Damasus pápa korában*, 366–384. [Poems and Martyrs. Bishop Damasus of Rome and The Cult of theMartyrs, A. D. 366–384.] (Budapest: Kairosz, 2003).

Where are the Christians in the Late Roman Cemeteries?

The Roman roads radiating from Sopianae were lined with tombs. The largest and earliest graveyard on a hillside in the North was opened in the second or third century, containing more than a thousand graves. The earliest burials took place in the eastern part of the cemetery, the later ones in the western section. The burial chambers and various sepulchral buildings are clustered in the western-northwestern corner.[11] The different groupings of graves, the sepulchral buildings and the various artefacts found in the cemetery reveals the history, the customs and rituals, and occasionally the ethnic characteristics of the population. Only a few artefacts and burial habits suggest, however, that the deceased was pagan or Christian. Christian grave goods and representations raise the question whether the deceased professed the Nicene Catholic or the Arian faith. How deeply did the Christians of Sopianae understand their faith? Did they profess it out of personal choice or conformism? What were their perspectives on life and life after death?

Inhumation of the dead was typical in the Late Roman period. The body was placed in an outstretched position, oriented to the West, in a coffin-like box. The lid was assembled from bricks, less often from stone slabs or stones (fig. 1). Wooden coffins must have been common, but they did not survive. Sarcophagi were rare (fig.2). In some cemeteries, earthen graves appear in differing proportions, when presumably the dead body was only rolled in a blanket. Among the grave goods, clothing, belts and fibulae, jewelry such as bracelets, rings and earrings are common. Dishes are typical grave goods, and a variety of other remains have been found, reflecting the rich fabric of Sopianae's Late Roman society.

Differentiating between pagan and Christian graves is not easy. The difficulty lies in the fact that the two burial cultures, pagan and Christian diverge in Pannonia, enduring pagan rites merge with early Christian burial practices. A general feature of Christian burials seems to be their "puritanism," a restraint in depositing grave goods. This may, however, be also connected with the economic background of the deceased or the sparse burial customs of the poorer layers of society. The clasping of hands and arms might indicate Christian belief, but without sufficient evidence, this posture hardly reveals the faith of the deceased. Pitchers and cups in the grave might symbolize the Eucharist, but these objects were frequent accessories in pagan graves as well and thus cannot be used as definitive proof of the presence of Christians. Unfortunately, inscriptions wane and nearly disappear the Late Roman period. Few fourth-century grave-

---

[11] Zsuzsa Katona Győr, „Temetkezési szokások a római kori Sopianaeban." (Burial customs in Roman Sopianae), In: *Pécs története*, 153–194; Olivér Gábor, „Sopianae ókeresztény temetőjének épületei." (Building Structures in Sopianae's Early Christian Cemetery) in *Pécs története*, 195–222. In this paper, I rely on Olivér Gábor's conclusions.

Figure 1. Brick grave with gabled roof and plastered interior. The grave was broken into in a later period. © O. Gábor

Figure 2. Burial Chamber XX, secondary burial with painted interior, trellis motif and a Christogram in a triangle, above the head of the deceased. © Zs. Visy

Figure 3. The single buried sarcophagus discovered in the cemetery of Sopianae.© Zs. Visy

Figure 4. Burial Chamber II, surviving foundation walls of the burial chapel built above the crypt. © A.Török

Figure 5. Burial chamber XX was plastered, but unpainted. The grave is against the back wall, two secondary graves to the right and left made with different building methods. © Zs. Visy

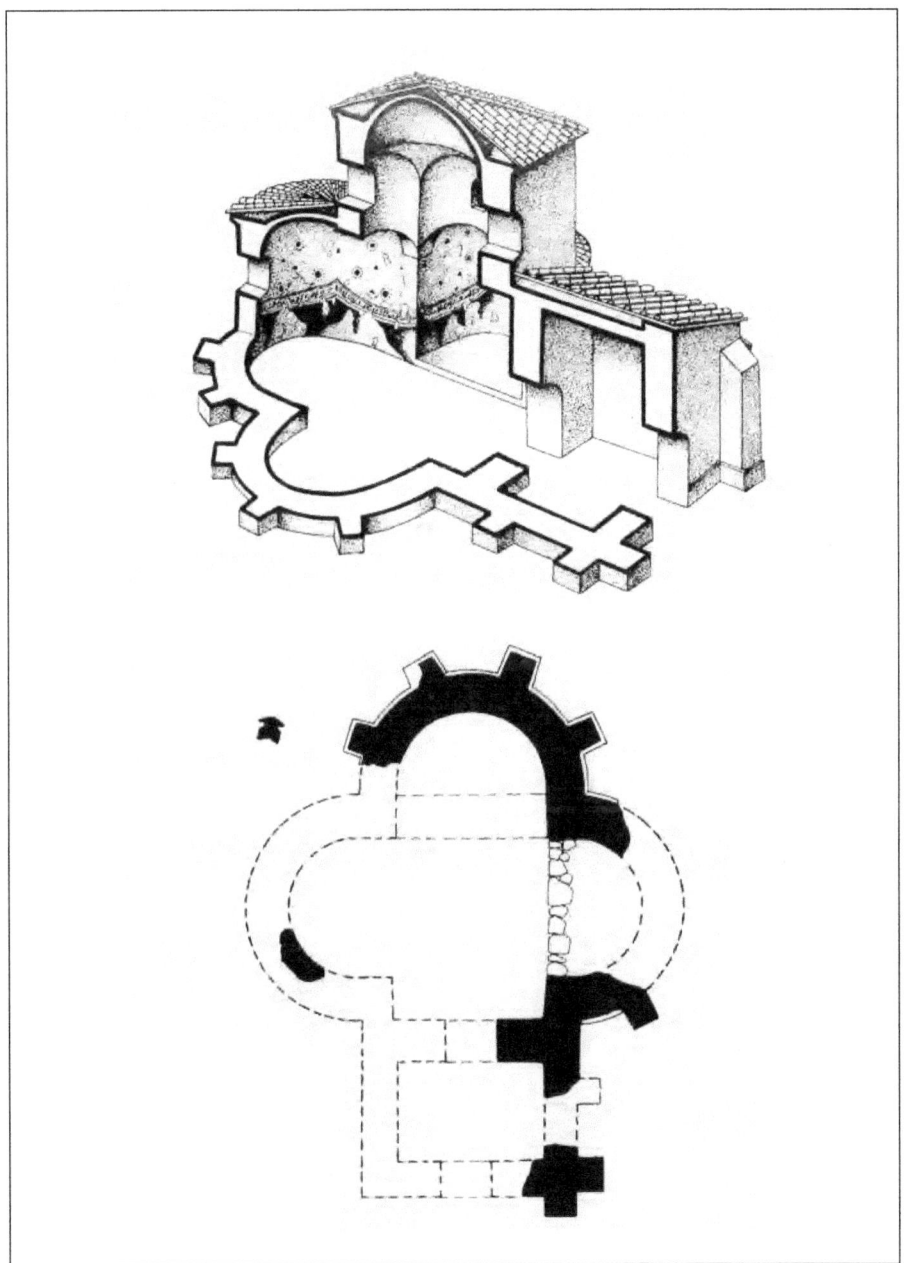

Figure 6. Ground plan and reconstruction of Burial Chamber XXXI (cella trichora.)
© Janus Pannonius Múzeum

Figure 7. Burial Chamber V with two secondary columns in the middle of the octagonal space, showing the brick foundation in the opposite corner and the vaulting rib partially covering an earlier wall niche. © Zs. Visy

Figure 8. Reconstruction of Burial Chamber XXXII (cella septichora). The building extends into the hillside to a depth of 2 to 5 meters. The drawing shows the 1.5-meter stairway down to the entrance on the western side.
© Zs. Visy– K. Szijártó

Figure 9. Burial Chamber XXXII (cella septichora), during excavation. The limestone floor is was created during the construction. On the left, the pile of lime in the apse was intended for plastering the interior, but this was never done. © Zs. Visy

Figure 10. Burial Chamber I (Saint Peter and Saint Paul burial chamber), back wall with niche and remains of the grave's side walls (later destroyed). The wall is decorated with garlands, in the center the Christogram is celebrated by Saint Peter and Saint Paul with outstretched arms. © A.Török

Figure 11. Burial Chamber I (Saint Peter and Saint Paul burial chamber), ceiling. The Garden of Eden with a Christogram in the middle and medallions with male busts in the four corners, amidst evergreens, vine and floral motifs, peacocks and doves.© A.Török

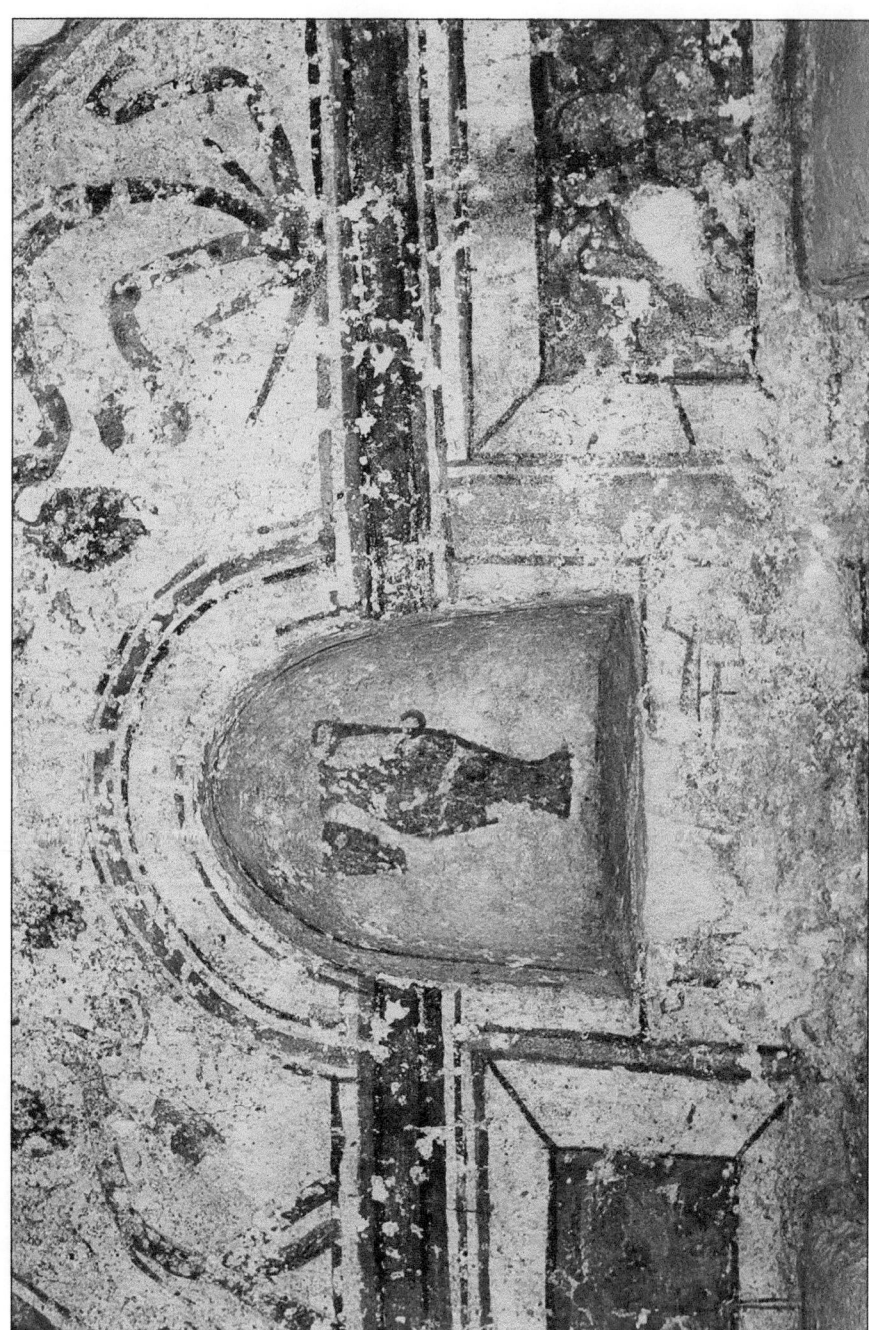

Figure 12. Burial Chamber II, back wall of the crypt with false marble, floral motifs, a jar and a cup. © I. Füzi

Figure 13. Burial Chamber XXXIII (mausoleum) northern wall, Adam and Eve under the Tree of Life with the snake.© I. Füzi

Figure 14. Burial Chamber XXXIII (mausoleum), northern wall, Daniel in the lions' den. © I. Füzi

stones and only a handful of Early Christian grave inscriptions were found in Pannonia, none in Sopianae. The dearth of written records makes extremely difficult to assess and interpret the cemeteries and graves. Most likely, those burials that contain objects with Christian symbols are Christian. The most common marker is the Christogram, appearing on fibulae, rings and wall paintings. This symbol was generally applied to the object when it was made, thus the person who bought and wore it was presumably Christian. The Christian identity of the owner is all the more certain if the symbol was engraved or etched on the item later because it reflects the owner's conscious decision Fibulae, spoons and dishes decorated with the bust of a youthful male form a separate category. This representation, rooted in the imperial cult as well as in biblical tradition, is sometimes a Christian marker, sometimes not.

Among the various funerary structures in Sopianae, the painted burial chambers are without exception Early Christian. The topographical context allows for linking the similarly structured and executed sepulchral buildings with the numerous excavated graves in the same section of the cemetery, filling in the space between the burial chambers. The western section of Sopianae's northern cemetery is to be considered an Early Christian cemetery, in contrast to the city's eastern cemetery, where no sepulchral buildings have been found. It seems that the city's Christian and non-Christian populations used different cemeteries and different sections in the cemeteries.

The interior of the brick or stone coffins in the sealed graves of Sopianae's northern cemetery is often plastered or whitewashed. The graves found in the burial chambers explain why it is so. The coffins were not only whitewashed but painted: a grave in Burial Chamber XX preserves a trellis motif and Christogram (fig. 3), just like in the twin-graves G/1–2.[12] These symbols allude to eternal happiness in Paradise after the resurrection in the closeness of Christ.[13] This practice cannot be found among pagan burials in Pannonia, consequently graves with a painted or whitewashed interior are considered Christian.

Christian Burial Chambers

The Early Christian cemetery of Sopianae contains a large variety of sepulchral buildings, classified according to size, style and function: one or two storey, made for the burial of one or more people, burial chambers, crypts, mausolea. As the walls of the burial chambers must have been painted, fresco decoration does not constitute

---

[12] Ferenc Fülep, "Sopianae," *Archaeologia Hungarica* 50 (1984): 76–77. Fig 23; Plate XLII.
[13] Zsolt Visy, "A Paradicsom Sopianae ókeresztény temetőjében" [The Paradise in the early Christian cemetery of Sopianae], in *Európé égisze alatt. Ünnepi tanulmányok Fekete Mária hatvanötödik születésnapjára barátaitól, kollégáitól és tanítványaitól.* László Vilmos, Ernő Szabó, Zoltán Csabai, Adrienn Vitári-Wéber *eds.((Pécs: L'Harmattan Kiadó, 2015), 421–437.

a distinguishing criteria. The orientation of the larger funerary buildings ones is along an east-west axis, with the entrance on the western side. The smaller ones—originally designed for just one corpse—are oriented north-south, with the entrance on the southern side. The entrance of unusual one-story structures with distinctive ground plans—octagonal or with multi-apsed—is also on the southern side. Since the orientation of the first graves in every burial chamber was east-west, unsurprisingly, most chambers had the same positioning. The strong southern slope of the area explains triggered the north-south orientation of the new burial chambers. As these were generally two-storied, the door of the surface burial chapel (*cella memoriae*) was directly above the crypt (hypogaeum); thus this alignment was the easiest and simplest. (fig. 4) It is important to emphasize that in these crypts, the coffin laid always along the east-west axis. (fig. 5) This is true for the octagonal chamber as well. Due to later disturbances in the ground, it is impossible to determine the original layout of the burial chambers with three apses. The entrance to Burial Chamber XXVII was to the east. This barrel-vaulted chamber, designed for two people, lies four meters below today's surface and has two recessed wall niches in its western wall. Its great depth suggests it had a *cella memoriae* above it, but no traces of it have been identified.

The majority of the burial chambers were designed for one person, but consisted of two units. A narrow descent dug into the ground led to the crypt, several square meters in size, and in some cases a narthex was built in front of the crypt's entrance. This descending passageway was refilled after the burial with loose rocks that prevented the earth from caving into the chamber.[14] Above the door to the crypt opened the entrance to the *cella memoriae*. The burial chapel was larger than the crypt, and each structure had its own walls. The burial chapels usually terminated in a semi-circular apse, some had a straight terminating wall. The interior of the crypt in many cases was plastered and whitewashed or painted with biblical scenes. Little remained of the walls of the surface structures, so it is impossible to know the way they were decorated: fresco fragments found nearby suggest that the upper chapels were also painted.

The mausoleum of Sopianae is an idiosyncratic construction. Oriented on an east-west axis, its burial chapel is much larger than the others. From the burial chamber, a stairway led to the narthex and crypt below. It must have been the burial place of a particularly distinguished person given not only its size but the exceptionally beautiful painting of the crypt, represent Adam and Eve under the Tree of Life (fig. 13) and the

---

[14] Zsolt Visy, "Újabb adatok a pécsi ókeresztény sírépítmények szerkezeti felépítéséhez" [New Evidence on the Structure of the Early Christian Burial Buildings at Pécs], *Archeologiai Értesítő* 132 (2007): 111–12; idem, "Recent Data on the Structure of the Early Christian Burial Buildings at Pécs," *Acta Classica Universitatis Scientiae Debreceniensis* XLIII (2007): 137–155.)

enormous marble sarcophagus placed in it during construction work. Unfortunately, the mausoleum, together with two later graves were destroyed during the Great Migration.[15]

The three-apsed structure excavated in the Rose Garden of Pécs was also two stories.[16] The upper burial chapel had a barrel vault and semi domes. The walls were reinforced with buttresses to support the weight and counteract sideway forces. The small crypt was presumably designed for one person, but disturbances to the soil have erased any traces. Excavation results show that there was no crypt under the three-apsed Burial Chamber XXXI. It was used in the early Middle Ages as a church. While the floor level of this burial chapel must have matched the exterior elevation at the southern entrance, the floor level of the three-apsed burial chamber was adjusted to the higher level near the northern wall. Due to the buttresses, these buildings rose above surface. In the light of this building, it is strange that the *cella trichora* unearthed in the south-western corner of Pécs Cathedral had no crypt beneath it (fig. 6).

The dead were buried deep underground in the one-story sepulchral structures with an interior space deep of 1.5 meters. The one-story regular octagonal building had to be entered by heading downwards to a level lower than the entrance way (fig. 7). Its walls extended beneath the upward slope, yet the building stood out from its surroundings. Despite later reconstructions, the grave at the base of the northern wall and the niche above—a typical feature of crypts—remained.

The seven-apsed Burial Chamber XXXII (*cella septichora*) as well as Burial Chamber XVI were designed for multiple burials, evidenced by the simpler one-story structure located to the south of the lavishly decorated burial chamber among the simpler graves. Positioned on a north-south axis, sunken beneath the ground to shoulder height, the barrel vaulted chamber contained fourteen graves in two rows.[17] The seven-apsed Burial Chamber is 23 meters long, this is the largest of Sopianae's known funerary buildings (figs. 8–9). Its distinctive ground plan is construed by a partial overlap of two pentagons. The entrance opens at the place of the eighth apse on the eastern side. Sunk 2–5 meters into the steep slope, an external stairway leading to the entrance was designed to bridge the 1.5-meter difference in elevation. The building is unfinished, as it is shown by its interior: the lack of roof bricks indicate that it has never been roofed. Consequently, no burial was found in this building.[18]

---

[15] The mausoleum was excavated by Ferenc Fülep, see Ferenc Fülep, Zoltán Bachman and Attila Pintér, *Sopianae-Pécs ókeresztény emlékei* (The Early Christian monuments of Sopianae-Pécs), (Budapest: Képzőművészeti Kiadó, 1988).

[16] Zsolt Tóth – Csaba Pozsárkó, "Újabb ókeresztény sírkápolna Sopianaeből" (A newly discovered early Christian burial chamber from Sopianae), Ókor (2012/I), 97–106.

[17] Ferenc Fülep, "Sopianae," *Archaeologia Hungarica* 50, Budapest: (1984): 79–81.

[18] Zsolt Visy, „Cella septichora. Előzetes beszámoló a Szent István téren, az ókeresztény temető területén folytatott régészeti kutatásokról" (Cella septichora. Preliminary report of the archaeological research in the territory of the early Christian cemetery under Szent István Square), PécsiSzemle IX/1 (2006) 3–13.; Csaba Pozsárkó et

The greatest attraction of the Early Christian cemetery of Sopianae are the painted burial chambers.[19] Several, if not all burial chambers must have been painted, but only the wall paintings of Burial Chambers I and II and the crypt of the mausoleum survived as a whole or in fragments. Burial Chamber I dedicated to the Apostles Saint Peter and Paul boasts with the most intact fresco decoration and a rich iconography. The lavish floral decoration on the entrance wall, the series of allegories of the Garden of Eden on the ceiling and the Christogram in the center, surrounded by the busts of four young men allude to the Resurrection and salvation in Heaven (fig. 10–11). The four young men, perhaps, stand for an allegory of the blessed. On the wall opposite the entrance, Saint Peter and Paul flank the niche in the wall and the Christogram above it. Three Biblical scenes decorate the lower half of the vaulting on both sides: seriously damaged, the images are barely discernible. The Fall (Adam and Eve with the snake), Daniel in the lions' den, and Jonah under the ivy tree are represented on the eastern wall; on the western wall, the Virgin Mary with Christ, the three Magi (or the three young men in the furnace), and Noah with the ark. The iconography of the fresco cycle focuses on the theology of resurrection and salvation, to prepare the deceased who died in the hope of the resurrection, for the joy of Heaven. Once the corpse was placed in the crypt, it was closed with stone slabs—still there at the discovery of the Burial Chamber in 1782[20]— never to be opened. The same is true for the paintings found in crypts or in the interior of the graves. The twin graves G 1/2 are a case in point.

As the ceiling of Burial Chamber II collapsed, only the paintings on the side walls survived: a trellis motif (perhaps alluding to the closure of the Garden of Eden), and two empty medallions suggesting that the decoration was not completed. In the niche, a pitcher and a cup are represented—this is perhaps the most debated painting in Sopianae. Elsewhere in the cemetery, real-life jars and cups were found placed in the graves. The representation of the jar in this prominent location may refer to the Eucharist (fig. 12) just as well as to pagan libations. If the fresco on its own cannot be interpreted as Christian, the topography of the burial chamber allows to identify it as Christian, because the tomb stands in the early Christian part of the cemetery. The burial chamber deploys the same techniques and structure as the other Early Christian monuments. The decorative motifs found in Burial Chamber II appear in the pictorial repertoire displayed in the other crypts.

The crypt of the mausoleum (Burial Chamber XXXIII) was lavishly decorated with wall paintings, the embedded columns (later torn down) and arch had colorful

---

al., "Sopianae: a cella septichora és környéke. Beszámoló a 2005–2006. évi régészeti feltárásról" (Sopianae: the cella septichora and its surroundings. Report of the archaeological excavation from 2005–2006.) *Ókor* VI/3 (2007), 84–90

[19] Hudák-Nagy, *A Fine and Private Place*.
[20] József Koller, Prolegomena in historiam episcopatus Quinqueecclesiarum, (Posonii, 1804) 25–26.

patterns. A sarcophagus was placed in the crypt before the fresco decoration, the area behind it remained unpainted. The northern wall, however, has well-preserved scenes of the Fall and Daniel among the lions (fig. 14). A Christogram was placed above the wall niche, next to it a fragment shows the foot of a (sitting?) figure—perhaps that of Christ?—in white clothes. The interpretation of the fragment is debated.

The analysis of the graves and grave goods shows that the cemetery was in use in the fourth and fifth centuries. Despite the lack of written evidence, it seems that the burial chambers were constructed the second half of the fourth century, perhaps as late as the last third of the century. There are discussions whether the representation of ivy leaves instead of gourd on the image of the resting Jonah can be used for the dating of Burial Chamber I. Saint Jerome replaced the traditional "gourd" with "ivy" in his new Latin translation of the Bible in 389/390–2. If the ivy in the crypt drew inspiration from Jerome's translation, the cycle should be dated to the very end of the fourth century.[21] Indirect evidence helps dating the cellaseptichora to this period as well. The building remained unfinished, its well-to-do commissioner either died or moved at the beginning of the fifth century, during the German raids ravaging the province.[22] If Valeria recovered,[23] Sopianae decayed: its impoverished citizens were unable to finish interrupted building projects. This hypothesis would date the burial chambers to the last decade of the fourth century.

Life in the burial chambers did not end with the funeral of the deceased. Funerary banquets and annual family commemoration of the dead followed. In Sopianae, almost each crypt contains additional burials, shown by the different material and structure of the coffins. At a later date, perhaps in the fifth century, the burial chambers were expanded and transformed into funerary chapels: a row of columns was built in front of Burial Chamber I and the neighboring octagonal Burial Chamber V. A tympanum topping the row of columns accentuated the entrance to the funerary structure. The interior of Burial Chamber V was revamped: two brick columns were erected in the center and four corners were narrowed to allow the construction of a brick cross vaulting. (fig. 7) A third phase of construction took place somewhat later when the vaulting collapsed: the columns were then torn down, and the floor was considerably raised. The

---

[21] Jonah 4:5–11. See György Heidl, "A pécsi 1. számú sírkamra Jónás-freskója és Szt. Jeromos Jónás-kommentárja" (The Jonah-fresco in Burial Chamber I in Pécs and Saint Jerome's Commentary on Jonah), *Katekhón* 2 (2005): 221–235; Krisztina Hudák, "The Iconographical Program of the Wallpaintings in the Saint Peter and Paul Burial Chamber of Sopianae (Pécs)," *Mitteilungen zur Christlichen Archäologie* 15 (2009): 47–76.

[22] András Mócsy, Pannonia. *Pauly-Wissowa Realencyklopädie des Altertumswissenschaft*, Suppl. IX, 1962, 580–582.

[23] Zsolt Visy, "Megjegyzések Valeria védelmi rendszereinek kérdéséhez." (Notes on the defence systems of Valeria) *Antik Tanulmányok* 25 (1978), 246–252; Zsolt Visy, "Adatok Valeria provincia katonai szervezetének kérdéséhez" (On the military organization of Valeria province) *Jelenkor* (2001): 1167–1168; Endre Tóth, "Sopianae a késő császárkorban" (Sopianae in the Late Empire), *Jelenkor* (2001): 1135.

date of the later construction periods is unknown, the last construction campaign might have taken place after the founding of the bishopric of Pécs in 1009 by King Stephen of Hungary. A painting on the foundation wall of the cella trichora, a burial chamber consecrated as a church in the eleventh century shows that the structure was in use at that time. The location of the Cathedral of Pécs in the north-western part of the Roman cemetery, in the vicinity of the ruined, but still standing early Christian burial chapels must have been a conscious choice of the leaders of the church and of the freshly Christianized Hungarian state. While the ruins of Sopianae were still standing above ground, the bishop chose the cemetery area at a distance from the Roman city as his headquarters, as if to reuse a once sacred place. This was, however, more than pragmatic spoliation and "ruin continuity." The decision to locate the bishopric in the cemetery as well as the choice of the patron saints of the bishopric of Pécs—Saint Peter and Saint Paul—might have been directly inspired by the fresco paintings in the burial chambers. What is more, the medieval cathedral was likely built upon a sizeable Roman sepulchral building, thereby it integrated spiritually as well as physically Sopianae's early Christian heritage into the ecclesiastical structure of medieval Quinqueeclesie.

SOPIANAE REVISITED: PAGAN OR CHRISTIAN BURIALS?[1]

Olivér Gábor and Zsuzsa Katona Győr

The Roman cemetery of Sopianae[2] (Pécs in Southern Hungary) is one of the few extant Late Antique burial sites in Europe.[3] Its intricate layout and the exquisite decoration of its burial chambers have intrigued scholars ever since its discovery in the late eighteenth century. Because of its fresco paintings—representing Christograms, the Virgin Mary, and the Apostles Saint Peter and Saint Paul—nineteenth-and twentieth-century scholarship identified the cemetery as 'Christian.'[4] Ongoing archaeological excavation and revisionist scholarship, however, triggered the reassessment of the site. Recent archaeological research estimates only a handful of the burial chambers Christian.[5] On the basis of research conducted on five hundred two Roman inhumation graves excavated in five groups in the northern cemetery of Sopianae and in the cemetery on Czindery Street,[6] this paper presents novel interpretations of the Roman graveyard along with new archaeological finds, focusing on the thorny problem of how

---

[1] The authors would like to express their gratitude to Marianne Sághy for her critical remarks and helpful suggestions during the successive stages of edition of this paper.

[2] Sopianae developed from several small Celtic settlements into a Roman town by the second century. At the beginning of the third century, it became an autonomous Roman *municipium* in Pannonia Province. At the end of the fourth century, when Pannonia was divided into four smaller provinces, Sopianae became the administrative capital of Valeria Province in the Northeastern part of Pannonia.

[3] Ferenc Fülep, *Sopianae. The History of Pécs during the Roman Era, and the Problem of the Continuity of the Late Roman Population*. Translated by Mrs. István Telegdy. (Budapest: Akadémiai Kiadó,1984); idem, „A pécsi későrómai ókeresztény mauzoleum feltárásáról." [On the Excavation of the Late Roman Early Christian Mausoleum of Pécs.] *Janus Pannonius Múzeum Évkönyvei* 32. 1987 31–44., Krisztina Hudák and Levente Nagy, *A Fine and Private Place*. Translated by Marianne Sághy. (Pécs: Örökség Ház, 2008), 7–8; Zsolt Visy (ed.), *Pécs története* [The History of Pécs], Pécs: Pécs Története Alapítvány–Kronosz Kiadó, 2013.

[4] Josephus Koller, Prolegomena, *Historiam Episcopatus Quinqueecclesiarum*. Posonii, 1804.

[5] Wolfgang Schmidt, "Spätantike Gräberfelder in den Nordprovinzen des Römischen Reiches und das aufkommen christlichen Bestattungsbrauchtums." *Saalburg Jahrbuch* (50) 2000, 213–440.

[6] These groups are not 'natural' groups: the excavations were limited by the size of the area available for digging.

to distinguish pagan and Christian burials at a site where inscriptions and written evidence are notoriously lacking.

Criteria of Research

To begin our research, we identified a number of criteria that archaeologists usually associate with religious belief. These criteria are as follows:

TOPOGRAPHY AND CHRONOLOGY

The Late Antique cemetery of Sopianae, once laying outside the Roman town, is now situated under and around the cathedral and the surrounding area that was once the site of the medieval town of Quinque Basilicae / Quinque Ecclesiae. Today, the cemetery area is delimited by Dóm Square– Szent István Square—Apáca Street—Széchenyi Square—Káptalan Street.[7] In the third and fourth century, the cemetery of Sopianae expanded from the southeast to the northeast (today's Széchenyi Square).[8] In 2002, archeologists discovered graves dated to the third century in the courtyard of the Nagy Lajos High School, where cremation and inhumation were both practiced. In the northern part of the cemetery (Székesfehérvár Street and Káptalan Street), however, only inhumations were found, thus this section was dated to the third-fourth centuries.[9] By the fourth century, the cemetery reached the southwest part of what is today Szent István's Square: the graves excavated near the cathedral date from the second half to the third quarter of the fourth century.[10] In addition to simple graves, gable-roofed brick burial structures—symbols of the *domus aeterna*, the eternal repose of the dead—stone sarcophagi and painted burial chambers were found here. The third-century southeastern cemetery must have been pagan, while the fourth-century northeastern cemetery was used by pagans and Christians alike. Christians might have sought to separate their graves from pagan ones, yet pagan and Christian graves lay next to each

---

[7] Zsuzsa Katona Győr, *Pécs (Sopianae) Early Christian Cemetery into the UNESCO World Heritage List. Management Plan*. Pécs, 2000–2001, 26. (hereafter: Katona Győr)

[8] Ferenc Fülep – Alice Burger, "Baranya megye a római korban." [Baranya County in the Roman Period] In: Gábor Bándi (ed.): *Baranya megye története az őskortól a honfoglalásig*. [The History of Baranya County from the Paleolithicum to the Hungarian Conquest] Pécs: Baranya megyei Levéltár, 1979, 223–328; Fülep 1984, 174; Katona Győr 2000–2001.

[9] Tibor Nagy, "Sopianae – Egy új városmonográfia margójára." [Sopianae—On a New Monography of a Roman Town] *Antik Tanulmányok* XXXIII (1987–88), 218–245. dated the graves around Burial Chambers VIII and IX at Szent István Square to the end of the third-beginning of the fourth century. Zsuzsa Katona Győr, however, dates an infant's tomb found in the segment of the cemetery on Székesfehérvár Street to the second century, on the basis of a coin minted in 138–143 and placed in the tomb (Katona Győr 2000–2001, 30).

[10] Fülep 1984, 159–161. János Kraft, *A pécsi ókeresztény temető geológiája és felszínének fejlődése*. [The Geology of the Early Christian Cemetery of Pécs]. Pécs: Örökségi Füzetek, 2006, 46–72.

other. At the beginning of the fourth century, Christians used only a small section of the cemetery, but within a century, the Christian graves expanded all over the graveyard.

CREMATION

Cremation is not a Christian burial custom.[11] In Sopianae, three different types of cremation burials came to light so far. Scattered cremation burials can be dated to the early phase of the cemetery, second and third centuries.[12] No grave goods were found in the graves. A *bustum* burial (on-the-site cremation) dated to the turn of the second and third century was unearthed under burial chamber XVII in Nagy Lajos High School on Széchenyi Square. Two fourth-century urn graves with crossbow brooches in them were excavated.[13] These three types of cremation graves seem to be the last archaeological remains of the pagan population that survived here until the fourth century. Due to the lack of scattered cremation burials and also the almost complete absence of burnished pottery, other objects (such as iron mounted wooden buckets[14]) and burial features (such as niche graves[15] and stone slab covered graves) need to be examined so as to identify the graves of different ethnic groups that arrived in the province from outside the Roman Empire in the fourth century.[16]

CROUCHED POSITION

This position was common in graves until the end of the Bronze Age, but by the fourth century, became rare. Skeletons buried in this position are thought to have been slaves from outside the Roman Empire. Several ethnic groups had settled in Pannonia during the fourth century, among them the Carpi coming from East of the Carpathian Mountains, who cremated their dead.[17] The crouched position was also common in the graves of Sarmatians. The graves found around Sopianae with skeletons in a crouched

---

[11] Jewish and Christian cremations are very ancient and very rare: David Noy, "Where were of the Jews of the Diaspora buried?" In: M. Goodmann (ed), *Jews in a Graeco–Roman world*. Oxford: Oxford University Press, 1998, 75–89; W. H. C. Frend, *The archaeology of early Christianity*. London: 1996 370; Volp 2002. 107. At the beginning of the second century, inhumation spread throughout the Roman Empire and cremation gradually disappeared. The number of inhumation burials increases in Pannonia from the beginning of the third century. Inhumation burials as such, however, cannot be considered exclusively Christian.

[12] The body was cremated elsewhere (*ustrinum*) and the ashes were subsequently scattered into a grave.

[13] In the northern outskirts of Sopianae two fourth-century urn graves came to light: Károly Sonkoly, "Római kori hamvasztásos urnasír Pécs belvárosában." [Roman Urn Grave in the center of Pécs.] In: *Janus Pannonius Múzeum Évkönyvei* 27 (1982), 117–123).

[14] Grave 108 in the yard of Nagy Lajos High School.

[15] Niche graves were rare in the cemeteries of Sopianae, only one was discovered in Czindery Street.

[16] János Dombay, *Későrómai temetők Baranyában*. [Late Roman Cemeteries in Baranya County] Pécs: Janus Pannonius Múzeum, 1957; Vera Lányi, "Die spätantiken Gräberfelder von Pannonien." *Acta Archaeologica Hungarica* 24 (1972), 53–213; Fülep, 1984.

[17] Gheorghe Bichir, "La civilisation des Carpes (Iie–IIIe siècle de n.È.)." *Dacia* 11 (1967). 177–224.

position may be connected to Germanic settlers or local servants. Crouched skeletons were found in fourth-century graves at the Nagy Lajos High School site in 2002 and at Kossuth Square in 2008.[18]

INHUMATED BODIES IN SUPINE POSITION

The practice of burying bodies in a supine position originates from the Eastern provinces and spread from the second century onwards. The orientation and the position of the body in the grave was held to be Christian.[19] In a few cases, grave goods do indicate Christian beliefs,[20] but both pagans and Christians used this burial rite, so it cannot be attributed to Christians alone.[21]

WEST-EAST ORIENTATION OF THE GRAVES

The dead were buried with their head to the West, their face to the East from the second half of the fourth century. In the Christian section of the Roman cemetery of Sopianae, ordinary graves had been oriented west-east.

NON-ORIENTED GRAVES

Non-oriented graves are Christian when the burial takes place inside burial chambers. Outside graves with orientations other than west-east are more likely to be pagan in the second half of the fourth century. This is not overruled by the *depositio ad sanctos* at Burial Chamber V, because the graves are oriented west-east even there.

DINING SETS[22]

Depositioning food and drink into graves reflect eastern influences in second-century Pannonia, as shown by the tripod-scenes on gravestones.[23] These carvings

---

[18] Zsolt Tóth, "Pécs, Kossuth tér." In: *Régészeti kutatások Magyarországon* (2009) 2010A Bp. 310; idem, *Pécs, Rákóczi út 52–56.* In: Régészeti kutatások Magyarországon (2009) 2010B Budapest. 310–311.

[19] Eszter B. Vágó – István Bóna, *Der spätrömische Südostfriedhof. Die Gräberfelder von Intercisa* I. Budapest: 1976, 207.

[20] Schmidt 2000, 288.

[21] Schmidt 2000, 321.

[22] Endre Tóth, "A pogány és keresztény Sopianae" [Sopianae Pagan and Christian] *Specimina Nova* XX (2006), 82. These items are spindle sticks (called earlier meat skewers): Zsuzsa Katona Győr, „Temetkezési szokások a római kori Sopianaeban." [Burial Customs in Roman Sopianae] In: *Pécs története* I, ed. Zsolt Visy. Pécs: Pécs Története Alapítvány-Kronosz Kiadó, 192.

[23] László Barkóczi, „A keletpannoniai sírsztélék ábrázolásainak délkeleti és keleti kapcsolatai" [The South-Eastern and Eastern Connections of the Images on Eastern-Pannonian Grave Stelae] *Archeológiai Értesítő* 109 (1982), 18–49; Peter Noelke – Bernd Kibilka – Dorothee Kemper, "Zu den Grabreliefs mit Darstellung des convivium coniugale im römischen Germanien und im benachbarten Gallien." *Bonner Jahrbücher* 205 (2005), 155–241; Endre Tóth, 2006, 76–78.

show funerary banquets with glasses raised to the dead. In a slightly faded wall painting of a third-century grave in Plovdiv, Bulgaria a burial feast can be seen: a woman with a wine jug (*oenochoe*) alongside with two men next to a sofa (*kline*).[24] The painting is dated to the third century, thus it cannot be early Christian. Christians often put food on the top of graves, a practice prohibited by the Synod of Braga in 572.

FUNERARY BANQUETS

Funerary banquets can only be considered pagan if they took place in the open air, not at the burial place. Eating and drinking at funerals was a symbolic act for Christians. Food prepared outside the cemeteries was consumed by the grave The ceremony was held at the place designated for this occasion. In contrast, pagans often cooked the banquet meal in the cemetery under the open sky (indicated by traces of fire smaller than cremation sites; no pit is connected to them and no burnt pieces of bones or grave goods were found). Several burnt areas, possibly traces of pagan funeral feast preparations, were discovered among the graves at the Nagy Lajos High School site.

PAGAN RELIGIOUS IMAGES

Do pagan religious images in the grave mean that these graves are not Christian? In a grave at Apáca Street (in the middle of the Roman cemetery, east of the Christian centre) a statuette of Mercury came to light. Is it an indicator of a non-Christian owner of the grave?[25]

CHRISTIAN IMAGES

The Christian meaning of an image is often questioned, even when the object was found in a Christian environment (such as the floral decoration in Burial Chamber I).[26] It is not always possible to define if a design is Christian or not. Christian symbols may appear in pagan environments. Non-religion specific symbols are as follow:

- Christogram (Burial Chamber I, Mausoleum, Cella Septichora)
- Peacock (Burial Chamber I).
- Dove (Burial Chamber I).
- Grapevine, garlands, floral motifs (Burial Chambers I–II).
- Painted wreaths, ribbons (Burial Chambers I. and XXXIII).
- Palm (Burial Chamber I and XXXIII).

---

[24] Renate Pillinger – Vanja Popova – Barbara Zimmermann, *Corpus der spätantiken und frühchristlichen Wandmalereien Bulgariens*. Wien: 1999. 42–46.
[25] Fülep 1984, 278.
[26] Schmidt 2000, 292.

- Painted jug and beaker (Burial Chamber II). These symbols were used in both pagan and Christian rites
- Painted candelabra (Burial Chamber I).
- Trellis/fence (Burial Chamber II, the eastern grave of Burial Chamber XX and the G/1–2 twin graves).[27]
- Geometric pattern (Burial Chambers I–II, X Cemetery building XXXIII).

PORTRAITS OF THE DEAD

Pagans and Christians alike represented their dead. Portraits abound on Graeco-Roman gravestones and banquet reliefs. In Sopianae, the sitting figure on the eastern wall of the mausoleum (Burial Chamber XXXIII) and the busts in medallions on the vault of the Saint Peter and Saint Paul burial chamber (Burial Chamber I) might be portraits of persons buried there. These portraits can only be considered Christian in this setting, otherwise nothing differentiates them from Classical portraiture.

GRAVE GOODS

Grave goods were discouraged by the Church Fathers, yet Christians also deposited grave goods in the graves of the deceased.[28]

CLOTHING

The dead were laid into their graves dressed up, decorated with jewels and dress accessories such as rings, bracelets, brooches, buckles, needles, combs. Unless decorated with Christian symbols, these objects are considered religiously neutral.

PITCHER AND DRINKING GLASS

Drinking vessels symbolize afterlife. Pitchers and glasses with the inscription 'pie zeses' (grave R/192 at Széchenyi Square)[29] can be either pagan or Christian.[30] Pottery objects or food containers cannot exclusively be regarded as pagan. In Sopianae, glass vessels are frequent grave goods, placed near the lower limbs. In fourth-century graves of Sopiane, several long scent bottles, empty or filled with some substance, were

---

[27] It could refer to either the borders of the pagan Elysium or the Christian Paradise, just like the phoenix or peacock allude to the afterlife.
[28] A large number of glass jugs and scent bottles came to light in west-east oriented graves around Burial Chamber XIII. Although these objects were also found in pagan graves, due to the close proximity to a Christian building Ferenc Fülep came to the conclusion that these graves were Christian. (Fülep 1984, 154).
[29] Fülep 1984, 67.
[30] Hudák – Nagy 2008, 13. In Pannonia, only one glass jug decorated with gold foil was found with a Christian inscription: *accipe vivas in Deo*. See Barkóczi László, *Pannonische Glasfunde in Ungarn*. 1988. Budapest. Nr. 304. Tóth E 2006 76.

Figure 1. Map of the cemeteries in Sopianae Pécs

Figure 2. Urn From Nagy Lajos School 2-3rd Century

Figure 3. Cremated Pagan Grave (Bustum) No 20 InSzéchenyi Tér 2nd Century

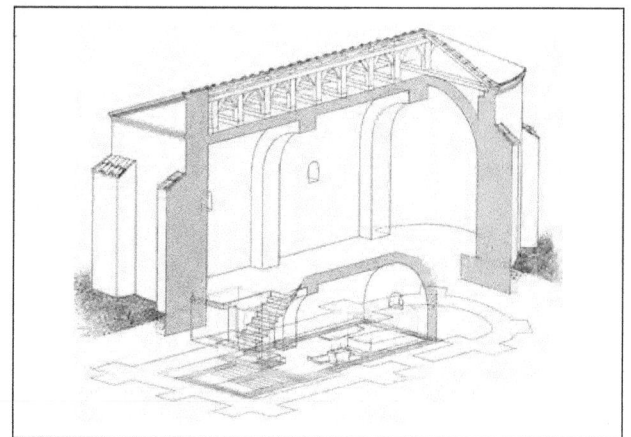

Figure 4. Mausoleum – Burial Chamber XXXIII

Figure 5. Mausoleum – Burial Chamber XXXIII

Figure 6. The Burial Chamber with the Jar

Figure 7. Brick Grave (No25)
In Széchenyi Tér 4th Century

Figure 8. Cemetery Building From Apáca Street 4th Century

found.[31] All graves of the burial chambers were robbed or disturbed, but we may hypothetise that they contained glass items. Glass objects were also found in a sarcophagus.[32] The jug and beaker fresco on the wall of Burial Chamber II can be considered Christian, as it comes from a Christian setting.

COINS

Coins as grave goods are considered a pagan habit.[33] The use of coins, however, continued way into the fourth and fifth centuries and had little to do with religion. In the early Christian cemetery of Sopianae, coins were found in burial chambers, too. Coins do not separate pagans from Christians.[34]

SHROUDS[35]

In the absence of valuable grave goods, nicely decorated gold-woven shrouds[36] may indicate status and wealth.[37] Textiles, decorated with gold were used by ordinary people who tried to imitate the funerary habits of the upper classes or the imperial family.[38] According to Vera Lányi, it was characteristic for the early Christians that dress accessories and jewellery (brooches, belt buckles, etc.) were not put into the graves where they were worn in life,[39] proving the use of shrouds in graves.[40] The objects were

---

[31] Fülep 1984 154. Perfume bottles do not indicate gender, woman and men equally used them: László Bartosiewicz – Anikó Bózsa, "Valami bűzlik Dániában – Kísérlet a szagok régészeti rekonstrukciójára." [Something smells in Denmark—An Attempt to Reconstruct Odors by Archaeological Methods] In: *Régészeti dimenziók* [Archeological Dimensions]. Alexandra Anders –Miklós Szabó –Pál Raczky (eds). Budapest: L'Harmattan, 2009, 55.

[32] Zsolt Visy, Előzetes kutatási beszámoló a Pécs, Szent István téren, az ókeresztény temető területén folytatott régészeti kutatásokról. [Preliminary Report of an Archaeological Excavations in the Early Christian Cemetery at Szent István Square in Pécs.] *Sopianae krónika* 1–2 (2007) 6–11.

[33] Adalbert G. Hamman, *La vie quotidienne des premiers chrétiens*, (Paris: Hachette, 1971); Schmidt 2000 176–177.

[34] Volker Zedelius, "Obolos oder Signum Christi?" In: *Spurenlese – Beiträgezur Geschichte des Xantener Raumes*. Köln: Rheinland Verlag, 1989, 175–178.

[35] Homer, *Iliad*, XVIII. 352–353, Lk 23,53 – Orazio Marucchi – Hubert Vecchierello, *Manual of Christian Archeology*. New Jersey: 1949, 103; Gyula Gosztonyi, *A pécsi ókeresztény temető*.[The Early Christian Cemetery of Pécs] Pécs, 1943, 42., Fülep 1984, 151; Endre Tóth 2006, 83.

[36] On textile remains: Gosztonyi 1943, 42; Fülep 1984 72, 151, 218, 220.

[37] Endre Tóth, 2006, 83.

[38] About similar Roman gold decorated shrouds see: Rodolfo Lanciani, *Pagan and Christian Rome*. Boston – New York: 1892, 203–204.

[39] Eszter B. Vágó, "Ausgrabungen in Intercisa (1957–1969)" *Alba Regia* 11 (1970), 116; Vera Lányi, "Villák és vidéki kőépületek" [Roman Villas and Stone Country Houses] In: András Mócsy– Jenő Fitz (eds.), *Pannonia régészeti kézikönyve* [Archaeological Manual of Pannonia]. Budapest, 1990, 222–226, 249–250.

[40] Fülep 1984 151., Endre Tóth, „Das Christentum in Pannonien bis zum 7. Jahrhundert nach den archäologischen Zeugnissen" In: *Das Christentum im bairischen Raum*. Köln – Weimar – Wien: De Gruyter, 1994, 251; Endre Tóth, 2006, 83.

put into the graves not as dress accessories, but for use in the afterlife. Shrouds can be seen in the scenes of resurrection of Lazarus and also in the incised scenes on the wall of the Commodilla-Catacomb in Rome, showing the undertaker burying a body wrapped in a shroud.[41] Shrouds were either put on the corpse as a winding sheet or the body was wrapped in it. As entrances to the burial chambers were narrow in Sopianae, it was probably easier to deposit the corpse tightly wrapped in a shroud.

STONES ON OR AROUND THE GRAVES

Stone covers on or around graves, used from the Neolithic Era,[42] survived in the fifth and sixth century among Christians.[43] In Sopianae, stone cover on graves started to appear at the beginning of the fourth century, but not necessarily under Christian influence. Stones were used to support the brick roof and the side of the grave. Stone covered graves seem to be religiously neutral.

FUNERARY AND ANNIVERSARY RITES

Remains of funeral banquets and *refrigeria* were found in the Roman cemetery of Sopianae. Funerary and anniversary rites originate from pagan custom, but Christians adopted them as well. Funeral banquets are considered pagan if prepared in the open air. Cemetery building XIII was purposely built for accommodating a funerary service, with a table (*mensa*) in the apse.

SECONDARY BURIALS

Family burial sites were used to deposit more than one member of a family. These graves had to be re-opened for new burials. The bodies interred earlier were pushed aside or poured over with lime or soil.[44] Secondary burial is not a Christian practice, but it occurred in early Christian burial chambers (Burial Chamber XXXIII). In Sopianae, secondary burials were found from the fourth century in the grave-group at 14 Apáca Street. Early Christians, if possible, avoided to disturb the dead, unless to collect relics or conduct secondary burials.

---

[41] Vincenzo Fiocchi Nicolai, Fabrizio Bisconti, and Danilo Mazzoleni, *The Catacombs of Rome*. Regensburg: Skira, 2002, 160.

[42] Diether Kramer, *Im Morgengrauen der abendländischen Zivilisation*. In: Galter – Kramer (ed). *Der Gräberfund von Klein im europäischen Kontext*. Graz: 2007, 186–188.

[43] Béla Miklós Szőke, "A Dunántúl lakossága és a honfoglaló magyarok" [The Magyar Conquerors and the Population of Transdanubian.] In: *Magyarok térben és időben*. Tata: Tudományos Füzetek 11, 1999, 90.

[44] Fülep 1984, 151.

CEMETERY BUILDINGS

The different types of cemetery buildings are the following: martyrium, cemetery basilica, two-storey burial chamber with upper-level *cella memoriae*. The community buildings are the *cellae trichorae* 1–2, and the *cella septichora*. The *cella septichora*, with a central space and seven apses, differs from its pagan model: the original purpose of the apse changed as it accommodated graves.[45]

SPOLIA

Architectural change in Roman cemeteries in the fourth century is connected with the rise of Christianity.[46] In Sopianae, the burial chambers and memorial chapels built after the middle of the fourth century reflect religious change. Burial Chamber V and cemetery building XIII were rebuilt, Burial Chamber IX was extended on the northern side when a new grave was added to it,[47] and the burial chamber of the Mausoleum (XXXIII) was altered. A shift in the function of the buildings was as significant as was any architectural change. The above ground memorial chapels in Sopianae are Christian buildings carrying on pagan tradition. The *cella memoriae* became memorial buildings, rather than venues for funeral banquets (Burial Chambers XIX and XX). Other architectural changes were the consequence of change in religious belief: placing new stone coffins into an existing burial chamber (Burial Chambers II, IV, VIII, IX, and XXVII), building new entrances to the burial chambers (VII?, XXXIII), erecting buildings above earlier graves (XIII, XXXIII?), and building new burial chambers on the ground of earlier graves (XXVIII, XXXV?).

PLASTERED GRAVES

The grave was the eternal home of the dead. For Christians, it symbolized Paradise.[48] In the cemetery of Sopianae, brick and stone built graves with plastered inner walls and painted graves are considered Christian burials. Fresco-painting and plaster on the walls appear in Pannonia with the rise of Christianity in the fourth century. It disappears during the third quarter of the fifth century.

---

[45] Gosztonyi 1943, 125–126.

[46] Thomas S. Burns – John W. Eadie (ed): *Urban Centers and Rural Contexts in Late Antiquity*. Michigan: 2001.

[47] Creating space for another grave inside the burial chambers was not a proper reconstruction (Burial Chambers II and IV), thus we cannot decide whether it was done by early Christians. However, in Burial Chamber XXVII the newly built grave destroyed the previous ones and this indicates a significant change. Erecting another building above the burial chamber of the mausoleum (Burial Chamber XXXIII) is a different matter. The burial chamber was already Christian, its addition was supposed to emphasize respect for the dead.

[48] For the theory that plastered buildings were Christian see Marko Kaplarević, Frühchristliche Malerei in Serbien. Diplomaarbeit, Universität Wien, 2011.

SUPPRESSION OF OLD HABITS

The tiny burial chambers of Sopianae were not suitable for accommodating large funeral banquets. There may have been some symbolic food or drink left in them for the afterlife (in *loculi*, niches, or on the grave), but the banquet or *refrigerium* was held *alfresco*, above ground. Providing room for the funerary ceremonies was the original reason behind the erection of memorial chapels above the burial chambers. Burial Chamber II, with a jug and a beaker—fresco may be the earliest Christian building in the cemetery referring to the place of drinking (*libatio*). Burial Chambers XIX and XX show the transformation of the burial chamber into burial monument with symbolic celebrations. Buildings above graves differ in size. This difference has nothing to do with the size of the congregation they were supposed to accommodate for banquets, but indicates that the size of the above ground buildings was adjusted to the size of the burial site below the surface. The *cella memoriae* above Burial Chamber XX is larger than that of Burial Chamber XIX, as the grave is also larger. The 3:2 ratio of the stone coffins is equivalent to the 1.5:1 ratio of the above surface buildings. These became burial monuments and their previous ritual role was pushed aside. The function of the *cella memoriae* above Burial Chamber XIX reminds of painted cemetery buildings: it had no entrance door, only a large window facing South.

CHRISTIAN SYMBOLS IN CEMETERIES

Christian symbols or inscriptions appeared on gravestones, wall paintings, mosaics, statuettes, reliefs, glasses, wooden chests, bricks, dress jewels and on other objects. In Sopianae only the Christogram, when depicted in the cemetery during the second half of the fourth century, can be considered a genuine Christian symbol (Burial Chambers I, IV, V, XX, and XXXIII).

NEUTRAL SYMBOLS IN CHRISTIAN ENVIRONMENT

Palm branch, flower, grapevine, bird, and trellis/fence are symbols used by pagans and Christians alike. These symbols are to be considered Christian if used together with indisputably Christian symbols. In Burial Chamber I, the presence of the Christogram alludes to Christian commissioners, thus the floral decoration on the walls is seen as Christian.

BIBLICAL THEMES

The following biblical scenes and themes are depicted in Sopianae:

- Adam and Eve (Burial Chambers I and XXXIII)
- Noah with the Ark (Burial Chamber I)
- Daniel in the lions' den (Burial Chambers I and XXXIII)
- Jonah and the whale (Burial Chamber I)

- The three Magi (Burial Chamber I)
- Virgin Mary with Child (Burial Chamber I)
- The Apostles Saint Peter and Saint Paul (Burial Chamber I)

ELEVATIO/TRANSLATIO

Graves were ritually re-opened so as to remove bones.[49] Relics of martyrs were removed from the tombs and were re-buried in a very special grave somewhere else, or in reliquiaires. In Sopianae, the tiny apse behind the niche on the northern wall of Burial Chamber I is considered to be a relic-holder (*fenestella*). Burial Chamber V might have been a martyrium and Burial Chamber XXXIII the final resting place of a confessor bishop.

SEPARATION OF CHRISTIAN GRAVES[50]

Until the end of the fourth century, Christians buried their dead in the northwestern section of the cemetery. This separation also can be seen as clustering of Christian graves, in Sopianae primarily around buildings. This may signal a burial to the saints (*depositio ad sanctos*). As Christian graves expanded towards the southeast, the orientation of the graves were not uniform.[51] It is possible that Christians did not always orient their graves, or that pagan graves were in the vicinity of the Christian graves.[52] Around the Christian community buildings the graves are always west-east oriented. These buildings might have included graves or relics of Christian martyrs and bishops (Burial Chambers I, V, and XXXIII). Around the cemetery buildings, only the west-east oriented burials are undoubtedly Christian, dated to the same time as the buildings. By the end of the fourth century, the northwestern section of the cemetery was used only by Christians. It cannot be proven, however, that pagans were pushed out, or that the new cemeteries of the poor in the southern and southeastern outskirts of Sopianae were used exclusively by pagans.

---

[49] The re-opening of graves for ritual purposes can be traced back to the middle Bronze Age in Hungary (János Dani – Gábor V. Szabó, *Temetkezési szokások a Polgár határában feltárt középsőbronzkori temetőben.* [Burial Rites in the Middle Bronze Age Cemetery Excavated at Polgár.] In: ΜΩΜΟΣ 3. 2004. 91–119; Mária Fekete, *Események és szemelvények* [Events and Excerpts.] Pécs, 2007, 42, but obviously for completely different reasons.

[50] Endre Tóth, 1994, 250; Mihály Nagy, "Typological Consideration on Christian Funerary Buildings in Pannonia." *Zalai Múzeum* 11 (2002), 21.

[51] Schmidt 2000, 321.

[52] In Poundbury (Dorset, United Kingdom) an irregularly positioned and separated group of graves came to light next to aligned rows of pagan burials. These may be Christian graves. They were oriented west-east, grave goods were scarce, and the dead were put into lead-lined stone coffins that were supposed to preserve the body: Keith Branigan, *Roman Britain. Life in an Imperial Province.* London, 1980, 273.

CEMETERY MAPPING [53]

The northwestern part (now Szent István Square) was the Christian hub of the Roman cemetery in Sopianae: the largest number of early Christian graves are to be discovered in this area.

Testing the criteria

Now our new task is to select the genuine Christian characteristics with the help of the Christian part of the cemetery. We should expect the presence of both pagan and Christian burials in the eastern part of the cemetery, under the grounds of the Nagy Lajos High School and in Apáca Street.

In this paper we have investigated the inhumation graves only, as the cremated ones obviously belonged to the pagan population. We have ignored the burial chambers and the wall paintings in our research because these do not provide any evidence to the Christian burial practice in ordinary graves. The following charts, using different colors, show the assumed religious characteristics. We have examined the data of 502 Roman graves excavated in five groups of graves in the northern cemetery of Sopianae and in a separated cemetery at Czindery Street, situated on the southeastern part of the town, as a reference group.[54]

3.1. Graves at 8 Apáca Street (34 graves)

	PAGAN ELEMENTS			COMMON ELEMENTS			EARLY CHRISTIAN ELEMENTS		
Grave no.	Abnormal position	Dinner set	Pitcher and/or glass	Obulus	Other gravegoods	Stone cover on grave	Orientation	Plastered grave walls	Crossed arms
1	double grave		pottery jug fagment		iron knife	no	W-E	yes	no data
			pottery jug fragment		iron nail	no			
2	double grave		glass fragment		iron knife	no	W-E	yes	no data
3	no data	no data	no data	no	glass fragment		W-E	yes	
4	BURIAL CHAMBER								
5	disturbed	no data	no data	no	no	no	W-E	yes	no data
6	no data	no data	no data	no	no	no	W-E	no data	no data

---

[53] Olivér Gábor, *Sopianae késő antik temetői épületei* [The Late Antique Cemetery Buildings of Sopianae.] Kaposvár, 2016, 151–169.

[54] These are not natural groups, because the excavations were limited by the size of the area available for digging.

	PAGAN ELEMENTS			COMMON ELEMENTS			EARLY CHRISTIAN ELEMENTS		
Grave no.	Abnormal position	Dinner set	Pitcher and/or glass	Obulus	Other gravegoods	Stone cover on grave	Orientation	Plastered grave walls	Crossed arms
7	no	no	no	no	no	no	W-E	no data	no
8	no		glass jar	no	animal bone iron nail	no	W-E	no data	no
9	no	no	no	no	jewellery	no	W-E	no data	no
10	no	no	no	no	no	no	W-E	no data	no
11	disturbed	no data	no data	no data	no data	no	W-E	no data	no data
12	no	no	no	no	no	no	W-E	no	no
13	no data	no	glass beaker	yes	jewellery glass bottle	no	W-E	yes	no data
14	no	no	no	no	no	no	W-E	yes	no data
15	double grave	no	no	no	no	no	W-E	yes	no data
16	double grave	no	no	no	no	no	W-E	yes	no data
17	no	no	no		jewellery	no	W-E	no	no data
					jewellery		W-E	no	no
18	no	no	no	no	jewellery	no	W-E	no	no
19	disturbed	no data	no data	no data	no data	no	W-E	no data	no data
20	disturbed	no data	no data	no data	no data	no	W-E	yes	no data
21	disturbed	no data	no data	no data	no data	no	W-E	no data	no data
22	disturbed	no data	no data	no data	no data	no	W-E	yes	no data
23	disturbed	no data	no data	no data	no data	no	W-E	yes	no data
24	disturbed	no data	no data	no data	no data	no	W-E	yes	no data
25	BURIAL CHAMBER								
26	disturbed	no data	no data	no data	no data	no	W-E	yes	no
27	disturbed	no data	no data	no data	no data	no	W-E	no	no
28	BURIAL CHAMBER								
29	disturbed	no	no	no	glass bottle	no	W-E	no	no
30	no	no	no	no	jewellery	no	W-E	yes	no data
31	no	no	no	no	jewellery	no	W-E	yes	no
32	no	no	no	no	jewellery	no	W-E	yes	no
33	no	no	no	no	jewellery	no	W-E	no	no
34	disturbed	no data	no data	no data	no data	no	W-E	no data	no data
35	disturbed	no data	no data	no data	no data	no	W-E	yes	no data
36	disturbed	no data	no data	no data	no data	no	no data	no data	no data
37	disturbed	no data	no data	yes	scent bottle	no data	W-E	no data	no data

3.2. Graves at 14 Apáca Street –12 St.István Square (104 graves)

	PAGAN ELEMENTS			COMMON ELEMENTS			EARLY CHRISTIAN ELEMENTS		
Grave. No.	Abnormal position	Dinner set	Pitcher and/or glass	Obulus	Other gravegoods	Stone cover on grave	Orientation	Plastered grave walls	Crossed arms
1	no data			no	ring	yes	W-E	yes	no data
					bracelet				
					hairpin				
					necklace				
					beads				
2	no data	no	no	no	no	no	W-E	yes	?
3	no	no	no	no	no	no	NW-SE	no	no
4	disturbed	no	no	no	grooch, br.	no	W-E	no	no data
					crossbow				
5	no	no	glass jug	no	glass scent bttle		NW-SE	yes	
			glass beaker		bottle				
6	decayed	no	glass cup	no	beads	no	W-E	yes	no
					bracelet				
					head jewel				
7	no data		pottery pitcher	no	gold	yes	SW-NE	no	?
			glass fragments		earring				
8	disturbed	no	no	no	no	no	no data	yes	?
9	no	no	no	no	no	no	W-E	yes	?
10	disturbed	no	glass beaker	no	glass scent bottle		NW-SE	yes	disturbed
			glass bottle		bracelet				
					gl. Vessel				
					jewellery	no			
11	disturbed	no	glass jug	no	glass scent bttle		NW-SE	yes	
			glass cup		bottle	no		no data	disturbed
12	disturbed	no	glass beakers	no	glass scent bttle		W-E	no data	no data
					bottle	no			
13	disturbed	no	no	no	no	no	W-E	no data	no data
14	yes	no	glass beaker	no	no	no	W-E	no data	no data
15	disturbed	no	glass beaker	yes	no	no	W-E	no data	no data
16	disturbed	no	glass beaker	no	glass scent bttle	no	W-E	yes	no data
			glass jug		bottle				
			glass cup						

Grave. No.	PAGAN ELEMENTS			COMMON ELEMENTS			EARLY CHRISTIAN ELEMENTS		
	Abnormal position	Dinner set	Pitcher and/or glass	Obulus	Other gravegoods	Stone cover on grave	Orientation	Plastered grave walls	Crossed arms
17	disturbed	no	no	no	glass scent bttle bottle jewellery	no	NW-SE	no	no data
18	disturbed		no	no	jewellery	no	NW-SE	no	? Maybe
19	disturbed		no	no	no	no	SW-NE	no	no data
20	disturbed		no	no	glass beaker	no data	NW-SE	yes	no data
21	disturbed		no	no	no	no	W-E	no data	no data
22	no data	no	glass jug	no	no	no	W-E	yes	no data
23	no data	no	no	no	no	no	W-E	no	no data
24	no data	no	glass bottle	no	no	no	NW-SE	yes	no data
25	no data	no data	no data	no	no data	no data	W-E	no data	no data
26	disturbed	no	glass bottle	no	jewellery	no	W-E	yes	no data
27	no data	no	glass bottle	no	no	no	W-E	yes	no data
28	disturbed	no	glass bottle	no	no	no	SW-NE	no data	no data
29	disturbed	no	glass beaker	no	no	no	SW-NE	no data	no data
30	disturbed	no	pottery jug glass beaker	no	no	no	W-E	no data	no data
31	no data	no	glass cups	no	no	no	W-E	no data	no data
32	disturbed	no	no	no	jewellery	no	no data	no data	no data
33	disturbed	no	no	no	no data	no data	W-E	no data	no data
34	no data		glass jug	yes	no data glass fragments glass scent bttle	no data	W-E	yes	no data
35	no data			no	glass fragment glass scent bttle	no	NW-SE	no	no data
36	no data		glass beaker	no		no	NW-SE	no data	no data
36/A			glass beaker			no	NW-SE	no data	no data
37	no data	no	no	no	jewellery	no	W-E	no data	no data
38	disturbed	no	no	no	glass scent bttle	no	W-E	no data	no data
39	disturbed	no	glass cup glass vessel	no			W-E	no data	no data
40	disturbed		no data	no	no data	no data	W-E	no data	no data
41	no data		glass beaker	no	jewellery	no data	no data	no data	no data
42	no		glass jug glass beaker	no	glass scent bttle	no data	NW-SE	yes	no data

	PAGAN ELEMENTS			COMMON ELEMENTS			EARLY CHRISTIAN ELEMENTS		
Grave. No.	Abnormal position	Dinner set	Pitcher and/or glass	Obulus	Other gravegoods	Stone cover on grave	Orientation	Plastered grave walls	Crossed arms
43	disturbed		glass vessel	no	glass scent bttle		W-E	yes	no data
			glass bottle		fragments				
44	no data		glass beaker	no		no data	NW-SE	yes	no data
45	disturbed		glass beaker	yes	jewellery	no data	W-E	yes	no data
46	disturbed		no	no	no	no data	W-E	no data	no data
47	disturbed		no	no	glass scent bttle	no data	W-E	yes	no data
48	no		no	no	glass scent bttle	no data	W-E	yes	no data
					jewellery				
49	disturbed		no	no	no	no data	NW-SE	no data	no data
50	disturbed		glass beaker	no	jewellery		W-E	yes	no
			glass bottles		glass plates				
51	disturbed		glass bottles	no		no	W-E	yes	yes
			glass beaker						
52	no			yes	buckle	no	W-E	yes	yes
53	disturbed		glass beaker			no data	W-E	yes	no data
54	disturbed		no		no	no data	NW-SE	no data	no data
55	no		no		no	no	SW-NE	no data	no data
56	yes		no	no	no	no	NW-SE	no data	no data
57	no data		no	no	glass scent bttle	no data	NW-SE	no	no data
58	disturbed		no	no	no	no	SW-NE	yes	no data
59	yes		no	no	no	no	W-E	no	no data
60	no		no	no	jewellery	no	W-E	yes	yes
61	no data		no	no	no	no	W-E	no	no data
62	no		glass beaker	no	no	no	W-E	no	no data
63	no data		no	no	no	no	W-E	no	no data
64	no		glass beaker	no	no	no	SW-NE	no	no data
65	disturbed		no	no	no	no	NW-SE	no	no data
66	no		no	no	no	no	W-E	no	no data
67	no		no	no	no	no	SW-NE	no	no data
68	no		glass cup	no			W-E	yes	no data
			glass beaker		no	no			
69	no		no	no	jewellery	no	W-E	no	no data
70	disturbed		no	no	glass scent bttle	no	SW-NE	no	no data
71	disturbed		no	no	no	no	NW-SE	no data	no data
72	no data		no	no	no	no	NW-SE	no data	no data

	PAGAN ELEMENTS			COMMON ELEMENTS			EARLY CHRISTIAN ELEMENTS		
Grave. No.	Abnormal position	Dinner set	Pitcher and/or glass	Obulus	Other gravegoods	Stone cover on grave	Orientation	Plastered grave walls	Crossed arms
73	no data		no	no	jewellery	no	W-E	no data	no data
74	disturbed		no	no	no	no	W-E	no data	no data
75	no data		glass beaker	no	no	no	SW-NE	no data	no data
76	no data		no	no	no	no	W-E	no data	no data
77	no		glass jug glass vessel	no	no data	no data	W-E	no data	no data
78	disturbed		no	no	jewellery	no data	SW-NE	no data	no data
79	disturbed		no	no	no	no data	SW-NE	no data	no data
80	no data		no	no	glass vessel	no data	W-E	no data	no data
81	disturbed		no	no	no	no data	W-E	no data	no data
83	no data		no	no	lead fragment	no data	W-E	no data	no data
84	no		glass bottles glass goblet	no	glass scent bttle	no data	W-E	no	no
85	no		glass cup	yes	glass scent bttle jewellery	no	E-W	no	no
86	disturbed		no	no	no	no	W-E	yes	no data
87	disturbed		no	no	no	no	W-E	no	no data
88	no		no	no	jewellery	no	W-E	yes	no
89	no		glass beaker glass jug	no	glass scent bttle	no	W-E	yes	no no
90	no		glass beakers	no	glass scent bttle	no	W-E	yes	no
91	disturbed			no	bulla glass scent bttle ring	no	NW-SE W-E	yes	no data
92	no		no	no	no		W-E	no	no data
93	no		no	no	clay spindle glass scent bttle	no	W-E W-E	no no	no data no data
94	was not excavated		no data	no data	no data	no data	W-E	no data	no data
95	was not excavated		no data	no data	no data	no data	W-E	no data	no data
96	disappeared		no	no	buckle	no	W-E	yes	no data
97	no		no	no	no	no	NW-SE	yes	no data
98	no data		glass jug fragment	no	glass scent bttle	no	W-E	yes	no data
99	yes		glass beaker	no		no	SW-NE	no	no data

	PAGAN ELEMENTS			COMMON ELEMENTS			EARLY CHRISTIAN ELEMENTS		
Grave. No.	Abnormal position	Dinner set	Pitcher and/or glass	Obulus	Other gravegoods	Stone cover on grave	Orientation	Plastered grave walls	Crossed arms
100	no data		glass beaker	no	jewellery	no	W-E	no	no data
101	disturbed		no	no	jewellery	no	W-E	no	no data
102	multiple burial			no	jewellery	no	NW-SE	yes	no data
103	no data		glass bottle	no	no	no	W-E	yes	no data
104	no		no	no	glass scent bttle	no	W-E	yes	no data

3.3. Graves at 3 Székesfehérvár (Vörösmarty) Street (114 graves)

	PAGAN ELEMENTS			COMMON ELEMENTS			EARLY CHRISTIAN ELEMENTS		
Grave. No.	Abnormal position	Dinner set	Pitcher and/or glass	Obulus	Other gravegoods	Stone cover on grave	Orientation	Plastered grave walls	Crossed arms
1	no data	no data	no data	no data	glass fragment	no	no data	yes	no data
					iron spear				
2	no	no	no	no	no	no	W-E	no	no
3	disturbed	maybe	glass jugs	yes	jewellery	yes	W-E	yes	no data
			glass beakers		gold rings				
			glass bowl		iron belt buckle				
					lead object				
					crossbow brooch				
4	disturbed	no	pottery jug	no	jewellery	yes	W-E	yes	no data
					pot				
5	no			yes	no	no	W-E	yes	no
6	no	no	no	yes	no	no	W-E	no	no
7	disturbed	no	no	no	crossbow brooch	yes	E-W	no	yes
8	no	no	no	yes	jewellery	yes	W-E	no	no
9	disturbed	no	no	no	no	no	W-E	no	no
10	disturbed	no	no	no	no	no	N-S	no	na data
11	no		pottery pot	no	pottery	yes	W-E	no	maybe
					glass fragment				
12	disturbed			yes	scent bottle	no	W-E		maybe
					needle case			no	
13	no	no	pottery jug	no	no	yes	W-E	no	yes
14	disturbed		no	yes	scrinium	no	W-E	yes	no
					jewellery				
15	disturbed	no	no	no	no	no	NW-SE	no	no

Grave. No.	PAGAN ELEMENTS			COMMON ELEMENTS			EARLY CHRISTIAN ELEMENTS		
	Abnormal position	Dinner set	Pitcher and/or glass	Obulus	Other gravegoods	Stone cover on grave	Orientation	Plastered grave walls	Crossed arms
16	disturbed		no	yes	jewellery	yes	E-W	yes	no
17	no	no	no	no	brooch	yes	W-E	yes	no
18	no	no	no	no	jewellery iron fragment	yes	E-W	no	no
19	disturbed		no	no	jewellery	yes	W-E	no	
20	yes		no	no	jewellery	yes	E-W		
21	disturbed	no	no data	no	jewellery	no	W-E	no	no data
22	yes	no	no	no	jewellery	no	E-W	no	no
23	no	no	no	no	jewellery	no	W-E	no	yes
24	no data	no data	no data	no data	no data	no	no data	no data	no data
25	no	no	glass beaker glass jug	no		yes	SW-NE	no	no
26	no	no	no	no	iron ring	no	NE-SW	no	
27	no	no	no	no	no	no	N-S	no	no
28	no	no	no	no	no	no	N-S	no	no
29	no	no	glass fragment	no	jewellery glass object	yes	E-W	no	no
30	disturbed	no data	no data	no data	no data	yes	W-E	no	no
31	no	no	no	no	jewellery	no	W-E	no	no
32	no	no	no	no	no	no	N-S	no	yes
33	no	no	no	no	no	no	W-E	no	no
34	disturbed	no	pottery jug	yes	jewellery gold jewellery pottery	no	W-E	no	no data
35	disturbed	no	no	no	seashell	no	no data	no	no
36	disturbed	no	no	no	no	no	E-W	no	no
37	yes		no	no	bronze buckle	no	W-E	no	no
38	no	no	no	no	no	no	W-E	no	no
39	yes	no	no	no	no	no	NE-SW	no	no
40	yes	no	no	no	no	no	SW-NE	no	no
41	no	no	no	no	scent bottle crossbow brooch	yes	W-E	no	no
42	no	no	glass cup pottery jug	no	pottery jewellery iron object scent bottle	no	NE-SW	no	yes
43	no	no	no	no	no	no	W-E	no	no

Grave. No.	PAGAN ELEMENTS			COMMON ELEMENTS				EARLY CHRISTIAN ELEMENTS		
	Abnormal position	Dinner set	Pitcher and/or glass	Obulus	Other gravegoods	Stone cover on grave	Orientation	Plastered grave walls	Crossed arms
44	disturbed	no data	glass cup	yes	bronze buckle	no data	no data	no	no
45	no	no	no	no	iron ring iron objects	no	E-W	no	no
46	no data	no	glass cup	yes	no data	no data	E-W	no data	no data
47	no	no	no	no	no	yes	E-W	no data	no
48	disturbed	no	glass beaker	coin	no jewellery	yes	E-W	yes	no data
49	disturbed	no data	no data	no data	no data	no data	no data	no	no data
50	no	no	no	no	no	no	W-E	no	no data
51	no	no	no	no	jewellery	yes	W-E	no	no
52	disturbed	no	no	no	no	no	E-W	no	maybe
53	disturbed	no	no	yes	jewellery	no	W-E	no	no data
54	no	no	no	no	no	no	W-E	no	no
55	no	no	glass bottle	no	jewellery	no	NE-SW	no	no
56	no	no	no		jewellery iron jewellery	no	NE-SW	no	no
57	no data	no data	no data	no data	no data	no data	NW-SE	no	no
58	no	no	no	no	no	no data	W-E	no	no
59	yes	no	no	no	no	no	SW-NE	no	no
60	disturbed	no data	no data	no data	no data	no data	NE-SW	no data	no data
61	no data	no	no	no	no	yes	W-E	yes	no
62	disturbed	no data	no data	no data	no data	no data	E-W	no data	no data
63	disturbed	no data	no data	no data	jewellery	no data	E-W	no	no
64	disturbed	no data	no data	no data	no data	no data	W-E	no data	no data
65	disturbed	no data	no data	no data	no data	no data	no data	no data	no data
66	disturbed	no data	no data	no data	jewellery	no data	W-E	no data	no data
67	no	no	no	yes	wooden bucket	no	E-W	no	no
68	disturbed	no data	no da	no data	no data	no data	W-E	no data	no data
69	disturbed	no	no	no	jewellery	no data	E-W	no	no
70	disturded	no data	no data	no data	no data	yes	W-E	no	no data
71	no	no	no	no	no	no	W-E	no	no
72	no	no	no	yes	jewellery scrinium bone pins	yes	W-E	yes	no
73	no data	no	glass cup	no	no	no	SW-NE	no	no
74	disturbed	no	glass cup	no	scent bttle	no	E-W	no	no
75	no	no	no	no	strap end	no	E-W	no	yes
76	no	no	no	no	jewellery	no	NE-SW	no	no
77	disturbed	no data	no data	yes	no	yes	NE-SW	no data	no data

	PAGAN ELEMENTS			COMMON ELEMENTS			EARLY CHRISTIAN ELEMENTS		
Grave. No.	Abnormal position	Dinner set	Pitcher and/or glass	Obulus	Other gravegoods	Stone cover on grave	Orientation	Plastered grave walls	Crossed arms
78	disturbed	no data	no data	no data	no	no data	no data	yes	no data
79	disturbed	no data	pottery jug pottery beaker	no data	no data	no data	no data	no data	no data
80	disturbed	no data	no data	no data	no data	no data	no data	no data	no data
81	no	no	no	no	jewellery	no	N-S	no	yes
82	no	no	no	no	crossbow brooch	maybe	NE-SW	no	no
83	no data	no	no	no	no	no	NW-SE	no	no data
84	no	no	no	no	crossbow brooch	no	NE-SW	no	no
85	no data	no	no	no	no	no	SW-NE	no	no
86	no	no	glass beaker	no	jewellery	no	NE-SW	no	no
87	no	no	glass cup pottery jug	yes	crossbow brooch	no	NE-SW	no	no
88	disturbed	no	no	no	no	no	W-E	no	no
89	disturbed	no	no	no	no	no	W-E	no	no
90	disturbed	no	no	glass beaker	no	no	W-E	yes	no
91	no	no	glass cup glass bttle	yes	crossbow br. iron knife	no	E-W	yes	no
92	no	no	glass cup glass jugs	yes	jewellery glass ring with MENORA hair pins iron knife	no	E-W	no	no
93	disturbed	no	no	no	no	no	SE-NW	no	no
94	disturbed	no data	no data	no data	no data	no data	W-E	yes	no data
95	no	no data	no data	no data	crossbow brooch	no data	N-S	no	no
96	disturbed	no data	no data	no data	no data	no data	NE-SW	yes	no data
97	no	no	no	no	no	no	W-E	no	no
98	disturbed		glass cup glass bottle	no	jewellery iron spear wooden chest	no	E-W	yes	no data
99	no	no	no	no	jewellery	no	NE-SW	no	no
100	disturbed	no	no	no	jewellery	no	NE-SW	no	no
101	no	no	glass cup	yes	jewellery iron object scent bottle	no	E-W	no	yes

	PAGAN ELEMENTS			COMMON ELEMENTS			EARLY CHRISTIAN ELEMENTS		
Grave. No.	Abnormal position	Dinner set	Pitcher and/or glass	Obulus	Other gravegoods	Stone cover on grave	Orientation	Plastered grave walls	Crossed arms
102	disturbed	no data	no data	no data	no data	no data	N-S	no	no data
103	no	pottery bowl	glass vessel	yes	no	no data	W-E	no	no
104	no	no	glass bottle glass cup	yes	bronze buckle jewellery iron buckle iron axe broze belt mounts	no	E-W	yes	no
105	no	no	no	yes	jewellery bone pins iron knife	no	E-W	no	no
106	disturbed	no data	no data	yes	jewellery	no	E-W	no	no data
107	no	no	glass cup	no	bronze earring jewellery	no	NE-SW	no	no
108	no	no	glass fragment	no	crossbow brooch jewellery	no	NE-SW	no	no
109	no	no	no	no	no	no data	SW-NE	no	no
110	disturbed	no	no	no	no	no	no data	no	no
111	disturbed	no	no	no	no	yes	no data	no	no
112	disturbed	no	no	no	no	no	NE-SW	no	no
113	disturbed	no	no	no	no	no	no data	no	no
114	no	no	bronze pitcher	no	no	no	no data	no	no

3.4 Graves under the grounds of the Nagy Lajos High School in Széchenyi Square (111 graves)

	PAGAN ELEMENTS			COMMON ELEMENTS			EARLY CHRISTIAN ELEMENTS		
Grave. No.	Abnormal position	Dinner set	Pitcher and/or glass	Obulus	Other gravegoods	Stone cover on grave	Orientation	Plastered grave walls	Crossed arms
1	no	no		no	no	no	NW-SE	yes	no
2	no	no	no	no	bronze bukle iron chain	no	E-W	no	no
3	disturbed	no data	no data	no data	no data	no	no data	no	no
4	no data	no data	no data	no data	bronze buckle	no	E-W	no data	no data
5	disturbed	no data	no data	no data	bronze buckle	no	W-E	no data	no data

	PAGAN ELEMENTS			COMMON ELEMENTS			EARLY CHRISTIAN ELEMENTS		
Grave. No.	Abnormal position	Dinner set	Pitcher and/or glass	Obulus	Other gravegoods	Stone cover on grave	Orientation	Plastered grave walls	Crossed arms
6	disturbed	no data	no data	no data	no	no data	no data	no data	no data
7	disturbed	no data	no data	no data	no data	no data	no data	no data	no data
8	no	no	glass bottle	yes	iron pin	no	SW-NE	yes	yes
9	no	no	no	no	bronze sheet	no	NE-SW	no	no
10	no	no	no	no	crossbow brooch	no	SE-NW	no data	yes
					bronze buckle			no	no
11	no	no	no		jewellery	yes	SW-NE	no	no
12	no	bronze bowl		yes	scent bottles	no	W-E	no	yes
					jewellery				
13	no	no	no	no	no	no	SW-NE	no	yes
14	no	no	no	no	no	no	SE-NW	no	no
15	disturbed	no data	no data	no data	bronze mount	no	SE-NW	no	no
					iron strap				
16	no	no	no	no	no	yes	NE-SW	no	no
17	no	no	no	no	iron buckle	no	NE-SW	no	no
18	no data	no data	no data	no data	no data	no data	no data	no data	no data
19	disturbed	no	glass beaker	yes	jewellery	no data	no data	no	no
20	no data	no data	no data	no data	no data	no data	no data	no data	no data
21	disturbed	no	no	no	no	yes	NE-SW	no	no
22	disturbed	no	no	no	no	yes	SE-NW	no	yes
23	disturbed	no data	no data	no data	legs pulled up	no	SW-NE	no data	no data
24	disturbed	no	no	no	jewellery	no	E-W	no	no
25	no	no	glass bottle	yes	jewellery	no	SW-NE	yes	no
26	no	no	glass beaker	no	jewellery	no	NE-SW	no	no
			pottery bottle		bone pin				
					hair pin				
					bronze sheet				
27	no	no	no	no	no	no	SE-NW	no	no
28	disturbed	no	no	no	no	no	SW-NE	no	no
29	no	no	no	no	no	no	NW-SE	no	no
30	no	no	no	no	no	no	no data	no	no
31	no	no	no	no	jewellery	no	SW-NE	no	maybe
32	no	no	no	no	bronze fragment	no	no data	no	no
					scent bottles				
33	no	no	no	no	bronze buckle	no	NE-SW	no	yes
34	disturbed	no	no	no	no	no	NE-SW	no	no

Grave. No.	PAGAN ELEMENTS			COMMON ELEMENTS			EARLY CHRISTIAN ELEMENTS		
	Abnormal position	Dinner set	Pitcher and/or glass	Obulus	Other gravegoods	Stone cover on grave	Orientation	Plastered grave walls	Crossed arms
35	no	no	no	no	no	no	W-E	no	no
36	no	no	no	no	no	no	SW-NE	no	no
37	on its side	no	no	no	wooden case	no	SW-NE	no	no
					oil lamp				
					Samian ware				
38	no	no	no	no	no	no	SE-NW	no	no
39	no	bronze bowl	no	yes	jewellery	no	W-E	yes	no
					scent bottles				
					iron knife				
					seashell				
40	no	no	glass cup	no	jewellery	no	W-E	no	no
41	legs pulled up	no	glass cup	no	jewellery	no	NE-SW	yes	no
42	no	no	no	yes	iron stick	no	W-E	no	no
					iron knife				
43	disturbed	no	no	no	no	no	NE-SW	yes	no data
44	no	no	no	no	no	no	W-E	no	no
45	disturbed	no	no	no	no	no	SW-NE	no	no data
46	no	pottery	no	no	jewellery	no	W-E	no	no data
					iron needle				
					iron fragment				
47	disturbed	no	no	no	no	no	SW-NE	no	no
48	no	no	glass beaker	no	iron belt	no	W-E	no	no
					jewellery				
49	no	no	no	no	crossbow brooch	no	SE-NW	no	no
50	disturbed	no	no	no	no	no	W-E	no	no
51	no	no	no	no	jewellery	yes	E-W	no	no
52	hands up	no	no	no	no	no	NW-SE	no	no
53	no	no	no	no	jewellery	no	SW-NE	no	no
					bronze buclke				
					iron piece				
					led piece				
54	no	no	no	no	bronze buckle	no	SW-NE	no	no
55	disturbed	yes	pottery jug	yes	bronze sheets	no	SW-NE	no	no
					bronze nails				
56	no data	no data	no data	no data	no data	no data	no data	no data	no data
57	no data	no data	no data	no data	no data	no data	no data	no data	no data
58	no	no	glass beaker	yes	jewellery	no	W-E	no	no

SOPIANAE REVISITED: PAGAN OR CHRISTIAN BURIALS?

Grave. No.	PAGAN ELEMENTS			COMMON ELEMENTS			EARLY CHRISTIAN ELEMENTS		
	Abnormal position	Dinner set	Pitcher and/or glass	Obulus	Other gravegoods	Stone cover on grave	Orientation	Plastered grave walls	Crossed arms
59	no	no	glass	yes	iron fragment	no	SW-NE	no	yes
60	no	no	no	no	bronz belt pieces crossbow brooch	no	NW-SE	no	yes
61	no	pottery bowl	no	no	no	no	SW-NE	no	no
62	no	no	no	no	jewellery	yes	E-W	no	no
63	no	no	no	no	jewellery comb ring	yes	W-E	no	no
64	no	no	no	no	no	no	E-W	no	no
65	no	no	no	no	scent bottles	no	W-E	yes	no
66	on its side	no	no	no	no	no	E-W	no	no
67	no	no	no	no	no	no	E-W	no	no
68	no	no	pottery jug	no	jewellery brooch ring	yes	SW-NE	yes	no
69	no	no	glass beaker	no	brooch	no	W-E	no	yes
70	no	no	no	no	jewellery	no	W-E	no	no
71	disturbed	no	no	no	no	no	S-N	no	no
72	no	no	no	no	pottery fragment	no	N-S	no	no
73	no	no	glass jug	no	jewellery		W-E	no	yes
74	no data	no data	no data	no data	no data	no	no data	yes	no data
75	no	no	no	no	pottery fragment	no	SW-NE	no	no
76	no	no data	no data	yes	bronze buckle	no	E-W	no	no
77	no	no	no	no	jewellery	no	W-E	no	yes
78	no	no	no	no	no	no	NE-SW	no	no
79	no	no	no	no	no	no	E-W	no	no
80	no	no	no	no	jewellery brooch	no	W-E	no	yes
81	no	no	no	yes	no	no	S-N	no	no
82	disturbed	no	no	no	no	no	SW-NE	no	no
83	no	pottery bowl	no	yes	no pottery jug	no	SW-NE	no	yes
84	no	no	no	no	crossbow brooch	no	S-N	no	yes
85	no	no	no	no	no	no	NW-SE	yes	no

Grave. No.	PAGAN ELEMENTS			COMMON ELEMENTS			EARLY CHRISTIAN ELEMENTS		
	Abnormal position	Dinner set	Pitcher and/or glass	Obulus	Other gravegoods	Stone cover on grave	Orientation	Plastered grave walls	Crossed arms
86	no	no	no	no	no	no	E-W	no	no
87	disturbed	no	no	37 coins	no	no	N-S	no	no
88	disturbed	no	no	no	brooch	no	W-E	no	no
89	no	no	no	yes	jewellery	no	W-E	yes	no
					bronze fragment				
90	no	pottery jar	no	no	brooch	no	E-W	no	no
91	no	no	no	no	no	no	E-W	no	no
92	no	no	glass cup	yes	no	no	E-W	no	no
93	no	no	glass cup	no	brooch	no	SW-NE	no	no
94	disturbed	no	pottery jug	yes	no	yes	NE-SW	no	no
95	no	no	glass cup	no	brooch	no	W-E	no	no
96	on its side	no	no	no	jewellery	no	SE-NW	no	no
97A	disturbed	pottery jar	no	no	jewellery	no	SE-NW	no	no
97B	no	no	no	no	no	no	SW-NE	no	no
98	no	no	no	no	no	no	S-N	no	no
99	no	no	no	no	iron object	no	W-E	no	no
100	no	no	no	yes	strap end	no	SW-NE	no	no
					crossbow brooch				
101	no data	no data	no data	no data	no data	no data	no data	no data	no data
102	no	no	no	no	no	no	SW-NE	no data	no data
103	no data	no data	no data	no data	no data	no data	no data	no data	no data
104	no	no	no	no	no	no	SW-NE	no	no
105	disturbed	no	no	no	glass object	no	W-E	yes	no data
					iron knives				
					iron clip				
106	disturbed	no	no	yes	no	no	SW-NE	no	no
107	disturbed	no	no	no	no	no	no data	no	no
108	disturbed	nno	pottery jug	yes	buckle	no	SW-NE	yes	no
			pottery cup		bucket				
			iron cup		jewellery				
			pottery jar		brooch				
					iron stick				
109	disturbed	no	no	no	brooch	no	SW-NE	no	no
110	no	no	no	no	pottery fragment	no	SW-NE	no	no
111	crouched	no	no	no	iron fragment	no	NE-SW	no	no

3.5. Graves at 13 Apáca Street (29 graves)

	PAGAN ELEMENTS			COMMON ELEMENTS			EARLY CHRISTIAN ELEMENTS		
Grave. No.	Abnormal position	Dinner set	Pitcher and/or glass	Obulus	Other gravegoods	Stone cover on grave	Orientation	Plastered grave walls	Crossed arms
1	no	no		no	iron object	no	NE-SW	no	no
2	no	no	no		no data	no	NE-SW	no	yes
3	no data	no data	no data	no data	no	no	no data	no data	no data
4	no data	no data	no data	no data	no data	no	no data	no data	no data
5	no data	no data	no data	no data	no data	no	no data	no data	no data
6	no	no	no	no	bracelets	no	W-E	no	no
7	disturbed	no	no	no	glass bangle iron knife	no	W-E	no	no
8	no	no	no	no	no data	no	W-E	yes	no
9	disturbed	no	no	no	no data	no	W-E	no	no data
10	disturbed	no data	no data	no data	no data	no	no data	no data	no data
11	no	no	no		jewellery	no	E-W	no	no
12	no	no		no	no	no	W-E	no	yes
13	disturbed	no data	no data	no data	no data	no	no data	no data	no data
14	disturbed	no	no		jewellery	no	no data	no	yes
15	disturbed	no	no		no	no	E-W	no	no data
16	no	no	no	no	no	no	W-E	no	yes
17	disturbed	no	no	no	jewellery	no	S-N	no	no
18	no	no	no	no	jewellery	no	W-E	yes	no
19	no	no	no	no	jewellery	no	W-E	yes	yes
20	disturbed	no data	no data	no data	no data	no	W-E	no	no data
21	no	no	no	no	no	no	W-E	yes	no
22	no	no	no	no	jewellery	no	W-E	no	yes
23	pulled up legs	no	no	no	jewellery	no	W-E	no	no
24	no	no	no	no	jewellery	no	W-E	no	yes
25	no	no	no	no	bronze belt	no	E-W	no	yes
26	no	no	no	no	bronze belt	no	E-W	no	no
27	no	no	no	no	no	no	W-E	yes	yes

Grave. No.	PAGAN ELEMENTS			COMMON ELEMENTS				EARLY CHRISTIAN ELEMENTS		
	Abnormal position	Dinner set	Pitcher and/or glass	Obulus	Other gravegoods	Stone cover on grave	Orientation	Plastered grave walls	Crossed arms
28	disturbed	no	no	no	no	no	W-E	no	no
29	disturbed	no data	no data	no data	no data	no	no data	no data	no data

3.6. Graves at Czindery Street (110 graves)

Grave. No.	PAGAN ELEMENTS			COMMON ELEMENTS				EARLY CHRISTIAN ELEMENTS		
	Abnormal position	Dinner set	Pitcher and/or glass	Obulus	Other gravegoods	Stone cover on grave	Orientation	Plastered grave walls	Crossed arms
1	yes	no	no	no	jewellery	no	NW-SE	no	no
2	no	no	no	no	jewellery	no	NW-SE	no	no
3	no data	no data	no data	no data	no	no	E-W	no	no data
4	no	no	no	no	no	no	NW-SE	no	no
5	no data	no	no	no	no	no	NW-SE	no	no data
6	no	no	no	?	no	yes	SE-NW	no	no
7	no	no	no	no	jewellery	no	NE-SW	no	no
8	no	no	no	no	no	no	E-W	no	no
9	no	no	no	no	jewellery	no	NW-SE	no	no
10	no data	no	no	no	iron, bronze	no	NW-SE	no	no
11	no	no	no	no	jewellery	no	NE-SW	no	yes
12	disturbed	no	no	no		maybe	NE-SW	no	no
13	no	no	no	yes	jewellery	no	SW-NE	no	no
14	no	no	no	no	jewellery	no	E-W	no	yes
15	disturbed	no data	no data	maybe	no	no	W-E	no	no data
16	no	no	no	no	no	no	W-E	no	no
17	no data	no data	no data	no data	no data	no data	no data	no data	no data
18	no data	no data	no data	no data	no data	no data	no data	no data	no data
19	disturbed	no data	no data	no data	no data	no data	no data	no data	no data
20	no data	no data	no data	no data	no data	no data	no data	no data	no data
21	no	no	no	no	iron obj.	no	NE-SW	no	no
22	no	no	no	no	no	no	NE-SW	no	no
23	no	no	no	no	jewellery	yes	NE-SW	no	no
24	no data	no data	no data	no data	no data	no data	NE-SW	no data	no data
25	disturbed	no	no	no		no	S-N	no	no
26	disturbed	no data	no data	no data	no data	no data	no data	no data	no data
27	disturbed	no data	no data	no data	no data	no		no data	yes
28	no	no	no	?		no data	NE-SW	no data	no data

Grave. No.	PAGAN ELEMENTS			COMMON ELEMENTS			EARLY CHRISTIAN ELEMENTS		
	Abnormal position	Dinner set	Pitcher and/or glass	Obulus	Other gravegoods	Stone cover on grave	Orientation	Plastered grave walls	Crossed arms
29	no	no	no	no	no	no data	E-W	no	no
30	no	no	no	no	no	no	E-W	no	no
31	no	no	no	no	jewellery	no	E-W	no	no
32	no	no	no	no	no	no	NE-SW	no	no
33	no	no	no	no	no	no	N-S	no	no
34	no	no	no	no	no	no	W-E	no	no
35	no	no	no	no	jewellery	no	W-E	no	???
36	disturbed	no data	no data	no data	no data	no	E-W	no	no data
37	yes	no	no	no	no	no	W-E	no	no
38	no	no	no	no	jewellery	no	E-W	no	yes
39	no	no	no	no	crossbow brooch bronze object	no	W-E	no	yes
40	no data	bo data	no data	no data	no data	no data	no data	no data	no data
41	no	no	no	no	jewellery	no data	E-W	no	no
42	disturbed	no data	no data	no data	crossbow brooch	no data	E-W	no data	no data
43	no data	no data	no data	no data	no data	no data	no data	no data	no data
44	no data	no data	no data	no data	no data	no data	no data	no data	no data
45	no data	no data	no data	no data	no data	no data	no data	no data	no data
46	disturbed	no	no	no	no	no data	E-W	no	no
47	disturbed	no	no	no	no	no	W-E	no	no
48	no	no	no	no	jewellery	no	E-W	no	no
49	no	no	no	no	jewellery	no	E-W	no	yes
50	no	no	no	no	jewellery	no	E-W	no	no
51	no data	no data	no data	no data	no data	no data	no data	no data	no data
52	disturbed	no	no	yes	jewellery	yes	W-E	no	no
53	no	no	no	no	jewellery	no	E-W	no	no
54	no	no	no	no	no	no	W-E	no	no
55	no	no	no	no	no	no	E-W	no	no
56	no	no	no	no	no	no	E-W	no	nono
57	no	no	no	no	no	no	E-W	no	no
58	disturbed	no	no	no	jewellery	no	E-W	no	yes
59	no data	no data	no data	no data	no data	no data	no data	no data	no data
60	no	no	no	no	jewellery	no	E-W	no	no
61	disturbed	no data	no data	no data	no data	no data	E-W	no data	no data
62	yes	no	no	no	crossbow brooch	no	W-E	no	no
63	no data	no data	no data	no data	no data	no data	E-W	no data	no data

	PAGAN ELEMENTS			COMMON ELEMENTS			EARLY CHRISTIAN ELEMENTS		
Grave. No.	Abnormal position	Dinner set	Pitcher and/or glass	Obulus	Other gravegoods	Stone cover on grave	Orientation	Plastered grave walls	Crossed arms
64	no	no	no	yes	iron piece	no	E-W	no	no
65	yes	no	no	no	no	no	E-W	no	no
66	no	no	no	no	jewellery	no	E-W	no	no
67	no data	no data	no data	no data	no data	no data	no data	no data	no data
68	disturbed	no data	no data	no data	no data	no data	E-W	no data	no data
69	disturbed	no data	no data	no data	no data	no data	E-W	no data	no data
70	no	no	no	no	knife	no	E-W	no	no
					crossbow brooch			no	no
					belt buckle				
71	disturbed	no	no	no	no	no	E-W	no	no
72	disturbed	no	no	no	no	no	E-W	no	no
73	no	no	no	no			W-E	no	no
74	no	no	no	no			W-E	no	no
75	no	no	no				NE-SW	no	no
76	disturbed	no data	no data	no data	no data		E-W	no	no
77	disturbed	no	no			no	E-W	no	no
					jewellery				
78	no	no	no		jewellery	no	W-E	no	no
79	no	no	no		jewellery	no	W-E	no	no
80	no	no	no		no	no	E-W	no	no
81	no	no	no		no	no	N-S	no	no
82	no	no	no		bronze object	no	E-W	no	no
83	no	no		yes	crossbow brooch	no	E-W	no	no
					bronze object				
84	no data	no data	no data	no data	no data	no	E-W	no data	no data
85	no	no	no	yes	jewellery	no	E-W	no	no
86	disturbed	no	no	no	jewellery	no	SE-NW	no	yes
					bronz belt				
87					earring		NW-SE		
88	no		pottery jug	yes	earring	partial	E-W	no	no
			pottery jar		bracelets				
					iron fragment				
					pot				
89	no	no	no	no	no		W-E	no	no
90	no	no	no	no	belt buckle	no	E-W	no	no
91	disturbed	no	no	no	no	no	NE-SW	no	no
92	disturbed	no	no	no	no	no	E-W	no	noyes
93	yes	no data	no data	no data	no	no	E-W	no	no data

	PAGAN ELEMENTS			COMMON ELEMENTS			EARLY CHRISTIAN ELEMENTS		
Grave. No.	Abnormal position	Dinner set	Pitcher and/or glass	Obulus	Other gravegoods	Stone cover on grave	Orientation	Plastered grave walls	Crossed arms
94	no	no	no	no	jewellery	no	E-W	no	no
95	disturbed	no data	no data	no data	no	no	W-E	no data	no data
96	disturbed	no	no	no	jewellery	no	E-W	no	no
97	no	no	no	no	iron object	no	E-W	no	no
98	disturbed	no data	no data	no data	no data	no	E-W	no data	no data
99	disturbed	no data	no data	no data	no	no	W-E	no	no
100	disturbed	no	no	no	jewellery	no	E-W	no	no
101	disturbed	no data	no data	no data	no data	no	E-W	no	no data
102	no	no	no	no	bronze belt	no	W-E	no	no
103	disturbed	no data	no data	no data	no data	no	E-W	no	no data
104	no data	no data	no data	no data	no data	no data	no data	no data	no data
105	disturbed	no data	no data	no data	no data	no	E-W	no	no data
106	no	no	no	no	no	no	W-E	no	no
107	disturbed	pot	no	yes	iron object	no	E-W	no	no
108	no	no	no	no	jewellery / crossbow brooch / iron spere	no	E-W	no	no
109	disturbed	no	no	no	no	no	E-W	no	no
110	no	no	no	no	jewellery	no	W-E	no	no

An Old–New Theory about Early Christian Burial Characteristics in Sopianae

GRAVES AT 8 APÁCA STREET

At 8 Apáca Street, three burial chambers, two double graves, and thirty-four other graves came to light in 1958 during the excavation of Ferenc Fülep.[55] The orientation of the graves is rather uniform. The main orientation is west-east with slight deviation towards the northwest and southwest in some graves. The lack of grave-goods is striking, especially if we compare this cemetery to the sites nearby, like the group of graves at 3 Székesfehérvár Street and at 14 Apáca Street, where many graves were found with rich grave goods (Tables II–III). Due to the extent of disturbance and destruction to the graves (all the burial chambers, the double graves, and fifteen of the thirty-four

---

[55] Ferenc Fülep, "Késő római temető Pécs – Geisler Eta u. 8. sz. alatt." *Archaeológiai Értesítő* 96 (1969), 3–42; Fülep, 1984. 76; Katona 2013, 158.

other graves came to light severely disturbed) and the low number of grave goods, this cemetery is unlikely to reveal much about the funerary habits of Sopianae or distinguish between pagan and Christian graves. There were no food containers in the graves and glass vessels came to light only in Graves 1, 8, 13, 29, and 37.[56] Fragments of a glass jug and beaker were found only in Grave 1. Coins were also scarce in the graves. Only one was found in Grave 13, which was a brick grave with plastered walls. As for the funerary rite altogether there were seventeen graves with plastered inner walls in this cemetery (Table I), but graves with stone cover above or around them are not known from this site at all. Due to insufficient data regarding the positions of the skeletons this element was not investigated.

GRAVES UNDER 14 APÁCA STREET AND 12 SZENT ISTVÁN SQUARE

Between 1968 and 1970, one hundred four roman graves were excavated around and under cemetery building no. XIII by Ferenc Fülep at 14 Apáca Street and the neighboring plot on 12 Szent István Square. Unfortunately, forty percent of the graves were damaged, destroyed, or disturbed and the human bones were severely decayed even in the undisturbed graves. Due to insufficient data concerning the position of the skeletons and particularly the position of the arms, in this part of the cemetery we can only research the rite, the grave-goods, and the orientation. The orientation of the graves is rather uniform. Ninety-one percent of them were directed west-east, several of them with a little deviation towards the north and south. There were just two graves with unidentifiable orientation.[57] Well built brick and stone graves with massive tile roofs are particularly characteristic to this cemetery. Their inner walls were very often plastered, but plastering occurred on the sidewalls of the simpler earthen graves as well (Table II. Graves 1, 2, 5, 6, 8–11, 16, 20, 22, 24, 26, 27, 34, 42–45, 47, 48, 50–53, 58, 60, 68, 86, 89–91, 96–98, 102–104). The simple earthen grave with a brick roof above the pit is also characteristic to this grave-group. Plastered graves represent some 37% (=38 graves) of the total number of graves. A striking feature of this site is the high number of secondary and multiple burials.[58] Strictly speaking nowhere else in the cemetery of Sopianae was this type of burial found so frequently. There was just one secondary burial at 3 Székesfehérvár Street (Table III. Graves 88 and 91, which were above each other) and at 13 Apáca Street (Table V. Grave 22) but none came to light at the other sites discussed in this article.

There were many grave goods in the graves despite the extensive destruction and disturbance. However, the number of coins in the graves is very low.[59] Ferenc Fülep

---

[56] Fülep 1969, 31 Figs. 48–49.
[57] Katona 2013, 171.
[58] Fülep 1984, 155.
[59] Fülep 1984, 153.

had already drawn our attention to the unusually high number of glass vessels in the graves.[60] Glass vessels that can be connected to drinking or water were often placed in the graves (Table III. Graves 5, 7, 10,11,16, 20, 22, 24, 26, 27, 29–31, 34, 39, 41–44, 50, 51, 53, 67, 77, 81, 84, 85, 89, 90, 99, and 103). Another type of glass vessel, the so-called long spindle-shaped scent bottles, came to light together with pots, jugs, and other glass objects, but obviously with a purpose other than containing water. Graves were generally lacking any objects that could contain food. There were no Christian symbols on the objects at all. In conclusion we may say that in this part of the cemetery the pagan, common, and Christian elements were discovered mixed in the graves, however, those elements that are considered Christian ones are more frequent. There were grave goods in west-east oriented graves, but very few coins were found, although in some cases coins were found in graves with plastered inner walls. Stone cover on graves is not characteristic to this part of the cemetery. For some reason glass vessels and glass scent bottles outnumber jewellery in the graves and these were often put as grave goods into west-east oriented graves. On the basis of all of this it is not possible to distinguish between pagan and Christian graves just on the grounds of the grave goods and funerary rites, despite the fact that there was actually a Christian cemetery building on the site. Also, it cannot be accidental that so many double, triple, and secondary burials came to light here. The earlier explanation that these were family tombs and were in use many times may be correct, but we can also consider another option. People who opened the brick graves again and again to put more bodies in them simply wanted to bury their dead as close to Burial Chamber XIII as possible.

GRAVES AT 3 SZÉKESFEHÉRVÁR (VÖRÖSMARTY) STREET

One hundred fourteen Roman graves were excavated between 1981 and 1983 during a rescue excavation at this site. Above the Roman graves remains of medieval and modern age houses, pits, wells, and kilns were found. We have only excavated inhumation graves here. Some 45 percent of the graves were disturbed, looted, or destroyed. The orientation and forms of the graves were rather diverse.[61] There was no dominant orientation in this part of the cemetery although the west-east alignment or slight deviation from this was very frequent. Also, the number of east-west directed graves were high, and seven north-south oriented graves were found in this part of the cemetery. Similarly, this unusual orientation appeared in many cases on the nearby plot at the yard of the Nagy Lajos High School.[62] The forms of the graves were also rather diverse.[63] There were more earthen graves and less brick built graves. Plastering on the

---

[60] Fülep 1984, 154.
[61] Katona 2013, 172.
[62] Katona 2013, 173.
[63] Katona 2013, 172.

inner grave walls (Table III. Graves 1, 3–5, 14, 16, 17, 48, 61, 72, 78, 90, 91, 94, 96, 98, and 104) is most characteristic to the brick graves, but also occurred on the walls of earthen graves. Similarly, both types of graves were plastered at 14 Apáca Street and at the Nagy Lajos High School site (Tables II–IV). Stone cover above and around the graves was very common in this group of graves. The highest percentage of graves that use stones in the burial practice seems to be here at Székesfehérvár Street. As we have already mentioned, stone cover on and around graves can be considered a part of the structure rather than part of the rite. The stones supported the roof tiles and the tiles or bricks that sealed the graves on the shorter ends. However, very interestingly in two parts of this cemetery, between Graves 24 and 33 and in an area around Graves 10, 11, 14, 19, and 72, we have found a large stone covered surface made of one layer of stones of irregular size. This stone layer was not a natural deposition, it could not be a pavement-like surface as it is too uneven for that. There was no building nearby so it is not rubble either. This surface was on the same level as the Roman graves, therefore, somehow it could have been in some kind of connection with the cemetery, with the burial process or with the rites.

Stones put on and around graves were part of the structure (Table III. Graves 3–5, 14, 16, 17, 47, 48, 55, 61, and 70). For example, during the excavation of Graves 47 and 55 we observed that the stones were put on the long walls of the grave and were supposed to support the roof. On Grave 61 not only were the roof and the sides covered with stones, but it expanded to the shorter end of the grave forming a half-circle shaped feature there. The inner walls of this grave were plastered, and there were no grave goods in the grave. At the excavation we have found only one grave that was properly "wrapped" in stones. This was Grave 29, with north-south orientation. A carefully placed circle of stones was found around the skeleton. It was a child's grave and some pieces of jewellery were found in it. There was no brick roof on the grave.

The position of the skeletons in Graves 20, 22, 37, 39, 40, and 59 was abnormal to some extent. In Grave 20 a child's skeleton was excavated on its side. The grave was disturbed, its orientation was east-west, and there were just a few glass beads in the grave. In the other graves the legs were pulled up or showed other abnormalities. Their orientation is diverse, and there was only one grave with grave goods. In Grave 37 one bronze belt buckle came to light (Table III. Graves 20, 22, 37, 39, 40, and 59).

The high number of coins is striking in this part of the cemetery, especially if we compare it to the neighboring sites, such as 8 Apáca Street or 14 Apáca Street, where coins were very scarce. In another cemetery nearby, at 13 Apáca Street, there were no coins in the graves at all. In our cemetery in Grave 4 we found a pair of pierced pendants, one of them was decorated with the Christ-monogram and was made out of a coin. We probably may say that the Christian population of the town was not keen to carry on with putting *oboli* into the graves but found an alternative use of the coin and made a piece of jewellery out of it.

Pagan, "common", and Christian elements appear mixed in some of the graves or there is an overlap of elements in others (Table III. Graves 3, 91, 92,98, and 104.) However, some features point out that the pagan presence was still strong in this part of the cemetery. The number of coins, which may have been used as *oboli* is high, there is at least one grave with stone cover on the site and the number of pottery and glass jugs as well as cups and beakers also increased. Further research will be necessary to establish the exact date of the graves. It would help us to create a timeline of the cemetery and would also help us to distinguish—if at all possible—between the manifestations of the different religions in the town of Sopianae during the Late Roman Period.

GRAVES UNDER THE GROUNDS OF THE CISTERCIAN NAGY LAJOS HIGH SCHOOL, PÉCS, SZÉCHENYI SQUARE

In the inner yard of the high school a large group of cremated and inhumated graves were excavated between 2002 and 2004 during a rescue excavation carried out by Gábor Kárpáti.[64] We do not discuss the cremated graves in this article. There were 111 inhumation graves excavated on the site and they were very diverse in every aspects of our research. There was no dominant orientation, although the majority of the graves were west-east oriented with a little deviation to the northwest or southwest in some graves.[65] A reasonably high percentage of the graves were directed to the opposite east-west direction or with slight deviation towards the north or south (Table IV). The walls of the graves were often plastered, but only the walls of west-east or northwest-southeast oriented brick built graves. At other sites, especially at 3 Székesfehérvár Street and 14 Apáca Street walls of earthen graves were often plastered too.

We have to be very careful when discussing the problem of stone covered graves. As was already mentioned by Ferenc Fülep, the graves were deepened into the pannon soil, which naturally contains pebbles and small stones. Therefore small stones naturally occurred around the graves. But in this site there were nine graves covered with stones of larger size mostly on the long walls and they had a proper function in the graves. They were supposed to support the roof tiles or the tiles on the shorter ends of the grave. Proper stone covered graves were not excavated here. On the other hand, this is not important at all, as we have already mentioned in the discussion of the Székesféhérvár Street cemetery, stones on and around graves —with very few exceptions—were not part of the rituals, but part of the grave structure.

At this site the skeletons were found in an abnormal position in six graves (Table IV. Graves 37, 41, 52, 66, 96, and 111). The orientation of Grave 52 (without grave goods) was almost exactly west-east, the other five were oriented towards the

---

[64] Gábor Olivér, "Three new finds of the Danubian horseman from Baranya county." In: *Pannonica provincialia et archaeologica*, I. Budapest, 2003, 449–466; Katona 2013 161.

[65] Katona 2013, 172.

southwest or northeast. Three of the skeletons were laid down on their sides, one in a slightly crouched position, one with pulled-up hands, and one with pulled-up legs. Grave goods were found in Graves 37 and 41. Grave 41 was a northeast-southwest oriented brick grave with plastered inner walls. There was a glass cup, a coin, and few pieces of jewellery in it. As we can see from this the pagan, common, and Christian elements came to light within the same grave. Why were these people buried in this prehistoric-like position in their graves? It was an equally unusual habit in both Roman-pagan and Christian graves. There were no grave goods in two of these graves, therefore we can assume that these were graves of the poor.

It is not always easy to figure out how the deceased was laid in the grave at the time of the funeral. Unless it was wrapped in a shroud or sheet or was put into a tight coffin, or the grave was filled up with some sort of filling the arms and legs may have moved during the decomposition of the body. Therefore the position of the arms is the less reliable element in establishing the religion of the deceased.[66]

We are emphasizing again that similarly to other grave groups in Sopianae many graves came to light with damage or disturbance on the site. The graves were rich in grave goods, but objects that can be connected to food (pots, plates, bowls) are very scarce. There are seven graves furnished with these objects, namely, Graves 12, 39, 61, 83, 90, and 97A. The latter grave was a west-east oriented brick grave with plastering on the inner wall. There was a bronze bowl and one coin in it. Objects that could be used as water containers such as glass or earthenware bottles, jugs, cups, and beakers were used as grave goods more often. These came to light in both brick and earthen graves (Table V. Graves 8, 19, 25, 26, 40, 41, 48, 55, 58, 68, 69, 73, 83, 93, 94, 95, and 108). Coins were also found in great number in the graves (Table V, 8, 12, 19, 25, 39, 42, 55, 58, 59, 76, 81, 83, 87, 89, 92, 94, 100, 106, and 108). This is similar to the neighbouring Székesfehérvár Street site where there were very many coins in the graves, too.[67]

It seems that in this part of the cemetery the pagan, common, and Christian elements came to light mixed in the graves, for example, in Graves 8, 12, 22, 25, 39, 59, 68, 89, and 108 (Table V). However, some graves may have belonged to the pagan population of the town. This is not surprising as this cemetery was also used for cremation burials in earlier times.[68] We will carry on with our research and analysis in the future to figure out the inner chronology of this cemetery and to find out more about this

---

[66] In Sopianae the brick and stone built graves were either not filled in with any substance or we simply do not have proof of it thus far, therefore the limbs may have not been in their original position at the time of the excavation. In Britannia Province late Roman graves came to light in York and Poundbury where the stone coffins were filled up with gypsum. [Alison Taylor: *Burial Practice in Early England*. Stroud, 2001, 129.]

[67] Katona 2013, 108.

[68] Gábor 2003.

interesting group of graves because at the present our analysis is not detailed enough to distinguish between the pagan and Christian graves.

GRAVES AT 13 APÁCA STREET

In 2004 twenty-nine Roman graves, remains of Roman and medieval buildings, pits, wells, and other features came to light during a rescue excavation at 13 Apáca Street.[69] The majority of the graves were disturbed, which puts a limit to our research regarding the evaluation of the grave goods and rites. West-east orientation is dominant fifteen graves (52 percent), four graves (14 percent) were oriented to the opposite direction, towards the east. Only one grave was oriented south-north. Due to disturbance it was not possible to figure out the orientation of seven graves (24 percent). Most of the graves are simple earthen graves, with brick roof above them. This type of grave is characteristic to the entire cemetery of Sopianae.[70] The inner walls of Graves 8, 18, 19, 21, and 27 were plastered, all of them were made of bricks and stones and were oriented west-east. In this part of the cemetery there was no plaster on the walls of the earthen graves. The bodies were on their back in their graves with one exception. In Grave 23 a skeleton with somewhat pulled-up legs was found and we can probably see it as an abnormal position. There were two skeletons in the west-east oriented Grave 22. It is the only double burial at this site. The bodies were not buried together, the one on the left hand side was put into the grave sometime later when the grave pit was enlarged in order to accommodate this body. Arms crossed over the middle part of the body occurred in nine graves (31 percent) (Table V. Graves 2, 12, 14, 16, 19, 22, 24, 25, and 27).[71]

In general there were very few grave goods in the graves, even if we take the high percentage of the disturbed graves into consideration, furthermore the objects are scarce even in the undisturbed graves. If there were objects in the graves they were mostly jewellery and pieces of belt mounts. There were no coins, pottery, or glass vessels. In conclusion we may say, that the pagan elements, such as dinner sets, *oboli,* or the abnormal position of the deceased were not characteristic to this part of the cemetery. As for the Christian elements, the west-east orientation and the presence of plastered grave walls were significant and in many cases so were the crossed arms above the middle part of the body. In this group of graves it is the early Christian elements that dominate and the occurrence of the pagan elements are less significant.

---

[69] For this research, we used the original documentation of the excavation kept in the Archive of the Archaeological Department of the Janus Pannonius Museum of Pécs, Inv. n.: 2058–2004.

[70] Katona 2013, 166.

[71] It is important to emphasize that the arms only remained in their original position if the deceased was wrapped in a shroud or sheet or was put into a narrow coffin, otherwise the limbs could have moved during the decomposition of the body, therefore it would be difficult to figure out the original position of the arms and legs.

GRAVES IN CZINDERY STREET (SOUTHERN PART OF SOPIANAE)

It is worthwhile to compare the data of the above discussed cemetery parts to the One hundred ten graves of the Czindery Street Roman cemetery that was excavated in 2002.[72] It is situated approximately one mile away from the northern cemetery. It is a separate cemetery not only because of its geographical position, but also because of the obvious archaeological differences. First of all, the difference in the orientation of the graves is striking. At this site the number of east-west oriented graves is much higher than in any part of the northern cemetery.[73] Simple earth graves predominated the site and there were no plastering on the walls of the graves. Stone covered graves were rare, there were just a few cases in this cemetery (Table VI. Graves 6, 23, and 88). We cannot see any difference in the position of the arms or the skeleton overall. At the Czindery Street site there were eight skeletons (Table VI. Graves 11, 14, 27, 38, 39, 49, 58, and 66) with crossed arms and there were seven similar graves at 3 Székesfehérvár Street (Table III. Graves 13, 23, 32, 42, 75, 81, and 101) and eight at 13 Apáca Street (Table V. Graves 2, 12, 14, 19, 22, 24, 25 and 27). Significantly more, twelve graves, were found with crossed arms at the Nagy Lajos High School excavation (Table V. Graves 8, 10, 12, 13, 22, 23, 33, 59, 60, 75, 80, 83, and 84). There were no glass vessels in the graves and both pottery and coins were also rare. Altogether there were only two pots and seven coins excavated in this cemetery, however jewellery was more frequently put into the graves. Pieces of jewellery and bronze or iron items came to light in 40 percent of the graves (44 graves).

Conclusions

It seems that those burial characteristics that were observed earlier and were considered theoretically to be early Christian are not applicable to the entire cemetery of Sopianae. Christian and pagan characteristics often came to light next to each other or in the same grave.

In the northwestern corner of Sopianae's fourth-century cemetery, Christians always oriented their graves west-east, but sometimes pagans did the same in other parts of the cemetery.

Upon moving further toward the east and southeast from this Christian section of the cemetery, the number of graves with west-east orientation gradually decreases and the number of graves with an orientation other than west-east increases.[74]

---

[72] Special thanks to Gábor Kárpáti for his permission to use of the original documentation in this research. Inv. no. 2069–2004, 2068–2004, 2077–2007, Department of Archaeology, Janus Pannonius Museum in Pécs.
[73] Katona 2013, 173.
[74] Katona 2013, 172.

Graves with west-east orientation predominated in the northwestern part of the cemetery. The result of the examination of the six grave groups (Tables I–V) shows that in the middle and eastern part of the cemetery, the number of west-east oriented graves decreased towards the east. In another cemetery nearby (Czindery Street, Table VI) the east-west orientation was the most frequent. The west-east orientation is a Christian characteristic in our classification, but obviously the orientation on its own cannot prove that the grave belonged to a Christian person.

Crossing the arms and positioning them on the middle part of the body is probably the least convincing Christian burial characteristic. This position of the arms was very rare even in west-east oriented, possibly Christian, graves of Sopianae.

Zsolt Visy recently suggested[75] that graves with plastered inner walls[76] can be Christian. According to his opinion the burial chambers and the graves were essentially the same, because both were the final resting place of the dead. Both had plastered walls and in some cases painted with frescoes. Based on his reasoning it seemed logical to accept plastered walls as a Christian characteristic and to include it in our criteria. From our charts it is obvious that most of the graves did not belong to this category and only the minority of the stone and brick graves were plastered inside. At 13 Apáca Street and Nagy Lajos High School sites only the walls of brick built graves were plastered, but at other sites, like at Székesfehérvár Street and 14 Apáca Street walls of earthen graves with brick roof were plastered, too. There were no plastered graves in the cemetery at Czindery Street. The orientation of the plastered graves is west-east in most cases, but there are exceptions, like Grave 3 at Székesfehérvár Street, which was oriented east-west.

Recent archaeological research offers a very colorful picture regarding many issues of the late Roman cemeteries of Sopianae, such as how they were opened and managed and also about the religion of those buried there.[77]

In Sopianae, the northwestern part of the cemetery belonged to Christians in the fourth and fifth centuries. By the end of the fourth century the Church might have been involved in cemetery matters to some extent, but because the architecture of the buildings and the appearance of the graves were very diverse, and also reflect the differ-

---

[75] We would like to thank Visy Zsolt for his permission to use his manuscript "Paradise in the Early Christian cemetery of Sopianae."

[76] Taylor, *Burial Practice in Early England*. Stroud 2001, 129.

[77] Éric Rebillard, *Religion et sépulture. L'Église, les vivants et les morts dans l'Antiquité tardive*. Parois : ÉHESS, 2003. Rebillard's theses are taken over by Nicola Denzey Lewis, "Reinterpreting "Pagans" and "Christians" from Rome's Late Antique Mortuary Evidence." In: M. R. Salzman – M. Sághy – N. L. Testa (eds.): *Pagans and Christians in Late Antique Rome*. Cambridge: Cambridge University Press, 2015, 273–290. The Greek word *koimeterion* means graves, not cemeteries. The Christian use of the Latin *coemeterium* from the second to the fourth centuries refers to burial sites above ground, certainly different from medieval graveyards (such as the German *Friedhof*) around churches: Ulrich Volp, *Tod und Ritual in den christlichen Gemeinden der Antike*. Leiden-Boston: De Gruyter, 2002, 112.

ences in the social and financial status of the families using the cemetery, it is most likely that the Church was only an organizer rather than the owner.[78] The role of the Church increased significantly in another aspect of the cemeteries in the fourth century, namely regarding saints'cults. Under the instructions of the bishops the majority of saints'relics were taken out of private ownership and were made available to everyone, first only in cemeteries, but later in churches too. This transition is palpable at Pécs, where the *fenestella* of Burial Chamber I was still strictly a place for private relics, but not far from it a mausoleum of a saint (or saints), managed by the Church, was already in existence.

Although certain written sources suggest that the cemeteries might have been managed by the Church even before 313 AD, by the end of the fourth century the clergy almost certainly was involved with the cemetery.[79] Otherwise it would be difficult to explain the sudden appearance of the newly opened early Christian cemeteries or portions of cemeteries, the development and supervision of the *depositio ad sanctos*, the increased number of cemetery buildings, which were built in carefully selected locations, the existence of communal funeral rites, the erection of buildings for community use and the encouragement to dispel earlier pagan rites. The fourth-century early Christian Church had no intention to control every aspect of life (and death). The takeover of cemeteries was a long process in late Roman times;[80] the Church kept an eye on

---

[78] In the Roman cemeteries and catacombs, the desire to bury family members together, often in case of popes, survived for a long time. In Sopianae, despite the difference in the landscape and surroundings between the different parts of the cemetery, the diversity of the architecture suggest similar traditions until the beginning of the fifth century. The number of communal buildings only increased in the last phase of the cemetery.
See Mark Joseph Johnson, "Pagan-Christian Burial Practices of the Fourth Century: Shared Tombs?" *Journal of Early Christian Studies* 5.1 1997. 37–59.41.). See also Vincenzo Fiocchi Nicolai, *Strutture funerary edifici di culto paleocristiani di Roma dal IV al VI secolo*. Città di Vaticano: Pontificia commissione di archeologia sacra, 2001. Just like the catacombs of Rome, the early Christian cemetery of Sopianae was managed by the Church by the end of the fourth century. Without the Church it would be difficult to explain the uniform Christian iconography and decoration of the buildings. Individual graves and buildings, however, belonged to private families. The very last building of the cemetery may be the poor quality Burial Chamber XXXV, a family burial site, built at the beginning of the fifth century: Zsolt Tóth, "Rómaikori sírépítmény a Széchenyi téren." [Roman Burial Building on Széchenyi Square.] *Pécsi Szemle* (2010), 16.

[79] Nammius Quintus, an undertaker (*custor cymiteri*) in Pannonian Savaria (present day Szombathely), who died at an extreme old age: Gábor Kiss- Endre Tóth – Balázs Zágorhidi Czigány, *Szombathely története a városalapításától 1526-ig* [History of Szombathely from the Beginning to 1526.] Szombathely, 1998, 64. Nagyné Hudák Krisztina, A kereszténység története a Kárpát-medencében 374–456 között./History of the Christianity in the Carpathian basin between 374–456. Dokt. dissz. manuscript, ELTE BTK, 2012.Budapest. 123.). Nammius Quintus' fifth-century gravestone came to light at Saint Martin Church in Savaria. His old age indicates that he might have worked in the cemetery as early as the end of the fourth century.

[80] Ireland, situated outside of the Empire, is a good example. Although Christianity appeared as early as the fourth century, the Church took control over cemeteries relatively late, from the end of the seventh century. We would like to thank Elizabeth O'Brien for this information. According to Ulrich Volp there were different stages in the Church's involvement in the funeral rites: first there were funeral services without any Church involvement, although there might have been some self-control on behalf of the bereaved, later the wake devel-

the cemetery and on the plots (though not necessarily a religious act), but it was not involved in individual burials. Officially they only regulated the prayers and the order of commemoration.[81] Sopianae, as the headquarter of Valeria Province, witnessed the slow expansion of the Church's role, but due to the arrival of the Huns at the beginning of the fifth century it could not see it completed.

In Sopianae first only the northeastern "quarter" of Northern Cemetery was managed entirely by Christians, later they control took over the whole cemetery. On the northeastern side the presence of large communal buildings (*Cella Septichora*, early Christian mausoleum) and other large buildings that were built earlier, but underwent some alteration by that time (Burial Chamber V,[82] and the XIII building at 14 Apáca Street[83]) suggest not only the existence of an already independent Christian cemetery, but also some kind of organized building activity and communal rites performed by the Christian community. The *depositio ad sanctos* was practiced exclusively by Christians and probably shows the existence of a martyr grave in the cemetery.

The uniformization of grave-goods in late Roman times, or the lack thereof, can be explained by widespread economic and political changes, the pauperization of the population, and certainly by some changes in funerals, as well as in the transformation of the religious beliefs of the people of Sopianae. To be able to draw a more accurate picture of the funerary habits of Sopianae in late Roman times and to make our observations more precise, we need to carry out more thorough research over the coming years. Our research continues—the revision of archaeological data has only begun.

---

oped into psalm singing, and finally efforts were made to unify the funeral services. As a result of this the impurity of death became part of the church's services—family funerals became church liturgy (the first evidence that proves that priests attended funerals comes from the second century—Tertullianus, *De Anima* LI), and the wake developed into the joy of the resurrection in heaven (Volp 2002 183–185 195–198).

[81] Mark Joseph Johnson, Pagan-Christian Burial Practices of the Fourth Century: Shared Tombs? *Journal of Early Christian Studies* 5.1 (1997), 43.

[82] Gábor Olivér, "Early Christian Buildings in the Northern Cemetery of Sopianae." *Studia Patristica* LXXIII. 2014, 39–42.

[83] Fülep 1984, 99–101.

IMPACT BEYOND THE EMPIRE:
PAGAN AND CHRISTIAN BURIAL IN IRELAND
(1ST–8TH CENTURIES)

Elizabeth O'Brien

Whilst contacts between Ireland, Britain, and continental Europe have been active since the Neolithic period,[1] the purpose of this paper is to draw attention to contacts with the Roman world, particularly with Roman and post-Roman Britain, during the Irish later Iron Age, that is, from the first to the eighth centuries AD, concentrating mainly on the fourth to eighth centuries, using archaeological evidence for burial practices in combination with primary documentary sources.

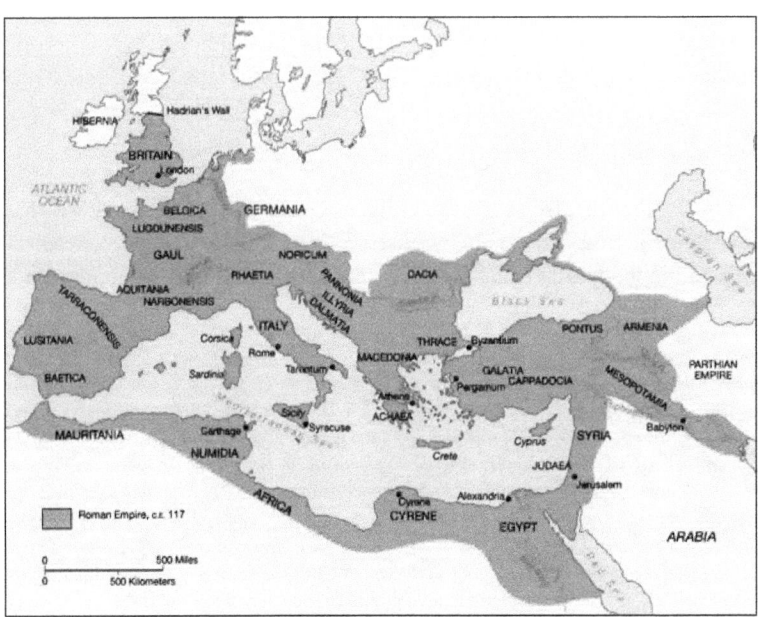

Figure 1. Map of Roman Empire c. AD 117.

---

[1] John Waddell, "The Irish Sea in Prehistory," *The Journal of Irish Archaeology* VI 1991/92 (1992): 29–40.

Ireland (known to the Romans as Hibernia), was located at the extreme western fringe of, but was never absorbed into, the Roman Empire. (fig. 1) However, the Roman world was not unaware of Ireland's existence, and while the island never became part of the Empire, absorbing it was contemplated. For instance, Tacitus records that Agricola, who was Governor of Britain AD 78–84, had given the matter some thought, but for whatever reason he did not act on it. Agricola was also very aware of maritime trading and traffic into Irish harbors:

> ...he also manned with troops that part of the British coast which faces Ireland, in hope of future action rather than out of fear; for Ireland, I believe, which lies between Britain and Spain and also commands the Gallic Sea, would unite, to their mutual advantage, the most effective portions of our Empire...we are better informed, thanks to the trade of merchants, about the approaches to the island and its harbours...I have often heard my father-in-law say that with one legion and a fair contingent of irregulars Ireland could be overpowered and held....[2]

Further evidence that Ireland was familiar to mariners, and undoubtedly to traders, in the second century AD can be deduced from the map of Ireland produced by Claudius Ptolemaeus as part of his map of Europe c. AD 150, which, although based on copies made in the medieval period, still retains place-names based on the language of Old Irish.[3]

Iron Age Burial Rites

During the Irish Iron Age, the indigenous burial rite in Ireland was that of cremation, with cremation deposits being inserted, probably in organic containers (never in ceramic containers),[4] into small pits, or spread directly onto the ground surface. These

---

[2] *Tacitus: Bk.1 Agricola*, trans. M. Hutton, rev. ed. R. M. Ogilvie (Massachusetts & London: Loeb Classical Library, Harvard University Press, 1970 edition), cap. 24, 70–71: *...eamque partem Brittaniae quae Hiberniam aspicit copiis instruxit, in spem magis quam ob formidinem, si quidem Hibernia medio inter Britanniam atque Hispaniam sita et Gallico quoque mari opportuna valentissimam imperii partem magnis in vicem usibus miscuerit...melius aditus portusque per commercia et negotiatores cogniti... Saepe ex eo audivi legione una et modicis auxiliis debellari obtinerique Hiberniam posse...*

[3] For details and context of early Irish place-names see Gregory Toner, "Identifying Ptolemy's Irish places and tribes," in *Ptolemy. Towards a linguistic atlas of the earliest Celtic place-names of Europe*, eds. D. M. Parsons and Patrick Sims-Williams (Aberystwyth: CMCS Publications, 2000), 73–82.

[4] At some point between 700 BC and 400 BC the Irish abandoned the use of pottery and adopted an aceramic culture, leading to a complete absence of ceramic containers for domestic or for funerary purposes. See Barry Raftery, "The Conundrum of Irish Iron Age Pottery," in *Sites and Sights of the Iron Age*, Oxbow Monograph 56, eds. Barry Raftery, Vincent Megaw, and Valery Rigby (vcially.Oxford, 1995), 152.

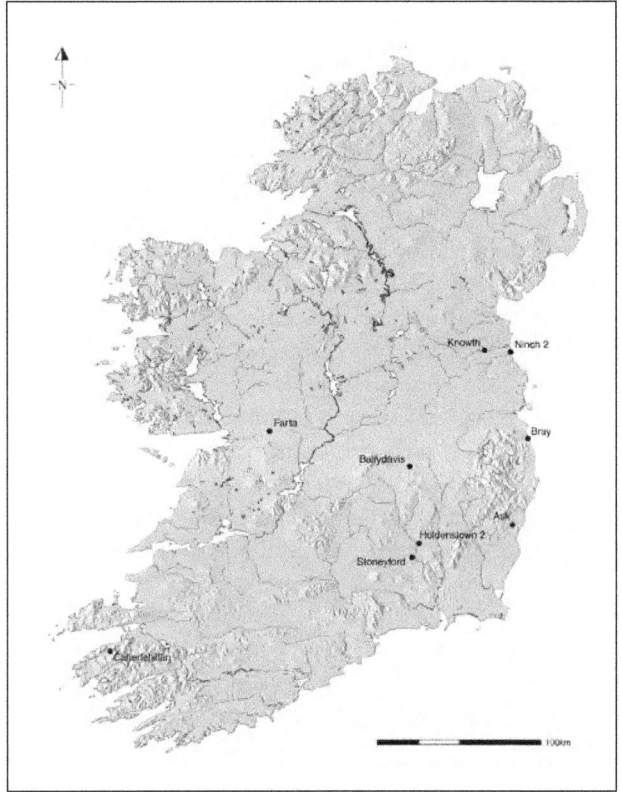

Figure 2. Map of Ireland showing location of places referred to in the text.
© The Discovery Programme & E. O'Brien

deposits were placed usually in the encircling fosse of ring-barrows, but sometimes in the interior, or, they were inserted into already existing burial monuments. Many cremation deposits are unaccompanied by grave goods, however, when grave goods are present they consist of items of personal adornment, for instance, glass beads, some of which are highly decorated, amber beads, iron or copper-alloy safety-pin type fibulae, and in one instance a small decorated circular bronze box recovered in a cremation deposit dated from the fourth to first century BC[5] at Ballydavis, Co. Laois (fig. 2).[6] These goods,

---

[5] GrA-13594: 2140±50BP. Calibrated at 2 sigma using OxCal 4.2 = 359–47 cal BC. Original date: Jan Lanting and Anna L. Brindley, "Dating Cremated bone: The Dawn of a New Era," *Journal of Irish Archaeology* IX (1998): 1–7.

[6] Valerie J. Keeley, "No. 173, Ballydavis. Early Iron Age complex," in *Excavations 1995*, ed. Isabel Bennett (Dublin: Wordwell, 1996), 51.

which are not of native manufacture, provide evidence for outside contacts, influences, or intrusions during this period, probably from Britain.[7] The small decorated circular bronze box, for instance, is paralleled by a similar box from a female cart burial (cart burial 2) at Wetwang Slack, Yorkshire,[8] and is dateable to a similar period.[9] Evidence for contact with the pagan Roman (or Romano-British) world is provided by a Roman type, first century cremation burial discovered at Stoneyford, Co. Kilkenny (fig. 2), beside the Kings River, a tributary of the major navigable River Nore. When this burial was unearthed in the mid-nineteenth century it was described as having been discovered within a circular enclosure. The burial, which is unique in an Irish context, consisted of a glass urn containing a cremation, covered by a bronze mirror, accompanied by a glass lachrymatory (*unguentarium*) and protected by stones.[10] The glass urn has been described as being of ordinary Roman table glass of the first century AD.[11] The location of Stoneyford close to a navigable river is important, for it indicates possible traders, probably from Roman Britain in the first century AD, whose presence would appear to have been accepted by the local indigenous population.

Further burial evidence for direct contact with the pagan Roman world is provided by a small group of inhumation burials discovered in 1835 above the high water line on the beach at Bray, Co. Wicklow by workmen (fig. 2). This event is recorded two years later, in 1837, when it is described as "several skeletons laid side by side with a stone at the head and feet, and accompanied by coins of Trajan 97–117 AD and Hadrian 117–138 AD found in the thoracic area of the skeletons."[12] (It is usual that coins

---

[7] Elizabeth O'Brien, *Post-Roman Britain to Anglo-Saxon England: Burial Practices Reviewed* (Oxford: BAR 289 (British Series), 1999), 26–27 (hereafter O'Brien, Post-Roman Britain); Original three volume PhD thesis available at http://ora.ox.ac.uk/objects/uuid:e415687f-4964-4225-8bc3-23e4ab8e5e78; Elizabeth O'Brien, "Burial Practices in Ireland; first to seventh centuries AD," in *Sea Change: Orkney and Northern Europe in the later Iron Age AD 300*–800, eds. Jane Downes and Anna Ritchie (Angus: Pinkfoot Press, 2003), 63–65, (hereafter O'Brien, "Burial Practices"); Elizabeth O'Brien, "Pagan or Christian? Burial in Ireland during the 5th to 8th centuries AD," in *The archaeology of the Early Medieval Celtic Churches* Society for Medieval Archaeology Monograph 29, Society for Church Archaeology Monograph 1, ed. Nancy Edwards (Leeds: Maney Publishing, 2009), 136 (hereafter O'Brien, "Pagan or Christian?").

[8] John Dent, "Three cart burials from Wetwang, Yorkshire," in *Antiquity* LIX (1985): 85–92, plates XVIII–XXI.

[9] OxA-14113: 2227±30BP. Calibrated at 2 sigma = 390-200 cal BC.

[10] From Edward Clibborn's scrapbook, "Relating to articles exhibited this 19th of May 1852," *Illustrated Notebook*, Royal Irish Academy MS24, E.34.

[11] Edward Bourke, "Stoneyford: a first-century Roman burial from Ireland," *Archaeology Ireland* 3, no. 2 (1989): 56–57; Edward Bourke, "Glass vessels of the First Nine Centuries AD in Ireland," *Journal of the Royal Society of Antiquaries of Ireland* 124 (1994): 163–209.

[12] Samuel Lewis, *A Topographical Dictionary of Ireland* (London: Lewis & Co., 1837), 223; William Hamilton Drummond, "On Roman coins found in Ireland," *Proceedings of the Royal Irish Academy* 2, 1840–1844 (1844): 185–90; J.D. Bateson, "Roman Material from Ireland: a reconsideration," *Proceedings of the Royal Irish Academy* 73C (1973): 21–79, especially 35 (hereafter Bateson, "Roman Material"); Elizabeth O'Brien, "Iron Age burial practices in Leinster: Continuity and Change," *Emania* 7 (1990): 37–42; Elizabeth O'Brien, "Pagan and

placed in the mouth will fall into the upper thoracic area with decomposition of the body). These burials at Bray represent a burial-rite that has been recognized in Romano-British contexts from the second century onwards.[13] These individuals were buried by their peers who were familiar with these burial rites, with the coins representing the Roman custom of including Charon's fee to enable the deceased to pay the ferryman in order to cross the River Styx,[14] a custom otherwise unknown in Ireland, which did not have a coin-based currency. As coastal erosion is a major problem in this area up to the present day, it is possible that when these burials were interred almost two thousand years ago the shore-line was very different to that of the present time, and the burials could have been part of a dry-land cemetery, the greater part of which has, over time, been eroded by the sea. Also, the fact that coins spanning the first half of the second century AD were used, implies a succession of burials, perhaps involving a couple of generations, rather than just one burial episode. The evidence suggests that these burials possibly represent the presence of a pagan Romano-British settlement or trading-post close to this location on the eastern coast during the early second century AD. These are the only known second century extended inhumation burials in Ireland, an indication that the rite did not spread further at that time.

During a comparatively short interlude spanning the final centuries BC and the first centuries AD the rite of crouched inhumation, where the body was placed on its side with the knees drawn up towards the abdomen, with varying orientation, was introduced into Ireland, but was confined to an area along the east coast stretching roughly from the River Liffey to the River Boyne. This type of burial, which remained a minority rite, eventually declined, and was not adopted by the native population.[15] Grave goods (mainly beads) accompanying crouched inhumations at Knowth, Co. Meath (fig. 2),[16]

Christian Burial in Ireland during the first Millennium AD: Continuity and Change," in *The Early Church in Wales and the West*, eds. Nancy Edwards and Alan Lane (Oxford: Oxbow Monograph 16, 1992), 132; O'Brien, "Pagan or Christian?," 138.

[13] Extended inhumation burials accompanied by coins (often placed in the mouth) are known in Britain from the mid and late second century onwards. For full details see: Robert Philpott, *Burial Practices in Roman Britain: A survey of grave treatment and furnishing, AD 43–410*, BAR British Series 219 (Oxford, 1991), 210–216 (hereafter Philpott, *Burial Practices*).

[14] See Philpott, *Burial Practices*, 214–216.

[15] O'Brien, "Burial Practices," 65; O'Brien, "Pagan or Christian?" 136–38; Tiernan McGarry, "The Knowth Iron Age burials in an Irish and wider context," in *The Archaeology of Knowth in the First and Second Millennia AD: Excavations at Knowth 5*, ed. George Eogan (Dublin: Royal Irish Academy, 2012), 689–94 (hereafter Eogan, *The Archaeology of Knowth*).

[16] Knowth, Co. Meath is the site of the famous Neolithic passage-grave complex constructed in the fourth/third millennium BC. George Eogan, "Excavations at Knowth, Co. Meath," *Proceedings of the Royal Irish Academy* 66C (1968): 299–400; George Eogan, "Report on the Excavations of some passage graves, unprotected inhumation burials, and a settlement site at Knowth, Co. Meath," *Proceedings of the Royal Irish Academy* 74C (1974): 11–112; Eogan, *The Archaeology of Knowth*.

match those found with some cremations of the same period, the exception being fibulae, which are not present with these inhumations. Strontium and oxygen isotopic analyses of teeth from several of these crouched inhumation burials at Knowth, Co. Meath, one of Ireland's most significant ancestral burial places, confirms that many of these individuals originated in northern Britain,[17] where this burial rite was a common native pre-Christian tradition at that time.[18]

Burials placed into existing indigenous ancestral burial monuments (known to the Irish as *ferta*) represent the presence of newcomers into an area, who are making a deliberate effort to create an impression of uninterrupted continuity, either by erecting new burial imitative monuments among those already present, or by burying selected persons from their own people into already existing monuments. This process can usually be understood as an attempt to legitimize claims to sovereignty by burying newcomers among the perceived ancestors of a displaced indigenous population in order to create new ancestors and/or to claim the indigenous ancestors as their own, thereby gaining their protection. It is also a method of laying claim to territory.[19] It is possible that these immigrants from Britain who were buried at Knowth were probably seeking to stake territorial claims. It is also possible that their specific burial-rite ceased because they became absorbed into the local indigenous populations.

Early Medieval Burials: Extended Inhumation

The rite of extended supine inhumation burial, where the body was placed on its back, with the head to the west, and normally unaccompanied by grave goods, was introduced into Ireland possibly during the later fourth century, but certainly during the early fifth century as a result of contacts with the western and northern fringes of Romanized Britain where, although the burial rite was Roman, grave goods were usu-

---

[17] Jacqueline Cahill-Wilson, H. Usborne, Christopher Taylor, Peter Ditchfield and Alistair W.G. Pike, "Strontium and oxygen isotope analysis on Iron Age and Early Historic burials around the great mound at Knowth," in Eogan, *The Archaeology of Knowth*, appendix 5, 775–88; Jacqueline Cahill-Wilson, Christopher Standish, and Elizabeth O'Brien, "Investigating Mobility and Migration in the later Iron Age," in *Late Iron Age and 'Roman' Ireland*, Discovery Programme Report 8 (Dublin: Wordwell, 2014): 127–149 (hereafter Cahill-Wilson et al., "Investigating Mobility and Migration in the later Iron Age").

[18] Rowan Whimster, *Burial practices in Iron Age Britain c. 700BC–AD43* (Oxford: BAR 90 (British Series), 1981), 194; O'Brien, *Post-Roman Britain*, 1.

[19] For a detailed explanation of Irish *ferta* see, Thomas Charles-Edwards, "Boundaries in Irish Law," in *Medieval Settlement: Continuity and Change*, ed. Peter H. Sawyer (London: Arnold, 1976), 83–87 (hereafter Charles-Edwards, "Boundaries in Irish Law"); Elizabeth O'Brien and Edel Bhreathnach, "Irish Boundary *Ferta*, their Physical Manifestation and Historical Context," in *TOME: Studies in Medieval Celtic History and Law, in honour of Thomas Charles-Edwards*, eds. Fiona Edmonds and Paul Russell (Woodbridge: Boydell Press, 2011), 53–64 (hereafter O'Brien, and Bhreathnach, "Irish Boundary *Ferta*").

ally omitted.[20] There is, however, some evidence in the far south/west of the country for some influence from the European mainland. The strong cultural and physical contacts that existed between Ireland and western Britain in this period are well documented.[21] For instance, there is evidence to suggest that in the fourth century a treaty existed between the Irish (known to the Romans as the *Scotti*) and the Roman authorities in Britain, which, according to the Roman historian Ammianus Marcellinus, was broken by the *Scotti* (and *Picti*) in AD 360 when they raided the frontiers of Britain.[22] Under the year AD 367 Ammianus Marcellinus also records incursions by the *Atacotti* and the *Scotti*.[23] It has been proposed that the *Atacotti* and the *Scotti* represent two Irish confederations, the former comprising Ulstermen (*Ulaid*) in north/east Ireland, the latter comprising Leinstermen (*Laigin*) in eastern Ireland.[24] Later tradition, and especially the *Historia Brittonum*,[25] suggests that the *Déisi* and *Uí Liatháin* from southeast and southern Ireland, established settlements on the Welsh coast, with the former founding the Welsh kingdom of Dyfed.[26] This latter evidence is, however, late, and should be approached with caution. It has also been argued on the basis of place-name evidence, and the possible borrowing from British-Latin into Old Irish poetry, that the Leinstermen (*Laigin*) of eastern Ireland had connections with the Llŷn peninsula in northern Wales, as the name *Llŷn* may derive from a declined form of *Laigin*.[27] Further important evidence for an Irish presence in Wales and south/west Britain (Devon and Cornwall) during the period

---

[20] Philpott, *Burial Practices*, discussion at p. 111; O'Brien, *Post-Roman Britain*, 26–27; O'Brien, "Burial Practices," 65–66; O'Brien, "Pagan or Christian?," 143–45.

[21] Bateson, "Roman material," 21–92; J. D. Bateson, "Further finds of Roman Material from Ireland," *Proceedings of the Royal Irish Academy* 76C (1976): 171–80; Charles Thomas, *Christianity in Roman Britain* (London: Batesford, 1981); Richard B. Warner, "Some observations on the Context and Importation of Exotic Material in Ireland, from the First Century BC to the Second Century AD," *Proceedings of the Royal Irish Academy* 76C (1976): 267–92; O'Brien, "Burial Practices," 66; O'Brien, "Pagan or Christian?," 143–144; Jacqueline Cahill Wilson, "Romans and Roman Material in Ireland: A Wider Social Perspective," in *Late Iron Age and 'Roman' Ireland*, Discovery Programme Reports 8 (Dublin: Wordwell, 2014), 11–58.

[22] Ammianus, *Res Gestae*, xx.1, ed. Wolfgang Seyfarth (Leipzig: Teubner, 1978) (hereafter Ammianus, *Res Gestae*); Thomas Charles-Edwards, *Early Christian Ireland* (Cambridge: CUP, 2000), 158–160 (hereafter Charles-Edwards, *Early Christian Ireland*); Thomas Charles-Edwards, *Wales and the Britons 350-1064* (Oxford: OUP, 2013), 33.

[23] Ammianus, *Res Gestae*, xxvii. 8..

[24] Charles-Edwards, *Early Christian Ireland*, 159–160.

[25] Nennius, "Chapter 14: History of the British," in *British History and the Welsh Annals*, ed. and trans. John Morris (London: Phillimore, 1980).

[26] Francis John Byrne, *Irish Kings and High Kings* (London: Batesford, 1973), 72, 183; Melville Richards, "The Irish Settlements in South-West Wales: a topographical approach," *Journal of the Royal Society of Antiquaries of Ireland* 90, pt. ii (Dublin, 1960): 133–162; Charles Thomas, *And shall these mute stones speak?* (University of Wales Press, 1994), 41–49; Wendy Davies, *Wales in the Early Middle Ages* (Leicester University Press, repr. 1989), 87–88 (hereafter Davies, *Wales in the Early Middle Ages*).

[27] James Carney, ed., "Three Old Irish Accentual Poems," *Ériu* 22 (1971): 23–80, 69–70.

in question is demonstrated by the occurrence in these regions of memorial stones with inscriptions, often containing Irish personal names, depicted in Latin and in Irish *ogam* characters.[28] When the Roman authorities finally withdrew from Britain in AD 410, the country became vulnerable to increased raiding from Ireland and elsewhere. The boy Patrick (later to become the patron saint of Ireland) was himself taken as a slave in an Irish raid on Britain in the early fifth century. That this raiding was not a one-way phenomenon is demonstrated in Patrick's own condemnation, in his letter to Coroticus, of a raid on Ireland from Britain in the fifth century when newly baptized Irish Christians were taken as slaves.[29]

Undoubtedly settlers moved in both directions bringing with them their own local customs and beliefs. Together with the new religion of Christianity, an important new custom introduced into Ireland in the later fourth-early fifth century was the burial rite of west-east extended supine inhumation. This was the burial-rite that had been adopted in the general Roman world from the mid-second century,[30] and soon became universal among all communities, including Christians, in the Romanized west. Because the rite was universal it cannot automatically be seen as a sign of Christian burial in Ireland, especially in the conversion period of the fifth century. Although this new burial rite soon replaced the rite of cremation in Ireland, there are indications that cremation was still sporadically practiced in parts of the country, for instance cremation deposits at Ask, Co. Wexford (fig. 2) have been dated as late as the seventh to eighth century AD.[31]

Extended supine inhumation burials, datable to the fifth-sixth centuries in Ireland include burials in slab-lined cists (fig. 3a), but more usually stone-lined, and unprotected dug graves (fig. 3b). Irish burials of this period were never placed in wooden or stone coffins. Close parallels for the slab-lined cists and dug graves are to be found in cemeteries in Somerset and Dorset in Roman Britain, and cemeteries in Wales have produced evidence suggesting their continuous use from the fourth to the eighth centuries.[32]

---

[28] Damien McManus, *A Guide to Ogam* (Maynooth: An Sagart, 1991), 61–64; Davies, *Wales in the Early Middle Ages*, 87–89; Elizabeth Okasha, *Corpus of Early Christian Inscribed Stones of South-west Britain* (London: Leicester University Press, 1993), 37–39.

[29] *Epistola ad Milites Corotici*, in *The Book of Letters of Saint Patrick the Bishop*, ed. and trans. David R. Howlett (Dublin: Four Courts Press, 1994), 26–39.

[30] Jocelyn M. Toynbee, *Death and Burial in the Roman World* (London: Thames and Hudson, 1971), 44; Philpott, *Burial Practices*, 53.

[31] SUERC-32851: 1330±30BP, calibrated at 2 sigma = cal AD649-767. Paul Stevens, "Burial and ritual in Early Medieval North Wexford; new evidence from Ask townland," in *Encounters between Peoples*, Archaeology and the National Roads Authority, Monograph Series No. 9, eds. Bernice Kelly, Niall Roycroft, and Michael Stanley (Dublin: National Roads Authority, 2012), 49–60.

[32] O'Brien, *Post-Roman Britain*, 32–38; David Longley, "Early Medieval Burial in Wales," in *The Archaeology of the Early Medieval Celtic Churches*, The Society for Medieval Archaeology Monograph 29, The Society for Church Archaeology Monograph 1, ed. Nancy Edwards (Leeds: Maney Publishing, 2009),105–32.

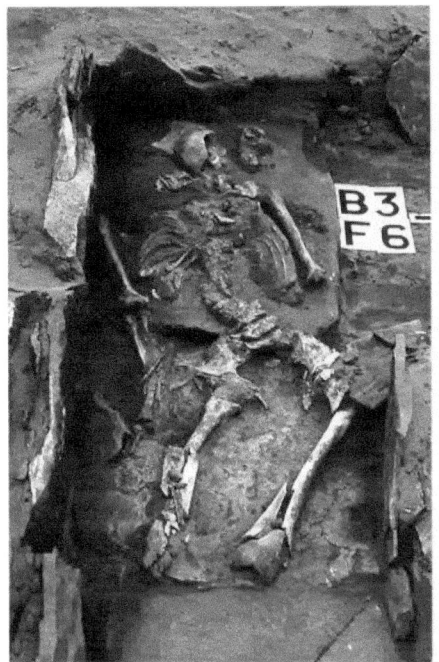 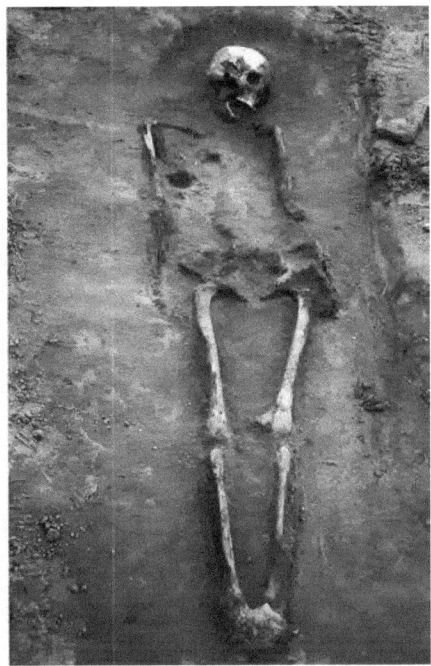

Figure 3a. Image of a burial in a slab-lined cist. © E. O'Brien
Figure 3b. Image of a burial in an unprotected dug grave. © E. O'Brien

It is impossible to differentiate between Christian and pagan burials during the fifth to eighth centuries in Ireland because all graves looked alike. The exception would be burials in recognizable ecclesiastical cemeteries. This difficulty with secular cemeteries is brought sharply into focus by both Muirchú and Tírechán who, writing in the late seventh century, refer to an incident whereby Patrick, while travelling along a road, reputedly stopped at two new graves, one of which was marked by a cross. When questioned by Patrick, a voice from the grave marked by the cross admitted that he was a pagan and that the cross had been placed in error on his grave instead of that of his Christian neighbor.[33] This reference was obviously meant as a warning to Christians to be careful about their place of burial. Admittedly this is an anachronistic reference to an incident that was reputed to have taken place during the fifth century when Patrick was active, but the fact that both Tírechán and Muirchú mention it indicates that they were still familiar with the concept in the late seventh century.

---

[33] Ludwig Bieler, ed. and trans., *The Patrician Texts in the Book of Armagh,* Scriptores Latini Hiberniae, Vol. X (Dublin: Dublin Institute for Advanced Studies, 1979), Muirchú, II.2, 114–15; Tírechán, §41, 154–57.

In Ireland while some early inhumation burials were isolated single burials, others became the foundation burials for secular familial cemeteries. Some of these secular cemeteries also contain evidence for settlement in the form of industrial activity, but with no evidence for an ecclesiastical presence. These are now referred to as "cemetery-settlements."[34]

One example of an early isolated single burial is that at Farta (an Anglicized version of *ferta*),[35] Co. Galway (fig. 2), where the extended inhumation of a female aged twenty to twenty-five years,[36] accompanied by a small horse aged about seven years,[37] had been inserted into the upper levels of a prehistoric burial mound, at the base of which was a Bronze Age urned cremation burial. This female inhumation was originally published in 1904 as being an accompaniment to the Bronze Age cremation,[38] but radiocarbon dates recently obtained by this writer place her death at cal AD 383–536,[39] and that of the horse at cal AD 388–536.[40] This burial fits into the period of the introduction of the rite of extended inhumation into Ireland, but the unusual grave accompaniment indicates that it is unlikely that this is the burial of a Christian. Strontium and oxygen isotope analyses of the female's teeth reveal that she was not of local origin.[41] While there is some possibility that she may have originated in the east of Ireland, her isotope signatures are also consistent with an origin in eastern Britain. Initial results of strontium and oxygen isotope analyses of a tooth from the horse indicate a signature similar to that of the female. Further research of this site is ongoing. This is a prime example of the reuse of an already existing ancestral burial mound (or *ferta*) by a new population-group, possibly from Britain.

By the sixth-seventh century, extended supine inhumation, oriented west-east (head west) and interred in organized cemeteries, normally unaccompanied by grave goods, had become the standard burial rite in Ireland. From approximately the seventh

---

[34] The term "cemetery-settlement" has been coined by Tomás Ó Carragáin, "Cemetery Settlements and Local Churches in Pre-Viking Ireland in Light of Comparisons with England and Wales," in *Anglo-Saxon/Irish Relations before the Vikings*, eds. James Graham-Campbell and Michael Ryan (Oxford: OUP, 2009), 329–66, especially 339.

[35] Irish place-names web site, www.logainm.ie.

[36] Laureen Buckley, "Farta Skeletal Report" (Unpublished osteo-archaeological report prepared for Elizabeth O'Brien, Mapping Death Project, 2012).

[37] Finbar McCormick, "The Farta Horse Burial" (Unpublished osteo-archaeological report prepared for Elizabeth O'Brien, Mapping Death Project, 2013).

[38] George Coffey, "On the Excavation of a Tumulus near Loughrea, Co. Galway," *Proceedings of the Royal Irish Academy* 25C (1904/1905): 14–20.

[39] OxA-X-2488.42; 1625±26BP. All radiocarbon dates cited in this paper have been calibrated at 2 sigma, using OxCal 4.2. (© C. Bronk Ramsey).

[40] UBA-23699; 1618±26BP. This date was obtained with the assistance of a grant from the Royal Irish Academy.

[41] Cahill-Wilson et al., "Investigating Mobility and Migration in the later Iron Age," 141–142.

century onwards skeletons often show indications that the body had been wrapped in a winding sheet or shroud: the legs and feet are very close together and the arms remain close to the body (see fig. 3b). The wrapping of a body in a winding sheet or shroud is regarded as a Christian custom, based on the description of Christ's burial as contained, for instance in Luke 23:53,[42] where the body is described as having been wrapped in a shroud before being laid in the tomb. Adomnán, who a century after the death of St. Columba (who died at Iona AD 597) describing the burial of the saint, states "...the venerable body of the holy and blessed patron was wrapped in clean fine cloths and laid in the appointed burial-place".[43] This was therefore regarded as the appropriate mode of burial for Christians in both Ireland and Britain by the seventh century. A panel on the shaft of the early tenth-century Cross of the Scriptures at Clonmacnoise, Co. Offaly, (amongst others) shows the Irish interpretation of this feature of Christ's burial.[44]

One of the organized secular cemeteries, with no evidence for settlement or ecclesiastical activity, is represented by the site excavated at Holdenstown 2, Co. Kilkenny (fig. 2).[45] This cemetery, which contained ninety-four extended inhumation burials, comprising males, females, and one infant, laid in rows, has produced dates spanning the fifth to seventh centuries.[46] The earliest dated burial at this site, a centrally placed young male (B59) in a grave partially lined with large stones, who is perhaps the foundation burial, has produced a date of cal AD 427–544.[47] Strontium isotope analysis of the teeth of this individual suggests that he originated in the north or west of Britain.[48] This burial was accompanied by an antler pick which has been dated to cal AD 257–410,[49] considerably older than the burial. The date for this object matches the date of similar antler objects unearthed in a ring-ditch at a nearby ancestral burial site (*ferta*) (Holdenstown 1). It would appear that the object with B59 was deliberately removed from the nearby *ferta* site and placed with this burial, perhaps to create a link with the ancestors of the indigenous population. This is a secular cemetery with no known church associa-

---

[42] Vulgate Gospel.

[43] Alan Orr Anderson and Marjorie Ogilvie Anderson, ed. and trans., *Adomnán's Life of Columba*, 2nd ed. (Oxford: OUP, 1991), Book 3.23, 230–31: *sancti et beati patroni ueneerabile corpus mundis inuolutum sindonibus et praeparata possitum in rata busta*.

[44] See illustration in Peter Harbison, *The High Crosses of Ireland; An Iconographical and Photographic Survey*, vol. 3 (Bonn, 1992), figure 909.

[45] Yvonne Whitty and Maeve Tobin, "Rites in transition: the story told by Holdenstown 1 and 2," *SEANDA, National Roads Authority Magazine* 4 (2009): 19–21; O'Brien and Bhreathnach, "Irish Boundary *Ferta*," 53–64.

[46] Full list of dates can be viewed under "Holdenstown 2," at www.mappingdeathdb.ie.

[47] UBA-13667; 1569±22BP.

[48] Janet Montgomery and Julie Milns, "Report on the strontium isotope analysis of four prehistoric and early medieval burials from the Holdenstown and Kilree areas of the Nore Valley," (Unpublished report prepared for Irish Archaeology Consultancy Ltd., 2010).

[49] UBA-20006; 1698±24BP. Date obtained under the auspices of the Mapping Death Project.

tions but the disposition of the skeleton suggests that the body may have been wrapped in a shroud, and as such possibly represents the burial of a Christian. If his is the foundation burial in this cemetery, this young man from post-Roman Britain may have been the progenitor of a new lineage in the region.

An example of a secular cemetery-settlement is provided by the site at Ninch 2, Co. Meath,[50] where the earliest (possibly foundation) burials are also not of native origin. The site is located on a low ridge overlooking the sea on the east coast (fig. 2), and consists of a series of super-imposed concentric enclosures containing evidence of industrial activity in the form of corn-drying kilns, animal enclosures, cobbled surfaces, etc. Towards the center of the site a discrete area within an encircling ditch was reserved for burial and contained ninety-two inhumation burials. Two burials from the earliest phase (male B856 and female B770) were selected for radiocarbon dating, and returned results for the male burial of cal 549–633 AD,[51] and for the female cal 607–659 AD.[52] Strontium and oxygen isotope analysis of a tooth from male B856 indicates that this person is not of Irish origin, and surprisingly the suggested place of origin is in central or eastern Europe. Strontium and oxygen isotope analysis of a tooth from female B770 indicates that while there is a slight possibility that she may have originated in Britain, it is possible that she also originally came from central or eastern Europe.[53] Further analysis of these results is ongoing but the implications are that these burials represent movement of peoples from the post-Roman European mainland into Ireland, possibly via Britain. It is not known whether or not these people represented pagans or Christians, but it is noted that at least some burials at this cemetery appear not to have been shroud wrapped, perhaps suggesting that it contained burials of both pagans and Christians.

There are, of course, instances of undeniably Christian burial in Ireland in the fifth-sixth centuries, and one example is the very interesting cemetery in a small Christian ecclesiastical site at Caherlehillan, Co Kerry[54] (on the south/west coast of Ireland) (fig. 2) where the primary feature was a small church, with a "special" grave, which was later covered by a stone shrine. Due to the lack of preservation of skeletal material at this site it was not possible to obtain radiocarbon dating for the burials. However, material

---

[50] Cia McConway, "Successive Early Medieval enclosed settlements at Ninch, Co. Meath," in *Death and burial in Early Medieval Ireland in the light of recent archaeological excavations*, eds. Christiaan Corlett and Michael Potterton (Dublin: Wordwell, 2010), 157–72.

[51] UBA-20055; 1404±19BP. These dates were obtained under the auspices of the Mapping Death Project.

[52] UBA-20056; 1479±20BP.

[53] Cahill-Wilson et al., "Investigating Mobility and Migration in the Later Iron Age," 144–145.

[54] John Sheehan, "A Peacock's Tale: Excavations at Caherlehillan, Iveragh, Ireland," in *The archaeology of the Early Medieval Celtic Churches*, Society for Medieval Archaeology Monograph 29, Society for Church Archaeology Monograph 1, ed. Nancy Edwards (Leeds: Maney Publishing, 2009), 191-206.

from the fill of the primary foundation trench produced a date of cal AD 437–649.[55] Also present at this site were decorated stone slabs, which have engraved Maltese crosses with a handle, reminiscent of a *flabellum*, above of which is the profile of a peacock. The excavator indicates a parallel for these designs in the Mediterranean Christian culture. Also retrieved at this site were fragments of imported pottery of north-eastern Mediterranean Bii type, dateable to the late fifth-mid sixth century. This raises the possibility that Christianity was introduced into this extreme south-western part of Ireland, not from Britain, but directly from mainland Europe.

The Influence of the Christian Church on Burials

Up until at least the eighth century, burial in the majority of Irish monastic cemeteries was reserved for kings, bishops, abbots, clerics, and patrons. Selected members of secular communities were buried among the ancestors in ancestral *ferta*, and the remainder in secular familial community cemeteries, which could contain both pagan and Christian burials, a practice tolerated by the Church because of the importance attached by the Irish to burial among their ancestors.[56]

When reflecting on burial in Ireland, especially in the period spanning the fifth to eighth centuries, one might be forgiven for assuming, given that Christianity had been introduced into Ireland by the early fifth century, that burial rites and place of burial would automatically be governed, or at the very least, be overseen by the Christian Church from the time of its introduction. It can now be demonstrated, using a combination of archaeological evidence and literary sources that the Church did not seek to actively influence burial practices until the end of the seventh–early eighth century, at least three centuries after the introduction of Christianity. The beginnings of this trend can be seen in the implicit warning contained in the late seventh-century reference to an incident regarding the burial of a pagan and a Christian, already referred to. The earliest rules relating directly to guidelines for the burial of Christians that we are aware of are included in the *Collectio Canonum Hibernensis*,[57] written in the early eighth century. That the Church was very conscious of the importance of ancestral graves and had to find ways to accommodate these changes, can be observed in the inclusion of several rules referring specifically to traditional burial practices. The following is an example of just two of these rules: It is evident in *HIB* LI, chapter 2, that ancestral cemeteries were not to be totally abandoned and Christians were still to be held in some way responsible for the upkeep of their ancestral burial place, when a rule under the heading *Concerning*

---

[55] GrA-24462; 1490±40BP.
[56] O'Brien, "Pagan or Christian?" 148–49.
[57] Hermann Wasserschleben, ed., *Die Irische Kanonensammlung* (Leipzig, 1885) (hereafter *HIB*).

the dead seen in dreams (De mortuis in sono visis) makes the point by including a warning "to remind mankind that respect should be given to a burial, though it may perhaps not be given to the dead, yet it is a matter for blame if [the burial] is neglected by those in the religious state".[58] The implication being that those who were in religious life were still being held responsible for the upkeep of their ancestors' graves. Another rule, *HIB* L, chapter 3, under the heading *Concerning the fact that martyrs*[59] *who are buried in desert places are more visited than [those] among evil men (De eo, quod magis visitantur martyres in deserto humati, quam inter malos homines)* rule (a) reads: "In the Lives of the Fathers we read: Martyrs buried among evil persons are visited by angels, but however, the angels return sorrowful,"[60] illustrating the point that Christians were still being buried in ancestral cemeteries among "evil men," presumably meaning their pagan ancestors. In order for their graves to be visited by angels this practice should be discontinued and their burial should be in "desert" places—which in an Irish context means an early ecclesiastical foundation.

Conclusion

That the Church was successful in its efforts to control the burial of Christians can be confirmed with evidence provided by radiocarbon-dated burials in twenty-one *ferta* sites indicating that by the eighth-ninth century, secondary burial in prehistoric ancestral burial mounds or *ferta* had ceased. However, the inclusion of *ferta* as boundary markers in Irish early law tracts[61] helped to prolong their memory in the general consciousness and ensured that they were still recognized as the burial places of ancestral guardians. That *ferta* continued to be remembered as important features in the landscape is also evident from place-name evidence. There are many recorded place-names throughout the country that include the element *fert* or *ferta*, for instance Ardfert and Clonfert,[62] both of which eventually became the location of major ecclesiastical foundations.

Radiocarbon-dated burials in secular cemeteries likewise reveal that the majority of non-ecclesiastic familial and settlement-cemeteries also ceased to be used during

---

[58] *HIB*, 209: *sive admonendo humano generi, ut sepulturae prebeatur humanitas, quae licet defunctis non opituletur, tamen culpator, si in religiositate neglegitur.* The translation of relevant material from *HIB* was undertaken some time ago by the author under the supervision of Prof. Thomas Charles-Edwards. However, the author accepts full responsibility for any errors or omissions in the translations.

[59] In an Irish context "martyrs" means all who have died as Christians. Ireland does not have any record of Christians who were killed for their faith thereby becoming "martyrs" in the normally accepted sense.

[60] *HIB*, 208: *In vitas partum legimus: Martyres inter malos sepultos ab angelis visitari, sed tamen tristes reversos angelos.*

[61] Charles-Edwards, "Boundaries in Irish Law"; O'Brien and Bhreathnach, "Irish Boundary *ferta*."

[62] The place-names database of Ireland, www.logainm.ie.

the eighth-ninth centuries. However, a limited number of these cemeteries continued to be used for burial up until the time of the Irish Church reforms of the late eleventh-early twelfth centuries,[63] indicating that some families were probably in a position to compromise with Church authorities whereby certain family members were buried in the local ecclesiastical cemetery, while others continued to be buried in the non-ecclesiastical familial cemetery.

Ultimately however, the increasing power of the Church, from the late seventh century onward, influenced the abandonment of burial among the pagan ancestors in favor of burial at ecclesiastical sites.

---

[63] For instance, the site at "Johnstown, Co. Meath," see www.mappingdeathdb.ie.

LIST OF CONTRIBUTORS

MIRIAM ADAN JONES (Vrije University, Amsterdam) is a PhD student working on a project entitled „*Catholics of the English Race*" that explores the overlap between ethnic and ecclesiological categories in England in the seventh and eighth centuries. On the basis of letters, histories, homilies and sermons, biblical commentaries and hagiographies, she aims to reconstruct a picture of the way ethnicity could function as an ecclesiological category in early medieval Britain.

IVAN BASIĆ (University of Split), assistant professor of history and vice president of the Croatian Society for Byzantine Studies, whose research interests include the late antique and medieval Adriatic, church history, urban history, historical geography, Early Christian and medieval art and architecture. He has published widely on the social, religious and cultural history of Dalmatia in the *longue durée*, such as *The Inscription of Gaius Orchivius Amemptus* (Split, 2015); *Diocletian's Villa in Late Antique and early medieval Historiography: A Reconsideration* (Split, 2014); and *Spalatensia Porphyrogenitiana. Some Issues Concerning the Textual Transmission of Porphyrogenitus' Sources for the Chapters on Dalmatia in the De administrando imperio* (Split, 2013).

OLIVÉR GÁBOR (Janus Pannonius Museum, Pécs) is a senior museologist and archaeologist working on the Roman cemeteries of Sopianae. He conducted excavations in Roman and Great Migration sites in Baranya county and published *Sopianae késő antik temetői épületei (Late Antique Funerary Constructions in Sopianae)* in 2016.

MAËL GOARZIN (Université de Lausanne/École Pratique des Hautes Études, Paris) is a PhD student in Ancient Philosophy working on the practical aspects of the philosopher's everyday life in Late antique Neoplatonism through the study of biographical texts. His blog is focused on practical ethics and philosophy as a way of life: https://biospraktikos.hypotheses.org/

Józef Grzywaczewski (Cardinal Stefan Wyszyński University, Warsaw), professor of patristic theology was Rector of the Polish Seminary in Paris, teaching in the Institut Catholique. His research focuses on the history and theology of the first four centuries. His latest book: *The Biblical Idea of Divine Mercy in the Early Church* (Warsaw, 2016).

LINDA HONEY, a philologist, historian, and Biblical scholar, received her doctorate with a specialization in women in the Christian Near East (4th-6th centuries) at the University of Calgary. She is keenly interested in travellers who crossed spatial and religious frontiers from Late Antiquity through the Early Modern Period including Thecla, Tryphaena, and Egeria. She has published several articles and is a popular conference speaker. Her interest is the history of the Middle East translates to the present in that she serves with Global Aid Network as an advocate for refugees and displaced people.

ZSUZSA KATONA-GYŐR (Janus Pannonius Museum, Pécs) is an archaeologist who excavated Altinum along the Dabube limes and published widely on the cemeteries and burial chambers of Sopianae.

DANIEL K. KNOX (CEU Budapest) is a PhD student focusing on the literary corpus of Bishop Ennodius of Pavia, and social ties in Ostrogothic Italy. He is interested in social network analysis and prosopography, as well as literary and historical analysis of Italian and Gallic letter collections in Late Antiquity. Daniel is originally from New Zealand where he completed his undergraduate (VUW) and master's (Auckland) degrees prior to moving to Budapest to pursue his doctoral thesis at the Central European University.

JÉRÔME LAGOUANÈRE (Université Paul-Valéry Montpellier 3/Institut d'Etudes Augustiniennes, Paris), associate professor of Latin Language and Literature, deals with the works of the Latin Church Fathers, particularly Tertullian and Saint Augustine. His research explores the relationship between ancient philosophy and Christianity. His works include *Intériorité et réflexivité dans la pensée de saint Augustin. Formes et genèse d'une conceptualisation* (Paris, 2012) and *Tertullianus Afer. Tertullien et la littérature chrétienne d'Afrique* (Turnhout, 2015).

ECATERINA LUNG (University of Bucharest), professor in the Department of Ancient History, Archaeology, and Art History, is the director of the Centre for Medieval Studies of the University of Bucharest. Her main research interests are medieval historiography, gender studies and cultural history.

BRANKA MIGOTTI (Croatian Academy of Sciences and Arts, Zagreb) is a scholarly adviser and head of the Archaeological Department of the Croatian Academy of Sciences and Arts, and collaborating professor in the doctoral program of the Archaeology Department of Zagreb University. Her main scholarly interest was for a long time in the Late Roman period and early Christianity of the Roman provinces of Dalmatia and Pannonia. In the last decade she has been mostly engaged in the research of Roman stone funerary monuments of Pannonia in their overall material, social and religious context.

LEVENTE NAGY (University of Pécs), head of the Department of Archaeology also teaches Latin and ancient history at the University of Pécs. He works on topics in ancient history, Late Antique archaeology and Early Christian hagiography and is involved in cultural heritage projects. He co-authored with Krisztina Hudák *A Fine and Private Place: Discovering the Early Christian Cemetery of Sopianae/Pécs* (Pécs, 2008). His recent publications include *Pannonian cities, martyrs, relics* (Pécs, 2012); "Zoltán Kádár and the Early Christian Iconography of Roman Pannonia." *Studia patristica* 2014: (LXXIII), 145-168; and „Bemerkungen zum ikonografischen Programm des frühchristlichen Kästchenbeschlags von Császár (Ungarn), *Mitteilungen zur Christlichen Archaeologie* 18 (2012).

ELIZABETH O'BRIEN (Society of Antiquaries, Dublin) is principal researcher of the Mapping Death Project, www.mappingdeathdb.ie, based at The Discovery Programme (Centre for Archaeology and Innovation Ireland), www.discoveryprogramme.ie

MONIKA PESTHY-SIMON (Budapest) is an independent scholar whose field of research includes early Judaism and Christianity, Christian apocrypha and patristic writings. Her most important publications are *Isaac, Iphigeneia, Ignatius: Martyrdom and Human Sacrifice* (Budapest – New York, 2017); *La théologie de la tentation dans le christianisme ancien* (Bern, 2011); and „Mulier est instrumentum diaboli: Women and the Desert Fathers", in: G. H. Van Kooten – A. Hilhorst (eds.), *The Wisdom of Egypt: Jewish, Early Christian & Gnostic Essays in Honour of Gerard Luttikhuizen* (Leiden, 2005).

HRISTO PRESHLENOV (National Institute of Archaeology, Bulgarian Academy of Sciences is an archaeologist of the Western Coast of the Black Sea. His research projects concern the urban, maritime, economic and social aspects of the Pontic cities as well as the Christianization of the cities. Excavation leader in Deultum, Mesambria Pontica, Scatrae and Agathopolis, he publishes archaeological surveys of the region and its cities, such as *Antique public spaces in Nessebar (VI c. BC – VI c. AD). II. Eastern coast* (Sofia, 2008) and participates in collaborative works, such as *The Bosporus: Gateway between the Ancient West and East (1st Millennium BC-5th Century AD)*. edited by Gocha R. Tsetskhladze, Sümer Atasoy, Alexandru Avram, Şevket Dönmez, James Hargrave (Oxford, 2013).

EDWARD M. SCHOOLMAN (University of Nevada, Reno) associate professor of history teaches courses on the ancient and medieval Mediterranean oikumené. His research primarily focuses on Italy and its cultural transformation in the post-Roman world. His book, *Rediscovering Sainthood in Italy: Hagiography and the Late Antique Past in Ravenna* appeared in 2016.

LUCIANA GABRIELA SOARES SANTOPRETE (Rheinische Friedrich-Wilhelms-Universität, Bonn) fellow of the Alexander von Humboldt Foundation in Germany and research associate in the Laboratoire d'Études sur les Monothéismes at the CNRS and in the Centre Jean Pépin in Paris is working on a French translation with commentaries of Plotinus' *Treatise 32* "On the Intellect". She co-edited, with Chiara O. Tommasi and Helmut Seng, the volume *Formen und Nebenformen des Platonismus in der Spätantike* for the « Bibliotheca Chaldaica » series (Heidelberg: Universitätsverlag Winter, 2016.)

JUANA TORRES (Universidad de Cantabria, Santander), professor of Classics at the Department of Historical Sciences of the University of Cantabria, teaches Latin, Early Christianity and Women's history in Late Antiquity, focusing on religious conflicts. Her research project *"Forms of polemic in Early Christian literature: from dialogue to altercatio"* explores the location of controversy in the Christian literary system, highlighting the reuse of literary forms inherited from Judaism and the Classics in Christian controversial literature.

ANNA JUDIT TÓTH (Budapest), research fellow at the Research Centre for the Humanities of the Hungarian Academy of Sciences, works on popular religion in Late Antique and medieval Byzantium.

MARGARITA VALLEJO-GIRVÉS (University of Alcalà, Madrid) is professor of Ancient History dealing with the history of the Eastern Roman Empire. Her publications include *Hispania y Bizancio. Una relación desconocida* (Madrid, 2012) and *Viaje y Visiones del Mundo* (Malaga, 2008). Her recent research project explores „Exile and Confinement in the Late Antique Mediterranean World."

ZSOLT VISY (University of Pécs), emeritus professor at the Department of Archaeology that he had founded, he directs the PhD program for ancient history and archaeology and an international academic program entitled *Corpus limitis imperii Romani*.

He is the leading archaeologist of the excavations at the Early Christian cemetery of Sopianae/Pécs that became a World Heritage Site in 2000. He is a project leader in the Sevso treasure-research and co-authored with Zsolt Mráv *The Sevso Treasure* (Pécs, 2013). Commissioned by the Prime Minister's Office, prepares a dossier on the „Frontiers of the Roman Empire in Hungary: the *Ripa Pannonica*" to candidate for the World Heritage Site recognition. Visy had conducted excavations along the Danube limes in Intercisa (Dunaújváros), Lussonium (Paks-Dunakömlőd), Inéaceni/Énlaka (Romania).

INDEX OF PERSONAL NAMES

A

Aba, 30, 34, 35, 36, 37, 38, 41
Acacius of Caesarea, 75
Accili Sabbatini, Maria Assunta, 8
Æthelbert, ing, 5, 152, 154, 159, 160, 161, 163
Agathias, 5, 60, 122, 123, 129
Agricola, 342
Agrypnius Volusianus, 109
Amalasuntha, 262, 264
Ambrose of Milan, 99, 101, 135, 275
Ammianus Marcellinus, 39, 74, 75, 241, 251, 252, 274, 275, 347
Ammianus Marcellinus, 39, 74, 75, 77, 109, 110, 111, 112, 113, 117, 241, 251, 252, 257, 274, 275, 347
Anastatius, 4
Anderson, Benedict, 119, 120
Anderson, William Blair, 203, 208
Androklea, 39
Apollonius of Tyana, 112, 114
Apuleius, 109, 112, 114
Arcadius, mperor, 47, 53, 78
Aretarchos, 30, 41
Aristotle, 12, 14, 110, 112, 232, 233, 237
Arnobius, 34, 225

Asmus, Rudolf, 44, 49, 55
Augustine, bishop of Hippo, 5, 11, 33, 59, 60, 105, 106, 107, 108, 109, 110, 111, 112, 113, 114, 115, 116, 117, 118, 135, 154, 160, 161, 162, 358
Augustus, 47, 64, 134, 207, 216, 254, 263
Aurelius Prudentius Clemens, 205

B

Baronio, Cesare, 74, 76, 77
Barth, Fredrick, 119
Basić, Ivan, 7, 241, 247, 251, 257, 259, 260, 261, 264, 265, 266, 269, 357
Basilicus, 4
Basil of Caesarea, 33
Bayliss, Richard, 243, 244, 247, 256
Bechtle, Gerald, 230, 233
Beierwaltes, W., 230
Bernardi, Jean, 71, 72, 77
Bidez, J., 70, 72, 229
Blanco, Antonino González, 235
Blumenthal, H. J., 17, 230
Bonamente, Giorgio, 2
Bouillet, M.-N., 233
Bowersock, Glen, 88, 255
Brandt, Hartwin, 2

Bréhier, Émile, 235
Brent, Allen, 39, 51, 88, 89
Brisson, Luc, 12, 13, 14, 220, 227, 228, 231, 232, 233
Broneer, Oscar, 165
Bulić, Frane, 242, 252, 257

C

Calandion, bishop, 56, 57
Cameron, Alan, 1, 2, 19, 49, 54, 55, 56, 59, 105, 109, 122, 123, 126
Candidus, 43, 46, 54
Canivet, 73
Chase, Michael, 128, 230
Cicero, 111, 112, 113, 114
Claudian Claudianus, 205
Claudius, 342
Constantine, emperor, 2, 5, 39, 47, 72, 128, 129, 133, 134, 135, 136, 142, 144, 145, 146, 147, 148, 149, 188, 202, 247, 248, 249, 253, 254, 256
Constantinus II, emperor, 78, 141, 142
Coutinho Figuinha, Matheus, 8
Cribiore, Raffaella, 2

D

Dagron, Gilbert, 27, 28, 32, 35, 36, 38, 39, 48, 51
Dalisandus, 51
Damascius, philosopher, 43, 44, 49, 52, 54, 55, 129, 222
Damasus, bishop of Rome, 103, 275
Daniel the Stylite, 31, 45
Dehandschutter, Boudewijn, 89, 90, 224
Deogratias, 109, 117
Dexianos, 30, 41
Dillon, John, 13, 14, 218, 222, 228, 230
Dodds, Eric R., 224, 228
Dubois, Jean-Daniel, 221, 232

E

Edwards, Marc, 11, 45, 97, 167, 230, 344, 345, 346, 347, 348, 352, 354
Elagabalus, emperor, 134, 146
Emmelia, 22
Eparchius Avitus, 206
Epicurus, 110, 112
Euplus, 85
Eupsychius of Caesarea, 74
Eusebius, bishop of Cibalae, 100
Evagrius Scholasticus, 43

F

Fatti, Federico, 73, 74
Felix III, pope, 53
Felix IV, 262, 264, 265
Fitz, Jenő, 136, 142, 143, 305
Fülep, Ferenc, 275, 289, 291, 295, 296, 297, 299, 300, 305, 306, 329, 330, 331, 333, 339

G

Gábor, Olivér, 7, 274, 276, 295, 310, 357
Galerius, emperor, 98, 248, 257, 274
Gibbon, Edward, 76, 77
Gillett, Andrew, 215
Giuseppe di Lampedusa, 67
Goarzin, Maël, 3, 11, 357
Gratian, emperor, 101, 253, 255
Gregory of Nazianzus, 71, 72, 73, 75, 76, 77, 78, 79, 254
Gregory of Nyssa, 3, 11, 12, 19, 20, 21, 22, 23, 24, 25, 59
Gregory of Tours, 5, 123, 124, 128, 176
Gregory the Great, 151, 152, 153, 154, 155, 156, 157, 159, 162
Grzywaczewski, Józef, 6, 203, 358

H

Hadot, Pierre, 14, 15, 220, 225, 226, 227, 228, 229, 230, 231, 233
Harder, Richard, 218
Heyman, George, 88, 89
Honey, Linda, 3, 27, 28, 29, 30, 32, 35, 36, 39, 42, 358
Honorius, emperor, 255, 263, 268
Hunger, Herbert, 121

I

Iamblichus, 12, 66, 226, 229
Ignatius of Antioch, 4, 83, 84, 87, 88, 89, 94, 359ez ugyanaz!
Illus, 3, 4, 43, 44, 49, 50, 51, 52, 53, 54, 55, 56, 58
Iordanes, 124, 125, 126, 127, 128
Irenaeus, bishop of Sirmium, 99

J

James, Liz, 44, 47
John of Antioch, 43, 44
John of Nikiu, 51
John of Ravenna, 249, 268, 269
John Talaia, 53, 56
John the Cappadocian, 61
Julian, emperor, 1, 4, 52, 66, 69, 71, 72, 74, 75, 76, 77, 78, 79, 116, 229, 253, 254
Julius Caesar, 254
Julius Nepos, emperor, 257, 264
Julius, bishop of Rome, 70
Justinian, 4, 60, 61, 64, 66, 126, 129, 184, 185, 186, 193, 258, 264, 267, 268

K

Kaldellis, Anthony, 60, 61, 62, 63, 122, 126
Karaman, Ljubo, 242, 252, 257
Katona Győr, Zsuzsa, 7, 274, 276, 295, 296, 298
Kerchove, Anna van den, 217, 220, 221, 222
Kimber Buel, Denise, 120
Knox, Daniel K., 6, 95, 203, 358
Kötting, Bernhard, 31

L

Lactantius, 225
Lagouanère, Jérôme, 5, 105, 358
Laniado, A., 43, 45
Lányi, Vera, 297, 305
Leo I, emperor, 45, 46, 47, 58, 124, 183, 209
Leo II, emperor, 47, 48
Leontius, emperor, 3, 43, 44, 52, 56, 57, 58
Libius Severus, 210
Liebeschuetz, Wolf, 2, 126, 127, 128
Wolf, 2, 32, 126

Linguiti, Alessandro, 14, 15, 16, 19, 230
Livius, 66
Longinianus, 106
Louis the Great, king, 8
Lucanus, 66
Lung, Ecaterina, 5, 119, 358
Lydus, John, 4, 59, 60, 61, 62, 63, 64, 65, 66, 67

M

Macrina, 3, 12, 13, 19, 20, 21, 22, 23, 24, 25, 26
Macrobius, 110
Majorian, 206, 209, 210, 213, 214, 215, 216, 250
Malalas, John, 5, 28, 43, 51, 55, 56, 57, 62, 63, 123, 124, 126, 129
Malchus, 43, 49, 50
Marcus Aurelius, 188

Maris of Chaldeon, 70, 75
Marius Victorinus, 59, 60, 228, 230
Mark of Arenthusa, 4, 11, 33, 45, 69, 70, 71, 72, 73, 74, 75, 76, 77, 79, 84, 86, 97, 106, 114, 155, 173, 248, 338, 339
Markus, Robert A., 8, 152, 153, 154, 157, 159, 263
Marsus Leontius, 52
Mathisen, Ralph W., 8
Maximinus II Daia, emperor, 188
Maximus of Madaura, 106
McKitterick, Rosamond, 125, 126
Mellitus, abbot, 151, 152, 153, 154, 155, 158, 161, 162
Meredith, Anthony, 12, 14, 18, 21, 23
fogalom, nem személy!
Migotti, Branka, 5, 100, 133, 135, 140, 143, 144, 145, 146, 147, 148, 149, 242, 359
Montanus of Singidunum, 99
Moreschini, Claudio, 225
Moss, Candida, 87, 89, 90, 91, 92, 95

N

Nagy, Levente, 8, 97, 149, 273, 295, 359
Narcissus of Neronias, 70
Nectarius, 106

O

O'Brien, Elizabeth, 7, 338, 341, 343, 344, 345, 346, 347, 348, 349, 350, 351, 353, 354, 359
Olympius, 19, 20, 183

P

Pamprepius, 4, 43, 44, 48, 49, 50, 51, 52, 53, 54, 55, 58
Perpetua, 84, 85, 86, 95
Pesthy-Simon, Monika, 4, 83, 87, 95, 99, 359

Peter III, 53
Phocas, 61, 63, 64, 263
Photius, 28, 61, 62
Plato, 1, 7, 12, 14, 32, 60, 65, 109, 217, 220, 223, 227, 228, 230, 231, 232, 233, 237
Plotinus, 3, 7, 12, 13, 14, 15, 16, 17, 18, 19, 20, 24, 26, 218, 219, 220, 221, 222, 223, 224, 225, 227, 228, 229, 230, 231, 232, 233, 234, 235, 236, 237, 360
Pollio, 5, 97, 99, 100, 101, 102, 103
Polycarp of Smyrna, 4, 89
Pow, Stephen L., 8
Preshlenov, Hristo, 6, 181, 189, 190, 191, 192, 194, 359
Proclus, 12, 48, 62, 66, 231, 233
Procopius of Caesarea, 60, 121, 125
Proklianos, 39
Puech, Henri-Charles, 50, 51, 53, 223, 224
Pythagoras, 12, 109, 116, 223

R

Rákos-Zichy, Johanna, 2, 8
Rasimus, Thuomas, 231, 233
Rhetorius, 44, 49, 55
Rihmer, Zoltán, 2, 99
Rist, John M., 230
Roberts, Michael, 205
Rousseau, Phillip, 12, 206, 209, 210, 214
Rufius Antoninus, 109
Rutilius Namatianus, 205

S

Saffrey, Henry Dominique, 13, 230
Sághy, Marianne, 1, 2, 19, 26, 97, 103, 149, 203, 273, 275, 295, 337
Salzman, Michelle R., 2, 8, 19, 107, 337
Scholer, David, 234
Schoolman, Edward, 1, 6, 165, 172, 360
Seleucia, 27

Seneca, 4, 89
Sidonius, 6, 203, 204, 205, 206, 207, 208, 209, 210, 211, 212, 213, 214, 215, 216, 256, 257, 261, 264
Sidonius Apollinaris, 203, 204, 256, 261, 264
Simplicianus, 59
Siricius, bishop of Rome, 103
Smith, Andrey, 230
Soares Santoprete, Luciana Gabriela, 217, 218, 220, 221, 236, 360
Socrates, 32, 70, 71, 75, 76, 91
Sozomen, 70, 71, 72, 73, 74, 75, 79
Stark, Karen L., 8
Stroumsa, Guy G., 222
Synerus, 5, 97, 98, 99, 103, 104
Syrianus, 66

T

Tacitus, 342
Tamás, Hajnalka, 100, 101, 102
Tardieu, Michel, 218, 221, 222, 223, 225, 226, 227, 228, 229, 230, 232
Tertullian, 85, 86, 95, 135, 143, 225, 358
Thecla, 3, 27, 28, 29, 30, 32, 33, 34, 35, 36, 37, 38, 39, 40, 41, 42, 53, 86, 95, 358
Theiler, W., 230
Theodore of Heraclea, 70
Theodoret of Cyrrhus, 72, 75, 76
Theodosius, emperor, 77, 206, 244, 250, 253
Theonilla, 39, 40
Theophanes Confessor, 43, 51
Thillet, Pierre, 235
Thomas of Spalato (also: Thomas, archdeacon of Split), 242, 249, 258, 268, 269
Tigriana, 35, 37
Torres, Juana, 4, 69, 71, 78, 79, 360
Trocundes, 52
Turner, John D., 227, 228, 231, 232

U

Udvardy, György, 8

V

Vaes, Jan, 243, 245, 269, 270
Valentina of Caesarea, 85
Valentinian I, emperor, 100, 101, 190, 254
Valentinian II, emperor, 77
Vallejo-Girvés, Margarita, 3, 4, 43, 360
Varro, 66, 105
Verina, 3, 4, 43, 44, 45, 46, 47, 48, 49, 50, 51, 52, 56, 57, 58
Vikan, Gary, 31
Virgil, 106, 110, 111, 112, 113, 127, 204
Visy, Zsolt, 7, 8, 273, 274, 275, 278, 279, 280, 282, 283, 289, 290, 291, 293, 295, 298, 305, 337, 360, 361
Volusianus, 106, 109, 110, 111, 112, 113, 114, 116, 117
Vulić, Hrvoje, 100

W

Wallis, Richard, 224, 230
Watson, Lynette, 13, 203, 204, 205, 206, 214, 215, 216
Wenskus, Reinhard, 119
Whittaker, John, 230
Williams, Sam K., 11, 12, 20, 23, 25, 88, 90, 93, 94, 342
Wolfram, Herwig, 69, 127

Z

Zacharias Scholastikos, 43, 52, 53, 54
Zambon, Marco, 230
Zeno, 3, 28, 43, 44, 45, 46, 48, 49, 50, 51, 52, 53, 54, 55, 56, 57, 58, 92
Znorovszky, Andrea-Bianka, 8
Zoticus, 62

INDEX OF GEOGRAPHICAL NAMES

A

Alexandria, 39, 44, 49, 53, 54, 70, 71, 75, 76, 85, 135, 160, 167, 245, 275
Anchialos (now: Pomorie), 181, 183, 185, 200, 202
Apamea, 121
Aphrodisias, 54, 232, 237
Apollonia/Sozopolis (now: Sozopol), 181, 183, 186, 191, 193, 196
Aqua Iasae (now: Varaždinske Toplice, Croatia, 134
Aquileia, 99, 101, 135
Aquincum (now: Budapest), 274, 275
Augusta Treverorum (now: Trier), 274

B

Black Sea, 6, 122, 181, 182, 183, 186, 187, 189, 192, 194, 196, 197, 198, 199, 201, 202, 359
Britain, 8, 141, 146, 154, 160, 309, 341, 342, 344, 345, 346, 347, 348, 350, 351, 352, 353, 357

C

Calama, 107
Carnuntum (now: Petronell), 146, 274
Cibalae (now: Vinkovci, Croatia), 99, 100, 275
Cilicia also: Silifke, Turkey, 27, 29, 38, 39, 51, 70, 243, 244, 247, 256
Constantinople, 4, 39, 45, 46, 47, 48, 49, 50, 51, 52, 53, 56, 58, 61, 62, 70, 75, 133, 147, 183, 184, 211, 213, 254, 257, 258, 263
Cyprus, 29, 41

D

Danube region, 181
Debeltos (now: Debelt), 181, 183, 197, 199, 200
Dionysopolis (now: Balchik), 181, 187, 189, 190
Dorset, 309, 348
Dulcissimus, 185

G

Galway (county), 350
Gaza, 52, 54, 79

H

Haemimontus, 6, 181
Hibernia, 8, 342

I

Ireland, 7, 13, 154, 338, 341, 342, 343, 344, 345, 346, 347, 348, 349, 350, 351, 352, 353, 354, 359

K

Kerry (county), 352
Kilkenny (county), 344, 351

L

Laois (county), 343

M

Meath (county), 345, 346, 352, 355
Mesembria (now: Nesebar), 181, 183, 190, 193, 194
Milan, 2, 99, 101, 102, 133, 135, 224, 235, 242, 249, 254, 261, 275
Moesia Secunda, 6, 181, 202
Mursa (now: Osijek), 274, 275

N

North Africa, 1, 8, 106, 107, 117, 169, 173, 243, 244

O

Odessos (now: Varna), 181, 183, 184, 185, 186, 187, 188, 189, 193, 194, 196, 197, 198, 199, 200, 201, 202
Offaly (county), 351

P

Pannonia, 5, 8, 97, 98, 99, 100, 102, 104, 136, 141, 142, 146, 148, 149, 208, 273, 274, 275, 276, 289, 293, 295, 297, 298, 300, 305, 307, 309, 359
Pannonia Superior, 5, 136, 146
Pécs, 2, 8, 98, 148, 149, 273, 274, 275, 276, 289, 290, 291, 293, 294, 295, 296, 297, 298, 301, 305, 309, 329, 333, 335, 336, 338, 357, 358, 359, 360, 361
Philadelphia (in Lydia), 12, 28, 32, 44, 60, 61, 121, 204
Poetovio (now: Ptuj), 136, 142, 275
Poreč, 264, 266, 268

R

Ravenna, 249, 258, 264, 265, 266, 267, 268, 269, 360
Rome, 1, 2, 6, 7, 14, 18, 19, 27, 48, 59, 70, 73, 84, 87, 88, 101, 105, 109, 110, 121, 122, 123, 126, 134, 136, 143, 146, 148, 152, 153, 154, 156, 162, 170, 175, 205, 206, 207, 208, 209, 211, 213, 220, 229, 234, 244, 246, 249, 250, 253, 254, 255, 256, 262, 263, 264, 265, 267, 270, 273, 275, 305, 306, 337, 338

S

Savaria (now: Szombathely), 275, 338
Scythia, 6, 8, 181, 187, 189, 202
Seleucia, 27, 28, 31, 32, 35, 38, 39, 40, 41, 42

Singidunum (now: Belgrade), 99, 275
Sirmium (now: Stremska Mitrovica), 70, 71, 97, 99, 100, 103, 104, 136, 275
Somerset, 348
Sopianae (now: Pécs, Hungary), 7, 148, 149, 273, 274, 275, 276, 279, 289, 290, 291, 292, 293, 294, 295, 296, 297, 298, 300, 301, 305, 306, 307, 308, 309, 310, 329, 330, 333, 334, 335, 336, 337, 338, 339, 357, 358, 359, 361
Split, 241, 242, 245, 246, 247, 248, 249, 251, 252, 253, 254, 257, 258, 259, 260, 261, 264, 265, 266, 267, 268, 269, 270, 357
Sufes, 107
Syrian Antioch, 39

T

Tarsus, 35, 36, 51, 53, 55, 56, 57, 254
Templum Iovis (now: Obzor), 181, 193
Tirissa/Acres, 181, 193, 197

W

Wexford (county), 348
Wicklow (county), 344

Y

Yorkshire, 344

For Product Safety Concerns and Information please contact our EU representative GPSR@taylorandfrancis.com Taylor & Francis Verlag GmbH, Kaufingerstraße 24, 80331 München, Germany

T - #0010 - 220426 - C0 - 229/152/21 - PB - 9789633862551 - Matt Lamination